Forensic Analytics

Methods and Techniques for Forensic Accounting Investigations

MARK J. NIGRINI,
B.COM.(HONS), MBA, PH.D.

WILEY

John Wiley & Sons, Inc.

Published by John Wiley & Sons, Inc., Hoboken, New Jersey.
Published simultaneously in Canada.

For general information on our other products and services or for technical support, please contact our Customer Care Department within the United States at (800) 762-2974, outside the United States at (317) 572-3993 or fax (317) 572-4002.

Wiley also publishes its books in a variety of electronic formats. Some content that appears in print may not be available in electronic books. For more information about Wiley products, visit our web site at www.wiley.com.

ISBN 978-0-470-89046-2; ISBN 978-1-1180-8763-3 (ebk); ISBN 978-1-1180-8766-4 (ebk); ISBN 978-1-1180-8768-8 (ebk)

Printed in the United States of America

16

To my daughter, Paige Nigrini.
Thank you for understanding that "the book"
needed many late nights and weekend afternoons.

Contents

Preface

THE BUSINESS OF OCCUPATIONAL and financial statement fraud is unfortunately alive and doing very well. There are regular reports of financial statement fraud in the financial press, and all types of financial fraud in the press releases section of the SEC's website. There are also regular reports of occupational fraud in the financial press. These reports might just be the tip of the iceberg. The 2010 *Report to the Nations on Occupational Fraud and Abuse* of the Association of Certified Fraud Examiners estimates that the typical organization loses 5 percent of its annual revenue to fraud. These statistics are confirmed in other fraud surveys such as *The Global Economic Crime Survey* of PriceWaterhourseCoopers (2009) and in reports published by the U.S. Government Accountability Office. Together with the losses from employee fraud, there are also other corporate and public sector losses from accounting errors such as underbilling or overpaying or duplicate payments.

Forensic analytics describes the act of obtaining and analyzing electronic data using formulas and statistical techniques to reconstruct, detect, or otherwise support a claim of financial fraud. In this book, forensic analytics is also used to detect accounting errors such as underbilling or overpayments. Forensic analytics also includes the detection of biases that come about when people aim for specific numbers or number ranges to circumvent actual or perceived internal control thresholds. The use of forensic analytics has been made easier with the continued increase in computing power available on laptop computers and access to inexpensive software capable of some rigorous data analysis on large data tables. The main steps in forensic analytics are (a) data collection, (b) data preparation, (c) the use of forensic analytics, and (d) evaluation, investigation, and reporting. The availability of computing power and the use of the Internet for many facets of forensic analytics have made all the steps in the process easier. All that is missing now is for forensic investigators, internal auditors, external auditors, and other data analysts to use the methods and techniques on their data.

The first three chapters in the book are an overview of using Microsoft Access, Excel, and PowerPoint for the analysis of data and the reporting of the forensic results. The next nine chapters describe forensic analytic methods and techniques that begin with high-level overviews and then drill deeper and deeper into the data to produce small sets of suspicious transactions. One high-level overview technique reviewed in depth is Benford's Law. Thereafter, two chapters show how correlation and time-series analysis can be used as detective or proactive continuous monitoring techniques. Chapters 15 and 16 discuss, with examples, a forensic risk-scoring technique that would work well in a continuous monitoring application. Chapter 17 reviews the detection of financial statement fraud. The chapter shows how Benford's Law can be used to detect such frauds and also includes a scoring technique to score divisions for financial reporting fraud. The final chapter reviews the use of forensic analytics to detect purchasing card fraud and possible waste and abuse in a purchasing card environment.

The methods and techniques in the book are discussed and described with results from real-world data. The chapters also include a detailed demonstration of how to run the tests in Access 2007 and Excel 2007. These demonstrations are supported by about 300 screen shots showing the steps used to run the tests. In a few cases, either Access or Excel is demonstrated when that alternative is clearly the way to go. Forensic investigators should have no problem in running these tests in Access 2010 or Excel 2010 using the screenshots in the book.

The companion site for the book is www.nigrini.com/ForensicAnalytics.htm. The website includes the data tables used in the book. Users can then run the tests on the same data and can then check their results against the results shown in the book. The website also includes Excel templates that will make your results exactly match the results in the book. One template is the *NigriniCycle.xlsx* template for all the tests in the Nigrini cycle. The templates were prepared in Excel 2007. The companion site also includes PowerPoint 2007 slides for all 18 chapters. The website also has exercises and problems typical of those found at the end of college textbook chapters. These materials could be used by college professors using the book in a formal college course. With time, more sections will be added to the website and these might include links to useful resources and questions from forensic investigators and my answers to the end-of-chapter questions.

Forensic Analytics is the result of many years of work on forensic analytic projects, starting with my Ph.D. dissertation titled "The Detection of Income Tax Evasion through an Analysis of Digital Distributions." The book was written so that it would be understood by most financial professionals. Ideally, most users will have some experience in obtaining transactional data and some experience with the basic concepts of data analysis, such as working with tables, combining (appending) or selecting (extracting subsets) data, and performing calculations across rows or down columns. Users should understand the basics of either Excel or Access. There are many books covering these basics and also many free resources on the Microsoft website. In addition to the technical skills, the ideal user should have enough creativity and innovation to use the methods as described, or to add twists and tweaks to take into account some distinctive features of their environment. Besides innovation and creativity, the target user will also have a positive attitude and the disposition to, at times, accept that their past few hours of work have all been the equivalent of barking up the wrong tree and after taking a deep breath (and a few minutes to document what was done) to go back (perhaps with new data) and start again. Much of forensic analytics is more like an art than a science and forensic investigators need a personality that matches the iterative process of modifying and refining the tests.

To this day I am still thankful to my Ph.D. dissertation committee for their guidance and supervision of my forensic-based dissertation that was a move into uncharted waters. I still remember the many Friday afternoon progress sessions with Martin Levy, a professor of Applied Statistics and Quantitative Analysis. A special thanks is also due to the first internal audit directors, Jim Adams, Bob Bagley, and Steve Proesel, that used my forensic analytic services in the mid-1990s. I needed their vote of confidence to keep going. I'd also like to thank the Wiley professionals, Timothy Burgard, Stacey Rivera, and Chris Gage, who turned my manuscript into a quality finished product.

Mark J. Nigrini, Ph.D.
Pennington, New Jersey, USA
February 18, 2011

About the Author

ARK NIGRINI, PH.D., IS an Associate Professor at The College of New Jersey in Ewing, New Jersey, where he teaches auditing and forensic accounting. He has also taught at other institutions, including Southern Methodist University in Dallas, Texas.

Mark is a Chartered Accountant and holds a B.Com. (Hons) from the University of Cape Town and an MBA from the University of Stellenbosch. His Ph.D. in Accounting is from the University of Cincinnati, where he discovered Benford's Law. His dissertation was titled "The Detection of Income Tax Evasion through an Analysis of Digital Distributions." His minor was in statistics and some of the advanced concepts studied in those statistics classes are used in this book.

It took a few years for his work to be noticed by corporate America. The breakthrough came in 1995 when his work was publicized in an article titled "He's got their number: Scholar uses math to foil financial fraud" in the *Wall Street Journal*. This was followed by several other articles on his work and on Benford's Law in the national and international media. A recent article on Benford's Law that discussed Mark's forensic work was published in Canada's *Globe and Mail* on December 22, 2010. Mark has also been interviewed on the radio and television. His radio interviews have included the BBC in London and NPR in the United States. His television interviews have included an appearance on NBC's *Extra*.

Mark has published papers on Benford's Law, auditing, and accounting in academic journals such as *The Journal of the American Taxation Association, Auditing: A Journal of Practice and Theory, The Journal of Accounting Education, The Review of Accounting and Finance, Journal of Forensic Accounting,* and *The Journal of Emerging Technologies in Accounting*. He has also published in scientific journals such as *Mathematical Geology* and pure mathematics journals such as the *International Journal of Mathematics and Mathematical Sciences*. Mark has also published articles in practitioner journals such as *Internal Auditor* and the *Journal of Accountancy*. Mark's current research addresses forensic and continuous monitoring techniques and advanced theoretical work on Benford's Law.

Mark has presented many academic and professional seminars for accountants in the United States and Canada with the audiences primarily comprising internal auditors, external auditors, and forensic accountants in the public and private sectors. Mark has presented a number of association conference plenary or keynote sessions with his talk titled "Benford's Law: The facts, the fun, and the future." The release date of *Forensic Analytics* is planned to coincide with a plenary session to be delivered by Mark at NACVA's Annual Consultants' Conference in San Diego, CA, on June 9, 2011. Mark has also presented seminars overseas with professional presentations in the United Kingdom, The Netherlands, Germany, Luxembourg, Sweden, Thailand, Malaysia, Singapore, and New Zealand. Mark is available for seminars and presentations and he can be contacted at ForensicAnalytics@gmail.com. Other contact information is given on his website www.nigrini.com.

CHAPTER ONE

Using Access in Forensic Investigations

F ORENSIC ANALYTICS IS THE procurement and analysis of electronic data to reconstruct, detect, or otherwise support a claim of financial fraud. The main steps in forensic analytics are (a) data collection, (b) data preparation, (c) data analysis, and (d) reporting. This book casts a wider net than simply the detection of financial fraud. Using computer-based analytic methods our goal is the detection of fraud, errors, and biases where biases involve people gravitating to specific numbers or number ranges to circumvent actual or perceived internal control thresholds. These analytic methods are directed at determining the likelihood or magnitude of fraud occurring. They would be a part of a fraud deterrence cycle that would include other steps such as employment screening procedures, including background checks. The techniques described in the book rely on the analysis of data, usually transactional data, but at times, other data such as statistical data or aggregated data of some sort.

The main workhorses for the preparation and analysis of data will be Microsoft Access and Microsoft Excel (or Access and Excel, for short). Other valuable and dependable and high-quality tools for data analysis include IDEA, Minitab, and SigmaPlot for preparing high-quality complex graphs. The reporting and presentation of the results is usually done using Microsoft Word and/or Microsoft PowerPoint. These results could include images cropped from various sources (including Access and Excel). Images can be copied and pasted into Word or PowerPoint by using a software tool called Snag-It.

This chapter introduces Access and the components and features of Access that are used in a forensic analytics environment. The next two chapters do the same for Excel and PowerPoint. In summary, Access has almost everything that is needed for a forensic analytics application with reasonably sized data sets, where there is not a high requirement for high security. Forensic-related applications can be created in Access and other users with little or no knowledge of Access could use the system. The chapter reviews the Access components and features that make it useful for forensic analytics.

AN INTRODUCTION TO ACCESS

Access is Windows-based and so, fortunately, all the basic Windows operations work in Access. Your trusted mouse works just like before with right clicks, left clicks, and double clicks. Access is launched just like any other program using a shortcut or the **Start** button. Copying, moving, naming, and deleting files are done as usual. There are some differences that are mainly related to the fact that Access is a database program that expects the data tables to be continually changed and updated.

Access differs from Word and Excel in that for most users there was no migration from other products. Microsoft did an excellent job in showing people how to do task *x* in Word given that you used to do task *x* following a set of procedures using perhaps WordPerfect or Wordstar. Microsoft also showed people how to do task *y* in Excel given that you used to do task *y* using a series of steps in perhaps Quattro Pro or Lotus 1-2-3. For example, you can still enter *@sum(B1..B5)* in cell **B6** in Excel (2007) and not only will it calculate the sum correctly, but it will convert the formula to = SUM(B1:B5) for you. There is no help in Access geared to making you more familiar with the program, because there was not a preceding product that users were used to. This makes the logic of Access a little tricky to follow at first. With practice comes familiarity, and it will not be too long before you will prefer to use Access for those projects that are more suited to Access than to Excel.

One reason for favoring Access over Excel for forensic analytics work is that Access forces some discipline onto the data analysis project. Excel is basically a large free-form rectangle divided into smaller rectangles (called cells). In these cells you can (a) paste images, (b) enter numbers, (c) enter formulas, or (d) display a graph (called a chart in Excel). When you view a number in Excel, unless you click on the cell itself, you are never really sure if this is a data point or the result of a formula (a calculation). Excel is (unfortunately) very forgiving in that a column heading can be repeated (you can call both columns A and B, *People*), Excel does not mind if you call a column *Dollars* and immediately below the field name you enter the word *Rambo*. Excel has some built-in documenting capabilities (including the ability to Insert Comment) but most of the structure and the integrity are left up to the user. Without clear documentation it is easy for another user to have no clue as to what is happening in a complex spreadsheet, and even the original developer might have trouble figuring out what is happening if they look at a complex spreadsheet six months later. The opening screen for Access 2007 is shown in Figure 1.1.

In contrast to Access, most computer programs will at least do something once opened. For example, in PowerPoint you can immediately click on the blank slide and type a title or some text. This is not the case with Access. To get Access to start working

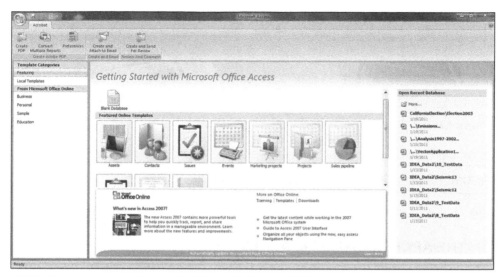

FIGURE 1.1 Opening Screen for Microsoft Access 2007

you either need to open an existing file or you need to create a new blank database. For a new forensic analytics project, the **New Blank Database** is the starting point. Clicking on **Blank Database** will start the series of dialog boxes creating a new Access database. The next step is shown in Figure 1.2.

Figure 1.2 shows the step needed to create an Access database named *Chapter1a. accdb* in a folder named *DataDrivenForensics*. Clicking the **Create** button will give the result in Figure 1.3.

The opening screen of the new database named *Chapter1a* is shown in Figure 1.3. *Table 1* is shown in the open objects panel and this is there so that the spot does not look empty. The table disappears once a new table is created and *Table 1* is closed. The navigation pane on the left lists all the Access objects and the details can be shortened or extended by selecting the drop down arrow and selecting **Object Type** or **All Access Objects**. The architecture of Access and the components of a database are discussed in the next section.

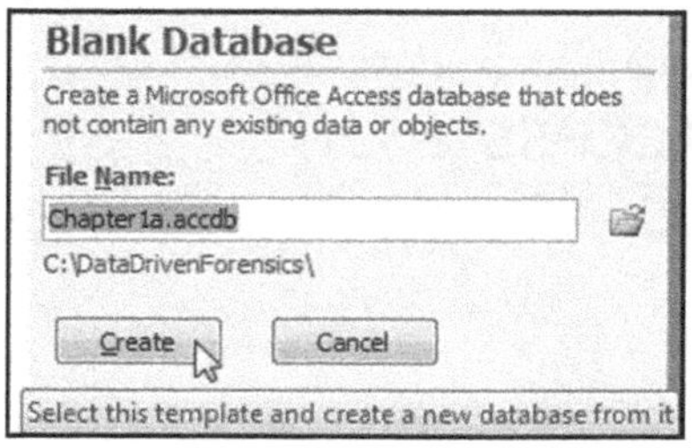

Blank Database

Create a Microsoft Office Access database that does not contain any existing data or objects.

File **N**ame:

Chapter1a.accdb

C:\DataDrivenForensics\

[Create]   [Cancel]

Select this template and create a new database from it

FIGURE 1.2 Creation of a New Blank Database in the *DataDrivenForensics* Folder

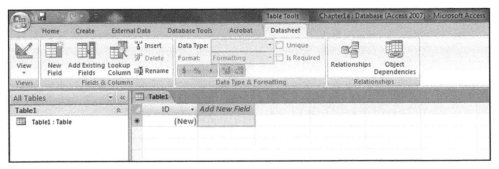

FIGURE 1.3 Opening Screen of a New Access Database Named *Chapter1a*

 ## THE ARCHITECTURE OF ACCESS

The Microsoft Access homepage at http://office.microsoft.com/en-us/access-help/ has lots of useful and reliable information on Access 2003, 2007, and 2010. The website's opening screen with Access 2007 selected is shown in Figure 1.4.

Extensive Microsoft Access information and help is available as can be seen in Figure 1.4. After selecting the appropriate version on the right (see the arrow in Figure 1.4) the site provides information and help related to using Access. A good starting place, irrespective of your Access version, is the Access Basics section in Access 2010. The *basics* are basically the same for each version except that Access 2007 and Access 2010 use the ribbon for the selection of tasks. There are also other websites with Access information and several of these are listed on the companion site for this book.

An Access database is a tool for collecting, storing, and analyzing data, and reporting information. A database consists of unprocessed data and other objects associated with collecting, editing, adding, deleting, processing, organizing, reporting on, and sharing the data. The objects listed below are of most interest from a forensic analytics perspective:

FIGURE 1.4 Microsoft Website with Access Information and Help

- **Tables.** Transaction data is stored in one or more tables. The layout of a table is the same as the layout of an Excel worksheet. Each row in the table is called a record and a record holds all the known information about one item or subject. These items or subjects could be employees, transactions, or books. The fields (columns) store similar data or facts for the various records. In a table of transactions, examples of possible fields are invoice date, invoice number, vendor number, invoice amount, and so on. In a table of census data by county examples of possible fields are county number, county name, state, area, count of people 2010, and projected count of people 2015. It is good practice to have an ID field in each table. This field is also called a primary key and holds a unique number for each record so that you can identify the record uniquely.
- **Queries.** Queries are fundamental to forensic analytics and many other Access-related tasks. Queries are often used to select a subset of records that meet certain criteria. For example, a query could retrieve all the counties in Texas with a population of less than 1,000 people. Every forensic question in Access will need a query. There are also other data-related tasks that require queries and these include appending data and updating data in tables. Queries are the workhorses of forensic analytics.
- **Reports.** Reports are used for the neat presentation of the results of the forensic analytics work. The reporting features and routines in Access allow for the creation of very neat and professional-looking reports. These reports can include conditional formatting for highlighting data. The reports can include professional-looking headings including company logos and other images. The report's footer also has many useful versatile features and capabilities. The reports can be previewed, printed on paper, viewed on a screen, exported to another program, and even converted to pdf files and sent as an attachment to an e-mail message.
- **Forms.** Forms are a user interface that can be used to enter data into tables or to edit existing data in tables. Forms can vary from being complex with command buttons and input controls to being just a basic screen with areas for data entry. Forms can also be used to neatly display the results of queries or to provide a neat way to input data. The form most often used in forensic analytics is called a switchboard. The switchboard has command buttons that can run queries or prepare reports with a single click. Switchboards allow users who are not familiar with Access to run a query or prepare a report.

Access databases can also include macros. Macros are generally time-saving objects. Macros can be used to automate tasks such as opening a report, running a query, or closing a database. The procedures for creating macros are reviewed on the Microsoft website or in any comprehensive Access book.

Access databases can also include modules that are procedures written in *Visual Basic for Applications* (VBA) that add functionality to a database. A module is a set of declarations, statements, and procedures that form a unit because they relate to one clearly defined task. Modules are flexible and we can do much more with modules than can be done by using the usual query design modes (using the design grid, SQL view, or a

Wizard). Getting started with VBA requires an upfront learning curve and the good news is that all the forensic analytics tests in this book can be done without modules.

For our forensic applications we always use tables and queries. Tables hold the raw data, and queries are used to analyze the data and also to update and manipulate tables (perhaps using append queries). Reports might, or might not, be needed for neatly formatted output, and the only form that fits well with data analysis is the switchboard.

A REVIEW OF ACCESS TABLES

Tables are the starting point for any forensic analytics project. Data is stored in tables and a database can be made up of many tables. An example of a database with several tables is shown in Figure 1.5.

The database included tables for data related to a large chain of restaurants. One goal in database design is to avoid storing duplicate information (also known as *redundant data*). This reduces storage costs, the chances of data inconsistencies, and

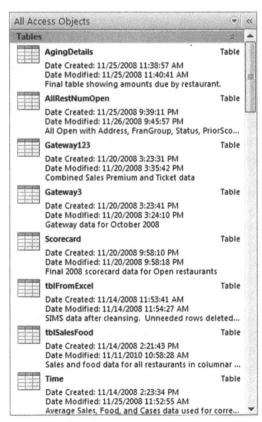

FIGURE 1.5 Access Database with Several Tables that Have Names, Descriptions, a Created Date, and a Modified Date

simplifies the task of updating records. Another principle of database design is that the database is divided into tables that each stores a relevant part of the total picture. A single table might work in some applications. Another goal is that the tables can be linked in some meaningful manner. Each restaurant in the example in Figure 1.5 has a unique restaurant number and that number (called a primary key) can be used for queries that use more than one table.

Tables are made up of records and fields. Each record contains all the information about one instance of the table subject. If the table has details about the books in a library, then each record would relate to a single book in the library. A field contains data about one aspect of the table subject. In the library example we might have a field for the book's title and another field for the acquisition date. Each record consists of field values which are also called facts. A field value might be *Lesa* or *Car* or $19.64. There are many data types of which numeric data, dates, and text data are most applicable to forensic analytics.

For most forensic applications the data will be imported into Access from another program or from a flat file. A file with more than one million records is quite normal. The desired properties of an imported data table or of a created table are listed below:

▪ Each field value should contain one value only such as one date, one amount, one census count, or one first name. Text fields can use more than one word if this describes an attribute of the record, such as *New Jersey* or *Loveland Supply Company* for vendor name. In contrast, F46bl could indicate that the person is a female, 46 years old, with blue eyes, but storing all this in one field value is not good practice. The investigator would then not be able to group by *Gender* and calculate descriptive statistics, or group by *Age* and calculate descriptive statistics. The correct practice would be to have one field for each of gender, age, and eye color.

▪ Each field should have a distinct name. Access allows users to add a caption in the Field Properties to more fully describe the field. This caption is very useful when using databases created by other people.

▪ All field values should hold a value for that field only and all the field values should be of the same data type (e.g., text, or numeric, or date). A blank field value is acceptable. For example, in a table of addresses, one field might be used for the apartment or suite number and in some cases this number would not be applicable and so the field value might be blank. A blank field value is also called a *null value* for numeric data, or a *zero-length string* for text, memo, or hyperlink fields.

▪ The order of the records in a table is not important and should have no effect on the results of any query.

▪ The order of the fields relative to each other is not important. Conventional practice is that the unique identifier field that identifies each record (the field usually called *ID*) is the first field in the table.

▪ Each record should be unique in that it differs from all the other records in the table. The record may differ on only one field such as the *ID* field, but nonetheless each row (record) should be unique. In a table of library books, a library with two identical books should be able to distinguish between the two books by a field called

Copy (or something similar) and the first copy of the book could have *Copy* = 1 and the second copy of the book could have *Copy* = 2.

■ A table should have a primary key that is unique and that contains no duplicate values so that each record (row) can be identified uniquely. A table can also have a foreign key, which is a way to link to the primary key in another table.

■ The field values must pertain to the subject matter of the table and must completely describe the contents of the table. A table for library books should hold all the data pertaining to each book, and should not contain superfluous data such as the home address of the last patron to read the book.

■ The preferred situation is that users should be able to change the data in one field without affecting any of the other fields. Access 2010 does allow users to have a calculated data type. This means that, for example, *ExtendedValue* could be equal to *Count* * *Amount*. If either *Count* or *Amount* is updated, then *ExtendedValue* is updated automatically.

If the data for the investigation is already in an Access format then the analysis can begin with little or no data preparation. When the data is in the form of a flat file (or files) then the data needs to be imported into Access. Some preparation work is also needed when the database was created in a prior version of Access. These prior-version databases can be converted to Access 2007 databases. The new Access 2007 file format is preferred because it has some new functions that were not previously available. Access 2007 is backward-compatible to Access 97.

 IMPORTING DATA INTO ACCESS

Importing data into Access is reasonably straightforward. Data is imported from Excel using ***External Data→Import→Excel*** as is shown in Figure 1.6.

FIGURE 1.6   Commands Used to Import Data from Excel into Access

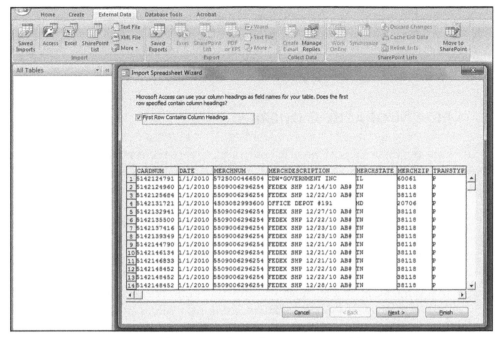

FIGURE 1.7 Import Spreadsheet Wizard Used to Import Data from Excel

Figure 1.6 shows the starting steps for importing data from Excel. Exporting data and results from Access to Excel can present some challenges when the data exceeds the size of the clipboard. One solution is to then use Excel to import the data from Access. The Import Spreadsheet Wizard for importing data from Excel is shown in Figure 1.7.

Importing data one sheet at a time from Excel is reasonably straightforward. It makes the importing procedure easier if the first row in Excel contains column headings. It is usually a good idea to format any field that will be used for calculations as the *Currency* data type. The imported data is shown in Figure 1.8.

Purchasing card data is shown in Figure 1.8 in a table that looks like a familiar Excel worksheet. A difference between Access and Excel is that in Access all calculations need

ID	CARDNUM	DATE	MERCHNUM	MERCHDESC	MERCHSTAT	MERCHZIP	TRANSTYPE	AMOUNT
1	5142124791	1/1/2010	5725000466504	CDW*GOVERN	IL	60061	P	106.89
2	5142124960	1/1/2010	5509006296254	FEDEX SHP 12/:	TN	38118	P	3.62
3	5142125684	1/1/2010	5509006296254	FEDEX SHP 12/:	TN	38118	P	3.67
4	5142131721	1/1/2010	4503082993600	OFFICE DEPOT	MD	20706	P	178.49
5	5142132941	1/1/2010	5509006296254	FEDEX SHP 12/:	TN	38118	P	3.62
6	5142135500	1/1/2010	5509006296254	FEDEX SHP 12/:	TN	38118	P	3.62
7	5142137416	1/1/2010	5509006296254	FEDEX SHP 12/:	TN	38118	P	3.74
8	5142139349	1/1/2010	5509006296254	FEDEX SHP 12/:	TN	38118	P	3.67
9	5142144790	1/1/2010	5509006296254	FEDEX SHP 12/:	TN	38118	P	11.29
10	5142146134	1/1/2010	5509006296254	FEDEX SHP 12/:	TN	38118	P	3.85
11	5142146833	1/1/2010	5509006296254	FEDEX SHP 12/:	TN	38118	P	3.62
12	5142148452	1/1/2010	5509006296254	FEDEX SHP 12/:	TN	38118	P	3.74
13	5142148452	1/1/2010	5509006296254	FEDEX SHP 12/:	TN	38118	P	3.74
14	5142148452	1/1/2010	5509006296254	FEDEX SHP 12/:	TN	38118	P	3.62
15	5142148452	1/1/2010	5509006296254	FEDEX SHP 12/:	TN	38118	P	3.62

FIGURE 1.8 Purchasing Card Data in Excel

to be done using queries. Another difference is that (almost) all changes to tables such as edits to records, deletions of records, additions of records, and deletions of fields are permanent. Excel has the ***Control+Z*** command to backtrack, but in Access there is no option to either backtrack or to exit without saving.

A REVIEW OF ACCESS QUERIES

Queries are the main focus in forensic analytics. A query is essentially a question, and forensic analytics is all about asking questions and scrutinizing or auditing the answers. The main types of queries are reviewed below:

- **Creating calculated fields.** Here we create one or more fields in the table that are calculated values using the data in the other fields. For example, with Benford's Law we need to calculate the first-two digits in every number and this first step is a query. The general rule is that any calculation is always based on other field values in that same record. For example, quantity times unit price will give us a total cost. Access can easily perform calculations using field values from the same row or record. It is difficult to perform a calculation that requires Access to use a field value from a preceding or succeeding row. An example of such a calculation is a cumulative sum. The problem with using preceding or succeeding rows is that if the table is resorted then the cumulative sums need to be recalculated and the order of the records in a table should not affect a calculated value.
- **Grouping records.** In these queries various parameters are calculated for each group in a field (e.g., *CardNum*, *MerchNum*, *Date*, or *MerchZip*). Examples of these parameters are the sum, average, count, maximum, minimum, first, last, or the standard deviation. Some forensic analytics tests simply involve calculating the sums or averages for selected groups of records.
- **Identifying duplicate records.** In these queries duplicate records are identified. This will usually be a selective identification of duplicates because one of the criteria in table design is that all the records are unique. This query will usually look for cases where we have duplicates on two or three fields only.
- **Filtering data.** Access has a powerful filtering function and many types of conditions can be used. A query could be used to show all the purchasing card transactions for employee *x* for a range of dates (perhaps a range when the employee was on vacation). The filter could be combined with a grouping command using the powerful *Where* criteria in Access.
- **Using a *Join* to query conditions in two or more tables.** A query that requires Access to use the data in two or more tables needs to include a *Join*. The most common type of Join is where we identify all our forensic units of interest at the start of the analysis and we want the next query to only give us the results for our selected vendors, merchants, or employees.
- **Appending data.** Append queries are important in forensic analytics because these queries can be used to retrieve data from one table and add it to another table.

This is a useful way to add (say) November's data to the year-to-date data table. Append queries are also useful to convert data from an Excel format where the data for each time period is in separate columns, to the table format in an Access database where the data for the various time periods are stacked on each other. An example is shown later in this chapter.

- **Crosstab queries.** Crosstab queries allow users to add another level of grouping. With the purchasing card data one could calculate the merchant totals for the year. A crosstab query could also add another layer of analysis to also include merchant totals per month.

- **Parameter query.** A parameter query returns all the records for a specified field value. This is useful for the risk-scoring models in Chapters 15, 16, and 17. A parameter query would be used to show all the card transactions for the *Crown Plaza Hotel* as is shown in Figure 1.9.

Figure 1.9 shows a parameter query in Design View. The "Enter Name of Merchant" in square brackets is an informative message that appears when the query is run. The query is run by clicking **Design→Results→Run**, and the dialog screen is shown in Figure 1.10.

Figure 1.10 shows the dialog box of a parameter query. The words *Crown Plaza Hotel* are entered and after clicking **OK** the results will show only the transactions for the Crown Plaza Hotel. A parameter query can have more than one parameter.

Queries are the workhorses of forensic analytics and the book shows many examples of queries from Chapter 4 through Chapter 18. Reports are either based on tables or queries. In a forensic environment the reports will usually be based on queries. The only real issue with Access is with calculations that are based on records that come before or after the record in question. Access has difficulty in looking up and down when performing calculations.

Field:	Date	CARDNUM	MERCHNUM	MERCHDESCRIPTION	MERCHSTATE	AMOUNT
Table:	PurchasingCards2010	PurchasingCards2010	PurchasingCards2010	PurchasingCards2010	PurchasingCards2010	PurchasingCards2010
Sort:	Ascending	Ascending				Descending
Show:	☑	☑	☑	☑	☑	☑
Criteria:				[Enter Name of Merchant]		
or:						

FIGURE 1.9 Parameter Query in Design View. The Query Is a Parameter Query Because of the "Enter Name of Merchant" in Square Brackets

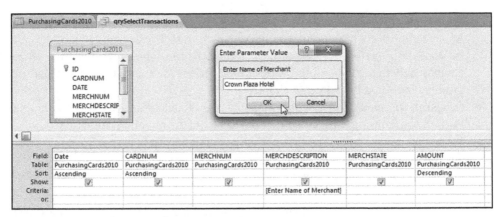

FIGURE 1.10   Dialog Box of a Parameter Query

Some forensic analytics tests will use several queries to get the final result. The general format for a query is to state which table (or tables or prior query) should be used, which fields (or columns) are to be queried, what calculations or comparisons should be done, which records should be returned, and how to format the output (sorting is one option). The usual method will be to use the ***Create→Other→Query Design*** sequence to create queries. The important features in Access supporting queries are:

- The ability to create queries using the wizards, Design View, or SQL view.
- The ability to query a combination of one or more tables or the results of prior queries.
- The ability to use SQL to change a query created in Design View.
- The Performance Analyzer (***Database Tools→Analyze→Analyze Performance***), which helps to make queries more efficient.
- The ability to format the output of the query (usually by displaying results to two digits after the decimal point).
- The ability to sort and resort query results without creating more queries.
- The extensive library of built-in functions for calculated fields.
- The built-in statistical operations such as Sum, Count, Average, Minimum, Maximum, First, and Last.
- The built-in Iif (Immediate If) function and the Switch function, which allows for multiple If statements, together with a full complement of operators including **And**, **Or**, and **Not.**
- The ability to work with empty (null) fields.
- The ability to easily export tables and the results of queries to Excel for further analysis or neat presentation.

Access was made to analyze data and the calculation speed is quite remarkable. With practice and patience the Access grid becomes quite logical. The next section demonstrates how to prepare Excel data for use in Access.

U.S. No. 2 Fuel Oil All Sales/Deliveries by Prime Supplier (Thousand Gallons per Day)											
Year	Jan	Feb	Mar	Apr	May	Jun	Jul	Aug	Sep	Oct	Nov	Dec
1983	65,251.4	63,848.0	62,375.4	53,049.0	36,302.8	40,598.8	35,802.6	41,119.8	38,150.2	41,636.8	54,958.2	78,119.2
1984	88,893.7	66,567.9	74,816.9	54,803.4	48,251.7	40,018.0	40,495.9	45,299.1	47,100.2	46,981.7	61,917.7	74,286.6
1985	87,392.1	77,660.0	67,731.4	55,829.4	45,673.8	40,889.3	41,082.0	44,985.2	45,262.7	54,954.8	58,369.5	80,912.0
1986	72,150.2	80,349.8	64,523.4	51,892.4	47,643.8	40,559.1	40,221.2	47,773.9	46,787.6	55,272.2	58,240.2	74,448.9
1987	78,148.0	73,292.2	65,579.3	52,600.1	46,028.2	43,426.8	44,110.6	41,079.7	47,423.7	60,538.5	62,190.7	78,371.5
1988	90,618.3	89,824.4	77,098.3	56,688.9	50,735.3	47,457.9	48,687.8	50,874.4	50,453.2	61,333.0	67,826.8	82,290.2
1989	79,098.6	79,580.9	75,144.4	55,264.5	46,260.3	45,547.3	39,889.0	50,778.4	50,742.5	56,433.0	64,378.7	92,250.9
1990	74,256.8	73,752.3	63,254.8	55,571.5	49,431.4	49,050.2	46,314.1	54,196.0	53,803.8	54,397.2	60,710.9	64,933.7
1991	81,366.5	68,472.4	60,802.5	53,574.6	46,538.5	42,699.6	43,889.8	46,724.4	46,882.3	53,013.5	55,807.4	68,245.1
1992	78,609.0	70,094.2	64,700.2	57,430.5	46,793.0	46,859.4	43,287.0	44,860.2	52,209.5	56,162.9	59,294.2	72,803.0
1993	62,959.1	69,927.9	65,619.9	49,032.0	38,744.9	41,405.4	38,368.4	40,131.1	41,414.2	32,073.2	38,875.9	51,627.7
1994	68,199.7	62,191.5	49,804.4	32,960.3	27,444.2	26,009.7	22,623.7	27,619.0	30,391.2	32,976.0	34,185.7	45,932.5
1995	47,443.4	54,852.4	41,434.2	31,347.5	26,195.3	24,322.2	21,676.0	24,859.5	26,625.0	29,076.7	38,986.2	53,054.9
1996	57,988.5	55,685.0	42,789.1	33,643.2	25,651.8	23,238.7	22,987.0	24,188.8	27,810.4	31,993.5	38,958.1	44,723.2
1997	52,887.5	46,281.0	39,457.7	33,128.7	25,986.1	24,433.3	23,436.9	23,967.5	27,152.4	30,358.4	35,005.9	45,200.0
1998	43,253.5	42,453.9	38,313.8	28,122.4	22,565.9	23,580.9	22,198.4	21,111.8	22,821.0	26,745.2	30,257.7	35,790.4
1999	45,674.2	42,867.5	40,885.0	25,178.0	20,491.4	19,771.7	19,443.3	20,478.6	20,686.4	26,551.8	31,225.7	39,182.7
2000	44,302.7	44,854.6	32,556.5	26,536.6	23,096.5	21,336.7	18,980.8	23,288.6	25,079.8	28,444.4	32,517.4	45,990.5
2001	53,025.9	47,172.5	41,607.6	31,383.8	22,890.0	20,873.6	20,666.7	21,538.4	22,254.6	26,139.6	29,756.8	34,409.8
2002	41,101.6	37,246.4	31,883.4	25,488.2	21,412.1	18,680.5	19,014.4	19,157.7	20,522.8	26,888.9	32,496.5	42,760.4
2003	48,363.6	44,799.6	35,392.1	27,697.4	20,906.8	18,965.7	18,912.4	19,226.8	22,797.1	26,763.4	26,669.6	37,965.0
2004	47,979.8	41,852.4	32,449.3	25,977.2	18,251.6	17,929.4	16,702.6	18,643.1	20,138.4	23,311.7	27,318.4	35,468.5
2005	38,673.1	37,556.4	33,096.5	21,996.3	19,922.3	18,032.3	15,622.7	18,866.3	19,670.4	20,815.7	25,978.4	34,780.1
2006	31,740.5	33,940.7	30,423.9	18,602.6	15,026.0	13,199.1	12,192.2	13,805.4	14,157.7	16,865.6	20,107.2	22,413.7
2007	28,370.3	35,872.9	26,326.4	18,745.5	12,724.6	9,494.8	8,344.7	8,942.9	8,861.3	10,809.0	17,532.6	24,448.1
2008	26,658.0	26,270.8	20,195.3	13,160.3	8,227.9	7,024.7	6,553.1	7,541.1	9,002.4	12,898.3	15,728.3	24,143.0
2009	29,853.1	25,136.2	19,550.3	12,196.2	7,314.3	6,297.5	5,262.4	5,057.2	7,518.7	10,975.7	11,797.9	20,549.5
2010	24,449.1	23,328.9	13,491.6	6,992.0	5,325.0	4,545.6	3,314.7	4,381.5	5,529.0	8,588.5		

FIGURE 1.11 U.S. Fuel Oil Sales from 1983 to 2010

CONVERTING EXCEL DATA INTO A USABLE ACCESS FORMAT

Data tables that are developed in Excel usually do not follow the rules and logic of database tables. These Excel tables need to be "converted" to a usable Access format. Quite often these Access conversions need to be performed on data downloaded from statistical agencies. An example of such a table is the Fuel Oil table of the EIA shown in Figure 1.11. This data was copied from the U.S. Energy Information Administration's website (www.eia.gov) by clicking through to *Petroleum→Prime Supplier Sales Volumes→No. 2 Fuel Oil* (1983–2010).

The fuel oil data in Figure 1.11 is accumulated row by row. As time progresses, more rows are added to the bottom of the table. In other Excel worksheets columns could be added to the right of the table as time progresses. This data was imported into Excel using the *Copy* and *Paste* commands. A portion of the Excel file is shown in Figure 1.12.

This data needs some preparatory steps because Access cannot work with time-related data when the time period is indicated in the field's name (e.g., Jan, Feb, or Mar).

	A	B	C	D	E	F	G	H	I	J	K	L	M
1	Year	Jan	Feb	Mar	Apr	May	Jun	Jul	Aug	Sep	Oct	Nov	Dec
2	1983	65,251.40	63,848.00	62,375.40	53,049.00	36,302.80	40,598.80	35,802.60	41,119.80	38,150.20	41,636.80	54,958.20	78,119.20
3	1984	88,893.70	66,567.90	74,816.90	54,803.40	48,251.70	40,018.00	40,495.90	45,299.10	47,100.20	46,981.70	61,917.70	74,286.60
4													
5	1985	87,392.10	77,660.00	67,731.40	55,829.40	45,673.80	40,889.30	41,082.00	44,985.20	45,262.70	54,954.80	58,369.50	80,912.00
6	1986	72,150.20	80,349.80	64,523.40	51,892.40	47,643.80	40,559.10	40,221.20	47,773.90	46,787.60	55,272.20	58,240.20	74,448.90
7	1987	78,148.00	73,292.20	65,579.30	52,600.10	46,028.20	43,426.80	44,110.60	41,079.70	47,423.70	60,538.50	62,190.70	78,371.50
8	1988	90,618.30	89,824.40	77,098.30	56,688.90	50,735.30	47,457.90	48,687.80	50,874.40	50,453.20	61,333.00	67,826.80	82,290.20
9	1989	79,098.60	79,580.90	75,144.40	55,264.50	46,260.30	45,547.30	39,889.00	50,778.40	50,742.50	56,433.00	64,378.70	92,250.90
10													
11	1990	74,256.80	73,752.30	63,254.80	55,571.50	49,431.40	49,050.20	46,314.10	54,196.00	53,803.80	54,397.20	60,710.90	64,933.70
12	1991	81,366.50	68,472.40	60,802.50	53,574.60	46,538.50	42,699.60	43,889.80	46,724.40	46,882.30	53,013.50	55,807.40	68,245.10
13	1992	78,609.00	70,094.20	64,700.20	57,430.50	46,793.00	46,859.40	43,287.00	44,860.20	52,209.50	56,162.90	59,294.20	72,803.00
14	1993	62,959.10	69,927.90	65,619.90	49,032.00	38,744.90	41,405.40	38,368.40	40,131.10	41,414.20	32,073.20	38,875.90	51,627.70
15	1994	68,199.70	62,191.50	49,804.40	32,960.30	27,444.20	26,009.70	22,623.70	27,619.00	30,391.20	32,976.00	34,185.70	45,932.50
16													
17	1995	47,443.40	54,852.40	41,434.20	31,347.50	26,195.30	24,322.20	21,676.00	24,859.50	26,625.00	29,076.70	38,986.20	53,054.90
18	1996	57,988.50	55,685.00	42,789.10	33,643.20	25,651.80	23,238.70	22,987.00	24,188.80	27,810.40	31,993.50	38,958.10	44,723.20

FIGURE 1.12 Fuel Oil Data in an Excel Worksheet

Many types of Excel layouts exist and they all need to be converted to an Access-friendly format. The blank rows can be deleted by highlighting the blank rows one at a time and then deleting the row because we only have six blank rows. Another option would be to sort the Excel table so that all the blanks are at the top of the table and then to delete the blank rows. You might need to copy the smaller table to a new Excel worksheet before importing this into Excel. This is because Excel seems to remember that the original table had (say) 35 rows and when it is imported into Access then Access imports 35 rows, even though the last six rows are blank. The Access table is shown in Figure 1.13.

Figure 1.13 shows the Access table with the Excel fuel oil data. The first step is to use Design View to change the name of the field *Year* to *YearTxt* (for year text). This is because the new table will have a field called *Year* with *Year* being a numeric field. The name change is shown in Figure 1.14.

The field name is changed to *YearTxt* in Design View in Figure 1.14. The table can now be converted to an Access format. The next step is to convert the numeric values to

ID	Year	Jan	Feb	Mar	Apr	May	Jun	Jul	Aug	Sep	Oct	Nov	Dec
1	1983	65,251.40	63,848.00	62,375.40	53,049.00	36,302.80	40,598.80	35,802.60	41,119.80	38,150.20	41,636.80	54,958.20	78,119.20
2	1984	88,893.70	66,567.90	74,816.90	54,803.40	48,251.70	40,018.00	40,495.90	45,299.10	47,100.20	46,981.70	61,917.70	74,286.60
3	1985	87,392.10	77,660.00	67,731.40	55,829.40	45,673.80	40,889.30	41,082.00	44,985.20	45,262.70	54,954.80	58,369.50	80,912.00
4	1986	72,150.20	80,349.80	64,523.40	51,892.40	47,643.80	40,559.10	40,221.20	47,773.90	46,787.60	55,272.20	58,240.20	74,448.90
5	1987	78,148.00	73,292.20	65,579.30	52,600.10	46,028.20	43,426.80	44,110.60	41,079.70	47,423.70	60,538.50	62,190.70	78,371.50
6	1988	90,618.30	89,824.40	77,098.30	56,688.90	50,735.30	47,457.90	48,687.80	50,874.40	50,453.20	61,333.00	67,826.80	82,290.20
7	1989	79,098.60	79,580.90	75,144.40	55,264.50	46,260.30	45,547.30	39,889.00	50,778.40	50,742.50	56,433.00	64,378.70	92,250.90
8	1990	74,256.80	73,752.30	63,254.80	55,571.50	49,431.40	49,050.20	46,314.10	54,196.00	53,803.80	54,397.20	60,710.90	64,933.70
9	1991	81,366.50	68,472.40	60,802.50	53,574.60	46,538.50	42,699.60	43,889.80	46,724.40	46,882.30	53,013.50	55,807.40	68,245.10
10	1992	78,609.00	70,094.20	64,700.20	57,430.50	46,793.00	46,859.40	43,287.00	44,860.20	52,209.50	56,162.90	59,294.20	72,803.00
11	1993	62,959.10	69,927.90	65,619.90	49,032.00	38,744.90	41,405.40	38,368.40	40,131.10	41,414.20	32,073.20	38,875.90	51,627.70
12	1994	68,199.70	62,191.50	49,804.40	32,960.30	27,444.20	26,009.70	22,623.70	27,619.00	30,391.20	32,976.00	34,185.70	45,932.50
13	1995	47,443.40	54,852.40	41,434.20	31,347.50	26,195.30	24,322.20	21,676.00	24,859.50	26,625.00	29,076.70	38,986.20	53,054.90
14	1996	57,988.50	55,685.00	42,789.10	33,643.20	25,651.80	23,238.70	22,987.00	24,188.80	27,810.40	31,993.50	38,958.10	44,723.20
15	1997	52,887.50	46,281.00	39,457.70	33,128.70	25,986.10	24,433.30	23,436.90	23,967.50	27,152.40	30,358.40	35,005.90	45,200.00

FIGURE 1.13 The Access Table with the Imported Excel Fuel Oil Data

OilSales	
Field Name	Data Type
ID	AutoNumber
YearTxt	Text
Jan	Number
Feb	Number
Mar	Number
Apr	Number
May	Number
Jun	Number
Jul	Number
Aug	Number
Sep	Number

FIGURE 1.14 Field Name Changed to *Yeartxt* in Design View

Currency. It is best to do this conversion at this early stage. The Currency conversions need to be done for each of the 12 numeric fields and the first conversion is shown in Figure 1.15.

This conversion needs to be done for all 12 numeric fields. The table needs to be saved before the changes take effect. Access gives a prompt that some accuracy might be lost with the currency format. When the table is viewed again in Datasheet View, the numbers will usually (but not always) be shown with leading dollar signs and negative numbers in parentheses. The currency format helps to prevent rounding errors in calculations.

OilSales	
Field Name	Data Type
YearTxt	Text
Jan	Currency
Feb	Number
Mar	Number
Apr	Number
May	Number
Jun	Number
Jul	Number
Aug	Number
Sep	Number
Oct	Number
Nov	Number
Dec	Number

General	Lookup	
Format	Standard	
Decimal Places	2	
Input Mask		

FIGURE 1.15 Conversion of the Field *Jan* to Currency with Two Decimal Places

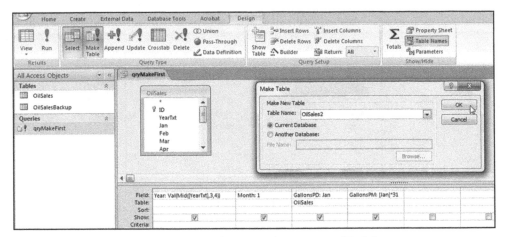

FIGURE 1.16 Make Table Query Used to Start the Process of Building a New Access Table

The next step is to create a table that will be the starting building block for our complete table. This is done with a Make Table query as is shown in Figure 1.16. The January data is used as a foundation to start the ball rolling. The new table is called *OilSales2*.

The conversion of a text field to a numeric value is sometimes tricky. In this case the *Year* field had two spaces to the left of the visible characters, which is not usually an issue with data formatted as text. The conversion to a numeric value required the use of the Val (value) and the Mid (middle) functions as shown below:

$$\text{Year}: \text{Val}(\text{Mid}([\text{YearTxt}], 3, 4))$$

The field *Month* was converted from *Jan* to the number *1*, which makes it easier to use in queries. The *GallonsPD* (gallons per day) field was formatted as currency using the field properties. The *GallonsPM* (gallons per month) field was automatically formatted as currency. The table is in gallons per day and the new table will include both the daily average and the monthly total. Even though **OK** is clicked in the dialog box in Figure 1.16, the query must still be run using **Design→Results→Run**. Access always gives a warning that you are about to paste *x* rows into a new table. This warning can be ignored if you are safely below the size limit of an Access database. Click **Yes** and the *OilSales2* table should be as is shown in Figure 1.17.

The next step is to Append the February data to this table and then to do the same for all the other months. The query to append February is shown in Figure 1.18.

The fields and data from *OilSales* are appended to *OilSales2*. The monthly total is a little complex because February sometimes has 28 days and sometimes the month has 29 days. The formula for *GallonsPM* is:

$$\text{GallonsPM}: \text{IIf}([\text{Year}] = 1984\,\text{Or}\,[\text{Year}] = 1988\,\text{Or}\,[\text{Year}]$$
$$= 1992\,\text{Or}\,[\text{Year}] = 1996\,\text{Or}\,[\text{Year}] = 2000\,\text{Or}\,[\text{Year}]$$
$$= 2004\,\text{Or}\,[\text{Year}] = 2008, [\text{Feb}]^*29, [\text{Feb}]^*28)$$

OilSales2

Year	Month	GallonsPD	GallonsPM
1983	1	$65,251.40	$2,022,793.40
1984	1	$88,893.70	$2,755,704.70
1985	1	$87,392.10	$2,709,155.10
1986	1	$72,150.20	$2,236,656.20
1987	1	$78,148.00	$2,422,588.00
1988	1	$90,618.30	$2,809,167.30
1989	1	$79,098.60	$2,452,056.60
1990	1	$74,256.80	$2,301,960.80
1991	1	$81,366.50	$2,522,361.50
1992	1	$78,609.00	$2,436,879.00
1993	1	$62,959.10	$1,951,732.10
1994	1	$68,199.70	$2,114,190.70
1995	1	$47,443.40	$1,470,745.40
1996	1	$57,988.50	$1,797,643.50
1997	1	$52,887.50	$1,639,512.50
1998	1	$43,253.50	$1,340,858.50
1999	1	$45,674.20	$1,415,900.20
2000	1	$44,302.70	$1,373,383.70
2001	1	$53,025.90	$1,643,802.90
2002	1	$41,101.60	$1,274,149.60
2003	1	$48,363.60	$1,499,271.60
2004	1	$47,979.80	$1,487,373.80
2005	1	$38,673.10	$1,198,866.10
2006	1	$31,740.50	$983,955.50
2007	1	$28,370.30	$879,479.30

Record: 1 of 28 No Filter Search

FIGURE 1.17   The First Table in the Creation of *OilSales2*

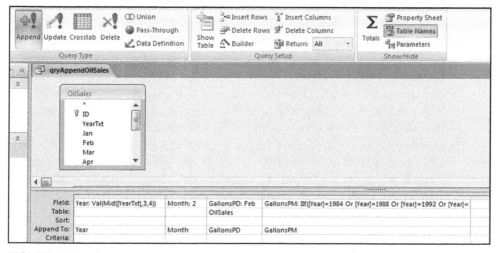

FIGURE 1.18   The Append Query Used to Build the *OilSales2* Table

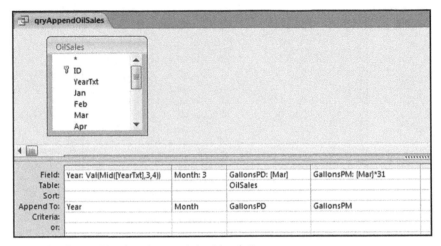

FIGURE 1.19 Query Used to Append the March Data

The formula uses the If function (IIf in Access for Immediate if) together with the Or function.

The query needs to be run using **Design→Results→Run**. Access gives a warning that you are about to append 28 rows. Once you have clicked **Yes**, the command cannot be undone. Run the query and click **Yes**. It is a good idea to make backup copies of your tables until you are quite familiar with the appending process. The query used for appending the March data is shown in Figure 1.19.

The Month is changed to "3" without any quotes, and the gallons per day and gallons per month formulas are also revised. The *GallonsPM* calculation for March is simply the gallons per day multiplied by 31. There is no leap year complication. This process is repeated for March through December. The final table is shown in Figure 1.20.

The record indicator at the bottom of the screen shows that there are 336 records in the table. This is correct because there are 28 years and 28*12 months equals 336 records. Access does not necessarily stack the tables one on top of the other in the order in which the append queries were run. One way to tidy up the table is to use another Make Table query to sort the data as you would like it to be sorted. It is good practice to check whether each month has been added just once. One or two queries can confirm this and the query in Figure 1.21 counts and sums the records for each month.

The query in Figure 1.21 tests whether there are 27 or 28 records per year and also whether the average of the numbers is logical. The results are shown in Figure 1.22.

The results of the query in Figure 1.22 confirm that the appending steps were done correctly. For each month there are either 27 or 28 records. September to December, 2010, did not have data at the time that the file was downloaded and the results show that months 9 to 12 have only 27 records. The average gallons per day has a seasonal pattern with high sales in the cold winter months (12, 1, 2, and 3 corresponding to December to March) and low sales in the summer months (5 to 8 corresponding to May to August). The table *OilSales2* can now be used for Access queries. This heating oil example is continued in Chapter 14 with the heating oil sales application.

Year	Month	GallonsPD	GallonsPM
1983	1	$65,251.40	$2,022,793.40
1984	1	$88,893.70	$2,755,704.70
1985	1	$87,392.10	$2,709,155.10
1986	1	$72,150.20	$2,236,656.20
1987	1	$78,148.00	$2,422,588.00
1988	1	$90,618.30	$2,809,167.30
1989	1	$79,098.60	$2,452,056.60
1990	1	$74,256.80	$2,301,960.80
1991	1	$81,366.50	$2,522,361.50
1992	1	$78,609.00	$2,436,879.00
1993	1	$62,959.10	$1,951,732.10
1994	1	$68,199.70	$2,114,190.70
1995	1	$47,443.40	$1,470,745.40
1996	1	$57,988.50	$1,797,643.50
1997	1	$52,887.50	$1,639,512.50
1998	1	$43,253.50	$1,340,858.50
1999	1	$45,674.20	$1,415,900.20
2000	1	$44,302.70	$1,373,383.70
2001	1	$53,025.90	$1,643,802.90
2002	1	$41,101.60	$1,274,149.60
2003	1	$48,363.60	$1,499,271.60
2004	1	$47,979.80	$1,487,373.80
2005	1	$38,673.10	$1,198,866.10
2006	1	$31,740.50	$983,955.50
2007	1	$28,370.30	$879,479.30

Record: I◄ ◄ 1 of 336 ► ►I ►⊞ 🚫 No Filter Search

FIGURE 1.20 Completed Heating Oil Table

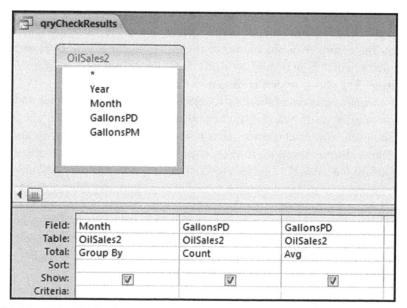

FIGURE 1.21 How to Check Whether the Append Queries Were Correctly Run

qryCheckResults		
Month ▾	CountOfGallonsPD ▾	AvgOfGallonsPD ▾
1	28	$56,739.58
2	28	$54,133.31
3	28	$46,832.27
4	28	$36,031.88
5	28	$29,494.13
6	28	$27,723.15
7	28	$26,431.48
8	28	$28,942.81
9	27	$31,322.94
10	27	$35,348.54
11	27	$40,410.84
12	27	$52,040.78

FIGURE 1.22 Results of the Query Designed to Test the Appending Operations

USING THE ACCESS DOCUMENTER

A forensic report is prepared after a forensic investigation is completed. This report should describe all the evidence gathered, the findings, conclusions, recommendations, and the corrective actions (if any) that were taken. The contents of this report should have a tone that is not inflammatory, libelous, or with prejudicial connotations. The report should include a description of the forensic analytics work that was done. The working papers should include a copy of the data analyzed on either a CD or a USB flash drive, and the results of the queries. A full description of the database should also be included in the report. A useful feature in Access is the **Database Documenter**. The database documenter is activated by using **Database Tools→Analyze→Database Documenter**. The dialog screen is shown in Figure 1.23.

For a complete documentation each object (in this case just Tables and Queries) needs to be selected using **Select All**. Click **OK** to run the documenter. The documentation is comprehensive and includes facts related to the database objects and the SQL code describing the queries. With the SQL code, the same query can be run on another computer using the same data table. The documenter also includes the time and date that the table was last updated giving a record of any changes to the table after a query was run. The Database Documenter does not meet the standards of absolute proof but it goes a long way to documenting and supporting a description of the tests that were run.

Another useful Access feature is the ability to describe tables and queries in the table and query properties. The **Table Properties** dialog box is activated by right clicking on the table names to give the dialog box shown in Figure 1.24.

The table description is entered using the Table Properties dialog box shown in Figure 1.24. The **Apply** and **OK** buttons are used after the description is typed. The fields can be described when the table is in Design View as is the case in Figures 1.14

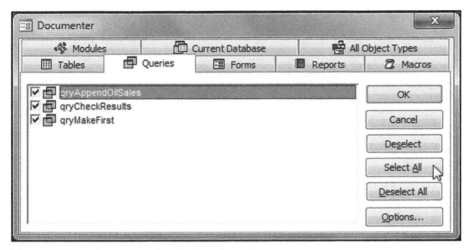

FIGURE 1.23 Dialog Screen for the *Database Documenter*

and 1.15. Access also allows for a complete description to be included for all queries. The **Query Properties** dialog box is activated using a right click on the query name and clicking **Object Properties**. An example is shown in Figure 1.25.

Access allows for a reasonably long description of each query using the Object Properties shown in Figure 1.25. The buttons **Apply** and **OK** are used to save the description. There is also a way to include a detailed description of the whole database using **Manage→Database Properties** as is shown in Figure 1.26.

The step to retrieve the database properties is shown in Figure 1.26. The details are shown across five tabs. A printout or an electronic jpg image of each of the tabs should be included in the working papers. The **Contents** tab is shown in Figure 1.27.

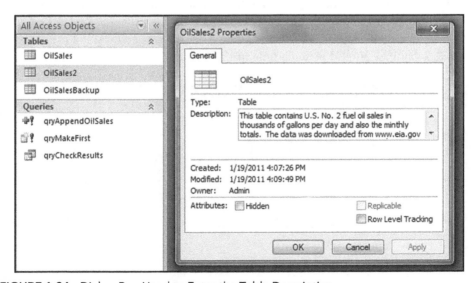

FIGURE 1.24 Dialog Box Used to Enter the Table Description

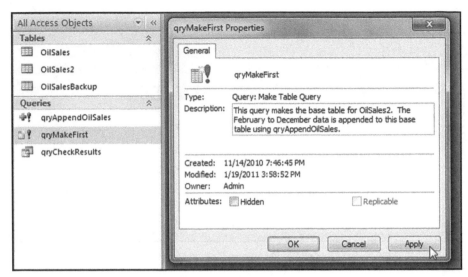

FIGURE 1.25   Dialog Box Used to Include a Description of a Query

The **Contents** tab lists the names of all the Access objects. The **Summary** tab is made up of details added by the forensic analyst. The database properties together with the documenter, the descriptions that can be included in the Design View of a table, and the tables and queries properties all make it easier for the analyst, or someone else, to understand the contents of the database. The table and query properties can be seen by expanding the details shown in the Navigation Pane. The procedure to see the properties is shown in Figure 1.28.

The procedure to view the object details is to right click on either the Tables or the Queries heading and then select **View By→Details**. The details will then be visible in the Navigation Pane. To return to the names only one would select **List**. The documentation options are valuable and allow other users to understand the contents when the database is used at some time in the future.

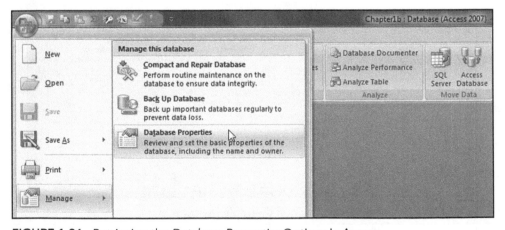

FIGURE 1.26   Retrieving the *Database Properties* Options in Access

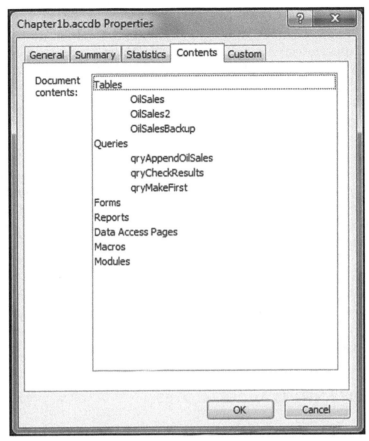

FIGURE 1.27   Database Properties Documentation Feature of Access

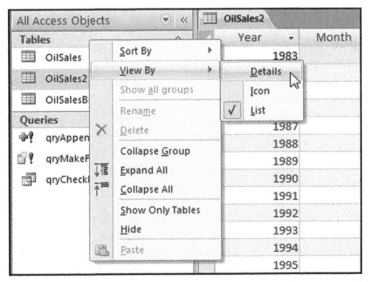

FIGURE 1.28   How to View the Access Object Details Instead of Just a List of the Objects

DATABASE LIMIT OF 2 GB

Access databases are limited to 2 gigabytes (2 GB). This limit applies to the database size when the database is saved and also while the database is being used. Assume that a database has one main table and the file size is 1.8 gigabytes. A query that selects most of the records would then double the size of the database to 3.6 gigabytes (the original table plus the query that selects most of the records). Access will not execute this query. The "size exceeded" error messages that Access displays do not clearly say "you have exceeded the Access maximum database size." The user is simply supposed to realize why the query is not executing properly. There is a solution to the 2 GB limit in that the data can be housed in multiple databases (each say one gigabyte in size) and the main Access database can then be linked to those tables. Linked tables do not add to the size of a database. Users still have to be aware that if one links to two 1.5 GB tables and then runs two queries that each selects most of the records in each table, then the second of those two queries will not run if the first query is still open.

There are a few more solutions to the database size limit. In a forensic investigations project the database size can be kept down by deleting fields that are not needed. Deleting text fields is a big help with reducing the size of the database. Another option is to upgrade to a data analysis software program and IDEA (www.caseware.com) works well in an environment with large data sets.

 MISCELLANEOUS ACCESS NOTES

This section reviews some miscellaneous aspects of Access that are relevant to forensic analytics. The list is based on personal experience and users should refer to one of the many comprehensive books on Access and/or the Microsoft website for more details.

- It is normal to format the output of a query for presentation purposes by (say) displaying only the significant digits of numbers. In Access all formatting must be done before the query is run. After the query is run the only formatting step that can be taken is to export the results to Excel and to format the results in Excel.
- Keep field names and table names short. Long field and table names cause extra work if these are used in calculated fields in queries.
- If a wrong field specification (e.g., define a date field as numeric) is entered when importing data into Access, then this issue cannot be corrected after the table has been created.
- It is good practice to create a backup copy of a table that will be queried frequently. Changes (deletions) to a table cannot be reversed. Access does not allow an "exit without saving" option.
- If a table is sorted immediately after creating the table then this sort is a "built-in" query that will run each time that the table is opened. This action can be undone.
- Dollar amounts should not be formatted as Double. The Currency data type should be used instead.

- It is a good practice to include a Primary key in tables. This optimizes computer performance for queries. The ***Database Tools→Analyze→Analyze Performance*** tool provides performance and other suggestions.
- To end a query that seems to have Access going in a loop use ***Control + Break***.
- Access has a password encryption feature. The tool is accessed through ***Database Tools→Database Tools→Encrypt with Password***. This tool is good enough to keep unsophisticated hackers at bay, but a determined tech-smart person could still work around the password.
- Including a switchboard with an application makes it look professional to another user and will allow users to create reports and to run queries with a single click. It is a good idea to practice creating a switchboard on a simple database with one or two tables and just a few queries. The Switchboard Manager helps with the process and it is accessed through ***Database Tools→Database Tools→Switchboard Manager***.

Access has many Access Options. It is a good idea to use the "Compact on Close" option. This saves hard drive space and helps with the 2 GB limit. With large databases the Compact on Close procedure might take a few minutes.

 ## SUMMARY

The chapter introduces Microsoft Access 2007 (Access) as a capable forensic analytics tool. Access is a Windows-based database program that keeps the tables, queries, and reports neatly compartmentalized. Access requires data to be housed in tables, calculations to be run as queries, and results to be shown in reports. Microsoft has a website for Access 2007, which contains excellent reference materials.

The usual forensic analytics starting point is to import the data into Access and to store it in a table. Tables are made up of fields, with each field storing one type of data for all the records. Records relate to one instance of a table subject, such as a book in a library's collection of books. Field values are a single number, date, or text value relating to a record. A table with eight fields and 1,000 records would have 8,000 field values. The data import procedure is usually quite straightforward especially if the data is being imported from an Excel file or from another Access database.

Queries are the workhorses used in forensic analytics. Queries are used to perform calculations or to select records with specific attributes (e.g., all the transactions for vendor #2204). Queries are also used to append tables to each other, to create tables, to delete data, and to update the data in tables. Queries are also used to group data and to run calculations on the groups (e.g., sums and averages). Queries can also be used to identify duplicate or near-duplicate records.

It is usually necessary to do some data cleansing and some data reorganizing work on data downloaded from the Internet. This is because the way that data is accumulated in Excel worksheets does not work well in an Access database. This chapter shows how to use a series of append queries to create an Access table that is compatible with the required attributes of a table and the logic of Access queries.

The chapter reviews the need for adequate documentation in a forensic analytics setting, and Access has tools available for this purpose. The Database Documenter creates a complete record of the contents of the database. Access also allows forensic investigators to fully describe tables, queries, and reports in the database documentation. There is also a way to describe in detail each field in an Access table. Access also allows users to document the database at a high level in the Database Properties section. Documentation is important so that someone can understand the contents and queries in a database months or years down the road. The chapter concludes with notes related to formatting, field names, data-type specifications, passwords, and switchboards.

CHAPTER TWO

Using Excel in Forensic Investigations

T HIS CHAPTER REVIEWS THE features of Excel 2007 (Excel) that make it an especially useful tool for forensic analytics. Excel is a software program that allows us to populate a rectangular grid called a worksheet with numbers, text, and images. Excel 2007 uses the new ribbon interface. Excel can perform many tasks and most users probably use less than 20 percent of the program's functionality. Even a forensic analytics project only requires some small part of all the capabilities of the program. Some of the main tasks that will be done with Excel in a forensic analytics environment are:

- Importing and accessing data from sources such as Access databases and government and corporate websites.
- Storing data in an easily retrievable format.
- Performing calculations related to the forensic analytic tests described in the later chapters.
- Grouping data and calculating statistics (such as sums or counts) on a per-group basis.
- Creating graphs that give insights into forensic matters.
- Interfacing seamlessly with Word and PowerPoint.

This chapter reviews some features that are useful in a forensic analytics context. These features include data import, worksheet formatting, protecting the worksheet's contents, and using Excel results in a Word document or a PowerPoint presentation. The formulas and techniques used to run the tests are described (with screenshots) in Chapters 4 through 17. The next section describes some pitfalls in using Excel.

PITFALLS IN USING EXCEL

The fact that Excel has several hundred million users supports the belief that Excel is an excellent product. In many cases Excel has been made to do a task that it was clearly not designed to do. One federal government agency used Excel to prepare a template for a purchasing order. Even though Excel is widely used, there are issues that we need to be aware of from a forensic analytics perspective. The start of the discussion is a review of the four major phases in a data-driven forensic investigation. The four main steps are:

1. **Data collection.** In this phase the relevant data are obtained (sometimes with difficulty from overprotective human resources or marketing departments), imported into Access or Excel, and stored. Obtaining data is often challenging and from time to time internal auditors and forensic auditors are faced with departmental managers using every stalling trick at their disposal.

2. **Data preparation.** This is where the data cleansing or data scrubbing takes place. This involves the detection and correction (or removal) of corrupt or inaccurate records from the data tables. The step identifies incomplete, incorrect, inaccurate, or irrelevant parts of the data and the replacement, modification, or deletion of some or all of the data. This step is usually done before data is sent to a data warehouse. An example of data cleansing is shown in the pollution statistics example in Chapter 13 where (a) subtotals were removed, as is commonly needed with government data, (b) countries with zero or very low emissions were removed because they were not really relevant to the research question (this step actually deleted about two-thirds of the countries in the table), (c) some geographic changes were made to keep the data consistent despite changes in national borders (e.g., by adding East and West Germany for 1988 and 1989 and naming the country "Germany"), (d) the data was put in a relational database table format as is shown in Chapter 1.

3. **Data analysis.** In this step the tests outlined in Chapters 4 through 18 are applied. The tests are designed to identify outlier records that stand out from the crowd in some way. These tests also involve various types of summaries, calculations, groupings, and comparisons.

4. **Reporting.** In the final phase the results of the analysis are reported to a select audience. The results could include tables, graphs, charts, and selected records. In a forensic setting, care needs to be taken to allow only the level of visibility that is appropriate for the audience and to prevent the audience from changing the contents of the reports.

Figure 2.1 shows a complex marketing spreadsheet prepared at a pharmaceutical company. The 42 MB Excel spreadsheet has four worksheets with thousands of rows and columns of data. The final results are shown on the worksheet that is currently visible.

A complex 42 MB Excel spreadsheet is shown in Figure 2.1. The spreadsheet used complex formulas including multiple IF statements combined with the AND function, Excel's graphing capabilities, totals and subtotals, grouping, pivot tables, and conditional

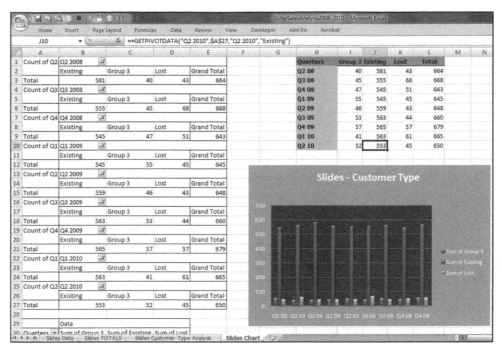

FIGURE 2.1 The Final Report of a Marketing Analysis Performed at a Pharmaceutical Company

formatting were among the functions used. This was an excellent piece of work but some issues need to be raised with respect to using Excel as the main tool in any complex application.

Excel is now limited to 1,048,576 rows and 16,384 columns. The rows and column limits are 2^{20} and 2^{14} for anyone who might be interested in the basis of the numbers. Although this might at first seem like all the rows and columns that anyone would ever need, it does present a scalability problem in some cases. Large data tables related to earth science data easily exceed 1 million records. Also, for data tables where the transactional amounts are small (e.g., coupon redemptions for a large consumer goods company) the number of records could easily exceed 10 million. Excel has size limitations and for applications that are likely to exceed this limit, it is best to start the forensic analytics project in Access or IDEA (see www.caseware.com). Even though all the rows and columns exist, it does not mean that they can all actually be used in the same project. The "Not Enough Memory" message will be displayed long before the data fills all of the 1 million rows and 16,000 columns. The memory limit for Excel is 2 GB. This memory limit is for all of Excel and so with two large Excel files open, a third (smaller) file might not function because of the combined resources exceeding the 2 GB limit.

Excel users generally love the flexibility of the program. The cells in Figure 2.1 contain labels, data, calculated fields, and a graph. An Excel worksheet can also include text and images and almost anything else that can make it into the clipboard. The other worksheets in Figure 2.1 include named ranges, complex IF formulas, pivot tables, filters, and Excel's grouping capabilities. The final result is a complicated system of dependent calculations, linked cells, hidden ranges, and conditional formatting that link together to form the final product. This complicated system has the drawback that there is no transparency of analytical processes. It is extremely difficult for someone else (or even the spreadsheet creator) to know what is actually happening in the spreadsheet. Auditing such a spreadsheet is extremely difficult and recent years have seen the introduction of the term *spreadsheet risk* to describe the risk of faulty decisions being made on the basis of errors that have crept into spreadsheets. Programs such as Access, SQL Server, and IDEA improve transparency by having tables, queries, and reports clearly separated. Those programs also have comprehensive documentation capabilities for the database objects.

Linked to the transparency issue is the fact that Excel mixes up the data and the results of the analysis. If the cursor was not in cell J10 and the formula was not visible in the formula bar, we would have no way of knowing whether the "553" was a data field value or the result of a calculation. As it stands, cell J10 is a formula that displays the "553" result. Access keeps tables, queries, and reports separate and we always know whether we are looking at data or the results of calculations.

Finally, as processes become more complex and more users want more information from the same Excel tool, it is inevitable that users will try to upgrade the spreadsheets to do just one more task. This will involve more creativity and even more complexity and more results will become interrelated adding to spreadsheet risk. Access allows users to add more tables, queries, and reports in a systematic way without disturbing the current calculations and relationships. Access databases can more easily accommodate additions and changes precisely because of the separation of tables, queries, and reports, and the required format of the database of tables.

One final situation where Access comes out ahead of Excel is that Access can support multiple users. It is quite unremarkable to see two librarians in a library each checking out and checking in books and logged on to exactly the same system. Excel was not designed with collaborative updating in mind. Admittedly though, collaborative updating is not really an issue in forensic analytics.

IMPORTING DATA INTO EXCEL

The normal situation in a forensic analytics environment is that transactional data is imported into Excel. This is generally an easy matter using the ***Data→Get External Data*** series of steps. Some caveats should be mentioned and the first of these is that the data set should be complete. It is a serious flaw in any analysis to be working with incomplete data. Forensic investigators should be especially wary of Excel data tables with exactly 16,284 or 65,536 rows. An example of this is shown in Figure 2.2.

A purchasing card data table with exactly 16,384 records is shown in Figure 2.2. Chapter 18 includes a case study of an analysis of purchasing card data. A data set with exactly 16,384 or 65,536 records occurs when the source system exports the data in an

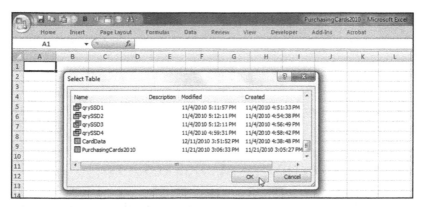

	A	B	C	D
16364		Q03	10.65	10/29/08
16365			11.07	10/31/08
16366			305.30	09/09/08
16367			25.71	09/25/08
16368		R	168.17	09/29/08
16369			243.04	09/30/08
16370		AB#	13.85	10/02/08
16371		GN	62.56	10/02/08
16372		AB#	51.58	10/03/08
16373			8.87	10/06/08
16374		S	289.48	10/07/08
16375			22.80	10/10/08
16376		AB#	28.32	10/14/08
16377			22.80	10/16/08
16378			165.90	10/16/08
16379		GN	121.32	11/03/08
16380			78.98	11/07/08
16381			32.23	11/07/08
16382		TH	1500.00	11/10/08
16383		TH	1201.47	11/17/08
16384			8.27	11/20/08
16385				
16386				
16387				
16388				

FIGURE 2.2 An Example of a Data Table with Exactly 16,384 Records

Excel format and that system is programmed to keep to either 16,384 or 65,536 records because that is what it thinks is the row limitation for Excel files. This limitation also occurs when the **Copy** and **Paste** sequence is used to copy from Access to Excel.

There are two solutions to the row-limitation problem. The first solution to the 16,384/65,536 problem is to have the source system download the data as a text file. The fields can be comma delimited (a .csv file) as long as none of the field values actually include commas (e.g., Boggs International, Inc.). If the field values do include commas, then tab delimited or fixed width should work fine. The second solution to the 16,384/65,536 problem is to import the data into Excel from Access as opposed to using a **Copy** and **Paste** to copy the data from Access and to paste it into Excel. This is done by using **Data→Get External Data→From Access**.

Figure 2.3 shows the step where a specific table is selected in the Access database. This process imports the Access data from Access into Excel. This process will import all the records that can fit into an Excel file (maximum of 1,048,576 rows). The data import

FIGURE 2.3 Importing Data into Excel from Access

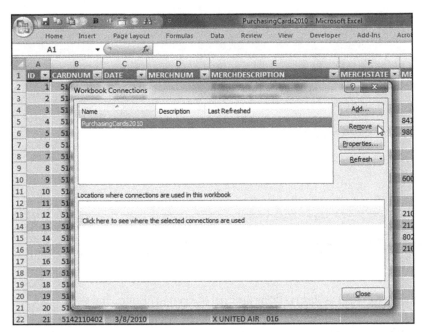

FIGURE 2.4 Removing the Connection to the Original Access Database

step also formats the data as an Excel table. Two further steps are needed in a forensic analytics environment. First, the data needs to be "disconnected" from the Access source so that the Excel file is independent of the Access source.

The step to remove the connection with the original database is shown in Figure 2.4. The sequence is **Data→Connections→Connections** followed by clicking the **Remove** button. Excel will give a warning and the step is finished with **OK** (to acknowledge the warning) and **Close**. While the table format is pleasing to the eye, it does create some issues for calculated fields. The last field in this table is column I and any simple formula in column J (e.g., **J2:** =I2*2) becomes

$$= \text{Table\_PurchasingCards2010.accdb}[[\#\text{This Row}], [\text{AMOUNT}]]^*2$$

even though the formula "I2*2" was entered in **J2**. It is easier to work with the data when it is not in this table format. The steps to undo the table format starts by selecting any cell in the table (e.g., **A2**) and then using a right click and the steps shown in Figure 2.5.

The procedure used to convert an Excel table to a normal range is shown in Figure 2.5. The commands are **Table→Convert to Range**. If a formula such as "I2*2" is now entered into cell **J2,** the formula will not be changed in any way.

REPORTING FORENSIC ANALYTICS RESULTS

Excel has several ways in which a worksheet can be formatted so as to help an analysis in a forensic environment. The EIA Fuel Oil data in Figure 1.12 will be used despite the

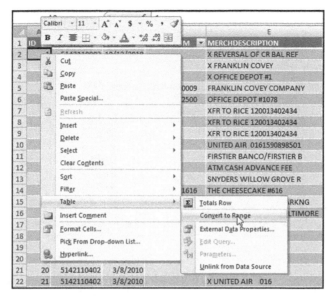

FIGURE 2.5 Procedure Used to Convert a Table Back to a Normal Range

format of the data. A calculated field will be added in column N that gives the average for the year. A quick way to copy a formula to the last row is to position the cursor at the bottom right corner of a cell so that the cursor changes to a cross. With a quick double-click on the left mouse button the formula will be copied to the last row. A screen shot of this is shown in Figure 2.6.

A series of two quick left double-clicks on the cross in Figure 2.6 will copy the formula to the last row. In this special case though we need to manually scroll to row 29 and copy the formula down for one more row. This is because cell M29 is blank because we do not yet have the data for December 2010. Excel has a host of conditional

	N2			*fx*	=AVERAGE(B2:M2)									
	A	B	C	D	E	F	G	H	I	J	K	L	M	N	O
1	Year	Jan	Feb	Mar	Apr	May	Jun	Jul	Aug	Sep	Oct	Nov	Dec	Average	
2	1983	65,251.40	63,848.00	62,375.40	53,049.00	36,302.80	40,598.80	35,802.60	41,119.80	38,150.20	41,636.80	54,958.20	78,119.20	50,934.35	
3	1984	88,893.70	66,567.90	74,816.90	54,803.40	48,251.70	40,018.00	40,495.90	45,299.10	47,100.20	46,981.70	61,917.70	74,286.60		
4	1985	87,392.10	77,660.00	67,731.40	55,829.40	45,673.80	40,889.30	41,082.00	44,985.20	45,262.70	54,954.80	58,369.50	80,912.00		
5	1986	72,150.20	80,349.80	64,523.40	51,892.40	47,643.80	40,559.10	40,221.20	47,773.90	46,787.60	55,272.20	58,240.20	74,448.90		
6	1987	78,148.00	73,292.20	65,579.30	52,600.10	46,028.20	43,426.80	44,110.60	41,079.70	47,423.70	60,538.50	62,190.70	78,371.50		
7	1988	90,618.30	89,824.40	77,098.30	56,688.90	50,735.30	47,457.90	48,687.80	50,874.40	50,453.20	61,333.00	67,826.80	82,290.20		
8	1989	79,098.60	79,580.90	75,144.40	55,264.50	46,260.30	45,547.30	39,889.00	50,778.40	50,742.50	56,433.00	64,378.70	92,250.90		
9	1990	74,256.80	73,752.30	63,254.80	55,571.50	49,431.40	49,050.20	46,314.10	54,196.00	53,803.80	54,397.20	60,710.90	64,933.70		
10	1991	81,366.50	68,472.40	60,802.50	53,574.60	46,538.50	42,699.60	43,889.80	46,724.40	46,882.30	53,013.50	55,807.40	68,245.10		
11	1992	78,609.00	70,094.20	64,700.20	57,430.50	46,793.00	46,859.40	43,287.00	44,860.20	52,209.50	56,162.90	59,294.20	72,803.00		
12	1993	62,959.10	69,927.90	65,619.90	49,032.00	38,744.90	41,405.40	38,368.40	40,131.10	41,414.20	32,073.20	38,875.90	51,627.70		
13	1994	68,199.70	62,191.50	49,804.40	32,960.30	27,444.20	26,009.70	22,623.70	27,619.00	30,391.20	32,976.00	34,185.70	45,932.50		
14	1995	47,443.40	54,852.40	41,434.20	31,347.50	26,195.30	24,322.20	21,676.00	24,859.50	26,625.00	29,076.70	38,986.20	53,054.90		
15	1996	57,988.50	55,685.00	42,789.10	33,643.20	25,651.80	23,238.70	22,987.00	24,188.80	27,810.40	31,993.50	38,958.10	44,723.20		
16	1997	52,887.50	46,281.00	39,457.70	33,128.70	25,986.10	24,433.30	23,436.90	23,967.50	27,152.40	30,358.40	35,005.90	45,200.00		
17	1998	43,253.50	42,453.90	38,313.80	28,122.40	22,565.90	23,580.90	22,198.40	21,111.80	22,821.00	26,745.20	30,257.70	35,790.40		
18	1999	45,674.20	42,867.50	40,885.00	25,178.00	20,491.40	19,771.70	19,444.30	20,478.60	20,686.40	26,551.80	31,225.70	39,182.70		
19	2000	44,302.70	44,854.60	32,556.50	26,536.60	23,096.50	21,336.70	18,980.80	23,288.60	25,079.80	28,444.40	32,517.40	45,990.50		
20	2001	53,025.90	47,172.50	41,607.60	31,383.80	22,890.00	20,873.60	20,666.70	21,538.40	22,254.60	26,139.60	29,756.80	34,409.80		

FIGURE 2.6 A Formula Is Copied Down to the Last Row Using a Left Double-Click on the Cross at the Corner of Cell N2

FIGURE 2.7 The Use of Data Bars to Visualize the Relative Sizes of the Averages

formatting options that can highlight interesting cells, emphasize unusual values, and visualize data using Data Bars, Color Scales, and Icon Sets using various criteria. Forensic analytics is about looking for interesting records and so highlighting unusual values with the formatting options is a useful tool in our toolbox. Excel's Data Bars can help us visualize the relative size of the averages.

Figure 2.7 shows the steps used to add Data Bars to a worksheet. The steps are *Home→Styles→Conditional Formatting→Data Bars* followed by selecting the Purple Data Bar. In the *More Rules* dialog box, Excel allows users to change the rules and the color schemes to suit almost any situation. Users should experiment with the conditional formatting rules and the color schemes. Users should also take into account whether the results will be included in a report that will be printed as black and white or as color. The Icon Sets have many different interesting cell formatting options.

Another useful Excel formatting option is the cell styles option where cells can be color coded according to their contents.

The selection of **Good-Bad-Neutral** cell styles is shown in Figure 2.8. Users would normally not color code an entire field as being *Bad* (or *Good* or *Neutral*) but the example is just an illustration. The **Data and Model** and the **Titles and Headings** styles allow users to prepare a worksheet with a professional and polished look to it with built-in visual guidance for users. The Excel formatting options are more than those available in Access. It might therefore be a good idea to sometimes import the Access results into Excel to use the special formatting.

PROTECTING EXCEL SPREADSHEETS

Maintaining confidentiality is especially important in a forensic analytics environment. Excel offers several protection options but none of these protections rivals Fort Knox and physical controls over the Excel file is just as important as the Excel-based protections.

FIGURE 2.8 The Cell Styles Options Available in Excel

The first protection option is to protect the Excel file itself. This is done with a password by clicking the ***Office*** button and then selecting ***Save As***. The next step is to select ***Tools→General Options*** at the bottom right section of the dialog box. Excel will then prompt for a password to open the file and a password to edit the file. In the example shown the password was made the same as the file name, but without the underscore.

Figure 2.9 shows the step used to access the dialog box used to create a password to open and to edit the file. If the file is saved and later reopened Excel calls for the password as is shown in Figure 2.10.

The opening dialog box for a password-protected Excel file is shown in Figure 2.10. Password-protected files can still be accessed by a determined and tech-savvy person and the password is only a good protection against most (but not all) people. Excel also has other levels of protection. These are activated through the ***Review*** group and examples include protecting the sheet (shown in Figure 2.11), protecting the workbook, and protecting and sharing the workbook.

The dialog box for protecting the worksheet is shown in Figure 2.11. These protections can be circumvented by a determined and tech-savvy user. One other simple method of hiding sensitive data is to simply ***Hide*** either the worksheet or selected rows or columns. This is done through the ***Home→Cells→Format→Hide & Unhide***. The command to hide a sheet is shown in Figure 2.12.

The command to hide rows, columns, or the entire worksheet is shown in Figure 2.12. These hidden sheets can easily be viewed again by using ***Home→Cells→Format*** and

FIGURE 2.9   The Step to the Dialog Box Used to Create a Password

then selecting the ***Unhide*** options. Although Excel does offer some security measures it is more important to control access to your confidential files.

 ## USING EXCEL RESULTS IN WORD FILES

Forensic work done in Excel will probably be included in a forensic report. Examples of this work could include a net-worth analysis, listings of fraudulent transactions, and graphs showing average prices paid or comparisons with other employees. The forensic

FIGURE 2.10   The Opening Dialog Box for a Password Protected Excel File

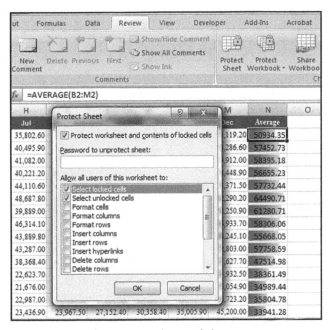

FIGURE 2.11   Dialog Box Used to Protect the Worksheet

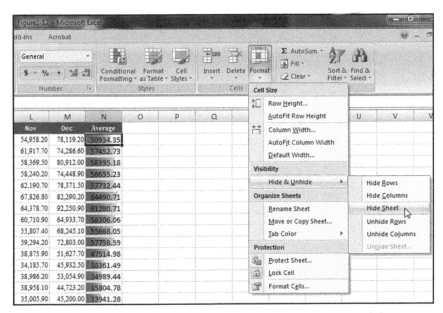

FIGURE 2.12   The Command to Hide Rows, Columns, or the Entire Worksheet

report should include all findings, conclusions, recommendations, and corrective actions taken. As an example, the headings after the title page could include:

- Background
- Executive Summary
- Scope
- Approach
- Findings
- Summary
- Financial Impact of the Fraud
- Recommendations
- End of Report
- Exhibits

Work done in Excel could be included in the Findings section and/or the Exhibits. Excel results can be sent to Word documents reasonably easily. The first step is to select the range that you would like to copy. As an example, the range could be **A1:M29** in the fuel oil worksheet. The procedure would be to click ***Home→Clipboard→Copy***. The next step would be to return to the Word document and to place the cursor where the table should be pasted. The paste command in Word is ***Home→Clipboard→Paste*** and ***Paste Special*** for the dialog box shown in Figure 2.13.

The dialog box used to paste an Excel table into a Word document is shown in Figure 2.13. The **Paste link** and **Microsoft Office Excel Worksheet Object** options are chosen. With this configuration all changes in the original Excel file are copied to the Excel table in the Word document. This could be useful when the data for September, October, November, and December become available. An update to the Excel file will be

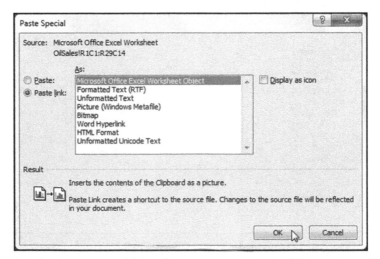

FIGURE 2.13   The Options Available When Pasting an Excel Table into a Word Document

immediately reflected in the Word file. To paste the table without having the updating option the selection would be:

- **Paste** (the radio button above **Paste link**)
- **Microsoft Office Excel Worksheet Object**

In addition to adding Excel tables to a Word document, the forensic report might require that an Excel graph (or chart) be embedded in the Word document. In this example an Excel chart of monthly purchasing card activity for a federal government agency (from Chapter 18) will be embedded into a Word document. The chart should be selected in Excel. The **Copy** command in Excel is activated using **Home→Clipboard→ Copy**. After switching to Word, the **Home→Clipboard→Paste→Paste Special** sequence is used to show the dialog box shown in Figure 2.14.

The dialog box used for embedding an Excel chart is shown in Figure 2.14. The options that should be chosen are:

- **Paste**
- **Microsoft Office Excel Chart Object**

After selecting the above options the next step is to click **OK**. The result is shown in Figure 2.15.

An Excel chart embedded in a Word document is shown in Figure 2.15. This chart can be updated from within Word by double-clicking the embedded chart in the Word document, and then clicking anywhere within the chart. A hatch-marked border will appear around the chart, and the embedded object will appear in an Excel workbook window. The object can now be edited by using the Excel chart-editing tools in Word. The editing process is ended by clicking outside the chart, anywhere in the Word document.

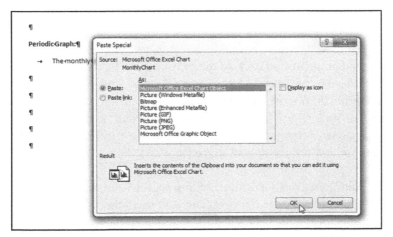

FIGURE 2.14 Dialog Box for Embedding an Excel Chart into a Word Document

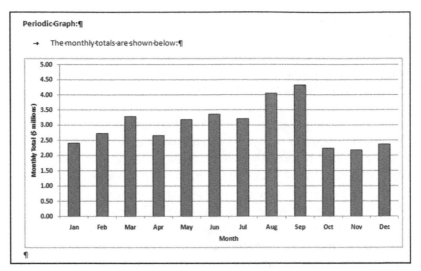

FIGURE 2.15 Excel Chart Embedded in a Word Document

If a Word document contains a table from an Excel file that is password protected then the password needs to be entered when the Word document is opened. If the password is not entered, then Word will not update the Excel table.

 EXCEL WARNINGS AND INDICATORS

During the course of a forensic analytics project users are almost sure to create a little green triangle in the top left corner of a cell. In the example shown (the source data for the chart in Figure 2.15), the "error" is an inconsistent formula. In each case column E equals column B, except for cell E9 where the formula is B9 minus 3102000. The adjustment was made because there was a large purchase in June in Mexican Pesos and this outlier amount was removed in the graph. In many cases the "error" will be something such as an inconsistent formula or the fact that "adjacent cells are ignored." The step to remove this minor eyesore is to select the down arrow to the right of the yellow exclamation point and click **Ignore Error** as is shown in Figure 2.16.

The procedure to remove the little green triangle in the top left corner of a cell is shown in Figure 2.16. The **Ignore Error** selection should not be made before considering whether there might be a real problem with a formula requiring perhaps an analysis of the precedents and dependents. Excel has an excellent formula auditing routine and an example of precedents and dependents for cell **J3** is shown in Figure 2.17.

Some results from Excel's formula auditing routines are shown in Figure 2.17. The formula auditing routines have many options and users should experiment a little with the available options. It is important in any forensic analytics project to correctly resolve all Excel's error messages. Any flaws in the analytics work could be exploited by defense counsel at a later stage.

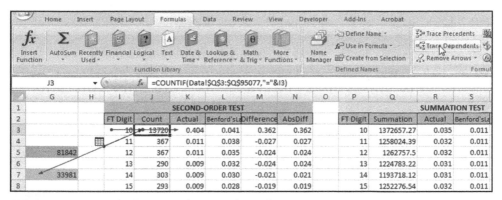

FIGURE 2.16 How to Remove the Green Triangle in the Top Left Corner of a Cell

FIGURE 2.17 Results from Excel's Formula Auditing Routines

 SUMMARY

Forensic analytics is the procurement and analysis of electronic data to reconstruct or detect fraud, errors, or biases. The main steps in forensic analytics are (a) data collection, (b) data preparation, (c) data analysis, and (d) reporting. Excel works well for the collection, preparation, and analysis steps. There are some caveats and these relate to (a) limitations on the number of records, (b) the lack of transparency between data, formulas, and the results of formulas, (c) the difficulty in adding more functions and reports to an existing application, and (d) the ability to use Excel in multi-user environments. Despite these caveats, Excel is still a favorite among accounting and auditing professionals. This chapter reviews some of the features of Excel that are relevant in a forensic investigations environment.

Importing data into Excel is usually not a problem. An issue can arise when the source system limits the output to either 16,384 or 65,536 records. Excel can import data seamlessly from Access and a host of other database programs. For data imported from Access it is best to remove the connection to Access (so that the Excel file does not update when the Access tables are changed) and also to convert the Excel table to a normal range.

Excel has many data-formatting options that help in interpreting and visualizing the data. Data bars resembling a very small graph can shade the cells allowing users to interpret the relative sizes without actually reading the numbers. Excel offers other cell styles such as *good*, *bad*, and *neutral* and other formatting options that might be useful in a forensic context.

Excel has some data-protection options. The first protection option is to password-protect the Excel file. A second level of protection is another password to write or change any cell contents in the workbook. Other levels of protection include the ability to hide rows or columns, or even the entire worksheet. Cells can also be protected with read-only privileges. Although the password protections are useful against an average Excel user they can be circumvented by a determined and tech-savvy person.

The results of tests and techniques performed in Excel are often included in forensic reports prepared in Word. These results could be extracts from Excel files and graphs and charts. Excel content can be easily copied over to Word documents and several copying options are available. The Excel data can be linked to the Word document, in which case the Word document is updated (changed) when the source data is changed. The Excel data can also be copied and pasted, in which case the Word document stays unchanged even when the source file is changed. Graphs and charts can also be copied from Excel to Word.

Excel has some built-in warnings related to formulas. Excel also gives users several ways to examine the precedents and dependents of formulas to uncover errors and other issues.

Despite the reservations related to having data, formulas, the results of formulas, and text and images all potentially on the same worksheet, Excel is a valuable tool for forensic analytics. Accountants and auditors are familiar with the tool and files can be sent to and received from other people with few, if any, issues in opening and reading the files.

CHAPTER THREE

Using PowerPoint in Forensic Presentations

THIS CHAPTER DISCUSSES ASPECTS of using PowerPoint 2007 for the presentation of the results of forensic analytic tests. PowerPoint has many features that make it a useful complimentary tool for forensic analytics. There are three activities related to forensic investigations where presentations come into play. The activities are:

1. Presenting the results of a forensic investigation to executive management.
2. Presenting the results of a fraud risk assessment study to managers and executive management.
3. Presenting the techniques and results of forensic or continuous monitoring techniques, methods, and systems to colleagues at an in-house retreat or to accounting professionals at a conference.

Even though each of these activities is related to forensic matters, the presentation dynamics differ quite markedly from each other. For example, some humor would be appropriate at an in-house retreat or at a presentation at a conference, but would usually be inappropriate when presenting the results of a forensic investigation to management. This chapter reviews considerations and techniques that are appropriate in these various scenarios. The PowerPoint review and the discussion section of this chapter are reasonably brief and additional coverage, with examples, is given in the companion site to this book.

OVERVIEW OF FORENSIC PRESENTATIONS

PowerPoint is an effective presentation tool because it has the flexibility to include (a) text, (b) complex diagrams (perhaps showing the internal control deficiency that was taken advantage of by the fraudster), and (c) images (photos and screenshots of scanned invoices or websites). The best situation is where PowerPoint enhances a presentation rather than PowerPoint being the presentation. The PowerPoint presentation should be subservient to the presenter. PowerPoint should not be the equivalent of the lights and smoke show at a rock concert.

The presenter should carefully consider the audience's gain and loss for each slide. The gain should be that they can find it easier to understand or appreciate some point. The loss related to a slide is not always so obvious. The loss is that the audience now has its attention divided between the presenter and the PowerPoint screen. There are now two focal points in the room. This "divided attention" issue is made more acute the greater the distance between the presenter and the screen. The audience has to decide when to look at the presenter and when to look at the screen.

One way to overcome the "divided attention" issue is for the presenter to "mute" the PowerPoint presentation when the audience should be looking at them. A screen with text or images will cause the audience to look at the screen even after the presenter has finished reviewing the contents of the screen and has moved ahead to another topic. The introduction to the new topic might be missed because the audience is still looking at the slide dealing with the prior topic. PowerPoint does not have an easy "one click" way to turn it off during a presentation and the presenter should look to see if the projection console has a "presentation mute" button. If this is not the case then a second person could mute the presentation when needed, or the presenter could use a blank slide as the transition from one topic to the next.

AN OVERVIEW OF POWERPOINT

PowerPoint is used for forensic presentations with information in the form of text, diagrams, and images being shown on slides. PowerPoint includes features for every aspect of the presentation, namely the slides themselves, presentation notes, an outline, and handouts. Microsoft has extensive help available on the Microsoft website. The page dedicated to PowerPoint help is http://office.microsoft.com/en-us/powerpoint-help/.

The PowerPoint window is similar to the Access window in that the window is divided into panes with each pane related to some aspect of the presentation. The PowerPoint window is shown in Figure 3.1.

The largest section is the **Slide pane,** which shows the current slide. The slide shown is the opening slide with the name of the presentation, an image below the title and the name of the author or presenter. The slide pane is the pane that is used most often for preparing a presentation and printed reduced-size slide panes are used as handouts or as a speaker aid during the presentation. The **Notes pane** is used for notes that function as presenter reminders during the presentation. The notes can be printed

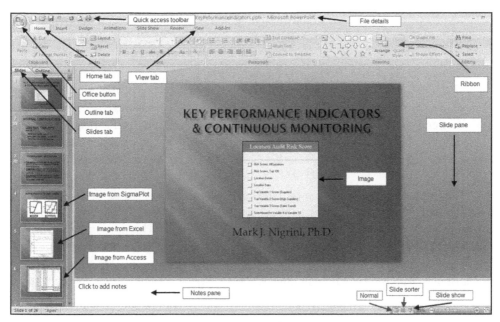

FIGURE 3.1 PowerPoint Window with a Prepared Presentation

as notes pages and they can also be displayed if the presentation is saved as a Web page. The **Slides tab** is visible when PowerPoint is opened. This tab shows the numbered slides as a column with thumbnails (small images) so that the user can see a small sequence of several slides at once. The **Outline tab** shows an outline of the text on each slide. The remainder of the PowerPoint window is fairly self-explanatory. The **Normal** view is usually the best environment for work on preparing and editing slides.

PLANNING THE PRESENTATION

Presentations, just like forensic analytic projects, need to be planned. The planning phase includes deciding whether PowerPoint is the best medium to use during the presentation. For example, neither differential calculus classes nor Japanese language classes are well-suited to PowerPoint. For a forensic report the planning phase should consider:

- The purpose of the presentation, which in a forensic case might be to inform management of a fraud and the results of the investigation.
- The message of the presentation would be to describe the fraud, the investigation, and corrective and planned future actions.
- The target audience would be selected members of management and other carefully chosen parties such as legal counsel. If the fraudster was a member of the management team then they would not be a part of the audience.

- The length of the presentation needs to be considered and the length should take into account audience questions.
- The presentation environment should be considered and in a forensic case the venue should be safe from casual eavesdropping.
- The presenter's characteristics should be taken into account including the experience level of the person and also whether they personally did the forensic work.
- Audience questions should be considered and anticipated. The planning phase should consider whether audience questions will be encouraged and allowed during the presentation or whether questions should be saved for the end.

The forensic topic could be a purchasing card fraud that was discovered during a forensic analytics project similar to that shown in Chapter 18. PowerPoint should be supported with other presentation aids, where appropriate. The primary presentation tool is the presenter, who should be appropriately dressed with a professional demeanor and body language. Other supporting aids could include physical objects (such as the employee's purchasing card) or documents evidencing the fraud (copies should be used for presentations and the originals kept under lock and key). Whiteboards and flipcharts can also be used but these are not recommended for a forensic presentation. Writing while talking is distracting and all documents and papers related to the case will inevitably be requested by the defense attorneys. Videos are also possible supplements to a presentation, but would probably not be too relevant in a forensic report. In addition to visual supplements, there are also auditory (acoustic or sound) supplements. The primary auditory tool is the presenter's voice and voice can impart the tone of the presentation and can emphasize certain parts or points in the presentation. Other auditory supplements would include recorded sounds or conversations and any soundtrack accompanying video.

 ## COLOR SCHEMES FOR FORENSIC PRESENTATIONS

Choosing an appropriate color scheme is an important early decision in the preparation of the PowerPoint part of the presentation. A consistent and appropriate color scheme sets the tone and the mood of the presentation. Microsoft has a large selection of templates available at http://office.microsoft.com/en-us/templates/?CTT=1.

The *Presentations* section of the resources has a large selection of PowerPoint presentations and slides available for download. A problem with most of the backgrounds and templates is that they are generally too flashy and bold for a forensic-related presentation. A flashy background or one that suggests drama is not really appropriate for a forensic presentation. The background colors set the mood of the presentation. Whatever colors are chosen, they should be consistent throughout the presentation. For example, bright neon colors (that indicate drama) should be avoided. Word documents are usually printed on white paper, but PowerPoint slides might never be printed at all. Microsoft has backgrounds for PowerPoint presentations that can be accessed at http://office.microsoft.com/en-us/templates/CT010117272.aspx.

TABLE 3.1 Background and Text Colors with Comments as to Their Suitability in a Forensic-Based Presentation

Background Color	Comments
Dark blue	First choice for a background color.
Black	Second choice for a background color. Black uses a lot of ink for printing as handouts.
Light blue	Third choice for a background color. Uses less ink for printing handouts and speaker notes.
Light gray	Fourth choice for a background color. Uses the least amount of ink for printing handouts and speaker notes.
White	Avoid white even though white is the background color in all printed books (except children's books).
Other colors	Other background colors such as red, orange, yellow, neon colors, green, brown, purple or pink are not appropriate for a forensic setting.
Text Color	
Yellow	First color choice for text on a dark background.
White	Second color choice for text on a dark background.
Black	Third color choice for text against a light blue or light gray background.
Red	Not recommended for text except for negative numbers.
Blue	Not recommended for text against a blue or black background.
Pastels, gray	Not recommended against black, blue, or gray backgrounds.
Green	Avoid green because of the chances that someone in the audience will not be able to see green.
Brown	Avoid brown for text.
Purple, pink	Avoid in a formal forensic setting.

The website has templates, backgrounds, and outlines for various types of presentations. A review of these backgrounds indicates that they are generally too flashy for a forensic presentation. A forensic presentation should have a completely neutral background precisely because we are not trying to create a mood of drama, excitement, or suspense. The suggested format is a plain background that tries to strike a balance between professionalism and attractiveness. Even a plain background has a color and Table 3.1 outlines some color considerations for a presentation based on a forensic report or a fraud risk survey.

Background and text color choices are shown in Table 3.1. In summary, dark blue is a good choice for a background and yellow would be a good choice for text. Microsoft has a good article on color choices on their website at http://office.microsoft.com/en-us/powerpoint-help/choose-the-right-colors-for-your-powerpoint-presentation-HA001012072.aspx.

The color choices can be put into action by opening PowerPoint and then by selecting **Design→Themes** followed by **Apex** as is shown in Figure 3.2.

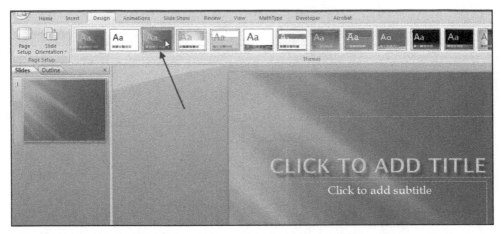

FIGURE 3.2   Selection of the Apex Theme for a PowerPoint Presentation

After selecting the Apex theme as is shown in Figure 3.2, that pattern will also be displayed in the Slides tab. The default color of the Apex theme is a light gray and we need to change the light gray to a darker blue. This is done by clicking on the Dialog box launcher in **Design→Background**. The Dialog Box launcher is the small icon in the bottom-right corner of a group, from which you can open a dialog box related to that group. The icon has two straight lines joined at 90 degrees and a small arrow pointing in a southeast direction. The dialog box can also be launched by right-clicking on the slide in the Slides tab and selecting **Format Background**. In the Format Background dialog box choose **Picture→Recolor** and then choose **Accent color 4 Dark** as is shown in Figure 3.3.

The original light gray is changed to a medium blue. Click **Accent color 4 Dark** and then click **Apply to All** followed by **Close**. The colors to the right of Accent color 4 Dark are closer to being purple than blue and blue is preferred to purple. The presentation now consists of just one (appropriately colored) slide. Since the presentation will consist of several slides the next step is to create a few working copies of the blank background. This is done by right-clicking on the slide and then clicking on **Duplicate Slide** twice. This will create a presentation with three blank title slides.

The next step is to add a layout to the second slide. This is done by clicking on the second slide and then selecting **Layout** followed by **Title and Content**. The final step is shown in Figure 3.4.

The layout of the second slide is changed to the **Title and Content** format in Figure 3.4. The same procedure should be applied to the third slide, but here the **Title Only** layout should be chosen. By using the **Duplicate Slide** command (activated by a right-click on the slide in the **Slides tab**) it is possible to duplicate any slide and the layouts in slides 2 and 3 should work well for most slides in a forensic presentation.

Not only are colors important but also the way that they are blended together. The predefined color schemes within PowerPoint have been well-chosen and it is usually

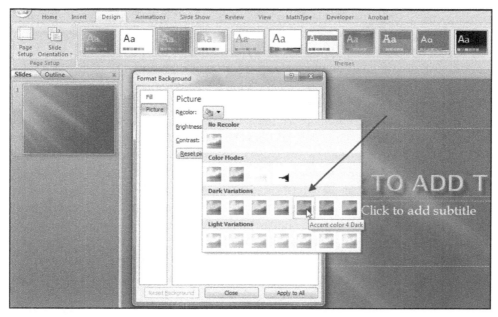

FIGURE 3.3 Selection of a Blue Color for a PowerPoint Background

best to use these as the color scheme unless circumstances are special (perhaps using the corporate logo colors is seen as a sign of loyalty). The colors and the way that they blend together might look different when projected onto a screen and it is a good idea to look at a presentation on the projection equipment before the actual presentation. When using graphs and charts in a presentation it is a nice touch to use one of the graph colors in the

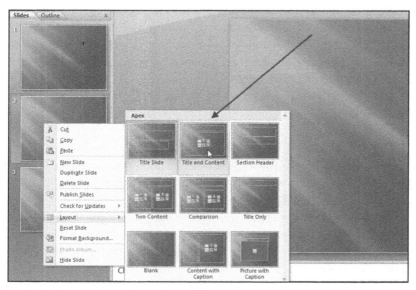

FIGURE 3.4 Selection of a *Title and Content* Layout for the Second Slide

heading text in PowerPoint. The color combinations will tie the elements of the slides together for a uniform look.

A general guide is to choose a background color (such as a blue or dark blue) together with up to three additional colors of text for maximum impact. The third color should be used quite sparingly. When choosing a background it is important to think about both the color and the texture of the color. A solid background color can look quite dull. The color texture option can be found at **Design→Background→Format Background→Texture**. The title text should be three to six words that are larger than the body text. Because the body text is smaller, the color contrast between the body text and the background should be more dramatic, because the body text is in a smaller font.

Some caveats to remember are that some colors have various associations in society. For example, red might mean "stop" or "danger," and green might mean "go." It is best to avoid using colors in contexts because these meanings might differ across various nationalities. Finally, the presenter should not rely too much on color to present the message, there should be a balance between professionalism and attractiveness, and everyone, including those who have sight challenges, should get all the information from the presentation, and not the color scheme.

 ## PROBLEMS WITH FORENSIC REPORTS

The presentation envisioned in this chapter is based on a forensic fraud report or a fraud risk assessment report. If the original study or the original document has issues or problems then the presentation will also have issues or problems. A dazzling presenter and a polished set of slides cannot convert a second-rate report into a noteworthy achievement. A good discussion of investigation reports is given in Golden, Skalak, and Clayton (2006). This section reviews some of the shortcomings and issues found in forensic reports that might influence the presentation.

Forensic reports should identify all of the relevant evidence that was used to conclude on the allegations under investigation. This report is important because the organization will use it as a basis for corporate filings, lawsuits, employment actions, and changes to accounting and financial systems. Forensic reports are discussed in the *Fraud Examiners Manual* of the Association of Certified Fraud Examiners (www.acfe.com). Some important considerations are:

- **Organization and work flow.** A good report flows from organizing each stage of the investigation from the initial allegation, to data gathering, and to the forensic analytics and corroboration.
- **Accuracy.** A high-quality report should be accurate with respect to the basic data, dates, events, monetary amounts, names, and places. In addition to factual accuracy, a good report should be well-written with no grammatical, typing, or spelling errors.
- **Clarity.** The report should be written in such a way so as to avoid any mis-understandings. This requires stating the facts and conclusions in language and terms that jurors can understand.

- **Impartiality.** A forensic report should be unbiased. The facts should speak for themselves and personal opinions and impressions should be avoided.
- **Relevance.** Only facts and other matters relevant to the investigation should be included in the report. It would be irrelevant to include details of a domestic dispute involving the accused in the forensic report.
- **Timeliness.** The report and the information gathered to support the fraud should be prepared in a timely manner. Written records of interviews should be prepared soon after the time of the interview.

The above points are good characteristics of a forensic report and the forensic presentation. Grisso (2010) examines several forensic reports and identifies the types of faults found in these forensic reports. Although these reports deal with forensic matters related to psychology, it would seem that these faults could fit quite well with forensic reports related to fraud. Grisso develops a set of prescriptive statements that have been slightly adapted to fit a fraud report. These prescriptive statements are:

- **Introductory material.** These should accurately identify the forensic investigator and all dates relevant to the investigation. The way in which the alleged perpetrator was informed of the purpose of the investigation should be documented. The sources of the data evaluated should be listed. The report should state the legal standard that permitted the analysis of the data and the interview process.
- **Organization and style.** The report should be organized in a way that is logical and that helps the reader to understand the fraud and the environment within which the act was committed. The data section should only report on the supporting data and should not include any inferences. Any inferences and conclusions should be stated in a section of the report that uses the earlier data but offers no new data. The language used should reflect no bias on the part of the investigator. The document should be professionally written with few, if any, typographical errors, grammatical errors, or colloquialisms.
- **Data reporting.** The investigation should obtain and use all the data that would be important to addressing the alleged fraud. The report should discuss only the data that is relevant to the investigation. The sources of the data should be clearly described. The report should document efforts to obtain data that was thought to be relevant but which was not forthcoming or was unavailable for some reason.
- **Interpretations and opinions.** The conclusions should address only the fraud investigation at hand. Each opinion or conclusion should be supported by a clear explanation. The report should describe any important ways in which the conclusions reached have some reasonable margin of error. With reference to those opinions or conclusions that require some specialized knowledge, the report preparer should only express opinions on those matters for which they are qualified and competent.

Other important issues include evidence considerations and the chain of custody because the evidence needs to be admissible and used at trial. The forensic report is an important document with serious implications for the accused if done right and implications for the prosecution if the document is flawed.

Copying from Word to PowerPoint

The Internal Revenue Service (IRS) has a summary of fraud examples in the *Examples of Corporate Fraud Investigations* of their website (www.irs.gov). The case below can be found by searching for "Charlene Corley" on the IRS website. The case is headed "South Carolina Woman Sentenced for Defrauding the Department of Defense of Over $20 Million." A summary of the case is given below:

> On March 2, 2009, in Columbia, S.C., Charlene Corley was sentenced to 78 months in prison, to be followed by three years of supervised release, and ordered to pay over $15 million in restitution. Corley pleaded guilty in August 2007 to conspiracy to commit wire fraud and conspiracy to commit money laundering. Information presented in court indicated that beginning in 1997 and continuing through September 2006, Corley and her sister, Darlene Wooten, owned C&D Distributors, LLC, a Lexington-based company that submitted electronic bids via computer to the Department of Defense to supply small hardware components, plumbing fixtures, electronic equipment, and various other items. Along with the cost of the items sold, C&D made claims for shipping costs. These shipping claims were processed automatically to stream-line the resupply of items to combat troops in Iraq and Afghanistan. The fictitious shipping costs ranged into the hundreds of thousands of dollars, despite the fact that the value of the items shipped rarely exceeded $100. As an example, in September 2006, C&D billed the Department of Defense $998,798 to ship two flat washers that cost $0.19 each. Over the course of the conspiracy, the defendants obtained approximately $20,576,925 in fraudulent shipping costs. The money was used to purchase beach houses, high-end automobiles, boats, jewelry, vacations, and other items. Darlene Wooten committed suicide last October, after being contacted by federal investigators about the fraud.

This high-profile fraud is reported on the IRS's website even though the case did not involve tax evasion. The court records include several actual examples of shipping charges, some of which were paid and other that were not paid. This is an example of a table that would be highly relevant in a forensic fraud report. The first 10 records are shown in Table 3.2.

An extract from the invoices and shipping charges exhibit in *U.S. v. Charlene Corley* is shown in Table 3.2. The table's format is a good example of what would be found in a forensic fraud report. This table, in whole or in part, would also be included in the forensic presentation. The table can be copied reasonably easily from Word to a PowerPoint slide. If the table is embedded in the slide then it can be edited using Word's table commands.

The way to copy a table to a slide begins with an open PowerPoint presentation with the relevant slide highlighted. In the example, the blank slide is Slide 4. The first step uses **Insert→Text→Object** to give the **Insert Object** dialog box. The usual

TABLE 3.2 The First 10 Items in the Table of Invoices and Shipping Charges in *U.S. v. Charlene Corley*

Contract #	Date	Item Description	Qty.	Cost of Items ($)	Shipping Amount ($)	Paid
SP070004MR0490001	11/7/2003	Pump Unit, centrifuge	11	924.00	41,076.00	No
SP070004MR049	11/11/2003	Pump Unit, centrifuge	11	924.00	41,923.00	Yes
SP041403MAD630000	3/26/2004	Longitudinal girder	19	75.81	402,074.81	No
SPM76004P08520001	4/2/2004	Valve, solenoid	1	89.90	40,300.90	No
SPM76004P0852	4/7/2004	Valve, solenoid	3	269.67	402,380.67	No
SPM76003P8429	4/22/2004	Tubing, nonmetallic	5	29.95	402,147.95	No
SP070004MR209	4/29/2004	Elbow, pipe to tube	1	8.75	445,640.75	Yes
SPE76004P0577	5/6/2004	Valve, check	1	51.99	40,289.99	No
SP041104WE358	7/23/2004	Plug, machine thread	1	10.99	492,096.99	Yes
SP074004MKM63	10/20/2004	Diaphragm	5	109.95	159,000.95	Yes

procedure would be to select ***Create from file*** and then to use the ***Browse*** button to open the Browse dialog box. The final step is to navigate to the Word file with the table. This transfer works best if the table is saved in a Word file by itself. The ***Link*** check box should not be selected. The dialog box is shown in Figure 3.5.

The dialog box used to insert a table from Word is shown in Figure 3.5. The table is copied from Word by clicking ***OK***. The result is shown in Figure 3.6.

The first version of the image is small and not exactly where it should be for a presentation. The table should be resized so that it is as big as possible and fits into the lower part of the slide without overlapping any other images or the slide title. The table is resized by dragging the corner sizing handles. The object border might have to be dragged beyond the edges of the slide to make the table clearly visible on the slide. It might be necessary to zoom out to (say) 30 percent or 40 percent to be able to drag the handles as far down as needed.

A second option to copy a Word table is to select the table in Word itself. This option involves clicking anywhere in the table and then using ***Layout→Table→Select→ Select Table***. The table is then copied to the clipboard using ***Home→Clipboard→ Copy***. After switching to PowerPoint and making the relevant slide the active slide, the table is inserted using ***Home→Clipboard→Paste***. The table will usually need some resizing and perhaps even some font color changes.

The first option using ***Insert Object*** is preferred. With this method it is easier to modify the embedded table by clicking anywhere in the shipping costs table while in PowerPoint. The embedded table object then becomes active in Word. After the changes have been made it is possible to leave Word and to get back to the PowerPoint file by using ***File→Close***, followed by ***Cancel*** to prevent getting out of PowerPoint entirely.

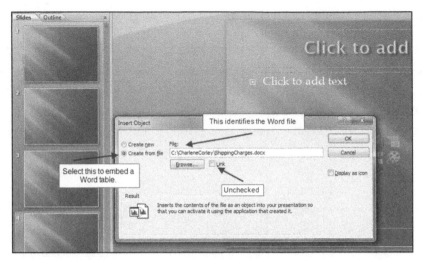

FIGURE 3.5 The Insert Object Dialog Box Used to Insert a Table from Word

Copying from Excel to PowerPoint

Chapter 18 includes a case study using forensic analytic tests on purchasing card data. These tests include a periodic graph showing that September has the highest monthly total and it would appear that employees might be spending the money "left in the budget." A related presentation should include the Excel graph (also shown in Figure 2.15 in Chapter 2). The graph is copied to PowerPoint by first opening Excel and then selecting the relevant graph. The selected graph will have three dots curving around the corners and the midpoint of each of the borders will have four dots visible.

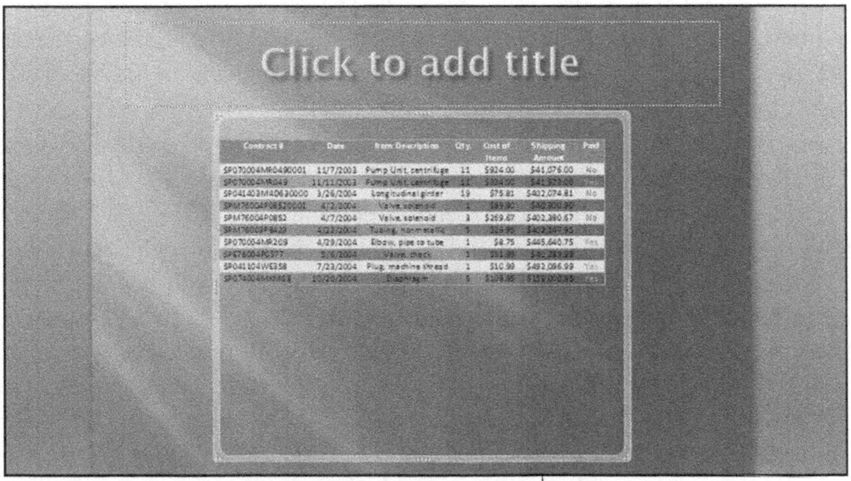

FIGURE 3.6 The Table Copied from Word into PowerPoint

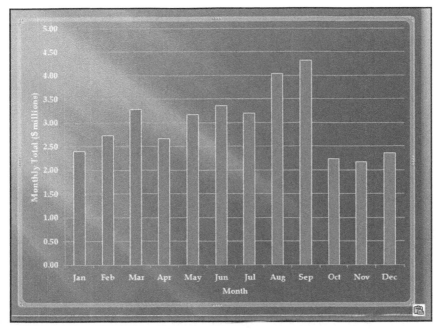

FIGURE 3.7 An Excel Graph that Has Been Copied to PowerPoint

The procedure to copy the graph is to click **Copy** in **Home→Clipboard→Copy** (while still in Excel). The next step is to move over to PowerPoint and then to highlight the relevant slide. The graph is pasted using **Home-Clipboard→Paste→Paste**. The result (for the purchasing card graph) is shown in Figure 3.7.

The result of the **Copy** and **Paste** operation is shown in Figure 3.7. This result is not exactly what was wanted because the graph is too big and it is also transparent. To format the graph requires the **Paste Options** dialog box that is visible in the bottom right-hand corner. The **Paste Options** dialog box has some options including **Paste as Picture**. The next step is to open the **Paste Options** dialog box and to choose **Paste as Picture**. The graph will then look just as it did in Excel. The procedure to reduce the graph's size is to right click on the graph and to use the **Size and Position** dialog box. A scale of 85 percent might work well. The result after adding a title might be as is shown in Figure 3.8.

The completed periodic graph slide is shown in Figure 3.8. The graph has been formatted as a picture and it has been resized. A title has also been added to the slide. With this transfer method the only way to now make changes to the graph is to make the changes in Excel and then to redo the **Copy** and **Paste** sequence. For a forensic presentation a little work on the borders would work well, and for a less formal presentation it might be appropriate to add some more pizzazz to the graph borders. The image's borders can be changed to one of many options by left double-clicking the graph which will activate the **Picture Styles** group on the **Format** tab. The result is shown in Figure 3.9.

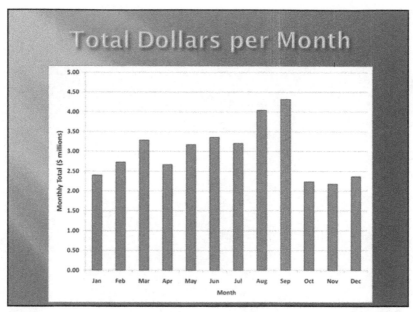

FIGURE 3.8 The Excel Graph after Tidying Up the Original *Copy* and *Paste* Procedure

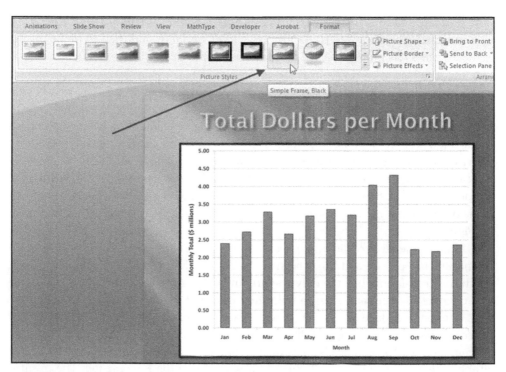

FIGURE 3.9 The Picture Styles Available in PowerPoint

Figure 3.9 shows the choice of "Simple Frame, Black," which would work well in a forensic fraud report. In presentations that are less formal, PowerPoint offers many other formats. For example, the *Picture Styles* group also has a set of *Picture Effects* options and the use of an effect such as *3-D Rotation* and *Perspective Right* makes for an interesting presentation. It is important to have the same theme for all the graphs and charts. The graphs should be prepared the same way in Excel (e.g., same color schemes and same fonts for the axes and same format for the legends) and they should have the same or similar *Picture Styles* (picture shapes, picture borders, and picture effects). All graphs should also be similarly formatted in the forensic fraud report.

Copying a Screenshot to PowerPoint

A forensic analytics presentation might include screenshots from a Web-based activity such as information gathering. It is always safer to rerun the tests and then to show screenshots of the computer screen than to access the Internet during the presentation. Moving from PowerPoint to Internet Explorer (and back again) will use valuable time, and the connection might not work or it might be slow, or it might need passwords to be activated. By way of an example, you might want to make the point that fraudsters do, in fact, get sentenced and do end up going to prison. This can be demonstrated by using the *Inmate Locator* on the website of the Federal Bureau of Prisons (www.bop.gov). Rather than running a live search for "Charlcne Corley" (the case discussed earlier in this chapter) you can run the search while preparing your presentation and you can then paste the results into your PowerPoint presentation. The procedure to copy the screen is to use *alt+Print Screen* to copy the current screen to the clipboard. The *Print Screen* key might be abbreviated "Prt Scr" or "Prt Sc" or something similar. The procedure to paste the image on a slide is either the *Paste* command or the shortcut for *Paste*, which is *Control + V*. The result of pasting the *Inmate Locator* screen is shown in Word in Figure 3.10.

After pasting the image into PowerPoint the image will usually be too big for the slide, and will contain additional details that should best be edited away. The *Size and Position* dialog box will help with both size and position. The dialog box can be accessed with a right-click on the image, or by using the dialog box launcher from the *Format→ Size* group. By using the *Scale* and *Crop from* options in the *Size* tab, and the options in the *Position* tab, the image can be resized, cropped, and repositioned perfectly. The final result is shown in Figure 3.11.

The cropped and resized image is shown in Figure 3.11. The Windows *Print Screen* key is useful for copying a basic screen image to a PowerPoint slide. If this task is going to be done repeatedly, then a program that can add some special effects (see the textboxes and arrows in Figure 3.1) is Snagit. The company's website is http://www.techsmith. com/snagit/.

Snagit is reasonably priced and works well. A free trial is available. The software also allows for some details to be blurred as is done in Figure 2.2 where the cardholder's names are blurred. The use of blurring is useful in a setting where you might not want the audience to see absolutely everything.

FIGURE 3.10 A Screenshot of the *Inmate Locator* Page of the Federal Bureau of Prisons

Notes on Graphs and Charts

Excel books use the words "chart" and "graph" interchangeably. In this book a *graph* is a function or a line, usually in the first quadrant (where both *x* and *y* are positive) drawn on the Cartesian plane (so named after Rene Descartes) or the coordinate plane. A *graph* therefore is a diagram representing a system of connections or interrelations among two

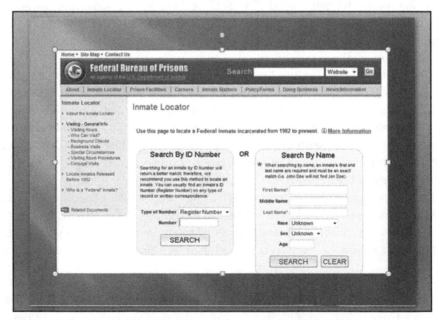

FIGURE 3.11 The Cropped and Resized Image on a PowerPoint Slide

or more phenomena or facts through the use of lines, bars, or points. In contrast, a *chart* is everything else that is a diagrammatic representation of one or more facts or phenomena. An often-used chart is a pie chart.

During the presentation each graph or chart should be discussed. Each graph should have the *x*-axis and the *y*-axis clearly labeled. The presenter should not expect the audience to immediately understand what is being shown on graph. A graph that took much time to prepare can probably not be understood by an audience in 15 seconds without any supporting explanations.

The starting point for a useful and relevant graph is to first determine the message, which is the point that you would like to make. The type of graph depends on the point that is being made or emphasized. The second step is to consider the phenomena or facts that are being compared. This will also influence the choice of the type of graph or chart. There are several types of comparisons. These comparisons are (a) a component comparison (customer *X* always favored cashier *Y*), (b) a ranking of items, (c) a time-series graph that shows changes over time, (d) a frequency distribution showing group membership, and (e) a pattern showing correlation or the lack thereof. For example, Figure 13.1 shows some highly correlated gasoline prices. The third step in graph preparation is to select the graph or chart form in Excel. A mismatch between the comparison being made and the graph form reflects poorly on the abilities of the forensic investigator.

Notes on PowerPoint Animations

PowerPoint has a large selection of animations. The *subtle* animations are highly appropriate to a formal forensic-related presentation, while the *exciting* animations are not well-suited to this type of presentation. For example, in a forensic presentation it is often appropriate to list the bullet points one at a time so that each can be briefly reviewed without the audience reading ahead. The abbreviated list of predictors in Figure 3.10 is drawn from the monthly reporting risk scoring application described in Chapter 17. The steps used to get the bullet points to appear one at a time on a mouse click are in the **Animations** tab in the **Animations** group. The procedure to use the animations is to highlight the bullet points and then to use **Animations→Animations** followed by the **Animate** drop down box to give several options. A good choice is **Fly In** and **By 1st Level Paragraphs**.

The way to animate the bullet points is shown in Figure 3.12. The **Animations** tab also includes an option for the transitions of the entire presentation in **Transitions to This Slide**. The best choice is a transition that is simple and the **Wipe Right** transition accomplishes this. It is important to use an appropriate transition and also to have all the transitions being consistent from slide to slide (use the **Apply To All** button).

Miscellaneous PowerPoint Notes

This section includes some miscellaneous presentation and PowerPoint notes. The observations were made from watching the presentations of others and also by reflecting back on my own work. The notes are listed below:

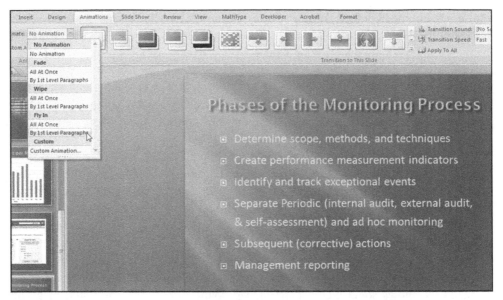

FIGURE 3.12   How to Animate the Bullet Points

- It is best not to read from PowerPoint slides especially when the presenter's back is turned to the audience. The audience can read the slides silently in their heads far quicker than any presenter can read out aloud. The presenter should talk about the point or points on the slide without reading the words out aloud.
- Slides should be kept simple with brief amounts of text, or only one diagram, or one or two images on each slide.
- PowerPoint's gimmicks should be avoided during a forensic-related presentation. These gimmicks have their time and place in perhaps a presentation to fifth graders.
- Include images only when they make an issue become more true to life. For example, in the sentencing hearing of Charlene Corley the prosecutor notes that,

> What did they do with that money? They each bought $96,000 matching Mercedes, they bought four beach houses, they bought luxury cars for their friends and their family. They bought a $250,000 box in Clemson stadium, they bought hundreds of thousands of dollars of jewelry. The list of assets that we gave you was ten pages, single spaced.

If the sentencing hearing was done with a PowerPoint presentation then the presentation would be made more true to life by including images of these assets. In a forensic fraud presentation the photos should be photos of the exact items. Photos of generic expensive cars or generic beach houses would not be appropriate. Avoid using low-quality (grainy) images unless the presentation is about the Kimberly Hole in 1872, in which case we would expect a low resolution.

- Presenters should avoid using cartoon images in forensic-related presentations. They will invariably set an incorrect tone for the presentation.
- Presenters should use sounds in a presentation only if they are important to delivering, complementing, or enhancing your message. Including sound in a presentation (e.g., 30 seconds from a recorded conversation) is tricky especially if the presentation is prepared on one computer and presented on another computer with the PowerPoint file on a USB flash drive. This is because the sound file might be in C:/Forensic on the presenter's computer but it is not in that location on the presentation computer.
- Presenters should spend time crafting the opening and closing remarks. Words should be chosen carefully in a forensic environment. For example, the investigator's job is not to call for justice, restitution, and a sentence that acts as a deterrent for future employees or customers. That is the public prosecutor's job.
- Keeping to the time limit is difficult for most presenters. One tactic is to divide the presentation into (say) four equal time segments. The presenter should make bold indications in their notes to the effect that slide #4 should be presented by 8:10, slide #10 by 8:20, slide #14 by 8:30, and concluding remarks should be started at around 8:40. These intermediate targets will help to ensure an on-time ending. It is often the case that presenters add unnecessary fluff at the start of a talk only to have to make a unflattering rush at the end to finish. This is an issue when it was the conclusions and suggestions for future work that drew the audience to the talk in question.

A well-prepared presentation will be well-received and people with presentation skills are in high demand in corporations. It is often the case that inexperienced presenters will spend 5 minutes answering a question on a tangential issue without realizing that those 5 minutes are squeezing the remaining points into an even more compressed time frame. With experience comes the ability to use all the presentation minutes for the maximum effectiveness. It is much easier to prepare a 90-minute presentation than it is to prepare a 20-minute presentation. The fast pace of corporate life does not allow for 90-minute marathons.

SUMMARY

PowerPoint causes the audience's attention to be divided between the presenter and the screen. The presenter should work to keep the focus on their persona and PowerPoint should be used to enhance the presentation. PowerPoint should not be the presentation. The chapter covered a number of issues related to using PowerPoint in a forensic-related presentation. The chapter also covered some common problems related to forensic reports mainly related to organization and style and interpretations and opinions.

In a forensic environment the first consideration is the color scheme and background colors. Dark background colors are preferred. PowerPoint is seamlessly compatible with Word and Excel. Files with images and content from the Office suite programs can be easily included in PowerPoint slides. The chapter concludes with a discussion of miscellaneous presentation issues, which have the general theme that a forensic-related presentation is a serious matter, the time constraints should be adhered to, the slides should enhance the presentation, and flashy gimmicks should be avoided.

4

High-Level Data Overview Tests

CHAPTERS 1 AND 2 introduced our quantitative forensic tools. Access is an effective and efficient software package that uses data tables, queries, and reports to store data, perform calculations, and neatly report the results of a series of analytic tests. Excel is an effective and efficient software package that can also store data, perform calculations, and report the results, although the lines among the three aspects of the analysis are not so clear cut. Most analytic tests can be performed using either Access or Excel. The tests that are described in the next chapters are demonstrated using both Access and Excel, unless one of these is not suitable for the task, or unless the steps in Excel are somewhat obvious. The results of the analytic tests can easily be included in a forensic report or a forensic presentation. The presentation of the forensic findings with a strong PowerPoint bias is reviewed in Chapter 3. Chapters 4 through 17 discuss various forensic analytic methods and techniques. These methods and techniques start with a high-level overview of the data.

This chapter reviews a series of three tests that form a good foundation for a data-driven forensic investigation. These three tests are the data profile, a data histogram, and a periodic graph. This chapter describes the tests and shows how these tests can be done in Access and Excel using a real-world data set of corporate invoices. There is no general rule as to whether Access or Excel is best for forensic analytics, although Access is usually preferred for large data sets, and Excel's graphing capabilities are better than those of Access.

The tests described in the chapter are there to give the forensic investigator an understanding and feel for the data. These high-level overview tests tell us how many records we have, and how the data is distributed with respect to amount and with respect to time. Chapter 9 will concentrate on how the current data compares to data from the prior period. These high-level overview tests should help the investigator to understand what it is that they are dealing with. This understanding should usually give some insights into possible processing inefficiencies, errors, questionable negative numbers, and time periods with excessive activity.

 ## THE DATA PROFILE

The data profile is usually the first test to be run on the data because this test might find serious issues that show that it is not a good idea to continue with the analysis. For example, we might find that a data table has exactly 16,384 records, which suggests that the original downloading procedure believed that it was exporting to Excel and there was a fixed limit of 16,384 records built into the routine. There is little point in continuing to work with incomplete data. We might also find that the data set does not contain any negative numbers and this might be an indicator that we have an accounts payable data set that is incomplete because we are lacking the credits. Again, there would be little point to continuing to work with an incomplete data table. The data profile is quite uncomplicated and the test divides the data into seven strata. For accounts payable data in U.S. dollars these strata usually are:

- Amounts equal to or larger than 10.
- Amounts from 0.01 to 9.99.
- Amounts equal to zero.
- Amounts from −0.01 to −9.99.
- Amounts equal to or smaller than −10.

The above strata or categories are described as the (1) large positive numbers, (2) small positive numbers, (3) zeroes, (4) small negative numbers, and (5) large negative numbers. Depending on the data under investigation, you might want to add extra strata or categories. A data profile of accounts payable data usually includes two extra strata as follows

- Numbers from 0.01 to 50.
- Numbers above 100,000.

These extra strata could point internal auditors to the low-value items (that cost money to process) and to the high-value items that would usually be material. It is usually more efficient in a statistical sampling context to sample from the high-dollar strata at a higher rate than from the low-dollar strata. The data profile of the *InvoicesPaid.xlsx* data is shown in Figure 4.1.

For some data sets it might be appropriate to use more strata (intervals) or to change the value of the low-value dollar range in the sixth stratum. In an analysis of the invoices paid by a major international conglomerate we used several strata for the large positive numbers (10 to 99.99, 100 to 999.99, 1,000 to 9,999.99, 10,000 to

	A	B	C	D	E	F	G	H	I	J
1						DATA PROFILE				
2										
3	Details			Count		% of Total		$		% of Total
4	Amounts	10.00 and over		177,763		93.82		$492,913,582.26		100.54
5	Amounts	0.01 to 9.99		7,320		3.86		$40,159.47		0.01
6	Amounts	equal to zero		123		0.06		$0.00		0.00
7	Amounts	-0.01 to -9.99		195		0.10		-$1,121.31		0.00
8	Amounts	-10.00 and under		4,069		2.15		-$2,674,995.52		-0.55
9				-------------		-------------		------------------		-------------
10				189,470		100.00		$490,277,624.90		100.00
11				=========		=========		=============		=========
12										
13	Low-value Amounts									
14	Amounts	0.01 to 50.00		43,253		22.83		$1,188,603.10		0.24
15				=========		=========		=============		=========
16										
17	High-value Amounts									
18	Amounts	100,000 and higher		370		0.20		$242,946,614.32		49.55
19				=========		=========		=============		=========

FIGURE 4.1 The Data Profile Shows the Counts and the Total Dollars in the Various Strata

99,999.99, and 100,000 and above). Changing the strata ranges would also be appropriate in countries where there are many units of the local currency to the U.S. dollar. Examples would include Japan, Norway, and South Africa. Different strata ranges would also be appropriate for other data sets with relatively large numbers (e.g., frequent flyer miles, hotel loyalty program points, or bank wire transfers).

Possible Findings from the Data Profile

The data profile helps us to understand the data being analyzed. Besides helping with an understanding, the data profile can provide some interesting initial results. Examples of these results in an accounts payable audit are:

■ **File completeness.** This test helps the investigator or auditor assess whether the file is complete. This is done by reconciling the total dollars in the table (in Figure 4.1 this amounts to $490,277,624.90) to the financial records. The reconciliation would help to ensure that we are working with a complete file (i.e., we have all the transactions for the period). In an external audit one of the management assertions is the assertion of *completeness*. With this assertion management are asserting that all the transactions that should be included in the financial statements are in fact included. In a forensic investigation there is no such assertion, but the investigator does need to know that all the transactions for the period are included in the data being analyzed. The data profile would also help the investigator to understand which transactions are included in the data set and which transactions are excluded. For example, in an analysis of health care claims the investigator might discover that certain types of claims (e.g., dental claims or claims by retired employees) are processed by another system and that a second, or third, separate analysis is also needed. By way of another example, some firms process "immediate and urgent" checks through a system separate from the usual accounts payable system, and government agencies also process contract payments and routine purchases through separate payables systems.

- **A high proportion of low-value invoices.** In accounts payable data it is usual to find that there is a high proportion of low-value ($50 and under) invoices. The normal proportion for low-value invoices is about 15 percent. Some company data profiles have shown a few cases where the low-value (under $50) invoices made up more than 50 percent of the count of the invoices. In one company in California the CFO called for a monthly report showing the percentage of low-value invoices. He was keen to see a continual reduction in that percentage. Internal auditors could suggest ways to cut down on the percentage or count of low-value invoices. These ways could include the use of closely monitored purchasing cards (see Chapter 18). The example in Figure 4.1 shows that about 43,000 invoices, or a little more than one-fifth of the invoices, were for $50 or less. This means that one-fifth of the entire accounts payable infrastructure was there to process low-value invoices and the total dollars for these invoices amounted to about $1.2 million. The other 80 percent of the time the accounts payable personnel were processing the larger invoices that totaled $489 million.

- **Zero invoices.** Many zero-dollar invoices would also be of interest to an investigator. An analysis done in Chicago (not the Figure 4.1 example) showed that the company had about 8,000 zero invoices. The follow-up work showed that these were warranty claims that were being processed as if they were normal purchases. It was therefore true that the company was buying something (a repair or replacement part) at a zero cost. However, processing 8,000 $0 invoices was inefficient. Processing and system inefficiencies are usually found in companies that have experienced high growth. A system that might have worked well when the company was younger and smaller becomes inefficient with large transaction volumes.

- **Number of credit memos.** The norm for credit memos as a percentage of invoices is about 3 percent. Percentages higher than 3 percent might indicate that an excessive amount of correcting is being made to invoices that have been entered for processing. Percentages lower than 3 percent might indicate that payments personnel are not thoroughly reviewing and correcting invoices prior to payments. Across a broad spectrum of companies the credit memo percentages would range from 1 percent all the way up to 6 percent. A low percentage (such as 1 percent) is a red flag that not much correcting is being done and, all things being equal, the payments data has a higher risk of overpayments.

- **Negative amounts.** The data profile is also useful for finding negative amounts in data sets that should not have negative numbers. Examples of data that should always be positive are perpetual inventory balances, gross or net pay payroll numbers, census counts, car odometer readings, and stream-flow statistics.

The data profile will not tell a story to us. We need to look carefully at the numbers and together with an understanding of the data we should develop some insights. It often helps to review the data profile with someone who is closely connected to the data. In a recent analysis of purchasing card transactions (see Chapter 18), I questioned why the largest dollar category had the highest number of transactions (the usual pattern is for high dollar amounts to occur less frequently than low dollar amounts). It turned out that their data profile range of $5,000 and higher referred not to single transactions above $5,000 but to cardholders with monthly purchases in excess of $5,000. After the data profile the next two tests are the data histogram and the periodic graph.

THE DATA HISTOGRAM

A data histogram shows us the pattern of our data with respect to size and counts by showing us the shape of the distribution. The histogram tells us something more about the properties of our data. We get to know how many small numbers there are, how many in-between numbers there are, and how many large numbers there are. The data histogram is shown graphically, whereas the data profile is a numeric table. In statistical terms this test is called a *descriptive statistic*. Descriptive statistics are graphical and numerical measures that are used to summarize and interpret some of the properties of a data table.

The histogram itself is a graph made up of vertical bars constructed on a horizontal line (the *x*-axis) that is marked off with intervals (e.g., $0 to $50). These intervals should include all the amounts in the data set and should not overlap (e.g., $0 to $50, and $40 to $90 do overlap because $45 or $47 would fall into either interval). Each record (usually a transaction) should belong to one interval only. The height of each bar in the histogram indicates the number of records in the interval.

The number of intervals in the histogram is at the discretion of the investigator. Some books suggest 14–20 intervals if there are more than 5,000 records. It seems that 14–20 intervals will give a crowded histogram especially when current and prior year histograms are being compared side-by-side (see Chapter 9 for comparing current data to prior period data). My experience in forensic environments suggests that 10 intervals works well. Each interval should have a neat round number as the upper bound (e.g., $250, $500, or $750) and should preferably contain enough records so that at least a small bar is visible for every interval. No real insights are obtained from a histogram that has one or two intervals with many records (say 90 percent of all the records) and the remaining intervals have few records. The final (10th) interval should be for all amounts greater than the prior upper bound (for example, $450 and higher). This makes the final interval width much wider than those of the first nine intervals and this interval should therefore be clearly labeled. Statistics books generally want each histogram bar to represent an equal interval but if we do this with financial data we will get about 70 percent of the records in the first interval and about 20 percent of the records in the second interval, and bars that are barely visible in the remaining intervals. This is because financial data usually has many small numbers and only a few large numbers.

Choosing the interval breakpoints involves some thought and perhaps repeated trials. This is not usually a problem because what we are trying to do is to get some

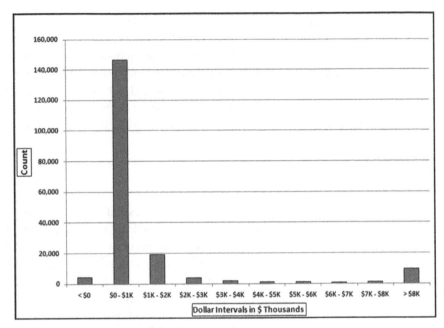

FIGURE 4.2 The Histogram of the Payments Data

insights on the distribution of the data and by redoing the intervals a few times over we are getting a good sense of the make-up or distribution of our numbers. Selecting the ranges is an iterative process. There is not usually a right answer and a wrong answer.

The histogram of the payments data is shown in Figure 4.2. The histogram shows that most of the invoices are in the $0 to $1,000 range. Note that the center eight ranges includes their lower limits ($1,000, $2,000, and so on) but excludes the upper limits ($2,000, $3,000, up to $8,000). The histogram shows that there are about 9,000 invoices of $8,000 and higher. The large bias toward many small numbers means that the data is positively skewed. Statisticians have a *skewness* measure that indicates whether the numbers are evenly distributed around the mean. Data that is positively skewed has many small amounts and fewer large amounts. This is usually the pattern found in the dollar amounts of invoices paid (expenses) as shown above and most financial and accounting data sets. In contrast, data with a negative skewness measure has many large numbers and fewer smaller numbers (as might be the case with student GPAs). The skewness of a data set with all numbers evenly distributed from (say) $0 to $8,000 is zero, which is neither positive, nor negative.

For example, a histogram over a short interval (perhaps $2,400 to $2,600) might help a forensic investigator to conclude that there are excessive purchases at or just below the limit of $2,500 for purchasing cards. This would be evidenced by a large spike in the (say) $2,475 to $2,500 interval. Chapter 18 shows several tests related to purchasing cards transactions.

THE PERIODIC GRAPH

The periodic graph is the last of the three high-level tests related to the distribution of the data. This test divides the data into time periods and shows the total per time period on a graph with time shown on the *x*-axis. This is useful for a better understanding of the data, and also to detect large anomalies. In the purchasing card example in Chapter 18 an example of such an anomaly was a single purchase for $3 million that was clear from an odd pattern on the periodic graph. In a purchasing card context this test has often showed increased card usage at the end of a fiscal year where cardholders try to spend the money in the budget. The periodic graph of the *InvoicesPaid.xlsx* data is shown in Figure 4.3.

The periodic graph shows relatively high totals for February and April. A review of the data shows that February had two large invoices (for $15.8 million and $14.5 million, respectively), and April had one large invoice for $26.8 million. These three large invoices explain the spikes. A forensic investigator could remove these three large invoices from the table (just for the purposes of this test) and redo the periodic graph. Any forensic report would show two periodic graphs, one with the three large invoices and one graph without the three large invoices.

These monthly totals (or weekly, or daily if relevant) are especially useful after a three or four year history has been built up, or if a history is available. The monthly totals could be used as inputs to a time-series analysis. The time-series analysis would give a forecast for the coming year. These forecasts could be used as a part of a continuous monitoring system. Time-series analysis and continuous monitoring is further developed in Chapter 14.

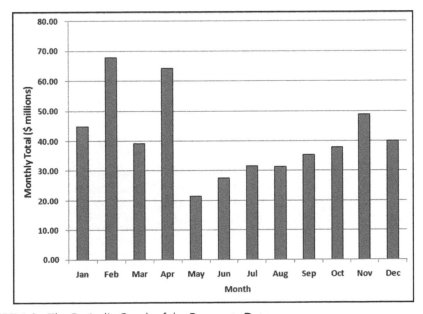

FIGURE 4.3 The Periodic Graph of the Payments Data

PREPARING THE DATA PROFILE USING ACCESS

In Access there is sometimes more than one way to get the same result, and the software demonstrations will show the way that fits in best with how the other tests are performed, or the way that is the easiest to adapt to other situations. The data profile queries are reasonably straightforward but before any queries can be run, the data needs to be imported into Access. The data files and the Excel template are available on the companion website. The invoices data for this chapter and also for chapters 5 through 12 are from a division of an electric power company. The invoices included all invoices from vendors and all payments to vendors and other entities. Vendor accounts were sometimes opened for odd situations, including giving customers refunds for some special situations. A view of the invoices table (imported using **External Data→ Import→Excel**) is shown in Figure 4.4.

The *InvoicesPaid* table (*tblInvoicesPaid*) is shown in Figure 4.4. The data was imported using the **External Data** tab and then **Excel** to import the *InvoicesPaid* data. The Excel file was imported using the **First row contains column headings** option. The *Date* field was formatted as *Date/Time* and the *Amount* field was formatted as *Currency*. The **Let Access Add Primary Key** option was accepted. The result is shown in Figure 4.4. The companion site includes a data profile template. The Excel template *DataProfile.xlsx* is shown in Figure 4.5.

In this section we use Access to run the calculations, and Excel for the neatly formatted reporting of the results. Each of the seven strata requires one (slightly different) query. The totals in row 10 and the percentages in columns F and J will be automatically calculated by Excel once the cells in columns D and H are populated. To get Access into its query creation mode we need to click **Create →Query Design** to give the screen shown in Figure 4.6.

This dialog box is used to select the table or tables, and also perhaps queries that will be used in the current query. Click **Add** and then **Close** to add the *tblInvoicesPaid* table to the top pane of the Query window. The first data profile stratum is for the large positive numbers, being amounts greater than or equal to 10. We need the count and the sum of these amounts. The first step in the query is to drag the *Amount* field from the table

All Access Objects ▼ «	tblInvoicesPaid				
Tables ▲	ID ▼	VendorNum ▼	Date ▼	InvNum ▼	Amount ▼
tblInvoicesPaid	1	2001	1/1/2010	4242J10	$25.19
	2	2001	1/1/2010	7899J10	$25.86
	3	2001	1/1/2010	3830J10	$26.57
	4	2001	1/1/2010	9514J10	$27.83
	5	2001	1/1/2010	6296J10	$28.09
	6	2001	1/1/2010	5884J10	$28.34
	7	2001	1/1/2010	6908J10	$32.12
	8	2001	1/1/2010	6882J10	$34.22
	9	2001	1/1/2010	2104J10	$34.97
	10	2001	1/1/2010	0496J10	$36.08

FIGURE 4.4 The *InvoicesPaid* Table in Access

	A	B	C	D	E	F	G	H	I	J
1						DATA PROFILE				
2										
3	Details			Count		% of Total		$		% of Total
4	Amounts	10.00 and over				#DIV/0!				#DIV/0!
5	Amounts	0.01 to 9.99				#DIV/0!				#DIV/0!
6	Amounts	equal to zero				#DIV/0!				#DIV/0!
7	Amounts	-0.01 to -9.99				#DIV/0!				#DIV/0!
8	Amounts	-10.00 and under				#DIV/0!				#DIV/0!
9				------------		------------		------------------		------------
10				0		#DIV/0!		0.00		#DIV/0!
11				=========		=========		=============		=========
12										
13	Low-value Amounts									
14	Amounts	0.01 to 50.00				#DIV/0!				#DIV/0!
15				=========		=========		=============		=========
16										
17	High-value Amounts									
18	Amounts	100,000 and higher				#DIV/0!				#DIV/0!
19				=========		=========		=============		=========

FIGURE 4.5 The Data Profile Excel Template

tblInvoicesPaid in the top pane of the Query window to the grid on the bottom pane of the Query window. This is done by highlighting the *Amount* field and dragging it down to the lower part of the Query window.

The *Amount* field needs to be dragged to the Query grid three times. *Amount* can also be moved to the Query grid by highlighting the field in the top part of the Query window and then double-clicking on *Amount*. The Access functions that we need (**Count**, **Sum**,

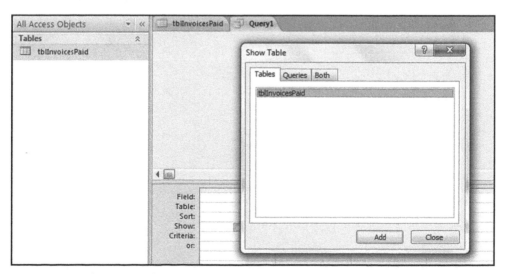

FIGURE 4.6 The First Dialog Box When Setting Up a Query in Access

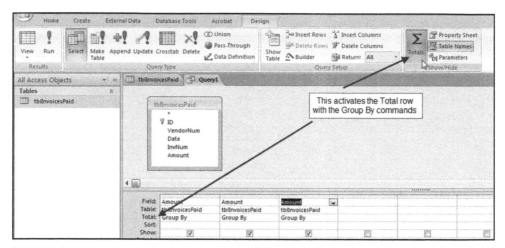

FIGURE 4.7   The Query Window with the Fields Selected and the Total Row Activated

and **Where**) only become visible in the lower pane of the Query grid after we click the **Totals** button (with the Greek sigma letter) using **Design→Show/Hide→Totals**.

Figure 4.7 shows that the fields have been selected and the **Total** row has been activated. The default command for the **Total** row is *Group By* and the data profile does not require a *Group By* command, but rather **Count**, **Sum**, and **Where**. The drop-down lists in the Totals row are used to select **Count**, **Sum**, and **Where**. For the first stratum we also need to insert the criteria **>=10**. The competed query grid, after saving the query as *qryDataProfile*, is shown in Figure 4.8. The three-letter prefix *qry* tells other Access users that the object is a query. Each of the descriptive words in the query name should be capitalized. There should not be any spaces in the query name.

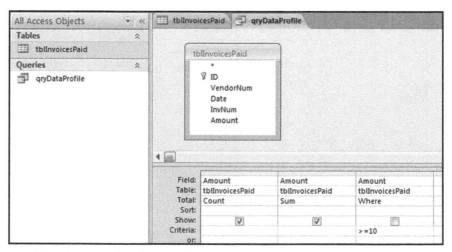

FIGURE 4.8   The Completed Query for the First Stratum of the Data Profile

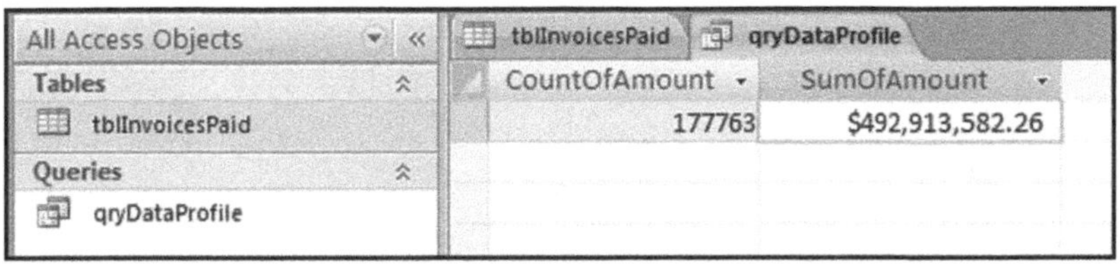

FIGURE 4.9 The Results of Running the First Data Profile Query

The completed query grid is shown in Figure 4.8. The query is run by clicking the **Run** button. This button is found at **Design→Results→Run**. The Run button has a large red exclamation point that makes it easy to see. The query results are shown in Figure 4.9.

It is usually necessary to widen the default column widths to see the full field names. The results tell us that the count of the amounts greater than or equal to 10 was 177,763 records, and the sum of the amounts greater than or equal to 10 was $492,913,582.26. We cannot format the output to a neatly comma delimited number of "177,763" after the query has run. All formatting must be done in the query Design View before running the query. The next step is to copy these results to the Excel template. The easiest way to do this is to highlight each result (separately) and to right-click and to use **Copy** and **Paste**. The Paste step in the Excel template is shown in Figure 4.10.

The **Copy** and **Paste** routine must be done for each of the 14 calculated values in the data profile (two calculated values per query). The other strata of the data profile have different bounds and different results and need to be calculated using a slightly different query. To get back to the Design View, right click on the **qryDataProfile** tab and select **Design View**. Once you are back in Design View, the only change that needs to be made for each strata is to change the **Criteria**. The Criteria for the next stratum is shown in Figure 4.11.

In Access "Between 0.01 And 9.99" means all numbers in the interval including 0.01 and 9.99. In everyday English we would use the words "from 0.01 to 9.99" to mean inclusive of 0.01 and 9.99. After the query in Figure 4.11 is run, the same **Copy**

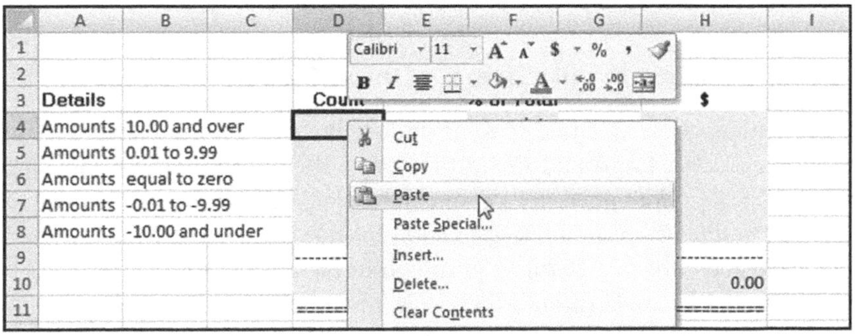

FIGURE 4.10 Pasting the Access Results into the Excel Template

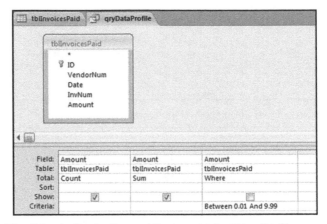

FIGURE 4.11 The Criteria for the Second Stratum in the Data Profile

and **Paste** routine should be followed to copy the results to the Excel template. The query can be reused for the remaining five strata and the criteria for these strata are shown below:

$$= 0$$
$$\text{Between} - 0.01 \text{ And} - 9.99$$
$$<= -10$$
$$\text{Between } 0.01 \text{ And } 50$$
$$>= 100000$$

The "Count-Sum-Where" query can be adapted to a number of useful situations. Functions other than Count and Sum could be used. For example, we might be interested in the average (**Avg**), the minimum (**Min**), or the Maximum (**Max**) for various ranges. If you require these statistics for the whole data table then the **Criteria** row should be left blank. We could only show some of our results and the check boxes in the **Show** row give us some options here. This section gives some good practice in using Access to calculate statistics for various strata. A shortcut using SQL and a Union query is shown in the next section.

Preparing the Data Profile Using a Union Query

In the previous section we used a somewhat tedious approach using seven Access queries together with **Copy** and **Paste** to prepare the data profile. In this section all seven queries will be combined to form one data profile query. To start we will make a copy of qryDataProfile and call it qryDataProfileAll. This is done by right-clicking qryDataProfile and choosing **Copy** as is shown in Figure 4.12.

The first step in making an exact copy of the data profile query is shown in Figure 4.12. After clicking **Copy** you now need to click **Paste**. At the prompt, name the new query, qryDataProfileAll.

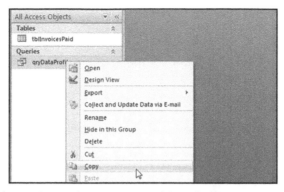

FIGURE 4.12 Making a Copy of an Existing and Saved Query

You now have two queries in your **Queries** group. Right click on *qryDataProfileAll* and open the query in Design View to show the familiar query grid. We are now going to enter the world of SQL (Structured Query Language) by using a right click on the query title (*qryDataProfileAll*) and then choosing *SQL View*. The SQL View screen is shown in Figure 4.13.

The good news is that SQL is quite readable. By simply changing the **Where** statement in the third line of code we can change the criteria. For example, changing the "10" in the third line to "100000" will give us the results for the largest strata in the last line of the data profile (where we looked at the high-value amounts). A query is run from SQL View exactly the same way as from Design View by clicking on the *Run* button. To get back to SQL View from the query result you click on the query title (*qryDataProfileAll*) and select SQL View.

With a union query we will run the seven strata queries at the same time by changing the criteria for each row. For example, the criterion for the first stratum is ">=10," and the criterion for the second stratum is "Between 0.01 and 9.99." To stack the queries on top of one another we need to (1) delete the semi colon and move it to the end of the query, (2) insert the word "Union" (without the quotation marks and preferably in capital letters) between each query, and (3) update the criteria.

The problem with the query as it stands is that the output is sorted based on the first field in ascending order. In this query it is clear which line in the results refers to which stratum. In other examples, it might not be so clear. We therefore need some way to keep the output in the same order as the strata in the data profile. To get Access to sort in the same order as the code we need to recognize that Access will sort on the first field ascending because we do not have an **Order By** statement in our code. We will use a little trick that leaves off any *Order By* statement and we will insert a new field at the left

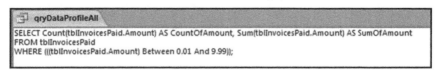

```
qryDataProfileAll
SELECT Count(tblInvoicesPaid.Amount) AS CountOfAmount, Sum(tblInvoicesPaid.Amount) AS SumOfAmount
FROM tblInvoicesPaid
WHERE (((tblInvoicesPaid.Amount) Between 0.01 And 9.99));
```

FIGURE 4.13 The SQL View of the Data Profile Query

```
qryDataProfileAll

SELECT "aLarge Positive" as Stratum, Count(tblInvoicesPaid.Amount) AS CountOfAmount, Sum(tblInvoicesPaid.Amount) AS SumOfAmount
FROM tblInvoicesPaid
WHERE (((tblInvoicesPaid.Amount)>=10))
UNION
SELECT "bSmall Positive" as Stratum, Count(tblInvoicesPaid.Amount) AS CountOfAmount, Sum(tblInvoicesPaid.Amount) AS SumOfAmount
FROM tblInvoicesPaid
WHERE (((tblInvoicesPaid.Amount) Between 0.01 and 9.99))
UNION
SELECT "cZeroes" as Stratum, Count(tblInvoicesPaid.Amount) AS CountOfAmount, Sum(tblInvoicesPaid.Amount) AS SumOfAmount
FROM tblInvoicesPaid
WHERE (((tblInvoicesPaid.Amount)=0))
UNION
SELECT "dSmallNegative" as Stratum, Count(tblInvoicesPaid.Amount) AS CountOfAmount, Sum(tblInvoicesPaid.Amount) AS SumOfAmount
FROM tblInvoicesPaid
WHERE (((tblInvoicesPaid.Amount) Between -0.01 And -9.99))
UNION SELECT "eLargeNegative" as Stratum, Count(tblInvoicesPaid.Amount) AS CountOfAmount, Sum(tblInvoicesPaid.Amount) AS SumOfAmount
FROM tblInvoicesPaid
WHERE (((tblInvoicesPaid.Amount)<=-10));
```

FIGURE 4.14 The SQL Code Used to Create the Data Profile with a Union Query

in such a way as to get the correct result. This new field will be a text field. Our new text field is created by inserting

"aLarge Positive" as Stratum,

in the first Select statement and using this pattern for all the other Select statements. The letter *a* before the words *Large Positive* is a little trick to get Access to show us this result first. The updated SQL code for the union query is shown in Figure 4.14.

By using **Copy** and **Paste** and by typing in the extra statements to correct the sort order we now have one query that will do the data profile calculations for five strata. The code to insert to correct the sort order is

"aLarge Positive" as Stratum,

"bSmall Positive" as Stratum,

"cZeroes" as Stratum,

"dSmall Negative" as Stratum,

"eLarge Negative" as Stratum,

The results of running the *qryDataProfileAll* query are shown in Figure 4.15.

The field names can be easily changed in the SQL code. For example, *Count of Amount* could simply be called *Count*. The entire field (all five numbers in *CountOfAmount* or all five numbers of *SumOfAmount*) can now be easily copied to the data profile template *DataProfile.xlsx*. Note that the query *qryDataProfileAll* is now a Union query and it cannot be viewed in Design View any more. Once the query has been saved and

Stratum	CountOfAmount	SumOfAmount
aLarge Positive	177763	$492,913,582.26
bSmall Positive	7320	$40,159.47
cZeroes	123	$0.00
dSmallNegative	195	($1,121.31)
eLargeNegative	4069	($2,674,995.52)

FIGURE 4.15 The Results of the Data Profile Union Query

	A	B	C	D	E	F	G
1	VendorNum	Date	InvNum	Amount			
2	2001	1/1/2010	0496J99	$36.08			
3	2001	1/1/2010	1726J99	$77.80			
4	2001	1/1/2010	2104J99	$34.97			
5	2001	1/1/2010	2445J99	$59.00			
6	2001	1/1/2010	3281J99	$59.59			

19	2001	1/1/2010	5793J99	$94.29			
20	2001	1/1/2010	5884J99	$28.34			
21	2001	1/1/2010	5991J99	$55.29			
22	2001	1/1/2010	6296J99	$28.09			
23	2001	1/1/2010	6585J99	$46.64			
24	2001	1/1/2010	6726J99	$49.91			
25	2001	1/1/2010	6882J99	$34.22			

⏮ ◀ ▶ ⏭ Tables ╱ DataProfile ╱ FirstOrder ╱ SecondOrder ╱ Summation ╱ LastTwoDigits ╲ **Data** ╱

FIGURE 4.16 The *Data* Tab of the *NigriniCycle* Template

closed you should see two silver rings to the left of the name *qryDataProfileAll* indicating that the query is a Union query.

PREPARING THE DATA PROFILE USING EXCEL

The data profile can also be prepared in Excel. This option works well when the original data is in an Excel file and when the number of records is less than the maximum row count in Excel (1,048,576 rows). The companion site to the book includes a file called *NigriniCycle.xlsx*. This template can be used for a number of tests including the data profile. For this example, the invoices data has been copied into the file into the *Data* tab. This is the default data location and if this convention is followed then the data profile is reasonably straightforward. The demonstration, though, is with a file named *NigriniCycle&InvoicesData.xlsx*. The *Data* tab is shown in Figure 4.16.

It is reasonably easy to import the data into the *NigriniCycle* template and the *Data* tab of that file is shown in Figure 4.16. The data profile is prepared in the *DataProfile* tab. The first COUNTIFS function can be entered into cell D4 as is shown in Figure 4.17.

D4	▾		f_x =COUNTIFS(Data!$D$2:$D$189471,">=10")						

	A	B	C	D	E	F	G	H	I	J
1					DATA PROFILE					
2										
3	Details			Count		% of Total		$		% of Total
4	Amounts	10.00 and over		177,763		100.00				#DIV/0!
5	Amounts	0.01 to 9.99				0.00				#DIV/0!
6	Amounts	equal to zero				0.00				#DIV/0!
7	Amounts	-0.01 to -9.99				0.00				#DIV/0!
8	Amounts	-10.00 and under				0.00				#DIV/0!
9				------------		------------		--------------		------------
10				177,763		100.00		$0.00		#DIV/0!
11				=========		=========		============		=========

FIGURE 4.17 The COUNTIF Function Used in the Data Profile

The first Excel formula used in the data profile is shown in Figure 4.17. The tab name in the function is followed by an exclamation point. This is followed by the range and the criteria. The criterion is entered in quotes. The **COUNTIFS** function is meant for two or more criteria and we only have one criterion for the $>=10$ strata. The **COUNTIF** function would have worked fine here. The **COUNTIFS** function is used to be consistent with the other strata. The formulas for all the cells in column D are shown below:

$$=COUNTIFS(Data!\$D\$2:\$D\$189471, ">=10")$$

$$=COUNTIFS(Data!\$D\$2:\$D\$189471, ">=.01",$$
$$Data!\$D\$2:\$D\$189471, "<=9.99")$$

$$=COUNTIFS(Data!\$D\$2:\$D\$189471, "=0")$$

$$=COUNTIFS(Data!\$D\$2:\$D\$189471, ">=-9.99",$$
$$Data!\$D\$2:\$D\$189471, "<=-0.01")$$

$$=COUNTIFS(Data!\$D\$2:\$D\$189471, "<=-10")$$

$$=COUNTIFS(Data!\$D\$2:\$D\$189471, ">=.01",$$
$$Data!\$D\$2:\$D\$189471, "<=50.00")$$

$$=COUNTIFS(Data!\$D\$2:\$D\$189471, ">=100000")$$

With the COUNTIFS function we state the range and a criterion, followed by a second range and another criterion, if applicable. For the second entry the first criterion was >-0.01 and the second criterion was $<=9.99$.

The SUMIFS function can be used for the calculations in column H. The SUMIFS function is a little bit more complex in that the range to be summed is entered first, followed by the ranges and criteria. The worksheet function for the cells in column H are shown below:

$$=SUMIFS(Data!\$D\$2:\$D\$189471, Data!\$D\$2:\$D\$189471, ">=10")$$

$$=SUMIFS(Data!\$D\$2:\$D\$189471, Data!\$D\$2:\$D\$189471, ">=.01",$$
$$Data!\$D\$2:\$D\$189471, "<=9.99")$$

$$=SUMIFS(Data!\$D\$2:\$D\$189471, Data!\$D\$2:\$D\$189471, "=0")$$

$$=SUMIFS(Data!\$D\$2:\$D\$189471, Data!\$D\$2:\$D\$189471, ">=-9.99",$$
$$Data!\$D\$2:\$D\$189471, "<=-0.01")$$

$$=SUMIFS(Data!\$D\$2:\$D\$189471, Data!\$D\$2:\$D\$189471, "<=-10")$$

$$=SUMIFS(Data!\$D\$2:\$D\$189471, Data!\$D\$2:\$D\$189471, ">=.01",$$
$$Data!\$D\$2:\$D\$189471, "<=50")$$

$$=SUMIFS(Data!\$D\$2:\$D\$189471, Data!\$D\$2:\$D\$189471, ">=100000")$$

H5			f_x	=SUMIFS(Data!$D$2:$D$189471,Data!$D$2:$D$189471,">=.01",Data!$D$2:$D$189471,"<=9.99")

	A	B	C	D	E	F	G	H	I	J	K
1						DATA PROFILE					
2											
3	Details			Count		% of Total		$		% of Total	
4	Amounts	10.00 and over		177,763		93.82		$492,913,582.26		100.54	
5	Amounts	0.01 to 9.99		7,320		3.86		$40,159.47		0.01	
6	Amounts	equal to zero		123		0.06		$0.00		0.00	
7	Amounts	-0.01 to -9.99		195		0.10		-$1,121.31		0.00	
8	Amounts	-10.00 and under		4,069		2.15		-$2,674,995.52		-0.55	
9				------------		------------		------------		------------	
10				189,470		100.00		$490,277,624.90		100.00	
11				=========		=========		=============		=========	
12											
13	Low-value Amounts										
14	Amounts	0.01 to 50.00		43,253		22.83		$1,188,603.10		0.24	
15				=========		=========		=============		=========	
16											
17	High-value Amounts										
18	Amounts	100,000 and higher		370		0.20		$242,946,614.32		49.55	
19				=========		=========		=============		=========	

FIGURE 4.18 The Data Profile Prepared in Excel

The data profile prepared in Excel is shown in Figure 4.18. Note that columns F and J already have the formulas needed for the calculation of the percentages.

The numbers in columns D and H have been neatly formatted. This file can be reused. As long as the amounts to be counted and summed are in column D of the *Data* tab then the data profile will be calculated correctly. Note, though, that the ranges (where the ending cell here is D189471) must be changed each time that the file is used.

CALCULATING THE INPUTS FOR THE PERIODIC GRAPH IN ACCESS

The periodic graph is a reasonably straightforward columnar graph prepared in Excel. Calculating the monthly totals is a little bit tricky but this can be done quite easily in Access. The Access route is the only one demonstrated in the chapter. The query logic in Access uses two queries. The first query calculates the month from the date and the second query sums the dollars per month. We need to calculate the month because the totals are monthly totals. The query to calculate the month from the date is shown in Figure 4.19.

The Access function used is **Month**. This function assumes that the date is correctly formatted as a date. The next query calculates the monthly totals and this is shown in Figure 4.20.

The query groups the records by month and then calculates the sum, maximum, average, and the count of the dollar amount of the records. The results are shown in Figure 4.21.

The monthly statistics are shown in Figure 4.21. It can be seen that the sums for months 2 and 4 are larger than the average monthly sum. The *SumOfAmount* field is the

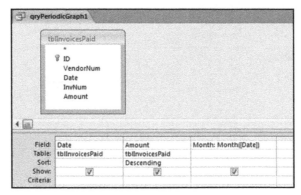

FIGURE 4.19 The Query Used to Calculate the Month from the Date

qryPeriodicGraph2

qryPeriodicGraph1

Date
Amount
Month

Field:	Month	Amount	Amount	Amount	Amount	Amount
Table:	qryPeriodicGraph1	qryPeriodicGraph1	qryPeriodicGraph1	qryPeriodicGraph1	qryPeriodicGraph1	qryPeriodicGraph1
Total:	Group By	Sum	Max	Min	Avg	Count
Sort:						
Show:	☑	☑	☑	☑	☑	☑
Criteria:						

FIGURE 4.20 The Query Used to Calculate the Monthly Statistics

qryPeriodicGraph2

Month ▾	SumOfAmount ▾	MaxOfAmount ▾	MinOfAmount ▾	AvgOfAmount ▾	CountOfAmount ▾
1	$44,805,166.31	$3,000,000.00	($10,076.40)	$2,138.37	20,953
2	$67,919,969.86	$15,779,215.20	($23,659.20)	$2,512.02	27,038
3	$39,168,956.51	$2,000,000.00	($17,311.34)	$1,998.62	19,598
4	$64,354,934.60	$26,763,475.78	($9,502.94)	$4,826.38	13,334
5	$21,475,272.57	$1,500,000.00	($28,656.99)	$1,838.79	11,679
6	$27,476,046.56	$1,500,000.00	($38,138.64)	$2,160.41	12,718
7	$31,477,426.38	$1,500,000.00	($3,830.00)	$2,549.40	12,347
8	$31,419,230.85	$1,500,000.00	($22,034.25)	$2,429.95	12,930
9	$35,366,425.11	$1,500,000.00	($24,670.76)	$2,878.83	12,285
10	$37,970,150.56	$1,500,000.00	($8,369.76)	$2,881.98	13,175
11	$48,831,160.25	$5,990,958.38	($6,951.01)	$3,677.05	13,280
12	$40,012,885.34	$846,000.00	($71,388.00)	$1,987.43	20,133

FIGURE 4.21 The Monthly Statistics of the Invoices Data

field graphed in Figure 4.3. The other calculated fields are there to gain a little more insight into the data. The next section calculates the inputs for the histogram.

PREPARING A HISTOGRAM IN ACCESS USING AN INTERVAL TABLE

We will use Access to do the calculations and we will use Excel to prepare the graphs. A Union query would work but it would get tiring to keep changing the intervals in the SQL code. With 10 Between statements it would be easy to make an error and to double-count or to omit some records.

For the histogram we will use a table called *IntervalBounds* to help with the calculation of the counts for the 10 intervals. As a start we need to find out what the minimum and maximum values are for our data. This is done by looking at the *MinOfAmount* and *MaxOfAmount* fields in Figure 4.21. We need the smallest minimum and the largest maximum.

We will use our minimum of –$71,388.00 and our maximum of $26,763,475.78 to set our histogram's intervals. The next step is to create an *IntervalBounds.xlsx* table in Excel. This table will hold what we believe to be a good starting point for the histogram intervals. In most cases the lower bounds are equal to the upper bounds of the previous interval. To avoid double-counting we will use greater than (>) for the lower bound and less than or equal to (< =) for the upper bound so that an amount such as $2,000 will only be counted in one interval. The lower and upper bounds should be formatted as currency with two decimal places because that is the format of our Access data. The *IntervalBounds.xlsx* table is shown in Figure 4.22.

This table should now be imported into Access using **External Data→Import→ Excel**. Select the **First Row Contains Column Headings** option and let Access add a primary key. The *SortOrder* field is used in Access to keep the output sorted in the "correct" order. The Access table should be named *tblIntervalBounds*. The calculations for the histogram are done with a reasonably complex Access query that is shown in Figure 4.23.

	A	B	C	D
1	SortOrder	Interval	LowerBound	UpperBound
2	1	Interval1	-$100,000.00	$0.00
3	2	Interval2	$0.00	$1,000.00
4	3	Interval3	$1,000.00	$2,000.00
5	4	Interval4	$2,000.00	$3,000.00
6	5	Interval5	$3,000.00	$4,000.00
7	6	Interval6	$4,000.00	$5,000.00
8	7	Interval7	$5,000.00	$6,000.00
9	8	Interval8	$6,000.00	$7,000.00
10	9	Interval9	$7,000.00	$8,000.00
11	10	Interval10	$8,000.00	$30,000,000.00

FIGURE 4.22 The Excel Table Used to Calculate the Values for the Histogram

FIGURE 4.23 The Query Used to Calculate the Values for the Histogram

The "Criteria" in the last column is

$>=$ [tblIntervalBounds]![LowerBound] And $<$ [tblIntervalBounds]![UpperBound]

The Figure 4.23 query uses two tables without a solid line or an arrow joining the two tables. This is a little Access trick that works well in certain very specific situations. The usual rule for queries is that two or more tables should be joined. The results of *qryHistogram* are shown in Figure 4.24.

It is a good idea to sum the *CountOfAmount* field to see that the total number of records agrees with the total number of records in the data profile. Save the query as *qryHistogram*. The *CountOfAmount* field is used to prepare a histogram graph as is shown in Figure 4.2. The companion site for the book includes an Excel template named *Histogram.xlsx*. This template can be used to prepare a histogram similar to Figure 4.2. Note that *qryHistogram* can be rerun with different upper and lower bounds by changing the numbers in *tblIntervalBounds*. The query can be rerun as many times as is needed to give meaningful insights. The updated table *tblIntervalBounds* should be saved before *qryHistogram* is rerun.

qryHistogram			
SortOrder ▾	LowerBound ▾	UpperBound ▾	CountOfAmount ▾
1	-$100,000.00	$0.00	4264
2	$0.00	$1,000.00	146548
3	$1,000.00	$2,000.00	19300
4	$2,000.00	$3,000.00	3897
5	$3,000.00	$4,000.00	2078
6	$4,000.00	$5,000.00	1201
7	$5,000.00	$6,000.00	937
8	$6,000.00	$7,000.00	883
9	$7,000.00	$8,000.00	965
10	$8,000.00	$30,000,000.00	9397

FIGURE 4.24 The Results of the Histogram Query

 **SUMMARY**

This chapter introduces forensic analytic tests with three high-level tests designed to give an overview of the data. These tests are designed to be the starting line-up in a series of tests. Chapter 18 gives an example of a series of tests (starting with these high-level overview tests) applied to purchasing card data. The first high-level overview test is the data profile. The data profile gives the investigator a first look at the data. In the data profile the data is grouped into seven groups. These groups are small and large positive amounts, small and large negative amounts, and zero amounts. The data profile also includes a "somewhat small" and a "relatively large" category. The ranges for the data profile can be adapted for numbers in different ranges. For example, grocery store prices are all relatively small numbers and economic statistics are usually very large numbers. The data profile gives the count and the sum for each stratum as well as percentages for the strata. In an accounts payable setting the data profile can suggest processing inefficiencies, and in other settings the data profile could point to data errors with perhaps negative numbers in data sets that should not have negative numbers. The steps taken to create the data profile and the work done to understand its contents all help to give the investigator a better understanding of the data.

The data profile calculations can be done using Access queries. The calculations for each data profile stratum can be done one at a time, or a Union query can be used to do the calculations all at once. The Access results are then copied to an Excel template for a neat presentation format. If the data set has less than 1,048,576 records then all the calculations can be done in Excel using the new COUNTIFS and SUMIFS functions.

The second test was the periodic graph. Here we look at the month-by-month trend. Large fluctuations tell us something about the data. This test is run using Access to perform the calculations and Excel to prepare the graph. This combination often works well in a forensic setting.

The third high-level test was the preparation of a histogram. The familiar histogram is a bar chart showing the counts of the amounts in various intervals. It seems that 10 histogram intervals would work well in most financial settings. The suggested approach is to do the calculations in Access and to prepare the graph in Excel. The histogram gives the investigator another view of the shape of the distribution. Histograms tell us which numeric ranges have the highest counts. A histogram for the current period is informative, but it is even more informative to compare the histograms for the current and the prior period to see whether conditions have changed. Chapter 9 shows how a histogram can be used to look for signs that conditions have changed. These changes might be red flags for errors or fraud.

Discussions with auditors have shown that they are keen to show that their audit provides some value above and beyond the audit report. These value-added discussions usually take place after the audit in the management letter meeting with the audit committee. Auditors indicated that the results of some forensic analytic tests using descriptive statistics (including a data profile, periodic graph, and histograms) showing some anomalies, would be something that they could use at these post-audit meetings. Other auditors suggested that they might suggest selected forensic analytic tests to management as tests that management could perform on an ongoing basis on their data in a continuous monitoring environment. They, the external auditors, would then use the results in the audit as evidence that the process was being regularly monitored by management. Chapters 5 to 14 review a number of forensic analytic tests that can be carried out on a regular basis. Chapters 15 and 16 show how several tests can be combined to score forensic units for risk. The concluding Chapter 18 shows how the tests can be used in a purchasing card environment.

CHAPTER FIVE

Benford's Law

The Basics

T HE BENFORD'S LAW–BASED TESTS signal abnormal duplications. The mathematics of Benford's Law gives us the *expected* or the *normal* duplications, and duplications above the norm are *abnormal* or *excessive*. Bolton and Hand (2002) state that the statistical tools for fraud detection all have a common theme in that observed values are usually compared to a set of expected values. They also say that depending on the context, these expected values can be derived in various ways and could vary on a continuum from single numerical or graphical summaries all the way to complex multivariate behavior profiles. They contrast supervised methods of fraud detection that use samples of both fraudulent and nonfraudulent records, or un-supervised methods that identify transactions or customers that are most dissimilar to some norm (i.e., outliers). They are correct when they say that we can seldom be certain by statistical analysis alone that a fraud has been perpetrated. The forensic analysis should give us an alert that a record is anomalous, or more likely to be fraudulent than others, so that it can be investigated in more detail. The authors suggest the concept of a *suspicion score* where higher scores are correlated with records that are more unusual or more like previous fraudulent values. Suspicion scores could be computed for each record in a table and it would be most cost-effective to concentrate on the records with the highest scores. Their overview of detection tools includes a review of Benford's Law and its expected digit patterns. Chapters 15 and 16 show how formal risk scores (like their suspicion scores) can be developed from predictors for the forensic units of interest.

Benford's Law gives the expected frequencies of the digits in tabulated data. As a fraud investigation technique Benford's Law also qualifies as a high-level overview. Nonconformity to Benford's Law is an indicator of an increased risk of fraud or error. Nonconformity does not signal fraud or error with certainty. Further work is always needed. The next four chapters add ever-increasing layers of complexity. The general goal, though, is to find abnormal duplications in data sets. The path from Chapter 4 to Chapter 12 is one that starts with high-level overview tests and then drills deeper and deeper searching for abnormal duplications of digits, digit combinations, specific numbers, and exact or near-duplicate records. Benford's Law provides a solid theoretical start for determining what is normal and what constitutes an abnormal duplication. The cycle of tests is designed to point the investigator toward (a) finding fraud (where the fraudster has excessively duplicated their actions), (b) finding errors (where the error is systematic), (c) finding outliers, (d) finding biases (perhaps where employees have many purchases just below their authorization level), and (e) finding processing inefficiencies (e.g., numerous small invoices from certain vendors).

The format of this chapter is to review Benford's original paper. Thereafter, the Benford's Law literature is reviewed. The chapter then demonstrates the standard set of Benford's Law tests. These tests concentrate only on a single field of numbers. The chapter continues with the invoices data from the previous chapter. The tests are demonstrated using a combination of Access and Excel.

AN OVERVIEW OF BENFORD'S LAW

Benford's Law gives the expected frequencies of the digits in tabulated data. The set of expected digit frequencies is named after Frank Benford, a physicist who published the seminal paper on the topic (Benford, 1938). In his paper he found that contrary to intuition, the digits in tabulated data are not all equally likely and have a biased skewness in favor of the lower digits.

Benford begins his paper by noting that the first few pages of a book of common logarithms show more wear than the last few pages. From this he concludes that the first few pages are used more often than the last few pages. The first few pages of logarithm books give us the logs of numbers with low first digits (e.g., 1, 2, and 3). He hypothesized that the worn first pages was because most of the "used" numbers in the world had a low first digit. The first digit is the leftmost digit in a number and, for example, the first digit of 110,364 is a 1. Zero is inadmissible as a first digit and there are nine possible first digits (1, 2, . . . , 9). The signs of negative numbers are ignored and so the first-two digits of −34.83 are 34.

Benford analyzed the first digits of 20 lists of numbers with a total of 20,229 records. He made an effort to collect data from as many sources as possible and to include a variety of different types of data sets. His data varied from random numbers having no relationship to each other, such as the numbers from the front pages of newspapers and all the numbers in an issue of *Reader's Digest*, to formal mathematical tabulations such as mathematical tables and scientific constants. Other data sets included the drainage areas of rivers, population numbers, American League statistics, and street numbers from an issue of *American Men of Science*. Benford analyzed either the entire data set at hand, or in the case of large data sets, he worked to the point that he was assured that he had a fair average. All of his work and calculations were done by hand and the work was probably quite time-consuming. The shortest list (atomic weights) in his list had 91 records and the largest list had 5,000 records.

Benford's results showed that on average 30.6 percent of the numbers had a first digit 1, and 18.5 percent of the numbers had a first digit 2. This means that 49.1 percent of his records had a first digit that was either a 1 or a 2. At the other end of the "digit-scale" only 4.7 percent of his records had a first digit 9. Benford then saw a pattern to his results. The actual proportion for the first digit 1 was almost equal to the common logarithm of 2 (or 2/1), and the actual proportion for the first digit 2 was almost equal to the common logarithm of 3/2. This logarithmic pattern continued through to the 9 with the proportion for the first digit 9 approximating the common logarithm of 10/9.

Benford then derived the expected frequencies of the digits in lists of numbers and these frequencies have now become known as Benford's Law. The formulas for the digit frequencies are shown below with D_1 representing the first digit, D_2 the second digit, and D_1D_2 the first-two digits of a number:

$$P(D_1 = d_1) = \log\left(1 + \frac{1}{d_1}\right) \quad d_1 \in \{1, 2, \dots, 9\} \tag{5.1}$$

$$P(D_2 = d_2) = \sum_{d_1=1}^{9} \log\left(1 + \frac{1}{d_1 d_2}\right) \quad d_2 \in \{0, 1, \dots, 9\} \tag{5.2}$$

$$P(D_1 D_2 = d_1 d_2) = \log\left(1 + \frac{1}{d_1 d_2}\right) \quad d_1 d_2 \in \{10, 11, \dots, 99\} \tag{5.3}$$

where P indicates the probability of observing the event in parentheses and log refers to the log to the base 10. The formula for the expected first-two digit proportions is shown in Equation 5.3. For the first-two digits, the expected frequencies are also highly skewed, and range from 4.139 percent for the 10 combination down to 0.436 percent for the 99 combination. The first-two digits of 110,364 are 11. Using Equation 5.3, the expected proportion for the first-two digits 64 would be calculated as follows:

$$P(D_1 D_2 = 64) = \log(1 + (1/64)) = 0.006733 \tag{5.4}$$

The expected frequencies for the digits in the first, second, third, and fourth positions is shown in Table 5.1. As we move to the right the digits tend toward being equally distributed. If we are dealing with numbers with three or more digits then for all practical purposes the ending digits (the rightmost digits) are expected to be evenly (uniformly) distributed.

TABLE 5.1 The Expected Digit Frequencies of Benford's Law

Digit	1st	2nd	3rd	4th
		Position in Number		
0		.11968	.10178	.10018
1	.30103	.11389	.10138	.10014
2	.17609	.10882	.10097	.10010
3	.12494	.10433	.10057	.10006
4	.09691	.10031	.10018	.10002
5	.07918	.09668	.09979	.09998
6	.06695	.09337	.09940	.09994
7	.05799	.09035	.09902	.09990
8	.05115	.08757	.09864	.09986
9	.04576	.08500	.09827	.09982

Source: Nigrini, M. J., 1996. "A taxpayer compliance application of Benford's Law." *The Journal of the American Taxation Association* 18 (Spring): 72–91.

The table shows that the expected proportion of numbers with a first digit 2 is 0.17609 and the expected proportion of numbers with a fourth digit 4 is 0.10002.

In the discussion section of his paper Benford noted that the observed probabilities were more closely related to "events" than to the number system itself. He noted that some of the best fits to the logarithmic pattern (of the digits) was for data in which the numbers had no relationship to each other, such as the numbers from newspaper articles. He then associated the logarithmic pattern of the digits with a geometric progression (or geometric sequence) by noting that in natural events and in events of which man considers himself the originator there are plenty of examples of geometric or logarithmic progressions. Benford concluded that nature counts e^0, e^x, e^{2x}, e^{3x}, and so on, and builds and functions accordingly because numbers that follow such a pattern end up with digit patterns close to those in Table 5.1. Figure 5.1 is an example of a geometric sequence of 1,000 numbers ranging from 10 to 100.

A geometric sequence such as is shown in Figure 5.1 is a sequence of terms in which each successive term is the previous term multiplied by a common ratio. The usual mathematical representation for such a sequence is given by

$$S_n = ar^{n-1} \tag{5.5}$$

where a is the first term in the sequence, r is the common ratio, and n denotes the nth term. In Figure 5.1, a equals 10, and r (the common ratio) equals 1.002305. There are 1,000 terms in the sequence shown in Figure 5.1. Using the assumption that the ordered (ranked from smallest to largest) records in a data set is made up of natural numbers from a geometric sequence, Benford then derived the expected frequencies of

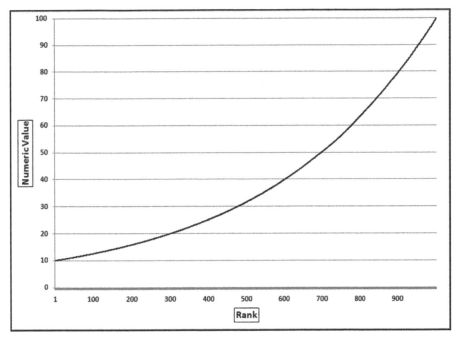

FIGURE 5.1 A Geometric Sequence of 1,000 Records with the Numeric Amounts Ranging from 10 to 100

the digits for tabulated "natural" data. The formulas are shown in Equations 5.1, 5.2, and 5.3 and the first through fourth digit frequencies are shown in Table 5.1.

Benford provided no guidance as to when a data set should follow the expected frequencies other than a reference to natural events and science-related phenomena developed by people. Benford gave examples of geometric progressions such as our sense of brightness and loudness. He also referred to the music scales, the response of the body to medicine, standard sizes in mechanical tools, and the geometric brightness scale used by astronomers. The strong geometric foundation of Benford's Law means that a data table will have Benford-like properties if the ranked (ordered from smallest to largest) records closely approximate a geometric sequence. Chapter 8 goes further with the discussion of the geometric basis of Benford's Law.

 FROM THEORY TO APPLICATION IN 60 YEARS

The first Benford's Law papers were published by Goudsmit and Furry (1944) and Furry and Hurwitz (1945). The 1944 paper suggests that Benford's Law is merely the result of the way that we write numbers and the 1945 paper is a mathematical discussion of Benford's formulas. Interestingly, Stigler (1945) wrote an unpublished working paper in which he challenged the basis of Benford's Law and gave an alternative distribution of the digits in lists of numbers. This was later called Stigler's Law. Nobel-laureate Stigler never published the paper. Stigler's logic is questioned in Raimi (1976) and it would therefore appear that to win a Nobel Prize, one should know what to publish and what to leave in working paper format.

The third Benford's Law paper was published in 1948 in *The Journal of General Psychology* (Hsu, 1948). Hsu apparently saw the link between Benford's results and human behavior. Hsu's only reference in his 1948 paper is to Benford's 1938 paper. Hsu had 1,044 faculty and students invent a four-digit number with the requirement that the number was *original* and should not represent an event, a fact, or a date. His results showed that the numbers did not follow Benford's Law and he believed that this was because Benford's Law did not apply to mental numbers. These results are an important early finding and shows that nonconformity to Benford's Law is not always an indicator of fraud or error.

The most significant advance in the 1960s was by Pinkham (1961). Pinkham posed the question that if there were indeed some law governing digital distributions then this law should be scale invariant. That is, if the digits of the areas of the world's islands, or the length of the world's rivers followed a law of some sort, then it should be immaterial if these measurements were expressed in (square) miles or (square) kilometers. Pinkham then proved that Benford's Law is scale invariant under multiplication. So, if all the numbers in a data table that followed Benford's Law were multiplied by a (nonzero) constant, then the new data table would also follow Benford's Law. A list of numbers that conform to Benford's Law is known as a Benford Set. What is notable is that Pinkham proved that it was *only* the frequencies of Benford's Law that were invariant under multiplication. So if a data set has digit frequencies other than those of Benford's Law, then multiplication by a (nonzero) constant will result in changed digital frequencies. It would seem logical that the closer the fit before multiplication (irrespective of the constant), then the closer the fit after multiplication. It is interesting that Pinkham's introduction states that any reader formerly unaware of Benford's Law would find an actual sampling experiment "wondrously tantalizing." Fifty years ago such an experiment would have required a great deal of effort. It is only now that such an experiment would really be wondrously tantalizing without being mentally exhausting.

Good (1965) was the first person to formally use Benford's Law. Good noted that certain random number tables had been formed by taking the middle three digits of the areas of English parishes. Good claimed that this would not produce random number tables because under Benford's Law the digits are not all equally likely, and such a table would have random numbers slightly biased toward the low digits.

There were two Benford developments in 1966. Feller (1966) developed an alternative proof for Benford's Law and Flehinger (1966) also developed an alternative proof for Benford's Law. Flehinger's proof has been criticized because she uses a special summation and averaging method (Holder sums), and mathematicians contend that using special tricks that end up with Benford's frequencies do not constitute a proof. That is, if the end result of your mathematical calculations equals Benford's Law, it does not mean that you have proved Benford's Law.

The first Asian contribution to the field came from the Indian Statistical Institute by way of Adhikari and Sarkar (1968) who developed a few theorems relating to numbers distributed uniformly over the range 0 to 1. They showed that after certain mathematical operations the numbers formed a Benford Set. In the next year Raimi (1969a) provided mathematical support for Benford's Law using Banach and other scale invariant measures. Raimi (1969b) is an excellent nonmathematical review of Benford's Law with some intuitive explanations of what later came to be called the *first digit phenomenon* in many papers. The second Raimi paper was the first time that Benford's Law made it into a widely circulated and highly respected medium (*Scientific American*). There was more to 1969 than the Woodstock rock festival because Adhikari (1969), now on a roll, followed his earlier paper with a few more theorems. Knuth (1969) completed the 1960s with a simplified proof of Flehinger's result and a reasonably in-depth discussion of Benford's Law.

The 1970s started with Hamming (1970) and an application of Benford's Law. Hamming considers the mantissa distribution of products and sums and gives applications of Benford's Law in round-off error analysis and computing accuracy considerations. The early 1970s also started a stream of articles by Fibonacci theorists who showed that the familiar Fibonacci sequence (1, 1, 2, 3, 5, 8, . . .) follows Benford's Law perfectly. The *Fibonacci Quarterly* journal became the first journal to publish six Benford's Law papers in the same decade. It is interesting that the Fibonacci sequence plays a role in *The Da Vinci Code*, the best-selling novel by Dan Brown. The Fibonacci sequence has also been featured in popular culture including cinema, television, comic strips, literature, music, and the visual arts. To see a reasonably good fit to Benford's Law the sequence should have about 300 or more elements. The more Fibonacci elements there are, the closer is the fit to Benford's Law. In the first of these papers Wlodarski (1971) shows that the first digits of the first 100 Fibonacci and the first 100 Lucas numbers approximates the expected frequencies of Benford's Law. Sentence (1973) tests the first 1,000 Fibonacci and Lucas numbers showing a close fit to Benford's Law. Several years later Brady (1978) tests the first 2,000 Fibonacci and Lucas numbers with an even closer fit to Benford's Law. Technically speaking, the Fibonacci sequence is an example of an asymptotically (approximate) geometric sequence with r (the common ratio) tending toward $(1 + \sqrt{5})/2$. These 1970s studies would have used reasonably complex computer programming because the Fibonacci numbers become very large very quickly and by the 100th Fibonacci number Excel has started to round the number to 16 digits.

By now researchers had begun to question whether Benford's Law had practical purposes and Varian (1972) questioned whether Benford's Law could be used to assess the reliability of forecasts. He tabulated the first-digit frequencies of a few sets of demographic data. The original data conformed quite closely to Benford's Law. He then checked the frequencies of forecasts made from the data. The forecasts also followed Benford's Law. Varian concluded that checking forecasts against Benford's Law was a potential test of the *reasonableness* of the forecasts. Another paper addressing the usefulness of Benford's Law appeared just two years later when Tsao (1974) applied Benford's Law to round off errors of computers.

Goudsmit (1977) delved into the Benford's Law past and shared the insight that the paper following Benford's paper in the journal was an important physics paper by Bethe and Rose. Physicists that read the Bethe and Rose paper saw the last page of Benford's paper on the left-hand page in the journal. They presumably found it interesting and went back to read all of Benford's paper. Goudsmit should know because he coauthored the first paper on the topic. It is amazing to think that had a stream of literature not been started by the readers of Bethe and Rose, that Benford's gem would not have been noted by academics or practitioners. It would seem that even if forensic analytic practitioners noted casually that more numbers began with a 1 than any other digit, they would probably not think that a precise expected distribution existed.

The most influential paper of the 1970s was Ralph Raimi's 1976 review paper published in *American Mathematical Monthly*. Raimi (1976) reviews the literature, which at that time came to 37 papers, including the original paper by Benford. Raimi also lists 15 other papers that mentioned Benford's Law in passing. According to Google Scholar, Raimi's 1976 paper has been cited by 160 Benford papers. Raimi starts with the digit frequency results from just a few data sets reinforcing the belief that data analysis prior to the 1990s was a labor-intensive process. Raimi includes an interesting result related to electricity usage. Raimi then continues with what he calls "a bit of philosophy." He then critiques some approaches to proving Benford's Law by noting that just because some mathematical method gives the Benford probabilities as their result, this does not prove Benford's Law. This is because there are many methods that will not result in the Benford probabilities. Raimi's concluding comments include a few gems such as the fact that he liked Varian's suggestion that Benford's Law could be used as a test of the validity of scientific data, and his belief that "social scientists need all the tools of suspicion they can find" (Raimi, 1976, 536).

The 1980s

The 1980s began with two Benford papers that addressed the potential usefulness of Benford's Law. Becker (1982) compared the digit frequencies of failure rate and Mean-Time-to-Failure tables with Benford's Law. He concluded that Benford's Law can be used to "quickly check lists of failure rate or MTTF-values for systematic errors." Nelson (1984) discussed accuracy loss due to rounding to two significant digits. He used Benford's Law to compute the average maximum loss in accuracy.

The Benford's Law literature has included some research that questions the validity of Benford's Law. Some questions should be expected, given the counterintuitiveness of the digit patterns. What is surprising in this case is the source of the challenge, namely Samuel Goudsmit (who published the first Benford's Law paper in 1944). Raimi (1985) discusses the basis and logic of Benford's Law and his 1985 paper concludes with an extract from a letter from Samuel Goudsmit (dated 21 July, 1978) in which Goudsmit claims that:

> To a physicist Simon Newcomb's explanation of the first-digit phenomenon is more than sufficient "for all practical purposes." Of course here the expression "for all practical purposes" has no meaning. There are no practical purposes, unless you consider betting for money on first digit frequencies with gullible colleagues a practical use. (Goudsmit as quoted in Raimi, 1985, 218)

Tax evasion, auditing, and forensic analytics research shows that there *are* practical uses of Benford's Law. It is interesting that Goudsmit published the first paper on Benford's Law after the publication of Benford's paper (Goudsmit and Furry, December, 1944), and Ian Stewart wrote a paper on Benford's Law that starts with a story about a trickster betting on first digits with the public at a trade fair in England (Stewart, 1993).

The 1980s also saw the first accounting application by Carslaw (1988). He hypothesized that when company net incomes are just below psychological boundaries, accountants would tend to round these numbers up. For example, numbers such as $798,000 and $19.97 million would be rounded up to numbers just above $800,000 and $20 million respectively. His belief was that the latter numbers convey a larger measure of size despite the fact that in percentage terms they are just marginally higher. Management usually has an incentive to report higher income numbers. Evidence supporting such rounding-up behavior would be an excess of second digit 0s and a shortage of second digit 9s. Carslaw used the expected second-digit frequencies of Benford's Law and his results based on reported net incomes of New Zealand companies showed that there were indeed more second digit 0s and fewer second digit 9s than expected.

Hill (1988) was the second Benford-based experimental paper after Hsu (1948). He provided experimental evidence that when individuals invent numbers these numbers do not conform to Benford's Law. Hill's 742 subjects had no incentive to bias their six-digit numbers upward or downward. Hill used the Chi-square and Kolmogorov-Smirnoff tests plus a little creativity to evaluate his results. His results showed that the first and second digits were closer to being uniformly distributed than being distributed according to Benford's Law. It is interesting that two subjects invented a six-digit string of zeroes (these results were discarded). Number invention has received much subsequent attention with results showing that autistic subjects were more likely to repeat digits (Williams, Moss, Bradshaw, and Rinehart, 2002). The papers on this topic include Mosimann, Wiseman, and Edelman (1995) who show that even with a conscious effort, most people cannot generate random numbers. Interestingly their results showed that 1, 2, and 3 were the most favored digits in number invention situations.

Carslaw's paper was soon followed by Thomas (1989). Thomas found excess second-digit zeros in U.S. net income data. Interestingly, Thomas also found that earnings per share numbers in the United States were multiples of 5 cents more often than expected. In a follow-on study Nigrini (2005) showed that this rounding-up behavior seems to have persisted through time. Quarterly net income data from U.S. companies showed an excess of second-digit zeroes and a shortage of second-digit 8s and 9s for both first quarters in 2001 and 2002. The second-digit zero proportion was slightly higher in 2002. This result was surprising given that this period was characterized by the Enron-Andersen debacle. An analysis of selected Enron reported numbers for 1997 to 2000 showed a marked excess of second-digit zeroes. The 1980s provided a strong foundation for the advances of the 1990s.

The 1990s

Benford's Law research was greatly assisted in the 1990s by the computing power of the personal computer and the availability of mainframe computers at universities for general research use (albeit with the complications of JCL, Fortran, and SAS). The 1990s advanced the theory, provided much more empirical evidence that Benford's Law really applied to real-world data, and also gave us the first major steps in finding a practical use for Benford's Law. Papers increasing the body of empirical evidence on the applicability of Benford's Law includes Burke and Kincanon (1991) who test the digital frequencies of 20 physical constants (a very small data set), and Buck, Merchant, and Perez (1993) who show that the digit frequencies of 477 measured and calculated alpha-decay half-lives conformed reasonably closely to Benford's Law.

A paper from the early 1990s dealt with tax evasion and used Benford's Law to support their statistical analysis. Christian and Gupta (1993) analyzed taxpayer data to find signs of secondary evasion. This type of evasion occurs when taxpayers reduce their taxable incomes from above a table step boundary to below a table step boundary. The table steps of $50 amounts occur in the tax tables in U.S. income tax returns that are used by taxpayers with incomes below $100,000 to calculate their tax liability. The tables are meant to help those people that would find it difficult to use a formula. A reduction in taxable income of (say) $4 (when the income is just above a table step boundary, at say $40,102) could lead to a tax saving of $50 times the marginal rate. Christian and Gupta assume that the ending digits of taxable incomes should be uniformly distributed over the 00 to 99 range, and Benford's Law is used to justify this assumption. Early papers such as this allowed later work such as Herrmann and Thomas (2005) to state casually as a matter of fact that the ending digits of earnings per share numbers should be uniformly distributed and then to test their hypothesis of rounded analyst forecasts.

Craig (1992) examines round-off biases in EPS calculations. He tested whether EPS numbers are rounded up more often than rounded down, indicating some manipulation by managers. Craig acknowledges that Benford's Law exists but he chose to ignore it in his analysis. It seems that Benford's Law would work in favor of his detecting manipulation. Since Benford's Law favors lower digits the probability of rounding down an EPS number to whole cents is larger than the probability of rounding up an EPS number. His roundup frequency of .551 was therefore perhaps more significant than he realized. Craig's work is followed by Das and Zhang (2003) who do not reference his 1992 paper.

The first forensic analytics paper using Benford's law was Nigrini (1994). He starts with the open question as to whether the digital frequencies of Benford's Law can be used to detect fraud. Using the numbers from a payroll fraud case, he compared the first-two digit frequencies to those of Benford's Law. The premise was that over time, individuals will tend to repeat their actions, and people generally do not think like Benford's Law, and so their invented numbers are unlikely to follow Benford's Law. The fraudulent numbers might stick out from the crowd. The payroll fraud showed that for the 10-year period of the $500,000 fraud the fraudulent numbers deviated significantly from Benford's Law. Also, the deviations were greatest for the last five years.

Nigrini suggests that the fraudster was getting into a routine and in the end he did not even try to invent authentic looking numbers.

By the mid-1990s advances were being made in both the theoretical and applied aspects of Benford's Law. The applied side strides were due to access to and the low cost of computing power. Also, by then Ted Hill had built up a high level of expertise in the field and his papers were about to provide a solid theoretical basis for future work. Boyle (1994) added to earlier theorems by generalizing the results of some earlier work from the 1960s. Boyle shows that Benford's Law is the limiting distribution when random variables are repeatedly multiplied, divided, or raised to integer powers, and once achieved, Benford's Law persists under all further multiplications, divisions, and raising to integer powers. Boyle concludes by asserting that Benford's Law has similar properties to the central limit theorem in that Benford's Law *is* the central limit theorem for digits under multiplicative operations.

Hill (1995) was the most significant mathematical advance since Pinkham (1961). Google Scholar shows that there are more than 200 citations of the Hill paper. After reviewing several empirical studies Hill shows that if distributions are selected at random (in any "unbiased" way), and random samples are then taken from each of these distributions, then the digits of the resulting collection will converge to the logarithmic (Benford) distribution. Hill's paper explains why Benford's Law is found in many empirical contexts, and helps to explain why it works as a valid expectation in applications related to computer design, mathematical modeling, and the detection of fraud in accounting settings. Hill showed that Benford's Law is the distribution *of all distributions*. It would be valuable future work if simulation studies drew random samples from families of common distributions to confirm Hill's theorem.

Nigrini (1996) applies Benford's Law to a tax-evasion setting. This paper is the first analysis of large data tables and the results of taxpayer interest received and interest paid data sets shown. These data tables ranged from 55,000 to 91,000 records. The interest-related data sets conformed reasonably closely to Benford's Law. The paper also reports the results of an analysis by the Dutch Ministry of Finance of interest received amounts. These numbers also conformed closely to Benford's Law. At this time there were relatively few published results of actual Benford's Law applications and it was not an easy matter to analyze even 100,000 records. A data set of that size required mainframe computing power and the personal computers of the mid-1990s struggled with data sets larger than 3,000 records. Nigrini (1996) also develops a Distortion Factor model that signals whether data appears to have been manipulated upward or downward based on the digit patterns. This model is based on the premise that an excess of low digits signals an understatement of the numbers and an excess of higher digits signals a potential overstatement of the numbers. The results showed that for interest received there was an excess of low digits suggesting an understatement of these numbers, and in contrast there was an excess of the higher digits in interest paid numbers, suggesting an overstatement of these numbers.

Nigrini and Mittermaier (1997) add to the set of papers advocating that Benford's Law could be used as a valuable tool in an accounting setting. They develop a set of Benford's Law–based tests that could be used by external and internal auditors. The paper shows that external auditors could use the tests to determine if a data set appears to be reasonable and to direct their attention to questionable groups of transactions. Internal auditors could also use the tests to direct their attention to biases and irregularities in data. The paper also indirectly showed that increased access to computing power had made Benford's Law a tool that could be employed at a reasonable cost without the need for specialist computing skills. The paper shows the results of an analysis of 30,000 accounts payable invoices amounts of an oil company and 72,000 invoice amounts of an electric utility. Both data tables showed a reasonable conformity to Benford's Law.

Hill (1998) is an excellent review of some empirical papers and the theory underlying Benford's Law. Hill writes that at the time of Raimi's 1976 paper, Benford's Law was thought to be merely a mathematical curiosity without real-life applications and without a satisfactory mathematical explanation. Hill believes that by 1998 the answers were now less obscure and Benford's Law was firmly couched in the mathematical theory of probability. With those advances came some important applications to society. Hill then restated his 1995 results in terms that nonmathematicians could understand and he also refers to Raimi's 1976 paper where Raimi remarks that the best fit to Benford's Law came not from any of the 20 lists that Benford analyzed but rather from the union (combination) of all his tables.

Busta and Weinberg (1998) add to the literature on using Benford's Law as an analytical procedure (a reasonableness test) by external auditors. They develop a neural network that had some success in detecting contaminated data, where contaminated refers to nonconformity with Benford's Law. The late 1990s also included Ettredge and Srivastava (1999) who linked Benford's Law with data-integrity issues. Their paper also noted that nonconformity to Benford's Law may indicate operating inefficiencies (processing many invoices for the same dollar amount) or flaws rather than fraud.

The 1990s ended with Nigrini (1999), which was a review article in a widely read medium. The *Journal of Accountancy* has more than 300,000 subscribers and this article marked the first time that a technical paper on Benford's Law had been circulated to such a wide audience. Also by the end of the 1990s Benford's Law routines had been added to the functionality of IDEA (a data analysis software program aimed at auditors). All of these developments set the stage for Benford's Law to be applied to many different environments by real accountants and auditors, not just accounting researchers. The technical issues (difficulty in obtaining data and performing the calculations) had largely been overcome and Benford's Law had been accepted as a valid set of expectations for the digits in tabulated data.

The main thrust of the current Benford's Law literature is that authentic data should follow Benford's Law and deviations from Benford's Law could signal irregularities of some sort. In each case Benford's Law functions as an expected distribution and the deviations calculated are relative to this expected distribution. The 2000s have also included several powerful theoretical advances and these will be discussed in later chapters where appropriate. One answer that is still somewhat elusive is a definitive test to decide whether a data table conforms to Benford's Law *for all practical purposes*. Unlike mathematical sequences such as the Fibonacci sequence, real-world data will have some departures from the exact frequencies of Benford's Law. How much of a deviation can one allow and still conclude that the data conforms to Benford's Law?

 ## WHICH DATA SETS SHOULD CONFORM TO BENFORD'S LAW?

Because of the relationship between geometric sequences and Benford's Law, data needs to form a geometric sequence, or a number of geometric sequences for the digit patterns to conform to Benford's Law. The general mathematical rule is therefore that you must expect your data, when ordered (ranked from smallest to largest), to form a geometric sequence. The data should look similar to Figure 5.1 when graphed. Also, the log of the difference between the largest and smallest values should be an integer value (1, 2, 3, and so on). These requirements are fortunately the requirements for a perfect Benford Set (a set of numbers conforming perfectly to Benford's Law). Experience has shown that the data needs only approximate this geometric shape to get a reasonable fit to Benford's Law. So, our beginning and end points need not be perfect integer powers of 10 (10^1, 10^2, 10^3, etc.), nor should the logs of the difference between the smallest and largest values be an integer (as in 40 and 400,000 or 81.7 and 81,700), nor do we need the strict requirement that each element is a fixed percentage increase over its predecessor. The graph of the ordered values can be a bit bumpy and a little straight in places for a reasonable level of conformity. We do, however, need a general geometric tendency.

Imagine a situation where the digits and their frequencies could not be calculated, but we could still graph the data from smallest to largest. If the data had the geometric shape, and if the difference between the log (base 10) of the largest amount, and the log (base 10) of the smallest amount was an integer (or close to an integer) then the data would conform to Benford's Law. Testing whether the shape is geometric might prove tricky until you remember that the logs of the numbers of a geometric sequence form a straight line, and linear regression can measure the linearity (straightness) of a line.

There are problems with graphing a large data set in Excel. The maximum number of data points that Excel will graph is 32,000 data points in a 2-D chart. Excel will simply drop all data points after the 32,000th data point. One solution is to graph every 20th data point in a data set of 600,000 records (thereby graphing just 30,000 records) or perhaps every 70th data point in a data set of 2,000,000 records (thereby graphing just 28,571 records). This solution would require you to create a data set of every 20th or 70th or *xth* record. The programming logic would be to keep the record if the ID value could be divided by 20 or 70 (or some other number) without leaving a remainder. These records would be exported to Excel to prepare the graph.

Three guidelines for determining whether a data set should follow Benford's Law are:

1. The records should represent the sizes of facts or events. Examples of such data would include the populations of towns and cities, the flow rates of rivers, or the sizes of heavenly bodies. Financial examples include the market values of companies on the major U.S. stock exchanges, the revenues of companies on the major U.S. stock exchanges, or the daily sales volumes of companies on the London Stock Exchange.

2. There should be no built-in minimum or maximum values for the data. An example of a minimum would be a stockbroker who has a minimum commission charge of $50 for any buy or sell transaction. The broker would then have many people whose small trades attract the $50 minimum. A data set of the commission charges for a month would have an excess of first digit 5s and second digit zeros. If we graphed the ordered (ranked) commissions, the graph would start with a straight horizontal line at 50 until the first trade that had a commission higher than $50 was reached. A built-in minimum of zero is acceptable. A data set with a built-in maximum would also not follow Benford's Law. An example of this could be tax deductions claimed for the child- and dependent-care credit in the United States. The limit for expenses for this credit is $3,000 for one qualifying person and $6,000 for two or more qualifying persons. If we tabulated these costs for all taxpayers, the digits patterns would be influenced by these maximums.

3. The records should not be numbers used as identification numbers or labels. These are numbers that we have given to events, entities, objects, and items in place of words. Examples of these include social security numbers, bank account numbers, county numbers, highway numbers, car license plate numbers, flight numbers, or telephone numbers. These numbers have digit patterns that have some meaning to the persons who developed the sequence. One clue that a number is an identification number or label is that we do not include the usual comma separator as is usually done in the United States. The general rule is that labels or identification numbers do not have comma separators, but they might have dashes (−) to improve readability.

An overall consideration is that there are more small items (data elements) than big items (data elements) for a data set to conform to Benford's Law. This is true in general in that there are more towns than big cities, more small companies than giant General Electrics, and there are more small lakes than big lakes. A data set with more large numbers than small numbers is student GPA scores (hopefully!).

THE EFFECT OF DATA SET SIZE

Close conformity to Benford's Law also requires that we have a large data set with numbers that have at least four digits. A large data set is needed to get close to the expected digit frequencies. For example, the expected proportion for the first digit 9 is .0457574906 (rounded to 10 places after the decimal point). If the data set has only 100 records we might get five numbers with a first digit 9. With 100 records we can only get from 0 to 100 occurrences of a specified first digit. This will end up being an integer percentage (e.g., 5 percent or 30 percent). The expected first digit percentages are all numbers with digits after the decimal point (see Table 5.1). With a small sample we cannot hit the Benford percentages on the nail and this fact, in and of itself, will cause deviations from Benford's Law. As the data set increases in size so we can come closer and closer to the expected percentages.

Benford's Law expects each numeric amount to have "many" digits. My research has shown that the numbers should have four or more digits for a good fit. However, if this requirement is violated the whole ship does not sink. When the numbers have fewer than four digits there is only a slightly larger bias in favor of the lower digits. So, if the two and three digit numbers are mixed with bigger numbers, the bias is not enough to merit an adjustment to the expected digit frequencies.

Another general rule is that the table should have at least 1,000 records before we should expect a good conformity to Benford's Law. For tables with fewer than 1,000 records, the Benford-related tests can still be run, but the investigator should be willing to accept larger deviations from the Benford's Law line before concluding that the data did not conform to Benford's Law. Experience has shown that NYSE data on 3,000 companies had a good fit to Benford's Law and census data on 3,141 counties also had a good fit to Benford's Law. At about 3,000 records we should have a good fit for data that conforms to the mathematical foundation of Benford's Law. The suggestion is to not test the digit frequencies of data sets with fewer than 300 records. These records can simply be sorted from largest to smallest and the pages visually scanned for anomalies.

Benford's Law is the basis of the data analysis tests described in Chapters 5 through 8. Benford's Law points to an abnormal duplication of digit and digit combinations in your data. The later tests search for abnormal duplications and drill deeper and deeper into the data to find these duplications.

THE BASIC DIGIT TESTS

The basic digit tests are tests of the (1) first digits, (2) second digits, and (3) first-two digits. These tests are also called the *first-order tests*. The first-order tests are usually run on either the positive numbers, or on the negative numbers. The positive and negative numbers are evaluated separately because the incentive to manipulate is opposite for these types of numbers. For example, management usually want a higher earnings number when this number is positive, but want a number closer to zero when earnings are negative. Taxpayers would tend to reduce income numbers, and to increase deduction numbers to minimize taxes. An optional filtering step is to delete all numbers less than 10 for the basic digit tests for transactional amounts. These numbers are usually immaterial for audit or investigative purposes. Also, numbers less than 10 might not have an explicit second digit. They might have an implicit second digit of 0 because 7 can be written as 7.0. Sometimes, though, the digits of the small numbers are relevant and they should then be included in the analysis.

The usual approach is to use Access for the digit calculations and Excel for the tables and the graphs (first digits, second digits, and first-two digits). Excel can be used for the digit calculations for data tables that fit within its row limitations. There are nine possible first digits (1, 2, . . . , 9), 10 possible second digits (0, 1, . . . , 9), and 90 possible first-two digits (10, 11, . . . , 99). The first-two digit graph shown in Figure 5.2 is from an analysis of the digit frequencies of the invoice amounts for 2007 for a city in the Carolinas. The city government had about 250,000 transactions for the year. The fit

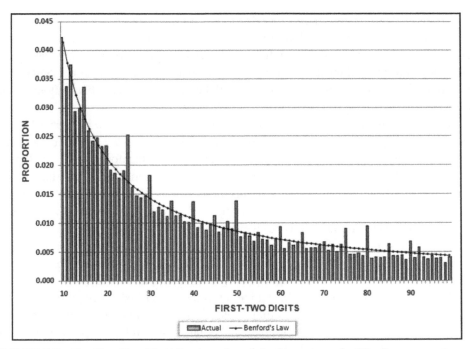

FIGURE 5.2 The First Two Digit Frequencies of the Payments of a City Government. The X-Axis Shows the First Two Digits and the Y-Axis Shows the Proportions. The Line Represents the Expected Proportions of Benford's Law and the Bars Represent the Actual Proportions

to Benford's Law is excellent. The spikes that are evident at some of the multiples of 5 (15, 25, 30, 40, 50, 75, and 80) are quite normal for payments data.

The *NigriniCycle.xlsx* template includes a *Tables* worksheet. The *Tables* details include (a) the actual count for each digit combination, (b) the actual proportion and the expected proportion for each digit combination, (c) the difference between the actual and expected proportions, and (d) the Z-statistic for each digit combination (Z-statistics above 1.96 indicate that there is a significant difference between the actual and expected proportions).

The first digit test (not included in the *NigriniCycle.xlsx* template) is a high-level test of reasonableness that is actually too high-level to be of much use. This test can be compared to looking out the window of the plane when you are descending to land in your home city. One or two landmarks and the look of the terrain would be a reasonableness check that you are indeed landing at your home city. The general rule is that a weak fit to Benford's Law is a flag that the data table contains abnormal duplications and anomalies. If an investigator is working with four data tables and three of them exhibit a good fit to Benford's Law, then the strategy would be to focus on the fourth nonconforming data table because it shows signs of having the highest risks for errors or fraud. Similarly, if a single company had three quarters of conforming data and one quarter of nonconforming data, then the nonconforming data has the higher risk of errors or fraud.

The second-digit test is a second overall test of reasonableness. Again, this test is actually too high-level to be of much use. For accounts payable data and other data sets where prices are involved, the second-digits graph will usually show excess 0s and 5s because of round numbers (such as 75, 100, and 250). This is normal and should not be a cause for concern. If the second-digit graph shows an excess of (say) 6s, the suggested approach is to go to the first-two digits graph to check which combination is causing the spike (excess). The result might be that 36 has a large spike in which case the investigator would select and review a much smaller sample of suspect records. An example of a spike at 36 is shown in Figure 18.5 in Chapter 18.

The first-two digits test is a more focused test and is there to detect abnormal duplications of digits and possible biases in the data. A bias is a gravitation to some part(s) of the number line due to internal control critical points or due to psychological factors with respect to numbers. Past experience with the first-two digits graph has given us eight guidelines for forensic analytics:

1. A common finding when analyzing company expenses is a spike at 24. A spike is an actual proportion that exceeds the expected (Benford) proportion by a significant amount. This usually occurs at firms that require employees to submit vouchers for expenses that are $25 and higher. The graph would then show that employees are submitting excessive claims for just under $25.

2. Spikes at 48 and 49 and 98 and 99 indicate that there are excessive amounts that are just below the psychological cutoff points of $100, $500, $1,000, $5,000, or $10,000.

3. Spikes that are just below the first-two digits of internal authorization levels might signal fraud or some other irregularity. For example, an insurance company might allow junior and mid-level adjusters to approve claims up to (say) $5,000 and $10,000. Spikes at 48, 49, 98, 99 would signal excessive paid amounts just below these authorization levels.

4. Several years ago forensic investigators at a bank analyzed credit card balances written off. The first-two digits showed a spike at 49. The number duplication test showed many amounts for $4,900 to $4,980. Most of the "49" write-off amounts were attributable to one employee. The investigation showed that the employee was having cards issued to friends and family. The employee's write-off limit was $5,000. Friends and family then ran up balances to just below $5,000 (as evidenced by the spike at 49) and the bank employee then wrote the balance off. The fraud was detected because there were so many instances of the fraud and the person was systematic in their actions.

5. An auditor ran the first-two digits test on two consecutive months of cost prices on inventory sheets. The results showed that the digit patterns were significantly different. The investigation showed that many of the items with positive cost values in the first month erroneously had zero cost amounts in the second month.

6. A finding by Inland Revenue in the United Kingdom was that there was a big spike at 14 for revenue numbers reported by small businesses. The investigation showed

that many businesspeople were "managing" their sales numbers to just below 15,000 GBP (pounds). The tax system in the United Kingdom allows businesses with sales under £15,000 to use the equivalent of a "Schedule C Easy" when filing.

7. Employee purchasing cards were analyzed at a government agency. The agency had a limit for any purchase by credit card of $2,500. The investigation showed a big spike (excess) at 24 due to employees purchasing with great gusto in the $2,400 to $2,499.99 range. This graph is shown in Figure 18.5. It was only because the proportions could be compared to Benford's Law that the investigators could draw the conclusion that the actual proportion was excessive. A result is only excessive when the investigator is able to compare the results to some accepted norm.

8. The accountants at a Big-4 audit firm tested their employee reimbursements against Benford's Law. The results for one employee showed a spike at 48. It turned out that the employee was charging his morning coffee and muffin to the firm every day, including those days when he worked in the office. One would think that an auditor would pay for his own breakfast!

The first-order test involves a set sequence of actions. The starting point is to calculate the first-two digits of each amount. Thereafter the first-two digits are counted to see how many of each we have. The results are then graphed and supporting statistics are calculated. The test is described in general terms in more detail below.

The first-two digit test is built into IDEA. In IDEA you would simply call up the routine and identify which field was the field of interest. To run the first-two digit test in Access or Excel requires a sequence of steps that are summarized below:

1. Use the *Left* function to calculate the first-two digits.
2. Use *Where* to set the >=10 criteria in the query. Because all numbers are >=10, we can use *Left* for the first-two digits. When analyzing negative numbers, we need to use the Absolute function to convert them to positive numbers.
3. Use a second query to count the number of times each first-two digit occurs. In Access this is done using *Group By* and in Excel this is done using *COUNTIF*.
4. If the calculations are done in Access, then the results need to be copied to the *NigriniCycle.xlsx* template so that the graphs and tables can be prepared. This template is also used if the calculations are done in Excel.

The above steps are an outline of how the tests would be run using Access or Excel. The actual mechanics are described in the next sections using the *InvoicesPaid.accdb* database. This database contains the invoices paid by a utility company. This is the same set of data that was used in Chapter 4.

 ## RUNNING THE FIRST-TWO DIGITS TEST IN ACCESS

In a forensic environment the first-order first-two digits test (hereinafter first-two digits test) would be run after the high-level overview tests of Chapter 4. Those tests were

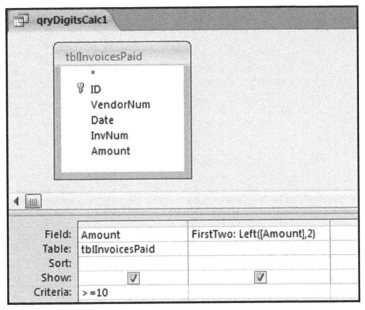

FIGURE 5.3 The Query Used to Calculate the First Two Digits of Each Number

the data profile, the periodic graph, and the histogram. We would use the same database to continue with our tests. The first step would therefore be to open the *InvoicesPaid .accdb* database.

When the database is opened we are given a security warning that "Certain content in the database has been disabled." Since we do not want the content to be disabled, the next step would be to click on the **Options** button. Thereafter select the radio button with the **Enable this content** option. Now click **OK** to get a database that is fully enabled and that does not have a security warning below the ribbon.

Our first query calculates the first-two digits of the *Amounts*. The first query is started with the usual **Create→Other→Query Design**. The invoices table *tblInvoices-Paid* is selected by selecting the table and then clicking **Add** followed by **Close**. The first-two digits of each number are calculated using a calculated field as is shown in Figure 5.3.

The query used to calculate the first-two digits of each number is shown in Figure 5.3. The field with the first-two digits is named *FirstTwo*. The formula is shown below:

$$\text{FirstTwo}: \text{Left}([\text{Amount}], 2)$$

The square brackets [ ] indicate that the formula is referring to the field called *Amount*. The >=10 criteria is used because we only do the tests on numbers that are 10 or greater because numbers less than 10 are usually immaterial. The **Left** function works correctly because it is operating on numbers that are positive and 10 or more. To

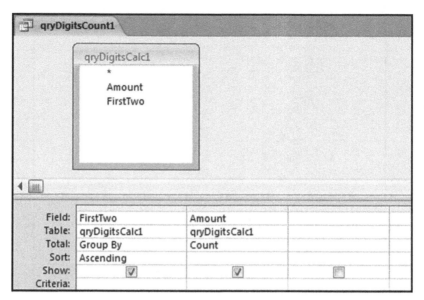

FIGURE 5.4   The Second Query Used for the First-Two Digits Test

calculate the digits of negative numbers we would have to include the Absolute (**Abs**) function in our formula. The result of running this query is an output data set with 177,763 records showing all the >=10 amounts and their first-two digits. The total of 177,763 records agrees with the data profile in Figure 4.1. Save the query as *qryDigitsCalc1* (an abbreviation for "digits calculate") with a right click on *Query1* and then by following the prompt for the query name. Close *qryDigitsCalc1*.

The second step is to count how many times each possible first-two digits combination occurred. The second query is a requery of *qryDigitsCalc1* and we set this up by using the usual **Create→Other→Query Design**. The query *qryDigitsCalc1* is selected by selecting the Queries tab and then selecting *qryDigitsCalc1* followed by **Add** and then **Close**. The query used for the counting function is shown in Figure 5.4.

This query groups the first-two digits and counts how many times each combination occurred. The query is run using **Design→Results→Run** and the results are shown in Figure 5.5.

The result shows us that we had 10,439 records that had first-two digits of 10 for the *Amount* field and 10,306 records that had first-two digits of 11. We can see that we do not have a good fit to Benford's Law. There is a steep drop-off from 10 and 11 to 12. Viewing these results on a graph would allow us to see the spikes on the graph. We will use the *NigriniCycle.xlsx* template to prepare the graph. Open this file and click the *Tables* tab.

The *CountOfAmount* field in Figure 5.5 needs to be copied using the usual Copy and Paste functions to column B of the template starting in cell B2. The result of the Copy and Paste is shown in Figure 5.6.

qryDigitsCount1	
FirstTwo ▾	CountOfAmount ▾
10	10439
11	10306
12	5966
13	5756
14	4462
15	5591
16	4391
17	3984
18	3830
19	3764
20	3920

FIGURE 5.5 The Results of the Second First-Two Digits Query

Columns C, D, E, and F as well as cell G5 is automatically recalculated. The template also automatically prepares the first-two digits graph. The graph is viewed by clicking on the *FirstOrder* tab. The first-two digits graph is shown in Figure 5.7.

The first-two digits graph in Figure 5.7 shows a major spike at 50, and two other significant spikes at 10 and 11. We also notice the two spikes at 98 and 99. Although these might not seem to be large spikes, the actual proportions of 0.009 and 0.008 are about double the expected proportion of 0.004. Also, these two-digit combinations (98 and 99) are just below a psychological threshold and we should check whether the digits are for amounts of $98 and $99 (which are not too material) or $980 to $999 (which are material). The graph shows that we have an excessive number of invoices that are just below psychological thresholds.

	B2		▾	f_x	CountOfAmount			
	A	B	C	D	E	F	G	H
1			FIRST-ORDER TEST					
2	FT Digit	untOfAmou	Actual	Benford'sLa	Difference	AbsDiff		
3	10	10439	0.059	0.041	0.017	0.017		
4	11	10306	0.058	0.038	0.020	0.020		
5	12	5966	0.034	0.035	-0.001	0.001	177763	
6	13	5756	0.032	0.032	0.000	0.000		
7	14	4462	0.025	0.030	-0.005	0.005	0	
8	15	5591	0.031	0.028	0.003	0.003		
9	16	4391	0.025	0.026	-0.002	0.002	0	
10	17	3984	0.022	0.025	-0.002	0.002		
11	18	3830	0.022	0.023	-0.002	0.002	0	
12	19	3764	0.021	0.022	-0.001	0.001		
13	20	3920	0.022	0.021	0.001	0.001		

FIGURE 5.6 Results of Pasting the Access Output into the Template

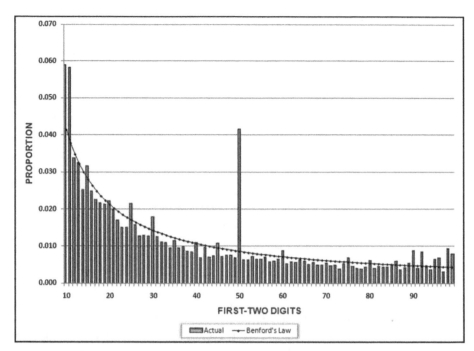

FIGURE 5.7 The First-Two Digits Graph of the *Invoicespaid* Data

___

The Excel template *NigriniCycle.xlsx* has some columns that are automatically calculated. The columns that relate to the first-order tests are columns A through F. An explanation for the columns that are automatically calculated is given below:

▪ **Column B.** The *Count* column shows the count of the numbers that had first-two digits of $d_1 d_2$. In this case there were 10,439 numbers with first-two digits of 10.

▪ **Column C.** The *Actual* column shows the actual proportion of numbers that had first-two digits of $d_1 d_2$. For the 10 combination the actual proportion of 0.059 is calculated as 10,439 divided by 177,763.

▪ **Column D.** The *Benford's Law* column shows the expected proportions of Benford's Law. The 90 Benford's Law proportions must sum to 1.000 and the 90 Actual proportions must also sum to 1.000. Small differences may occur due to rounding.

▪ **Column E.** The *Difference* column shows the difference between the actual proportion and the Benford's Law proportion. The difference is calculated as Actual minus Benford's Law. Positive differences tell us that the actual proportion exceeded the Benford's Law proportion.

▪ **Column F.** The *AbsDiff* column is the absolute value of the *Difference* in column E. These absolute values are used to calculate the Mean Absolute Deviation (MAD), which measures the goodness of fit to Benford's Law. The MAD is discussed further in Chapter 6.

Assessing the conformity (the goodness of fit) to Benford's Law is reviewed in Chapter 6. This case study is also continued in Chapter 6 and in others chapters that follow where we will home in on the suspect or suspicious transactions. For now, our conclusion is that our first order test has shown some large spikes at 10, 11, 50, 98, and 99. Running the tests in Excel is shown in a later chapter.

SUMMARY

Benford's Law gives the expected frequencies of the digits in tabulated data. These expected digit frequencies are named after Frank Benford, a physicist who published the seminal paper on the topic (Benford, 1938). Benford analyzed the first digits of 20 lists of numbers with a total of about 20,000 records. He collected data from as many sources as possible in an effort to include a variety of data tables. His results showed that on average 30.6 percent of his numbers had a first digit 1, and 18.5 percent of his numbers had a first digit 2. Benford's paper shows us that in theory and in practice that the digits are not all equally likely. For the first (leftmost) digit there is a large bias in favor of the lower digits (such as 1, 2, and 3) over the higher digits (such as 7, 8, and 9). This large bias is reduced as we move from the first digit to the second and later digits. The expected proportions are approximately equal from the third digit onwards.

The Benford's Law literature started with three papers in the 1940s. A significant advance came in the 1960s when it was discovered that Benford's Law was scale invariant. This means that if the digits of the areas of the world's islands, or the length of the world's rivers followed a law of some sort, then it should be immaterial which measurement unit was used. Benford's Law was found to be scale invariant under multiplication and so if all the records in a table that conformed to Benford's Law were multiplied by a (nonzero) constant, then the new list would also follow Benford's Law. A list of numbers that conform to Benford's Law is known as a Benford Set.

Another significant theoretical advance came in the 1990s when Hill showed that if distributions are selected at random, and random samples are then taken from each of these distributions, then the digits of the resulting collection will converge to the logarithmic (Benford) distribution. Hill's paper explained why Benford's Law is found in many empirical contexts, and helps to explain why it works as a valid expectation in applications related to computer design, mathematical modeling, and the detection of fraud in accounting settings. The 1990s also saw practical advances in the use of Benford's Law. An early fraud study showed that the digit frequencies of the invented fraudulent numbers did not follow Benford's Law. The increased ease of computing allowed for more research on larger and larger data sets showing Benford's Law to be valid in a variety of financial and accounting contexts. In 1999 a Benford's Law paper was published in a widely circulating accounting journal and Benford's Law was then introduced to the accounting and auditing community.

A few general tests can be used to see whether Benford's Law is a valid expectation. The general considerations are that the data set should represent the sizes of facts or events. Examples of such data would include the populations of towns and cities, or the market values of listed companies. Also, there should be no built-in minimum or maximum values in the data table, except that a minimum of zero is acceptable. Finally, the data table should not represent numbers used as identification numbers or labels. Examples of these numbers are social security numbers, bank account numbers, and flight numbers. A final consideration is that there should be more than 1,000 records for Benford's Law to work well.

The chapter shows the queries used in Access to run the first-two digits test. An Excel template is used to prepare the graphs. The first-two digits test is a high-level overview. A weak fit to Benford's Law suggests a heightened risk of errors or fraud. The first-two digits test is also effective in identifying biases in the data. These biases could be excessive purchases just below a control threshold of (say) $2,500, or an excess of taxpayers reporting sales amounts just below 15,000 British pounds where this is the cutoff amount to file a simplified tax return.

6

Benford's Law

Assessing Conformity

C HAPTER 5 REVIEWED THE history of Benford's Law, some possible uses for the results of our tests, and how to run the first-two digits test in Access. The focus of this chapter is on ways to assess the conformity of a data set to Benford's Law. The focus of our attention is Benford's Law, but these methods can be used for conformity to other expected values. We have many statistical methods and the concept of significance so it would seem that assessing the goodness of fit of our data to Benford's Law is a straightforward matter. However, our task is complicated by the fact that we are usually dealing with large data sets where even small deviations from the expected pattern are statistically significant.

Prior to the mid-1990s there was not much of a need to address conformity criteria. Most research papers used relatively small data sets. An exception to this rule was Thomas (1989) who analyzed 69,000 positive earnings numbers and 11,000 negative earnings numbers. In his study the Z-statistic worked well for the test of the first-two digits. The chapter reviews the tests described in most statistics books that would work well for smaller data sets. Thereafter we examine some of the mathematical properties of Benford's Law and the "best" test is suggested based on these properties. The conformity tests are demonstrated using both Access and Excel.

For the first-two digit test there are two ways to look at conformity. The first way is to test whether a specific first-two digit combination follows Benford's Law. The second way is to test whether the digit combinations (10, 11, 12, . . . 99) combined follow Benford's Law. This distinction is the subject of an excellent paper by Cleary and Thibodeau (2005). There are, however, issues with each of these methods. This chapter reviews the Z-statistic, chi-square test, Kolmogorov-Smirnoff test, the Mean Absolute Deviation, the basis of Benford's Law, and a test called the *mantissa arc test* (which is only slightly less complicated than it sounds).

ONE DIGIT AT A TIME: THE Z-STATISTIC

The Z-statistic is used to test whether the actual proportion for a specific first-two digit combination differs significantly from the expectation of Benford's Law. The formula takes into account the absolute magnitude of the difference (the numeric distance from the actual to the expected), the size of the data set, and the magnitude of the expected proportion. The formula adapted from Fleiss (1981) is shown in Equation 6.1:

$$Z = \frac{|AP - EP| - \left(\frac{1}{2N}\right)}{\sqrt{\frac{EP(1 - EP)}{N}}} \tag{6.1}$$

where EP denotes the expected proportion, AP the actual proportion, and N the number of records. The $(1/2N)$ term is a continuity correction term and is only used when it is smaller than the first term in the numerator.

From the numerator of Equation 6.1 we can see that the Z-statistic becomes larger as the difference between the observed (actual) proportion and expected proportion becomes larger. In the invoices table, the first-two digits 50 has an expected proportion of 0.009 and an actual proportion of 0.041. With 177,763 records in the table, the Z-statistic is calculated (using exact values) to be 149.333. At a significance level of 5 percent, the cutoff score is 1.96 and our calculated Z of 149.333 exceeds this cutoff score leading us to conclude that the actual proportion differs significantly from the expected proportion. At the 1 percent significance level our cutoff score would be 2.57, and we would have a significant difference if the calculated Z exceeded 2.57.

The second term in the Equation 6.1 numerator $(1/2N)$ is a continuity correction factor and it usually has little impact on the calculated Z-statistic. The effect of N in the denominator is that as the data set becomes larger, so the Z-statistic becomes larger. So our difference of 0.033 becomes more and more significant as the data set increases in size. Using the same actual proportion, if the data set had 500,000 records the calculated Z-statistic would be 250.463. The number of records almost tripled, but the Z-statistic showed a much smaller increase because N is inside the square root sign.

The expected proportion, EP, appears twice in the denominator. The effect of EP is that for any given difference, a larger expected proportion gives a smaller Z-statistic. In the above example we have a 3.3 percent difference $(0.041 - 0.009)$. If the expected proportion was (say) 50 percent, and the actual was 53.3 percent, we would still have a 3.3 percent difference. However, with a data set of 177,763 records the Z-statistic would be lower at 27.825, which is still above the cutoff score for a significant difference at the 1 percent level.

The effect of *EP* is quite logical. A 3.3 percent difference when *EP* is 4.1 percent means that the actual proportion is 3.80 times the expected proportion. However, when the expected proportion is 0.500 and the actual proportion is 0.533 there is a smaller relative difference between the two numbers. So any difference of *x* is more significant for the higher digits (which have lower expected proportions) than for the lower digits (which have higher expected proportions).

The Z-statistic tells us whether our actual proportion deviates significantly from the expected proportion. We usually use a significance level of 5 percent. The Z-statistic suffers from the excess power problem. For large data sets, even a small difference is likely to be flagged as significant. For example, for the *InvoicesPaid* data, 85 of the 90 first-two digit combinations have differences that are statistically significant. The large number of records makes small differences significant. The nonsignificant differences are for 13, 21, 40, 85, and 93. The Z-statistics taken together signal an extreme case of nonconformity.

For a larger data set of 1,000,000 records we might have an expected percentage of 10 percent for the second digit 4. If our actual percentage is 10.018 percent (a really small difference) the result is significant at the 0.05 level. With an expected percentage of 4 percent, an actual percentage of just 4.008 percent would be significant at the 0.05 level. This is indeed an insignificant difference from a practical perspective.

One solution is to ignore the absolute size of the Z-statistics. For the first-two digits there would be 90 Z-statistics (one for 10 through 99). Investigators would concentrate on which Z-statistics were both largest and associated with positive spikes (where the actual proportion exceeds the expected proportion). For the *InvoicesPaid* data the seven largest Z-statistics were for the 50, 11, 10, 98, 90, 92, and 99. These results will be considered in Chapter 8 in the number duplication test.

It is possible to calculate upper and lower bounds. These are the proportions at which the calculated Z-statistics equal 1.96. Any spike that protruded above the upper bound, or fell beneath the lower bound, would be significant at the 0.05 level. However, with the excess power problem we know that as the data table becomes larger, so the Z-statistic tolerates smaller and smaller deviations. Therefore, for large data tables, the upper and lower bounds will be close to the Benford's Law line. For very large data tables the lines will be so close to the Benford line that the upper and lower bounds might be indistinguishable from the Benford's Law line.

The Z-statistics cannot be added or combined in some other way to get an idea of the overall extent of nonconformity. So, a natural extension to the Z-statistic is a combined test of all the first-two digits. The well-known chi-square test and the Kolmogorov-Smirnoff test are discussed next.

THE CHI-SQUARE AND KOLMOGOROV-SMIRNOFF TESTS

The chi-square test is often used to compare an actual set of results with an expected set of results. Our expected result is that the data follows Benford's Law. The null hypothesis is that the first two digits of the data follow Benford's Law. The chi-square statistic for the digits is calculated as is shown in Equation 6.2:

$$\text{chi-square} = \sum_{i=1}^{K} \frac{(AC - EC)^2}{EC} \tag{6.2}$$

where *AC* and *EC* represent the Actual Count and Expected Count respectively, and *K* represents the number of bins (which in our case is the number of different first-two digits). The summation sign indicates that the results for each bin (one of the 90 possible first-two digits) must be added together. The number of degrees of freedom equals $K - 1$ which means that for the first-two digits the test is evaluated using 89 degrees of freedom. The chi-square statistic (the sum of the 90 calculations) for the *InvoicesPaid* data equals 32,659.05.

The calculated chi-square statistic is compared to a cutoff value. A table of cutoff scores can be found in most statistics textbooks. These cutoff values can also be calculated in Excel by using the CHIINV function. For example, CHIINV(0.05,89) equals 112.02. This means that if the calculated chi-square value exceeds 112.02 then the null hypothesis of conformity of the first-two digits must be rejected and we would conclude that the data does not conform to Benford's Law. The higher the calculated chi-square statistic, the more the data deviate from Benford's Law. If our calculated chi-square statistic was 100, then in statistical terms we would conclude that there is not enough evidence to reject the null hypothesis. The null hypothesis is that there is no significant difference between the actual proportions and those of Benford's Law.

From Figure 5.7 we can see that the actual proportions of the *InvoicesPaid* data deviate quite radically from the expected proportions. We need not really use the Z-statistic results (that there are 85 significant differences) to quickly assess the situation. The chi-square statistic also suffers from the excess power problem in that when the data table becomes large, the calculated chi-square will almost always be higher than the cutoff value making us conclude that the data does not follow Benford's Law. This problem starts being noticeable for data tables with more than 5,000 records. This means that small differences, with no practical value, will cause us to conclude that the data does not follow Benford's Law. It was precisely this issue that caused the developers of IDEA to build a maximum N of 2,500 into their Benford's Law bounds. Their Benford's Law graphs show an upper and a lower bound (above or below which we have a significant difference) that is based on the actual number of records, or 2,500, whichever is smaller. This ensures that the graphical bounds are not too close to the Benford's Law line so that all digits and digit combinations show significant differences. The chi-square test is also not really of much help in forensic analytics because we will usually be dealing with large data tables.

Another "all digits at once" test is the Kolmogorov-Smirnoff (abbreviated K-S) test. This test is based on the cumulative density function. In Figure 5.6 we can see that the expected proportions for the first digits 10, 11, and 12 are 0.041, 0.038, and 0.035, respectively. The cumulative density function is the cumulative sum of these values, which is 0.041 (the first proportion), 0.079 (the sum of the first two proportions), and

0.114 (the sum of the first three proportions), and so on to the 90th proportion. The third cumulative sum means that the expected probability of 10s, 11s, and 12s taken together is 0.114. For the *InvoicesPaid* data the sum of the actual 10, 11, and 12 proportions is 0.150. We get this by adding the actual proportions for 10, 11, and 12. At 12, we have an expected cumulative proportion of 0.114 and an actual cumulative proportion of 0.150. The difference between the expected and the actual cumulative proportions is 0.036. The K-S test takes the largest of the absolute values of these 90 possible first-two digit differences (called the *supremum* in statistical terms). The formula to determine whether the result is significant is shown in Equation 6.3:

$$\text{Kolmogorov-Smirnoff} = \frac{1.36}{\sqrt{N}} \qquad (6.3)$$

where 1.36 is the constant for a significance level of 0.05, and N is the number of records.

For the *InvoicesPaid* data there are 177,763 records and so the calculated K-S cutoff value is 1.36/sqrt(177763), which equals 0.00323. From the previous paragraph we know that the difference between the expected and actual cumulative proportion at 12 is 0.036. We need not go any further. Our difference of 0.03632 exceeds the K-S cutoff of 0.00323 and we have only looked at one cumulative difference. The null hypothesis that the data follows Benford's Law is rejected. A line graph of the actual and expected cumulative density functions is shown in Figure 6.1.

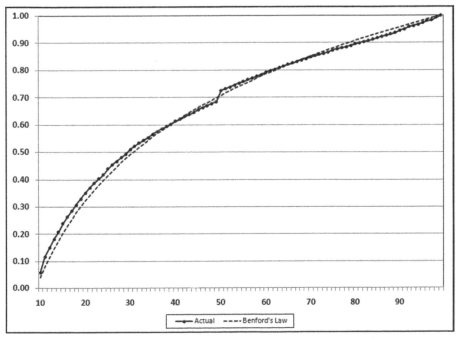

FIGURE 6.1 The Cumulative Density Function of Benford's Law and the Cumulative Density Function of the Invoices Data

The two cumulative density functions in Figure 6.1 seem to track each other closely. Once again the excess power problem means that while matters might look quite good visually, only small deviations are tolerated when the number of records becomes large. The supremum (the largest difference) occurs at 11. The kink upward at 50 is because of the large spike at 50. Both cumulative density functions end at 1.00. The inclusion of *N* in the formula makes the K-S a weak choice in a forensic analytics setting.

 ## THE MEAN ABSOLUTE DEVIATION (MAD) TEST

The Mean Absolute Deviation (MAD) test ignores the number of records, *N*. The MAD is calculated using Equation 6.4:

$$\text{Mean Absolute Deviation} = \frac{\sum_{i=1}^{K} |AP - EP|}{K} \tag{6.4}$$

where *EP* denotes the expected proportion, *AP* the actual proportion, and *K* represents the number of bins (which equals 90 for the first-two digits).

A version of the MAD (based on the percentage error) is used in time-series analysis where it is used to measure the accuracy of fitted time-series values. A low level of error indicates that the fitted time series values closely approximate the actual values and that the forecast can be seen to be reliable. Minitab calculates the MAD and also two other accuracy measures for time-series analysis. Since the MAD measures the accuracy in the same units as the data (in our case the proportions) it is easier to understand this measure. The number of records is not used in Equation 6.4.

There are three parts to the MAD. The numerator measures the difference between the actual proportion and the expected proportion for each first-two digit proportion. For the *InvoicesPaid* data we have an actual proportion of 0.059 for the 10 and an expected proportion of 0.041 for the 10. The deviation is the difference between the two numbers, which is 0.017. The absolute function means that the deviation is given a positive sign irrespective of whether the deviation is positive or negative. The absolute deviation of 0.017 can be seen in column **F** of Figure 5.6. The numerator of Equation 6.4 calls for us to sum the 90 first-two digit absolute deviations. The denominator tells us to divide by the number of bins, which is 90. This will give us the average (or mean) absolute deviation. When we apply the formula to the *InvoicesPaid* data we get a MAD of 0.00243. The MAD is therefore the average deviation between the heights of the bars in Figure 5.7 and the Benford line in Figure 5.7. The higher the MAD, the larger the average difference between the actual and expected proportions.

The *NigriniCycle.xlsx* template calculates the absolute deviations in column **F**. The MAD can be calculated by calculating the average for cells **F2:F92**. The MAD seems to be our answer. Unfortunately there are no objective statistically valid cutoff scores. We do not know what constitutes a *big* MAD that signals that our data does not conform to Benford's Law. Drake and Nigrini (2000) offer some suggestions based on their personal experiences. Their guidelines are based on everyday data sets that were tested against Benford's Law. Their table is due for an update and Figure 6.2 shows the Excel spreadsheet summarizing the MAD results of an analysis of 25 diverse data sets.

	A	B	C	D	E	F	G	H	I	J
1	Data#	Data Description	FTD	>= $10	Records	Notes				
2	2	Streamflow Data, Mathematical Geology	0.0001	0	457,440	Near perfect natural data				
3	20	Seismic signals, January 2010	0.0005	0	160,090,478	Assumed perfect				
4	16	Taxpayer, Balance Due 1989	0.0006	0	93,582	Expected to conform				
5	18	Ledger dump, Positive amounts	0.0008	0	151,202	Assumed good				
6	3	Conglomerate, invoices in source currency	0.0009	1	706,106	No fraud or errors suspected				
7	4	Conglomerate, invoices in US dollars	0.0009	1	704,390	No fraud or errors suspected				
8	19	Ledger dump, Negative amounts	0.0009	0	136,987	Assumed good				
9	23	Utility, KWH credits	0.0009	0	86,279	Surprisingly Benford				
10	8	Streamflow Data, 1998-2002	0.0011	0	37,879	Expected perfection here				
11	9	Invoice, Software company 1996	0.0012	1	36,515	This is a typical financial data set				
12	13	Invoice, North Carolina	0.0012	1	247,811	No fraud or errors suspected				
13	24	Census, 2000, county populations	0.0014	0	3,141	Assumed good				
14	25	Invoices, Transport company	0.0014	0	198,955	Assumed good				
15	5	Census, 1990, county populations	0.0015	0	3,141	Assumed good				
16	12	Federal Govt., purchasing cards	0.0015	1	81,842	Should be a good fit				
17	17	Conglomerate, travel reimbursements	0.0015	1	160,057	Sime issues expected				
18	11	Utility, purchasing cards	0.0019	1	44,614	Should be a good fit				
19	22	Utility, KWH billed	0.0019	0	10,669,357	Clear non-Benford pattern				
20	10	Conglomerate, legal fees	0.0023	0	14,667	This is quite a weak fit				
21	1	California Accounts Payable	0.0024	1	177,763	Data seems to have much by way of fraud or errors				
22	14	Internet site, balances	0.0025	1	40,060	Clear issues in this data				
23	15	Invoices, Texas	0.0026	1	1,887,958	Some issues				
24	21	Tobacco, Sales numbers	0.0030	0	34,716	Highly questionable data				
25	7	California, Special Election Governor	0.0033	1	3,112	Still a weak fit				
26	6	California, Special Election Governor	0.0101	0	6,384	Weak fit to Benford				
27										
28					1 = numbers less than 10 were deleted					

FIGURE 6.2 An Analysis of 25 Diverse Data Sets Where Conformity to Benford's Law Ranged from Near Perfect to Nonconformity

Based on these results a new set of first-two digits cutoff values was developed. These MAD cutoff values are shown in Table 6.1.

The MAD of the *InvoicesPaid* data is 0.00243 and the conclusion is therefore that the data set does not conform to Benford's Law. This is a reasonable result given that we can see several large spikes in Figure 5.7 and the clear nonconformity signals from the Z-statistics, the chi-square test, and the K-S test.

TESTS BASED ON THE LOGARITHMIC BASIS OF BENFORD'S LAW

Figure 5.1 in Chapter 5 showed that the mathematical basis of Benford's Law is that the data, when ranked from smallest to largest, forms a geometric sequence. A geometric

TABLE 6.1 The Cutoff Scores and Conclusions for Calculated MAD Values

First-Two Digits MAD Range	Conclusion
0.0000 to 0.0012	Close conformity
0.0012 to 0.0018	Acceptable conformity
0.0018 to 0.0022	Marginally acceptable conformity
Above 0.0022	Nonconformity

sequence is one where each term after the first term is a fixed percentage increase over its predecessor. The usual mathematical representation for such a sequence is given by

$$\text{Geometric sequence: } S_n = ar^{n-1} \qquad (6.5)$$

where S denotes the sequence, a is the first term in the sequence, r is the common ratio, and n denotes the nth term. In Figure 5.1, a equals 10, r (the common ratio) equals 1.002305, and there are 1,000 terms in the sequence.

Raimi (1976) notes that the data need only approximate a geometric sequence. For example, the Fibonacci sequence (1, 1, 2, 3, 5, 8, . . .) conforms closely to Benford's Law if the data table is large enough. A little bit of arithmetic and some knowledge of logarithms (to the base 10) is needed over here. The log of a number (base 10) is derived as follows:

$$\text{If } x = 10^y \text{ (e.g., } 100 = 10^2) \qquad (6.6)$$

$$\text{Then } y = \log_{10}(x) \qquad (6.7)$$

Equations 6.6 and 6.7 show us that 2 is the log (base 10) of 100 because 10^2 equals 100. Also, 2.30103 is the log (base 10) of 200 because $10^{2.30103}$ equals 200. Note that 0.30103 is the expected probability of a first digit 1 (see Table 5.1). Also, 2.47712 is the log (base 10) of 300 because $10^{2.47712}$ equals 300. Note that 0.47712 is the combined (cumulative) probability of the first digit being either a 1 or a 2. A well-known property of logarithms is shown in Equation 6.8:

$$\log(xy) = \log(x) + \log(y) \qquad (6.8)$$

The result of the property in Equation 6.8 is that the logs (base 10 will always be used unless stated otherwise) of a geometric sequence will form a straight line. In an arithmetic sequence the difference between any two successive numbers is a constant. In our case these differences will be the log of r, the common ratio. As a preliminary test of this property and the "Benfordness" of our *InvoicesPaid* data we will graph the logs of the sequence that is formed by ordering our data from smallest to largest. We will need a two-step procedure because we cannot graph 177,763 data points in Excel. Excel's graphing limit is 32,000 data points. Our strategy is therefore to calculate the logs of the numbers in the *Amount* field and then to plot every sixth record, which will give us a good enough picture of the logs of our data.

The above is quite straightforward except for the wrinkle that Access cannot directly calculate the log (base 10) of a number. Access can calculate the log to the base e (abbreviated ln). We therefore need to use Equation 6.9 below to convert the natural logarithms to logs to the base 10.

$$log_{10}(x) = \frac{\ln(x)}{\ln(10)} \qquad (6.9)$$

A final consideration is that the log of a negative number is undefined (it does not exist) and the general approach for accounts payable data is to ignore numbers less than $10 for the first-order test. We will also ignore these small amounts on our log graphs. We therefore need to restrict the log calculations to amounts $>=10$. A minimum value

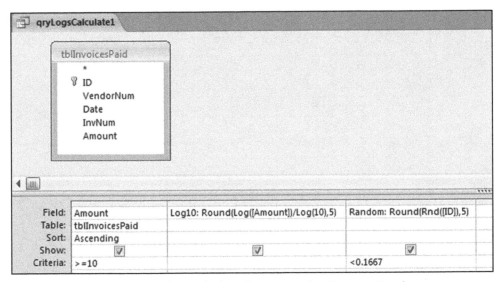

FIGURE 6.3 The Query Used to Calculate the Logs and to Extract a Random Sample of Records

that is an integer power of 10 (10^1, 10^2, 10^3, and so on) should not upset the digit patterns or the log graph. The first query calculates the log (base 10) using Equation 6.9 and it adds a new field that is a random number from 0 to 1. This query is shown in Figure 6.3.

The query to calculate the logs and to extract a random sample of about one-sixth of the records is shown in Figure 6.3. The query only calculates the logs for amounts >=10. The calculated fields are:

$$\text{Log}10 : \text{Round}(\text{Log}([\text{Amount}])/\text{Log}(10), 5)$$
$$\text{Random} : \text{Round}(\text{Rnd}([\text{ID}]), 5)$$

The *Log10* field calculates the log of each amount. The log is rounded to five places to keep the results tidy. The second calculated field, *Random*, creates a random number, rounded to five places, using the *ID* field as a seed value. The < 0.1667 criteria randomly keeps about one-sixth of the records (1/6 is about 0.1667). The query would also work if the criteria was a range such as "Between 0.40 and 0.5667." This query will produce the same random sample each time Access is started and the *InvoicesPaid* database is opened and the query is run. After the query is run Access recalculates the random numbers and so the random numbers in the output are once again random (from 0 to 1) and are not all less than 0.1667. Save the query as *qryLogsCalculate1*. The query returns a table of 29,662 records. This number might or might not differ from computer to computer and from Access version to Access version. The result will, however, always be close to 29,662 records.

The next step is to graph the logs in Excel. The shape of the graph of 29,662 records should closely mimic the patterns in the full data set of 177,763 records. Copy the contents of the *Log10* field (using **Copy** and **Paste**) from Access to the *Logs* tab in

	A	B	C	D	E	F	G	H	I	J
1	Rank	Log10								
32	180	1								
33	186	1								
34	192	1								
35	198	1								
36	204	1								
37	210	1								
38	216	1								
39	222									
51	294	1.00346								
52	300	1.00475								
53	306	1.00647								
54	312	1.00775								
55	318	1.00903								
56	324	1.00903								
57	330	1.00903								
58	336	1.0103								
59	342	1.0103								

Tables / DataProfile / FirstOrder / SecondOrder / Summation / LastTwoDigits / Data / OrderedLogs / **Logs**

FIGURE 6.4 The Log and Rank Data Used to Graph the Ordered Logs

column B of the *NigriniCycle.xlsx* template. Populate the *Rank* field with a series of numbers starting with 1 and ending with 29,662 at the last record (on row 29,663). The result is shown in Figure 6.4.

The ordered log data is shown in Figure 6.4. The logs should now be graphed using Excel's graphing capabilities. The first step is to highlight the range containing the data to be graphed, namely B2:B29663. The graph is then prepared using **Insert**→ **Charts**→**Line**. The resulting graph after a little bit of formatting is shown in Figure 6.5.

The graph shows a reasonably straight line through to rank 150000, after which we get another (almost) straight line with a steeper slope through to the end. The sharp upward curve on the right side of the graph is due to a handful of items that would have little impact on any goodness of fit test. We can see a horizontal segment at about 1.70 and again at 3.00. These are due to excessive duplications of $50 and numbers around $1,000 and higher. The horizontal segment at around 1.7 is associated with the large spike visible at 50 in Figure 5.7.

If the data followed Benford's Law closely we would see either a single straight line, or a series of straight lines with varying slopes from integer value to integer value. That is, from 1.00 to 2.00, from 2.00 to 3.00, from 3.00 to 4.00, and so on up the *y*-axis. The graph need not be straight (linear) from the first record to the Nth record, it need only be linear between the integer values on the *y*-axis. Also, if a linear segment has relatively few records (such as 4.00 to 5.00) then its effect on the digit frequencies is quite minor. For the invoices data the convex curved pattern from 1.00 to 2.00 probably has the most pronounced effect on the digit frequencies, followed by the 3.00 to 4.00 segment. Converting the logs back to numerical values this means that the biggest nonconforming segments are amounts from 10.00 to 99.99 and 1,000.00 to 9,999.00, respectively.

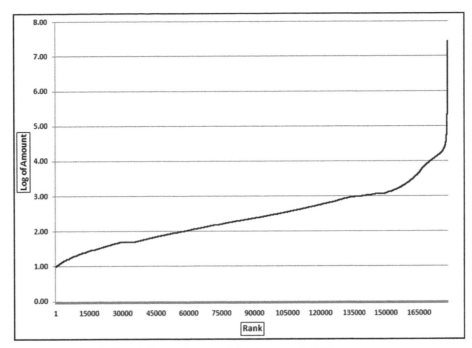

FIGURE 6.5 The Ordered (Sorted) Logs of the *InvoicesPaid* Data

We are almost ready to use the logarithmic basis of Benford's Law to test for conformity. For the next step we need to go back to the 1880s to the very first paper on digital frequencies written by Newcomb (1881). Newcomb states that the frequency of the digits is based on the fact that their mantissas are equally probable. This is almost equivalent to our prior statements that the logs of the ordered data should follow a straight line. By way of example, we could have the logs forming a straight line from 1.302 to 1.476 on the *y*-axis. This data set would not conform to Benford's Law because all the numbers would range from 200 to 300 and we would have no numbers with a first digit 1, 3, 4, 5, 6, 7, 8, and 9. The requirement that the mantissas are uniformly distributed is more comprehensive (except that it ignores the negative numbers that we encounter in private and public data). The mantissa is described in Equations 6.10 and 6.11.

$$\log_{10}(200) = 2.30103 \tag{6.10}$$

$$mantissa[\log_{10}(200)] = 0.30103 \tag{6.11}$$

The mantissa is the fractional part of the log of a number. The *mantissa* is the part of the logarithm to the right of the decimal point and the *characteristic* is the integer part to the left of the decimal point. The characteristic is 2 in Equation 6.10. Mantissas can span the range [0,1). The square bracket and round bracket mean that zero is included in the range together with all values up to, but not including, 1. A set of data that conforms to Benford's Law is known as a Benford Set. A test of the mantissas can therefore be used as

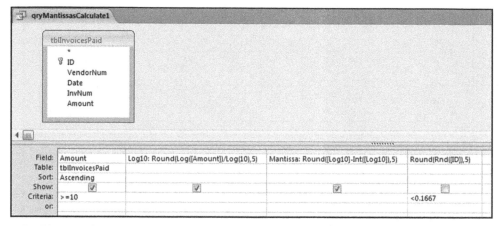

FIGURE 6.6 The Query Used to Calculate the Mantissas and to Extract a Random Sample of the Records

a test for a Benford Set. We need to test whether the mantissas are uniformly (evenly) distributed over the [0,1) interval. If the mantissas are distributed U[0,1) then the data conforms to Benford's Law. The query to calculate the mantissas uses the same logic as the query to calculate the logs. The query to calculate the mantissa is shown in Figure 6.6.

The query used to calculate the mantissas and to extract a random sample of one-sixth of the records is shown in Figure 6.6. This query follows the query in Figure 6.3 and includes a calculation of the mantissa. The mantissa formula is

$$\text{Mantissa}: \text{Round}([\text{Log10}]-\text{Int}([\text{Log10}]), 5)$$

The *Random* field is not shown in the results because it is not needed in the result. The **Round** function is used to keep the results neat and tidy.

The data needs to be copied to Excel and the mantissas need to be sorted from smallest to largest. The graph of the ordered mantissas is prepared in Excel. The result for the *InvoicesPaid* data is shown in Figure 6.7 together with the dashed line that would be the plot for uniformly distributed mantissas.

A necessary condition to test the mantissas for U[0,1) is that the mean is 0.50 and that the variance is 1/12. These conditions are, however, not sufficient conditions. Data sets that satisfy only the mean and variance requirements might have little or no conformity to Benford's Law. The basis of any mantissa-based model is that the ordered (ranked) mantissas should form a straight line from 0 to 1 (or more precisely $(N-1)/N$, which is fractionally less than 1) with a slope of $1/N$. This is the dashed line in Figure 6.7. It is tempting to use regression to assess the goodness of fit. The quantile (Q-Q) plots of Wilk and Gnanadesikan (1968) also look promising. For a regression test we would only need to test the intercept (which would equal zero for perfect conformity), the slope (which would equal $1/N$ for perfect conformity, and the R-squared (which would equal 1 for perfect conformity). This test is the subject of research in progress. The

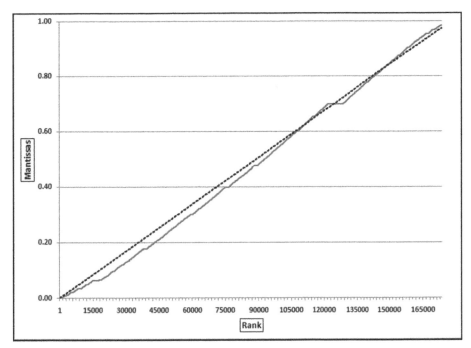

FIGURE 6.7 The Ordered Mantissas of the Data and a Straight Line from 0 to 1

next approach is the Mantissa Arc solution based on mantissas and another graphical approach. The Mantissa Arc test is described after we discuss how one can create a perfect Benford Set.

 ## CREATING A PERFECT SYNTHETIC BENFORD SET

Evaluating the possible goodness-of-fit tests for Benford's Law means that we should be able to create a perfect Benford Set against which to compare our results. From the previous section we know that the mantissas of a Benford Set are distributed uniformly (evenly) over the [0,1) range. One way to create a Benford Set is to create a set of uniform [0,1) mantissas and then to create a set of numbers from the mantissas.

Let us assume that we want to create a table with 1,000 numbers that range from 10 to 1,000. The lower bound is 10 and the upper bound is 1,000. To start we need to calculate *d*, which is the difference between the logs of the upper and lower bounds. This calculation is shown in Equation 6.12. Note that this difference must be an integer value (1, 2, 3, . . .) to give a Benford Set.

$$d = \log(ub) - \log(lb) \tag{6.12}$$

$$d = \log(1000) - \log(10) = 2$$

The mathematical representation for a geometric sequence is given in Equation 6.13.

$$S_n = ar^{n-1} \tag{6.13}$$

B2	▼	f_x	=10*(10^(2/1000))^(A2-1)

	A	B	C	D	E	F
1	**N**	**Sn**				
2	1	10.00000				
3	2	10.04616				
4	3	10.09253				
5	4	10.13911				
6	5	10.18591				
7	6	10.23293				
8	7	10.28016				
9	8	10.32761				
10	9	10.37528				
11	10	10.42317				

FIGURE 6.8 The Creation of a Synthetic Benford Set

where a is the first term in the sequence (in this case 10), r is the common ratio, and n denotes the nth term.

We need to calculate r, the common ratio that will give us a geometric sequence of exactly 1,000 terms that will start at 10 and end at 1,000. This is done using Equation 6.14.

$$r = 10^{\frac{d}{N}} = \sqrt[N]{10^d} \qquad (6.14)$$

Substituting $N=1000$ and $d=2$ in Equation 6.14 we get a calculated r of 1.00461579. The sequence can then be created in Excel as is shown in Figure 6.8.

The first 10 records of the synthetic Benford Set is shown in Figure 6.8. The "10" in the formula bar is the a in Equation 6.13, the "10^(2/1000)" term is r from Equation 6.14, and the "A2-1" term is $n - 1$ from Equation 6.13. The synthetic (simulated) Benford Set has all the required attributes. The sequence stops just short of 1,000. As N gets larger, so the upper bound tends toward, but never exactly touches, the stated upper bound (of 1,000). A graph of the sequence will be a perfect geometric sequence. A graph of the logs will be a straight line from 1 to 3, and a graph of the mantissas will be a perfect straight line from 0 to 1. The Z-statistics will all be insignificant (some deviations will occur because 1,000 records cannot give us some of the exact Benford probabilities), the sequence will conform to Benford's Law using the chi-square test (where the calculated chi-square statistic is 7.74) and the K-S test (where the largest difference equals 0.00204). The MAD equals 0.00068, which is clearly close conformity. Our synthetic Benford Set is about as good as it can get for a table of 1,000 records. As N increases, so the fit will tend to be an even closer level of perfection.

 THE MANTISSA ARC TEST

Figure 6.7 shows the mantissas ordered from smallest and plotted as a straight line. If the data formed a Benford set the mantissas would be uniformly (evenly) distributed

over the [0,1) range. No formal test related to the mantissas was proposed. Alexander (2009) proposes a test based on the mantissas, which we call the Mantissa Arc (MA) test.

In Figure 6.7 each mantissa is given a rank with the smallest value given rank #1 and the largest value given rank #N. The numeric value of the mantissa is plotted on the y-axis. In contrast, in the MA test each numeric value is plotted on the unit circle and for a Benford Set we would have a set of points uniformly distributed on the circle with radius 1 and centered on the origin (0,0).

Without showing the calculations just yet, the result that we would get for the Benford Set in Figure 6.8 would be as is shown in Figure 6.9.

In Figure 6.9 the uniformly distributed mantissas have been converted (using formulas) to a set of uniformly distributed points on the unit (radius = 1) circle centered on the origin (0,0). Alexander then takes this concept further. He calculates the "center of gravity" inside the circle and then he calculates whether this center of gravity differs significantly from (0,0). This is very clever. If the center of gravity differs significantly

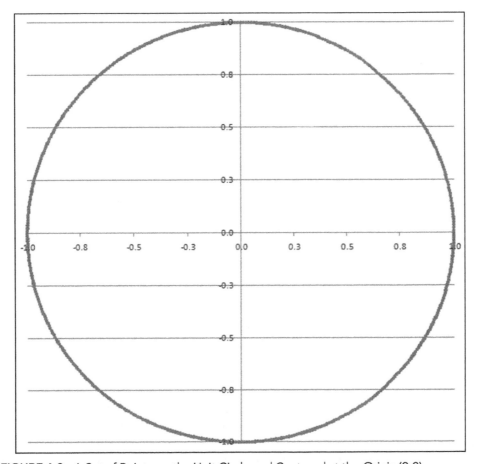

FIGURE 6.9 A Set of Points on the Unit Circle and Centered at the Origin (0,0)

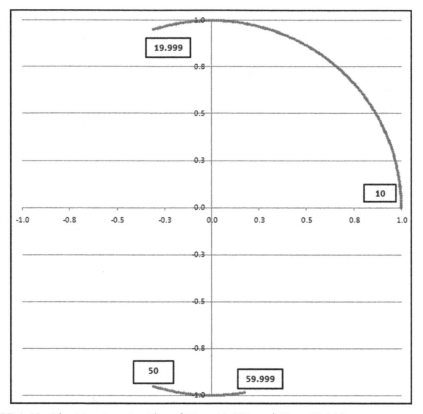

FIGURE 6.10 The Mantissa Arc Plot of 10 to 19.999 and 50 to 59.999

from (0,0) then the points are not evenly distributed on the unit circle and the data is then not a Benford Set. The center of gravity must lie somewhere within the circle. An exception would be if we had a single point, in which case the center of gravity would also be that point. But with a single point we would not really even have a part of a circle. It would just be a point. To see what would happen if we had sections completely missing from our geometric sequence, the MA result is shown in Figure 6.10 for the case where we have a subset of a Benford Set, these being all the numbers from 10 to 19.999 and 50 to 59.999.

The circumference of a circle is $2\pi r$ and because we are dealing with the unit circle (where r equals 1) our circumference is simply 2π. This circumference of 2π equals 6.2832. The length of the arc in the top right quadrant (usually called quadrant I) extending into quadrant II is 1.8914, which equals (not by coincidence) 0.30103 (the first digit 1 probability) times 6.2832 (the circumference). The length of the arc in the neighborhood of (0, −1) that extends from quadrant III to quadrant IV is 0.4975, which is 0.07918 (the first digit 5 probability) times 6.2832. The MA method plots the uniformly distributed mantissas uniformly on the unit circle centered at the origin (0,0). A mantissa of 0 (which corresponds to a log of 1.000 or 2.000 and consequently a number equal to 10 or 100) is plotted at (1,0). A number such as 17.783 (or 177.83) would have its mantissa of 0.25 plotted at (0,1). A number such as 31.623 (or 3,162.3) would have its mantissa of 0.50 plotted at (−1,0). A number such as 56.234 (or 562,234) would have its mantissa of 0.75 plotted at (0,−1).

If the mantissas are uniformly distributed on the circle, then the center of gravity is the origin (0,0). Let our table of N records be denoted $x_1, x_2, x_3, \ldots, x_N$. Each number must be converted to a point on the unit circle. The x-coordinate and the y-coordinates of the point are calculated as is shown in Equations 6.15 and 6.16.

$$x\text{-}coordinate = \cos(2\pi^*(\log(x_i) mod 1)) \tag{6.15}$$

$$y\text{-}coordinate = \sin(2\pi^*(\log(x_i) mod 1)) \tag{6.16}$$

where cos and sin refer to the trigonometric functions cosine and sine. The log is taken to the base 10 and mod 1 means that we only take the fractional part (the part to the right of the decimal point) of the log. For example, 11.03 mod 1 equals .03. The x-coordinate is sometimes called the abscissa and the y-coordinate is sometimes called the ordinate.

The center of gravity is also called the mean vector (MV) and its x and y coordinates are calculated as is shown in Equations 6.17 and 6.18.

$$x\text{-}coordinate = \frac{\sum_{i=1}^{N} \cos(2\pi^*(\log(x_i) mod 1))}{N} \tag{6.17}$$

$$y\text{-}coordinate = \frac{\sum_{i=1}^{N} \sin(2\pi^*(\log(x_i) mod 1))}{N} \tag{6.18}$$

The length of the mean vector, L^2, is calculated as is shown in Equation 6.19 (which uses Equations 6.17 and 6.18).

$$L^2 = (x\text{-}coordinate)^2 + (y\text{-}coordinate)^2 \tag{6.19}$$

Finally, the p-value of L^2 is calculated using either Equation 6.20 or its algebraic equivalent in Equation 6.21.

$$p\text{-}value = 1 - e^{-L^2 N} \tag{6.20}$$

$$p\text{-}value = 1 - \frac{1}{e^{L^2 N}} \tag{6.21}$$

Equation 6.21 shows us that as L^2 or N get larger (mathematicians would say as they tend to infinity) so the p-value tends to 1.00. This is because as either L^2 or N gets larger, the right-hand term tends toward zero and 1 minus zero equals 1.00. The p-value calculation is based on the tail of the chi-squared distribution with 2 degrees of freedom.

The calculations in Equations 6.17 to 6.21 were done in the lower part of the same Excel spreadsheet shown in Figure 6.8.

The mean vector and p-value calculations are shown in Figure 6.11. The Excel formulas are not too complicated especially when we realize that Equations 6.17 and

	F1010	▾	f_x	=1-EXP(-F1007*1000)		
◢	A	B	C	D	E	F	G
995	994	968.27786		2.98600	0.986	0.99613	-0.08785
996	995	972.74722		2.98800	0.988	0.99716	-0.07533
997	996	977.23722		2.99000	0.99	0.99803	-0.06279
998	997	981.74794		2.99200	0.992	0.99874	-0.05024
999	998	986.27949		2.99400	0.994	0.99929	-0.03769
1000	999	990.83194		2.99600	0.996	0.99968	-0.02513
1001	1000	995.40542		2.99800	0.998	0.99992	-0.01257
1002							
1003						Equation 6.17	Equation 6.18
1004						0.00000	0.00000
1005							
1006						Equation 6.19	
1007						0.00000	
1008							
1009						Equation 6.20	
1010						0.00000	
1011							

FIGURE 6.11 The Mean Vector and P-Value Calculations

6.18 are simply telling us to take the average, and the mathematical constant e is the EXP function in Excel. The Excel formulas are

$$\mathbf{F1004}: \quad = \text{AVERAGE(F2 : F1001)}$$
$$\mathbf{G1004}: \quad = \text{AVERAGE(G2 : G1001)}$$
$$\mathbf{F1007}: \quad = \text{F1004}^2 + \text{G1004}^2$$
$$\mathbf{F1010}: \quad = 1 - \text{EXP}(-\text{F1007}^*1000)$$

Since the calculated p-value in **F1010** is less than 0.05, the null hypothesis of uniformly distributed mantissas is not rejected and we conclude that the data conforms to Benford's Law.

Going back to our *InvoicesPaid* data we would do the calculations by extracting a sample of about one-sixth of the records using the query in Figure 6.6. For this test we would only need to keep the field *Amount* in the result. The next step would be to paste the 29,662 amounts into an Excel spreadsheet and to calculate the mean vector and the p-value as is done in Figure 6.11. The calculations for the *InvoicesPaid* data are shown in Figure 6.12.

The length of the mean vector (the center of gravity) is 0.00443. This is based on a sample, but for a sample of 29,662 records the sample mean is for all practical purposes equal to the mean. The p-value of 1.00 indicates that the data does not conform to Benford's Law (which is in agreement with the Z-statistics, chi-square, K-S, and the MAD). If the p-value was less than 0.05 we would have to redo the calculations based on the whole population to see whether the p-value stays below 0.05 with a larger N.

The mantissa arc graph for the *InvoicesPaid* data together with the mean vector is shown in Figure 6.13. The graph was prepared in Excel.

	K29672	▾	fx	=1-EXP(-K29669*29662)	
	I	J		K	L
29652	$850,000.00			0.90327	-0.42908
29653	$858,690.00			0.91483	-0.40385
29654	$1,000,000.00			1.00000	0.00000
29655	$1,088,096.11			0.97358	0.22835
29656	$1,200,000.00			0.87877	0.47724
29657	$1,500,000.00			0.44787	0.89410
29658	$1,500,000.00			0.44787	0.89410
29659	$1,500,000.00			0.44787	0.89410
29660	$1,605,161.30			0.27586	0.96120
29661	$3,069,846.95			-0.99673	0.08086
29662	$15,779,215.20			0.32044	0.94727
29663	$26,763,475.78			-0.89815	0.43970
29664					
29665				Equation 6.17	Equation 6.18
29666				0.06515	0.01378
29667					
29668				Equation 6.19	
29669				0.00443	
29670					
29671				Equation 6.20	
29672				1.00000	

FIGURE 6.12 The Mean Vector and p-Value Calculations for the *InvoicesPaid* Data

From the uniformity of the circle the data would seem that we have a good fit. However, what the graph actually shows us is that we are using all the points on the circle, or that all the mantissas seem to be used. There seem to be no open spaces between the markers (Excel terminology for points or dots) on the graph. If we used a fine marker (very small dots) we might see some open space. Unfortunately our markers are quite large and because we are plotting in two dimensions we cannot see how many markers are plotted on the same spot. The number 50.00 is used abnormally often in this data set. This corresponds to the point $(-0.315, -0.949)$ in quadrant III. In this two-dimensional graph we cannot see that this point is plotted excessively often. Future research might point us in the direction of a three-dimensional graph.

The problem with the mantissa arc approach is that the length of the mean vector (equation 6.19) needs to be very small for the test to signal conformity through a p-value less than 0.05. For example, all the hypothetical situations in Table 6.2 would have a p-value in excess of 0.05 (signaling nonconformity).

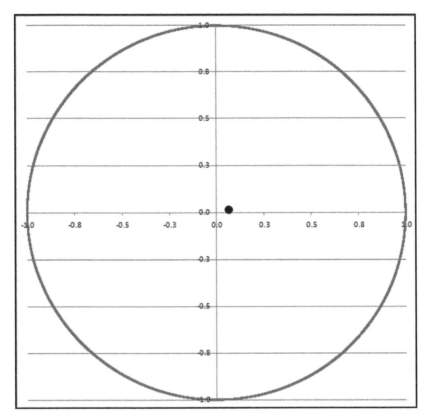

FIGURE 6.13   The Mantissa Arc Graph and the Mean Vector for the *InvoicesPaid* Data

The mantissa arc test is offered as an interesting alternative test and also because it offers some interesting insights into the mathematical basis of Benford's Law. Future research in the area should address the very small tolerance for deviations from a mean vector length of zero. Perhaps using some rules of thumb much like was done with the Mean Absolute Deviation and Figure 6.2 and Table 6.1 we could end up with a Mantissa Arc table similar to Table 6.1. Alternatively researchers could leave the mantissa arc logic and method intact and substitute $\sqrt{N}$ or $\sqrt[3]{N}$ or some smaller root to take account of the practical issues encountered with real world data sets.

TABLE 6.2   A Series of Hypothetical Results and the Mantissa Arc Test's Conclusions

Hypothetical L^2	Hypothetical N	p-Value	Notes
0.00006	1,000	0.058	*L*-squared is very close to zero
0.00003	2,000	0.058	*L*-squared is even closer to zero
0.00002	3,000	0.058	*L*-squared is zero for all practical purposes
0.00001	5,000	0.049	Data barely passes with *L*-squared close to zero
0.00001	10,000	0.095	Data fails with *L*-squared close to zero

 **SUMMARY**

Several valid goodness of fit tests are discussed in statistics textbooks. A major issue with each of these methods is that they work well for small data tables. When working with Benford's Law we often have large data tables and the usual test statistics always signal nonconformity. The basis of the classical tests is that we have a table of data that conforms to Benford's Law and from this we then extract a sample of x records. As the sample size increases so this mythical sample will tend towards conforming exactly to Benford's Law because the sample was drawn from a population that conformed to Benford's Law. These classical statistical methods "tolerate" only small deviations from perfection for large data sets.

We can assess conformity of a data set one digit at a time or all digits taken together. The Z-statistic is used to evaluate the digits one at a time. The test is based on both the absolute magnitude of the deviation and N, the number of records. As expected, this test suffers from the excess power problem in that even small deviations are statistically significant for large N. Both the chi-square and Kolmogorov-Smirnoff (K-S) tests evaluate all the digits at the same time. The chi-square test indirectly takes N into account. The K-S test incorporates N in the assessment of the significance of the result. In both cases the tests tolerate only small deviations from Benford's Law for large N making them only useful for comparing similarly sized data sets across time.

The Mean Absolute Deviation (MAD) test ignores N in its calculations thereby overcoming the problem related to large data sets. A problem with this test is that there are no objective cutoff values. A set of guidelines is offered based on an analysis of 25 real-world data sets.

The chapter reviewed the logarithmic basis of Benford's Law, which is that the mantissas (the fractional part of the logs) of the numbers are expected to be uniformly (evenly) distributed over the range [0,1). The square bracket means that the range includes 0 and the rounded bracket means that the range gets close to, but never actually touches 1. Some tests might be developed at some time in the future based on the logarithmic basis and the tools of linear regression. The chapter reviewed the mechanics of creating a synthetic (simulated) Benford Set being a set of numbers that conforms to Benford's Law. These data sets can be used by practitioners and researchers wanting to test various conformity methods, and for recreational Benford's Law research. The Mantissa Arc (MA) test of Alexander (2009) was reviewed. This clever technique transforms each number to a point on the unit circle centered at (0,0). The fit to Benford's Law is based on the distance of the center of gravity from (0,0) and N. Unfortunately this theoretically sound test is also sensitive and tolerates only very small deviations from Benford's Law.

Further research into conformity tests for large data sets is encouraged. The best solution seems to be the Mean Absolute Deviation (MAD). The cutoff values given in the chapter were based on the deviations found in several large real-world data tables.

7

Benford's Law

The Second-Order and Summation Tests

C HAPTERS 5 AND 6 dealt with forensic analytic situations where we expected our data to follow Benford's Law. Those chapters included guidelines for assessing which data sets should follow Benford's Law and a review of methods for measuring conformity to Benford's Law. In contrast, this chapter deals with two Benford's Law tests that do not rely on the data conforming to Benford's Law. One of these tests is called the second-order test. This relatively new test can be applied to (almost) any set of data. The second-order test looks at relationships and patterns in data and is based on the digits of the differences between amounts that have been sorted from smallest to largest (ordered). The digit patterns of the differences are expected to closely approximate the digit frequencies of Benford's Law. The second-order test gives few, if any, false positives in that if the results are not as expected (close to Benford), then the data do indeed have some characteristic that is rare and unusual, abnormal, or irregular.

The second of these new tests is called the summation test. The summation test looks for excessively large numbers in the data. The summation test is an easy extension to the usual first-two digits test and it can be run in either Access or Excel. This chapter also introduces Minitab as a possible tool for forensic analytics. The second-order test uses some of the mathematics from the prior chapter. The summation test uses some of the logic from Chapter 5. Both the second-order tests and the summation tests are run on the first-two digits. As is usual for the Benford's Law tests, the tests are run on the entire data table. Data is only ever sampled as a work-around to graphing a data table to stay within Excel's graphing limit of 32,000 data points.

A DESCRIPTION OF THE SECOND-ORDER TEST

A set of numbers that conforms closely to Benford's Law is called a *Benford Set*. The link between a geometric sequence and a Benford Set is discussed in the previous chapter. The link was also clear to Benford who titled a part of his paper "Geometric Basis of the Law" and declared that "*Nature* counts geometrically and builds and functions accordingly" (Benford, 1938, 563). Raimi (1976) relaxes the tight restriction that the sequence should be perfectly geometric, and states that a close approximation to a geometric sequence will also produce a Benford Set. Raimi then further relaxes the geometric requirement and notes that, "the interleaving of a number of geometric sequences" will also produce a Benford Set. A mixture of approximate geometric sequences will therefore also produce a Benford Set. This equation for a geometric sequence, S_n, is given in the prior chapter and is restated here again for convenience:

$$S_n = ar^{n-1} \tag{7.1}$$

where a is the first term in the sequence, r is the common ratio of the $(n+1)^{st}$ element divided by the nth element, and n denotes the nth term. In a graph of a geometric sequence (see Figure 5.1), the rank $(1, 2, 3, \ldots, N)$ is shown on the x-axis, and the heights on the y-axis are ar^{n-1}.

The digits of a geometric sequence will form a Benford Set if two requirements are met. First, N should be large and this vague requirement of being "large" is because even a perfect geometric sequence with (say) 100 records cannot fit Benford's Law perfectly. For example, for the first-two digits from 90 to 99, the expected proportions range from 0.0044 to 0.0048. Because any actual count must be an integer, it means that the actual counts (either 0 or 1) will translate to actual proportions of either 0.00 or 0.01. As N increases the actual proportions are able to tend toward the exact expected proportions of Benford's Law. Second, the difference between the logs of the largest and smallest numbers should be an integer value. The geometric sequence needs to span a large enough range to allow each of the possible first digits to occur with the expected frequency of Benford's Law. For example, a geometric sequence over the range [30, 89.999] will be clipped short with no numbers beginning with a 1, 2, or a 9.

The remainder of the discussion of the second-order test draws on Nigrini and Miller (2009). The algebra below shows that the differences between the successive elements of a geometric sequence give a second geometric sequence D_n of the form

$$\begin{aligned} D_n &= ar^n - ar^{n-1} \qquad \text{(with } n = 1, 2, 3, \ldots, N-1) \\ &= a(r-1)^* r^{n-1} \end{aligned} \tag{7.2}$$

where the first element of the sequence is now $a(r-1)$, and r is still the ratio of the $(n+1)$th element divided by the nth element. Since the elements of this new sequence form a geometric series, the distribution of these digits will also conform to Benford's Law and the $N-1$ differences will form a Benford Set.

The *second-order test* of Benford's Law is based on the digit patterns of the differences between the elements of ordered data and is summarized as follows:

- If the data is made up of a single geometric sequence of N records conforming to Benford's Law, then the $N - 1$ differences between the ordered (ranked) elements of such a data set gives a second data set that also conforms to Benford's Law.
- If the data is made up of nondiscrete random variables drawn from any continuous distribution with a smooth density function (e.g., the Uniform, Triangular, Normal, or Gamma distributions) then the digit patterns of the $N - 1$ differences between the ordered elements will be *Almost Benford*. Almost Benford means that the digit patterns will conform closely, but not exactly, to Benford's Law.
- Some anomalous situations might exist when the digit patterns of the differences are neither Benford nor Almost Benford. These anomalous situations are expected to be rare. If the digit patterns of the differences is neither Benford nor Almost Benford it is an indicator that some serious issue or error might exist in the data.

Miller and Nigrini (2008) describe and develop the mathematical proofs related to the second-order test. One odd case where the differences do not form a Benford Set exists with two geometric sequences where, for example, N_1 spans the $[30,300)$ interval and the second geometric sequence N_2 spans the $[10,100)$ interval. The combined sequence therefore spans the range $[10,300)$. The *differences* between the elements do not conform to Benford's Law even though the digit frequencies of the source data (N_1 and N_2) both individually and combined (appended) all conform perfectly to Benford's Law. The differences between the ordered elements of the two geometric sequences when viewed separately also form Benford Sets. However, when the two sequences are interleaved, the $N_1 + N_2 - 1$ *differences* do not conform to Benford's Law. This odd situation would be rare in practice.

The differences are expected to be Almost Benford when the data is drawn from most of the continuous distributions encountered in practice. A continuous distribution is one where the numbers can take on any value in some interval. To formally describe these differences, let Y_1 through Y_n be the X_i's arranged in increasing order (Y_1 is the smallest value and Y_n the largest); the Y_i's are called the order statistics of the X_i's. For example, assume we have the values 3, 6, 7, 1, and 12 for X_1 through X_5. Then the values of Y_1 through Y_5 are 1, 3, 6, 7, and 12, and the differences between the order statistics are 2, 3, 1, and 5. The second-order Benford test is described as follows:

> Let $x_1, \ldots, x_N$ be a data table comprising records drawn from a continuous distribution, and let $y_1, \ldots, y_N$ be the x_i's in increasing order. Then, for many data sets, for large N, the digits of the differences between adjacent observations ($y_{i+1} - y_i$) is close to Benford's Law. A pattern of spikes at 10, 20, $\ldots$, 90 will occur if these differences are drawn from data from a discrete distribution. Large deviations from Benford's Law indicate an anomaly that should be investigated.

Since most distributions satisfy the conditions stated above, the expectation is that we will see Almost Benford results from most data tables. There is only a small difference between the Benford and Almost Benford probabilities, and these differences depend only slightly on the underlying distribution. The suggested approach to assessing conformity in the second-order test is to either look at the data and make a subjective judgment call, or to use the mean absolute deviation (MAD). The formal tests such as Z-statistics, the chi-square test, or the K-S test are not appropriate because we will usually be dealing with large data sets and the expectation is Almost Benford, so we are not even expecting exact conformity.

To demonstrate Almost Benford behavior, the results of four simulations from very different distributions are shown. The data was simulated in Minitab 16 using the **Calc→Random Data** commands. The numbers in fields C1, C3, C5, and C6 were then sorted using **Data→Sort**. The differences between the numbers were calculated using **Calc→Calculator**.

The simulated data and the calculated differences are shown in Figure 7.1. The next step was to prepare histograms of the four data sets to see how different the distributions actually are. The four histograms in Figure 7.2 show (a) a normal distribution with a mean of 5000 and a standard deviation of 1000, (b) a uniform distribution over the [0,10000) interval, (c) a triangular distribution with a lower endpoint of 0 and an upper endpoint of 10000 and a mode of 5000, and (d) a Gamma distribution with a shape parameter of 25 and a scale parameter of 5000. Each of the data tables had 50,000 records. The four distributions in Figures 7.1 and 7.2 were chosen so as to have a mixture of density functions with positive, zero, and negative

	C1	C2	C3	C4	C5	C6	C7	C8
	Normal		Uniform		Triangular		Gamma	
1	841.10256761	*	0.04726847	*	45.12224549	*	49356.53300549	*
2	1053.75896052	212.65639291	0.42560981	0.37834134	50.94378152	5.82153603	49503.58403974	147.05103425
3	1081.66678956	27.90782904	0.45981089	0.03420108	57.48228827	6.53850675	51808.83215161	2305.24811188
4	1113.52315394	31.85636438	0.67226828	0.21245738	63.26269071	5.78040243	52079.30154825	270.46939664
5	1200.10599906	86.58284513	0.75946148	0.08719320	69.28564850	6.02295780	52123.25253331	43.95098505
6	1236.49365964	36.38766057	1.01170067	0.25223919	70.01551665	0.72986815	52274.14874080	150.89620750
7	1250.18451318	13.69085354	1.19054753	0.17884686	74.88033249	4.86481584	52434.96318478	160.81444397
8	1290.62273922	40.43822604	1.28995016	0.09940263	82.06455598	7.18422349	52570.22788341	135.26469863
9	1298.50246924	7.87973002	1.54652262	0.25657246	92.18152080	10.11696482	53004.14070007	433.91281666
10	1394.75913704	96.25666780	1.75248864	0.20596602	92.35328430	0.17176350	53251.26002541	247.11932534
11	1416.79602366	22.03688662	1.81624097	0.06375234	94.01611898	1.66283467	54344.04611085	1092.78608544
12	1427.59574604	10.79972238	1.90170385	0.08546288	94.16341252	0.14729354	54390.61953415	46.57342330
13	1434.32311646	6.72737042	1.93533934	0.03363549	102.72358211	8.56016959	54735.22281181	344.60327766
14	1445.33524725	11.01213079	1.97967172	0.04433238	108.12491349	5.40133138	56329.69980268	1594.47699087
15	1453.40324904	8.06800179	2.12314789	0.14347617	115.21017727	7.08526378	56390.87833112	61.17852844

FIGURE 7.1   The Minitab Calculations for the Second Order Test

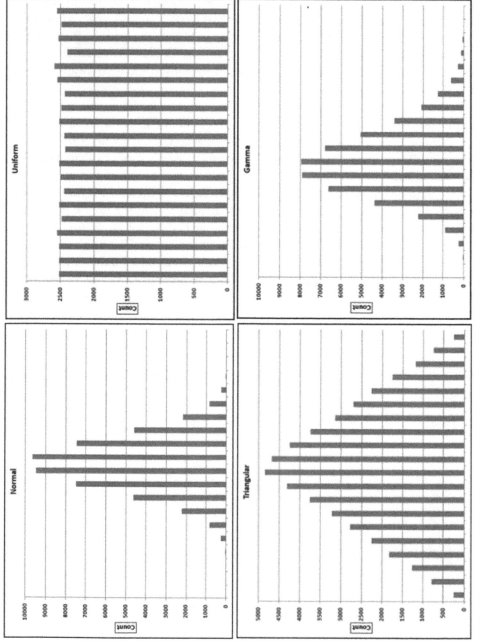

FIGURE 7.2 The Histograms of Four Simulated Data Tables of 50,000 Records Each

slopes as well as a combination of linear and convex and concave sections in the density functions. The scale parameters (the means) have no effect on the differences between the ordered records. The shape parameters (the standard deviations) do impact the sizes of the differences, as do the number of records (N). The four histograms are shown in Figure 7.2.

The next step in the second-order test was to analyze the digit patterns of the differences between the ordered (ranked) amounts for each distribution. Because each data table had 50,000 records there were 49,999 differences per data table. In Figure 7.1 the first three differences for the normal distribution in column C2 are 212.656, 27.908, and 31.856. The differences for the other distributions are in columns C4, C6, and C8. Before calculating the first-two digits for each table of differences, the smallest difference was calculated for each table. These minimums were 0.00000021, 0.00000013, 0.00000807, and 0.00001013 respectively. Each of the difference amounts (in all four columns) was multiplied by 100,000,000 if the amount was less than 1.00, so that all numbers had two digits to the left of the decimal point (0.00000021*100000000 equals 21.0). The four differences columns were then imported into Access. The first-two digits queries (see Figures 5.3 and 5.4) were run and the graphs were prepared. The results for each data table are shown in Figure 7.3.

The first-two digits of the differences, hereinafter called the *second-order test*, are all Almost Benford despite the fact that their densities in Figure 7.2 have completely different shapes. *Almost Benford* means that in one or two sections of the graph the actual proportions will tend to be less than those of Benford's Law, and in one or two sections the actual proportions will tend to exceed those of Benford's Law. The "over" and "under" sections are easier to see with larger data sets but we generally have either two "over" sections and one "under" section, or two "under" sections and one "over" section. If the simulations were repeated with larger data sets and the results aggregated, then these "over" and "under" sections would be easier to see. The differences between the ordered records of numbers drawn from a continuous distribution will exhibit Almost Benford behavior, but they will seldom conform perfectly to Benford's Law even with N tending to infinity (Miller and Nigrini, 2008). These differences should be close to Benford's Law for most data sets, and an analysis of the digits of the differences could be used to test for anomalies and errors. What is quite remarkable is that when all four data tables of 49,999 differences were appended to each other (to create one big data table of 199,996 records) the large data table had a MAD of 0.000294, which according to Table 6.1 is close conformity.

Running the Second-Order Test in Excel

The second-order test was run on the *InvoicesPaid* data set from Chapter 4. The data profile showed that there were 189,470 invoices. The first-order test in Chapter 5 showed that the data did not conform to Benford's Law using the traditional Z-statistics and chi-square tests. However, there was the general Benford tendency in that the low digits occurred more frequently than the higher digits. Again, the second-order test does

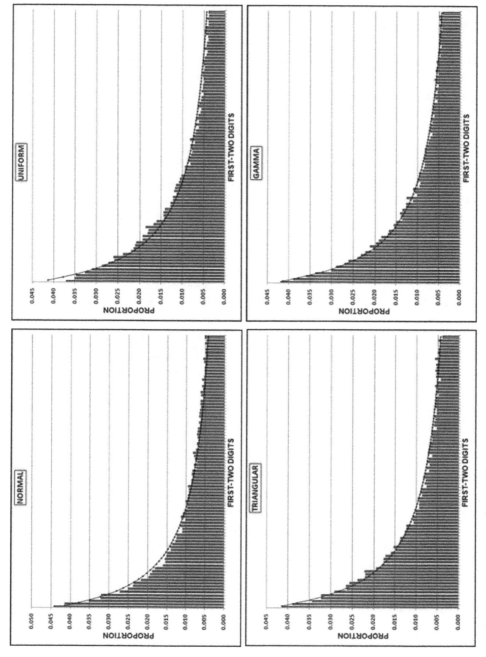

FIGURE 7.3 The First-Two Digits of the Differences

not require, or assume, conformity to Benford's Law. This test is usually run on all the numbers (including negative numbers and small positive numbers).

The second-order test cannot be run in Access. Access cannot easily calculate the differences between the sorted records. So if the 1,000th record was for $2,104 and the 1,001st record was for $2,150, Access cannot easily calculate that the difference is $46. This is because of the database concept that both row order and column order are unimportant in the design of tables in relational databases. Access has a domain aggregate function called *DLookUp*. The *DLookUp* function can be used to show the *Amount* from the preceding row. These domain aggregate functions are slow to execute and are impractical with large tables. The suggested approach is to use Excel to sort the records and to calculate the differences. Another approach would be to use IDEA, which includes the second-order test as a built-in routine.

The procedure in Excel would be to use the *NigriniCycle.xlsx* template and to sort the *Amount* ascending. The sort is done using **Home→Editing→Sort&Filter→Custom Sort**.

The sort procedure is shown in Figure 7.4. Click **OK** to sort the *Amount* field from smallest to largest. The next step is to create a new field, which we call *Diffs* (for differences) in column F. The blank column E is there to have a dividing line between our source data and our calculated values. The formula for the calculation of the differences for cell F3 is,

$$\textbf{F3: } = (D3 - D2) * 1000$$

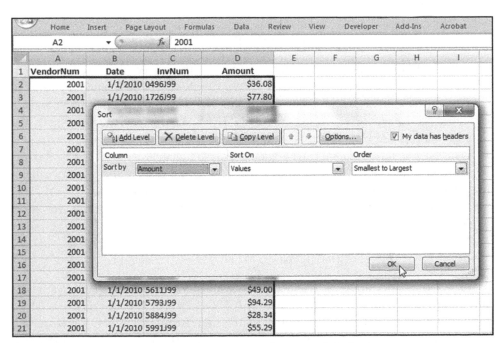

FIGURE 7.4 The Sort Procedure Used to Start the Second-Order Test

	Home	Insert	Page Layout	Formulas	Data	Review	View	Developer	Add-Ins	Acrobat
	G3	▾	f_x	=VALUE(LEFT(ROUND(F3,2),2))						

	A	B	C	D	E	F	G
1	VendorNum	Date	InvNum	Amount		Diffs * 1000	First-Two
2	2018	12/16/2010	217390394	-$71,388.00			
3	5806	6/14/2010	CM76475	-$38,138.64		$33,249,360.00	33
4	5806	5/18/2010	CM75887	-$28,656.99		$9,481,650.00	94
5	5806	5/18/2010	CM75887	-$28,656.99		$0.00	0
6	5806	5/18/2010	CM75886	-$27,680.52		$976,470.00	97
7	5806	5/18/2010	CM75886	-$27,680.52		$0.00	0
8	2013	9/23/2010	59175-01ADJ	-$24,670.76		$3,009,760.00	30
9	5806	5/18/2010	CM75881	-$23,701.18		$969,580.00	96
10	5806	5/18/2010	CM75881	-$23,701.18		$0.00	0
11	3630	2/14/2010	X4278701	-$23,659.20		$41,980.00	41
12	3630	8/5/2010	YJB73701	-$22,034.25		$1,624,950.00	16
13	5806	5/18/2010	CM75883	-$19,651.66		$2,382,590.00	23
14	5806	5/18/2010	CM75883	-$19,651.66		$0.00	0
15	5806	5/18/2010	CM75889	-$19,624.71		$26,950.00	26

FIGURE 7.5 The Calculation of the First-Two Digits of the Differences

The multiplication by 1,000 is so that amounts such as 0.01 become 10.00 and we can then use the **Left** function to calculate the first-two digits. The formula needs to be copied down to the last row of the data. The next step is to format column **F** as **Currency**. We will always have one blank (null) cell because a data set with N records only gives us $N-1$ differences. The next step is to calculate the first-two digits of each difference in column G. The formula in cell G3 is,

$$\textbf{G3:} = \text{VALUE(LEFT(ROUND(F3,0),2))}$$

The **ROUND** function is to be sure that we get the correct first-two digits. Excel might store a number such as 20 as 19.99999999999, which is fine for most calculations, except to identify the first-two digits. The comma 2 in the **LEFT** function indicates that we want the leftmost two digits. The **VALUE** part of the function means that we want the result as a number. The results are shown in Figure 7.5.

The calculation of the digits of the differences is shown in Figure 7.5. The next step is to count how many of the differences have 10, 11, 12, and so on as their first-two digits. In Access this would be a Group By query. In Excel this task is done with the **COUNTIF** function in the *Tables* worksheet. The **COUNTIF** formula in cell J3 of the *Tables* worksheet is

$$\textbf{J3:} = \text{COUNTIF(Data!\$G\$3:\$G\$189471,"="\&I3)}$$

The formula essentially looks at the first-two digits calculations in the *Data* worksheet and counts all the occurrences of 10, 11, 12, and so on. The reference to cell **I3** is to the number 10 in **I3** and cell **J3** counts the number of 10s. When the formula is copied down to cell **J92** the counts are for the numbers 10, 11, 12, and so on to 99. The results are shown in Figure 7.6.

	Home	Insert	Page Layout	Formulas	Data	Review	View	Developer	Add-Ins	Acrobat	

J3   *fx*   =COUNTIF(Data!$G$3:$G$189471,"="&I3)

	A	B	C	D	E	F	G	H	I	J	K	L	M	N
1			FIRST-ORDER TEST									SECOND-ORDER TEST		
2	FT Digit	untOfFirstT	Actual	Benford'sLa	Difference	AbsDiff			FT Digit	Count	Actual	Benford's	Difference	AbsDiff
3	10	10439	0.059	0.041	0.017	0.017			10	24712	0.367	0.041	0.326	0.326
4	11	10306	0.058	0.038	0.020	0.020			11	1099	0.016	0.038	-0.021	0.021
5	12	5966	0.034	0.035	-0.001	0.001	177763		12	1016	0.015	0.035	-0.020	0.020
6	13	5756	0.032	0.032	0.000	0.000			13	914	0.014	0.032	-0.019	0.019
7	14	4462	0.025	0.030	-0.005	0.005	67246		14	764	0.011	0.030	-0.019	0.019
8	15	5591	0.031	0.028	0.003	0.003			15	799	0.012	0.028	-0.016	0.016
9	16	4391	0.025	0.026	-0.002	0.002	0		16	712	0.011	0.026	-0.016	0.016
10	17	3984	0.022	0.025	-0.002	0.002			17	632	0.009	0.025	-0.015	0.015
11	18	3830	0.022	0.023	-0.002	0.002	0		18	645	0.010	0.023	-0.014	0.014
12	19	3764	0.021	0.022	-0.001	0.001			19	557	0.008	0.022	-0.014	0.014
13	20	3920	0.022	0.021	0.001	0.001			20	8874	0.132	0.021	0.111	0.111
14	21	3520	0.020	0.020	0.000	0.000			21	467	0.007	0.020	-0.013	0.013
15	22	3021	0.017	0.019	-0.002	0.002			22	413	0.006	0.019	-0.013	0.013
16	23	2656	0.015	0.018	-0.004	0.004			23	434	0.006	0.018	-0.012	0.012
17	24	2657	0.015	0.018	-0.003	0.003			24	365	0.005	0.018	-0.012	0.012
18	25	3798	0.021	0.017	0.004	0.004			25	418	0.006	0.017	-0.011	0.011

FIGURE 7.6 The Results of the Second-Order Test

The *NigriniCycle.xlsx* template works in much the same way as for the first-order test. The record count for the second-order test is shown in cell **G7** in the *Tables* worksheet. Since the original data table had 189,470 records we expect 189,469 $(N-1)$ differences. We only have 67,246 numbers with valid digits because the data table contained excessive duplication and there are only 67,247 different numbers being used in the data table of 189,470 records. When two successive numbers are equal (e.g., 50.00 and 50.00) then the difference between these numbers is zero and zero is ignored in the analysis of the digits of the differences. The excessive duplication will be clearer from the first-two digits graph. The graph is prepared in the template and can be seen by clicking on the *SecondOrder* tab.

The result of the second-order test of the *InvoicesPaid* data is shown in Figure 7.7. The first-order result in Chapter 5 showed five large spikes, and aside from that, the fit was at least reasonable from a visual perspective. For most of the higher first-two digit combinations (51 and higher) the difference between the actual and expected proportions was only a small percentage. The *InvoicesPaid* data did not conform using the conformity criteria. The deviations are comparable to those of the accounts payable data analyzed in Nigrini and Mittermaier (1997).

The results of the second-order test in Figure 7.7 are based on 67,246 nonzero differences. Differences of zero (which occur when the same number is duplicated in the list of ordered records) are not shown on the graph. The second-order graph in Figure 7.7 seems to have two different functions. The first Benford-like function applies to the first-two digits of 10, 20, 30, . . . , 90, and a second Benford-like function applies to the remaining first-two digit combinations (11 to 19, 21 to 29, . . . , 91 to 99). The groups are called the prime and the minor first two-digits:

1. **Prime:** First-two digits: 10, 20, 30, 40, 50, 60, 70, 80, and 90. $\{d_1 d_2 \bmod 10 = 0\}$
2. **Minor:** First-two digits: 11, 12, 13, . . . , 19, 21, 22, 23, . . . , 29, 31, . . . , 99. $(d_1 d_2 \bmod 10 \neq 0)$

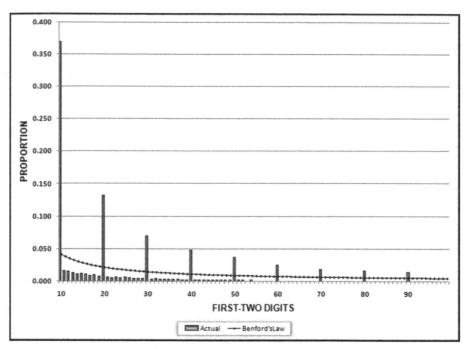

FIGURE 7.7 The Second-Order Test of the Invoices Data

The *InvoicesPaid* numbers are tightly clustered. For example, there were 139,105 records with an *Amount* field from $10.00 to $999.99. There are 99,000 different numbers from 10 to 999.99. A test showed that 39,897 of the available numbers between 10 and 999.99 were used. This suggests that the differences between the numbers in the 10 to 999.99 range are generally small and are probably 0.01, 0.02, and 0.03. Another test showed that there are 21,579 differences of 0.01, 7,329 differences of 0.02, and 3,563 differences of 0.03. The decrease in the counts is dramatic and there are only 464 differences of 0.08. The largest difference in this range is 0.47. The numbers in the 10 to 999.99 range are indeed tightly packed.

A difference of 0.01 has first-two digits of 10 because this number can be written as 0.010. A difference of 0.02 has first-two digits of 20 because 0.02 can be written as 0.020. The reason for the prime spikes in Figure 7.7 is that the numbers are tightly packed in the $10.00 to $999.99 range with almost three-quarters of the differences being 0.01 or 0.02. The mathematical explanation for the systematic spikes on the prime digits is that the *InvoicesPaid* table is not made up of numbers from a continuous distribution. Currency amounts can only differ by multiples of $0.01. The second-order results are caused by the high density of the numbers over a short interval and because the numbers are restricted to 100 evenly spaced fractions after the decimal point. The prime spikes should occur with any discrete data (e.g., population numbers) and the size of the prime spikes is a function of both N and the range. That is, we will get larger prime spikes for larger data tables with many records packed into a small range.

This pattern of spikes does not indicate an anomaly; it is a result of many numbers restricted to being integers or to fractions such as 1/100, 2/100, 3/100 being fitted into a tight range that restrict the differences between adjacent numbers.

An Analysis of Journal Entry Data

The next case study is an analysis of the 2005 journal entries in a company's accounting system (the second-order test was not known at the time). The external auditors did the usual journal entry tests, which comprised some high-level overview tests for reasonableness (including Benford's Law), followed by some more specific procedures as required by the audit program. The journal entries table had 154,935 records of which 153,800 were for nonzero amounts. The dollar values ranged from $0.01 to $250 million and averaged zero since the debits were shown as positive values and the credits as negative values. The dollar values were formatted as currency with two decimal places. The results of the first-order test are shown in Figure 7.8.

The results show a reasonable conformity to Benford's Law as would be expected from a large collection of transactional data. The calculated MAD was 0.001163, which just squeaks in with a "close conformity" score using Table 6.1. There is a spike at 90, and a scrutiny of the actual dollar amounts (e.g., 90.00, 9086.06) reveals nothing odd except for the fact that 111 amounts with first-two digits of 90 were for amounts equal to 0.01. The reason for this will become clear when the second-order results are discussed. The second-order results are shown in Figure 7.9.

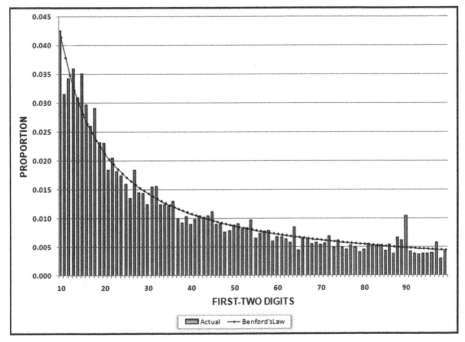

FIGURE 7.8 The First-Order Results for the Corporate Journal Entries

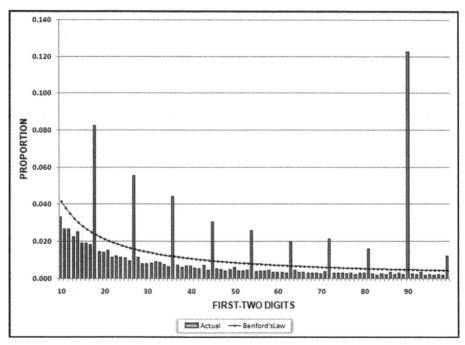

FIGURE 7.9 The Second-Order Results for the Corporate Journal Entries

The second-order test results in Figure 7.9 show that there are anomalous issues with the data. First, there is no spike at 10 and a large spike is expected for data representing dollars and cents in tightly clustered data due to differences of 0.01, which have first-two digits of 10 (since 0.01 is equal to 0.010). Second, there is a large spike at 90 and while spikes are expected at the prime digits, the largest of these is expected at 10 and the smallest at 90. Third, there is an unusual spike at 99. The 99 is a minor combination and 99 has the lowest expected frequency for both the first-order and second-order tests.

Further work showed that while the data was formatted as currency with two digits to the right of the decimal point (e.g., $11.03), there were amounts that had a mysterious nonzero third digit to the right of the decimal point. The extra digits can be seen if the data is formatted as a number with three digits to the right of the decimal point. A data extract is shown in Figure 7.10.

The journal entry data was originally housed in an Access database. The data was imported into the *NigriniCycle.xlsx* template using Excel's data import function. The import function is activated using **Data→Get External Data→From Access**. The file and the specific table are then selected. This method is better than using the clipboard, which is limited in size. Using this data import method causes the rows to be shaded and the original Access formatting is lost (which helped to see the data issue).

Transactional data can have a third digit as long as the third digit is a zero. For example, 11.030 can be shown as $11.03. To evaluate how many times a nonzero third digit occurred, all amounts were multiplied by 100 and the digits to the right of the

	B41688	▼	f_x =(A41688-A41687)*10000		
⊿	A	B		C	D
41683	9.99	$0.00	0		
41684	9.99	$0.00	0		
41685	9.99	$0.00	0		
41686	9.99	$0.00	0		
41687	9.99	$0.00	0		
41688	9.999	$90.00	90		
41689	9.999	$0.00	0		
41690	9.999	$0.00	0		
41691	9.999	$0.00	0		
41692	10.017	$180.00	18		
41693	10.017	$0.00	0		
41694	10.017	$0.00	0		
41695	10.017	$0.00	0		
41696	10.035	$180.00	18		
41697	10.035	$0.00	0		

FIGURE 7.10 A Sample of the Journal Entry Data

decimal point were analyzed. Approximately one-third of the amounts in the data table had a digit of zero to the right of the decimal point. The digits 1 through 9 appeared to the right of the decimal point with an average frequency of 7.3 percent and the percentages ranged from 6.2 percent for the digit 3 to 8.4 percent for the digit 2.

Follow-up work was done to see whether the extra digit occurred more frequently in any particular subset of the data, but the extra digit occurred with an almost equal frequency across the four quarters that made up the fiscal year. No systematic pattern was evident when the data was grouped by *source* (a field in the table). The proportion of numbers with third digits was about the same for the four largest sources (payroll, labor accrual, spreadsheet, and XMS).

The third digit explains why amounts displayed as $0.01 were shown to have first-two digits of 90. This was because unformatted numbers of 0.009 rounded to $0.01 when formatted as currency. In the journal entry data the second-order test showed a data inconsistency that was not apparent from the usual Benford's Law tests and also not apparent from any other statistical test used by auditors. While the dollar amounts of the errors were immaterial and did not affect any conclusions reached, this might not be the case for data that could be required to be to a high degree of accuracy.

The second-order test is a recent development. With the second-order test the data can contain errors and anomalies and we would still expect the second-order results to approximate Benford's Law. We can therefore get "good" results (such as Figure 7.3 or Figure 7.7) from bad data. On the other hand, when the second-order test signals an issue (because it is neither Almost Benford nor does it have the pronounced spikes at the prime digits) then the data really does have some issue. Simulations have shown that the test can detect excessive rounding (these results will look just like Figure 7.7 though). In another simulation the second-order test was run on data that was not ranked in ascending order. The situation could be where the investigator was presented with data that should have a natural ranking such as the number of votes cast in precincts ranked from the earliest report to the last to report, or miles driven by the taxis in a fleet ranked by gasoline usage. The second-order test could be used to see whether the data was actually ranked on the variable of interest. The general rule is that if the data is not correctly sorted then the second-order results will not be Almost Benford.

THE SUMMATION TEST

The summation test has been dormant for nearly 20 years and it is time to put it to good use. Benford's Law is based on the counts of the number of numbers with first-two digits 10, 11, 12, . . . , 99. In contrast, the summation test is based on sums rather than counts. The summation test seems particularly useful when viewed in the light of an article in the *Wall Street Journal* (1998):

> Kenneth L. Steen of Chattanooga, Tenn., was expecting a $513 tax refund. Instead he got a letter from the Internal Revenue Service informing him that he owes the government $300,000,007.57. "It's mind-boggling," Mr. Steen says. "I thought they had become the new, friendlier, more efficient IRS, and then this happens." Mr. Steen has plenty of company. An IRS official says about 3,000 other people around the nation got similar erroneous notices, each showing a balance-due of "three hundred million dollars and change."

The important facts are that all the erroneous amounts had first-two digits of 30 and all the amounts are very large when compared to normal balance-due notices. The Treasury is a bit lucky that the errors were balance-due notices and not taxpayer refunds. Had the Treasury issued 3,000 treasury checks for $300 million each it is quite possible that they would still be looking for some of the taxpayers and their money! To get an idea of just how big these erroneous amounts are, we could sum all 3,000 of the $300 million errors. The answer would be an amount equal to approximately 10 percent of the Gross Domestic Product of the United States of America (in 1998, which was when the error occurred). It is surprising that an accounting error equal to 10 percent of GDP was not detected internally prior to the notices being sent out to taxpayers.

With about 125 million tax returns per year an additional 3,000 amounts with first-two digits 30 would probably not cause anything resembling a spike on the IRS's first-two digits graph. Using the expected probability of the 30 we would expect about 1.8 million tax returns to have a balance-due or a refund amount with first-two digits of 30. An increase to 1.83 million would not affect the graph even slightly if we only compare a count of 1.80 million to 1.83 million. The ability to detect the errors improves dramatically of we look at the sum of these numbers.

I developed the summation theorem as a Ph.D. student. I still remember walking home from classes one day and asking myself what the relationship was between the sums of all the numbers with first-two digits 10, 11, 12, . . . , 99 in a Benford Set. Do the sums have the same pattern as the counts? It did not take long to simulate a synthetic Benford Set and then to calculate the sums. I was quite surprised by the result that the sums were approximately equal. The proof and the underlying mathematics require a little calculus as is shown in Equation 7.3.

$$
\int_{\log(ft)*N}^{\log(ft+1)*N} ar^{n-1} dn
$$

$$
= \frac{a}{r} * \left. \frac{r^x}{\ln(r)} \right|_{\log(ft)*N}^{\log(ft+1)*N} \tag{7.3}
$$

$$
= \frac{a}{r\ln(r)} * \left(r^{\log(ft+1)*N} - r^{\log(ft)*N} \right)
$$

$$
= \frac{a}{r\ln(r)}
$$

The first line of the equation calculates the area under the curve for an unspecified first-two digit combination abbreviated ft. The number of records is N, and the function is the sequence described by Equation 7.1. To keep the sequence neat we can restrict a to being equal to 10^k with $k \geq 0$, and k integer. This means that the starting point will be 10, or 100, or 1,000 or some similarly neat number. In the last step, the entire second term disappears. This is because of a neat substitution of $10^{(1/N)}$ for r (as in Equation 6.14), which makes the second term equal to $(1 - 0)$ or 1, and a "multiplication by 1" term can be dropped in the equation. In this example the log of the upper bound (say 100) minus the log of the lower bound (say 10) equals 1. This simplifies the mathematics above and the result can be generalized to cases where the difference between the logs exceeds 1.

The implication of ft disappearing from Equation 7.3 tells us that the areas under the curve do not depend on which first-two digits we are talking about. The areas under the curve are independent of ft and this means that they must be equal.

As a test of the mathematics we will create a synthetic Benford Set of 20,000 records with a lower bound of 10 and an upper bound of 1,000, just to make things a little more complex than Equation 7.3. We do not want too few records in the data table because the pattern will then not be clear. Also, too many records will make the pattern too neat. We will follow the logic in equations 6.12, 6.13, and 6.14, and Figure 6.8. We need to calculate the value of r that will give us a geometric sequence from 10 to 1,000 with $N = 20,000$ using Equation 6.14.

$$
r = 10^{\frac{2}{20000}} = \sqrt[10000]{10^1} = 1.00023029 \tag{7.4}
$$

We will use the *Data* worksheet in the *NigriniCycle.xlsx* template to create our synthetic Benford Set.

	Home	Insert	Page Layout	Formulas	Data	Review
	B2		▾	f_x =10*(10^(1/10000))^(A2-1)		

◢	A	B	C	D	E
1	n ▾	Sn ▾	FirstTwo ▾		
2	1	10.000000	10		
3	2	10.002303	10		
4	3	10.004606	10		
5	4	10.006910	10		
6	5	10.009215	10		
7	6	10.011520	10		
8	7	10.013825	10		
9	8	10.016131	10		
10	9	10.018438	10		
11	10	10.020745	10		
12	11	10.023052	10		
13	12	10.025361	10		
14	13	10.027669	10		
15	14	10.029978	10		

FIGURE 7.11 The Synthetic Benford Set with 20,000 Records

The data table that will be used for the summation test is shown in Figure 7.11. The formula in cells **B2** and **C2** are,

$$\textbf{B2}: = 10^*(10\,^{\wedge}(1/10000))\,^{\wedge}(A2 - 1)$$

$$\textbf{C2}: = \text{VALUE(LEFT(B2,2))} \text{ (first-two digits calculation)}$$

In the geometric sequence in column **B** we have a equal to 10 (the starting value) and the common ratio r equal to $10^{(1/10000)}$. The **B2** and **C2** formulas are copied down to row 20001. There are 20,000 records and one row is used for headings. The next step is to calculate the sums in the *Tables* worksheet. The formula and the results are shown in Figure 7.12.

The summation test's sums are calculated in column **J** of the *Tables* worksheet. The formula for column **J** is shown below.

$$\textbf{J5}: = \text{SUMIF(Data!\$C\$2:\$C\$20001,}" = "\&\text{P3, Data! \$B\$2:\$B\$20001)}$$

The first term in the formula states the column that we are filtering on. The second term is our condition (which is to equal 10, 11, or 12, or whatever the case may be). The third term is the range that we want to add (sum).

For the summation test all the Benford's Law proportions are equal amounts because we expect the sums to be equal. Also, the 90 possible (equal) proportions must add up to 1.00 because every valid number has a first-two digit combination. The expected sum stated as a proportion for the first-two digits is equal to 1/90. The summation graph is automatically prepared in the template and it can be seen by clicking on the *Summation* chart sheet.

	Home	Insert	Page Layout	Formulas	Data	Review	View	Developer	Add-

Q3 ▼ f_x =SUMIF(Data!$C$2:$C$20001,"="&P3,Data!$B$2:$B$20001)

	O	P	Q	R	S	T	U	V	W	X
1				**SUMMATION TEST**						
2		FT Digit	Summation	Actual	Benford'sLaw	Difference	AbsDiff		LT Digit	Count
3		10	47675.743	0.011	0.011	0.000	0.000		00	
4		11	47782.796	0.011	0.011	0.000	0.000		01	
5		12	47823.142	0.011	0.011	0.000	0.000		02	
6		13	47796.713	0.011	0.011	0.000	0.000		03	
7		14	47670.493	0.011	0.011	0.000	0.000		04	
8		15	47893.299	0.011	0.011	0.000	0.000		05	
9		16	47721.578	0.011	0.011	0.000	0.000		06	
10		17	47725.817	0.011	0.011	0.000	0.000		07	
11		18	47809.426	0.011	0.011	0.000	0.000		08	
12		19	47823.929	0.011	0.011	0.000	0.000		09	
13		20	47799.314	0.011	0.011	0.000	0.000		10	
14		21	47767.576	0.011	0.011	0.000	0.000		11	
15		22	47762.355	0.011	0.011	0.000	0.000		12	

FIGURE 7.12 The Calculated Sums of the Summation Test

The summation test results are shown in Figure 7.13. The bars are all very close to the expected values of 0.0111. Some variability can be seen as we move from left to right. This is because the actual and expected counts are lower for the higher digits and sometimes the simulation generates slightly fewer than expected or slightly more than expected records with a (say) first-two digits of 85. Since we are dealing with sums it

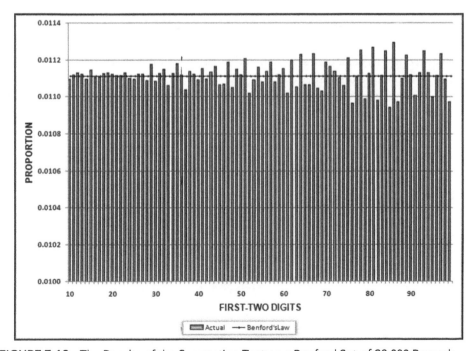

FIGURE 7.13 The Results of the Summation Test on a Benford Set of 20,000 Records

looks like a large effect. Also, note the calibration of the y-axis where the minimum value is 0.01 and the actual sums are actually all close to the 0.111 expectation.

Running the Summation Test in Access

For the summation test the calculations could be done in Access but the graph still needs to be prepared in Excel. The steps for the *InvoicesPaid* data are shown. The first stage (or step) is to make a table that includes only the positive amounts. No other fields are needed in the table. The table is created with the query shown below and the >0 criteria for the field named *PosAmount*. The Make Table query is created by selecting **Make Table** in the **Query Type** group. Enter the table name as *tblPosAmounts*. Click **OK**. Click **Run**.

The query used to create a table of the positive invoice amounts is shown in Figure 7.14. Click **Yes** after the warning that you are about to paste 185083 rows into a new table. At this stage we could import the data into Excel and then use the *NigriniCycle.xlsx* template because the table has less than 1,048,576 records. Note that in Excel we would not simply use the LEFT function because the leftmost two characters of 4.21 are "4." We would have to use LEFT(B2*1000,2) for the first-two digits and then we would have to look for accuracy issues (where 20 is perhaps held in memory as 19.99999999). It is easier to do the summation calculations in Access. The query to calculate the first-two digits is shown in Figure 7.15.

This query is similar to the usual query for the first-order test except that the query is run against all positive amounts. The formula in *qryDigitsCalc2* is,

$$\text{FirstTwo: Val(Left([PosAmount]}^*1000, 2))$$

The second query calculates the required sums of the numbers. This query differs from the query used in the first-order test.

The second summation test query is shown in Figure 7.16. The first-order test counts the amounts whereas the summation test sums the positive amounts. The sums

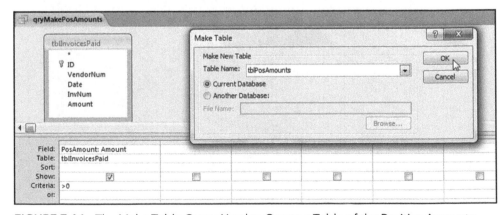

FIGURE 7.14 The Make Table Query Used to Create a Table of the Positive Amounts

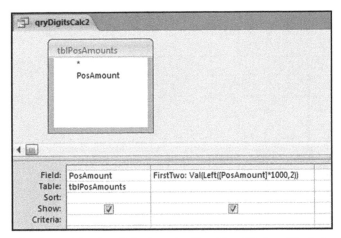

FIGURE 7.15 The Query Used to Calculate the First-Two Digits of Each Amount

are grouped by the first-two digits. The result can be copied and pasted using **Copy** and **Paste** into the *NigriniCycle.xlsx* template also using column Q as is shown in Figure 7.12. The summation graph can be accessed by again simply clicking on the *Summation* chart sheet. The results are shown in Figure 7.17.

The summation graph shows little conformity to Benford's Law. The graph shows that we have an excess of large numbers with first-two digits 10, 11, 14, 15, 26, and 50. These results will be investigated further in Chapter 8.

Experimentation with the summation theorem has shown that real-world data sets seldom show the neat straight-line pattern shown on the graph even though this is the

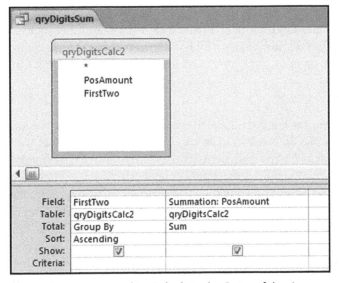

FIGURE 7.16 Shows the Query Used to Calculate the Sums of the Amounts

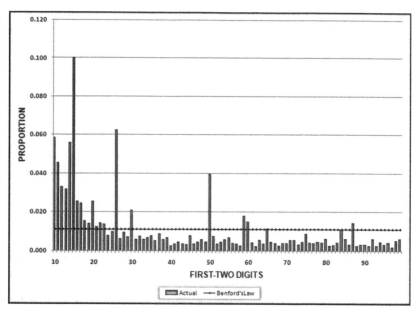

FIGURE 7.17   The Results of the Summation Test for the Invoices Data

correct theoretical expectation. This is because in the real world we do have abnormal duplications of large numbers. At this stage we cannot say whether the spikes are caused by a handful (one, two, or three) of *very* big numbers or an abnormal duplication of a few hundred moderately big numbers. The usual Benford's Law result in Chapter 5 had spikes at 10, 11, 50, 98, and 99, indicating high counts for these digit combinations. This suggests that the numbers at 98 and 99 are small because they do not affect the summation result. The numbers at 10, 11, and 50 are moderately large because the count and the sums are high. The numbers for 14, 15, and 25 are probably very large because they affect the summation, but not the graph based on the counts. This is a new test and results, findings, and comments from users are welcomed.

Discussion

The second-order test analyses the digit patterns of the differences between the ordered (ranked) values of a data set. In most cases the digit frequencies of the differences will closely follow Benford's law irrespective of the distribution of the underlying data. While the usual Benford's Law tests are usually only of value on data that is *expected* to follow Benford's law, the second-order test can be performed on any data set. This second-order test could actually return compliant results for data sets with errors or omissions. On the other hand, the data issues that the second-order tests did detect in simulation studies (errors in the download, rounding, and the use of statistically generated numbers) would not have been detectable using the usual Benford's Law tests.

The second-order test might be of use to internal auditors. In ACFE, AICPA, & IIA (2008) the document focuses on risk and the design and implementation by management of a fraud risk program. It is important to distinguish between *prevention*, which focuses on policies, procedures, training, and communication that stops fraud from occurring, and *detection*, which comprises activities and programs that detect frauds that have been committed. The second-order test would be a detection activity or detective control.

ACFE, AICPA, & IIA (2008) notes that a "Benford's Law analysis" can be used to examine transactional data for unusual transactions, amounts, or patterns of activity. The usual suite of Benford's Law tests are only valid on data that is expected to conform to Benford's Law whereas the new second-order test can be applied to any set of transactional data. Fraud detection mechanisms should be focused on areas where preventive controls are weak or not cost-effective. A fraud detection scorecard factor is whether the organization uses data analysis, data mining, and digital analysis tools to "consider and analyze large volumes of transactions on a real-time basis." The new second-order and summation tests should be included in any suite or cycle of data analysis tests.

In a continuous monitoring environment, internal auditors might need to evaluate data from a continuous stream of transactions, such as the sales made by an online retailer or an airline reservation system. Unpublished work by the author suggests that the distribution of the differences (between successive transactions) should be stable over time and consequently the digits of these differences should also be stable across time. Auditing research could address how the second-order test could be adapted so that it analyzes the differences between successive transactions. Future research that shows potential benefits of continuously running the second-order tests on the differences between the (say) last 10,000 records of transactional data might be valuable. Such research could show what patterns might be expected under conditions of "in control" and "out of control." Research on the detection of anomalies is encouraged given the large penalties for external audit failures.

SUMMARY

This chapter introduced two new reasonably advanced forensic analytic tests related to Benford's Law. The second-order test is based on the fact that if the records in any data set are sorted from smallest to largest, then the digit patterns of the differences between the ordered records are expected to closely approximate Benford's Law in all but a small subset of special circumstances.

The chapter showed four different data sets with markedly different distributions. However, the digit patterns of the differences between the successive numbers of the ranked data all showed the same pattern. That pattern was a reasonably close conformity to Benford's Law, which is called Almost Benford. When the second-order test is used on data that is made up of integers or currency amounts then a somewhat different pattern can emerge. These results are a Benford-like pattern on the prime combinations (10, 20, 30, . . . , 90) and another Benford-like pattern on the remaining (minor) digit combinations. The second-order test was demonstrated in Excel.

For the invoices data, the second-order test results did not conform to Benford's Law because of the amounts being in dollars and cents with a large number of records spanning a small range of values. The invoices data showed the patterns that could normally be expected from transactional data. The second case analyzed journal entries and the second-order test identified errors that presumably occurred during the data download. The second-order test could be included in the set of data diagnostic tools used by internal auditors and management as detective controls. The second-order test has the potential to uncover errors and irregularities that would not be discovered by traditional means.

The summation test is another new Benford's Law test. The chapter shows an example related to taxation where the summation tests would have detected 3,000 erroneous amounts for $300 million each. In this test the amounts with first-two digits 10, 11, 12, . . . , 99 are summed and graphed. This test can be run reasonably easily in either Excel or Access using the *NigriniCycle.xlsx* template to produce the graphical results. The summation test would signal to forensic investigators that the data table contains either a few very large amounts, or a larger amount of moderately large numbers each with the same first-two digits. The invoices data showed that there were an excess of large numbers with first-two digits of 10, 11, 14, 15, 26, and 50. These results are further investigated in Chapter 8 in the final set of tests in the Nigrini Cycle.

CHAPTER EIGHT

Benford's Law

The Number Duplication and Last-Two Digits Tests

THE DATA PROFILE, PERIODIC graph, histogram, first-order test, second-order test, and the summation test gave us valuable insights into the internal diagnostics of our data. The data profile and the histogram gave us insights into the distribution of the numbers. The periodic graph showed us the distribution of the amounts across time. The first-order test on the *InvoicesPaid* table showed that there were abnormal duplications of five first-two digit combinations. Although there was the general tendency toward more numbers with low first-two digits, the visual pattern of the graph and mean absolute deviation showed that the data did not conform to Benford's Law. The second-order test confirmed that much of the data was tightly packed into a small range, a fact that was also evident from the histogram. The summation test showed that there were abnormal duplications of some high-value amounts. The remaining tests in this chapter complete the *Nigrini Cycle*. This cycle of eight tests should be the minimum set of forensic analytic tests run on data tables. The first of the final two tests drill down into the data table to identify the exact transactions that were causing the spikes on our first-order and summation graphs. The second test identifies abnormal duplications on the right side of the numbers in the data table. These duplications could indicate errors, invented numbers, or excessive rounding.

Running the number duplications test is quite straightforward in Access and a little complex in Excel. Running the last-two digits test uses the same approach and logic as for the first-order tests. Running the round numbers test is a little bit tricky because we have to specify what we mean by "round."

THE NUMBER DUPLICATION TEST

The number duplication test is a drill-down test and is essentially a numbers hit parade. This test identifies which specific numbers were causing the spikes on the first-order graph and on the summation test graph. Spikes on the first-order graph are linked with some specific numbers occurring abnormally often while any spikes on the summation graph are associated with abnormally large numbers. For example, a large spike at 50 on the first-order graph could be caused by many $50s and on the summation graph it could be caused by a single $50 million.

The number duplication test was developed as a part of my Ph.D. dissertation when I was looking for amounts that were duplicated abnormally often by taxpayers. I believed that these abnormal duplications were there because taxpayers were inventing numbers and since we as humans think alike, we would gravitate toward making up the same numbers. There were some interesting results especially for deduction fields such as charitable contributions. The result of the number duplication test is a table in the form of a report showing (a) a rank, (b) the amount that was duplicated, and (c) count for each amount. The table would usually be sorted by the count descending so that the amount that occurred most often in the data table is listed first.

The number duplication test is run on each of the five main strata in the data profile. That is, we analyze the large positive, small positive, small negative, and large negative numbers separately. This makes it important that the strata in the data profile have some logic behind the break points.

The number duplication test has yielded some valuable findings. The usual candidates for a review in a forensic analytic setting are:

- **Numbers linked to large positive spikes on the first-order graph.** For the invoices data these would be amounts with first-two digits of 10, 11, 50, 98, and 99. The largest spikes are those first-two digits with the largest Z-statistics and an actual proportion that exceeds the expected proportion. We are usually only interested in positive spikes (i.e., excesses of first-two digits).
- **Numbers associated with large positive spikes on the summation test.** For the invoices data these would be amounts with first-two digits 10, 11, 14, 15, 26, and 50. Again, the largest spikes would be those digits with the largest Z-statistics. However, since the expected proportions are all equal, the largest spikes are simply the largest actual proportions.
- **Numbers just below psychological thresholds or just below control amount levels.** These would include amounts such as $24.50, $99, $990, and $4,950.
- **Large round numbers.** Round numbers are usually dollar amounts that have been negotiated. Examples of negotiated amounts are fees for professional services or donations, both of which are open to fraud and abuse. In one forensic investigation the data showed an excess of numbers equal to $5,000 and $10,000. The findings were that many of these numbers were for donations by company vice presidents to organizations that were of importance to them (and of not too much importance to the company).

- **Odd numbers that have occurred unusually often.** Examples of odd numbers in the invoices data include $1,153.35, $1,083.45, and $1,159.35.
- **Numbers that have occurred relatively more times than any other number.** In the invoices data $50 occurs more than twice as often as the next most frequently occurring number.
- **Numbers associated with inefficiencies.** This would occur when a certain type of transaction for a small dollar amount is processed many times over by a company. In one forensic investigation the auditors discovered that the company had processed 12,000 invoices for $8.20 each. These were for purchases of business cards by the head office employees.

The *InvoicesPaid* data is made up of transactions in dollars and cents. The number duplication test is not limited to currency units. Airline auditors ran the number duplication test against the mileage deposits to passenger frequent-flyer mileage accounts for a calendar year. The test showed that (not surprisingly) 500 miles was the most frequently deposited number, this being the minimum award for a flight of any distance. The second most frequent number was 802 miles. That number was the distance between the airline's two main hubs. This number was used repeatedly because the airline had many daily flights between its two main hubs.

A company in Tennessee used forensic analytics and the number duplication test to test for fictitious employees. They used the payroll file and tested whether there were duplications in the bank account numbers of employees (from the *Direct Deposit Details* field). More than two employees having their pay amounts deposited to the same bank account number could be an indicator of fraud. They found cases of multiple deposits in a single pay period to the same checking account and the forensic investigation showed that in most cases this duplication was because two employees were married (to each other). They also found other strange duplications where two or three (younger) employees shared an apartment and also a checking account. The explanation for this was that some of their employees did not qualify for a checking account (perhaps due to prior histories of bouncing checks) and shared a bank account with an employee who was a friend.

The number duplication test has also been run on employee credit cards and the results showed that there was very little number duplication. That is, the most frequently used number was not all that frequently used. These results made sense because there is no real reason that any amount for corporate purchases (other than perhaps courier fees) should occur abnormally often.

This test has also been used with varying levels of success on inventory counts, temperature readings, health care claims, airline ticket refunds, airline flight liquor sales, electricity meter readings, and election counts.

RUNNING THE NUMBER DUPLICATION TEST IN ACCESS

This test is not too complex to run in Access. It is a little complex in Excel because the standard Excel worksheet was not meant to group records and then to count the number of records in each group. In this test (and all the tests in the Nigrini Cycle) only one field is being analyzed. The tests will get more complex later when we analyze two or more fields at the same time. The logic for the number duplication test in Access is shown below:

- Identify the numeric field that will be analyzed.
- Use a criteria (>=10, or between 0.01 And 9.99) to correspond to the data profile strata.
- Use **Group By** in the query to group the numeric values.
- Use **Count** to count the numeric values in each group.
- **Sort** by the Count descending and then sort by the numeric field descending.
- Add the Rank to the output (this is tricky in Access). The rank is 1 for the highest count, 2 for the second highest rank, and so on.

The Access method is shown using the *InvoicesPaid* data from Chapters 4 to 7. The first number duplication query is shown in Figure 8.1. Change the query from the usual select query to a Make Table query by selecting **Query Type→Make Table** and naming the table *tblNumberDupsLP*. The LP at the end indicates Large Positive.

The first step in the number duplication test is shown in Figure 8.1. Save the query as *qryNumberDupsLP*. Run the query and click **Yes** after the warning about pasting 64579 rows into a new table. Open the table in Datasheet View to get the results shown in Figure 8.2.

The rank needs to be added to the table. The first step in this process is to change the view in the table from Datasheet View to Design View as is shown in Figure 8.3.

To add the Rank we need to first insert an extra row in the first position. The next step is to add an extra field called *Rank* and to make the Data Type **Auto Number** as is shown in Figure 8.4. The changes need to be saved at the prompt.

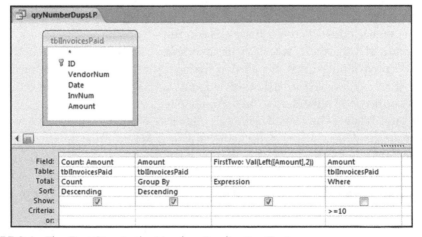

FIGURE 8.1 The First Step in the Number Duplication Test

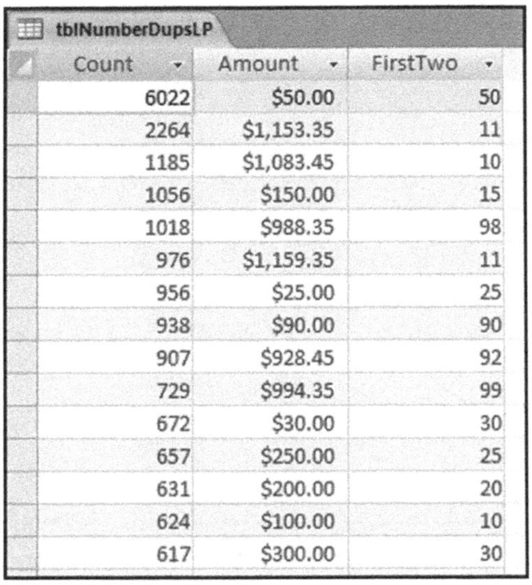

tblNumberDupsLP

Count	Amount	FirstTwo
6022	$50.00	50
2264	$1,153.35	11
1185	$1,083.45	10
1056	$150.00	15
1018	$988.35	98
976	$1,159.35	11
956	$25.00	25
938	$90.00	90
907	$928.45	92
729	$994.35	99
672	$30.00	30
657	$250.00	25
631	$200.00	20
624	$100.00	10
617	$300.00	30

FIGURE 8.2 The Table Listing the Amounts that Were Duplicated, and Their Counts

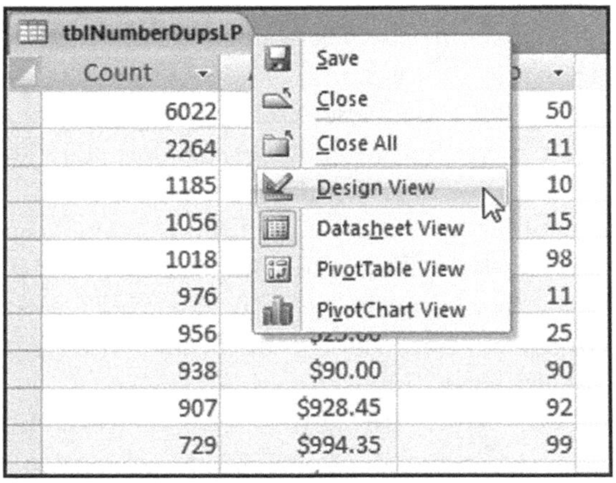

FIGURE 8.3 The Design View Command

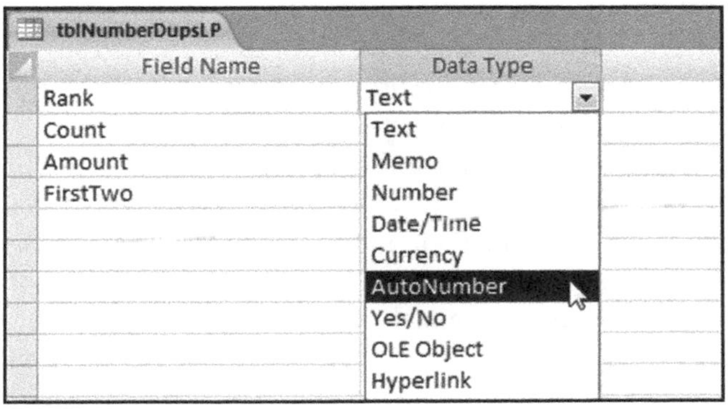

FIGURE 8.4 An Extra Field Named *Rank* Being Added to the Table

tblNumberDupsLP			
Rank	Count	Amount	FirstTwo
1	6022	$50.00	50
2	2264	$1,153.35	11
3	1185	$1,083.45	10
4	1056	$150.00	15
5	1018	$988.35	98
6	976	$1,159.35	11
7	956	$25.00	25
8	938	$90.00	90
9	907	$928.45	92
10	729	$994.35	99
11	672	$30.00	30
12	657	$250.00	25
13	631	$200.00	20
14	624	$100.00	10
15	617	$300.00	30

FIGURE 8.5 The Results of the Number Duplication Test. The Results Include Fields Showing the Rank and the First-Two Digits

To see the final result we have to look at the *tblNumberDupsLP* table in Datasheet View. The result is shown in Figure 8.5.

The first row shows that there were 6,022 invoices for exactly $50 each. This means that something that cost $50 was purchased 6,000 times. In a later chapter we will take the test one step further to see if all these invoices were all from one vendor. For now we will assume that they were from different vendors. This is an opportunity for an efficiency improvement. We have about 190,000 invoices for 2010, so this means that about 3 percent of the accounts payable department's workload was processing these $50 payments over and over again. The $50 duplication in the first row also explains the spike at 50 on the first-order graph.

At Rank #2 and Rank #3 there is a high count of numbers with first-two digits of 10 and 11. These numbers go a long way to explaining the spikes at 10 and 11 on the first-order graphs. These transactions should be selected and reviewed. The query result for $1,153.35 is shown in Figure 8.6.

The $1,153.35 transactions are shown in Figure 8.6. The drill-down showed that there was a clustering of dates and that 2,263 of the $1,153.35 transactions were from two vendors with one lone transaction with a third vendor. An in-depth audit would be warranted in a forensic investigations setting.

Another noteworthy fact from the number duplications is that we have $988.35 at rank #5 and $994.25 at rank #10. From Benford's Law we know that 98 is the second least likely first-two digit combination, and 99 is the least likely first-two digit combination. We would therefore *not* expect to see amounts beginning with 98 and 99 so close to the top of the rankings. Their high rankings go against all that we have learned about Benford's Law. The first-order test showed spikes (excesses) at 98 and 99. The $988.35 and the $994.35 are the causes of the spikes. An in-depth audit would be warranted in a forensic investigations setting.

qryViewTransactions

VendorNum	Date	InvNum	Amount
6661	1/4/2010	044901LA	$1,153.35
6661	1/4/2010	044927LA	$1,153.35
6661	1/5/2010	044721LA	$1,153.35
6661	1/5/2010	044758LA	$1,153.35
6661	1/5/2010	044766LA	$1,153.35
6661	1/5/2010	044826LA	$1,153.35
6661	1/5/2010	044842LA	$1,153.35
6661	1/5/2010	044868LA	$1,153.35
6661	1/5/2010	044873LA	$1,153.35
6661	1/5/2010	044876LA	$1,153.35
6661	1/5/2010	044877LA	$1,153.35
6661	1/5/2010	044881LA	$1,153.35

FIGURE 8.6 The Details for the $1,153.35 Amounts

There is one more noteworthy fact about the number duplication table, but we will save it for later in the chapter. As a clue you can look at the ending digits in Figure 8.5.

The last step in the number duplication test is to identify which amounts caused the spikes on the summation graph. To do this we need to sort the table by the first-two digits. Unfortunately in Access, if you sort a table once this becomes an automatic built-in sort every time that the table opens. Since we are really only interested in the spikes we can write a query to get our result. The query to sort and to only extract the amounts associated with a specified first-two digit combination is shown in Figure 8.7.

The criterion limits the results to numbers with first-two digits equal to 26. The two sort commands give us the largest amounts followed by the largest counts. Access first sorts on the leftmost sorted field. The results of the query are shown in Figure 8.8.

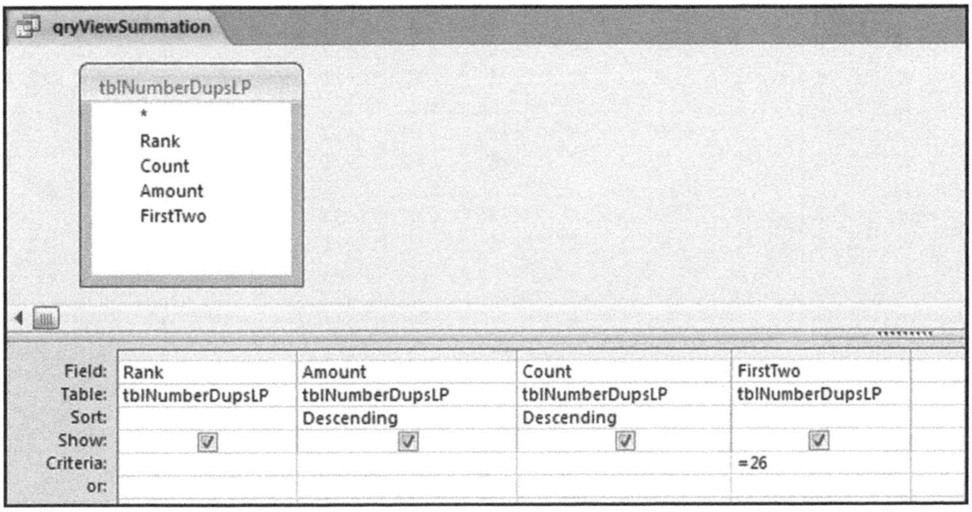

FIGURE 8.7 The Query to Drill Down to the Summation Transactions

qryViewSummation			
Rank ▾	Amount ▾	Count ▾	FirstTwo ▾
20918	$26,763,475.78	1	26
21037	$263,674.47	1	26
21038	$261,673.33	1	26
21039	$260,599.30	1	26
21875	$26,974.99	1	26
21876	$26,961.39	1	26
11255	$26,961.25	2	26
21877	$26,940.31	1	26
21878	$26,937.89	1	26
21879	$26,931.62	1	26
21880	$26,920.71	1	26
21881	$26,915.31	1	26

FIGURE 8.8 The Amounts with the First-Two Digits 26

The large amounts associated with the first-two digits 26 are shown in Figure 8.8. The largest dollar amounts are listed first. The table shows that the spike at 26 was caused by one large amount of $26,763,475.78. This transaction is probably neither an error nor a fraud. The transaction is nevertheless a high-value outlier and the payment should be reviewed. An amount of $26.8 million is rare for a cash payment. The summation test also showed a large spike at 50. These transactions are also extracted using the same *qryViewSummation* query by changing the criterion from 26 to 50. These results are shown in Figure 8.9.

qryViewSummation			
Rank ▾	Amount ▾	Count ▾	FirstTwo ▾
20980	$509,093.70	1	50
20981	$506,971.52	1	50
20982	$504,580.62	1	50
20983	$504,334.56	1	50
20984	$502,132.16	1	50
391	$500,000.00	30	50
21333	$50,934.86	1	50
21334	$50,850.30	1	50
21335	$50,814.00	1	50
21336	$50,759.80	1	50
21337	$50,430.00	1	50
21338	$50,409.60	1	50
21339	$50,187.34	1	50
21340	$50,112.00	1	50
21341	$50,105.70	1	50
21342	$50,006.06	1	50
21343	$50,000.00	1	50
31491	$5,098.77	1	50

FIGURE 8.9 The Amounts with the First-Two Digits 50

The large amounts associated with the first-two digits 50 are shown in Figure 8.9. These results differ from the 26 results. The 50 spike is mainly caused by a count of 30 for the amount of $500,000. These transactions should be reviewed. It was a high count of $50 that caused the spike at 50 on the first-order graph and the count of 30 for $500,000 that caused the spike at 50 on the summation graph.

The next number duplication test is an analysis of the small positive numbers. The Access approach would be the same as for the large positive numbers. The first step would be to create a new table of the small positive numbers. The query in Figure 8.1 can be reused except that the criterion would be "Between 0.01 and 9.99" and the table name would be *tblNumberDupsSP*.

The small positive number duplication results are shown in Figure 8.10. The goal of this test with accounts payable data is to look for processing inefficiencies. The results show duplications of small dollar amounts such as $0.29, $0.59, and $0.91. It is difficult to imagine what any company could be purchasing for such low amounts and also to be processing the payments through the accounts payable system. Note that the first-two digits are shown as single digits. This is because the leftmost two characters of $5.25 are "5" and because the query converts this to a value it is shown as 5. Note also that 0 is not a valid first-two digits combination. If we really wanted the first-two digits of the small positive numbers we could use **Left**([*Amount*]*1000,2). This would multiply 0.01 to 10.00 and the Left function would then extract the correct first-two digits for each small positive number. The left function would normally work well.

The final number duplication test is a test of the large negative numbers, which includes a comparison to the large positive numbers. The idea to include a comparison came about during a forensic investigation of ticket refunds for an airline. The investigators took the position that since the most frequently flown segment for the airline was from Dallas to Chicago that we should expect the most frequently refunded segment to be "Dallas to Chicago." Similarly, if the best-selling item for a fast-food restaurant was its double hamburger for $3.99, followed by its medium fries for $0.99, then we would expect most of the voids (sales amounts cancelled by the cashier) to be for $3.99

tblNumberDupsSP			
Rank	Count	Amount	FirstTwo
1	204	$5.25	5
2	152	$9.38	9
3	145	$6.45	6
4	144	$0.29	0
5	130	$5.00	5
6	118	$2.35	2
7	110	$4.40	4
8	100	$6.25	6
9	100	$0.59	0
10	91	$0.91	0

FIGURE 8.10 The Number Duplication Results for the Small Positive Numbers

followed by $0.99. It seems logical that refunds, corrections, and voids (all negative numbers) should be correlated with the original sales amounts. You need to sell something before you can refund or void it and the items that are most often sold are the ones most likely to be refunded or voided. We would therefore expect a relationship between the invoice amounts (large positive number duplications) and the credit memos (large negative number duplications).

The creation of the table for the large negative amounts follows the usual logic with just a few changes. The query in Figure 8.1 can be reused with some modifications. First, the criteria should be changed to $<=-10$. The less than sign is used to retrieve "large" negative numbers. Second, the first-two digits calculation needs to be changed because of the negative sign, which is the first character of a negative number. The calculated field needs to be changed to

$$\text{FirstTwo}: \text{Val}(\text{Left}(\text{Abs}([\text{Amount}]), 2))$$

The calculation shown above will ensure that we take the leftmost two characters of the absolute value of the *Amount*. The table name needs to be changed to *tblNumberDupsLN*. The query can then be run to create the number duplication table of large negative numbers. The *Rank* needs to be added as is shown in Figure 8.4. The *Rank* turns out to be useful for the final analysis.

The Access query to show the combined number duplication output is set up in a few of stages. The first step is to create a new query in the query Design View. Add both the *tblNumberDupsLP* and the *tblNumberDupsSP* tables to the query grid. The next step is to rename the fields so that we know what we are looking at once the query has run. The renaming step is needed because Access will not allow the same field name to be shown twice in a query result. The first step is shown in Figure 8.11.

The next step is to join the tables in *qryNumberDupsCompare* so that we have Rank #1 for large positive on the same row as Rank #1 for large negative. The first step in the join is to link the two fields by clicking on *Rank* for large positive and holding down the left click button and moving the cursor over to *Rank* for large negative. The result will be a thin straight line from *Rank* on the left to *Rank* on the right.

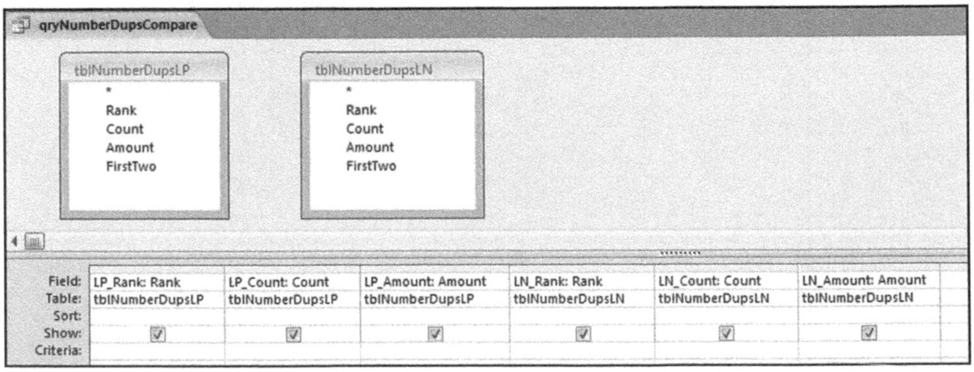

FIGURE 8.11 Comparing the Positive and Negative Number Duplications

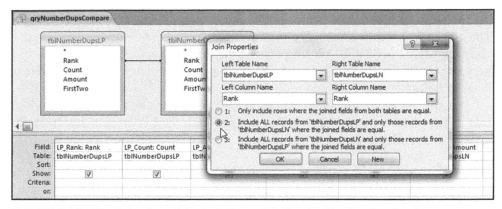

FIGURE 8.12 The Selection of the Left Outer Join for the Number Duplications

The final step is to change the default join to a left outer join. To do this we need to left click the line from *Rank* to *Rank*. The line will then become bold. The next step is to right click the bold line and to select **Join Properties**. The final step is to select the radio button for Option #2, which is a left outer join.

The final step in the comparison of the number duplications is shown in Figure 8.12. Click **OK** to accept the left out join (Option #2). The result will be a right-facing arrow in *qryNumberDupsCompare*. Run the query using the usual **Design→ Results→Run**. The number duplication comparison result is shown in Figure 8.13.

The number duplication results in Figure 8.13 are very interesting. There is no relationship between the top nine positive numbers and the top nine negative numbers. Indeed, the positive numbers that occurred abnormally often ($50.00, $1,153.35, $1,083.45, and $988.35) are nowhere near the top of the negative number duplication table. A search of the negative numbers shows that these amounts were corrected 8, 15, 5, and 7 times respectively. This level of transaction processing accuracy is highly

qryNumberDupsCompare

LP_Rank ▾	LP_Count ▾	LP_Amount ▾	LN_Rank ▾	LN_Count ▾	LN_Amount ▾
1	6022	$50.00	1	160	($119.80)
2	2264	$1,153.35	2	111	($139.80)
3	1185	$1,083.45	3	108	($29.95)
4	1056	$150.00	4	88	($239.60)
5	1018	$988.35	5	86	($359.40)
6	976	$1,159.35	6	78	($994.35)
7	956	$25.00	7	74	($479.20)
8	938	$90.00	8	67	($599.00)
9	907	$928.45	9	60	($150.00)
10	729	$994.35	10	60	($838.60)
11	672	$30.00	11	54	($34.95)
12	657	$250.00	12	52	($718.80)

FIGURE 8.13 The Number Duplications for the Positive and Negative Amounts

questionable for excessively recurring transactions. The results are also inconsistent. The other excessive duplication of $994.35 was corrected or voided 78 times giving a correction rate of about 10 percent. Four of the amounts with first-order spikes had very few corrections and one amount with a first-order spike was corrected at a rate of 1 in 10 times.

Another number duplications pattern will become evident when we look at the last-two digits. The low level of corrections and the high level of corrections should be reviewed further in a forensic environment.

RUNNING THE NUMBER DUPLICATION TEST IN EXCEL

These tests can also be run in Excel. We will not use Excel's pivot table function for now. We will import the data into Excel from Access because the Copy and Paste clipboard cannot hold 189,470 records. The first step is to open an Excel file and to save the workbook as *NumberDuplication.xlsx*. Import the Access data using **Data**→**Get External Data**→**Access Data** and then selecting the Access file and the table as is shown in Figure 8.14. The Access database *InvoicesPaid* should be closed while the Excel import procedure is taking place.

Click **OK** to select the *tblInvoicesPaid* data and click **OK** again to import the data. Excel's default options usually work well. The data is imported into Excel quickly and

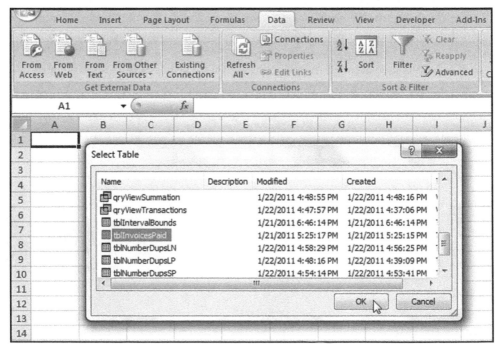

FIGURE 8.14   The Selection Screen for the Data Import

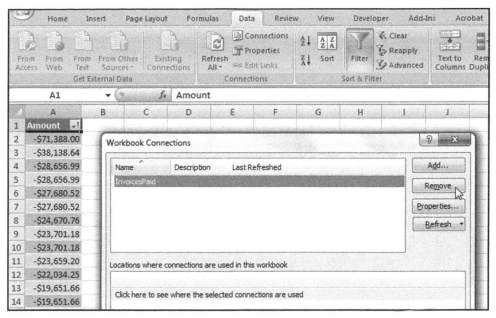

FIGURE 8.15 The Removal of the Connection with the Access Database

accurately. Once the data has been imported uncheck the Autofilters using *Home*→ *Editing*→*Sort & Filter* and uncheck *Filter*. Since we are only interested in the dollar amounts we should also delete the fields *ID*, *VendorNum*, *Date*, and *InvNum* by selecting the fields (columns) and clicking *Delete* from the right click option. The next step is to sort the *Amounts* ascending by selecting cell *A1* and using *Data*→*Sort & Filter*→*Sort* to sort *Amount* from *Smallest to Largest*. Finally, format the *Amount* field as Currency with two decimal places.

The final step is to sever (break) the connection to the Access database. Select *Data*→*Connections*→*Connections* and then *Remove* as is shown in Figure 8.15. Click *Remove* and click *OK* to note the warning about database updates.

The final formatting step is to remove the table formatting. This is done by placing the cursor in cell **A1**. Right click on cell **A1** and click *Table*→*Convert to Range*. Click *OK* and the data will now be a normal range.

The number duplications can now be calculated using indicator variables. The first indicator variable counts the number of equal amounts. The second indicator variable indicates when the highest count for a particular number has been reached. Both indicator variables use the IF function in Excel. The first "formula" is there just to start the sequence off at 1.

The indicator formulas are shown in Figure 8.16. The formulas for columns B and C are:

$$B2 : 1$$
$$B3 : \ = IF(A3 = A2, B2 + 1, 1)$$
$$C2 : \ = IF(B2 < B3, 0, B2)$$

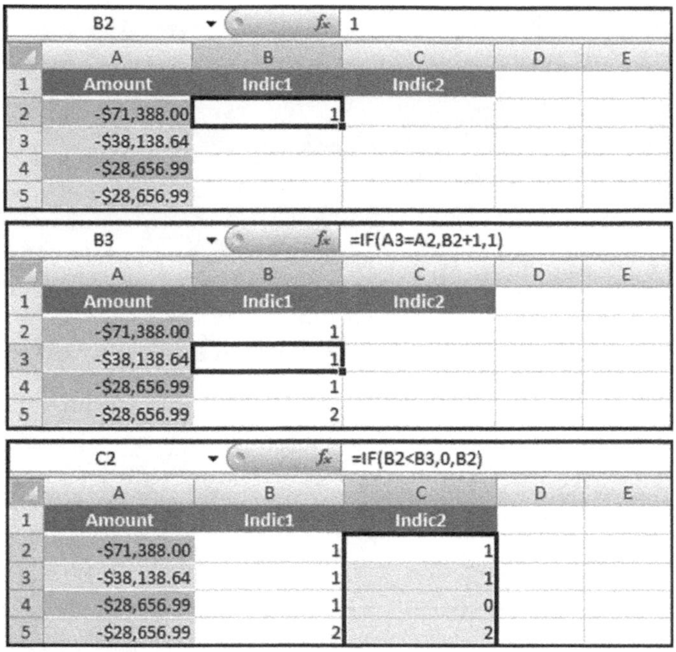

FIGURE 8.16 The Formulas Used for the Number Duplication Test

The formulas in B2 and C1 need to be copied down to the last row (in this case row 189471). The formulas *then* need to be converted to values. Select the cells with the calculations by using **F5** (the Go To button) and entering **B2:C189471** and clicking **OK**. Then use the right click sequence of **Copy→Paste Special→Values** and **OK** to convert the formulas to values.

The data now needs to be sorted by *Indic2* descending and then by *Amount* descending as the second sort. The commands are started with **Data→Sort** followed by the directions in Figure 8.17.

The final step is to do a little cleaning up. First delete the field *Indic1*, which is no longer needed. One way to get rid of some rows that we do not need is to scroll down to where *Indic2* shows 0s (row 67249). Delete the first zero row and all other subsequent rows by highlighting groups of rows and clicking **Delete**. The final Excel results are as shown in Figure 8.18.

The number duplication results are shown in Figure 8.18. In these results we do not have a *Rank* column as is seen in Figure 8.5. This is easy to add in Excel. Also, the large positive, small positive, zeroes, small negative, and large negative are all intermingled. Filters can be added to the results. This is done using **Home→Editing→Sort&Filter→Filter**. Excel's powerful filtering capabilities can be used to show only selected results in either or both of the *Amount* and *Indic2* fields. The results can be filtered to show only the large positive numbers or the large negative numbers or any other number range. The final step could be to rename the *Indic2* field to *Count*.

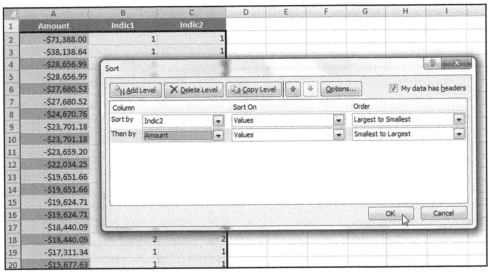

FIGURE 8.17 The Sort to Create the Number Duplication Table

 THE LAST-TWO DIGITS TEST

The last-two digits test completes the Nigrini Cycle. This test is a powerful test for number invention. The test is most appropriate when we do not want number invention or number creativity.

The number invention tests (which include a test for round numbers) are usually not all that valuable for accounts payable data. This is because any odd last-two digits results will be noticeable from the number duplication test. Also, for invoices amounts (in the U.S. in U.S. dollars) this test will usually simply show that many numbers end with "00." This fact should also be evident from the number duplication test.

	A	B	C	D	E	F	G
1	Amount	Indic2					
2	$50.00	6022					
3	$1,153.35	2264					
4	$1,083.45	1185					
5	$150.00	1056					
6	$988.35	1018					
7	$1,159.35	976					
8	$25.00	956					
9	$90.00	938					
10	$928.45	907					
11	$994.35	729					
12	$30.00	672					

FIGURE 8.18 The Results of the Number Duplication Test

The test is a little bit challenging in both Access and Excel because mathematically speaking there is no such thing as the last-two digits of a number. Irrational (which does not mean illogical in this case) numbers such as π, e, $\sqrt{2}$, and $1/7$ do not have a set of last-two digits. Furthermore, a number such as 1,103 could have 03 or 00 (as in 1103.00) as the last-two digits. The question in forensic analytics would be to ask what we are trying to find, and based on this, to determine what last-two digits (if any) are appropriate for the analysis. Experience has shown that for dollars and cents (i.e., currency) the cents (the two digits to the right of the decimal point) are appropriate, and for data consisting of integers (population numbers and election results), the 10s and units digits are appropriate. So for \$1,103.00 we would use 00 as the last-two digits, and for a population number or election result count of 1,103 we would use 03 as the last-two digits.

The suggested data-cleansing step is to follow the logic in the first-order test and to delete numbers less than 10 to avoid having small numbers influence the results. We also want to avoid the situation where we try to get the last-two digits of 7 or 0.02 and end up with incorrect results because of errors in the programming logic.

For the last-two digits test it is important that the data be formatted as **Currency** or **Integer** in Access to be sure that we are really getting the last-two digits. It is a good idea to randomly check some calculations to see that the query is correctly identifying the last-two digits.

The last-two digit test is generally run on data tables where we are looking for signs of number invention in data tables where we do not really want number invention. Examples of such applications might include:

- Census population numbers (quite relevant in 2010).
- Election results.
- Inventory counts.
- Odometer readings at the time of warranty claims.
- Weights of fish catches by trawlers (an early Benford's Law project).
- Temperature readings at automated weather stations (another project from the early days of digital analysis).
- Deduction numbers on individual tax returns (an application from my dissertation).
- Website hit statistics or banner ad clicks.
- Coupon redemption counts (a recent application).

The last-two digits and round numbers tests could also be useful in royalty situations where licensees have to report production numbers, sales numbers, or usage numbers to the licensor. An analysis of the number patterns might signal number invention.

The challenge from a programming perspective is to correctly identify the last-two digits. The logic includes being creative with multiplication (usually by 100) so that the last-two digits are those to the left of the decimal point. The procedures generally follow the same logic as is used in the first-order test. There are 100 possible last-two digits (00, 01, . . . , 99) and the expected proportions are equal at 0.01 for each possible

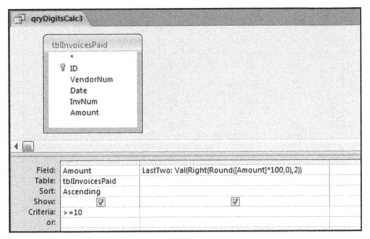

FIGURE 8.19 The Query Used to Calculate the Last-Two Digits

last-two digit combination. Table 5.1 shows that as we move the right in a number, that the digits are expected to be uniformly (evenly) distributed. Since there are 100 possible last-two digits, our expected proportion is uniform at 1/100 (0.01) each. The graph will look a bit like the graph of the summation test.

Running the Last-Two Digits Test in Access

The last-two digits test will be run on the *Amount* field of the *tblInvoicesPaid* table. The demonstration will also show how to calculate the last-two digits for data made up of integers (whole numbers such as 10, 11, 12, . . .). Figure 8.19 shows the query used to calculate the last-two digits.

The formula for the digits is more complex than usual and is shown below:

$$\text{LastTwo: Val(Right(Round([Amount]}^*100, 0), 2))$$

In the formula the **Val** function changes the result to a numeric value, the **Right** function takes the rightmost two characters, and the **Round** function rounds the number to an integer value before any calculations are done. The comma 2 means that we want the rightmost two characters. The result shows 177,763 *Amounts* that are greater than or equal to 10 together with the last-two digits for each of the numeric values. The next step is to count how many of each possible last-two digit combinations (00, 01, 02, . . . , 99) we have using the query shown in Figure 8.20.

It is a good idea to check that there are 100 records in the output (from 00 to 99 equals 100 records). We want to have a count for each possible digit combination, which might not be the case for small data sets. A data set of 500 records could easily not have a number ending with (say) 64. The last-two digits are graphed in the same way as with the other digit tests in the Nigrini Cycle. Copy the *CountOfLastTwo* field from Access and paste the result in column X in the *NigriniCycle.xlsx* template. The result is shown in Figure 8.21.

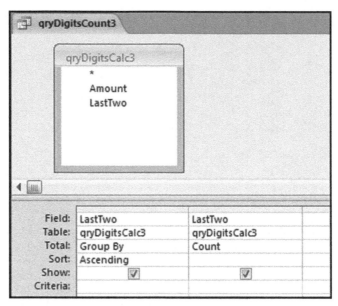

FIGURE 8.20 The Query Used to Calculate the Counts

The last-two digits graph is automatically prepared in the Excel template and can be accessed by clicking on the *LastTwoDigits* chart sheet.

The last-two digits results are shown graphically in Figure 8.22. The graph shows that about 23 percent of the amounts ended with 00. These numbers were whole dollars with no cents. This is common for corporate accounts payable data. The most interesting result is the spiking at multiples of 5 with large spikes at 35, 40, 45, and 50. This is an unusual result and we can also see this pattern from the numbers in the number duplication table in Figure 8.13. Another interesting result is that the last-two

	X2			f_x	CountOfLastTwo			
	V	W	X	Y	Z	AA	AB	AC	AD
1				LAST-TWO DIGITS				
2		LT Digit	ntOfLast	Actual	Benford's	Difference	AbsDiff		
3		00	40673	0.229	0.010	0.219	0.219		
4		01	982	0.006	0.010	-0.004	0.004		
5		02	1016	0.006	0.010	-0.004	0.004		
6		03	937	0.005	0.010	-0.005	0.005		
7		04	1014	0.006	0.010	-0.004	0.004		
8		05	1355	0.008	0.010	-0.002	0.002		
9		06	935	0.005	0.010	-0.005	0.005		
10		07	1036	0.006	0.010	-0.004	0.004		
11		08	1135	0.006	0.010	-0.004	0.004		
12		09	910	0.005	0.010	-0.005	0.005		
13		10	1593	0.009	0.010	-0.001	0.001		
14		11	935	0.005	0.010	-0.005	0.005		
15		12	1065	0.006	0.010	-0.004	0.004		

FIGURE 8.21 The Last-Two Digit Results in Excel Worksheet

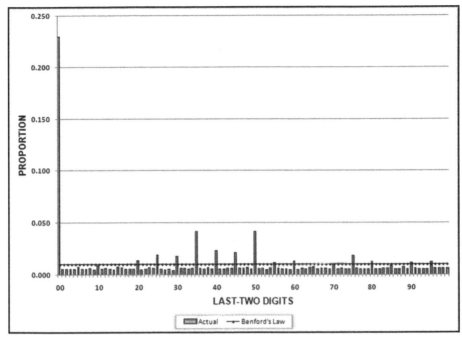

FIGURE 8.22 The Last-Two Digits Graph

digits for the negative numbers also show a clustering at multiples of 5, but at higher numbers in the neighborhood of 80. The clustering around multiples of 5 is an anomaly as is the clustering around 40 for the positive numbers and 80 for the negative numbers.

If our data was made up of integers (e.g., population counts or election results) we would have numbers such as 1,103. In this case we would want to have the 03 as our last-two digits. The formula that would calculate this is

$$\text{LastTwo: Val(Right(Int(Round([Amount], 0)), 2))}$$

The formula assumes that *Amount* is the field being analyzed. If not, then *Amount* should be changed to *People* or *Miles* or whatever the case may be.

For integer (whole numbers) data the last-two digits test can point to excessive rounding. An excess of numbers with 00 as the last-two digits (in a number such as 6,400) could signal excessive rounding. We would expect 0.01 of all numbers (election results or odometer readings) to have last-two digits of 00. If our actual proportion exceeds 0.01 it could indicate that we are looking at numbers that include estimates of some sort.

Running the Last-Two Digits Test in Excel

These tests are reasonably straightforward to run in Excel assuming that you have run the usual first-order test in Excel too. Figure 7.5 shows how to do the first-two digits calculation in Excel. The formula for the last-two digits would be

$$\text{H2: } = \text{VALUE(RIGHT(ROUND(D2*100, 2), 2))}$$

If we were dealing with integers we would simply adapt the formula. After calculating the last-two digits for each amount we would use the COUNTIF formula shown in Chapter 7 in the last-two digits of the *NigriniCycle.xlsx* template. With some practice it will probably take just a few minutes to run the test in either Access or Excel.

SUMMARY

The number duplication and the last-two digits test complete the Nigrini Cycle. These tests should be the starting blocks for any forensic analytics project. The starting tests were the data profile, periodic graph, histogram, first-order test, second-order test, and the summation test. These tests gave valuable insights into the internal diagnostics of our data. The data profile and the histograms gave us insights into the distribution of the numbers. The periodic graph gave us an insight into the distribution of the amounts across time. The number duplication test drills down to find the source of the spikes on the first-order and summation graphs. The last-two digits test looks for signs of number invention and rounding.

The number duplication test is essentially a numbers hit parade. The report shows us which numbers occurred most often and how often they occurred. The test gives us insights into the spikes on the first-order and the summation graphs. This test can also detect possible processing inefficiencies. These would occur when a small transaction was processed over and over again. The last part of the numbers duplication test is to see if we have a match between the patterns of our credit memos (corrections and voids) and our positive numbers. We would expect a close association between the positive numbers (sales numbers) and voided, corrected, or refunded amounts.

The goal of the last-two digits test is to detect number invention in data sets where we do not really want to see signs of people inventing numbers. Because we are looking at the right-hand side of the numbers we expect the digits (00, 01, 02, . . . , 99) to be evenly distributed. With 100 possible last-two digit combinations we expect each combination to occur about 1 percent of the time. We use this test to look for rounding or number invention in forensic situations such as election results, coupon or rebate check counts, odometer readings, or website statistics. The invoices data had an abnormal duplication of amounts ending in 35, 40, 45, and 50. This test has given many interesting findings and it can be easily run in either Access or Excel.

CHAPTER NINE

Testing the Internal Diagnostics of Current Period and Prior Period Data

C HAPTERS 4 THROUGH 8 reviewed the suite of tests in the Nigrini Cycle. These tests should be included in every forensic analytics project. The tests included the high-level overview tests, four digit-based tests, and the number duplication tests. Some tests used all the transaction data whereas a few of the tests (the first-order tests and the last-two digits test) used only the amounts greater than and equal to 10.00. The first test to do a comparison was the comparison of the positive and negative number duplications. The tests described in this chapter are a comprehensive comparison of two data tables to determine whether there has been some significant change in the events being measured.

Bolton and Hand (2002) state that fraud detection tools all have a common theme in that actual data is usually compared with a set of expected values. Depending on the context, these expected values can be derived in various ways and could vary on a continuum from single numerical or graphical summaries all the way to complex multivariate behavior profiles. Their discussion of expected values includes a discussion of Benford's Law. They contrast supervised methods of fraud detection, which uses samples of both fraudulent and legitimate records, and unsupervised methods, which identify transactions or customers that are most dissimilar to some norm (i.e., outliers). They correctly note that we can seldom be certain by statistical analysis alone that a fraud has been perpetrated. Rather, the analysis should give us an alert that a record is anomalous, or more likely to be fraudulent than others, so that it can be investigated in more detail. They suggest the concept of *suspicion scores* where higher scores are associated with records that are unusual or more like previous fraudulent values. Suspicion scores could be calculated for each record in a data table and it would then be most cost-effective to concentrate only on the records with the highest scores. The focus of this chapter is on an entire data table and the goal is to investigate whether there are significant differences between the current data and the data from prior periods. The prior data taken as a whole is seen to be the norm and the current data is being compared to that norm. Deviations from the norm could be due to fraud or error, or could be due to some change in the events (e.g., individual sales) being measured.

Golden, Skylak, and Clayton (2006) list four analytic techniques in their review of red flags and fraud detection techniques. One of these techniques is a comparison of the detail of a total balance with similar detail for the preceding year(s). Their hypothesis is that if no significant changes in the operations have occurred, then much of the detail (the individual amounts making up the totals) of the account balances in the financial statements should also stay unchanged. For example, if an analysis of customer accounts receivable balances shows a significant increase in the number of accounts that have balances below the threshold for a written confirmation, then such a change might warrant further analysis. Their comparison of detail tests are directed at accounts such as long-term assets or liabilities. This chapter extends this concept to revenue and expense transactional amounts, and asset and liability individual amounts. The underlying principle is that the distribution and internal makeup or structure of transactional amounts should be similar over time and that deviations from prior patterns are red flags for fraud or error.

The situation envisioned in the chapter is one where the forensic investigator or internal auditor proactively sets out to evaluate the risk of fraud or error. Alternatively, the situation could be one where an external auditor is concerned with the risks of a material misstatement in the financial statements. Statement on Auditing Standards (SAS) No. 106 requires auditors to obtain audit evidence to assess the risks of material misstatements in the financial statements and to detect these at the financial statement and assertion levels (AICPA, 2006). Audit procedures performed for this purpose include substantive analytical procedures. The SAS notes that when information is in an electronic form, then auditors may perform these audit procedures using Computer Assisted Audit Techniques (CAATs). Also, for external auditors the use of analytical procedures is required in the planning and review stages of all audits according to SAS No. 56 (AICPA, 1988). In the planning stages the objective is to, among other things, identify unusual transactions that might suggest matters that have audit planning ramifications. SAS No. 99 requires the auditor to consider whether any unexpected or unusual relationships that arise from comparing recorded amounts with expectations might be due to fraud (AICPA, 2002). Daugherty and Pitman's (2009) analysis of Public Company Accounting Oversight Board (PCAOB) inspection reports shows that deficiencies related to analytical procedures are common for smaller and larger accounting firms. Gramling and Watson's (2009) analysis of peer reviews also highlights deficiencies related to analytical procedures. The comparison techniques discussed in this chapter are not currently used by external auditors but it seems that these tests could be a useful set of additional methods and techniques for detecting errors and fraud.

This chapter suggests a set of tests called a *Nigrini parallel scan* for comparing current period data to prior period data. The prior period could be a prior month, quarter, or year. The tests are called a Nigrini parallel scan because we will use two parallel columns of statistics in a statistical examination of both sets of data. Scanning is a type of audit procedure aimed at detecting large and unusual transactions. The parallel scan is a structured approach to analyzing the detail in a set of transactions or the line items making up an account balance. The parallel scan is made up of numerical descriptive statistics related to a data overview, followed by measures of central tendency, variability, and the shape of the distribution. The parallel scan includes a histogram (from Chapter 4) and an analysis of digit patterns (a first-order test), which will be called *My Law*. The chapter includes a case study of college alumni gift amounts and the results show that the parallel scan would be useful to uncover errors or frauds that are major and significant. Also, running the parallel scan would give forensic investigators and internal and external auditors a better understanding of the organization and its environment.

The next section describes descriptive statistics that are made up of numerical and graphical descriptive statistics. Thereafter a case study of college alumni gift amounts is reviewed. The case study has a "no fraud" and a "fraud" situation. These sections are followed by a review of how the parallel scan can be run using Excel, Access, and Minitab. The chapter concludes with a discussion aimed mainly at external and internal auditors.

A REVIEW OF DESCRIPTIVE STATISTICS

Newbold, Carlson, and Thorne (2010) review graphical and numerical methods of describing data. *Parameters* are numerical measures that describe a specific character-istic of a population, and *statistics* do the same for a sample. Descriptive statistics are those graphical and numerical measures that are used to summarize and interpret some of the properties of a data set from which they were derived. In contrast, inferential statistics focus on using the data to make predictions, forecasts, and estimates to assist in decision making. The forensic goal is to use descriptive statistics to help to assess whether the data contains fraud or errors, or whether there has been a change in the events being measured. In an audit context an auditor could look at the detail making up general ledger accounts as evidence to assess whether the financial statements are free of material misstatement or error. This detail could be the individual sales transactions making up the detail of the sales account.

The first set of descriptive statistics in the parallel scan (see Table 9.1) give us an overview of the data, much like the data profile gives us an overview in the Nigrini Cycle. The overview consists of the sum, the number of records, and the number of missing records. In a forensic analytic project the sum should agree with, or should be recon-cilable with the trial balance to ensure that all the account details are included in the analysis. Missing records might indicate fraud, or processing or internal control issues.

The second set of descriptive statistics relates to measures of central tendency. The mean, median, and the mode are often used in the financial press and are understood by most forensic investigators. A large change in either of these values should be investi-gated. The difference between two means can be formally tested using the two-sample

TABLE 9.1 The Descriptive Statistics of Alumni Gifts for Two Consecutive Years

	Current	Prior	Change
Sum	$992,960	$923,005	+7.6%
Number of Records	2,959	2,531	+16.9%
Number of missing records	0	0	no change
Mean	$336	$365	−$29
A significant difference between the means?	No, α = 0.05		
Test used	Two-sample t-test		
Median	$100	$100	no change
Mode	$100	$100	no change
Minimum	$10	$10	no change
Quartile 1	$50	$50	no change
Quartile 3	$200	$250	−$50
Maximum	$54,780	$50,000	+$4,780
Range	$54,770	$49,990	+$4,780
Interquartile range	$150	$200	−$50
Standard deviation	1,343	1,449	−106.00
A significant difference between the variances?	No, α = 0.20		
Test used	Levene's test		
Coefficient of Variation (CV)	4.00	3.97	+0.03
Skewness	26	21	+5.00
Is the data normally distributed?	No, α = 0.05		
Anderson-Darling Test statistic	733	640	+93.00

t-test. The auditing concept of materiality and statistical significance are not the same, and a significant difference should not be seen to be a material difference. In Chapter 6 we saw that with large data sets even small differences between the actual and expected proportion give us statistically significant differences due to the excess power problem. We will have to carefully interpret the results of our descriptive statistics.

The third set of descriptive statistics measures the variability or the spread of the numbers. This includes the minimum and maximum, the interquartile range, and the range (the maximum minus the minimum amount). The interquartile range measures the spread in the middle 50 percent of the data and is the difference between the 75th percentile and the 25th percentile. The range is the difference between the 100th percentile and the minimum. This set of values includes the minimum amount that might yield investigative insights if the number was negative in a data set that should not contain negative numbers (e.g., wages, inventory counts, coupon or rebate amounts, or odometer readings). The variability measures also include the standard deviation that measures the average deviation about the mean. Large changes in the variability values could be a red flag for fraud or error. There could be changes in variability even though the measures of central tendency are largely unchanged. The difference between the standard deviations can be formally tested by testing the difference between the variances using Levene's test. To assess whether the standard deviation is big or small we use the coefficient of variation (CV), which gives us the standard deviation as a percentage of the mean. This is a useful measure because it allows us to interpret the standard deviation in the context of the mean.

The final set relates to the shape of the distribution of the data. The first such measure is skewness, which tells us whether the numbers are evenly distributed around the mean. Data that is positively skewed consists of many small amounts and fewer large amounts. This is usually the pattern found in the dollar amounts of invoices paid (expenses) or sales invoices (sales). Most financial data are positively skewed because we usually have many small numbers and only a few large numbers. In contrast, data with a negative skewness measure has many large numbers and fewer smaller numbers. These cases are relatively rare. Another shape measure is the Anderson-Darling test statistic that measures the closeness of fit to the normal distribution. A calculated test statistic of 0.80 would signal that the data is normally distributed. Financial data seldom conform to the normal distribution except possibly for salaries or wages data. The Anderson-Darling statistic can be used to test that the departure from normality is approximately the same from period to period. More information on the statistical terms and tests in this section can be found in the NIST/SEMATECH e-Handbook of Statistical Methods at www.itl.nist.gov/div898/handbook.

The first graphical method of describing data is the histogram. Newbold, Carlson, and Thorne (2010) describe a histogram as a graph consisting of vertical bars constructed on a horizontal line that is marked off with intervals. These intervals should be inclusive and should not overlap. Each record should belong to one and only one interval. The height of each bar in the histogram is proportional to the number of records in the interval. Chapter 4 discusses histograms and also how the histogram values can be calculated in Access and graphed in Excel.

The number of intervals used in a histogram is at the discretion of the forensic investigator. Newbold, Carlson, and Thorne (2010) suggest 14–20 intervals if there are more than 5,000 records. This will give a very crowded histogram especially when current and prior year histograms are being compared side by side. In forensic analytics it seems that 10 intervals would work well. Each interval should have a neat round number as the upper bound (e.g., $50, $100, $150) and should preferably contain enough records so that at least a small bar is visible for every interval. No real insights are obtained from a histogram that has one or two intervals containing most of the records. The final (10th) interval should be for all amounts greater than the prior upper bound (for example, $450 and higher). This makes the final interval width much wider than those of the first nine intervals and this interval should therefore be clearly labeled.

The second graphical method of describing data is through an adaptation of Benford's Law, which we will call *My Law*. The My Law concept was developed when an airline changed its pilot payroll systems. The logic in using the test was that the digits and number patterns from the new system should be the same (or at least similar) to those from the old system since nothing had changed except the processing system.

AN ANALYSIS OF ALUMNI GIFTS

The case study involves alumni gifts to a college. Alumni gifts are an important and significant source of revenue for most higher education institutions. The funds are used to support student services, academic programs, athletics, and other extracurricular activities. The college in this case is a liberal arts college that draws its students from the surrounding region. Each gift amount was a contribution from a past student. The contributions are for two consecutive years. The numerical descriptive statistics for the parallel scan are shown in Table 9.1.

Table 9.1 shows the numerical descriptive statistics of the gift data. The statistics give an overview of the data, show measures of central tendency and variability, and describe the shape of the distribution. In the current year the college received a total of $992,960, which was an increase of 7.6 percent over the prior year. In dollar terms the increase amounted to about $70,000. In the current year they received 2,959 gifts from past students, which was a 17 percent increase over the prior year. The increase in the total dollars was because of an increased number of phone calls and letters asking for donations. The data contained no null (missing) amounts.

With respect to central tendency, the mean decreased from $365 to $336. The decrease in the mean agrees with the fact that the percentage increase in the number of gifts was greater than the percentage increase in the total dollars. The decrease in the average gift amount might signal that funds are being misappropriated. The review revealed that there was a special effort to get more donations and past students were encouraged to make a gift even if it was small. Once someone made some contribution, there was a good chance of a bigger gift next time. The two-sample t-test was used for a comparison of the means and the difference between the means was not found to be significant. The mean was greater than the median of $100 indicating that the data was positively skewed. In both periods the minimum, maximum, and the range are comparable and no red flag is raised from an investigation perspective. Both the quartile 3 amount and the interquartile range differ by $50. The effort to get more gifts, even if they were small, also explained the decrease in the quartile 3 amount and the interquartile range. The mode (the most frequently occurring amount) was unchanged at $100 for both periods.

The measures of variability show that the standard deviation was largely unchanged. The standard deviation paints a more complete picture of dispersion than does the range. Two data tables may have the same range, but the amounts in one may be concentrated near the center of the range and in the other they may be concentrated in the tails of the distribution. Levene's test for the difference between the variances gave a test statistic of 0.31, which translates to a p-value of 0.577. This means that the difference between the variances is not significant. Experience with Levene's test has shown that the difference between the variances must be quite large before the test indicates a significant difference even at a significance level of 0.20. The coefficient of variation is little changed. The standard deviations are quite large when compared to the means in each period indicating that there is a large spread compared to the average values. The variability measures show no major change from period to period.

The shape measures show that the skewness measure increased from 21 to 26. This was also because of the additional small ($10 to $50) gifts. The Anderson-Darling test was used to assess conformity to the familiar bell-shaped Gaussian distribution. With the large skewness measures, a close fit to the normal curve is unlikely because the normal distribution is symmetric. The Anderson-Darling test statistics of 733 and 640 indicate large departures from normality (the bell-shaped curve) but the extent of the departure from normality is approximately equal.

The histograms of the gift amounts are shown in Figure 9.1. Using 10 intervals and a width of $50 for each interval gives a final 10th interval for amounts of $450 and higher. The y-axis (the count) for the current and prior year should be comparably calibrated (from 0 to 1,200 in this case) so that the histograms can be compared visually. For the gift data the histograms are similar except for the first two intervals (0 to $50, and $50.01 to $100), which have noticeably higher counts in the current period. The explanation for this difference was the increased effort to get more gifts in the current year (however small they might be).

The gift amounts were not expected to follow Benford's Law because gifts are influenced by human thought since the donor thinks of an amount to give. This number invention process usually sees a gravitation toward round numbers that are psychological thresholds. Also, donor recognition levels also influence the gift amounts. The first-order results for both years are shown in Figure 9.2.

Chapter 6 discussed assessing conformity to Benford's Law and the list of possible conformity tests included the chi-square and K-S tests, the Mean Absolute Deviation (MAD), and the mantissa arc test. The tests were geared toward assessing conformity to Benford's Law. In this case the goal is to compare the current and prior data. The prior period's first-order graph takes the place of Benford's Law. In the first application of this concept, the prior period data was called *My Law*. A large difference between the current data and My Law indicates that something has changed and the change could be due to errors or fraud, or a change in circumstances.

The MAD as shown in Equation 6.4 is the suggested statistic for measuring conformity. In this application the MAD is calculated in the same way except that the EP (Expected Proportion) is now the prior data. An extract from the table with the MAD calculation is shown in Figure 9.3.

The MAD for the current and the prior period data is 0.0015. The guidelines for assessing conformity in a My Law application are set out in Table 9.2.

Table 9.2 sets out ranges for the My Law application that are twice as wide as those for the usual first-order test. The prior distribution is not as stable as that of Benford's Law. There is some room for error and some judgment is used. The forensic investigator will need to evaluate whether the immediately prior period is the best benchmark. Another possible benchmark would be to look at two or three prior periods and then to average the results. Given the instability of the prior distribution we should allow for larger differences before we reach a nonconformity conclusion. The MAD for the gift data is 0.0015 and this gives us a comfortable *close conformity* conclusion.

The numerical and graphical descriptive statistics of the parallel scan show that the current data detail is reasonably similar to the prior data detail. The overview measures,

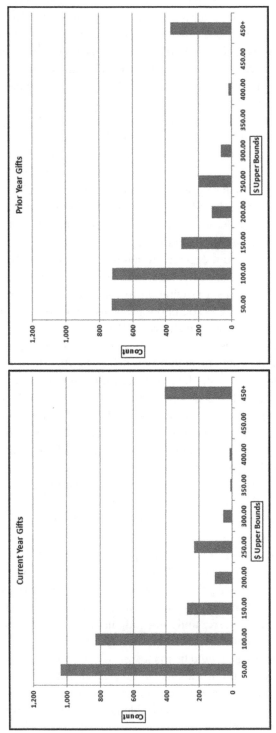

FIGURE 9.1 The Histograms of the Current and Prior Year Gift Amounts

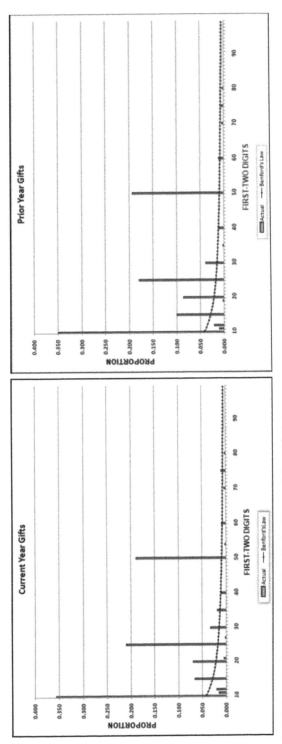

FIGURE 9.2 The Results of the First-Order Tests of the Gift Data

	A	B	C	D	E	F
1			FIRST-ORDER MAD			
2	FT Digit	Count	Current	Prior	Difference	AbsDiff
3	10	1050	0.355	0.347	0.008	0.008
4	11	43	0.015	0.009	0.005	0.005
5	12	57	0.019	0.021	-0.002	0.002
6	13	0	0.000	0.000	0.000	0.000
7	14	0	0.000	0.000	0.000	0.000
8	15	192	0.065	0.100	-0.035	0.035
9	16	0	0.000	0.000	0.000	0.000
10	17	0	0.000	0.000	0.000	0.000
11	18	0	0.000	0.000	0.000	0.000
12	19	0	0.000	0.000	0.000	0.000
13	20	202	0.068	0.085	-0.017	0.017
14	21	12	0.004	0.000	0.004	0.004
15	22	0	0.000	0.000	0.000	0.000
16	23	0	0.000	0.000	0.000	0.000
17	24	0	0.000	0.000	0.000	0.000
18	25	619	0.209	0.178	0.031	0.031

FIGURE 9.3 An Extract from the Worksheet Calculating the MAD

TABLE 9.2 The Mean Absolute Deviation Cutoff Values for a My Law Application

MAD range	Conclusion
0.0000 to 0.0024	Close conformity
0.0024 to 0.0036	Acceptable conformity
0.0036 to 0.0044	Marginally acceptable conformity
Above 0.0044	Nonconformity

together with the statistics relating to central tendency, variability, and the shape of the distribution show that the detail is consistent from year to year. The drive for additional gifts (however small) explains all of the main time-related differences. The histogram and the digit patterns show a consistency from year to year, except for some differences due to the drive for additional gifts. These results suggest a reduced risk of errors or fraud.

AN ANALYSIS OF FRAUDULENT DATA

The current data was seeded with fraud. The realistic, but hypothetical, fraud is based on the recognition that donors receive from the college based on the amount of the gift. Donor names and recognition levels are listed in various college publications, and formal events are held for members of various recognition levels. It is normal for donors to give an amount that would just qualify for some recognition level. The fraud in this case was that the accountant diverted funds for his personal use, constrained by the fact that the donor would complain if they were given an inferior recognition level at college events. With the *recognition level* constraint only about one-half of the gifts had any dollars that could be "skimmed off the top." An example of the fraud is recording $7,000 as $5,000 to siphon off $2,000 leaving the donor still a member of the "Platinum Society," which recognizes gifts from $5,000 to $9,999. There was no skimming (theft) of amounts under $150 because the theft of such small amounts was not worth the risk. This $150 lower limit meant that only about 16 percent of the gift amounts were subject to skimming. The largest gift was reduced by $40,000 to $14,780 since the accountant would still want an odd number here and there to account for gifts of appreciated stock. The fraudulent data is therefore the table of old current data with each "skimable number" over $150 reduced to the lower threshold for its recognition level. The number of records is unchanged, but one-sixth of the gift amounts have been reduced and the rest are unchanged from the data analyzed in Table 9.3.

TABLE 9.3 The Descriptive Statistics of the Fraudulent Data

	Fraudulent	Prior	Change
Sum	$857,895	$923,005	− 7.1%
Number of records	2,959	2,531	+ 16.9%
Number of missing records	0	0	no change
Mean	$290	$365	− $75
A significant difference between the means?	Yes, α = 0.05		
Test used	Two-sample t-test		
Median	$100	$100	no change
Mode	$100	$100	no change
Minimum	$10	$10	no change
Quartile 1	$50	$50	no change
Quartile 3	$125	$250	− $125
Maximum	$14,780	$50,000	− $35,220
Range	$14,770	$49,990	− $35,220
Interquartile range	$75	$200	− $125
Standard Deviation	745	1,449	− 704.00
A significant difference between the variances?	Yes, α = 0.20		
Test used	Levene's test		
Coefficient of Variation (CV)	2.57	3.97	− 1.40
Skewness	7	21	− 14.00
Is the data normally distributed?	No, α = 0.05		
Anderson-Darling Test statistic	676	640	+ 36.00

Table 9.3 shows the descriptive statistics of alumni gifts for the current fraudulent year and the prior year together with the change for the year. The abbreviation α refers to the significance level of the test.

The descriptive statistics of the fraudulent data and the prior data are shown in Table 9.3. The overview shows that the number of records has increased and the explanation of the increased drive for gifts of any size is an acceptable explanation for the higher count. The sum shows a decrease and this should raise a red flag from a fraud perspective because the college made a concerted effort to raise more gift dollars than the prior year. The change in the sum is consistent with the presence of fraud (or error).

The central tendency statistics show that the mean decreased by $75. This change is consistent with the presence of fraud. The difference between the means is now statistically significant at the 0.05 level and can therefore not be attributed to random fluctuations. The total amount skimmed from the gifts was $135,000 and this loss was large enough to cause a significant difference between the means. Table 9.3 also shows that the quartile 3 value of $125 and the maximum value of $14,780 are both much less than the comparable numbers for the prior period.

The variability statistics show that the standard deviation decreased from about 1,450 to 750. The fraudulent data had far less dispersion (spread) about the mean. This reduction in variability was directly because of the fraud. The accountant siphoned off large amounts from the large gifts (above $10,000) in that they had almost all of their excesses (the amount needed to be in the top gift tier) diverted. The large reductions in the large amounts caused the standard deviation to decrease. The decrease was large enough to cause a significant difference between the variances using Levene's test. This test requires a reasonably dramatic difference to be significantly different and past experience suggests using a significance level of 0.20 for this test. The fraud caused the standard deviation to halve and so the CV was also notably reduced by about one-third. The reductions in skewness, standard deviation, and CV, all indicate large decreases in dispersion. The decrease in dispersion is evident from the decrease in the range. The variability measures indicate that the account detail has changed.

The skewness measure decreased from 21 to 7. The amounts siphoned off from the large gifts made the distribution more symmetric. The skewness measure can be highly influenced by just a few large amounts. The Anderson-Darling statistic is virtually unchanged and it is therefore not overly influenced by a small group of large numbers. The skewness measure correctly indicates that the shape of the distribution has changed.

The statistical overview and measures of central tendency can be calculated with Excel. The data analysis functions are found using **Data→Analysis→Data Analysis→Descriptive Statistics**. The descriptive statistics of the fraud data is shown in Figure 9.4.

The descriptive statistics are shown in Figure 9.4. The Excel results should be formatted to zero or two decimals where appropriate. The quartile 1 and quartile 3 values can be calculated in Excel using the Large function. Excel's output includes the standard deviation and the skewness measure. Access can compute some of the descriptive statistics but Access is limited in what it can do in this arena. For example,

	A	B	C
1	*Fraud*		
2			
3	Mean	289.93	
4	Standard Error	13.69	
5	Median	100.00	
6	Mode	100.00	
7	Standard Deviation	744.86	
8	Sample Variance	554817.82	
9	Kurtosis	87.18	
10	Skewness	7.26	
11	Range	14770.00	
12	Minimum	10.00	
13	Maximum	14780.00	
14	Sum	857895.00	
15	Count	2959	
16	Largest(1)	14780	
17	Smallest(1)	10	
18	Confidence Level(95.0%)	27	
19			

FIGURE 9.4 Descriptive Statistics Produced by Excel

calculating the median is possible in Access but it does require some reasonably nimble Access gymnastics.

Minitab does an excellent job with descriptive statistics. This software package is developed by the Pennsylvania State University. A free trial version can be downloaded from the Minitab website. The Minitab steps to calculate the descriptive statistics are **Stat→Basic Statistics→Display Descriptive Statistics**. The fraud data results are shown in Figure 9.5.

The Minitab results are shown in Figure 9.5. The Anderson-Darling test is run in Minitab using **Stat→Basic Statistics→Graphical Summary** and the comprehensive results are shown in the third panel in Figure 9.5. Levene's test for equal variances is run using **Stat→Basic Statistics→2 Variances**. Minitab is user-friendly, and easy to use and to understand. Data can be imported into Minitab using the familiar **Copy** and **Paste** steps. Extensive help is available in Minitab to explain the results and the formulas used in the program. Minitab is the preferred tool for the calculation of descriptive statistics.

The histograms of the fraudulent and the prior data are shown in Figure 9.6. The results show that the counts for the lower values for the fraudulent data are higher than the counts for the lower values in the original data.

The increased drive for gifts of any size is a plausible explanation for the higher counts in the $50 and $100 intervals in the fraud data. The histogram gives us no indication that the sum has decreased by 14 percent because histograms measure counts and not sums. Most of the siphoning off by dollar value took place in the bin for $450+, and while the dollar amounts were reduced (in one case by $40,000 and in another case by $17,895), the counts (which is what a histogram is all about) were not

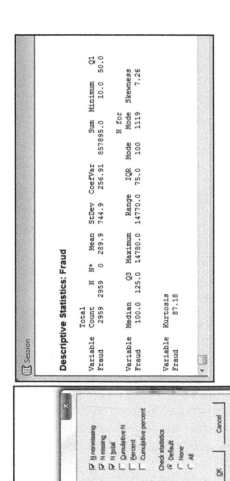

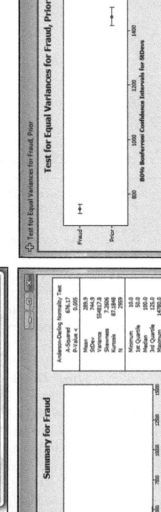

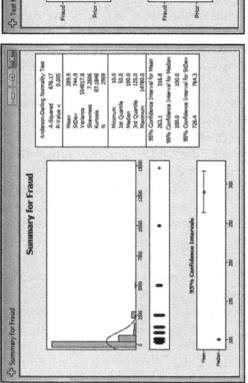

FIGURE 9.5 A Minitab Dialog Screen and the Descriptive Statistics

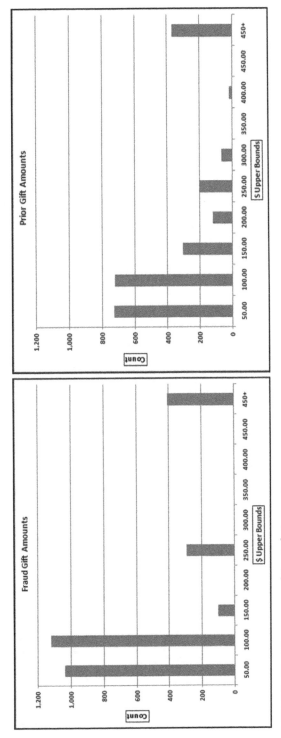

FIGURE 9.6 The Histograms of the Gift Amounts

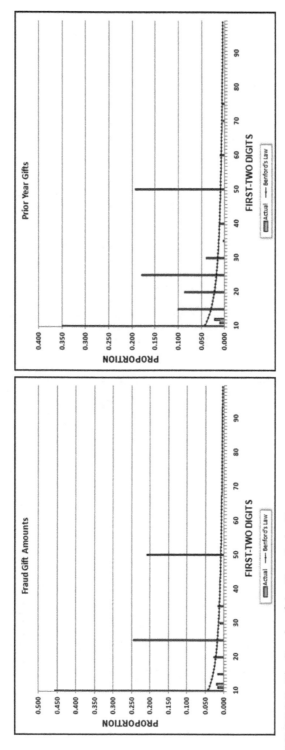

FIGURE 9.7 The Results of the First-Order Tests

noticeably affected. This reminds us that each descriptive statistic or graph only looks at one characteristic of the data. The fraud histogram shows that the fraud data has counts of zero for the $200, $300, $350, $400, and $450 intervals whereas most of these intervals had small bars (positive counts) in the prior year. The newly empty intervals are quite suspicious and correctly signal a change in the data detail. The next test is a comparison of the first-order tests in Figure 9.7.

The first-order tests in Figure 9.7 show a surprising result. The focus is on a comparison of the first-order results between the current and the prior year, with the Benford proportions included only as reference points. The digit patterns of the fraudulent data and the prior data are not too different. The y-axes are calibrated equally from 0 to 0.50 so that the differences are easier to see. The MAD of 0.00451 signals nonconformity or that there is a large difference between the two years. The fact that the distributions are not wildly different is somewhat surprising. This could be because there were only 470 skims (about 16 percent of the amounts) and in some cases the skims did not affect the first digit (e.g., amounts in the $150 to $199 range were reduced to $100) or the changes might have cancelled each other. These results themselves are a bit anomalous in that we have a nonconformity conclusion using the MAD even though the fraud only affected a small percentage of the detail in the data table.

The second-order test of Benford's Law was not performed on the data because the data was not drawn from a continuous distribution with a smooth density function as is a requirement of this test. The type of data (alumni gifts) was such that there were unused intervals of numbers that were entirely missing from the data set, followed by clusters of numbers at certain favored gift amounts. The data sets contained about 3,000 records each but there were too few different numbers being used to get any useful pattern from the second-order test.

The last-two digits, the summation test, and the number duplication tests are not seen to be very useful in a comparison of current data and prior period data. The suite of current and prior data tests only includes descriptive statistics, histograms, and the first-order test.

 ## SUMMARY AND DISCUSSION

The forensic analytic tests in the chapter relate to a comparison of the transaction details of the current period to the transaction details of the prior period. These tests would help to assess the risk of fraud or errors. The tests are made up of numerical statistics related to a data overview, and measures of central tendency, variability, and the shape of the distribution. The tests also include two graphical methods related to the shape of the distribution and the first-order test.

The case study dealt with gift amounts given to a college over a period of two consecutive years. The descriptive statistics and the graphical methods showed that there were differences between the two data sets. The explanation for the differences was that the college embarked on a special drive to get more people to donate, even if the gift amounts were small. In the second analysis the current year gift data was seeded with a fraud where the accountant siphoned off dollar amounts from about one-sixth of the gifts. The new fraud descriptive statistics showed some substantial differences between the fraudulent data and the gifts from the prior year. The numerical descriptive statistics signaled a change in the details. For the graphical methods, the histogram signaled that the detail had changed. The first-order test also signaled a noticeable change in the account detail. The current set of digit patterns were compared to the digit patterns for the prior year and this application was called *My Law*. In some cases the changes were evident from some tests and in other cases the fraud or errors were evident from other tests. Even in the absence of errors or fraud, the analysis of the detail gives insights into the entity and its environment that might prove to be useful in a forensic investigations environment.

Discussions with external auditors indicated that most practicing auditors would understand the overview statistics and some of the central tendency measures. The use of the other numerical and graphical methods would have to be preceded by some training on understanding and interpreting these statistics. Auditors and forensic investigators would have to understand that some numeric and graphical values will have small changes from period to period due to normal changes in conditions that are unrelated to fraud or error. Forensic users will have to identify what makes up a substantial change and one worthy of further investigation. The "investigate further" decision is similar to what auditors already do with the familiar profitability and liquidity ratios.

Auditors also indicated that they are keen to show that their audit provides some value above and beyond the audit report. These value-added discussions usually take place after the audit in the management letter meeting with the audit committee. The results of an analysis using these descriptive statistics, with some anomalous results detected, would be something that they could use at these post-audit meetings. These tests could even be suggested to management as tests that they (management) could perform on an ongoing basis on their data. The auditors would then use the results in the audit as evidence of the monitoring of controls.

CHAPTER TEN

Identifying Fraud Using the Largest Subsets and Largest Growth Tests

T HE NIGRINI CYCLE LOOKED at the data in a single field only. The data profile and the histogram gave us information on the distribution of the numbers. The periodic chart gave us the monthly totals. The first-order, summation, second-order, and last-two digits tests all analyzed the digit patterns in a single field. The number duplication test also looked at the duplications of specific numbers in a single field. In the parallel scan we also looked at a single field of data but we compared the numerical and graphical statistics over two time periods. In the next four chapters the forensic tests will analyze two or more fields at a time. These tests are drill-down tests that will give us small samples of highly suspicious records. The tests in the next four chapters are called the advanced tests because of the use of more than one field in the analysis.

The first test described is the *largest subsets* test. The test uses two fields, one with transaction or balance numbers (such as dollars, inventory counts, vote counts, population counts) and another field to indicate the subset (e.g., vendor number, credit card number, or branch number). The word subset is borrowed from mathematics where we know a *set* to be a collection of distinct objects and a *subset* to be a set whose members are all contained in another set. In our case our *subset* is a group of records that have something in common. This could be all the sales rung up by a cashier or all the purchasing card expenses for a cardholder for the fourth quarter of 2011.

Choosing the subsets requires some imagination. The data can often be divided into several subset groupings. For example, purchasing card data can be grouped by cardholder, or it can be grouped by merchant (the entities that sell the goods or services, e.g., the local car rental agency). The data can also be grouped by time period (e.g., by month) or by the merchant classification.

Accounts payable data could be grouped by vendor or by the type of purchase (purchase order, no purchase order) or by time. There are often a few different ways that data can be divided into subsets. For frequent-flyer miles the grouping could be by customer account number. For inventory data the grouping could be by location. For health care claims the groupings could be providers, employees, or Current Procedural Terminology (CPT) codes. For airline ticket refunds or retail customer refunds the groupings could be the credit card that received the refund. The goal in a forensic investigation is to think of subsets where abnormal duplications could signal errors, fraud, or processing inefficiencies.

The largest subset test has worked well as an error-detecting and a fraud-detecting test. This is particularly so when the data has not yet been the subject of a proactive fraud audit. The first analysis of any data set need not use sophisticated mathematics or statistics. The largest subsets test will usually show valuable results. The goal of the test is to find subsets that are highly inflated due to the error or fraud. Had the largest subsets test been run on the IRS data at the time when 3,000 taxpayers were each billed $300 million, the errors would have been found quite easily. A listing of employees by overtime dollars might point to suspicious behavior, a listing of retail stores authorizing the largest refund totals, or in banking, those employees with the most transactions in their personal accounts might point to suspicious behavior. An example of the largest subsets test is shown in Figure 10.1.

The largest subsets table in Figure 10.1 shows the vendor number, the invoice count, and the total dollars invoiced by the vendor in 2010. The table shows that the largest vendor (#16721) invoiced 51 times for a total amount of $48,945,037.31. The next section reviews some findings from the largest subsets test.

qryLargestVendors		
VendorNum ▾	InvoicesCount ▾	InvoicesSum ▾
16721	51	$48,945,037.31
2088	62	$33,969,172.65
2508	1697	$22,255,032.87
2817	43	$19,067,059.18
17141	3	$17,839,333.34
2786	1396	$17,283,574.49
16059	3	$16,528,575.56
14728	115	$16,174,568.28
3630	13973	$15,288,401.29
2001	4736	$12,207,770.41
6118	46	$10,678,566.27
16637	30	$10,638,664.03
2101	14	$10,230,544.38

FIGURE 10.1 The Largest Vendors for 2010

FINDINGS FROM THE LARGEST SUBSETS TEST

The largest subsets test has produced interesting and useful results. Experience has shown that fraudsters (at least, the ones that were caught) do not know when to stop. They keep up with the scheme to the point that they are likely to show up as a large subset. This is the pattern from the hotel check-in clerk that put their own Hotel Club points on the invoice for everyone that checked in and was not a member of the hotel's loyalty program, to the vice chairman of a major retail company that pled guilty to purchasing card improprieties of $500,000 (including CDS, beer, and a customized dog kennel).

This test should be included on every forensic analytics project. The findings from the test have been very valuable and examples of these forensic findings are described here:

- A company was processing 35,000 invoices per year from a single supplier (Hewlett-Packard). By coincidence another analysis about a year later showed another company processing 42,000 invoices from Hewlett-Packard. This is an efficiency issue in that if any company is transacting in large volumes with another entity then these transactions should be done as efficiently as possible. It would be very inefficient to have 35,000 paper invoices submitted for processing and 35,000 checks mailed to the supplier. Eliminating the paper and streamlining these transactions would result in large savings.
- A controller in Phoenix, Arizona, running the largest subsets test against overtime dollars found that the employee at the top of the list was "working" 1,300 overtime hours in a year. Experience has shown that when employees have figured out how to manipulate the system they do not know when to stop. Even if a finding of 1,300 hours turns out not to be fraud it would still show that staffing levels were inadequate and that the company would benefit from improved planning.
- A company in Chicago, Illinois, found 12,000 invoices each for $8.20 from a printing shop down the road from the head office. The printer supplied business cards for head-office employees and each invoice was being processed individually by accounts payable.
- A company in Dallas, Texas, found that the company was processing 100,000 FedEx invoices per month. The review showed that the courier was used for expedited shipments to customers and that these charges (plus a healthy markup) were recovered from customers. The auditors found that the invoices were being entered electronically and that the transactions were not being entered manually by accounts payable personnel. The problem though with adding 100,000 records to the AP file *every month* was that this bloated the invoices table. The larger file required more mainframe storage space. Queries against the invoices table took more CPU seconds, which was a waste of valuable resources.
- A Texas-based airline used credit card numbers as the subset variable and then tested passenger ticket refunds using the largest subsets test. The results showed that some credit cards were getting thousands of dollars of refunds every year.

No fraud was found after a number of these high-refund cards were reviewed. However, in a related case (also in Texas) a university bookstore employee (a student) repeatedly processed refunds against his own personal credit card. A largest subsets test of the refunds and credit card numbers would have detected his scheme. The fraud was detected by other means after having run its course for a few years and the employee did not graduate from the university.

▪ A company in Orlando, Florida, used the largest subsets test against perpetual inventory records and identified the locations with the most dollars of *negative* inventory. The auditors ran the test against the extended values (quantity times cost) in the inventory table. A number of locations (by coincidence all in the Dallas-Fort Worth area) had high levels of negative inventory. The review showed that this was because managers were invoicing customers for goods before the goods were received into inventory. As a result of the pre invoicing the quantity on hand was negative. Experience has shown that managers that get up to tricks like pre-invoicing are prone to later on move ahead to bigger and grander accounting mischief.

▪ A company in Ventura, California, used the largest subsets test as a purely exploratory test against the checks written to vendors. The results showed that two vendors were each being paid 100 checks per month, which would sum to 2,400 checks per year to each of the two vendors. The vendors were local telephone companies and the company had about 100 branches in each telephone company's calling area. Processing 2,400 telephone bills individually was inefficient. The modern day equivalent is for companies to process employee cell phone bills individually.

▪ A company in the Dallas-Fort Worth area ran the largest subsets against employee reimbursements. The results showed that one employee was reimbursed for a total of $620,000 for the year. The investigation showed that a check was erroneously made out to the employee for $608,000. Accounts payable personnel confirmed that the check was prepared but that the error was detected before the check was given to the employee. The investigators suggested that flags be put into the system to flag potential high dollar errors *before* the checks were printed.

▪ An analysis of employee purchasing cards at a government agency in Washington, DC, showed a number of merchants on the list that violated the rules of the purchasing cards. For example, the cards were not supposed to be used for motor vehicle expenses. The largest subsets analysis includes running the test by cardholder, by merchant, and by date. The investigation was undertaken in response to an employee who used the card repeatedly for personal use at an x-rated video store.

▪ An analysis of motor vehicle expenses at a company based in San Diego, California, showed a vendor for car batteries appearing near the top if the list. The investigator then calculated how many car batteries each car in the fleet was using. It turned out that each car in their fleet was using two car batteries per year!

This test is a relatively simple test that has given very good results. Several employee frauds were detected at an airline where the test looked to see which "passengers" were accumulating the most frequent-flyer miles in a year. The employee fraud had annual totals way in excess of the 400,000 or so miles accumulated by the most loyal frequent flyers. The frauds had annual totals that were almost impossibly high unless someone was flying every day.

Running the largest subsets test is quite straightforward in Access. The largest subsets test is quite straightforward using Excel's pivot table capabilities. The largest growth test is somewhat complicated in Excel and it gives us some good practice with Excel's computational capabilities.

RUNNING THE LARGEST SUBSETS TEST IN ACCESS

The logic in Access is to (a) identify the subset field and the numeric field that will be counted and summed, (b) to use the *Group By, Count,* and *Sum* functions to identify the largest subsets, and (c) to sort by *Sum* or *Count* descending. Adding some bells and whistles requires some design grid gymnastics. We will continue with the *InvoicesPaid* data from Chapter 4 using vendors as our subset variable with a sum and count of the *Amount* field.

The largest subset's Access query is shown in Figure 10.2 and the result was shown earlier in Figure 10.1. The result is a listing of the largest subsets ranked by total dollars. The results can be changed to list the vendors with the largest counts at the top of the report. The fields are named *InvoicesCount* and *InvoicesSum* to slightly shorten the field names. The field names will be used in subsequent queries.

The Figure 10.2 query gives a listing of 26,166 vendors each with a count of the invoices and the total dollars. A look at the bottom of the table shows that there are about 3,000 vendors with total dollars of less than $10. The creation of a vendor

qryLargestVendors

tblInvoicesPaid

*
ID
VendorNum
Date
InvNum
Amount

Field:	VendorNum	InvoicesCount: Amount	InvoicesSum: Amount	
Table:	tblInvoicesPaid	tblInvoicesPaid	tblInvoicesPaid	
Total:	Group By	Count	Sum	
Sort:			Descending	
Show:	☑	☑	☑	
Criteria:				

FIGURE 10.2 The Access Query Used to Identify the Largest Subsets

Property Sheet	✕
Selection type: Query Properties	

General	
Description	
Default View	Datasheet
Output All Fields	No
Top Values	All
Unique Values	No
Unique Records	No
Source Database	(current)
Source Connect Str	
Record Locks	No Locks
Recordset Type	Dynaset
ODBC Timeout	60
Filter	
Order By	
Max Records	
Orientation	Left-to-Right
Subdatasheet Name	
Link Child Fields	
Link Master Fields	
Subdatasheet Height	0"
Subdatasheet Expanded	No
Filter On Load	No
Order By On Load	Yes

FIGURE 10.3 The Query Property Sheet

account for such small amounts is very inefficient. Also, every valid vendor account could be used to commit a fraud and also each unnecessary vendor number could be the recipient of an unintentional payment in error. The largest subset results can be kept to a manageable size by using the **Top Values** property. Use ***Design→Show/ Hide→Property Sheet*** to give the property sheet shown in Figure 10.3.

The **Top Values** option is shown in Figure 10.3. This control (the fourth line on the sheet) allows us to have Access only return the (say) top 100 values. Change the **All** default to 100 and then close the property sheet. There is no message from Access saying that the changes have been accepted. This will only be clear when the query is run. The result of running the query with the 100 top values selected on the invoices data is shown in Figure 10.4.

The results are limited to the 100 largest vendors in Figure 10.4. The results are easier to interpret when the output includes vendor names as well as numbers. A recent analysis of purchasing card data included a restaurant on a largest subsets list for $31,000. Although the total dollars were not particularly high, the fact that it was a small hole-in-the-wall restaurant next to their factory raised more than just a few eyebrows. The auditor knew that this was not an eatery used to conduct company business. It was a lunchtime eatery for employees. In another analysis of purchasing

qryLargestVendors		
VendorNum ▾	InvoicesCount ▾	InvoicesSum ▾
16721	51	$48,945,037.31
2088	62	$33,969,172.65
2508	1697	$22,255,032.87
2817	43	$19,067,059.18
17141	3	$17,839,333.34
2786	1396	$17,283,574.49
16050	3	$16,528,575.56
5806	22...	$ 5,287.6
2676	746	$4,845,889.28
6661	4947	$4,011,179.46
2372	342	$3,809,420.35
2657	13	$3,785,566.17
17637	2948	$3,265,928.44

Record: ◄ ◄ 1 of 100 ► ►► �filter No Filter Search

FIGURE 10.4 The 100 Largest Vendors

card data an electronics store was on the largest subsets list with a total of $87,000. This total was also not especially high, but in a corporate setting, purchases from electronics stores are very suspicious. The largest subsets analysis sometimes also requires a review of the medium-size totals for suspicious items.

RUNNING THE LARGEST GROWTH TEST IN ACCESS

This test uses some of the logic of the current period and prior period comparisons and some of the logic of the largest subsets test from this chapter. This test identifies cases where a subset had a growth spurt over some period of time. This growth spurt could be due to fraud, error, or simply a change in circumstances. A purchasing cardholder might have new job responsibilities requiring more travel than before. In forensic work we are not only interested in growth. A large decrease in dollars might also signal fraud. For example, a hotel might report substantially lower sales for tax purposes or a franchisee might report substantially lower sales to the franchise holder.

This test has been used successfully by a consumer goods company looking at coupon redemptions by merchants (stores). A large increase in coupons redeemed was found to be due to fraud. A fast-foods franchising company reviewed large decreases in sales by individual restaurants to determine whether it was due to sales underreporting.

This would be an easy test to run in Access if every subset in period 0 (the prior period) also had sales in period 1 (the current period). This is not always the case. Stores open and stores close and restaurants open and restaurants close. Purchasing

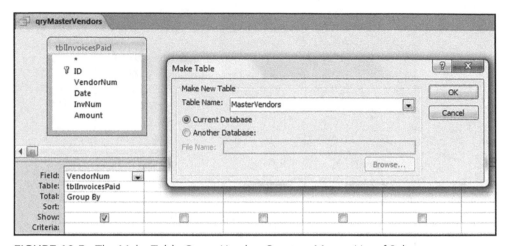

FIGURE 10.5 The Make Table Query Used to Create a Master List of Subsets

cardholders become purchasing cardholders in some periods and stop being cardholders in other periods. The challenge in Access is to change a null (missing) total for a period to a zero for the period.

The first step in the largest growth test is to create a master list (as a table) of all the subsets that had activity in either period. This is done with a make-table query as is shown in Figure 10.5.

The make table query dialog screen shown in Figure 10.5 is accessed by using **Design→Query Type→Make Table**. Click **OK**. The query will create a table of all the vendors. The query must be run using **Design→Results→Run**. Click **Yes** for the warning message about pasting 26,166 rows into a new table. This result of the *qryMasterVendors* query is a table called *MasterVendors*.

For the largest growth test we will use the invoices data and the comparison will be between the totals for each vendor for the first half and the second half of the year. We will use the abbreviations H1 and H2 to refer to the first period (the first six months) and H2 to refer to the second period (the last six months) of our 2010 data. The next step is to calculate the total for each vendor for each of H1 and H2. The query to calculate the total for H1 is shown in Figure 10.6.

The query to calculate the H1 totals in Figure 10.6 uses number signs # at the start and the end of each date. This tells Access that the reference is to a date. The result of running *qryTotalH1* is a sum for each vendor for the first six months for all the vendors that had transactions in the first six months. There were 20,339 such vendors. A query for the last six months also needs to be created. The date range will be #7/1/2010# to #12/31/2010# when written as an Access criterion. This query would be named *qryTotalH2*. The results should show that there were transactions for 9,952 vendors in the last half of the year. When we are likely to reuse queries it is better to use short names. The first stage of the query to get the totals for both H1 and H2 is shown in Figure 10.7.

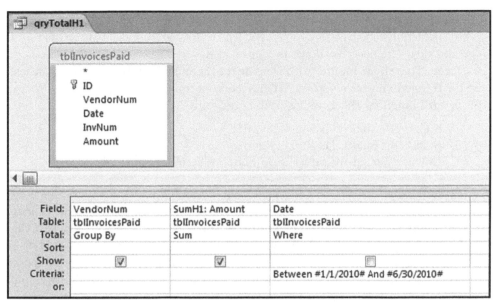

FIGURE 10.6   The Query Used to Calculate the H1 Sum

To get the H1 and H2 totals for each vendor side by side we need to set up a query as is shown in Figure 10.7 with a left outer join. The join is from *MasterVendors* to *qryLargestH1* and also from *MasterVendors* to *qryLargestH2*.

The next step is to change the null (blank) values to zeroes, and then to calculate the change from H1 to H2. Because we cannot have two fields with the same name *SumH1* and *SumH2* need to be renamed when we do the calculations. The *Change*

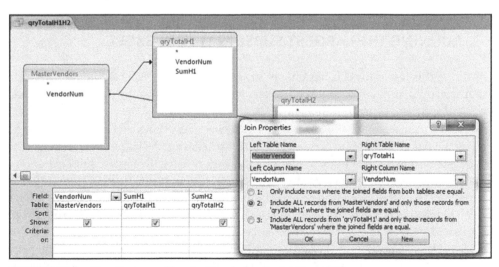

FIGURE 10.7   The Query to Get the Totals for Both H1 and H2

formula needs to avoid any division by zero. A vendor with no transactions in H1 is given a percentage increase of 200 percent. The results are rounded to keep the results nice and tidy. The query is shown in Figure 10.8.

Figure 10.8 shows the query to calculate the H1 and H2 totals. The calculated fields use the **If** function, which is spelled **Iif** in Access (for Immediate If). The query also uses the **Is Null** function. The formulas in the query are

Sum1: Iif([SumH1] Is Null,0,[SumH1])
Sum2: Iif([SumH2] Is Null,0,[SumH2])
Change: Round(Iif([Sum1] > 0,([Sum2] − [Sum1])/[Sum1], 2) ∗ 100,2)

From time to time Access balks at sorting the results when the query has many calculated fields and the sort is run on a calculated field. It is generally good practice to use another query to sort the results. In this case the query would be called *qryTotalSorted*. The query selects the *VendorNum*, *Sum1*, *Sum2*, and *Change* fields from *qryTotalH1H2* and sorts on *Change* descending. *Change* should be renamed to *ChangePct* and formatted as Standard with 1 decimal place for neat and tidy results. The results are shown in Figure 10.9.

This largest growth results in Figure 10.9 needs to be carefully reviewed. We are interested in large percentage increases, but not necessarily when the base is small. For example, an increase from $6.00 to $667.00 is an 11,017 percent increase, but the base is small. However, in this case it is a possibility that the second period amount was really for $6.67 (which sounds like a better match to $6.00) and the amount was incorrectly entered as $667.00 and not $6.67.

Also, the 200 percent section of the results is in reality all those cases of zero activity in H1 and activity in H2. In addition to the percentage increases *qryTotalH1H2* can be revised to show the absolute dollar amount as the increase. For example, the increase for the first row would be $16,165,938.28, which is the H2 total minus the H1 total.

RUNNING THE LARGEST SUBSETS TEST IN EXCEL

Running this test in Excel is reasonably straightforward. We will use the invoices data that was used for the Access tests. The test will use vendors as the subset variable and we will sum and count the *Amount* field.

In the number duplication test we counted how many times each number occurred. We could use an adaptation of those indicator variables for the largest subsets tests. The choice here is to use pivot tables. Pivot tables work well for the largest subsets test. We will use a new spreadsheet as opposed to adding yet more sheets to the *NigriniCycle.xlsx* template. The Excel spreadsheet with the *InvoicesPaid* data is shown in Figure 10.10.

The data was imported from Access using **Data→Get External Data→From Access**. The Excel table was converted to a range and this removed the filters in the first row and the connection to the source data in Access. The next step is to use the pivot table function using **Insert→Tables→Pivot Table→Pivot Table**. This will give the dialog box shown in Figure 10.11.

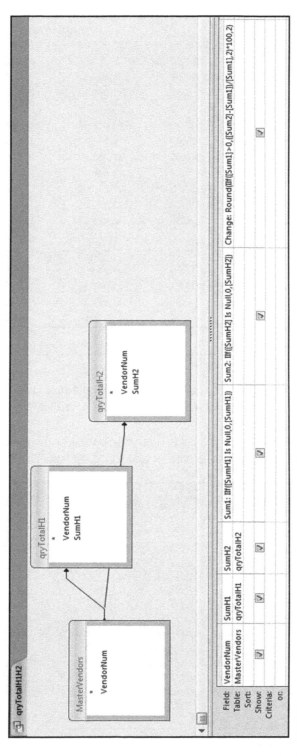

FIGURE 10.8 The Query to Calculate the Amounts for Each Period

qryTotalSorted			
VendorNum ▾	Sum1 ▾	Sum2 ▾	ChangePct ▾
14728	$4,315.00	$16,170,253.28	374,645.2
4967	$805.00	$379,739.42	47,072.6
2879	$300.00	$81,169.50	26,956.5
5769	$83.75	$21,966.03	26,128.1
5843	$18.00	$4,195.16	23,206.4
2098	$1,622.70	$360,050.00	22,088.3
6547	$69.40	$12,673.80	18,162.0
16731	$70.00	$11,058.86	15,698.4
3719	$175.00	$24,445.00	13,868.6
5778	$137.50	$17,578.62	12,684.5
2764	$1,915.00	$243,100.00	12,594.5
2493	$376.50	$46,466.14	12,241.6
20914	$6.00	$667.00	11,016.7
6854	$20.00	$2,040.00	10,100.0
4251	$276.00	$27,534.00	9,876.1
14390	$21.01	$1,861.47	8,759.9
15510	$20.00	$1,738.28	8,591.4
11893	$200.00	$14,603.00	7,201.5

FIGURE 10.9 The Results of the Largest Growth Test

Excel has correctly identified the data source and the preferred choice is to show the output on a new worksheet. Click **OK** to give the next dialog box as is shown in Figure 10.12.

The next step is to identify the fields that will be used in the pivot table and then placing the fields in the boxes at the bottom of the field list box. The first step is to drag

	A	B	C	D	E
1	ID	VendorNum	Date	InvNum	Amount
2	1	2001	1/1/2010	4242J10	$25.19
3	2	2001	1/1/2010	7899J10	$25.86
4	3	2001	1/1/2010	3830J10	$26.57
5	4	2001	1/1/2010	9514J10	$27.83
6	5	2001	1/1/2010	6296J10	$28.09
7	6	2001	1/1/2010	5884J10	$28.34
8	7	2001	1/1/2010	6908J10	$32.12
9	8	2001	1/1/2010	6882J10	$34.22
10	9	2001	1/1/2010	2104J10	$34.97
11	10	2001	1/1/2010	0496J10	$36.08
12	11	2001	1/1/2010	4325J10	$37.31
13	12	2001	1/1/2010	8045J10	$38.68
14	13	2001	1/1/2010	4697J10	$40.55
15	14	2001	1/1/2010	4812J10	$41.79
16	15	2001	1/1/2010	8185J10	$42.56

FIGURE 10.10 The Invoices Data in an Excel Worksheet

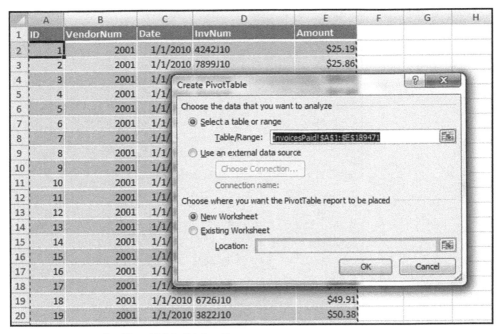

FIGURE 10.11 The Pivot Table Dialog Box

the field *VendorNum* to the **Row Labels** box and *Amount* to the **Sum Values** ($\sum$ Values) box. The subsets and their sums are shown in columns A and B. These results now need to be sorted by *Amount* descending and the *SumOfAmount* field needs to be formatted as currency with two decimal places. To run the sort command use **Home→Editing→Sort&Filter** with the cursor in cell **B4**. The tidying up steps include closing the pivot table dialog box and deleting the top two rows. The final result is shown in Figure 10.13.

The largest subsets result in Figure 10.13 agrees with the Access result in Figure 10.4. The last row of the Excel output (row 26168) shows the grand total and this grand total agrees with the data profile total in Figure 4.1. Excel's pivot tables are a useful tool for forensic analytics.

 ## RUNNING THE LARGEST GROWTH TEST IN EXCEL

This test identifies subsets that have shown large increases in the past. In this section we use a little sleight of hand with pivot tables to get our required result. With Excel we do not need to create a master list of the subsets that had activity in either period. We do need to use an indicator variable to indicate whether the invoice belongs to H1 (the first half of the period) or H2 (the second half of the period). This is done using the IF function and the function and the result is shown in Figure 10.14.

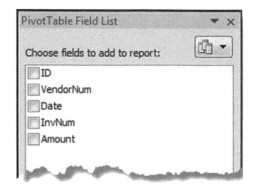

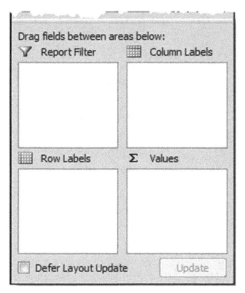

FIGURE 10.12 The Pivot Table Field List

The formula used to identify the period is shown in Figure 10.14. The formula is shown below:

$$=IF(MONTH(C2)<=6,1,2)$$

With each transaction now coded as to H1 or H2 we can run the largest subset growth test in Excel using pivot tables. The goal is to get the result shown in Figure 10.9. Calculating the change percentage and formatting the table will take some additional work after the pivot table has run. The pivot table is created using **Insert→Tables→ Pivot Table→Pivot Table**. The default settings are usually appropriate for the largest subsets test or the largest growth test. Click **OK** to activate the pivot table dialog box.

The pivot table is set up as is shown in Figure 10.15. The result needs a bit of tidying up work. The first step is to close the Pivot Table Field List box. The next step is to delete

⊿	A	B	C
1	Row Labels ▾	Sum of Amount	
2	16721	$48,945,037.31	
3	2088	$33,969,172.65	
4	2508	$22,255,032.87	
5	2817	$19,067,059.18	
6	17141	$17,839,333.34	
7	2786	$17,283,574.49	
8	16059	$16,528,575.56	
9	14729	$16,174,568	

⊿	A	B	C
24	23.2	,5,809,420.35	
25	2657	$3,785,566.17	
26	17637	$3,265,928.44	
27	2318	$3,182,804.50	
28	2735	$3,151,334.95	
29	2679	$2,778,167.64	
30	3141	$2,627,342.57	

⏮ ◀ ▶ ⏭ LargestSubsets InvoicesPaid

FIGURE 10.13 The Results of Running the Largest Subset Test Using Pivot Tables

the first two (blank) rows of the spreadsheet. Put the cursor in cell A2. With the pivot table results being the active sheet use **Options→Pivot Table→Options→Options** to get to the pivot table options dialog box shown in Figure 10.16.

The **Pivot Table Options** dialog box is shown in Figure 10.16. In the **Layout & Format** tab (the visible tab in Figure 10.16) use the **Format** section to show 0 for empty cells. This is done by entering a zero (0) in the third line from the bottom in Figure 10.16. In the **Totals & Filters** tab unselect both boxes related to the grand totals. In the

⊿	A	B	C	D	E	F
1	ID	VendorNum	Date	InvNum	Amount	Period
2	1	2001	1/1/2010	4242J10	$25.19	1
3	2	2001	1/1/2010	7899J10	$25.86	1
4	3	2001	1/1/2010	3830J10	$26.57	1
5	4	2001	1/1/2010	9514J10	$27.83	1
6	5	2001	1/1/2010	6296J10	$28.09	1
7	6	2001	1/1/2010	5884J10	$28.34	1
8	7	2001	1/1/2010	6908J10	$32.12	1
9	8	2001	1/1/2010	6882J10	$34.22	1
10	9	2001	1/1/2010	2104J10	$34.97	1
11	10	2001	1/1/2010	0496J10	$36.08	1
12	11	2001	1/1/2010	4325J10	$37.31	1
13	12	2001	1/1/2010	8045J10	$38.68	1

FIGURE 10.14 The Indicator Variable Used to Indicate Whether the Period Is H1 or H2

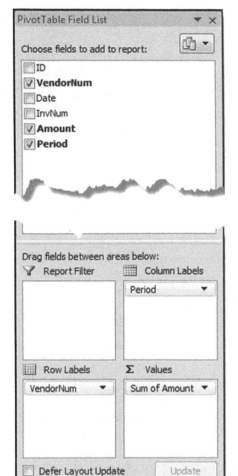

FIGURE 10.15 The Pivot Table Setup for the Largest Subsets Growth Test

Display tab unselect **Display field captions and filter drop downs**. Click **OK** to activate the changes and to exit from the **Pivot Table Options** dialog box.

The next step is to calculate the percentage change. Insert the column heading *ChangePct* in cell **D2**. The formula for cell **D3** is

$$\textbf{D}3:\ =\ \mathrm{Round}(\mathrm{If}(B3>0,(C3-B3)/B3,2)*100,2)$$

We then need to get the results into a format that is not constrained by pivot table formatting. This is a little bit tricky because Excel does not really want to add our *ChangePct* field in column D to the pivot table report. The quickest way to do things is to add a formula in F3, which is = A3. Copy this formula across to I3. We now have a copy of the first row in cells **F3:I3**. Copy down as far as is needed (to the bottom of the pivot

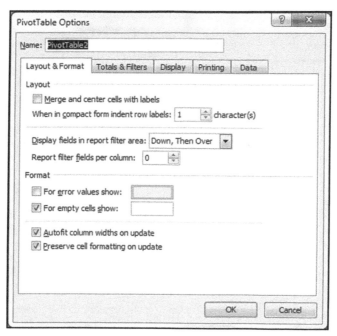

FIGURE 10.16 The Pivot Table Options Dialog Box

table report). Highlight the entire set of formulas (**F3:I26168**) and use the Paste Special feature to convert the formulas to values. Now delete the entire pivot table. Remove the extra header row, add the field names, and format the range neatly. Sort the data by *ChangePct* descending (largest to smallest).

The subsets with the largest percentage growth numbers are shown in Figure 10.17. For the subsets growth test we are interested in subsets that have a large percentage growth and also subsets that have a large growth measured in dollars. The step to convert the changes to dollars and to sort the results requires changing the formula in column D and then sorting the data from largest to smallest. Creating a copy of the worksheet means that both sets of results are easily accessible.

The largest growth subsets as measured by the change in dollars are shown in Figure 10.18. More sophisticated methods are available to calculate the growth in subsets. For example, each month could be given a numeric value of 1 to 12. Thereafter, the total dollars per month would be calculated much like the H1 and H2 totals. The next step would be to use regression to calculate the slope of the best fitting line. Subsets with positive slopes would be subsets that show an increase from month-to-month. The slope would be the average monthly increase in dollars. The subsets with the largest positive slopes would be those subsets with the largest increases (as measured by total dollars). Excel has a built-in regression function that can be activated using **Data→Analysis→Data Analysis**. The regression tool will analyze subsets one at a time (vendor by vendor) and what we really want is an analysis of all vendors at the

	A	B	C	D
1	VendorNum	H1	H2	ChangePct
2	14728	$4,315.00	$16,170,253.28	374645.15
3	4967	$805.00	$379,739.42	47072.6
4	2879	$300.00	$81,169.50	26956.5
5	5769	$83.75	$21,966.03	26128.1
6	5843	$18.00	$4,195.16	23206.44
7	2098	$1,622.70	$360,050.00	22088.33
8	6547	$69.40	$12,673.80	18161.96
9	16731	$70.00	$11,058.86	15698.37
10	3719	$175.00	$24,445.00	13868.57
11	5778	$137.50	$17,578.62	12684.45
12	2764	$1,915.00	$243,100.00	12594.52
13	2493	$376.50	$46,466.14	12241.6
14	20914	$6.00	$667.00	11016.67
15	6854	$20.00	$2,040.00	10100
16		$276.00	$27,584.00	9976.09
26	17202	$2,000.00	$114,000.00	5600
27	7538	$1,334.42	$75,594.18	5564.95
28	8738	$91.04	$5,030.38	5425.46
29	4424	$50.00	$2,740.00	5380

◄ ◄ ► ► LargestSubsets / InvoicesPaid / **LargestGrowthPct** / Largest

FIGURE 10.17 The Excel Results for the Subset Growth Test

	A	B	C	D	E	F
1	VendorNum	H1	H2	ChangeDollars		
2	14728	$4,315.00	$16,170,253.28	$16,165,938.28		
3	2786	$2,766,074.69	$14,517,499.80	$11,751,425.11		
4	7172	$0.00	$5,485,583.00	$5,485,583.00		
5	6118	$2,750,319.84	$7,928,246.43	$5,177,926.59		
6	3142	$1,488,343.87	$6,047,390.38	$4,559,046.51		
7	2001	$4,952,998.10	$7,254,772.31	$2,301,774.21		
8	3141	$252,284.26	$2,375,058.31	$2,122,774.05		
9	5806	$1,542,846.07	$3,582,441.62	$2,039,595.55		
10	3547	$0.00	$1,747,913.27	$1,747,913.27		
11	2892	$2,368,206.47	$3,504,619.94	$1,136,413.47		
12		$1,486,715.10	$2,322,705.25	$835,990.15		
25	2098	$1,622.70	$360,050.00	$358,427.30		
26	2569	$745,017.98	$1,078,304.53	$333,286.55		
27	3244	$10,087.50	$340,427.57	$330,340.07		
28	2733	$84,322.22	$397,146.27	$312,824.05		
29	2053	$164,504.39	$475,986.85	$311,482.46		

◄ ◄ ► ► LargestSubsets / InvoicesPaid / LargestGrowthPct / **LargestGrowthDollars**

FIGURE 10.18 The Subsets Sorted by the Growth in Dollars

same time followed by an evaluation of all the results (sorted by slopes descending). This issue will be looked at in Chapter 13.

The data could also be analyzed using dates as the subset variable. The test is useful for purchasing card irregularities and prior work has found excessive purchases at or near the end of the fiscal year and also excessive purchases around the holiday season. Excel allows us to create a pivot table and a chart at the same time. Place the cursor in cell **A2** of the data table and then click ***Insert→Tables→Pivot Table→Pivot Chart***. Excel should correctly see where your data is located. Accept the default selection of the data. The pivot table setup would be as shown in Figure 10.19.

The pivot table dialog box is shown in Figure 10.19. The pivot chart is created on the same sheet as the pivot table. The chart can be moved by right clicking in the chart and using ***Move Chart*** and then ***New Sheet***. The graphical result after a little formatting here and there is shown in Figure 10.20.

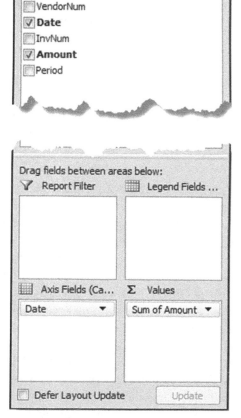

FIGURE 10.19 The Creation of a Pivot Chart

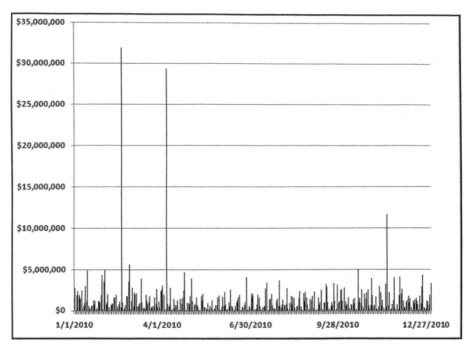

FIGURE 10.20 The Pivot Chart Showing Total Dollars per Day

 SUMMARY

The tests in Chapters 4 through 9 looked at the data in a single field only. In this chapter the complexity of using a second field was added. The chapter described two tests and findings from these tests together with the steps to running the tests in Access and Excel.

The *largest subsets* test uses one field with transaction or balance numbers and another field to indicate subset membership. Examples of transaction or balance numbers include invoiced dollars, inventory counts, vote counts, and population counts. Examples of subset fields include vendor numbers, credit card numbers, branch numbers, or customer numbers. The word *subset* is borrowed from mathematics where a *set* is a collection of distinct objects and a *subset* is a set whose members are all contained in another set. In our forensic tests a *subset* is a group of records that have something in common. All the sales rung up by a cashier have that cashier in common. Similarly, all the purchasing card expenses for a cardholder have that cardholder in common.

Findings from the largest subsets test have included fraudulent overtime payments, fraudulent customer refunds, and fraudulent mileage awards by airline employees. The findings have also included processing inefficiencies and the inefficient use of database resources. In the data cleansing stage the largest subsets test has also detected data errors where some subsets showed unrealistically high totals.

The *largest growth* test identifies subsets that have had very high growth over two or more time periods. The growth can be measured as a percentage or in absolute dollar terms. The largest subsets and the largest growth tests can be run in Excel using the pivot table function. Running the tests in Access uses some reasonably straightforward queries.

Identifying relevant subsets requires some creativity. The data can usually be divided into several subset groupings. For example, purchasing card data can be grouped by cardholder, by merchant, by merchant category, or by date. Accounts payable data could be grouped by vendor. This data could also be grouped by the type of purchase (purchase order, no purchase order) or by time. For frequent-flyer miles the subset could be account number. For inventory data the subsets could be location. For health care claims the subsets could be providers, employees, or CPT codes. The goal in forensic analytics is to think of subsets such that abnormal duplications for a subset could signal errors, fraud, or processing inefficiencies.

CHAPTER ELEVEN

Identifying Anomalies Using the Relative Size Factor Test

T HE PREVIOUS CHAPTER INTRODUCED tests to identify abnormally large subsets and subsets that had experienced explosive growth. The tests concluded with a test of the dollar totals for all the days in a year. The focus in the previous chapter was on size. In this chapter we compare large amounts to a benchmark to see how large they are relative to some norm, hence the name the *relative size factor test*. The relative size factor test is a powerful test for detecting errors. The test identifies subsets where the largest amount is out of line with the other amounts for that subset. This difference could be because the largest record either (a) actually belongs to another subset, or (b) belongs to the subset in question, but the numeric amount is incorrectly recorded.

The relative size factor (RSF) test is an important error-detecting test. An airline auditor reported at an IATA conference that his airline had found errors that amounted to around $1 million as a result of running this test on their accounts payable data. This test was developed in the mid-1990s after I learned of a case where a company in Cleveland wired $600,000 in error to the bank account of a charity. The $600,000 was supposed to have gone to a vendor. Once the "wrong bank account" error was discovered the company contacted the charity, which claimed that the money had already been spent and was largely unrecoverable. The $600,000 was significantly more than any amount that had been donated to the charity before. Had the company run a reasonableness test before authorizing the transfer, it would have seen that the $600,000 was much more than the $3,000 it donated to the charity every quarter.

The RSF test identifies subsets where the largest amount is significantly larger than the other items in the subset. The largest amount would be significantly larger if the numbers were (say) $8,000, $200, $200, and $150. The RSF calculation uses the ratio

	A	B	C	D	E
1	VendorNum ▾	Amount ▾	SecondLargest ▾	Count ▾	RSF ▾
2	2398	$731,546.00	29.95	4	24425.58
3	2450	$53,649.13	20.45	3	2623.43
4	2971	$5,028.20	7.08	2	710.20
5	5003	$1,607.29	3.47	3	463.20
6	5769	$21,941.44	53.25	4	412.05
7	3430	$4,451.13	25	3	178.05
8	2865	$46,459.31	313.04	8	148.41
9	3458	$1,509.50	11.3	2	133.58
10	2135	$42,922.10	345.82	17	124.12
11	16469	$9,530.73	80.6	3	118.25
12	6547	$12,565.80	108	4	116.35
13	20914	$667.00	6	2	111.17
14	13604	$4,330.00	42.87	2	101.00
15	4948	$500.00	5	2	100.00
16	2567	$823.96	9.28	2	88.79
17	8687	$764.47	9.5	2	80.47
18	4302	$424.48	5.6	2	75.80
19	7080	$1,385.00	19.05	2	72.70
20	2900	$6,041.43	84.5	2	71.50
21	12198	$3,500.00	50	2	70.00

FIGURE 11.1 The Relative Size Factors of the *InvoicesPaid* Data

of the largest amount ($8,000) to the second largest amount ($200) to give a ratio of 40. The RSF formula is shown in Equation 11.1.

$$\text{Relative Size Factor} = \frac{\text{Largest Record in a Subset}}{\text{Second Largest Record in a Subset}} \quad (11.1)$$

The formula in Equation 11.1 divides the largest amount by the second largest amount to give a ratio that is greater than or equal to 1.00. The output table usually includes some additional information to help the investigator to identify suspicious or questionable transactions. The additional information could include (a) the subset name or number, (b) the largest amount for the subset, (c) the second largest amount for the subset, (d) the record count for the subset, and (e) the relative size factor. The results for the *InvoicesPaid* data table are shown in Figure 11.1.

RELATIVE SIZE FACTOR TEST FINDINGS

This forensic analytics test has most often been run using the largest and second largest numbers in the various subsets. Forensic investigators can adapt this formula to bring attention to the outliers, depending on what is seen to be an outlier. Examples of adaptations include (a) the largest amount divided by the average amount, (b) the largest divided by the average where the average excludes the largest number, and (c) the smallest number divided by the average (which is used when looking for understatements). Some notes and findings from the use of the RSF test are outlined here:

- A frequent finding is the detection of the *decimal point error* in accounts payable data. This happens when an amount such as $3200.00 is entered into the system as $320000 (the decimal point is omitted) and the vendor is paid 100 times the actual invoice amount. One telltale sign of this error occurring is an amount paid that has no cents to the right of the decimal point. If $421.69 is entered as $42,169 then the amount paid has no cents. This error might only occur once in every 5,000 transactions but in a data set of 200,000 records there would be a good return from identifying 40 such errors. This error is reasonably easy to detect and the *InvoicesPaid* data shows some likely candidates. A partial decimal point error could occur if $421.69 is paid as $4216.90 and the telltale sign here is a RSF of 10 for the vendor.
- Large RSFs are more indicative of error when the subset has many records. The more records in the subset, the more the largest amount stands out from a large crowd. The general rule is that the larger the crowd, the more suspicious the RSF.
- This test showed some valuable findings in a forensic audit of purchasing card transactions in Washington, DC, where the merchant was the subset variable and the numeric field was the amount charged. Investigators found interesting and suspicious items, and possible errors where the RSFs were equal to 10, 5, 4, 3, 2, and 1. An RSF of 1.00 occurs when the largest and second largest items are equal.
- An investigation of perpetual inventory records in Toronto, Ontario, using the extended inventory value (cost times quantity) as the *Amount* and the location as the *Subset*, showed an RSF of 800 for one location. A review of the data showed that this very large amount was a $500,000 error. The error would have caused the location's profits to have been overstated and would have earned the local manager a performance bonus based on the incorrect profit number.
- The RSF test gave some valuable findings in an investigation of insurance claims in Houston, Texas. In the investigation the subset variable was the insurance adjuster (a person in the company who approves claims payments) and the approved claim was the numeric amount. Two adjusters were found to have RSFs of 6.00 and claims authorized of around $30,000 each where the $30,000 amount was far in excess of their authorized limits.
- An investigation of health care payments by a company in Cleveland, Ohio, showed some interesting results. The subset variable was the CPT code (a five digit code describing the tasks and services provided by medical practitioners). The test was run twice using two different numeric amounts. Using the *Amount claimed* as the numeric amount gave RSFs as high as 200, and with *Amount paid* as the numeric amount gave RSFs as high as 6. This means that for some identical procedures the amount paid to a medical practitioner was up to six times as high for the largest payment when compared to the second largest payment. Both the largest and second largest numbers could be excessive, so for this type of data, a modified RSF could be calculated using the largest and the average amount for each subset.

- An investigation of onboard beverage sales by an airline based in Texas showed some interesting findings. These beverage sales have few controls because the beverages in the first-class cabin are free and the beverages in the economy-class cabin are sold to passengers. The analysis used the flight number as the subset variable because a Friday evening flight from LAX to Las Vegas would have a higher alcohol consumption than a Monday morning flight from New York City to Washington, DC. The investigators looked for understatements and the formula used was the minimum amount of sales for a flight number divided by the average amount of sales for the flight number.

- An investigation of sales data at a sportswear manufacturer in Oregon showed some interesting results. The subset variable was the SKU (stock keeping unit) number and the numeric variable was the selling price per unit. The goal was to find sales of goods at prices much below the average price. The investigators were concerned that internal salespeople might be selling goods to "friends" at a discount to the usual selling price. As with the beverage sales, the formula was the minimum amount per unit for an SKU divided by the average selling price per unit for the SKU. The results showed some sales at prices close to zero dollars.

RUNNING THE RSF TEST

The test seems just like the largest subsets test with a complication or two. This test is actually quite difficult to program. One complication is that a subset with only one record cannot have an RSF because there is no second largest number. It is usually a good idea to delete all records less than 1.00, or 10.00 to avoid small numbers influencing the results. Including negative numbers could give us a negative RSF, which is quite meaningless. Also, small positive numbers might give highly inflated RSFs if we (say) divided $8,000 by $0.50.

It is quite difficult to identify the second largest amount in each subset. The main steps in running the test are to delete the small and irrelevant numbers, and then to delete all the subsets with only one record. We then need to identify the largest and second largest numbers for each subset. We also need to establish a rule that would apply if the largest and the second largest numbers were both equal. The logic that could be used with any data analysis program is:

1. Sort the data by *Subset* and by *Amount* descending and delete all numbers less than (say) 1.00.
2. Identify the subsets that have only one numeric record and delete these records.
3. Identify the largest *Amount* for each subset and also calculate the **Count** for each subset.
4. Identify those cases where any *Amount* appeared more than once in a subset.
5. Identify those subsets where the count of the largest amount was two or more and calculate the RSF of those subsets to be 1.00. Save these results.
6. Delete all the subsets with RSFs equal to 1.00 from the main data table.

7. Identify and remove the maximum *Amount* from each subset.
8. Identify the maximum *Amount* of the remaining records (which will be the second largest number).
9. Calculate the RSF and the other statistics to be included in the results table (e.g., the *Subset* number, the largest *Amount*, the second largest *Amount*, the count, and the RSF itself).

It might be possible to run the RSF test in Access with fewer than 11 queries. However, 11 queries make it easier to follow the logic of each query. Several queries include the **Join** command and the series of queries ends with a Union query to tidy things up. The tests can be run in Excel and surprisingly this test is easier to program in Excel than it is to program in Access.

RUNNING THE RELATIVE SIZE FACTOR TEST IN ACCESS

In this section, we use the *InvoicesPaid* data table. This goal is to identify subsets where the largest *Amount* is much larger than the other numbers in the subset. The *VendorNum* field will be the subset field and *Amount* will be the numeric field. The first step is to sort the data and to only keep the records that are greater than or equal to $1.00. This is done with the query shown in Figure 11.2.

The *qryRSF1* query (results not shown) gives us the largest, the second largest, and all the other records for each subset. The second step is to create a master list of those vendors that have more than one record. Any subset with only one record cannot possibly have a second largest amount.

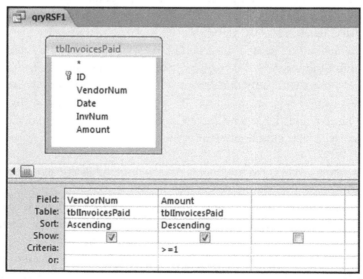

FIGURE 11.2 This Step Sorts the Data and Keeps Those Records that Are $1.00 and Larger

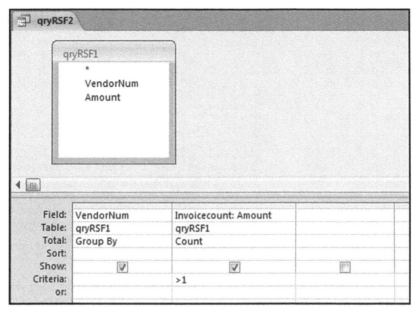

FIGURE 11.3 The Creation of a Master List of Subsets with More than One Record

The query to create a master list of vendors with valid RSFs is shown in Figure 11.3. The result of this query is a master vendor list of 6,457 vendors. This vendor count is much less than the vendor count for the largest subsets test shown in Figure 10.2. The largest subsets test included all vendors (26,166 vendors) whereas *qryRSF2* limits the results to vendors with two or more transactions of $1.00 or more. There were about 20,000 vendors with only one transaction (one record) or where the second transaction was for less than $1.00.

The next step is to keep only the records in *qryRSF1* that match a subset listed in *qryRSF2*. This will give a data table of *Amounts* ≥ 1.00 for vendors with more than one record. This is done using a **Join** and *qryRSF3*; Figure 11.4 shows the details.

Figure 11.4 shows the query used to keep only those subsets with more than one record and only amounts greater than or equal to 1.00. The **Join** used is an inner join and this is the default join unless an outer join is specified by using the second or third radio button. The **Join Properties** dialog box is shown only for informational purposes. The results of *qryRSF3* are shown in Figure 11.5.

Figure 11.5 shows that there were 165,257 records remaining after deleting amounts less than 1.00 and those subsets with only one record. The next step is to identify the maximum amount for each subset. The maximum and the second largest amounts might be equal in some cases.

The query in Figure 11.6 calculates the largest amount for each subset using the **Max** function in Access. The query is run against *qryRSF3* and the maximum field is named *MaxAmount*. This name is shorter than the default name assigned by Access. This query will take longer to run than the preceding queries because the three queries

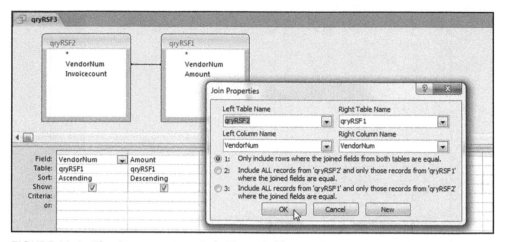

FIGURE 11.4 The Query to Keep Only Those Subsets with More than One Record

that precede this query need to be run first. The record count should match the record count for *qryRSF2*. The count of *Amount* is included in the final results. The next step is to identify the second largest amount in each subset. This would be straightforward if the second largest number was never equal to the largest number. The goal now is to identify the cases where the largest and second largest are equal and to calculate an RSF of 1.00 for these cases. The query to see whether any amounts are duplicated at all in the subset is shown in Figure 11.7.

The query in Figure 11.7 produces a table of all the duplicates in all the subsets. The last page of the results is shown in Figure 11.8.

VendorNum	Amount
2001	$330,596.59
2001	$283,969.14
2001	$112,211.04
2001	$109,857.21
2001	$109,857.21
001	$103,352.5

001	3,839.72
2001	$33,336.73
2001	$32,645.40
2001	$32,089.92
2001	$31,750.98
2001	$31,449.75
2001	$30,091.06

Record: ◄ ◄ 1 of 165257 ► ►ı 🔍 No Filter

FIGURE 11.5 The Data that Will Be Used to Calculate the RSFs

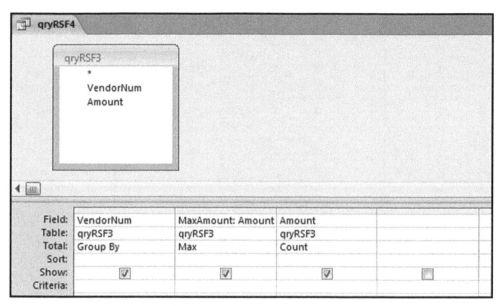

FIGURE 11.6 The Query Used to Identify the Largest (Maximum) Amount

The result of *qryRSF5* in Figure 11.8 shows all the cases of number duplication. The cases of interest are those cases where the maximum amount is duplicated. Our results in *qryRSF4* gives the maximum for each subset. The next step is to find all those instances where it was the maximum amount that was duplicated. It is here

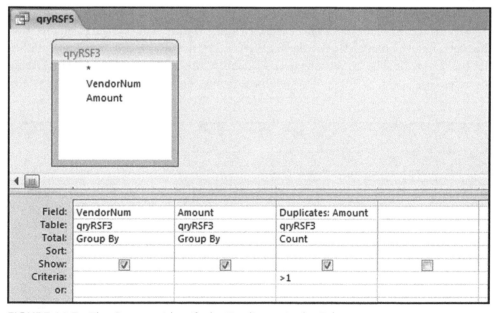

FIGURE 11.7 The Query to Identify the Duplicates in the Subsets

qryRSF5		
VendorNum ▾	Amount ▾	Duplicates ▾
21756	$100,000.00	2
21757	$25.00	3
21802	$219.00	4
21818	$173.20	2
21843	$129.00	4
21844	$250.00	2
21850	$2,739.00	2
21862	$26.07	2
21863	$235.87	3
21879	$384.00	2
21888	$30.00	5
21896	$199.95	2
21899	$250.00	2
21932	$500.00	2
21969	$114.54	3
22004	$5.76	3

FIGURE 11.8 The Last Page of the Query Identifying the Number Duplications

that our RSFs will equal 1.00 because the largest and second largest amounts are equal. This query takes some fancy footwork with a **Join** in Access.

The query to identify the subsets with RSFs of 1.00 is shown in Figure 11.9. The calculated field *RelativeSize* should be formatted as **Fixed** with two decimal places to keep the results neat and tidy. There are two joins in the query and both are the inner joins that are the first (default) option in **Join Properties**. This query needs to run all five of the prior queries.

Figure 11.10 shows a listing of vendors with RSFs equal to 1.00. The calculated RSF has been neatly formatted to two decimal places. The next step is the calculation of RSFs for the rest of the subsets. We now need to identify "the rest" of the subsets. This is done by removing the 1,313 RSF = 1.00 subsets (shown in Figure 11.10) from the data.

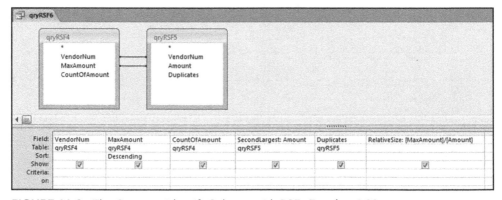

FIGURE 11.9 The Query to Identify Subsets with RSFs Equal to 1.00

qryRSF6					
VendorNum	MaxAmount	CountOfAmount	SecondLargest	Duplicates	RelativeSize
5806	$611,841.09	2198	$611,841.09	2	1.00
5710	$306,320.44	170	$306,320.44	2	1.00
2735	$283,125.00	68	$283,125.00	2	1.00
17256	$151,550.00	24	$151,550.00	2	1.00
2098	$150,000.00	6	$150,000.00	2	1.00
7005	$120,250.00	31	$120,250.00	8	1.00
2023	$102,648.06	40	$102,648.06	3	1.00
2175	$100,00	2	$100		
1571	$18,1		$1 .00	2	1.00
5241	$16,250.00	30	$16,250.00	2	1.00
15142	$14,847.92	12	$14,847.92	2	1.00
17836	$13,617.73	7	$13,617.73	2	1.00
2229	$13,130.00	31	$13,130.00	2	1.00
2478	$12,500.00	4	$12,500.00	2	1.00
3808	$11,211.46	3	$11,211.46	2	1.00
5640	$10,917.72	17	$10,917.72	5	1.00

Record: 1 of 1313 ▸ No Filter Search

FIGURE 11.10 Vendors with RSFs Equal to 1.00

The query to remove the subsets is still called a **Join**. The result of this **Join** will be a smaller data set.

Figure 11.11 shows the query used to remove the RSF = 1.00 vendors and their transactions from the data. The criteria **Is Null** is made up of two words separated by a space. The join is an outer join combined with the **Is Null** criteria. The **Show** box is unchecked for the third field, which means that our results will only show two fields. Running *qryRSF7* query leaves 153,167 records (result not shown). This record count equals the 165,257 records from *qryRSF3* minus the 12,090 records that were removed with *qryRSF7*. To calculate the number of records removed with *qryRSF6* requires a new query (not shown) that sums the *CountOfAmount* field in *qryRSF6*.

The next step is to calculate the RSFs for the subsets with RSFs larger than 1.00. The maximum *Amount* for each subset was calculated in *qryRSF4*. The next step is to

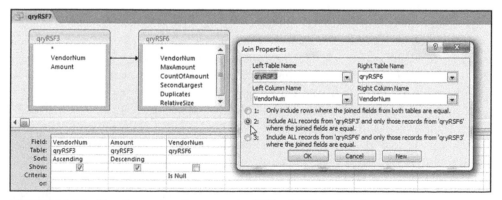

FIGURE 11.11 The Query that Removes the RSF = 1.00 Vendors from the Data

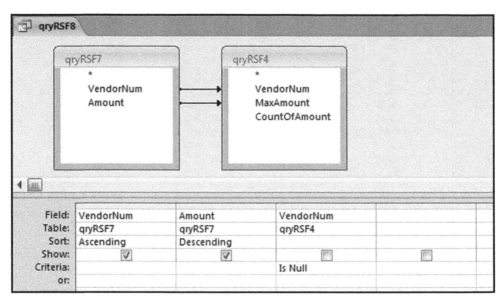

FIGURE 11.12   The Query that Removes the Maximum for Each Subset

remove all the maximums so that we can recalculate the maximum. The second maximum will be the second largest *Amount*. The query *qryRSF8* to remove the maximum (again involving a *Join*) is shown in Figure 11.12.

The query *qryRSF8* has two right-facing arrows and uses the **Is Null** criteria. The result is a table of 148,023 records (not shown), which reconciles with the previous queries. The query correctly removed the maximums of the subsets where the second largest amount was not equal to the maximum.

The next step is to identify the second largest number for each subset. We have removed the largest number, so the second largest number is the maximum amount for each subset. The query to extract the maximum, *qryRSF9*, is shown in Figure 11.13.

The query *qryRSF9* shown in Figure 11.13 calculates the second largest amount. The **MAX** function can be used because the largest *Amounts* were removed in the prior query. The results of *qryRSF9* are shown in Figure 11.14.

The second largest amounts for each subset are shown in Figure 11.14. The first entry agrees with Figure 11.5, which shows that the second largest amount for vendor 2001 is $283,969.14. There are only two more steps. The next query *qryRSF10* calculates the RSF for each subset. The setup and the formula is shown in Figure 11.15.

Figure 11.15 shows the query to calculate the RSFs for those subsets with RSFs larger than 1.00. The *RelativeSize* formula is quite simple being the maximum amount divided by the second largest amount. There is no need to cater for division by zero because the zero amounts were deleted quite early in the process. The *RelativeSize* field is formatted as Fixed with two decimal places. Access seems to accept sorting on this field even though it is a calculated field. This query will take a while to run because all the prior steps are run before the results can be displayed.

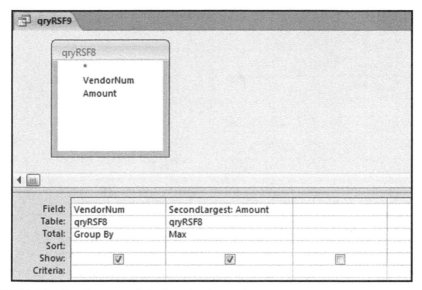

FIGURE 11.13 The Query to Calculate the Second Largest *Amount*

Figure 11.16 shows us the (almost final) set of results. The RSFs are sorted from largest to smallest and the maximum *Amount*, the second largest *Amount*, and the count for the subsets are shown as additional information.

We need one query to combine the results from *qryRSF10* (RSFs greater than 1) with *qryRSF6* showing the RSFs equal to 1.00. This is done with *qryRSF11*, which is constructed in two parts shown in Figure 11.17. The first step is to prepare a normal

qryRSF9	
VendorNum ▾	SecondLargest ▾
2001	$283,969.14
2002	$1,277.63
2004	$3,323.21
2005	$189.40
2006	$479.58
2007	$3,924.25
2008	$3 89.3
2022	$58,880.85
2026	$755.67
2027	$397.01
2028	$61.75
2029	$1,641.92
2030	$25,619.84

Record: I◀ ◀ 1 of 5144 ▶ ▶I ▶ No Filter Search

FIGURE 11.14 The Results of the Query that Calculates the Second Largest *Amount*

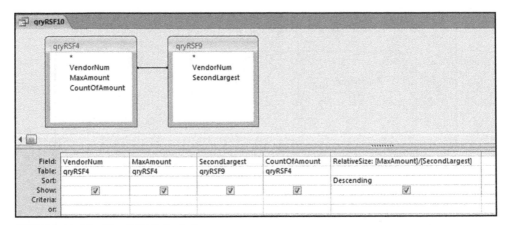

FIGURE 11.15 The RSF Calculation

Select query as is shown in the top panel, and then after switching to SQL view, the text in the box is updated.

Figure 11.17 shows the query used to combine the *qryRSF6* and *qryRSF10* results. The *RelativeSize* field in the top panel should be formatted as **Fixed** with 2 decimal places

VendorNum	MaxAmount	SecondLargest	CountOfAmount	RelativeSize
2398	$731,546.00	$29.95	4	24425.58
2450	$53,649.13	$20.45	3	2623.43
2971	$5,028.20	$7.08	2	710.20
5003	$1,607.29	$3.47	3	463.20
5769	$21,941.44	$53.25	4	412.05
3430	$4,451.13	$25.00	3	178.05
2865	$46,459.31	$313.04	8	148.41
3458	$1,509.50	$11.30	2	133.58
2135	$42,922.10	$345.82	17	124.12
16469	$9,530.73	$80.60	3	118.25
6547	$12,565.80	$108.00	4	116.35
20914	$667.00	$6.00	2	111.17
13604	$4,330.00	$42.87	2	101.00
4948	$500.00	$5.00	2	100.00
2567	$823.96	$9.28	2	88.79
8687	$764.47	$9.50	2	80.47
4302	$424.48	$5.60	2	75.80
7080	$1,385.00	$19.05	2	72.70
2900	$6,041.43	$84.50	2	71.50
12198	$3,500.00	$50.00	2	70.00
3524	$205,242.00	$3,025.00	3	67.85
13560	$352.10	$5.55	3	63.44
4863	$1,575.00	$25.00	4	63.00
13656	$508.78	$8.65	2	58.82
4388	$179.97	$3.06	2	58.81

Record: 1 of 5144   No Filter   Search

FIGURE 11.16 The Relative Size Factor Results

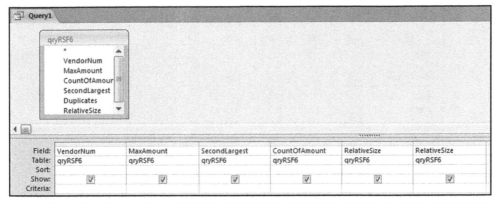

FIGURE 11.17 The Query to Combine the Results

before switching to SQL view. The SQL text added to the select query from the grid in the top panel is

```
UNION
SELECT qryRSF10.VendorNum, qryRSF10.MaxAmount, qryRSF10.SecondLargest,
    qryRSF10.CountOfAmount, qryRSF10.RelativeSize
FROM qryRSF10
ORDER BY RelativeSize DESC;
```

The results are the same as can be seen in Figure 11.16 except that the record count is now 6,457 records because we have combined the results from two queries. As a final touch another query can be used to select the records for a specified subset.

Figure 11.18 shows the query that is used to select all the transactions for a specified vendor. This type of query is called a parameter query. When the query is run, the user will be prompted to enter the vendor number ("Enter the Vendor Number" as is shown on the Criteria line). The records returned after entering 4863 are shown in Figure 11.19.

The follow-up investigations showed that the first vendor in Figure 11.16 was a payment for a land purchase. The large dollar amount was the cost of the land as paid to the title company and the other costs were small incidentals related to the purchase. The results in Figure 11.16 show a number of possible decimal point errors. These include the vendors with maximum amounts of $667.00, $4,330.00, $500.00, $1,385.00, $3,500.00, $205,242.00, and $1,575.00. There are also possible overpayments where the RSFs are exactly 10, 5, 4, 3, and 2. Also, any investigation should at least on a test basis look at the cases where the RSFs are

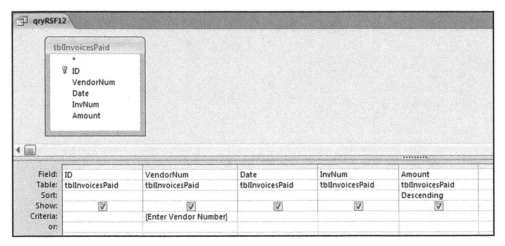

FIGURE 11.18 The Query to Select the Data for a Vendor

ID	VendorNum	Date	InvNum	Amount
79824	4863	2/7/2010	20710	$1,575.00
79825	4863	6/15/2010	61510	$25.00
79823	4863	1/31/2010	13100	$25.00
79822	4863	1/5/2010	10310	$20.00
(New)				

FIGURE 11.19 The Transactions for Vendor 4863

slightly above 1.00 (e.g., 1.01 or 1.02). The two largest invoices for a vendor could actually be the same invoice. The first invoice might include a shipping charge or a late fee and the second invoice might not have included the small additional amount.

Forensic investigators should focus on relatively large RSFs (usually shown at the top of the results table), RSFs where the dollar amount of the largest item is relatively high, and cases where the RSFs are a round number such as 100, 10, 5, 4, 3, 2, and 1.

 RUNNING THE RELATIVE SIZE FACTOR TEST IN EXCEL

It would seem that this test is more difficult to run in Excel than it is to run in Access. The test is only moderately complex in Excel mainly because Excel has the ability to look up (to the previous row) and down (to the next row) when performing calculations. This makes it quite easy to identify the largest and second largest amounts for a vendor provided that the table is sorted correctly. It is best to start with a new worksheet with only the invoices data. The worksheet sheet will look just like Figure 10.10. The first step

	VendorNum	Date	InvNum	Amount	E
184394	51219	3/1/2010	261433298013	$1.07	
184395	2001	7/14/2010	210938399207!	$1.06	
184396	2022	9/30/2010	580 2452J99	$1.06	
184397	7248	1/7/2010	05AT5300	$1.06	
184398	16559	8/4/2010	NV-38921	$1.05	
184399	4558	1/16/2010	1750696B00	$1.04	
184400	51134	3/1/2010	261537198416	$1.03	
184401	51495	2/1/2010	220162056414	$1.03	
184402	51889	5/1/2010	270951535748	$1.03	
184403	9293	1/26/2010	12610	$1.02	
184404	2004	6/4/2010	071105803001	$1.01	
184405	3136	1/18/2010	15235	$1.01	
184406	5063	6/8/2010	07117287/002	$1.01	
184407	3870	5/31/2010	53110	$1.00	
184408	6384	2/16/2010	639014	$1.00	
184409	6384	10/14/2010	626094	$1.00	
184410	12952	5/5/2010	050510	$1.00	
184411	16272	1/20/2010	11448	$1.00	
184412	20739	11/30/2010	R400523	$1.00	
184413	20794	12/22/2010	110810	$1.00	
184414	8294	11/18/2010	111810	$0.99	
184415	2004	7/6/2010	072881152/00:	$0.98	
184416	3630	10/26/2010	J3616501	$0.98	
184417	4132	4/10/2010	040700-C	$0.98	
184418	5848	3/8/2010	5295647	$0.98	
184419	14507	8/2/2010	072710	$0.98	
184420	6204	7/18/2010	268031	$0.96	
184421	6942	1/27/2010	12710	$0.96	
184422	8740	1/4/2010	10410	$0.96	
184423	3630	3/6/2010	AM852902	$0.95	

FIGURE 11.20 The Sorted *InvoicesPaid* Data

is to delete all the Amounts less than $1.00. This is done by sorting by *Amount* descending and then finding the first row where we have amounts equal to $0.99.

The row where the *Amounts* are less than $1.00 is shown in Figure 11.20. We will only run the RSF test using records that are ≥ 1.00. To keep only the $>=\$1.00$ records we simply delete the records less than $1.00. This is done by highlighting rows 184414 to 189471 and then deleting them.

The next step is to sort the worksheet so that we have the largest and second largest amounts as the first two amounts shown for every vendor. This is done using **Home→Editing→Sort&Filter→Custom Sort** followed by the options shown in Figure 11.21.

The sort procedure shown in Figure 11.21 lists the largest *Amount* for each vendor followed by the second largest *Amount*. The RSF calculation is now fairly straightforward except for the possibility that a vendor only has one record. The calculations will use several indicator variables along the way. The process will be started by adding a heading *Indic1* to column E. The first entry is the numeric value 1 in cell E2. The next step is to enter the formula shown in cell E3 in Figure 11.22 and then to copy this formula down to the last record (E184413).

The formula to count the number of records for each subset is shown in Figure 11.22. The formula used in E3 is

$$\textbf{E3:} = \text{IF}(\text{A3} = \text{A2}, \text{E2} + 1, 1)$$

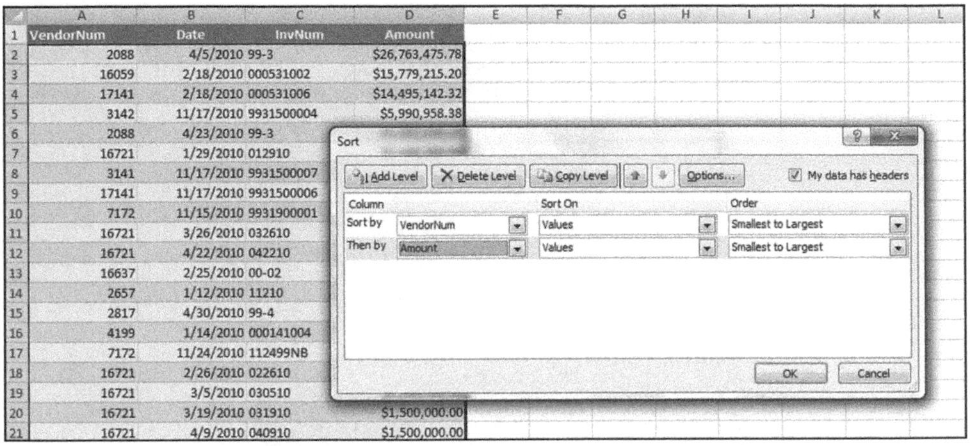

	VendorNum	Date	InvNum	Amount
2	2088	4/5/2010	99-3	$26,763,475.78
3	16059	2/18/2010	000531002	$15,779,215.20
4	17141	2/18/2010	000531006	$14,495,142.32
5	3142	11/17/2010	9931500004	$5,990,958.38
6	2088	4/23/2010	99-3	
7	16721	1/29/2010	012910	
8	3141	11/17/2010	9931500007	
9	17141	11/17/2010	9931500006	
10	7172	11/15/2010	9931900001	
11	16721	3/26/2010	032610	
12	16721	4/22/2010	042210	
13	16637	2/25/2010	00-02	
14	2657	1/12/2010	11210	
15	2817	4/30/2010	99-4	
16	4199	1/14/2010	000141004	
17	7172	11/24/2010	112499NB	
18	16721	2/26/2010	022610	
19	16721	3/5/2010	030510	
20	16721	3/19/2010	031910	$1,500,000.00
21	16721	4/9/2010	040910	$1,500,000.00

FIGURE 11.21 The Sort Procedure for the RSF Calculations

The *Indic1* formula gives us the count for each subset. The count is the largest *Indic1* value for the subset. We will use the *Indic1* count in the results. The next step is to copy the *Indic1* field and use the **Paste Special** feature to paste the formulas as values. We can now resort the field and still keep the maximums correctly calculated. This step converts the *Indic1* formulas to values. The next step is to sort the data table on *Vendor* Ascending and *Amount* Descending. The effect of these steps is that the largest and second largest amounts for each subset are shown first. The formula in column F will identify the largest and second largest amounts. The largest value for the first subset is always on the second row and so we can simply enter "1" in cell **F2**.

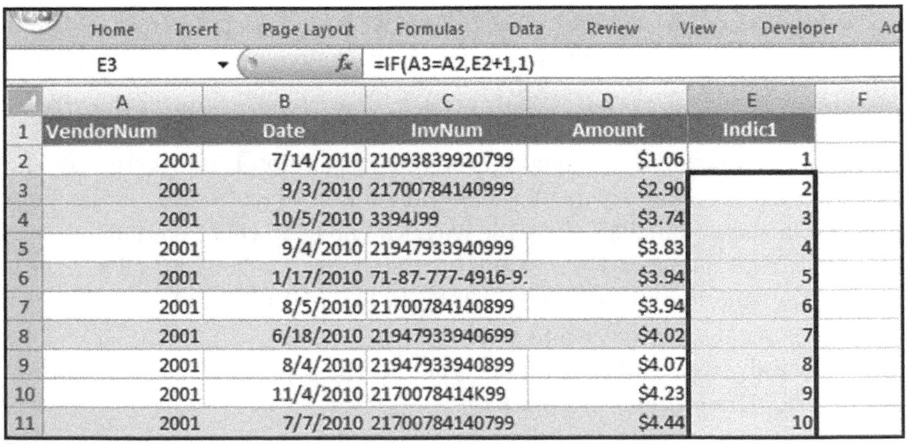

	VendorNum	Date	InvNum	Amount	Indic1
2	2001	7/14/2010	21093839920799	$1.06	1
3	2001	9/3/2010	21700784140999	$2.90	2
4	2001	10/5/2010	3394J99	$3.74	3
5	2001	9/4/2010	21947933940999	$3.83	4
6	2001	1/17/2010	71-87-777-4916-9:	$3.94	5
7	2001	8/5/2010	21700784140899	$3.94	6
8	2001	6/18/2010	21947933940699	$4.02	7
9	2001	8/4/2010	21947933940899	$4.07	8
10	2001	11/4/2010	2170078414K99	$4.23	9
11	2001	7/7/2010	21700784140799	$4.44	10

FIGURE 11.22 The Formula to Calculate the Count

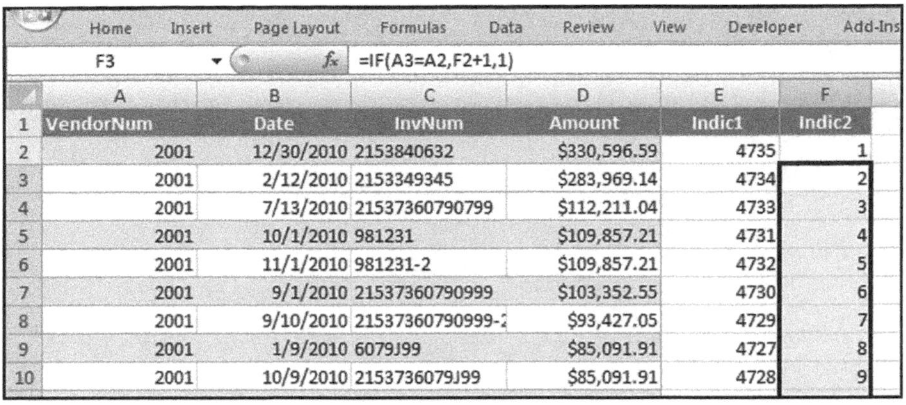

FIGURE 11.23 The Formula to Identify the Largest and Second Largest Amounts

The formula to identify the largest and second largest amounts is shown in Figure 11.23. The formula used in F3 is

$$\mathbf{F3}: =\mathrm{IF}(A3=A2,F2+1,1)$$

The rows of interest are those rows where *Indic2* equals 1 and the very next row if the *Indic2* value equals 2. Two 1s in succession in *Indic2* indicate that we have a subset with only one record. The second largest value can be identified by using a slightly complex AND function. This formula is shown in Figure 11.24.

Figure 11.24 shows the procedure to "lift" the second largest amount to the same row as the largest amount. The formula for column G in Figure 11.24 is

$$\mathbf{G2}: =\mathrm{IF}(\mathrm{AND}(A2=A3,F3=2),D3,"\ ")$$

The **G2** formula has actually been copied to the last row (cell G184413) in Figure 11.24. The reason that nothing is visible in cells G3:G11 above is that the

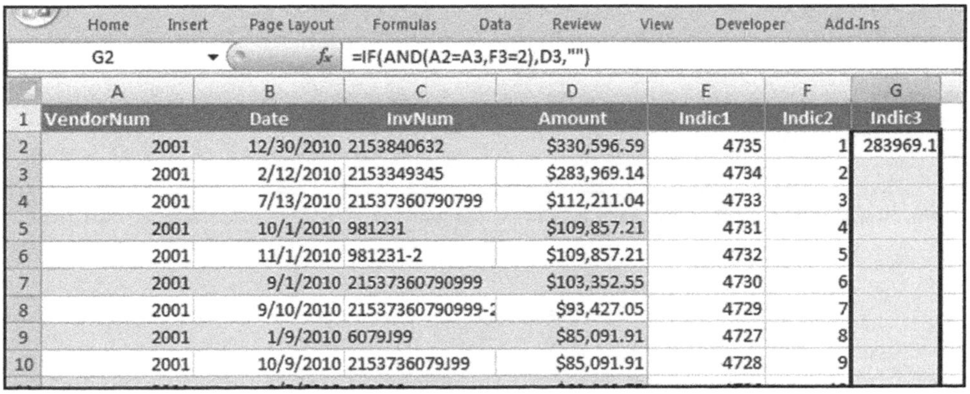

FIGURE 11.24 The Formula for the Second Largest *Amount*

	Home	Insert	Page Layout	Formulas	Data	Review	View	Developer	Add-Ins
	G2	▾		fx	1.02				

	A	B	C	D	E	F	G
1	VendorNum	Date	InvNum	Amount	Indic1	Indic2	Indic3
2	9293	8/2/2010	072710	$1.59	2	1	1.02
3	8779	3/17/2010	031600	$7.13	2	1	1.09
4	9291	7/14/2010	071310	$15.22	2	1	1.4
5	22015	4/3/2010	40300	$10.71	2	1	1.44
6	8271	12/16/2010	121610	$4.09	2	1	1.49
7	6796	3/11/2010	031110	$1.62	3	1	1.52
8	7042	12/9/2010	120610	$3.38	2	1	1.53
9	21293	2/28/2010	121310	$1.72	2	1	1.56
10	8241	11/24/2010	102610	$39.23	2	1	1.66

FIGURE 11.25 The Subsets and Their RSFs

formula shows a blank cell if the row is not the first row of a subset with more than one record. We have what we need. All the subsets of interest have a numeric value in column G. All the rows that are irrelevant have blanks (null values) in column G. The final steps involve some tidying up. We need to first change the formulas in column G to values using **Copy** and **Paste Special**. The data then needs to be sorted so that all the relevant results are shown first. This is done by sorting on column G and sorting from A to Z (this will put the blank cells at the bottom of the table).

Figure 11.25 shows the results of those subsets with valid RSFs at the top of the worksheet. The next step is to find the first blank cell in column G and delete all the rows in the table that are below this row. This is shown in Figure 11.26.

Figure 11.26 shows the first blank record that needs to be deleted. A quick way to highlight from row 6459 all the way down to the end is to use

	Home	Insert	Page Layout	Formulas	Data	Review	View	Developer	Add-Ins
	A6459	▾		fx	2001				

	A	B	C	D	E	F	G
6452	16637	2/25/2010	00-02	$1,755,217.76	30	1	1086001
6453	2817	4/30/2010	99-4	$1,631,560.69	43	1	1208343
6454	3142	11/17/2010	9931500004	$5,990,958.38	3	1	1488344
6455	7172	11/15/2010	9931900001	$2,000,000.00	7	1	1500000
6456	16721	1/29/2010	012910	$3,000,000.00	51	1	2000000
6457	17141	2/18/2010	000531006	$14,495,142.32	3	1	2209187
6458	2088	4/5/2010	99-3	$26,763,475.78	62	1	3069847
6459	2001	2/12/2010	2153349345	$283,969.14	4734	1	
6460	2001	7/13/2010	21537360790799	$112,211.04	4733	2	
6461	2001	10/1/2010	981231	$109,857.21	4731	3	
6462	2001	11/1/2010	981231-2	$109,857.21	4732	4	
6463	2001	9/1/2010	21537360790999	$103,352.55	4730	5	
6464	2001	9/10/2010	21537360790999-2	$93,427.05	4729	6	
6465	2001	1/9/2010	6079J99	$85,091.91	4727	7	

FIGURE 11.26 The End of the Relevant RSF Data

	A	B	C	D	E
1	VendorNum ▾	Amount ▾	SecondLargest ▾	Count ▾	RSF ▾
2	2398	$731,546.00	29.95	4	24425.58
3	2450	$53,649.13	20.45	3	2623.43
4	2971	$5,028.20	7.08	2	710.20
5	5003	$1,607.29	3.47	3	463.20
6	5769	$21,941.44	53.25	4	412.05
7	3430	$4,451.13	25	3	178.05
8	2865	$46,459.31	313.04	8	148.41
9	3458	$1,509.50	11.3	2	133.58
10	2135	$42,922.10	345.82	17	124.12
11	16469	$9,530.73	80.6	3	118.25
12	6547	$12,565.80	108	4	116.35
13	20914	$667.00	6	2	111.17
14	13604	$4,330.00	42.87	2	101.00
15	4948	$500.00	5	2	100.00
16	2567	$823.96	9.28	2	88.79
17	8687	$764.47	9.5	2	80.47
18	4302	$424.48	5.6	2	75.80
19	7080	$1,385.00	19.05	2	72.70
20	2900	$6,041.43	84.5	2	71.50
21	12198	$3,500.00	50	2	70.00
22	3524	$205,242.00	3025	3	67.85
23	13560	$352.10	5.55	3	63.44
24	4863	$1,575.00	25	4	63.00
25	13656	$508.78	8.65	2	58.82
26	4388	$179.97	3.06	2	58.81
27	7713	$1,169.34	20.02	2	58.41
28	8614	$3,444.76	60.7	69	56.75
29	6906	$489.35	8.71	2	56.18
30	3432	$17,375.62	312.64	7	55.58

I◀ ◀ ▶ ▶I InvoicesPaid

FIGURE 11.27 The Final RSF Results

Control+Shift+Down Arrow. A right click and Delete is all that is then needed to delete all that we do not need. It is possible to apply a filter to column G to display only the rows with numeric values greater than $0.99. Deleting the rows makes it easier to report the results in a very neat format. With a filter the unneeded rows are still there.

The worksheet includes some columns that can now be deleted. The next step is to rename *Indic1* to *Count*. *Indic3* should be renamed *SecondLargest*. *Amount* should be renamed *Largest*. The date and invoice number fields should be deleted. The *Indic2* field can also be deleted. The RSF needs to be calculated using equation 11.1.

The final results are shown in Figure 11.27. The table has been formatted using **Home→Styles→Format As Table** with a Table Style Medium 2 applied. This style automatically adds the filters on the first row. The table was also formatted as Calibri 11 points throughout.

SUMMARY

This chapter introduces, discusses, and demonstrates the Relative Size Factor (RSF) test. This test is a powerful test for detecting errors and fraud. The test identifies subsets where the largest (and perhaps the smallest) amounts seem to be out of line with the other amounts for that subset. The large difference could be because the record either (a) actually belongs to another subset, or (b) belongs to the subset in question, but the numeric amount was incorrectly recorded.

The RSF test was developed as a result of a case where a company wired a large amount of money to the bank account of a charity in error. The funds were supposed to go to a vendor. The amount was significantly more than any amount that had been donated to the charity before. Had the company run a reasonableness test before initiating the transfer, it would have seen that the amount was way out of line with any amount previously sent to the charity. This test has led to large recoveries in accounts payable audits. The test has also found interesting forensic results in an investigation of sales numbers, insurance claim payments, inventory numbers, and health care claims.

The RSF test identifies subsets where one amount is significantly larger than the other items in the subset. The formula identifies the largest amount in a subset and divides it by the second largest amount. The RSF report usually includes (a) the subset name or number, (b) the largest amount for the subset, (c) the second largest amount for the subset, (d) the record count for the subset, and (e) the relative size factor. This test has most often been run using the largest and second largest numbers in the various subsets. Investigators can adapt this formula to (a) the largest amount divided by the average amount, (b) the largest divided by the average where the average excludes the largest number and (c) the smallest number divided by the average (which is used when looking for understatements).

The RSF test can be run in Access. The process is a bit tedious and it takes a series of 11 queries. The first steps delete all amounts less than 1.00 and those subsets with only one transaction. The next step is to identify all the subsets where the largest amount is also coincidentally also the second largest amount. These subsets have RSFs equal to 1.00. The next step is to identify both the largest and the second largest *Amounts* for the remaining subsets. The final steps involve calculating the RSFs, preparing the final report, and combining the RSF equal to 1.00 and the RSFs greater than 1.00 reports. The Access queries can be reused on other data tables with the same field names. The RSF test is surprisingly easier to program in Excel.

CHAPTER TWELVE

Identifying Fraud Using Abnormal Duplications within Subsets

T HE TESTS IN THIS chapter are based on the assumption that excessive duplications within subsets are indicators of fraud and errors. Because there is always going to be some amount of *normal duplication*, and some level of *abnormal duplication* we have to review our results carefully to find the duplications that are there because of errors or fraud. Another way to focus on important results is to only look at duplications above a dollar threshold. The goal is to run tests where abnormal duplications are reasonably reliable indicators of fraud or errors.

The first test described in the chapter is a straightforward test to find duplicate records. Although duplicate payments with all fields being the same are rare in accounts payable, it is possible for duplicates to arise in other situations. For example, an employee might duplicate a purchase using a purchasing card. The second test is a little more complex in that we are looking for partial duplicates. The most valuable results from the partial duplicates test has been from identifying cases of the (a) same dollar amounts, (b) same date, (c) same invoice number, and (d) different vendors. These errors occur when the wrong vendor is paid first and the correct vendor is paid later. The third test quantifies the level of duplication within a subset. Subsets are then ranked according to their duplication measures. A formula is used to calculate the duplication measure.

The tests in this chapter are all are aimed at finding duplicates or near-duplicates within subsets. The subset duplication tests are demonstrated using the *InvoicesPaid* data table. The Access and the Excel steps needed to run the tests are demonstrated with explanations and screen shots. The tests are easier to run in Excel even though Access has some helpful duplication-related wizards.

THE SAME-SAME-SAME TEST

The *same-same-same* test is the most basic of the within-subset duplication tests. The goal of this test is to identify exact duplicates. The test is called the same-same-same test regardless of how many fields are used to determine whether the records are duplicates. In the *InvoicesPaid* data table, the test was used to identify:

> The same *Amount*
> The same *Date*
> The same *Invoice Number*
> The same *Vendor*

Some creativity by the forensic investigator is needed to identify what would be an odd match. In one project an odd match could be an inventory file with the same product number and the same quantity on hand. In another project it could be the same frequent-flyer number getting the same mileage amount deposited twice in the same day (and not equal to the 500-mile minimum). In another project it could be a member of a hotel's preferred guest club staying at different hotels on the same date. In a warranty claims table it could be the same car showing the same odometer reading on two different dates. In an airline baggage claims table it could be multiple claims from the same address (although this was found to be normal in Puerto Rico where entire streets of people all have their mail delivered to one address, being the equivalent of a very big mailbox for the whole street). In another project it could be two candidates in an election getting the same number of votes in a precinct. In purchasing card data it could be cases where the same card has the same dollar amount charged more than once on the same date (which usually turns out to be a split purchase to keep under the control threshold). The person running the forensic analytics tests needs some creativity to create a test to identify duplicates that are anomalies. The same-same-same test, together with a little creativity, has been used to find abnormal duplicates in data tables relating to:

- Accounts payable
- Health insurance payments
- Property and casualty insurance payments
- Employee reimbursements
- Customer refunds
- Inventory
- Fixed assets
- Payroll files

Financial managers often claim that their systems have built-in checks for duplicate payments. Even if this is so, it is still important to actually test the controls. Duplicate payments could be frauds and are more likely to occur when the company has just started a new fiscal year, has changed accounts payable (AP) systems, or has acquired an entity and assumes responsibility for the AP function after the date of acquisition.

One international conglomerate had several unconnected SAP systems for accounts payable. It was possible that one system processed the payment correctly and that payment was duplicated on another one of their systems.

 ## THE SAME-SAME-DIFFERENT TEST

The same-same-different test is a powerful test for errors and fraud. This test should be considered for every forensic analytics project. A few years ago an airline auditor reported at an IATA conference that his airline had found errors of about $1 million as a result of running this test on their accounts payable data. This was the same auditor mentioned in Chapter 10. His results were therefore $1 million from the RSF tests and another $1 million from the same-same-different test. In a recent forensic investigation of purchasing cards at a utility company this test showed several instances where two employees split the same purchase using *different* cards. This was a clever twist to the usual splitting the purchase and putting the charge on the same card. In the *InvoicesPaid* data table the test was used to identify:

The same *Amount*
The same *Date*
The same *Invoice Number*
Different *Vendors*

The test is called the same-same-different (abbreviated SSD) test regardless of how many fields are used to determine whether the records are near-duplicates. The usual test is run such that the *different* field is a subset field. We are therefore looking for transactions that are linked to two different subsets. The assumption is that one of the transactions is an error and should not have been linked to the second (different subset). The usual SSD report is to have each matching case on two rows in the results table. Some notes on the results and findings are outlined below.

- This test always detects errors in accounts payable data. The largest single error detected to date was for $104,000.
- The errors detected by the SSD test occur because the wrong vendor is paid first and then the correct vendor is paid afterwards (presumably after calling and asking for payment). Most system controls check to see whether that exact invoice was paid to the correct vendor but they seldom check the details against payments to other vendors.
- Organizations are at a higher risk for this type of error when vendors have multiple vendor numbers. Multiple vendor numbers are a control weakness and open the door for duplicate payments to that vendor.
- The likelihood of having detected duplicate payments is higher when the two vendor numbers are similar. For example, vendor #78461 and vendor #78416 suggests a keypunch error.

- Increasing the number of *sames*, to perhaps SSSSD is useful for very large data files where SSD or SSSD yields thousands of matches and forensic investigators want a smaller initial sample of highly likely errors. In a forensic investigation at a large conglomerate, an additional field (purchase order #) was added to the test to keep the number of matches to a manageable size.
- If an investigation shows many such duplicate payments, the forensic report should suggest system improvements to reduce the chances of this happening again.
- This test also works well to detect the same invoice being paid by different payment processing locations. Here the *different* field would be a processing location indicator.

The longer the time period, the higher the chances of SSD detecting errors. For any short period (say July 2011) it is possible that one payment was made in the month of July and the second payment was made in either June or August.

The logic to running these tests is not overly complex in Access. It is a little bit challenging to keep the relevant records together in the report. The match could be that we have two invoices for $1,964 on 11/03 for Vendor #83 and one invoice for $1,964 on 11/03 for vendor #34. The report should show that there are two invoices for Vendor #83 and one invoice for Vendor #34. This is a little complex in Access.

 THE SUBSET NUMBER DUPLICATION TEST

The Subset Number Duplication (SND) test identifies excessive number duplication within subsets. This test works well in situations where excessive number duplication might signal that the numbers have been invented which might be a red flag for fraud. For example, assume that we have 30 state lotteries that require players to choose 6 numbers out of 49. In a data table of the winning numbers for each state we would expect an equal amount of number duplication in each of the 30 subsets. Each possible number should occur with a frequency of 1/49 for each subset. Abnormal duplications of any single number would indicate that the winning numbers were not random. The SND test could also be used with inventory data sets or election results where an excess of specific numbers might signal double-counting. This test uses the Nigrini Number Frequency Factor (NFF), which measures the extent of number duplication for each subset. This test was developed in my Ph.D. dissertation and was used to identify excessive duplications on tax returns. The formula is shown in Equation 12.1:

$$\text{Number Frequency Factor} = \frac{\sum c_i^2}{n^2} \qquad (12.1)$$

where c_i is the count for a number where the count is greater than 1 (a count of 1 shows no duplication, only numbers that occur more than once are duplicated), and n is the number of records for the subset. Assume that a subset had the following numeric values, 505, 505, 505, 505, 505, 1103, 1103, 64, 37. The NFF would then be calculated as

$$\text{Number Frequency Factor} = \frac{5^2 + 2^2}{9^2} \tag{12.2}$$

The calculation in Equation 12.2 shows 5^2 and 2^2 in the numerator. This is because 505 occurred five times and 1103 occurred twice in the data, hence the $5^2 + 2^2$. There were nine records in the subset, which is why the denominator is 9^2. The more the tendency toward all the numbers being the *same* (by increasing the 505s) the more the NFF will tend toward 1.00. If all the numbers are the same, the NFF will equal 1.00. If all the numbers were different, then the NFF would equal zero because the numerator will equal zero.

This test has detected a situation where an oil refinery's purchasing department purchased boots for employees (for around $40) repeatedly from the same supplier. Not only was boot use excessive but this was a case where the items could have been purchased in bulk and withdrawn from supplies as and when needed. In the same forensic investigation, the test detected excessive duplication in a vendor providing $600 helicopter rides to an oil rig. The view of the investigators was that employees that enjoy helicopter rides should pay for the rides with their own funds.

The SND test always finds repeated payments to the same supplier. In many cases these repeated payments are not always frauds or errors. For example, the test identified vendors where child support or alimony was paid to collection agencies (after being deducted from employee paychecks). The investigators then checked that the deductions were in fact being made from the employee paychecks. It would be a clever fraud if an employee in accounts payable got the company to pay their alimony payments without any deductions from their paychecks.

This test is open to some innovative twists. In one case it was used with purchasing card data where the card number and the date were concatenated (merged into one field). In Access the calculated field would, for example, be [CardNumber] & [Date]. The test identified cases where an employee made repeated purchases for the same dollar amount on a specific date. The most extreme case was an employee that made four payments of $2,500 to the same vendor (a hotel) on the same date. The amount of $2,500 was the dollar limit for card purchases and the four $2,500 purchases was really one $10,000 purchase.

A national office supplies and office services retailer ran this test against their sales data. The subset variable was employee number and the numeric amount was the total sales amount for each individual sale. The goal was to find employees who were repeatedly ringing up sales for (say) $0.10 and pocketing the difference between the real sales amount (say $16.00) and $0.10. The test identified several fraudulent cashiers.

Running the SND test is complicated in Access and requires a Join and the use of the Min and Max functions. Running this test in both Access and Excel is good practice for other complicated tests and queries. The test requires the forensic investigator to (a) Group By subset and also to identify the Minimum, Maximum, Count, and Sum for each subset, (b) to Count the number of times that each *Amount* occurs in each subset, (c) to square the count only when the count is greater than 1, (d) to Sum the squared counts for each subset, and (e) to link (a) and (d) using a Join. The final step is to sort the results in the report.

RUNNING THE SAME-SAME-SAME TEST IN ACCESS

Access has a *Find Duplicates Query Wizard*, which works well for this reasonably straightforward test. A problem with this wizard is that the duplicates are shown on two lines, and the triplicates on three lines and so forth. This causes a large results table for large data sets. The preferred method is to use **Group By** routines that will be good practice for other similar tests. The tests will be run on the *InvoicesPaid* data table. The test is designed to identify:

The same *Amount*
The same *Date*
The same invoice number (*InvNum*)
The same vendor (*VendorNum*)

Figure 12.1 shows the Access query that highlights the cases of the same vendor, date, invoice number, and amount. This query is preferred over the Find Duplicates Query Wizard and it also allows us to enter criteria such as ≥100 to keep the results table to a manageable size. We also have greater control on how the results are displayed (the order of the fields and the sort). The results are shown in Figure 12.2.

qrySSS1

tblInvoicesPaid

ID
VendorNum
Date
InvNum
Amount

Field:	VendorNum	Date	InvNum	Amount	Amount	Amount
Table:	tblInvoicesPaid	tblInvoicesPaid	tblInvoicesPaid	tblInvoicesPaid	tblInvoicesPaid	tblInvoicesPaid
Total:	Group By	Group By	Group By	Count	Group By	Where
Sort:				Descending	Descending	
Show:	✓	✓	✓	✓	✓	
Criteria:				>1		>=100
or:						

FIGURE 12.1 The Query to Identify the Same Vendor, Date, Invoice Number, and Amount

VendorNum ▾	Date ▾	InvNum ▾	CountOfAmount ▾	Amount ▾
20885	12/8/2010	120810	4	$178.92
4239	1/13/2010	GOM011599	4	$154.39
16804	1/1/2010	LV RENTS	3	$38,710.36
17256	1/20/2010	44004	3	$9,220.01
17256	12/20/2010	43749	3	$9,145.76
7492	1/16/2010	20153	3	$1,546.98
5063	11/20/2010	580338901	3	$1,338.83
3630	9/13/2010	D7519401	3	$1,009.88
5930	3/9/2010	532090	3	$964.40
5178	7/26/2010	042907JJ	3	$300.00
5178	7/26/2010	E4-2314	3	$285.00
6718	3/7/2010	30700	3	$283.38
5063	11/23/2010	48140858	3	$248.59
5063	11/10/2010	57235729	3	$230.47
2865	3/20/2010	78279A	3	$212.64
3833	2/8/2010	19616	3	$203.89

Record: ◄ ‹ 1 of 1597 ► ► ◄ No Filter | Search

FIGURE 12.2 The Results of the Same-Same-Same Test

The results in Figure 12.2 show a large number of duplications. The results are sorted by the *Count* descending and then by the *Amount* descending. Amounts less than $100 are not included in the results to keep the results table to a manageable size.

RUNNING THE SAME-SAME-DIFFERENT TEST IN ACCESS

Access has a *Find Unmatched Query Wizard* that works reasonably well for the same-same-different test. A problem with this wizard is that we get some strange results when we have a group of three invoices with two of them being for the same vendor and the third invoice being for a different vendor. For example, we might have a pattern of *x-y-z*, *x-y-z*, and *x-y-k* in that we have three transactions of which two are Same-Same-Same and the third one differs in a Same-Same-Different (SSD) way from the first two invoices. The Access wizards do not report the whole story. The preferred method is to use Group By and Join routines that will be good practice for other similar tests. The test shown below is designed to identify

The same *Amount*
The same *Date*
The same invoice number (*InvoiceNum*)
Different vendors (*VendorNum*)

The first query identifies all the cases where we have the same *Amount*, the same *Date*, and the same *InvNum*. The *VendorNum* field will be used in the next query. The first query is shown in Figure 12.3.

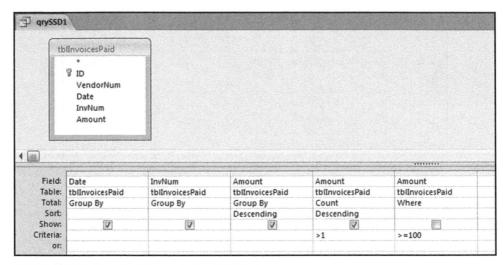

FIGURE 12.3 The First Query in the SSD Test

The query *qrySSD1* in Figure 12.3 identifies all the groups of interest as the first step in the SSD test. The results show that we have 2,111 cases where we have the same *Date*, the same *InvNum*, and the same *Amount*. In some of these groups the vendors will be the same and in some cases the vendors are different (in which case they are exactly what we are looking for in this SSD test). The next query lists all of the transactions of these groups. The query to do this uses a somewhat complex **Join**. The second query is shown in Figure 12.4.

Figure 12.4 shows the transactions of the groups with the same amounts, dates, and invoice numbers.

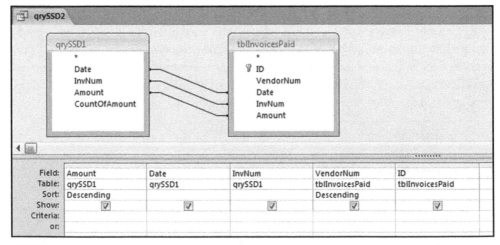

FIGURE 12.4 The Transactions that Match on Date, Amount, and Invoice Numbers

Amount	Date	InvNum	VendorNum	ID
$718,765.79	1/31/2010	00-01	16637	170735
$718,765.79	1/31/2010	00-01	16637	170736
$611,841.09	12/23/2010	587102	5806	112231
$611,841.09	12/23/2010	587102	5806	112232
$518,518.78	1/31/2010	99-12A	16637	170734
$518,518.78	1/31/2010	99-12A	16637	170733
$339,631.30	2/4/2010	351001	6118	122239
$339,631.30	2/4/2010	351001	6118	122238
$306,320.44	3/4/2010	171801221	5710	104942
$306,320.44	3/4/2010	171801221	5710	104943
$151,550.00	2/7/2010	44145	17256	172952
$151,550.00	2/7/2010	44145	17256	172953
$120,250.00	2/1/2010	020110A	7005	137101
$120,250.00	2/1/2010	020110A	7005	137100
$118,933.35	1/27/2010	171417141	5710	104897
$118,933.35	1/27/2010	171417141	5710	104898
$102,648.06	11/4/2010	170575615	5710	105026
$102,648.06	11/4/2010	170575615	5710	105025
$102,648.06	11/23/2010	170794026	5710	105031
$102,648.06	11/23/2010	170794026	5710	105032
$100,000.00	3/15/2010	31500	21756	181040
$100,000.00	3/15/2010	31500	21756	181039
$87,217.56	6/24/2010	62410	3288	34018
$87,217.56	6/24/2010	62410	3287	34017
$63,418.32	10/1/2010	100110	7005	137121

Record: I◄ ◄ 1 of 4355 ► ►I ⟩ ☒ No Filter | Search

FIGURE 12.5 The Results of the Matching Transactions

The second query *qrySSD2* has extracted all the transactions of interest and the results are shown in Figure 12.5. In some cases the vendor numbers are the same and in some cases, they are different. In Figure 12.5 it can be seen that the first case of the vendor numbers being different is for the amount of $87,217.56, which is shown near the bottom of the table in Figure 12.5.

The next step is to get Access to identify those cases where the vendor numbers are different. This would be reasonably straightforward if we always had groups of two transactions and the vendor numbers were either always the same or always different. The issue, though, is to also identify cases where we have groups of three (or more) and two (or more) of the vendor numbers are the same and one is different. The programming logic will use the fact that for groups of three or more the first vendor number will differ from the last vendor number. The next step is to look at the groups and to identify the first vendor, the last vendor, and to indicate if they are equal. This is shown in Figure 12.6.

The query uses the First and Last functions in Access. The field names *VNF* and *VNL* are abbreviations for "Vendor Number First" and "Vendor Number Last." The next step is to check whether the first and last vendor numbers are equal. This is done using an indicator variable in *qrySSD4* as is shown in Figure 12.7.

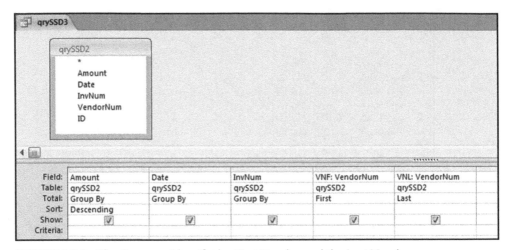

FIGURE 12.6   The Query to Identify the First Vendor and the Last Vendor

The query *qrySSSD4* in Figure 12.7 uses an indicator variable to indicate whether the transaction groups have different starting and ending vendor numbers. The groups with different starting and ending numbers are our subsets of interest. The result of *qrySSD4* is a table with 537 records. Each of these records represents a transaction group. The final query gets back to the original transactions so that we can see the details for the groups on successive lines (some groups have three records and others might even have four records).

The final step is the *qrySSD5* query shown in Figure 12.8. This query goes back to the second query and "fetches" the transaction details. The results are shown in Figure 12.9.

The results of the SSD test in Figure 12.9 show many possible recoverable errors. The sum of the *Amount* field for all 1,173 records is $1.65 million and on the basis that

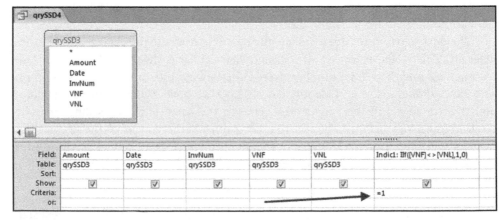

FIGURE 12.7   The Query to Calculate Whether the First and Last Vendor Numbers Are Equal

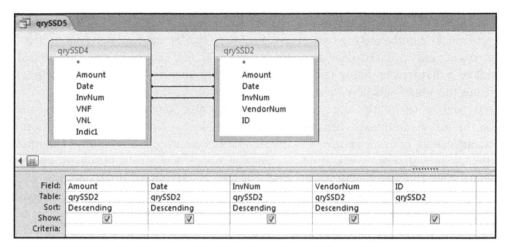

FIGURE 12.8 The Final Query to Find the Same-Same-Different Transactions

one payment is probably correct and the other payment in each group is possibly an error, we have identified about $800,000 in possible overpayments. There is a duplication of $23,500 with invoice WSTC49 and a duplication of $16,650 with invoice

Amount	Date	InvNum	VendorNum	ID
$87,217.56	6/24/2010	62410	3288	34018
$87,217.56	6/24/2010	62410	3287	34017
$44,783.42	6/8/2010	121800	5698	104648
$44,783.42	6/8/2010	121800	3013	30868
$29,689.42	12/31/2010	501	6297	124420
$29,689.42	12/31/2010	501	4404	66612
$26,153.00	7/1/2010	Q506190	3323	34161
$26,153.00	7/1/2010	Q506190	3012	30806
$23,500.00	10/1/2010	WSTC049	4277	64485
$23,500.00	10/1/2010	WSTC049	4276	64429
$18,446.00	6/21/2010	6963782	3323	34155
$18,446.00	6/21/2010	6963782	3012	30803
$16,650.00	10/5/2010	WSTC52	4277	64486
$16,650.00	10/5/2010	WSTC52	4276	64431
$15,000.00	7/8/2010	3248-02	3428	34574
$15,000.00	7/8/2010	3248-02	2716	25405
$14,861.00	6/26/2010	6973550	3323	34156
$14,861.00	6/26/2010	6973550	3012	30804
$14,018.58	12/7/2010	323447	8995	146226
$14,018.58	12/7/2010	323447	6020	120280
$13,023.78	8/3/2010	100630	5290	95376
$13,023.78	8/3/2010	100630	4449	71770
$11,237.52	5/8/2010	V595994	3013	30852
$11,237.52	5/8/2010	V595994	2922	29798
$10,975.04	4/30/2010	5519392	4449	71753

Record: I◄ ◄ 1 of 1173 ► ►I ✝ No Filter Search

FIGURE 12.9 The Results of the Same-Same-Different Test

number WSTC52. These errors seem to be related and it seems that accounts payable personnel might be making several errors between two similar looking vendors. These errors are easy to make when a vendor is perhaps an international conglomerate with different divisions operating out of the same building (hence the same street address), using the same stationery, and selling similar products. If the invoice image can be retrieved then identifying the errors is made much easier. Some of the duplications could be the result of a fraud where an accounts payable employee purposefully pays the wrong vendor (who they know) and then pays the correct vendor. To look for abnormal duplications of vendors would require another query. The results of this query (not shown) are that one vendor does indeed appear in the results 17 times and two other vendors appear in the results 16 times. The transactions for these vendors require some additional scrutiny.

RUNNING THE SUBSET NUMBER DUPLICATION TEST IN ACCESS

The SND test requires a series of queries. Our results table will show some subset details together with the calculated NFF for each subset. Those subsets with the most duplication (where all the numbers are the same) are shown at the top of the results table. The first query shown in Figure 12.10 collects some of the statistics shown in the results table.

The results of query *qryNFF1* in Figure 12.10 show that there are 9,424 vendors with amounts $\geq\$100$. The $>=100$ criteria limits the results to duplications that might be worth investigating. Other forensic investigations using this test on small dollar amounts in purchasing card data found that the duplications were related to cafeteria meals for $6.25 and parking charges when employees at another location came to the head office building for meetings. Small dollar duplications are discarded in large data tables to keep the results to a manageable size. The next query starts

qryNFF1

tblInvoicesPaid

* ID
VendorNum
Date
InvNum
Amount

Field:	VendorNum	MinAmount: Amount	MaxAmount: Amount	Count: Amount	Sum: Amount	Amount
Table:	tblInvoicesPaid	tblInvoicesPaid	tblInvoicesPaid	tblInvoicesPaid	tblInvoicesPaid	tblInvoicesPaid
Total:	Group By	Min	Max	Count	Sum	Where
Sort:					Descending	
Show:	☑	☑	☑	☑	☑	☐
Criteria:						>=100
or:						

FIGURE 12.10 The Query that Calculates the Statistics for the Final Results Table

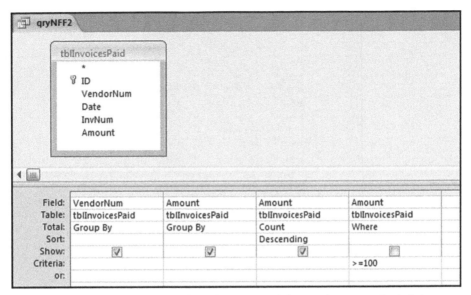

FIGURE 12.11 The Query to Calculate the Extent of the Duplication in Each Subset

the work needed to calculate the NFF values using the formula in Equation 12.1. The first step is to count how many times each different amount is used in a subset and this query is shown in Figure 12.11.

The query *qryNFF2* in Figure 12.11 calculates the count for each *Amount* in a subset. The results are sorted by the *Count* descending, which gives us an early view of the duplications.

Figure 12.12 shows the duplications in the subsets. These results tie in with some previous findings. The first-order test in Chapter 5 indicated that we had an excess of number with first-two digits 50, 11, 10, 98, 90, and 92 with a slightly smaller spike at the psychological threshold of 99. The results in Figure 12.12 show many amounts with these first-two digits. The results in Figure 12.12 show the exact numbers and also show that many of these duplications occurred in the same subset. The last-two digits test indicated that we had an excess of numbers ending in 00, 50, 35, 40, 45, and 25. The results in Figure 12.12 show many numbers with last-two digits of 35, 40, and 45. These early results also show that we have lots of duplications for vendor 6661 with five of the first six rows having duplications for this vendor.

To calculate the NFF we need to square the *CountOfAmount* when the count is larger than 1 for the c^2 term in the numerator of Equation 12.1. This condition requires the use of the Immediate If function and the query is shown in Figure 12.13.

The Counts are squared using the *qryNFF3* query in Figure 12.13. The formula is as follows:

$$\text{CountSq: } \text{IIf}([\text{CountOfAmount}] > 1, [\text{CountOfAmount}]^{\wedge}2, 0)$$

qryNFF2		
VendorNum ▾	Amount ▾	CountOfAmount ▾
17637	$1,153.35	1373
6661	$1,159.35	940
6661	$1,153.35	890
6661	$988.35	690
6661	$994.35	619
6661	$1,318.35	560
3690	$1,018.30	500
17637	$1,118.40	364
16513	$1,083.45	337
17637	$988.35	320
3657	$150.00	287
16542	$898.50	278
17637	$1,083.45	275
5564	$1,054.25	271
16513	$928.45	263
3690	$1,024.30	261
17487	$868.55	243
5956	$1,083.45	242
5928	$928.45	234
5930	$964.40	233
3690	$1,120.30	202
14720	$1,118.40	176
16492	$928.45	171
5928	$934.45	160
17637	$1,013.55	127

Record: I◄ ◄ 1 of 83209 ► ►I ☒ No Filter | Search

FIGURE 12.12 The Largest Counts for the Subsets

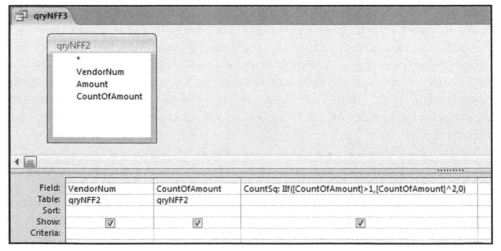

FIGURE 12.13 The Query to Square the Counts

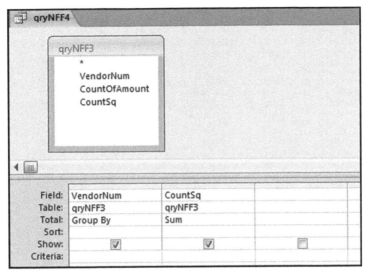

FIGURE 12.14 The Query to Sum the *CountSq* Values

The result of the *CountSq* formula will be a *CountSq* of zero for a count of 1 and a *CountSq* of the count squared for counts larger than 1. The next step is to Sum the *CountSq* values. This is done using the query shown in Figure 12.14.

The sums of the *CountSq* values are calculated using the query *qryNFF4* shown in Figure 12.14. The query works well because there is a record for each vendor, even if the sum is zero. The results show 9,424 vendors, which agrees with the results of *qryNFF1*. It is important to check that no subsets or records get lost along the way in a series of queries. The final NFF calculation is to combine the results of the first and fourth queries and this is done in Figure 12.15.

The query to calculate the final NFF scores is shown in Figure 12.15. The NFF calculation is as follows:

$$\text{NFF: } [\text{SumOfCountSq}]/[\text{Count}]^{\wedge}2)$$

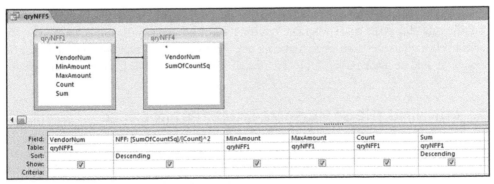

FIGURE 12.15 The Query to Calculate the Final NFF Scores

qryNFF5					
VendorNum ▾	NFF ▾	MinAmount ▾	MaxAmount ▾	Count ▾	Sum ▾
21756	1.000	$100,000.00	$100,000.00	2	$200,000.00
15817	1.000	$25,000.00	$25,000.00	2	$50,000.00
6092	1.000	$3,266.00	$3,266.00	15	$48,990.00
4720	1.000	$3,000.00	$3,000.00	16	$48,000.00
6091	1.000	$2,870.83	$2,870.83	16	$45,933.28
9508	1.000	$3,203.70	$3,203.70	14	$44,851.80
16732	1.000	$3,800.00	$3,800.00	11	$41,800.00
6102	1.000	$2,600.00	$2,600.00	16	$41,600.00
4186	1.000	$2,318.75	$2,318.75	16	$37,100.00
4514	1.000	$1,800.00	$1,800.00	16	$28,800.00
4234	1.000	$3,600.00	$3,600.00	8	$28,800.00
5605	1.000	$8,084.29	$8,084.29	3	$24,252.87
5536	1.000	$1,250.00	$1,250.00	16	$20,000.00
5355	1.000	$1,900.00	$1,900.00	10	$19,000.00
4556	1.000	$1,125.00	$1,125.00	15	$16,875.00
5158	1.000	$1,000.00	$1,000.00	16	$16,000.00
3767	1.000	$990.00	$990.00	16	$15,840.00
3953	1.000	$7,822.56	$7,822.56	2	$15,645.12
7453	1.000	$7,750.00	$7,750.00	2	$15,500.00
6259	1.000	$7,680.00	$7,680.00	2	$15,360.00
4826	1.000	$900.00	$900.00	16	$14,400.00
3072	1.000	$7,143.00	$7,143.00	2	$14,286.00
3071	1.000	$1,350.00	$1,350.00	9	$12,150.00
14793	1.000	$6,000.00	$6,000.00	2	$12,000.00
6738	1.000	$742.00	$742.00	16	$11,872.00
Record: ◄ 1 of 9424 ► ►| 🔾 No Filter Search					

FIGURE 12.16 The Results of the Number Duplication Test

The results are shown in Figure 12.16. There is one record for each subset (each vendor). The results are limited to vendors with one or more amounts greater than or equal to $100.

The results of the SND test are shown in Figure 12.16. The subsets with a NFF of 1.00 are shown at the top of the list. There are 311 subsets with NFFs equal to 1.00. This is a large list to scan and audit. The second sort is by Sum descending. The results where the Count equals 2 are not terribly interesting and *qryNFF5* could be updated to omit these subsets in the final results. Also, subsets with NFFs equal to zero (meaning that all the numbers were different) could also be omitted from the results. Counts of 12 are common for annual data. Perhaps the most anomalous results above are those cases with counts of 16 and this might be the starting point in a forensic investigation. The remaining duplications can be selectively audited because overpayments are quite likely with repetitive purchases. The review would be made easier if the vendor name and address was included in the results.

RUNNING THE SAME-SAME-SAME TEST IN EXCEL

It would seem that Excel's pivot table capabilities would be well-suited to running the Same-Same-Same test. This is not true because of the long processing time when Excel has to group by more than one field and also the fact that pivot table output is produced in a rather inflexible pivot table format. It is easier to use some cleverly thought out calculated fields. Using the *InvoicesPaid* data the test is designed to identify:

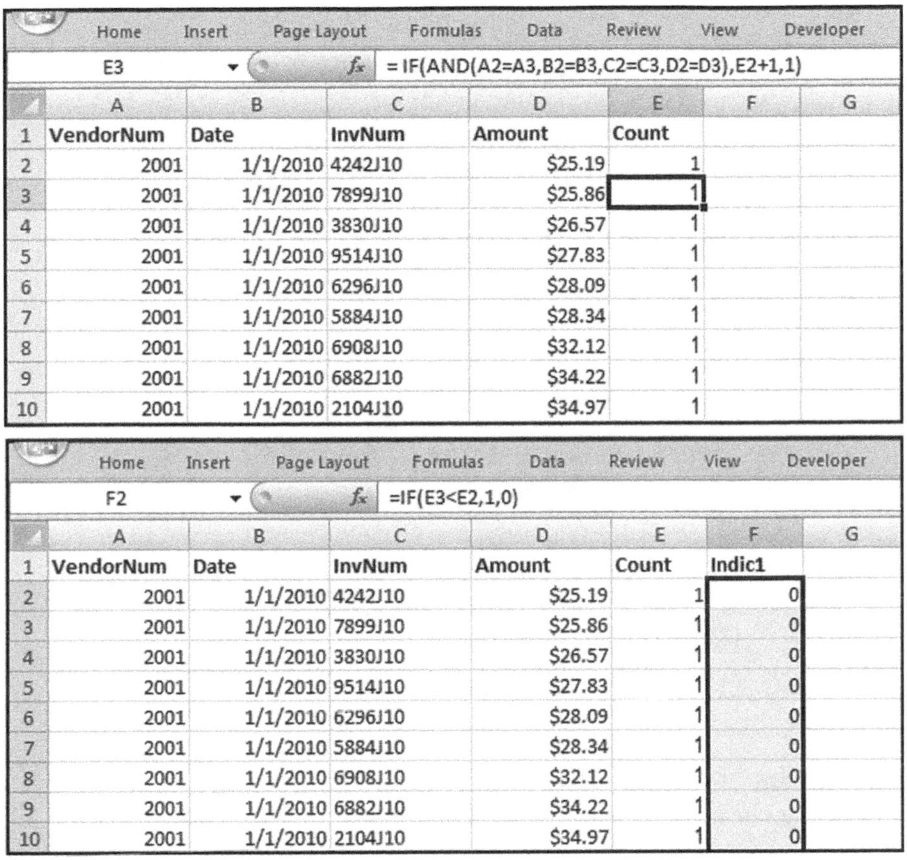

	A	B	C	D	E	F	G
1	VendorNum	Date	InvNum	Amount	Count		
2	2001	1/1/2010	4242J10	$25.19	1		
3	2001	1/1/2010	7899J10	$25.86	1		
4	2001	1/1/2010	3830J10	$26.57	1		
5	2001	1/1/2010	9514J10	$27.83	1		
6	2001	1/1/2010	6296J10	$28.09	1		
7	2001	1/1/2010	5884J10	$28.34	1		
8	2001	1/1/2010	6908J10	$32.12	1		
9	2001	1/1/2010	6882J10	$34.22	1		
10	2001	1/1/2010	2104J10	$34.97	1		

	A	B	C	D	E	F	G
1	VendorNum	Date	InvNum	Amount	Count	Indic1	
2	2001	1/1/2010	4242J10	$25.19	1	0	
3	2001	1/1/2010	7899J10	$25.86	1	0	
4	2001	1/1/2010	3830J10	$26.57	1	0	
5	2001	1/1/2010	9514J10	$27.83	1	0	
6	2001	1/1/2010	6296J10	$28.09	1	0	
7	2001	1/1/2010	5884J10	$28.34	1	0	
8	2001	1/1/2010	6908J10	$32.12	1	0	
9	2001	1/1/2010	6882J10	$34.22	1	0	
10	2001	1/1/2010	2104J10	$34.97	1	0	

FIGURE 12.17 The Calculations to Identify the Duplicates in the Data

The same *Amount*
The same *Date*
The same invoice number (*InvNum*)
The same vendor (*VendorNum*)

The initial step is to sort the data by *VendorNum*, *Date*, *InvNum*, and *Amount* ascending (smallest to largest). Once this is done, the first series of formulas to run the test are shown in Figure 12.17.

The formulas in Figure 12.17 identify the duplicates in the *Invoices* data. The formula in column E is basically a counter that counts how many times a row has been duplicated. The formula in column F indicates when the highest number in the series has been reached. The formulas are as follows:

E2: =1
E3: =IF(AND(A2=A3,B2=B3,C2=C3,D2=D3),E2+1,1) [copied to the last row]
F2: =IF(E3<E2,1,0) [copied to the last row]

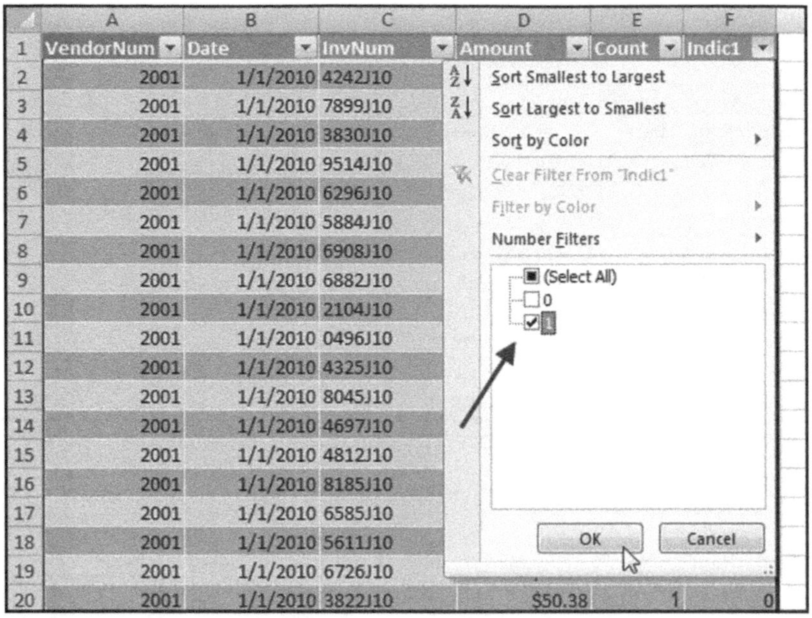

FIGURE 12.18   The Filter to Display Only the Records Equal to 1.00

The formula in the *Count* column starts counting upward (1, 2, 3, . . .) when it sees that the current row is the same as the prior row. The formula in the *Indic1* column indicates when the highest count has been reached for a particular group. Our duplicates will be those cases where the current row is equal to a prior row and we have reached the highest count for the group. These cases will have *Indic1* equal to 1.

The formulas in columns E and F need to be converted to values. This is done by highlighting the columns and then using the familiar **Copy** and **Home→ Clipboard→Paste→Paste Values**. Even though the zeroes in column F are now just in the way, we do not have to delete the column F zeroes. We can use a filter to show only the nonzero records. This is done by highlighting cell **A1**. Then click **Insert→Tables→Table**. Excel automatically senses the location of the data. Click **OK**. The filter is activated by clicking on the drop-down arrow in *Indic 1* and we can now use a filter as is shown in Figure 12.18.

Select the check box for the records equal to 1.00. Click **OK**. The next step is to sort by *Count* descending and then by *Amount* descending using **Home→Editing→Sort & Filter→Custom Sort**. The final step is to filter on *Amount*, keeping only the records where the *Amount* is ≥100.00. This is shown in Figure 12.19.

The final filter to display only *Amounts* ≥$100.00 is shown in Figure 12.19. The final result is shown in Figure 12.20. The results match the Access results in Figure 12.2.

The Excel procedure seems like more work than would be the case in Access using the duplicates wizard. It is true that the Excel procedure must be started with a sort,

	A	B	C	D	E	F	G
1	VendorNum ▾	Date ▾	InvNum ▾	Amount ▾	Count ▾	Indic1 ▾	
5692	20885	12/	Sort Smallest to Largest		4	1	
6514	4239	1/1	Sort Largest to Smallest		4	1	
7036	6870	12/2	Sort by Color ▸		4	1	
7530	16804	1/	Clear Filter From "Amount"		3	1	
8806	17256	1/2	Filter by Color ▸		3	1	
10015	17256	12/2			3	1	
19120	7492	1/1	Number Filters ▸		Equals...		
19124	5063	11/2	☑ (Select All)		Does Not Equal...		
19126	3630	9/1	☑ -$28,656.99		Greater Than...		
20294	5930	3/	☑ -$27,680.52		Greater Than Or Equal To... ⬉		
20612	5930	3/	☑ -$23,701.18				
22783	15759	10/1	☑ -$19,651.66		Less Than...		
22786	10277	9/	☑ -$19,624.71		Less Than Or Equal To...		
23466	12817	4/1	☑ -$18,440.09		Between...		
23472	3630	9/1	☑ -$13,023.78		Top 10...		
23474	5063	12/	☑ -$7,920.93				
23476	9288	12/2	☑ -$4,471.62		Above Average		
23478	7492	1/3			Below Average		
23480	5063	11/4/2010 56873849	$335.32		OK Cancel	Custom Filter...	
23482	5178	7/26/2010 042907JJ	$300.00	3	1		

FIGURE 12.19 The Filter to Display Only *Amounts* ≥$100.00

whereas the Access wizard does not need to work on sorted data. The formulas in Figure 12.17 do require some work to see that they are correct and are copied down to the last row. The remaining Excel steps consist mainly of formatting the output and keeping only the higher value records in the final result. These are formatting steps that would still need to be run after using the Access wizard. The fact that the Excel results can be easily manipulated (e.g., by changing the high-value dollar amount) make Excel the preferred way to run this test.

	A	B	C	D	E	F
1	VendorNum ▾	Date ▾	InvNum ▾	Amount ▾	Count ▾	Indic1 ▾
5692	20885	12/8/2010	120810	$178.92	4	1
6514	4239	1/13/2010	GOM011599	$154.39	4	1
7530	16804	1/1/2010	LV RENTS	$38,710.36	3	1
8806	17256	1/20/2010	44004	$9,220.01	3	1
10015	17256	12/20/2010	43749	$9,145.76	3	1
19120	7492	1/16/2010	20153	$1,546.98	3	1
19124	5063	11/20/2010	580338901	$1,338.83	3	1
19126	3630	9/13/2010	D7519401	$1,009.88	3	1
20294	5930	3/9/2010	532080	$964.40	3	1
20612	5930	3/9/2010	531049	$934.45	3	1
22783	15759	10/11/2010	260301163	$718.15	3	1

FIGURE 12.20 The Final SSS Results in an Excel Table

RUNNING THE SAME-SAME-DIFFERENT TEST IN EXCEL

It would seem that this would be a difficult test to run in Excel. The test uses five queries in Access and Access has some powerful **Group By** and **Join** capabilities that Excel does not have. The answer is that Excel can run this test quite easily because of its ability to do calculations that involve the preceding and succeeding rows. The test makes use of that fact and the IF, AND, and OR functions. Using the *InvoicesPaid* data the test is designed to identify

The same *Amount*
The same *Date*
The same invoice number (*InvNum*)
Different vendors (*VendorNum*)

The first set of formulas are similar to those for the Same-Same-Same test, except that we are looking for matches on three columns. The first step is to move the *VendorNum* field to the last column and to do a sort by,

Date Ascending
InvNum Ascending
Amount Ascending.
VendorNum Ascending

Once the data has been sorted the first series of formulas to run the test are entered. These formulas are shown in Figure 12.21.

The first set of formulas for the same-same-different test is shown in Figure 12.21. The SSS (for same-same-same) indicator in column E starts a count for the number of same-same-same cases ignoring the *Vendor* field. A count of 2 or more in the SSS field means that we have one or more duplicates. The *Group* field in column F starts numbering the groups with a 1, 2, 3, and so on. If group #78 has 4 records the formula would show 1, 2, 3, and 4 on four successive rows. The formulas are as follows:

> **E2:** =1
> **E3:** =IF(AND(A3=A2,B3=B2,C3=C2),E2+1,1) [Copy down to the end]
> **F2:** =1
> **F3:** =IF(E3>E2,F2,F2+1) [Copy down to the end]

The next formula indicates whether there are different vendors in any *Group*. If the vendors do change then this is exactly what we are interested in because we are identifying groups with different vendors. The formulas for column G are shown in Figure 12.22.

The formula in Figure 12.22 indicates whether there has been a change in the vendor for a specific group. The formulas are

> **G2:** =0
> **G3:** =IF(AND(E3>E2,D3<>D2),1,0) [Copy down to the end]

E3 =IF(AND(A3=A2,B3=B2,C3=C2),E2+1,1)

	A	B	C	D	E	F	G
1	Date	InvNum	Amount	VendorNum	SSS		
2	1/1/2010	59	$73.50	5953	1		
3	1/1/2010	136	$791.92	15868	1		
4	1/1/2010	139	$2,443.50	15868	1		
5	1/1/2010	829	$1,950.00	7690	1		
6	1/1/2010	963	$124.00	4243	1		
7	1/1/2010	1000	$160.00	9894	1		
8	1/1/2010	1019	$20.00	3773	1		
9	1/1/2010	1146	$335.00	12820	1		
10	1/1/2010	1160	$60.00	6620	1		

F3 =IF(E3>E2,F2,F2+1)

	A	B	C	D	E	F	G
1	Date	InvNum	Amount	VendorNum	SSS	Group	
2	1/1/2010	59	$73.50	5953	1	1	
3	1/1/2010	136	$791.92	15868	1	2	
4	1/1/2010	139	$2,443.50	15868	1	3	
5	1/1/2010	829	$1,950.00	7690	1	4	
6	1/1/2010	963	$124.00	4243	1	5	
7	1/1/2010	1000	$160.00	9894	1	6	
8	1/1/2010	1019	$20.00	3773	1	7	
9	1/1/2010	1146	$335.00	12820	1	8	
10	1/1/2010	1160	$60.00	6620	1	9	

FIGURE 12.21 The Excel Formulas for the Same-Same-Different Test

At this stage a "1" in the *VenChange* field means that we have a group with one or more duplicates and that the vendor number has changed. We have a group that has the same dates, invoice numbers, amounts, and a change in vendors. The vendor change can occur with the second record for any group or it can happen with the last

G3 =IF(AND(E3>E2,D3<>D2),1,0)

	A	B	C	D	E	F	G
1	Date	InvNum	Amount	VendorNum	SSS	Group	VenChange
2	1/1/2010	59	$73.50	5953	1	1	0
3	1/1/2010	136	$791.92	15868	1	2	0
4	1/1/2010	139	$2,443.50	15868	1	3	0
5	1/1/2010	829	$1,950.00	7690	1	4	0
6	1/1/2010	963	$124.00	4243	1	5	0
7	1/1/2010	1000	$160.00	9894	1	6	0
8	1/1/2010	1019	$20.00	3773	1	7	0
9	1/1/2010	1146	$335.00	12820	1	8	0
10	1/1/2010	1160	$60.00	6620	1	9	0

FIGURE 12.22 The Formula to Identify a Change in the Vendor Field

H2 =IF(F2<>F1,G2,H1+G2)

	A	B	C	D	E	F	G	H
1	Date	InvNum	Amount	VendorNum	SSS	Group	VenChange	SumVC
2	1/1/2010	59	$73.50	5953	1	1	0	0
3	1/1/2010	136	$791.92	15868	1	2	0	0
4	1/1/2010	139	$2,443.50	15868	1	3	0	0
5	1/1/2010	829	$1,950.00	7690	1	4	0	0
6	1/1/2010	963	$124.00	4243	1	5	0	0
7	1/1/2010	1000	$160.00	9894	1	6	0	0
8	1/1/2010	1019	$20.00	3773	1	7	0	0
9	1/1/2010	1146	$335.00	12820	1	8	0	0
10	1/1/2010	1160	$60.00	6620	1	9	0	0

FIGURE 12.23 The Formula to Indicate the Last Record for Each SSD Group

record. The fact that the vendor change can happen at any record after the first record makes it difficult to extract all the groups of interest. The next formula causes the last record for each group to have the "1" if there is a vendor change. The formula is shown in Figure 12.23.

Figure 12.23 makes sure that there is an indicator on the same row as the last record for a group if that group has a vendor change. The formula for the *SumVC* field in column H is

H2: =IF(F2<>F1,G2,H1+G2) [Copy down to the end]

Figure 12.24 shows the formula in the *SSSD* field in column I for showing an indicator only in the last row of any group that has a vendor switch. The prior formula could have had indicators in the last row and in some of the other rows of any group (where there was a vendor change).

I2 =IF(AND(OR(F3>F2,F3=""),H2>0),1,0)

	A	B	C	D	E	F	G	H	I
1	Date	InvNum	Amount	VendorNum	SSS	Group	VenChange	SumVC	SSSD
2	1/1/2010	59	$73.50	5953	1	1	0	0	0
3	1/1/2010	136	$791.92	15868	1	2	0	0	0
4	1/1/2010	139	$2,443.50	15868	1	3	0	0	0
5	1/1/2010	829	$1,950.00	7690	1	4	0	0	0
6	1/1/2010	963	$124.00	4243	1	5	0	0	0
7	1/1/2010	1000	$160.00	9894	1	6	0	0	0
8	1/1/2010	1019	$20.00	3773	1	7	0	0	0
9	1/1/2010	1146	$335.00	12820	1	8	0	0	0
10	1/1/2010	1160	$60.00	6620	1	9	0	0	0

FIGURE 12.24 The Formula to Make an Indicator Only in the Last Row of Each Group

	Home	Insert	Page Layout	Formulas	Data	Review	View	Developer	Add-Ins		
	J2	▼	fx	=IF(OR(I2=1,AND(F2=F3,J3=1)),1,0)							

	A	B	C	D	E	F	G	H	I	J
1	Date	InvNum	Amount	VendorNum	SSS	Group	VenChange	SumVC	SSSD	Matches
2	1/1/2010	59	$73.50	5953	1	1	0	0	0	0
3	1/1/2010	136	$791.92	15868	1	2	0	0	0	0
4	1/1/2010	139	$2,443.50	15868	1	3	0	0	0	0
5	1/1/2010	829	$1,950.00	7690	1	4	0	0	0	0
6	1/1/2010	963	$124.00	4243	1	5	0	0	0	0
7	1/1/2010	1000	$160.00	9894	1	6	0	0	0	0
8	1/1/2010	1019	$20.00	3773	1	7	0	0	0	0
9	1/1/2010	1146	$335.00	12820	1	8	0	0	0	0
10	1/1/2010	1160	$60.00	6620	1	9	0	0	0	0

FIGURE 12.25 The Formula to Insert Indicators on All the Rows

The formula in Figure 12.24 is used to make sure that we only have an indicator in the last row of any group of interest. The formula is

I2: $=IF(AND(OR(F3>F2,F3=""""),H2>0),1,0)$ [copy down to the last row]

The final calculating step is to place indicators in all the rows of any group of interest.

Figure 12.25 shows the formula used to enter a "1" in the *Matches* field in column J on each row of each group of interest. The formula is

J2: $=IF(OR(I2=1,AND(F2=F3,J3=1)),1,0)$

The calculations are now done and the next steps are to report the results neatly without unneeded columns or rows. The next step is to copy the entire data table to a new worksheet. The creation of a copy is done by right clicking on the worksheet tab and then clicking **Move or Copy** and then checking **Create a Copy**. Once the copy has been created then all the formulas should be converted to values using the familiar **Copy** and **Home→Clipboard→Paste→ Paste Values**.

The next step is to delete the unneeded columns E, F, G, H, and I. The worksheet should then be sorted by

Matches Descending
Amount Descending
Date Ascending
InvNum Ascending
VendorNum Ascending

To tidy up the result we should format the worksheet as a table using **Home→ Styles→Format As Table→Table Style Medium 2**.

	A	B	C	D	E
1	Date	InvNum	Amount	VendorNum	Matches
2	6/24/2010	62410	$87,217.56	3287	1
3	6/24/2010	62410	$87,217.56	3288	1
4	6/8/2010	121800	$44,783.42	3013	1
5	6/8/2010	121800	$44,783.42	5698	1
6	12/31/2010	501	$29,689.42	4404	1
7	12/31/2010	501	$29,689.42	6297	1
8	7/1/2010	Q506190	$26,153.00	3012	1
9	7/1/2010	Q506190	$26,153.00	3323	1
10	10/1/2010	WSTC049	$23,500.00	4276	1
11	10/1/2010	WSTC049	$23,500.00	4277	1
12	6/21/2010	6963782	$18,446.00	3012	1
13	6/21/2010	6963782	$18,446.00	3323	1
14	10/5/2010	WSTC52	$16,650.00	4276	1
15	10/5/2010	WSTC52	$16,650.00	4277	1
16	7/8/2010	3248-02	$15,000.00	2716	1
17	7/8/2010	3248-02	$15,000.00	3428	1
18	6/26/2010	6973550	$14,861.00	3012	1
19	6/26/2010	6973550	$14,861.00	3323	1
20	12/7/2010	323447	$14,018.58	6020	1
21	12/7/2010	323447	$14,018.58	8995	1
22	8/3/2010	100630	$13,023.78	4449	1
23	8/3/2010	100630	$13,023.78	5290	1
24	5/8/2010	V595994	$11,237.52	2922	1
25	5/8/2010	V595994	$11,237.52	3013	1
26	4/30/2010	5519392	$10,975.04	4448	1
27	4/30/2010	5519392	$10,975.04	4449	1
28	12/15/2010	364461	$10,920.00	2569	1
29	12/15/2010	364461	$10,920.00	2569	1
30	12/15/2010	364461	$10,920.00	6881	1

|◄ ◄ ► ►| Results InvoicesPaid

Ready   1173 of 189470 records found

FIGURE 12.26 The Excel Results of the Same-Same-Different Test

The final step is to filter on *Matches* $=1$, and *Amount* ≥ 100.00 to give the result in Figure 12.26.

The same-same-different results of Excel are shown in Figure 12.26. The information bar at the bottom of the page shows that the record count agrees with the Access results in Figure 12.9. The Excel procedure again seems like much more work than would be the case in Access using the duplicates wizard. There are six calculated fields that need to be carefully entered and copied down to the last row. The remaining Excel steps consist mainly of sorting and formatting the output and keeping only the higher value records in the final result. Once again, the fact that the Excel results can be easily manipulated (e.g., by changing the high-value dollar amount) makes Excel the preferred way to run this test. Also, the Excel results can be sent to internal audit or corporate risk management and they can be viewed without the user needing Access or needing to know how to run an Access report.

RUNNING THE SUBSET NUMBER DUPLICATION TEST IN EXCEL

This test generally only uses *Amounts* ≥ 100 to keep the results to a manageable size. Any dollar filter for this test should be applied at the start. An efficient way to do this is to

	A	B	C	D
119946	21627	3/3/2010	30200	$100.00
119947	21628	3/20/2010	32000	$100.00
119948	21638	3/8/2010	120371088	$100.00
119949	21758	3/15/2010	31500	$100.00
119950	21761	3/16/2010	120435401	$100.00
119951	21813	3/2/2010	21700	$100.00
119952	21876	3/9/2010	30900	$100.00
119953	21993	3/27/2010	120270433	$100.00
119954	21998	3/23/2010	1568618-2000	$100.00
119955	22027	4/5/2010	120222212	$100.00
119956	22032	4/5/2010	130022298	$100.00
119957	2373	5/24/2010	526105395	$99.99
119958	3630	1/31/2010	V9554601	$99.98
119959	3812	4/8/2010	IN00014427	$99.98
119960	5865	10/2/2010	95637X-409	$99.98
119961	16683	1/20/2010	150481	$99.97
119962	4436	2/9/2010	491946158	$99.96
119963	5828	1/27/2010	12710	$99.96
119964	2003	9/28/2010	1481089	$99.95
119965	4413	10/27/2010	102710	$99.95
119966	4632	11/17/2010	69059	$99.95
119967	4632	12/2/2010	69110	$99.95
119968	4984	9/15/2010	487946	$99.95
119969	5683	1/5/2010	10510	$99.95
119970	17849	7/15/2010	1121100	$99.95
119971	4201	1/3/2010	386-004415	$99.93
119972	3742	4/12/2010	5438	$99.90
119973	21797	2/16/2010	21600	$99.90
119974	4925	11/11/2010	9402	$99.89
119975	13685	5/28/2010	R213529	$99.88

H ◀ ▶ H InvoicesPaid

FIGURE 12.27 The Step to Delete All Records Less than $100.00

sort the data table by *Amount* descending and then to delete all the records less than $100.00.

Figure 12.27 shows the method used to delete all the records less than $100.00. The records from row 119957 to the end of the page are highlighted using **Control+Shift** and the **Down Arrow**. Press **Delete** to delete the records.

The next step is to delete the *Date* and *InvNum* fields. These are not used for the calculations and our worksheet will have a neater format and smaller file size.

The next step to begin the calculations is to re-sort the data by

VendorNum Ascending
Amount Ascending

The first calculation is to enter "1" in **C2** and then to enter a formula in **C3** that counts the number of records in each subset. The second calculation is to enter "1" in cell **D2** and then to start a count in **D3** when duplicate numbers are found. The formulas are shown in Figure 12.28.

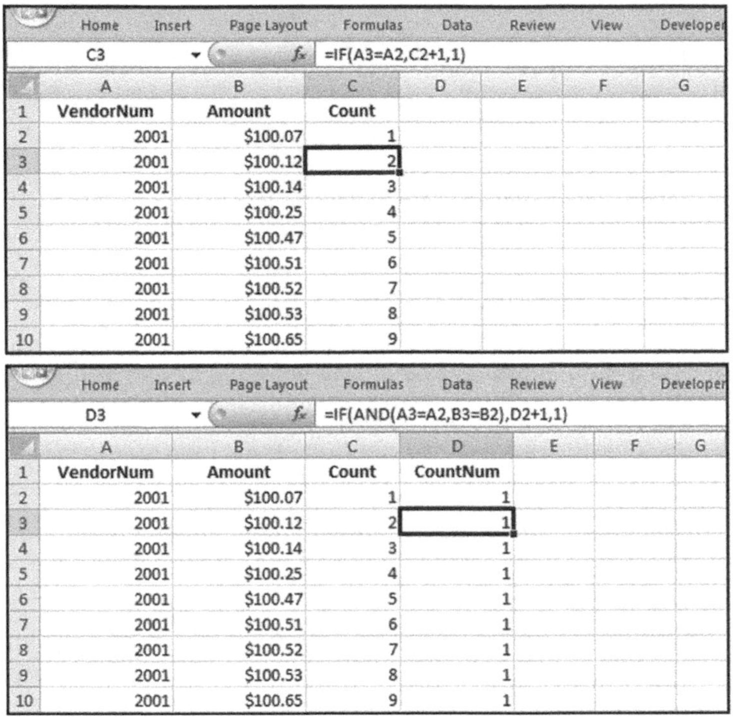

	A	B	C
1	VendorNum	Amount	Count
2	2001	$100.07	1
3	2001	$100.12	2
4	2001	$100.14	3
5	2001	$100.25	4
6	2001	$100.47	5
7	2001	$100.51	6
8	2001	$100.52	7
9	2001	$100.53	8
10	2001	$100.65	9

	A	B	C	D
1	VendorNum	Amount	Count	CountNum
2	2001	$100.07	1	1
3	2001	$100.12	2	1
4	2001	$100.14	3	1
5	2001	$100.25	4	1
6	2001	$100.47	5	1
7	2001	$100.51	6	1
8	2001	$100.52	7	1
9	2001	$100.53	8	1
10	2001	$100.65	9	1

FIGURE 12.28 The Formulas to Count the Records and the Duplications

The two counters are shown in Figure 12.28. The formulas are

C1: =1
C2: =IF(A3=A2,C2+1,1)
D1: =1
D2: =IF(AND(A3=A2,B3=B2),D2+1,1)

The next steps are to square the counts and to sum the squared counts. The numerator in Equation 12.1 shows that the counts must be squared and the squared counts must be summed.

The formulas used to square the counts and to sum the square counts are shown in Figure 12.29. Care needs to be taken to square only the largest count for each duplicated number. The formulas are

E2: =IF(AND(D2>1,D3<D2),D2^2,0)
F2: =E2
F3: =IF(A3=A2,E3+F2,E3)

The formulas above square the counts and sum the squared counts. The E2 and F3 formulas need to be copied down to the last record. The remaining part of the formula is the denominator in Equation 12.1. This formula needs to square the count for each subset.

Home Insert Page Layout Formulas Data Review View Developer

E2 f_x =IF(AND(D2>1,D3<D2),D2^2,0)

	A	B	C	D	E	F	G
1	VendorNum	Amount	Count	CountNum	CountSq		
2	2001	$100.07	1	1	0		
3	2001	$100.12	2	1	0		
4	2001	$100.14	3	1	0		
5	2001	$100.25	4	1	0		
6	2001	$100.47	5	1	0		
7	2001	$100.51	6	1	0		
8	2001	$100.52	7	1	0		
9	2001	$100.53	8	1	0		
10	2001	$100.65	9	1	0		

Home Insert Page Layout Formulas Data Review View Developer

F3 f_x =IF(A3=A2,E3+F2,E3)

	A	B	C	D	E	F	G
1	VendorNum	Amount	Count	CountNum	CountSq	SumCountSq	
2	2001	$100.07	1	1	0	0	
3	2001	$100.12	2	1	0	0	
4	2001	$100.14	3	1	0	0	
5	2001	$100.25	4	1	0	0	
6	2001	$100.47	5	1	0	0	
7	2001	$100.51	6	1	0	0	
8	2001	$100.52	7	1	0	0	
9	2001	$100.53	8	1	0	0	
10	2001	$100.65	9	1	0	0	

FIGURE 12.29 The Formulas Used to Square the Counts and to Sum the Squared Counts

The formula used to square the count for each subset is shown in Figure 12.30. The formula is

G2: =IF(A3<>A2,C2^2,0)

Home Insert Page Layout Formulas Data Review View Developer Add-I

G2 f_x =IF(A3<>A2,C2^2,0)

	A	B	C	D	E	F	G
1	VendorNum	Amount	Count	CountNum	CountSq	SumCountSq	NSq
2	2001	$100.07	1	1	0	0	0
3	2001	$100.12	2	1	0	0	0
4	2001	$100.14	3	1	0	0	0
5	2001	$100.25	4	1	0	0	0
6	2001	$100.47	5	1	0	0	0
7	2001	$100.51	6	1	0	0	0
8	2001	$100.52	7	1	0	0	0
9	2001	$100.53	8	1	0	0	0
10	2001	$100.65	9	1	0	0	0

FIGURE 12.30 The Formula to Square the Count

| H3 | | | f_x | =IF(A3=A2,MIN(B3,H2),B3) | | | | | |

	A	B	C	D	E	F	G	H	I	J
1	VendorNum	Amount	Count	CountNum	CountSq	SumCountSq	NSq	Min	Max	Sum
2	2001	$100.07	1	1	0	0	0	$100.07		
3	2001	$100.12	2	1	0	0	0	100.07		
4	2001	$100.14	3	1	0	0	0	100.07		
5	2001	$100.25	4	1	0	0	0	100.07		
6	2001	$100.47	5	1	0	0	0	100.07		
7	2001	$100.51	6	1	0	0	0	100.07		

| I2 | | | f_x | =IF(A3<>A2,B2,0) | | | | | |

	A	B	C	D	E	F	G	H	I	J
1	VendorNum	Amount	Count	CountNum	CountSq	SumCountSq	NSq	Min	Max	Sum
2	2001	$100.07	1	1	0	0	0	$100.07	0	
3	2001	$100.12	2	1	0	0	0	100.07	0	
4	2001	$100.14	3	1	0	0	0	100.07	0	
5	2001	$100.25	4	1	0	0	0	100.07	0	
6	2001	$100.47	5	1	0	0	0	100.07	0	
7	2001	$100.51	6	1	0	0	0	100.07	0	

| J3 | | | f_x | =IF(AND(A3=A2),B3+J2,B3) | | | | | |

	A	B	C	D	E	F	G	H	I	J
1	VendorNum	Amount	Count	CountNum	CountSq	SumCountSq	NSq	Min	Max	Sum
2	2001	$100.07	1	1	0	0	0	$100.07	0	$100.07
3	2001	$100.12	2	1	0	0	0	100.07	0	200.19
4	2001	$100.14	3	1	0	0	0	100.07	0	300.33
5	2001	$100.25	4	1	0	0	0	100.07	0	400.58
6	2001	$100.47	5	1	0	0	0	100.07	0	501.05
7	2001	$100.51	6	1	0	0	0	100.07	0	601.56

FIGURE 12.31 The Formulas for the Descriptive Statistics

The formula needs to be copied down to the last row. The next series of formulas calculates descriptive statistics that will be included in the output. The formulas calculate the minimums, maximums, and sums for each subset. The formulas are more complex than normal because a vendor can have one record or it could have more than one record.

The formulas used for the descriptive statistics are shown in Figure 12.31. The formulas are as follows:

H2: =B2
H3: =IF(A3=A2,MIN(B3,H2),B3)
I2: =IF(A3<>A2,B2,0)
J2: =B2
J3: =IF(AND(A3=A2),B3+J2,B3)

The formulas in **H3, I2,** and **J3** should be copied down to the last row, which in this case is row 119956. The final two steps are to calculate the NFF as shown in Equation 12.1 and also to place an indicator in the last row for each subset. The formulas are shown in Figure 12.32.

The formula used for the NFF calculation and the formula to indicate the last record for each subset is shown in Figure 12.32. The formulas are

$$K2: \; =IF(G2>0,F2/G2,0)$$
$$L2: \; =IF(A3<>A2,1,0)$$

K2 =IF(G2>0,F2/G2,0)

	H	I	J	K	L
1	Min	Max	Sum	NFF	EndSub
2	$100.07	0	$100.07	0	
3	100.07	0	200.19	0	
4	100.07	0	300.33	0	
5	100.07	0	400.58	0	
6	100.07	0	501.05	0	
7	100.07	0	601.56	0	

L2 =IF(A3<>A2,1,0)

	H	I	J	K	L
1	Min	Max	Sum	NFF	EndSub
2	$100.07	0	$100.07	0	0
3	100.07	0	200.19	0	0
4	100.07	0	300.33	0	0
5	100.07	0	400.58	0	0
6	100.07	0	501.05	0	0
7	100.07	0	601.56	0	0

FIGURE 12.32 The Formula for the NFF Calculation

The formulas should be copied down to the last row, which in this case is row 119956. The worksheet now has everything needed to report the NFFs. The next steps all involve preparing the NFF report. The starting step could be to format K2:K119956 as numeric showing 3 decimal places. The next step is to convert all the formulas in C2:L119956 to values by using the familiar ***Copy*** followed by ***Home→ Clipboard→Paste→Paste Values***.

The next step in the report's preparation is to delete the unneeded columns. These unneeded columns are C, D, E, F, and G.

It is possible to filter the results so that only those rows are displayed where *EndSub* equals 1. The preferred step is to actually delete the rows that are not needed. This will give a smaller file size if the results are being sent by e-mail or are included in a set of working papers. To delete the unneeded rows, the results should be sorted by *EndSub* descending and the rows where *EndSub* = 0 should be deleted. This will give a final table with 9,425 rows.

	A	B	C	D	E	F
1	VendorNum	Amount	Min	Max	Sum	NFF
2	21756	$100,000.00	$100,000.00	$100,000.00	$200,000.00	1.000
3	15817	$25,000.00	$25,000.00	$25,000.00	$50,000.00	1.000
4	6092	$3,266.00	$3,266.00	$3,266.00	$48,990.00	1.000
5	4720	$3,000.00	$3,000.00	$3,000.00	$48,000.00	1.000
6	6091	$2,870.83	$2,870.83	$2,870.83	$45,933.28	1.000
7	9508	$3,203.70	$3,203.70	$3,203.70	$44,851.80	1.000
8	16732	$3,800.00	$3,800.00	$3,800.00	$41,800.00	1.000
9	6102	$2,600.00	$2,600.00	$2,600.00	$41,600.00	1.000
10	4186	$2,318.75	$2,318.75	$2,318.75	$37,100.00	1.000

FIGURE 12.33 The NFF Table in Excel

The next step is to delete the *EndSub* field, which is column G. The field is no longer needed because all the rows have *EndSub* = 1.00.

The final step moves the most important results to the top of the table. This is done by first sorting on *NFF* descending, followed by *Sum* descending. As a final touch, the results can be formatted as a table using ***Home***→***Styles***→***Format*** as ***Table***→***Table*** style Medium 2. This will give the result in Figure 12.33, which matches Figure 12.16.

The NFF results are shown in Figure 12.33. The results can be saved to a file for the forensic working papers or the results could be e-mailed to accounts payable or corporate risk personnel for follow-up work. It is more complex to run this test in Excel.

 ## SUMMARY

This chapter described three tests related to finding excess duplications within subsets. The assumption underlying these tests is that excessive duplications could be due to fraud or error or some other type of anomaly. The tests can be designed so that the discovery of a duplicate does signal an issue of some sort. It is not abnormal for the same person to charge two equal amounts to a credit card for courier charges on the same day (especially if it is a minimum flat-rate amount), but it would be unusual to charge exactly $113.64 twice for gasoline in the same day or to pay two hotel bills from different hotels on the same day.

The first test looked for exact duplicates and in an accounts payable context this might indicate a duplicate payment. In a purchasing card context this might indicate a split purchase (which is a contravention of an internal control), and in an "election results" context it might mean that that one person's votes were erroneously entered again as the votes of some other person.

The second test was called the same-same-different test and this test looked for near duplicates. In an accounts payable context this would occur if an invoice was erroneously paid to one vendor and then correctly paid to another vendor. In a purchasing card context a near-duplicate might indicate a split purchase where the purchase was split between two cards. This test, in carefully thought out circumstances, usually delivers valuable results.

The third test described in the chapter quantifies the level of duplication within a subset. The subsets are then ranked according to their duplication measures. A formula is used to calculate the Number Frequency Factor duplication measure.

The tests in this chapter are all aimed at finding duplicates or near-duplicates within subsets. The Access and the Excel steps needed to run the tests are demonstrated using explanations and screen shots. The tests are slightly easier to run in Excel even though Access has some helpful duplication-related wizards. One advantage of Excel is that the results can be viewed by another user without that user having access to Access.

CHAPTER THIRTEEN

Identifying Fraud Using Correlation

U SING CORRELATION TO DETECT fraud is a relatively recent event. The first application of correlation in a forensic setting was at a fast-food company where correlation was used to identify restaurants with sales patterns that deviated from the norm. These odd sales patterns played an important part in identifying sales numbers that were influenced by fraud. The next correlation application was at an electric utility where correlation was used to identify customers with electric usage patterns that differed from the seasonal norm. The usage patterns together with other red flags were successful at detecting some large-scale electricity theft. A recent correlation application was at a consumer goods manufacturer where correlation was used to identify retailers with coupon redemption patterns that differed substantially from the norm. Again, the redemption patterns together with other red flags were successful at identifying highly suspect patterns in coupon submissions.

Correlation is usually used to detect fraud on a proactive basis. According to the IIA (2004), controls may be classified as *preventive*, *detective*, or *corrective*:

- **Preventive controls.** These controls are there to prevent errors, omissions, or security incidents from occurring in the first place. Examples include controls that restrict the access to systems by authorized individuals. These access-related controls include intrusion prevention systems and firewalls, and integrity constraints that are embedded within a database management system.
- **Detective controls.** These controls are there to detect errors or incidents that have eluded the preventative controls. Examples include controls that test whether authorization limits have been exceeded, or an analysis of activity in previously dormant accounts.

▪ **Corrective controls.** These controls are there to correct errors, omissions, or incidents after detection. They vary from simple correction of data-entry errors, to identifying and removing unauthorized users from systems or networks. Corrective controls are the actions taken to minimize further losses.

The most efficient route is to design systems so as to prevent errors or fraud from occurring through tight preventive controls. In some situations, tight preventive controls are difficult to achieve. For example, it is difficult to have watertight controls in situations where customer service plays a large role. These situations include airline, hotel, or rental car check-in counters. Customer service personnel need some leeway to handle unusual situations. Other low-control environments include situations where the transactions are derived from third-party reports such as sales reports from franchisees, warranty claims reported by auto dealers, baggage claims reported by passengers at airports, and reports of coupons or rebates redeemed by coupon redemption processors. In cases where preventive controls are weak, detective controls have additional value.

The use of correlation as a detective control is well suited to situations where there are, (a) a large number of forensic units (departments, divisions, franchisees, or customers, etc.), (b) a series of time-stamped revenues, expenses or loss amounts, and (c) where a valid benchmark exists against which to measure the numbers of the various forensic units. The requirements above are open to a little innovation. For example, election results are well-suited to correlation studies, but here there is no series of time-stamped transactions. An example of time-stamped revenue amounts would be sales dollars on a month-by-month basis for fiscal 2011.

Correlation tests are usually done together with other fraud detection techniques, with the correlation tests being only one part of a suite of tests used as a detective control. This chapter reviews correlation itself and includes four case studies showing its use in a forensic analytic setting. The chapter shows how to run the tests in Access and Excel.

THE CONCEPT OF CORRELATION

Correlation measures how closely two sets of time-related numbers move in tandem. In statistical terms *correlation* measures how well two sets of data are linearly related (or associated). A high degree of correlation would occur when an x percent increase (or decrease) in one field is matched with an x percent increase (or decrease) in another field. For example, at gasoline stations there is a high level of correlation between the posted prices for low-, mid-, and high-octane gasoline. A change of (say) 10 cents in the price of one grade is almost always matched with a 10 cents change in the other two gasoline grades. Figure 13.1 shows the weekly retail pump prices of the three gasoline grades (regular, mid-, and high-octane) for 2009 for the New England region.

The three series of gasoline prices in Figure 13.1 track each other very closely. The middle grade is on average about 4.6 percent more expensive than the regular grade,

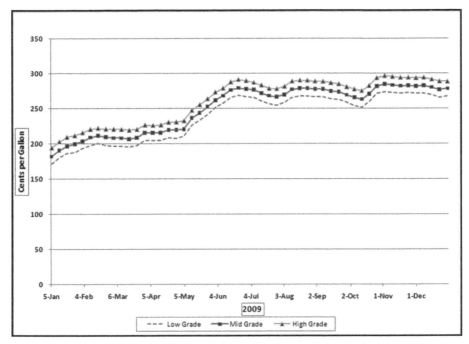

FIGURE 13.1 The Weekly Retail Pump Prices of Gasoline in 2009 in New England

Source: Department of Energy (www.eia.gov: Retail Gasoline Historical Prices)

and the high grade is on average also about 4.6 percent higher than the middle grade. The stable price differences indicate that the prices move in tandem. A change in one price is matched with an almost identical change in the other. The statistical technique used to measure how well the prices track each other is called *correlation*. The numerical measures of correlation range from −1.00 to +1.00.

It is important to emphasize that correlation does not imply causation. Two data fields can be highly correlated (with correlations at or near +1.00 or −1.00) without the numbers in one field necessarily causing the other field's numbers to increase or decrease. The correlation could be due purely to coincidence. For example, the winning times in one-mile races are positively correlated with the percentage of people who smoke. This does not mean that quicker one-mile races causes people to smoke less. The ranges of the correlation coefficient are discussed in the next paragraph.

When the correlation is equal to zero, there is no correlation between the two data fields. An increase in the value of one of the data series is matched with an equal chance of either an increase or a decrease in the second data series. Similarly, a decrease in the value of one of the data series is matched with a 50/50 chance of either an increase or a decrease in the second data series. A correlation of zero also occurs when the values in the series are unchanged over time and the second series shows a set of values that are either increasing or decreasing or some other pattern of changes. Examples of zero or near-zero correlations are shown in Figure 13.2.

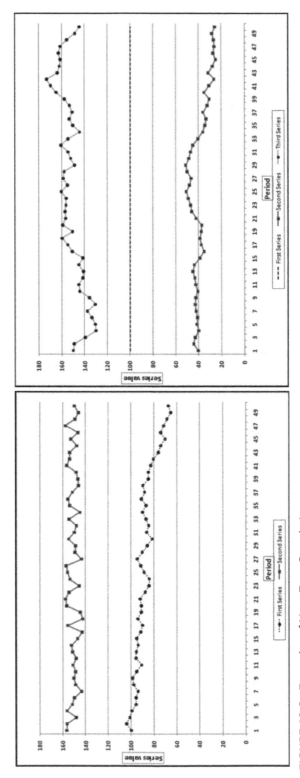

FIGURE 13.2 Examples of Near-Zero Correlations

The correlations between the first and second series in the graph on the left is close to zero. The data points in the two series move in the same direction for one-half of the time and move in opposite directions for the remainder of the time. The calculated correlation is fractionally above zero. In the graph on the right, the first series (the middle set of dashes) starts at 100 and randomly ticks up by 0.0001 or down by 0.0001. The first record is 100 and all subsequent values are either 100.0001 or 99.9999. The second series (the bottom series of values) starts at 40 and randomly drifts downward to 25. The third series starts at 150 and randomly drifts downward to 145. Even though the second and third series both ultimately drift downward the calculated correlation between the first and second series is small and positive and between the first and third series is small and negative. When one series is exactly constant the correlation between it and another series cannot be calculated because the correlation formula would then include a division by zero, which is undefined. The general rule is that if one series is almost unchanged then the correlation between it and any other series will be close to zero.

A correlation of 1.00 says that there is a perfect, positive, linear relationship between the two series. The positive +1.00 does not mean that one series is always increasing. A positive correlation has little to do with a positive slope. A correlation of 1.00 happens when a percentage increase in one field is matched with exactly the same percentage increase in the other field. A correlation of 1.00 would also happen when an increase (or decrease) in the value of one field is matched with exactly the same absolute value change in the other field. A correlation of 1.00 does not imply that the change in one field causes the change in the other field. Figure 13.3 shows two examples of correlations equal to 1.00.

Figure 13.3 shows two examples of correlations equal to 1.00. In the graph on the left the percentage changes in both series are identical. For example, the second data point in each series is 10.125 percent greater than the first data point. Both series show an overall decrease of 81.375 percent, but the effect is most noticeable for the larger (topmost) series. In the graph on the right each series oscillates by the same absolute amount. For example, in each case the second data point in the series is 4.05 units larger than the first unit in the series. The vertical distance between all three series is constant. In the first panel the percentage changes are equal, and in the second panel the absolute changes are equal. The correlation is also equal to 1.00 with a combination of percentage and absolute value changes. The correlation is equal to 1.00 if the second series is a linear combination of the first series through multiplication by a constant, addition of a constant, or both multiplication by and addition of constants.

A correlation of −1.00 indicates that there is a perfect, negative, linear relationship between the two series. An increase in the value of one series is matched with a decrease in the second series. Figure 13.4 shows examples of correlations equal to or close to −1.00.

Figure 13.4 shows two examples of perfect and near-perfect negative correlations. The graph on the left shows the case where an *increase* in one series is matched with a *decrease* in the other, and a *decrease* in the value of one series is matched with exactly the

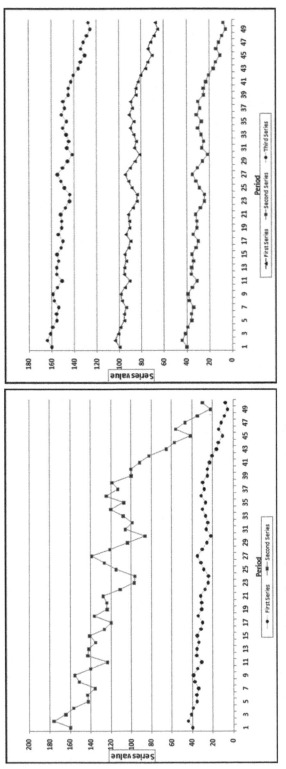

FIGURE 13.3 Some Examples of Perfect, Positive Linear Correlations

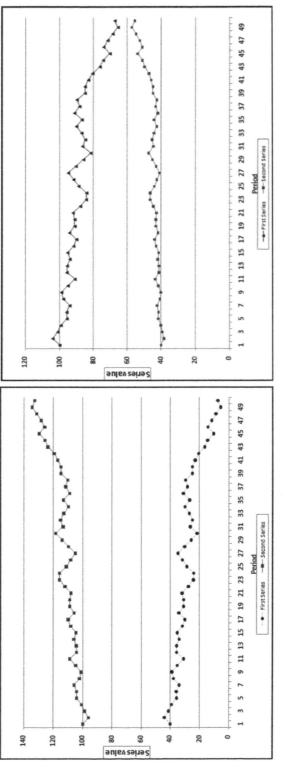

FIGURE 13.4 Examples of Negative Linear Correlations

269

same absolute value *increase* in the other. The correlation here is −1.00 because each increase or decrease is matched with an opposite change of exactly the same absolute value and this pattern continues throughout. In the graph on the right the increase of 4.05 percent in the lower series is matched with a decrease of 4.05 percent in the upper series. The absolute values of the percentages are equal but the directions are opposite. The percentages in the lower series cause much less of an upward or downward gyration because the absolute values are smaller than those of the second series. If the starting value for the lower series was (say) 5.00, then the changes would hardly be noticeable with the naked eye, but the correlation would still be a near-perfect −0.984. If one series started at 100 and the changes were easily noticeable, and a second series started at (say) 5.00 and had identical percentage changes (perhaps in the same direction and perhaps in the opposite direction) it would be impossible to tell visually whether the correlation was perfectly positive, near zero, or almost perfectly negative. The magnitude of the correlation is not visually obvious when one series plots as an almost straight line.

Correlations between 0 and 1.00 indicate that the correlation, or association, is positive and the strength of the relationship. A correlation of 0.80 says that the association is strong in that a positive increase (or decrease) in the one series is most often matched with a positive increase (or decrease) in the other. A correlation of only 0.30 means that an increase in the value of one series is matched with an increase in the other for slightly more than one-half of the data pairs. Similarly, correlations between 0 and −1.00 tell us that the correlation, or association, is negative and the strength of the relationship. Some more examples of positive and negative correlations are shown in Figure 13.5.

Figure 13.5 shows some examples of weak and strong positive and negative correlations. It is quite difficult to estimate correlations by just looking at them. In the graph on the left the correlation between Series 1 (the middle series) and Series 2 (the upper series) is 0.80. It is therefore strong and positive. Both series have a general downward drift and because they move in the same direction, the correlation is positive. The correlation between Series 1 and Series 3 (the lower series) is 0.30. This is a weak positive correlation. The direction changes are the same for just over one-half of the data points. In the graph on the right the correlation between Series 1 (the middle series) and Series 2 (the upper series) is −0.80. The general tendency for Series 1 is a decrease and the general tendency for Series 2 is an increase. The change is in the opposite direction for about two-thirds of the data points. The correlation between Series 1 and Series 3 (the lower series) is −0.30. This is a weak negative correlation. The general tendency for Series 1 is a decrease and for Series 2 is a very mild increase. The direction changes are the same for about one-half of the data points. It might be possible to visually distinguish between correlations of 0.80. 0.30. −0.80, and −0.30. The task is more difficult for correlations that are closer together in value and also where the changes in the series are not so easy to see as would happen if one series had values that ranged between 4.5 and 5.5 on a graph scaled from 0 to 180 on the *y*-axis.

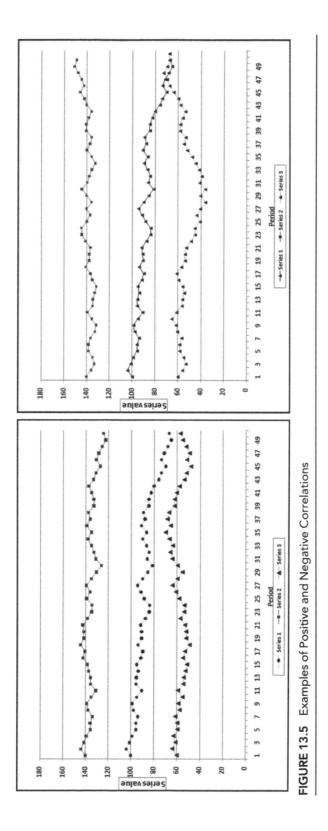

FIGURE 13.5 Examples of Positive and Negative Correlations

CORRELATION CALCULATIONS

The correlations calculated in Figures 13.1 to 13.5 are the Pearson product-moment correlations. The formula is shown in Equation 13.1.

$$\text{Correlation} = \frac{n\sum x_i y_i - \sum x_i \sum y_i}{\sqrt{n\sum x_i^2 - \left(\sum x_i\right)^2}\sqrt{n\sum y_i^2 - \left(\sum y_i\right)^2}} \qquad (13.1)$$

where x_i and y_i are the records in the fields whose correlations are being calculated.

This correlation equation in Equation 13.1 includes summations, which means that the calculations will require a series of queries in Access. Excel offers three options when it comes to calculating correlations. The first two options are to use the CORREL function or the Correlation tool in the Data Analysis tools. The Correlation tool calculates the correlations between all the records in all the fields. If a data table contains 10 fields then the Correlation tool will calculate the correlations among all 10 fields, which would give a 10 by 10 matrix as a result. The CORREL function allows more control because the results can be limited to the correlations of interest. The third Excel option is to calculate the correlation using the formula in Equation 13.1.

Excel is the efficient solution when a correlation calculation is needed for one forensic unit for only two data fields. The CORREL function or the Correlation tool is impractical when many forensic units are being compared to a single benchmark. The solution is to use Access when many forensic units are being compared to a single benchmark. With many forensic units IDEA is also an excellent option because it has correlation included as a built-in function. This chapter shows how to run the Access queries.

USING CORRELATION TO DETECT FRAUDULENT SALES NUMBERS

This section describes the use of correlation by an international company with about 5,000 franchised restaurants. The franchisees are required to report their monthly sales numbers in the first three days of a month. For example, the sales numbers for November should be reported by the third day of December. Based on the reported sales numbers, the franchisor bills the franchisee for royalty and advertising fees of 7 percent of sales. The sales reports are processed by the accounts receivable department and time is needed to follow up on missing values and obvious errors. By the end of the second week of a month the sales file for the preceding month has undergone all the major internal testing procedures. By the end of the third week of a month the forensic auditors are in a position to review the sales file. There is, however, a continual revision process that occurs because of sales adjustments identified by the franchisees and the franchisor. The forensic auditors have only a short window during which to review the sales numbers before the next wave of monthly reports becomes the current month. Reporting errors by franchisees could be either intentional or unintentional.

Reporting errors (intentional or unintentional) are usually in the direction of understated sales and result in a revenue loss for the franchisor. Using the Vasarhelyi (1983) taxonomy of errors, these errors could be (a) computational errors, (b) integrity errors (unauthorized deletion of transactions), (c) timing errors (incorrect time period), (d) irregularities (deliberate fraud), or (e) legal errors (transactions that violate legal clauses) such as omitting nonfood revenues. The cost of a revenue audit on location is high, and the full cost is not only borne by the franchisor, but also partially by the franchisee in terms of the costs related to providing data and other evidence. A forensic analytics system to identify high-risk sales reports is important to minimize the costs of auditing compliant franchisees. The available auditor time should be directed at high-risk franchisees. This environment is similar to many others where audit units self-report dollar amounts and other statistics, and the recipient has to evaluate which of these might contain errors (e.g., individual tax returns, pollution reports, airline baggage claims, and insurance claims).

The sales audit system included forensic analytics that scored each restaurant based on the perceived risk of underreported sales. In the Location Audit Risk System, each restaurant was scored on 10 indicators. For each indicator a score of 0 suggested a low risk of underreported sales, while a score of 1 suggested a high risk of underreported sales. The 10 indicators included a correlation test.

The reported monthly sales number from each franchisee is the only number reported to the franchisor and is the only sales-related information that is processed, thereby precluding tests based on more explanatory variables (such as cash register reports or sales tax returns). In developing the sales expectations the assumption was made that the seasonal and cyclical patterns of the franchisee sales numbers should closely follow those of the company-owned restaurants.

The first step in the development of the analytic tests was to calculate and graph the pattern of monthly sales for the company-owned restaurants. The results are shown in Figure 13.6.

Figure 13.6 shows the monthly sales pattern. There is a seasonal pattern to the sales numbers and a general upward trend. February has low sales presumably because of the winter cold and the fact that it only has 28 days. The highest sales are in the summer vacation months of July and August, and the holiday period at the end of the year.

The assumption of this test was that the average sales pattern shown in Figure 13.6 should be the same for the franchised restaurants unless there were errors in reporting or some other unusual situation. Deviations from the benchmark (or the "norm") signal possible reporting errors. An example of a hypothetical pattern is shown in Figure 13.7.

In Figure 13.7 the average sales pattern is the line with the diamond-markers and the hypothetical restaurant #1000 is the line with the circular markers. Restaurant #1000 shows an increase for February and has two abnormally low sales months (months 11 and 12). Also, the July sales number is lower than the June sales number, which differs from the average pattern. The correlation between the sales for #1000 and the average sales line is 0.279. Figure 13.7 also shows a linear regression line for restaurant #1000, which has a downward slope, whereas the regression line for the average (not shown) would have an upward slope.

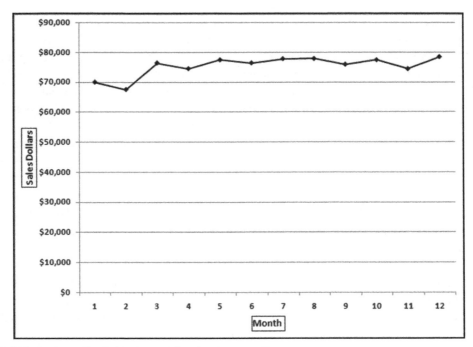

FIGURE 13.6 The Sales Pattern for the Average Restaurant

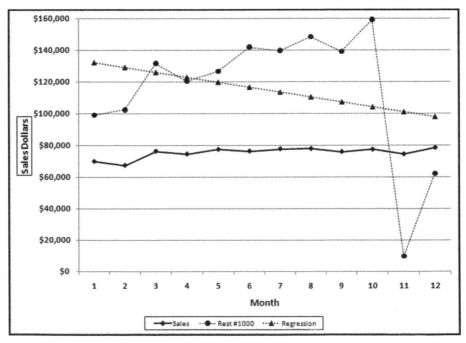

FIGURE 13.7 The Average Sales Pattern and the Sales for a Hypothetical Restaurant

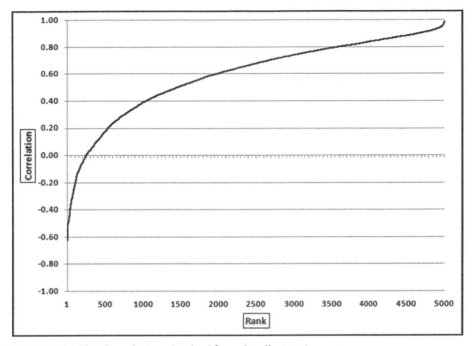

FIGURE 13.8 The Correlations Ranked from Smallest to Largest

The forensic analytics system was based on 10 predictors. Each predictor was seen to be a predictor of sales errors or irregularities. Each predictor was scored between 0.00 and 1.00, with 1.00 indicating a high risk of error or fraud. One predictor was based on the correlation between the sales for that particular restaurant, and the average sales pattern (in Figure 13.6). The correlation was calculated for each restaurant (their sales numbers against the average pattern) and the correlations were then ranked from smallest to largest.

The correlations were sorted from smallest to largest and the results are shown in Figure 13.8. The lowest correlation was about −0.60 and the highest correlations were close to 1.00. It is quite remarkable that there were about 250 restaurants with negative correlations. The results showed that correlation worked well at detecting anomalies because the locations with negative correlations did have odd sales patterns. There were many cases, though, where the anomalies were caused by factors other than errors. For example, locations at university campuses had weak correlations because universities are generally empty in July (with zero or low sales) and full of hungry students in February (generating relatively high sales). Also, restaurants that were located near a big annual sporting event also had weak correlations. For example, horse racing season in Saratoga Springs is in July and August and there are a few big annual events at the Indianapolis Motor Speedway. The sharp upward spike in sales at the time of these big events impacted the correlation score. New restaurants also usually had low correlation scores. The zero sales months prior to opening, followed by a steady upward trend in sales after opening, gave rise to a weak correlation score. Weak correlation scores could be due to explainable factors other than fraud or error. The scoring of forensic units for fraud risk is further discussed in Chapter 15.

USING CORRELATION TO DETECT ELECTRICITY THEFT

An electric utility company in South America suspected that electricity in certain locations was being consumed and not billed. Calculations by their forensic auditors confirmed this by comparing the kilowatt hour (kWh) records for production with the kWh records for billing. The loss was large enough to merit a special forensic investigation. Access was used to calculate the average billing pattern for the average customer. The average electric usage is shown in Figure 13.9.

The first step in the analysis was to assess how realistic the billing pattern was. For this country the monthly average temperatures varied only slightly and so air-conditioning usage would have varied only slightly from month to month. Also, with a low average income, electric air conditioning was not going to amount to much to begin with. The first conclusion was that the seasonal pattern in Figure 13.9 was not accurate. Despite the issues with the benchmark, the correlations were calculated between each meter and the average monthly pattern. The ordered correlations are shown in Figure 13.10.

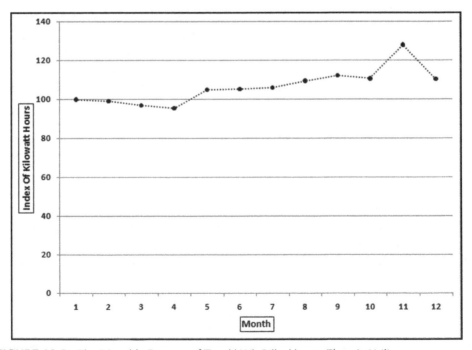

FIGURE 13.9 The Monthly Pattern of Total kWh Billed by an Electric Utility

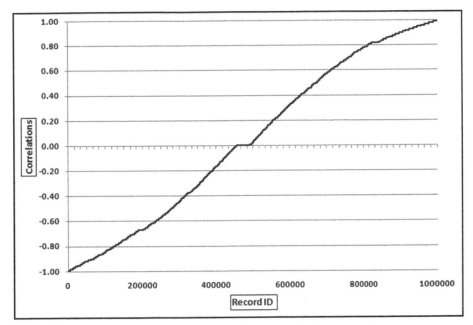

FIGURE 13.10 The Ordered (Ranked) Correlations of the Electric Utility

Figure 13.10 shows that the ranked correlations ranged from −0.99 to +0.99. The correlations were pretty much evenly spread over the range. The strange monthly pattern and the spread of the correlations indicated that correlation would not identify a small subset of odd meter patterns. The pattern actually indicates that one-half of the meter patterns were odd. With one million meters even a sample of 2 percent would give an audit sample of 20,000 units. Subsequent work showed that the meters were read every 28 days and so a specific meter might get read twice in one month and once in all the other months of the year.

Despite the issues with the correlations the correlations were still used to select an audit sample because the general trend in Figure 13.9 showed an increase. A negative correlation for a meter would mean that there was a declining trend for the year. A decrease in consumption is one indicator of electricity theft. An "extreme meter" test (called *Extreme Medidor*) was developed, which combined three predictor elements. These were (a) a large negative correlation (−0.75 or smaller), (b) a large percentage decrease from the first six months to the last six months of the year, and (c) a large decrease in absolute kWh terms. The forensic analytic test produced a sample of 1,200 highly suspect customers. The results also included a report showing customers with large credits (journal entries that simply reduced the number of kWh billed). These were red flags for internally assisted fraud by employees in the billing departments. The forensic investigation resulted in the recovery of several million dollars from customers and the prevention of further losses. Chapters 15 and 16 discuss in more detail the development of forensic risk scoring models for the detection of frauds and errors.

USING CORRELATION TO DETECT IRREGULARITIES IN ELECTION RESULTS

In October 2003 the state of California held a special election to decide on the incumbency of the governor in office. This election was unusual in that there were 135 candidates on the ballot (plus some write-in candidates) to replace the current governor. The candidate list included several actors (including Arnold Schwarzenegger and Gary Coleman) and others from all walks of life including a comedian, a tribal chief, and a publisher (Larry Flynt). The election results can be found by clicking on the links for *Election Results* from the Secretary of State's page for elections (www.sos.ca.gov/elections/).

The assertion in this application is that each candidate's votes in each county should be in proportion to the total votes cast in the county. For example, 22.65 percent of the total votes cast were cast in Los Angeles County and 9.43 percent of the total votes cast were cast in San Diego County. For every candidate we would expect 22.65 percent of their total to come from Los Angeles and 9.43 percent of their total to come from San Diego. That is, we would expect the vote count for any candidate to be 2.4 times higher in Los Angeles as compared to San Diego (22.65/9.43 = 2.4). So, if a candidate received 10,000 votes then we would expect 2,265 votes (10,000 * 22.65 percent) to be from Los Angeles and 943 votes (10,000 * 9.43 percent) to be from San Diego. The proportion of votes cast in each county is shown in Figure 13.11.

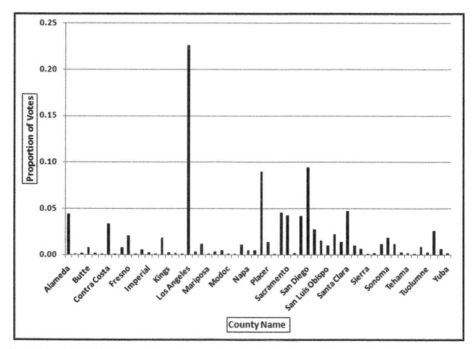

FIGURE 13.11   The Proportion of Votes Cast in Each County in the 2003 Election in California

The proportion of votes cast on a county-by-county basis is shown in Figure 13.11. There are 58 counties but Figure 13.11 only shows every second county name so that the names are readable. The proportion for each county is calculated by dividing the number of votes cast in the county by the total number of votes cast in the election. In Los Angeles County there were 1,960,573 votes cast out of a total of 8,657,824 votes cast in the state giving a Los Angeles proportion of 0.2265. In San Diego County, there were 816,100 votes cast and the San Diego County proportion is therefore 0.0943. The expectation is that the votes received by each candidate follows the pattern that most of their votes were received in Los Angeles and San Diego and few votes were received in Alpine or Sierra (which had about 500 and 1,500 voters in total). The correlations were calculated for each candidate between their voting patterns and the patterns shown in Figure 13.11. The correlations were then sorted from smallest to largest and the results are shown in Figure 13.12.

Figure 13.12 shows that the correlations ranged from 0.06 to 0.99. The lowest correlation was for candidate Jerry Kunzman and the highest correlation was for candidate Tom McClintock. The correlation for the winner, Arnold Schwarzenegger, was 0.98. In Figure 13.12 it seems that Arnold Schwarzenegger has the highest correlation but that is simply because the labels on the x-axis only show every fourth label to keep the labels readable. Even though the correlation for Jerry Kunzman is 0.06 this does not automatically signal fraud or error. The low correlation signals that this candidate's pattern differs significantly from the average pattern. The voter patterns for

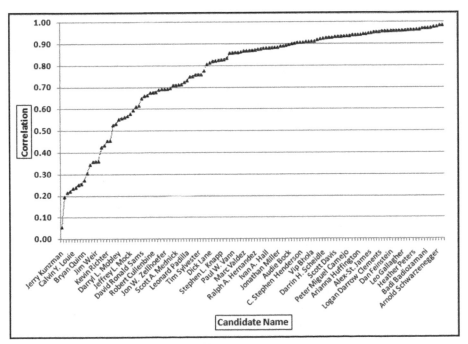

FIGURE 13.12 The Correlations for the Election Candidates

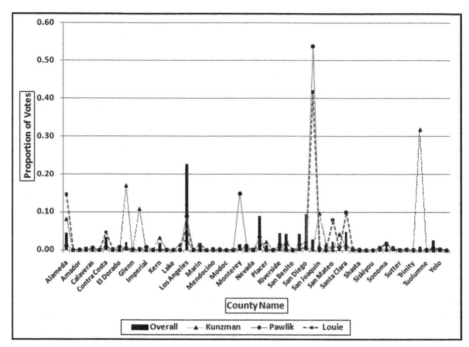

FIGURE 13.13 The Voter Patterns for Three Candidates with Low Correlations

the two lowest correlations (Jerry Kunzman at 0.06 and Gregory Pawlik at 0.20) and another candidate, Calvin Louie, are reviewed in Figure 13.13.

The voting patterns in Figure 13.13 show that the low correlations come about when a candidate gets a high proportion of their votes in a single county and very few votes in the counties that, on average, gave many votes to other candidates. For example, Kunzman got 32 percent of his votes in small Tulare County where the average percentage for this county was generally very low. It is a coincidence that Pawlik and Louie both got very high percentages in San Francisco.

The two lowest correlations were 0.056 and 0.196 for Kunzman and Pawlik. Pawlik only received 349 votes in total (about 6 votes per county). Pawlik received zero votes in 29 counties and any string of equal numbers will contribute to a low correlation. Pawlik received 188 votes in one county, and the string of zeroes together with one county providing about one-half of the total Pawlik votes caused a very weak correlation. In an investigative setting, the count of 188 votes in that single county would be reviewed.

Kunzman is a more interesting candidate with a near-zero correlation of 0.056. Kunzman received single digit counts for 42 counties giving a near-zero correlation for those 42 counties. He then received 736 votes in Tulare, a county with about 73,000 votes cast in total. Most of Kunzman's votes came from one small county. The correlation of near-zero is a true reflection of the voting pattern. In an investigative setting, the 736 votes in Tulare would be reviewed.

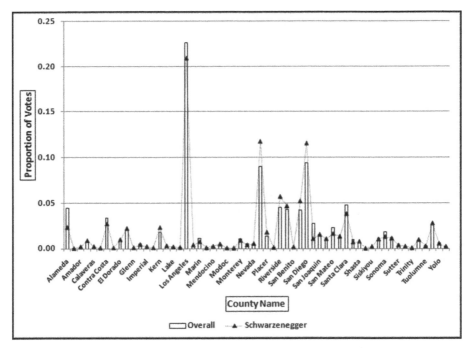

FIGURE 13.14 The County-by-County Results for the Winner, Arnold Schwarzenegger

It is interesting that the correlation for the winner, Arnold Schwarzenegger, was 0.98. With such a high correlation his vote pattern should closely follow the overall pattern in Figure 13.13 (the bars). This is indeed the case and these results are shown in Figure 13.14.

Figure 13.14 shows that the overall proportions and Schwarzenegger's proportions track each other quite closely to give a correlation of 0.98. The high correlation indicates that he was almost equally well liked across all counties. He did score low percentages in some counties but the overall picture was one of equal popularity throughout California. The graph shows that, for example, 22.6 percent of all votes cast were cast in Los Angeles, and 20.9 percent (slightly less) of Schwarzenegger's votes came from Los Angeles. Also, 9 percent of the total votes came from Orange County (the bar approximately in the middle of the x-axis) and 11.7 percent of Schwarzenegger's votes came from Orange County. For a correlation of 0.98 high percentages are needed in one series (total votes in California) and these should be matched with high percentages in the second series (votes for the candidate).

There were no candidates with negative correlations. Negative correlations would mean that a candidate would receive high counts in counties with low totals and low counts in counties with high totals. This would be very odd in election results. Correlation should provide similarly interesting results for other elections.

DETECTING IRREGULARITIES IN POLLUTION STATISTICS

In this section carbon dioxide emissions are analyzed for signs of errors or fraud. With global warming, countries have incentives to understate their emissions, and scientists, in general, have incentives to want accurate data with which to assess the issues and propose solutions. Data for the past 20 years are analyzed for signs of errors and fraud and also to assess what useful information is provided by the correlation calculations. The data was obtained from the U.S. Energy Information Administration's website and an image of the website with some of the data is shown in Figure 13.15.

The U.S. Energy Information Administration (EIA) is the statistical and analytical agency within the U.S. Department of Energy. The agency collects, analyzes, and disseminates independent and impartial energy information to promote sound policy making, efficient markets, and public understanding of energy and its interaction with the economy and the environment. The carbon dioxide emissions data for 1989 to 2008 was downloaded and a partial view of the file is shown in Figure 13.16.

Some data-cleansing steps were needed before the data could be analyzed. First, region totals (such as North America in row 5, and Central and South America in row 12 need to be removed). Second, countries with zero or very low emissions should be removed from the analysis. The inclusion of these countries in the analysis will complicate any interpretations from the data. The deletion of small countries will keep the results focused on the significant polluters. Third, some geographic changes needed to be made to the data such as adding East Germany and West Germany for 1988 and 1989 and including these numbers in the statistics for "Germany" (as in the united West and

U.S. Energy Information Administration
Independent Statistics and Analysis

Glossary   search

> International > International Energy Statistics

International Energy Statistics

| Petroleum | Natural Gas | Coal | Electricity | Renewables | Total Energy | Indicators | Country |

All Flows | Production | Consumption | Reserves | Imports | Exports | Carbon Dioxide Emissions | Heat Content

Country: All Countries by Region   Start Year: 1989 End Year: 2008   Update

Product: CO2 from the Consumption of Coal   Unit: Million Metric Tons

CO2 Emissions from the Consumption of Coal (Million Metric Tons)   Units Conversion   Download Excel

	1989	1990	1991	1992	1993	1994	1995	1996	1997	1998	1999	200(
North America	1,936.552	1,948.865	1,938.944	1,959.871	2,013.915	2,025.380	2,051.484	2,139.240	2,198.799	2,229.498	2,229.003	2,332.7
Bermuda	0	0	0	0	0	0	0	0	0	0	0	
Canada	125.223	111.927	117.144	122.599	113.741	114.980	118.998	120.323	134.137	139.848	139.311	149.4
Greenland	0	0	0	0	0	0	0	0	0	0	0	
Mexico	16.022	15.533	14.542	15.350	17.758	17.160	19.384	23.471	24.774	25.193	27.295	27.8
Saint Pierre and Miquelon	0	0	0	0	0	0	0	0	0	0	0	
United States	1,795.308	1,821.405	1,807.258	1,821.923	1,882.416	1,893.240	1,913.102	1,995.447	2,039.888	2,064.457	2,062.397	2,155.4
Central & South America	62.389	52.239	62.130	59.507	61.057	61.271	60.631	66.497	74.635	76.205	71.357	70.6
Antarctica	0	0	0	0	0	0	0	0	0	0	0	
Antigua and Barbuda	0	0	0	0	0	0	0	0	0	0	0	
Argentina	3.185	2.060	2.595	2.957	2.551	4.128	3.501	3.496	3.505	3.533	2.375	2.4

FIGURE 13.15 An Extract of Carbon Dioxide Emissions Data

Source: U.S. Energy Information Administration, www.eia.doe.gov.

	A	B	C	D	E	F	G	H	I	J
1	Table: CO2 Emissions from the Consumption of Coal (Million Metri									
2										
3			1989	1990	1991	1992	1993	1994	1995	1996
4										
5	North America		1937.97902	1932.10181	1920.96109	1941.24291	2002.42182	2014.62674	2039.69263	2126.90405
6	Bermuda		0	0	0	0	0	0	0	0
7	Canada		126.48745	113.05748	118.32716	123.83688	114.88984	116.14127	120.19997	121.53801
8	Greenland		0	0	0	0	0	0	0	0
9	Mexico		16.18364	15.68958	14.68845	15.50471	17.93787	17.33339	19.57981	23.70759
10	Saint Pierre and Mique		0	0	0	0	0	0	0	0
11	United States		1795.30793	1803.35474	1787.94548	1801.90131	1869.59411	1881.15209	1899.91285	1981.65846
12	Central & South Americ		63.0191	52.76627	62.75776	60.10769	61.67383	61.88942	61.24376	67.22555
13	Antarctica		0	0	0	0	0	0	0	0
14	Antigua and Barbuda		0	0	0	0	0	0	0	0
15	Argentina		3.19696	2.07021	2.62084	2.98671	2.57667	4.16731	3.627	3.52151
16	Aruba		0	0	0	0	0	0	0	0
17	Bahamas, The		0	0	0	0	0	0	0	0
18	Barbados		0	0	0	0	0	0	0	0
19	Belize		0	0	0	0	0	0	0	0
20	Bolivia		0	0	0	0	0	0	0	0
21	Brazil		36.57057	32.02667	37.84747	34.36368	34.92142	34.45539	35.87395	37.81518
22	Cayman Islands		0	0	0	0	0	0	0	0

FIGURE 13.16 The File with Carbon Dioxide Emissions from Coal

Source: U.S. Energy Information Administration, www.eia.doe.gov.

East). Fourth, the data need to be reconfigured in a table where all fields contain the same data. The statistics of 134 countries were deleted (leaving 90 countries) and the combined emissions of the deleted countries equaled about 0.05 percent of the world total. The data was imported into Access and an extract of the emissions table is shown in Figure 13.17.

The world total for each year from 1989 to 2008 was calculated from the emissions data in Figure 13.17. Thereafter the correlation for each country was calculated between the emissions for the specific country and the world total. Over the 20-year period the world total increased by 53.8 percent. The increase was, however, not uniform across the years. There were three years where the total decreased. These years corresponded to the economic slowdowns of 1991, 1992, and 1998. The results included some high positive correlations and quite a few negative correlations. Because the world trend is upward, upward-trending countries would have positive correlations while negative correlations occur because of a decreasing trend or some other anomaly. A table with the 15 highest and the 15 lowest correlations is shown in Figure 13.18.

The low correlation countries generally have a downward trend. In a few cases this was because of a poor country becoming even poorer and in so doing consuming less coal in total. In three cases the low correlations were because the national boundaries were created or changed (Belarus, Czech Republic, and Moldova). In general, the low correlations were because less energy was created through the burning of coal. A negative correlation indicates a difference between the world trend and the trend for a particular country. Some of the high and low correlation patterns are shown in Figures 13.19 and 13.20. Figure 13.19 shows the world trend and the annual numbers for three high-profile high correlation countries. The emission numbers were indexed with the 1989 values set equal to 100. Without indexing the world total would be very large relative to the other values and it would be difficult to see small up and down changes.

EmissionsData			
ID	Year	Name	Carbon
1	1989	China	$1,916.7674
2	1990	China	$1,924.2031
3	1991	China	$1,994.1440
4	1992	China	$2,063.5755
5	1993	China	$2,189.1307
6	1994	China	$2,376.3344
7	1995	China	$2,373.9000
8	1996	China	$2,395.9535
9	1997	China	$2,524.8705
10	1998	China	$2,410.5575
11	1999	China	$2,288.3151
12	2000	China	$2,178.3897
13	2001	China	$2,280.4695
14	2002	China	$2,740.7201
15	2003	China	$3,322.1505
16	2004	China	$4,206.8119
17	2005	China	$4,578.1733
18	2006	China	$4,823.5192
19	2007	China	$5,139.8615
20	2008	China	$5,381.9981
21	1989	United States	$1,795.3079
22	1990	United States	$1,803.3547
23	1991	United States	$1,787.9455
24	1992	United States	$1,801.9013
25	1993	United States	$1,869.5941

Record: I◄ ◄ 1 of 1800 ► ►I ►▪ ▼ No Filter | Search

FIGURE 13.17 The Access Table with the Pollution Statistics

Figure 13.19 shows the world pattern and the patterns for three countries as index values starting at 100. The world pattern is the solid line generally trailing at the bottom of the graph that shows an increase of 53.8 percent over the 20 year period. The patterns for both China and India each show increases of about 180 percent over the period. The pattern for South Africa shows a slightly smaller increase of 42.3 percent over the period. The correlations of China, India, and South Africa are 0.9891, 0.8934, and 0.8492 respectively. The patterns for China and India shows that the series needs to only match each other approximately to give a high correlation. The low correlation patterns are shown in Figure 13.20.

Figure 13.20 shows the world emissions pattern as the solid line with an increasing pattern. The graph also shows three well-known countries with relatively low correlations. The emissions pattern for Finland is the dashed line that ends marginally lower than 100 at 98.8. The overall pattern showed a marginal decrease whereas the world pattern shows an increase. The pattern for Finland is choppy with jagged up and down movements. The absolute numbers are small coming in at about 0.17 percent of the world total. The sharp increase from 2002 to 2003 is suspect. The absolute numbers show an increase of about 10.5 million tons. European Union publications show an increase for Finland of only 3 million tons due to a very cold winter and declining

qrySortedCorrelations	
Name	Corr
China	0.9891
Malaysia	0.9847
Pakistan	0.9648
Indonesia	0.9608
Puerto Rico	0.9516
Vietnam	0.9447
Korea - South	0.9213
Mauritius	0.9118
Peru	0.9088
India	0.8934
Japan	0.8925
Thailand	0.8925
Guatemala	0.8845
Turkey	0.8788
Congo (Kinshasa)	0.8747

Name	Corr
Germany	-0.3769
Korea - North	-0.4021
Moldova	-0.4263
Norway	-0.4317
United Kingdom	-0.4342
Czech Republic	-0.4805
Belarus	-0.4983
France	-0.5092
Denmark	-0.5196
Ireland	-0.5593
Hungary	-0.5947
Luxembourg	-0.6070
Poland	-0.6617
Zimbabwe	-0.7969
Belgium	-0.8808

FIGURE 13.18 The Results Showing the Highest and the Lowest Correlations with the World Trend

electricity imports and increased exports. The EIA increase of 10.5 million tons might be due to an error of some sort (perhaps correcting a prior year number?). The low correlations for Belgium and Germany (-0.8808 and -0.3769) are because their emissions decreased while the world total increased. This general decline in European emissions is supported by the data on the website of the European Environment Agency. A noteworthy pattern is the sharp decline in German pollution in the early 1990s. Intuitively, this might seem to be an error. However, the sharp (but welcome) decline in pollution from the former East Germany is documented in a scientific paper published in *Atmospheric Environment* (1998, Volume 32, No. 20).

Given the interesting European results the correlation studies suggest several research questions. The first being an assessment of the correlation between the U.S. figures of the EIA and the European figures of the European Environment Agency. The second being an assessment of the correlations between the emission numbers of the European countries using the European totals as the benchmark.

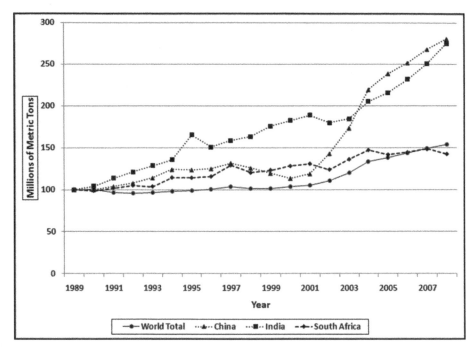

FIGURE 13.19 The World Pattern and the Pattern for Three High Correlation Countries

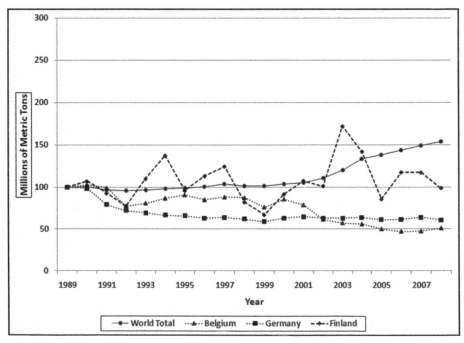

FIGURE 13.20 The World Pattern and the Pattern for Three Low Correlation Countries

CALCULATING CORRELATIONS IN ACCESS

Access is the preferred software when we need to calculate correlations for many locations or individuals. The calculations will be demonstrated on the hypothetical sales of three restaurants and a series of average sales numbers. In each case we are calculating the correlations between the sales for a single restaurant and the average. The calculations are calculated using Equation 13.1. Because of the summations and the use of x^2, y^2, and xy, the analytics will require a series of queries. The data for the three restaurants are in *tblSalesData* and the average numbers are in *tblAverage*. The Access table is shown in Figure 13.21.

Figure 13.21 shows the sales data and the table format needed for the correlation calculations. The sales data needs to have a location identifier (*RestNum*) and a time period identifier (*Month* and *Year*). The calculations are much easier if the table contains only the data that will be used for the calculations with no missing (or null) values. The table *tblAverageSales* has only 12 rows, one row for each month, similar to the first 12 rows of *tblSalesData*, without the *RestNum* field. The sales numbers field in *tblAverageSales* is named *AvgSales* so as not to use the same field name as in the main

ID	RestNum	Sales	Month	Year
1	1000	$99,090	1	2011
2	1000	$102,484	2	2011
3	1000	$131,734	3	2011
4	1000	$120,518	4	2011
5	1000	$126,630	5	2011
6	1000	$142,014	6	2011
7	1000	$139,739	7	2011
8	1000	$148,518	8	2011
9	1000	$139,220	9	2011
10	1000	$159,278	10	2011
11	1000	$9,821	11	2011
12	1000	$62,174	12	2011
13	2000	$15,055	1	2011
14	2000	$17,998	2	2011
15	2000	$16,880	3	2011
16	2000	$18,764	4	2011
17	2000	$14,361	5	2011
18	2000	$9,891	6	2011
19	2000	$8,815	7	2011
20	2000	$11,955	8	2011
21	2000	$24,312	9	2011
22	2000	$27,631	10	2011
23	2000	$26,053	11	2011
24	2000	$17,031	12	2011
25	3000	$100,976	1	2011

Record: I◄ ◄ 1 of 36   ► ►I ►▭   ℀ No Filter | Search

FIGURE 13.21   The Sales Numbers in the Table *tblSalesData*

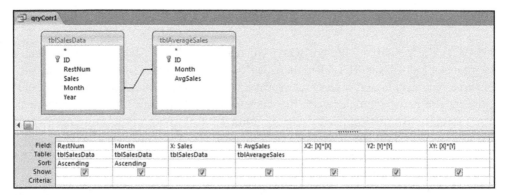

FIGURE 13.22 The First Query to Calculate the Correlations

tblSalesData table. The sales numbers are formatted as Currency because this formatting avoids some of the errors that occur with the use of floating-point arithmetic operations. The correlations use a series of four queries. The first query *qryCorr1* is shown in Figure 13.22.

The first correlation query *qryCorr1* combines the microdata and the average data in a single table, and calculates the squared and multiplied values that are needed for Equation 13.1. The use of the join matches up the sales of each restaurant against the average sales. The average sales will be pasted next to the sales numbers for each location. The sales numbers are also renamed *X* and *Y* so that these shorter names tie in with Equation 13.1 and because it is easier to use short names in formulas. The *X2* stands for *x*-squared and similarly *Y2* stands for *y*-squared. The calculated fields have also been formatted as Currency with zero places after the decimal point making the results a little easier to read. The next query calculates the sums required and this query is shown in Figure 13.23.

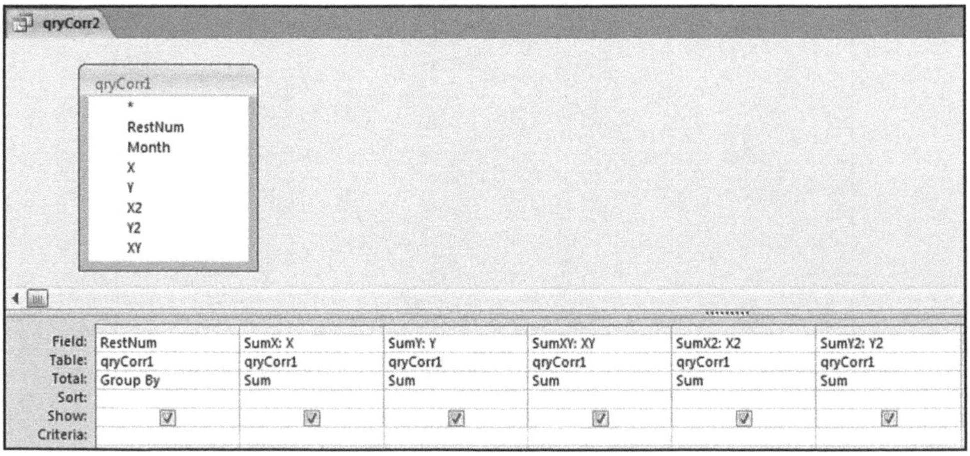

FIGURE 13.23 The Second Query to Calculate the Correlations

RestNum	SumX	SumY	SumXY	SumX2	SumY2
1000	$1,381,220	$904,272	$104,521,131,673	$178,701,698,978	$68,267,071,914
2000	$208,746	$904,272	$15,702,918,181	$4,035,658,852	$68,267,071,914
3000	$1,431,085	$904,272	$108,234,946,497	$172,407,416,005	$68,267,071,914

qryCorr2

FIGURE 13.24 The Results of the Second Query to Calculate the Correlations

The query in Figure 13.23 uses only the data and calculations from the first query. The query *qryCorr2* calculates the summations needed for the correlations. The correlation equation uses the sums of the xs and ys and the x and y-squared terms and well as the cross multiplication of x and y. The summations need to be done separately for each restaurant (or country, or candidate, or meter, as in the chapter case studies). This example has only three restaurants and so there are three rows of output. The results of *qryCorr2* are shown in Figure 13.24.

The results in Figure 13.24 show one row of sums for each location. The results for this step for the election candidates in the prior case study had one row for each candidate, giving 135 rows for that *qryCorr2*. The next step is to calculate how many records we have for each restaurant (or location, or candidate, or country). This will usually be known to the forensic investigator (e.g., 12 months, 58 counties, 20 years) but it is better to calculate the number with a separate query and then to use the results in the final query. The query needed to count the records in the *tblAverageSales* table is shown in Figure 13.25.

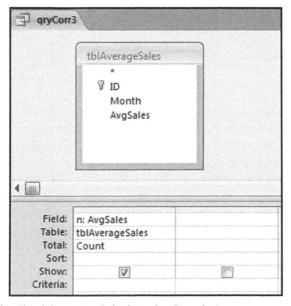

FIGURE 13.25 The Third Query to Calculate the Correlations

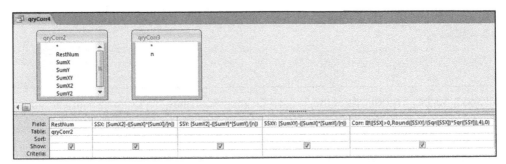

FIGURE 13.26 The Fourth Query to Calculate the Correlations

Figure 13.25 shows the query that counts the number of records for each unit. This count is named n to match up with Equation 13.1. In the final query, the correlations are calculated and *qryCorr4* is shown in Figure 13.26.

In the final query, the correlations are calculated and *qryCorr4* is shown in Figure 13.26. The calculated numbers are broken down into parts known as the sum of squares. The "SS" in *SSX*, *SSY*, and *SSXY* refers to the sum of squares. The correlation calculation uses these sums of squares. The formulas used in *qryCorr4* are:

SSX: [SumX2]-([SumX]*[SumX]/[n])
SSY: [SumY2]-([SumY]*[SumY]/[n])
SSXY: [SumXY]-([SumX]*[SumY]/[n])
Corr: IIf([SSX]>0,Round([SSXY]/(Sqr([SSX])*Sqr([SSY])),4),0)

The query *qryCorr4* is algebraically equivalent to Equation 13.1. The revised formula is shown in Equation 13.2.

$$\text{Correlation} = \frac{\sum x_i y_i - \frac{\sum x_i \sum y_i}{n}}{\sqrt{\sum x_i^2 - \frac{(\sum x_i)^2}{n}}\sqrt{n\sum y_i^2 - \frac{(\sum y_i)^2}{n}}} \quad (13.2)$$

The next step is to sort the correlations. Since the calculated field *Corr* is based on three other calculated fields in the same query, the best option is to use another query for the sort. Also, if the calculated *Corr* results in an error condition for any record then this will give issues with the sort. The error message will seem to relate to the sort and not to the original *Corr* calculation. The query for the sort is shown in Figure 13.27.

The query used to sort the correlations is shown in Figure 13.27. The results of the query are shown in Figure 13.28.

The results in Figure 13.28 show that the numbers for restaurant #3000 track the average pattern quite closely. The sales numbers for restaurant #1000 have a very weak correlation with the average. This pattern can be seen in Figure 13.7. The correlation for restaurant #2000 is weak and negative. This sales pattern was adapted from the sales numbers from a restaurant on a college campus where the sales numbers were low in July, August, and December because of the summer and winter breaks.

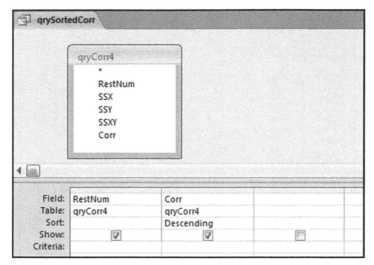

FIGURE 13.27 The Query to Sort the Correlations

FIGURE 13.28 The Correlations Sorted from Largest to Smallest

 CALCULATING THE CORRELATIONS IN EXCEL

Excel has three ways of calculating correlations. The first method is to use the **Data→Data Analysis→Analysis Tools→Correlation** tool. The second alternative is to use the CORREL function. The third alternative is to use either Equation 13.1 or Equation 13.2. Excel is the preferred alternative if we only have to calculate one correlation between two sets of data because we can use the CORREL function. Excel becomes a bit cumbersome when we have to calculate the correlations for many locations, countries, candidates, or other unit of interest. The number of records is not usually an issue with Excel because the data tables used with correlation applications are usually well within the Excel limit. The correlation calculations will be demonstrated using the same data as in the previous section.

The preferred Excel option when there are many forensic units (locations, candidates, countries, or other units) is to use the CORREL function. To do this, each forensic unit should have exactly the same number of rows and the row count should match the

	A	B	C	D	E
1	RestNum ▼	Sales ▼	Month ▼	Year ▼	AvgSales ▼
2	1000	$99,090	1	2011	$70,000
3	1000	$102,484	2	2011	$67,537
4	1000	$131,734	3	2011	$76,451
5	1000	$120,518	4	2011	$74,539
6	1000	$126,630	5	2011	$77,466
7	1000	$142,014	6	2011	$76,408
8	1000	$139,739	7	2011	$77,799
9	1000	$148,518	8	2011	$77,888
10	1000	$139,220	9	2011	$75,912
11	1000	$159,278	10	2011	$77,425
12	1000	$9,821	11	2011	$74,392
13	1000	$62,174	12	2011	$78,455
14	2000	$15,055	1	2011	$70,000
15	2000	$17,998	2	2011	$67,537
16	2000	$16,880	3	2011	$76,451
17	2000	$18,764	4	2011	$74,539
18	2000	$14,361	5	2011	$77,466
19	2000	$9,891	6	2011	$76,408
20	2000	$8,815	7	2011	$77,799
21	2000	$11,955	8	2011	$77,888
22	2000	$24,312	9	2011	$75,912
23	2000	$27,631	10	2011	$77,425
24	2000	$26,053	11	2011	$74,392
25	2000	$17,031	12	2011	$78,455
26	3000	$100,976	1	2011	$70,000
27	3000	$96,762	2	2011	$67,537
28	3000	$112,794	3	2011	$76,451
29	3000	$117,258	4	2011	$74,539
30	3000	$114,941	5	2011	$77,466

|◄ ◄ ► ►| SalesData

FIGURE 13.29 The Layout of the Sales Numbers in Excel

Average series or whatever is being used as a benchmark. The Excel file for the sales numbers is shown in Figure 13.29.

Figure 13.29 shows the data table in an Excel format. Each location has 12 records and the benchmark numbers are duplicated next to the 12 records for each restaurant. The months should match exactly. Each record should show the sales for a specified month and the benchmark for that same month. The Excel data was formatted as a table using **Home→Styles→Format as Table** with Table Style Medium 2. The CORREL function is shown in Figure 13.30.

The *Correlation* field should be formatted to show only four digits after the decimal place. The CORREL function should also be copied down so that the calculation is run for all restaurants.

Figure 13.31 shows the **Copy** and **Paste** steps used to apply the CORREL function to every forensic unit. The first 12 rows are highlighted (even though 11 of these rows are blank) for the **Copy** command and all the rows are highlighted for the **Paste** command.

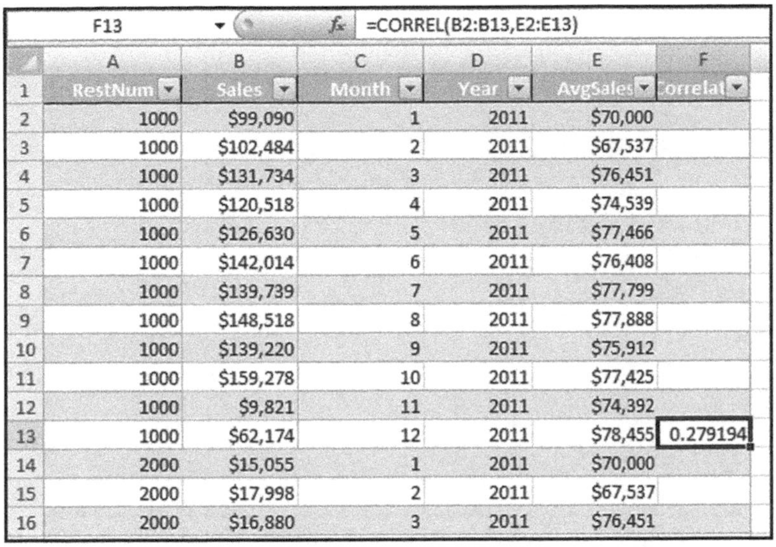

FIGURE 13.30 The Use of the CORREL Function to Calculate Correlation

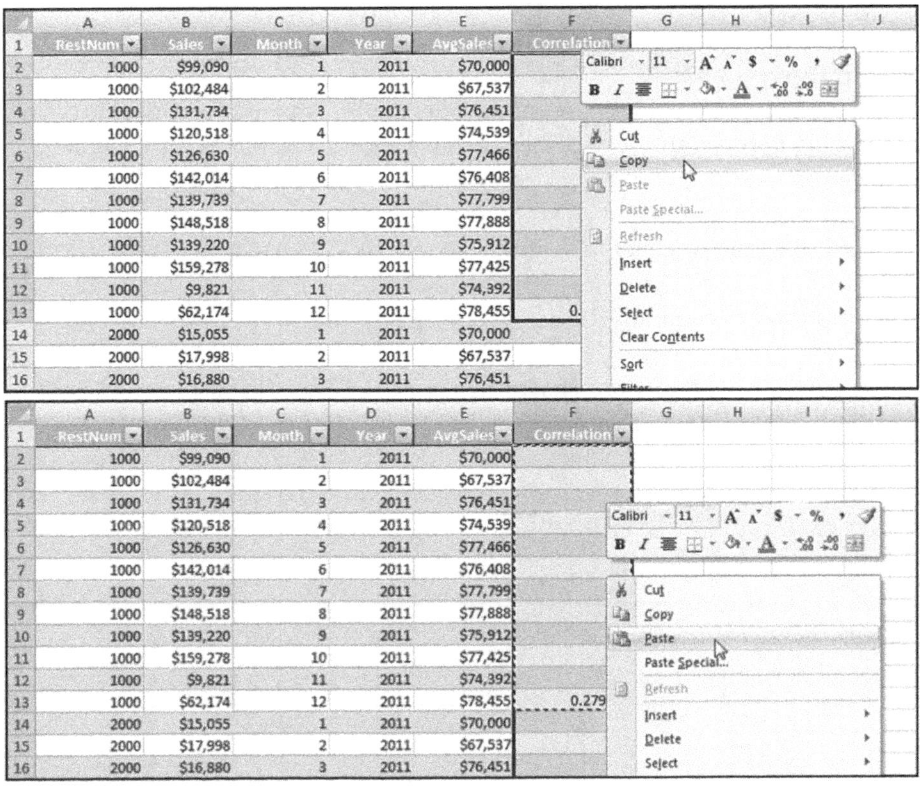

FIGURE 13.31 The *Copy* and *Paste* Steps to Calculate the Correlation for Each Forensic Unit

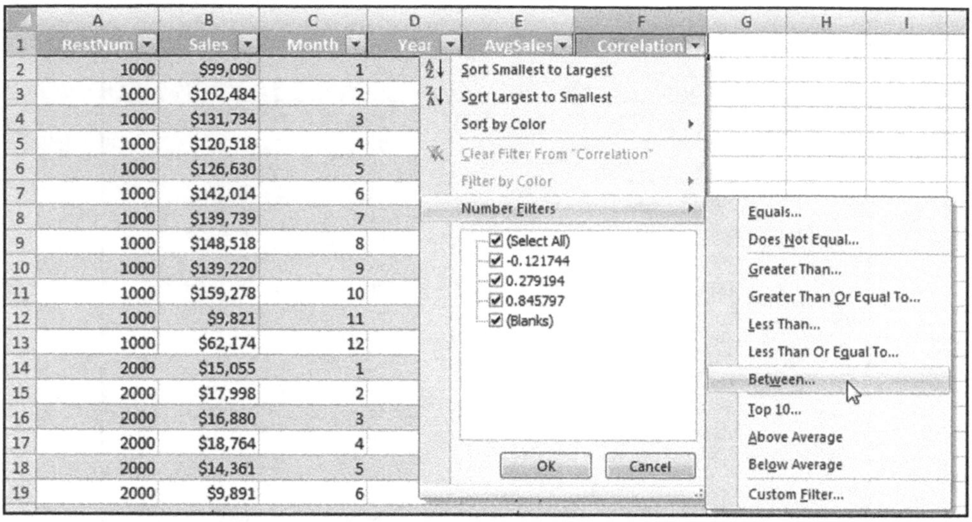

FIGURE 13.32 The Filter to Extract Only the Correlations for the Forensic Units

The result will be one correlation at the last row of the data for every forensic unit. The last step is to apply a filter so that we only show one row for each forensic unit. This is shown in Figure 13.32.

The filter used to extract only the correlations is demonstrated in Figure 13.32. After clicking ***Between*** the next step is to complete the dialog box by entering the upper and lower bounds,

"is greater than or equal to" −1.00
And,
"is less than or equal to" 1.00

The correlation results are shown in Figure 13.33. All that remains is for the correlations to be sorted. This is easily done using ***Home→Editing→Sort&Filter***. Using Excel is probably a little quicker than Access because of the CORREL function in Excel. The upside to using Access is that the queries and the entire setup can be reused on other data.

F37 =CORREL(B26:B37,E26:E37)

	A	B	C	D	E	F
1	RestNum	Sales	Month	Year	AvgSales	Correlation
13	1000	$62,174	12	2011	$78,455	0.279194
25	2000	$17,031	12	2011	$78,455	-0.121744
37	3000	$131,565	12	2011	$78,455	0.845797

FIGURE 13.33 The Correlation Results in Excel

SUMMARY

This chapter reviewed how correlation could be used to identify errors and frauds. Correlation measures how closely two sets of time-related data move in tandem. In the United States the prices of gasoline for regular, mid-, and high-octane fuel are highly correlated. A price move for one grade is closely matched by a price move in the other grades. Correlation results range from -1.00 to $+1.00$. A correlation of 1.00 indicates that there is a perfect, positive, linear relationship between the two series. A change in the value of one variable is matched with an exact percentage change in the second variable, or an exact absolute value change in the second variable. When the correlation is zero there is no correlation between the two series of data. A correlation of -1.00 (which is rare) means that there is a perfect negative relationship between two sets of data.

Four case studies are reviewed and in the first application correlation was used to identify sales patterns that differed from a benchmark. These differences could be red flags for intentional or unintentional errors in sales reporting. Correlation by itself was an imperfect indicator because there were many valid reasons for having weak correlations. The correlation tests were combined with other tests to examine the trend in sales. A weak correlation matched with a strong *increasing* trend in sales was some assurance that sales were not being underreported. The use of correlation helps investigators to understand the entity and its environment.

The second correlation application was to identify electricity theft. A weak correlation between the patterns for a specific user and the average pattern was an indicator that the user might be stealing electricity. In this application the benchmark average pattern was questionable. However, since the average trend was increasing, a weak correlation meant that the customer had a decreasing trend. The tests combined correlation, a test for a decreasing trend, and a test for abnormally high credits for each customer.

The third application was to find anomalies in election results. The 2003 California election results were tested. The assumption was that if 23 percent of the total votes came from Los Angeles, and 10 percent of the votes came from San Diego, then each candidate should get 23 percent of their votes from Los Angeles, and 10 percent from San Diego. Low correlations would result when a candidate got an abnormally large percentage of their votes from one or two counties. The results showed some odd voting patterns. The winner, Arnold Schwarzenegger, had a correlation of 0.98, which means that his votes in each county closely tracked the totals for the counties.

The final application used carbon dioxide emission statistics for about 90 countries for 20 years. Total world emissions increased by 53.8 percent over the past 20 years. Several countries had high correlations, meaning that their emissions increased in line with the world increase. The countries with low correlations were countries with strange issues such as extreme poverty in Zimbabwe and North Korea. A negative correlation occurs when the emissions for a country show a decrease in the face of the world total showed an increase. The green drive in Europe also gave rise to negative correlations. Other negative correlations came about because of significant geographical changes (e.g., Czechoslovakia splitting into two parts). Correlation also correctly signaled the sharp decrease in emissions from East Germany after unification.

Correlations can be calculated in Access using a series of four queries. These queries can be reused in other applications provided that the table names and the field names are unchanged. The correlation graphs are prepared in Excel. The correlations can also be calculated in Excel using the CORREL function.

Correlation provides an informative signal that the data for a specific location, country, candidate, or other forensic unit differs from the average pattern or some other benchmark. The use of correlation combined with other techniques, could be useful indicators of errors or fraud.

CHAPTER FOURTEEN

Identifying Fraud Using Time-Series Analysis

A TIME-SERIES ANALYSIS EXTRAPOLATES the past into the future and compares current results to those predictions. Large deviations from the predictions signal a change in conditions, which might include fraud. A time-series is an ordered sequence of the successive values of an expense or revenue stream in units or dollars over equally spaced time intervals. Time-series is well suited to forensic analytics because accounting transactions usually include a time or date stamp. The main objectives with time-series analysis are to (a) give the investigator a better understanding of the revenues or expenditures under investigation, and, (b) to predict the revenues or expenses for future periods. These predicted values will be compared to the expected results and large differences investigated.

The comparison of actual to predicted results is closely related to a continuous monitoring setting. Time-series analysis has been made easier to use over the past few years by user-friendly software and the increased computing power of personal computers. An issue with time-series is that the diagnostic statistics are complex and this might make some forensic investigators uncomfortable in drawing conclusions that have forensic implications. For example, there are usually three measures to measure the accuracy of the fitted model and users might not know which measure is the best.

The usual forensic analytics application is forecasting the revenues for business or government forensic units, or forecasting items of an expenditure or loss nature for business or government forensic units. *Forensic units* are units that are being analyzed from a forensic perspective and are further discussed in Chapter 15. A forensic unit is basically the subunit used to perpetrate the fraud (a cashier, a division, a bank account number, or a frequent flyer number). For example, in an audit of the small claims paid by insurance agents in 2011, the 2011 claims would be predicted using time-series and the

2008–2010 claims. A large difference between the actual and the predicted claim payments would indicate that conditions have changed.

In a continuous monitoring environment time-series could be used to compare the actual revenues against forecasts for the current period. Time-series could be used to forecast the monthly revenues for each location for restaurant chains, stores, or parking garages. Large differences between the actual and the forecast numbers are signs of possible errors in the reported numbers. Time-series could also be used as a control of expenditure or loss accounts that have high risks for fraudulent activity. Loss accounts are costs that have no compensating benefit received and examples of these losses include (a) merchandise returns and customer refunds at store locations, (b) baggage claims at airport locations, (c) payroll expenses classified as overtime payments, (d) credits to customer accounts at utility companies, (e) warranty claims paid by auto manufacturers, or (f) insurance claims paid directly by agents.

Extrapolation (time-series) methods and econometric methods are the main statistical methods used for the analysis of time-series data. The choice of methods depends on the behavior of the series itself and whether there is additional data (besides just the revenue or expense numbers) on which to base the forecast. Time-series methods generally use only the past history of a time-series to forecast the future values. Time-series methods are most useful when the data has seasonal changes and the immediate past values of the series are a useful basis for the forecast. The original motivation for using time-series in forensic analytics was an application to see whether the divisional controllers were booking higher than usual sales at the end of each quarter. This quarter-end excess was called the quarter-end *sales pad*.

Time-series is a more sophisticated form of regression analysis where the forecasts include seasonal increases and decreases. In a forensic investigation setting time-series could be used by:

- A franchisor, to see which locations are showing a decrease in sales compared to past trends.
- An airline, to see which airports are showing a large increase in cases of baggage theft.
- A bank, to see which branches are showing the largest increases in loans written off.
- A school district, to see which schools are using more electricity than the amount extrapolated from past trends.
- An insurance company, to see which agents are paying claims in excess of their predicted values.
- A cruise ship or hospital, to see which ships or departments have food consumption in excess of their predicted values.
- A courier service, to see which locations are showing the largest increases in fuel expenses.
- A church district, to see which churches are showing decreasing trends in income.

This chapter reviews four time-series case studies to show how the technique works in practice. The case studies include heating oil sales, stock market returns, construction numbers, and streamflow statistics. The chapter includes a review of running the time-series tests in Excel.

TIME-SERIES METHODS

To extrapolate means to extend the curve beyond the known values in a way that makes sense. These extended values would be our forecasts. Forecasting methods are usually based on (a) the simple average of past data values, or (b) a weighted average of the past data values with higher weights on more recent values, or (c) a simple or weighted average of past values together with an adjustment for seasonal patterns or cyclical patterns. A seasonal pattern is one that varies with some regularity in the past data. For example, heating oil sales are seasonal with high sales in the cold winter months and low sales in the hot summer months. A cyclical pattern is one that cycles up and down over long unequal time periods; for example, stock market bull or bear cycles, or housing boom or bust cycles.

The first step in the process is to fit a function (a line) to the series of past values. This is quite easy if the past values are close to being a straight line. The better the fit of the line to the past values, the more confidence can be shown in the predicted values. The fit between the past data and the fitted line is measured by the mean absolute percentage error (MAPE). The MAPE is a close cousin of the mean absolute deviation (MAD) discussed in Chapter 6.

Because time-series is entirely based on the past values in a series we need to consider the random variation in the past time-series. If the random variations are large then the past data values will only be a noisy basis for predicting the future. For example, in an elementary school in a remote part of the country the enrollments could be forecast with a high degree of accuracy because the population would be much the same from year to year. In other situations the future is affected by highly variable external factors. High levels of random variation would be characterized by higher MAPE measures.

AN APPLICATION USING HEATING OIL SALES

Heating oil is a low viscosity, flammable liquid petroleum product used as a heating fuel for furnaces or boilers in buildings. Heating oil use is concentrated in the northeastern United States. The demand for heating oil makes it highly seasonal. Heating oil data was obtained from the U.S. Census Bureau (Census Bureau) and the U.S. Energy Information Administration (EIA). The time-series graph in Figure 14.1 shows heating oil sales from 2005 to 2010.

The EIA data used is the "U.S. No. 2 Fuel Oil All Sales/Deliveries by Prime Supplier." The data is the detail supplied from the "Prime Supplier Sales Volumes" page. The EIA data has been converted from thousands of gallons per day to a monthly number. The

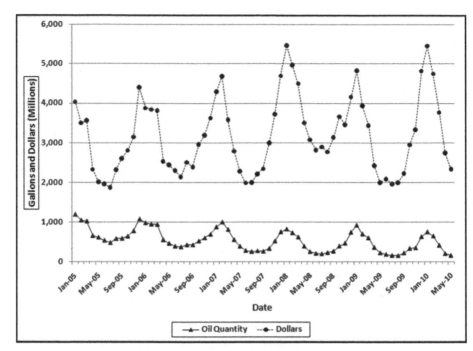

FIGURE 14.1   U.S. Heating Oil Sales in Dollars and Gallons

reported number for January 2009 was 29,853.1. This number was multiplied by 31 to give a January volume of 925.4461 million gallons.

The heating oil sales data in Figure 14.1 shows that the demand is highly seasonal with a low demand in the warm summer months and a high demand in the cold winter months. The seasonal pattern repeats every 12 months. The lower line represents the sales in millions of gallons and the upper line shows the sales in millions of dollars. The two series are highly correlated since the seasonal pattern exists for both total gallons and total dollars. The peak is during the cold period and the valley is at the warmest time of the year. The correlation between the two series is 0.67. The correlation is less than 1.00 because (a) both series are subject to some measurement error, and (b) the price per gallon was not constant over the period. The price varied from a low of $1.808 per gallon at the start of the period to $2.716 at the end of the period with a high of $4.298 near the middle of the series in July 2008. Since the sales dollars series is affected by quantity and price, the sales in gallons will be used for time-series analysis. The time-series analysis is shown graphically in Figure 14.2.

Figure 14.2 shows the actual heating oil data in millions of gallons from Figure 14.1 together with the fitted line and the 12 forecasts for 2010. The forecasting method used is based on Ittig (2004). This method is a decomposition method that also takes the trend into account. The method first calculates the effect of the seasons on the data (e.g., month 1 is 69.2 percent higher than average, and month 7 is 46.2 percent lower than average). The data is then deseasonalized, which basically removes the seasonal factors (e.g., month 1 is reduced by 40.9 percent and month 7 is increased by 85.9 percent to

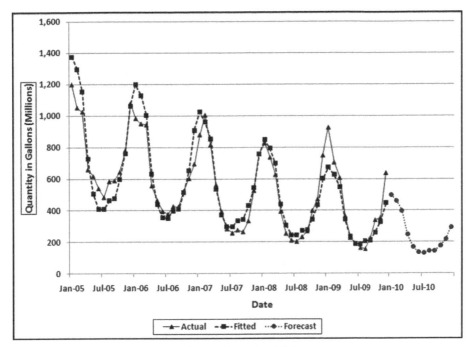

FIGURE 14.2 The Time-Series Analysis of Heating Oil Data

get back to the baseline). A regression is run on the logs of the quantities and the seasonal factor is then put back into the data. The Ittig (2004) method works well for financial data because it takes into account the seasonal factors, the trend, and also whether the seasonal pattern is becoming more or less pronounced. In the heating oil data it seems that the seasonal pattern is becoming less pronounced as the series is trending downward. The trend refers to the general upward or downward tendency over the five-year range.

There is more than one method for measuring how "good" a forecast is. One useful metric is how well the fitted values match the actual values for the past data. In the heating oil data this would be the 2005 to 2009 numbers. The closer the fitted values track the actual numbers, the easier it was for the technique to fit a function to the past data. Our assessment of the fit of the function is similar to our assessment of the fit of the actual proportions to the proportions of Benford's Law in Chapter 6. The metric for assessing the goodness-of-fit for time-series data is the MAPE and the formula is shown in Equation 14.1.

$$\text{MAPE} = \frac{\sum_{i=1}^{K} \left| \frac{(AV - FV)}{AV} \right|}{K} \times 100 \tag{14.1}$$

where AV denotes the actual value, FV denotes the fitted value, and K is the number of records used for the forecast. The MAPE calculation in Equation 14.1 is invalid for an AV value (or values) of zero, because division by zero is not permissible. For AV values of zero

TABLE 14.1 A Short Example of the Goodness-of-Fit Calculations

Actual	Fitted	Absolute Difference (AD)	AD Divided by Actual
100	97	3	.0300
105	110	5	.0476
106	111	5	.0472

the MAPE should be reported as N/A (not applicable) or the MAD in Equation 6.4 should be used. In the case of the heating oil data we have 12 records for each year giving us a K of 48 (12 times 4).

The MAPE in Equation 14.1 is closely related to the MAD in Equation 6.4. The MAPE gives us the goodness-of-fit as a percentage. The MAPE for the heating oil data in Figure 14.2 is 12.7 percent, which means that the fitted line is, on average, 12.7 percent "away" from the actual line. This high MAPE is even more troublesome because the fit is worse for the most recent year. A simple example with only three actual and fitted values (as opposed to 48 actual and fitted values for the heating oil data) is shown in Table 14.1.

An example with only three data points and three fitted values is shown in Table 14.1. The average of the absolute differences is 0.0416 and after multiplying by 100 we get a MAPE of 4.16.

There is no benchmark for a "large" MAPE. Each application should be looked at individually. If the stakes are high and a high degree of confidence is needed in the results then we would like to see a low MAPE, which indicates that the past seasonal patterns and the past trend is stable. For forensic applications where there might be legal implications, a low MAPE would be needed before using the data in a case against an individual or entity. For marketing situations where forecasts are mingled with intuition a large MAPE might be tolerated. The heating oil forecasts and the actual numbers (as far as was known at the time of writing) are shown in Figure 14.3.

The forecast in Figure 14.3 is the dashed line that shows the strong seasonal trend with high values for the winter months and low values for the summer months. The graph in Figure 14.2 shows a downward trend over the four-year period and this trend is continued for the fifth year (the forecast year). The results show that the actual numbers for January and February exceeded the forecast while the actual numbers for March to June were on target. The June numbers were the latest available at the time of writing. A review of the actual numbers in Figure 14.2 shows that there was a surge in demand in December 2009 and this surge carried forward to the first two months of 2010. The National Oceanic and Atmospheric Administration (NOAA at www.noaa.gov) in its *State of the Climate* report dated March 10, 2010, noted that for the 2009–2010 winter more than one-half of the country experienced below normal temperatures. This trend was not uniform across the whole country and the areas that had a colder than usual winter contributed to the above-trend heating oil consumption in December to February. The analysis correctly indicated that conditions were different in December to February.

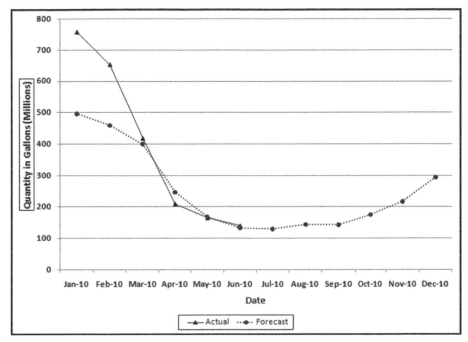

FIGURE 14.3 The 2010 Forecasts and the Actual Numbers for January to June

AN APPLICATION USING STOCK MARKET DATA

A search for "best months for stock market" or "timing the market" will show a number of articles suggesting that stock returns in some months are historically better than others. This case study will use stock market data from 1988 to 2009 to calculate whether there is a seasonal effect. Data for the S&P 500 was downloaded from the Investing section of Yahoo! Finance (http://finance.yahoo.com) using the symbol ^GSPC. The monthly return was calculated as a percentage. An extract from the spreadsheet is shown in Figure 14.4.

The return for each month is calculated in Figure 14.4. The formula for the monthly return is shown in Equation 14.2.

$$\text{Return} = \left(\frac{(t_0 - t_{-1})}{t_{-1}} \right) \times 100 \qquad (14.2)$$

where t_0 is the closing value of the index for the current month and t_{-1} is the closing value of the index for the prior month. The calculated return is a percentage return rounded to five decimal places to keep the spreadsheet neat. The return for the first month (January 1980) uses the closing index value from December 1979. The December 1979 values are not included on the spreadsheet. The actual returns and the fitted values of a time-series analysis are shown in Figure 14.5.

			Home	Insert	Page Layout		Formulas	Data	Review	
		F3		▼		ƒx	=ROUND(((E3-E2)/E2)*100,5)			

	A	B	C	D	E	F
1	Date	Open	High	Low	Close	Return
2	1/2/1980	107.94	117.17	103.26	114.16	5.76246
3	2/1/1980	114.16	120.22	111.33	113.66	-0.43798
4	3/3/1980	113.66	114.34	94.23	102.09	-10.1795
5	4/1/1980	102.09	106.79	98.95	106.29	4.11402
6	5/1/1980	106.29	112.72	103.5	111.24	4.65707
7	6/2/1980	111.24	117.98	109.77	114.24	2.69687
8	7/1/1980	114.24	123.93	113.54	121.67	6.50385
9	8/1/1980	121.67	127.78	119.42	122.38	0.58355
10	9/2/1980	122.38	132.17	121.79	125.46	2.51675
11	10/1/1980	125.46	135.88	124.66	127.47	1.6021
12	11/3/1980	127.47	141.96	127.23	140.52	10.2377
13	12/1/1980	140.52	140.66	125.32	135.76	-3.38742
14	1/2/1981	135.76	140.32	128.57	129.55	-4.57425
15	2/2/1981	129.48	132.02	124.66	131.27	1.32767
16	3/2/1981	131.27	138.38	128.56	136	3.60326
17	4/1/1981	136	137.72	131.58	132.81	-2.34559
18	5/1/1981	132.81	134.92	128.78	132.59	-0.16565
19	6/1/1981	132.59	135.67	128.77	131.21	-1.0408
20	7/1/1981	131.21	131.78	125.96	130.92	-0.22102
21	8/3/1981	130.92	135.18	122.29	122.79	-6.2099
22	9/1/1981	122.79	124.58	110.19	116.18	-5.38317
23	10/1/1981	116.18	123.28	115	121.89	4.91479
24	11/2/1981	122.35	126.97	119.13	126.35	3.65904
25	12/1/1981	126.35	127.32	121.04	122.55	-3.00752
26	1/4/1982	122.55	123.72	113.63	120.4	-1.75439
27	2/1/1982	119.81	119.81	110.03	113.11	-6.05482
28	3/1/1982	113.11	114.8	104.46	111.96	-1.01671
29	4/1/1982	111.96	119.33	111.48	116.44	4.00143
30	5/3/1982	115.96	119.92	111.66	111.88	-3.91618

◄ ◄ ► ►│ S&P500

FIGURE 14.4 The Monthly Data Used to Analyze S&P 500 Returns

Figure 14.5 shows the actual stock market returns (as the highly volatile series) and the fitted time-series values (as the stable series just above the 0 percent line). The actual returns vary widely with no noticeable pattern or trend except that there seems to be periods of high volatility (a large spread) followed by periods of low volatility. The fitted values, while difficult to see clearly, have some features that are noticeable. The fitted values are trending downward meaning that over the 30-year period the average returns were trending downward. The fitted values are not a straight line, which means that the model did detect a seasonal pattern. However, the fitted values straighten out as we move ahead in time indicating that the seasonal pattern became less pronounced as time moved forward. Finally, the MAPE was 200.2 percent, meaning that the model is not very reliable. The predicted and actual values will tell us if there is a seasonal effect and these are shown in Figure 14.6.

The actual and predicted returns for 2010 are shown in Figure 14.7. The predicted numbers would have been of little use to any investor. The correlation between the actual returns and the fitted values was −0.13. The time-series model is essentially

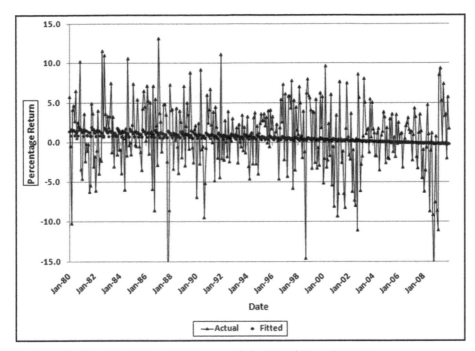

FIGURE 14.5 The Stock Market Returns and the Fitted Time-Series Line

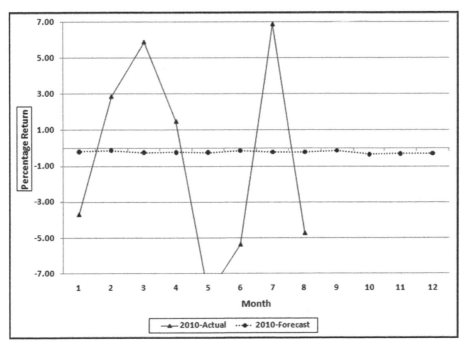

FIGURE 14.6 The Actual and the Predicted Returns for 2010

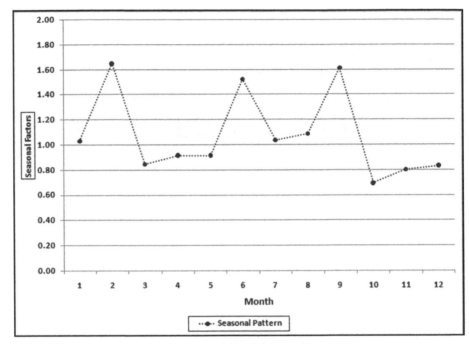

FIGURE 14.7 The Seasonal Pattern in the Stock Market Data

predicting a straight line. Because the returns were steadily decreasing over time the model predicted negative returns for every month. The negative correlation means that the small seasonal (monthly) adjustments are more often in the wrong direction than in the right direction. In essence, these results tell us that movements in the stock market are random and there are no easily detectable patterns that can be reliably traded on. The seasonal factors are shown in Figure 14.7.

The seasonal pattern in Figure 14.7 (which is essentially Figure 14.6 without the actual values) shows that the months with the highest returns were February, June, and September. The months with the lowest returns were October, November, December, and March. The poor showing of October was due in large part to the crash of October 1987 and also a large negative return in October 2008. These results suggest that the saying "sell in May and go away" is not really true. A search of this term, or a look at the review in Wikipedia also shows that this is not one of the best market tips. Any stock market regularity (day of the week, time of the day, before or after presidential elections) that is regular and large enough to cover occasional losses and trading costs could be very valuable.

 ## AN APPLICATION USING CONSTRUCTION DATA

Construction spending is an important part of the economy. Economists look at construction spending to gauge the overall health or optimism in the economy. The construction industry is one of the first to spiral downward in a recession and is one of the first industries to recover during the recovery phase. This section shows the application of time-series analysis to different sectors in the construction industry. It will be seen that some sectors are more amenable to time-series analysis than others. The applications will use historical data for 2005 to 2009 (60 months) for (a) residential construction, (b) highway and street, (c) healthcare, and (d) educational. The data was obtained from the U.S. Census Bureau website (www.census.gov) in the section devoted to construction spending tables. The 2010 data shown was the latest available at the time of writing. Figure 14.8 shows the results for residential construction.

The left panel of Figure 14.8 shows total residential construction (public and private) from 2005 to 2009 (60 months) and the forecasts for 2010. The left panel shows a seasonal pattern from year to year with the annual low being in February and the annual high being in July. The graph shows a downward trend over the five-year period. This is in line with the decline in economic conditions from 2005 to 2009. The panel on the right shows the forecasts for 2010 (which is the same as the right side of the graph in the left panel) and the actual results for 2010.

The MAPE of the construction data is 8.3 percent. The 2005 and the 2006 numbers are roughly equal, and this is followed by a sharp decline. Time series analysis struggles with a change in the trend (level followed by a decline) and works best when the long-term trend is consistent. In this case, a solution could be to drop the 2005 data and to only use 2006 to 2009 for the fitted values and the forecast. An analysis of the 2005 to 2009 data (not shown) shows a MAPE of just 5 percent. The model is therefore able to create a better fit between the past data and the fitted line. Because the trend is so negative the model actually forecasts some negative values for 2011 and the entire series of forecasts for 2012 is made up of negative numbers. Time-series analysis is more of an art than a science and the results should be carefully interpreted and used. The Highway and Street construction results are shown in Figure 14.9.

The Highway and Street ("highway") results in Figure 14.9 have some notable features. First, the numbers are highly seasonal with the August peak being more than double the January low. The long-term trend is upward with an average monthly increase of about $31 million over the five-year period. Finally, the seasonal pattern and the trend are both regular meaning that the model can work well with this data. The MAPE is 3.4 percent, which means that the model could fit a close-fitting line.

The 2010 actual and forecast numbers are shown in the right side panel of Figure 14.9. The model captures the seasonal pattern and the seasonal trend is being closely followed in 2010. However, the trend is slightly off. The model forecasts 2010 numbers that are about 5 percent higher than the fitted 2009 numbers. However, the actual numbers are about 11 percent below the forecasts for 2010. Not only did the increase not materialize, but the trend was reversed with a decrease in 2010 as compared to 2009 (at least for the year-to-date). The most recent month shows the largest shortfall for the year-to-date. The large 11 percent difference between the actual and the forecast numbers correctly signals that conditions have changed and the long-term trend has been disrupted. These findings agree with numbers posted by the American Road and Transportation Builders Association, although it should be noted

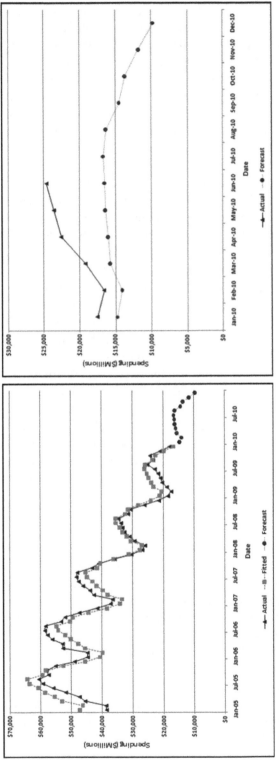

FIGURE 14.8 A Time-Series Analysis of Residential Construction Data

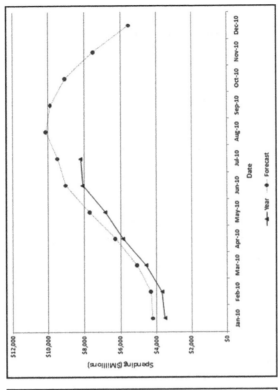

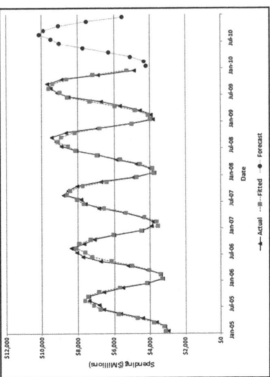

FIGURE 14.9 A Time-Series Analysis of Highway and Street Construction Data

that the construction categories covered by that Association are more than just the highway category of the Census Bureau. The healthcare construction results are shown in Figure 14.10.

The healthcare construction ("health care") results in Figure 14.10 have some notable features. First, the numbers are seasonal with the October peak being about 17 percent more than the January low. This seasonal pattern is less extreme than the pattern for construction spending. The long-term trend is upward with an average monthly increase of about $20 million over the five-year period. Finally, the seasonal pattern and the trend are both stable until the last six months of the period when it seems that healthcare spending falls off a cliff. The MAPE is 4.4 percent, which is usually a good fit, except for this case where most of the error is in the last six months of the last period.

The 2010 actual and forecast numbers are shown in the right side panel of Figure 14.10. The results show that the model captures the seasonal pattern and that the seasonal pattern is being reasonably closely followed in 2010. The trend is off because the forecasts are about 25 percent higher than the actual numbers. The upward trend has reversed itself to a decline in 2010 as compared to 2009 (at least for the year-to-date). The 25 percent difference between the actual and the forecast numbers correctly signals that things have changed, and for the worse. These findings echo the sentiments and numbers in the 2010 Hospital Building Report of the American Society for Healthcare Engineering. The educational construction results are shown in Figure 14.11.

The educational results in Figure 14.11 are similar to the healthcare results. The numbers are highly seasonal. The August peak is about 51 percent more than the February low. This seasonal pattern is more extreme than healthcare spending, which seems logical given that the school year starts around the end of August. The long-term trend is upward with an average monthly increase of about $45 million over the period. Finally, the seasonal pattern and the trend are both stable until the last six months of the period when it seems that educational spending falls off a cliff. The MAPE is 3.7 percent, which under normal circumstances is a good fit, except for this case where much of the error is in the last six months of the last period.

The 2010 actual and forecast numbers are shown in the right side panel of Figure 14.11. The model captures the seasonal pattern and the seasonal trend is being reasonably closely followed in 2010. Again, however, the trend is slightly off. The model forecasts 2010 numbers that are about 26 percent higher than the actual 2010 numbers. The upward trend has reversed to a decline in 2010. The large difference between the actual and the forecast numbers once again signals that conditions have changed. These findings echo the sentiments and numbers in the 2010 School Construction Report, a supplement to *School Planning & Management*.

The construction data shows that time-series analysis can accurately detect a seasonal pattern, when one exists. The technique falls somewhat short when the long-term trend is not consistent, as was the case with the residential construction data. Also, the technique relies on mathematics that is quite capable of predicting negative construction numbers. Negative numbers are just not possible for construction data. Time-series also struggled with an accurate forecast when the numbers showed a sharp

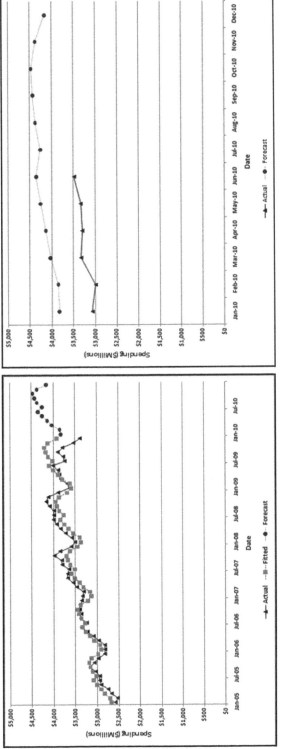

FIGURE 14.10 A Time-Series Analysis of Healthcare Construction Data

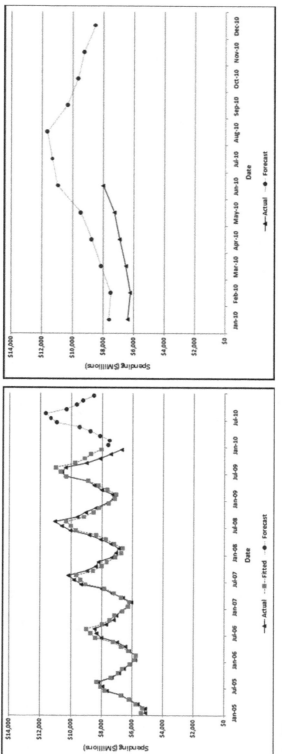

FIGURE 14.11 A Time-Series Analysis of Educational Construction Data

decrease in the last six months. The results correctly signaled that the long-term trends had been disrupted, and that the past patterns in the past data were not being continued.

 ## AN ANALYSIS OF STREAMFLOW DATA

Nigrini and Miller (2007) analyze a large table of earth science data. The results showed that streamflow data conformed closely to Benford's Law and that deviations from the Benford proportions in other earth science data could be indicators of either (a) an incomplete data set, (b) the sample not being representative of the population, (c) excessive rounding of the data, (d) data errors, inconsistencies, or anomalies, or (e) conformity to a power law with a large exponent.

There are several reasons for the collection of accurate, regular, and dependable streamflow data. These are:

- **Interstate and international waters.** Interstate compacts, court decrees, and international treaties may require long-term, accurate, and unbiased streamflow data at key points in a river.
- **Streamflow forecasts.** Upstream flow data is used for flood and drought forecasting for improved estimates of risk and impacts for better hazard response and mitigation.
- **Sentinel watersheds.** Accurate streamflow data is needed to describe the changes in the watersheds due to changes in climate, land, and water use.
- **Water quality.** Streamflow data is a component of the water quality program of the USGS.
- **Design of bridges and other structures.** Streamflow data is required to estimate water level and discharge during flood conditions.
- **Endangered species.** Data is required for an assessment of survivability in times of low flows.

This section analyzes data prepared by Tootle, Piechota, and Singh (2005) whose study analyzes various influences on streamflow data. Their study used unimpaired streamflow data from 639 stations in the continental United States. This data set is particularly interesting because the Nigrini and Miller (2007) study showed near-perfect conformity to Benford's Law for streamflow data. The advantage of their data over the Nigrini and Miller (2007) data is that the data is in a time-series format and each station has a complete set of data for the period under study. An additional reason for studying streamflow data is because the methods used for measuring flow at most streamgages are almost identical to those used 100 years ago. Acoustic Doppler technology is available but has yet to provide accurate data over a wide range of hydrologic conditions more cost-effectively than the traditional current meter methods. For this application 60 months of data (1997 to 2001 inclusive) was used to provide a forecast for 2002. Each record is an average monthly streamflow from a station from 1997 to

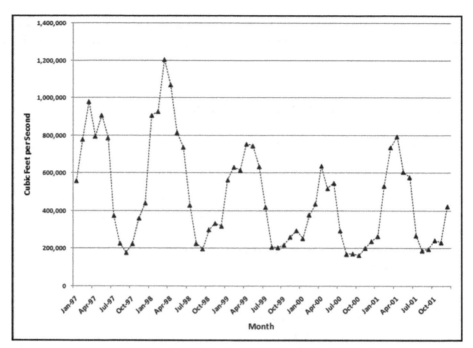

FIGURE 14.12 The Sum of the Streamflows from 1997 to 2001

2001 measured in cubic feet per second. The monthly flows ranged from 0 to 74,520 cubic feet per second. The data was highly skewed with the average monthly flow being 749 cubic feet per second. The monthly totals for the period are shown in Figure 14.12.

The data is highly seasonal with the annual maximum being recorded in either March or April of each year, and the annual minimum being recorded in August, September, or October of each year. The 1998 calendar year had the highest annual total streamflow and the 2000 calendar year had the lowest annual streamflow. The fact that an "early" year had the highest annual sum, and a "later" year had the lowest sum means that the time-series model will forecast a declining trend. The time-series results are shown in Figure 14.13.

The actual and the fitted values (together with the 2002 forecasts) are shown in the left panel and the forecasts and the actual numbers are shown in the right panel. The data for 1997 to 2001 is highly seasonal. The September low is about 27 percent of the March high. Streamflows are apparently not regular and consistent from year to year. Dettinger and Diaz (2000) include an interesting discussion of streamflow seasonality. They note that seasonality varies widely from river to river and is influenced by rainfall, evaporation, the timing of snowmelt, travel times of water to the river, and human interference. Summer rainfall contributes less to streamflow. So streamflow is influenced not only by the amount of rainfall, but the timing thereof. The next step in the analysis is to compare the forecasts to the actual numbers for the 639 stations. The distribution of the MAPEs is shown in Figure 14.14.

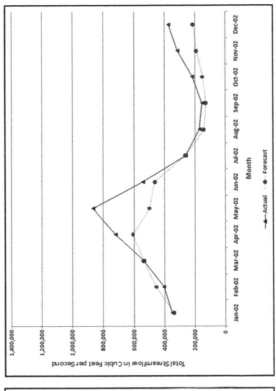

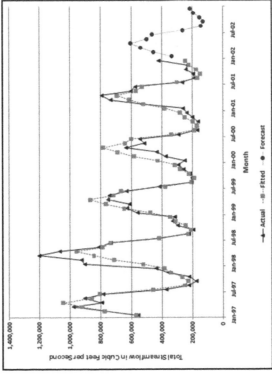

FIGURE 14.13 A Time-Series Analysis of Streamflow Data

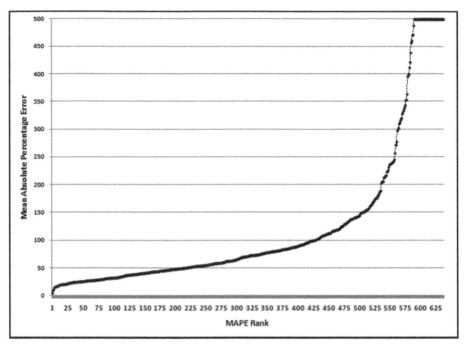

FIGURE 14.14 The Ordered MAPEs for the Streamflow Stations

Only about one-third of the MAPEs are less than 50 percent (the left side of the graph). About one-quarter of the MAPEs exceed 100 percent. The MAPE numbers have been capped at 500. These high MAPEs indicate that the time-series model is struggling to fit a neat curve to the past data and suggests that the forecasts will not be too reliable. The results for a station with a low MAPE and a station with a high MAPE are shown next. The results for station 4124000 are shown in Figure 14.15.

This station is on the Manistee River, near Sherman, Michigan. This station had the second lowest MAPE (8.3 percent). The actual numbers and the fitted lines are shown in the left panel. Even though the MAPE was comparatively low, the graph shows that there was much variability in the flow from year to year. The actual numbers have a downward trend for the first four years followed by an upward jump in the last year. This gives a slope of near zero which is what we would expect in a river over a short period of time. The results for 2002 (the forecasts and the actual numbers) are shown in the right panel of Figure 14.15. Here the seasonal pattern is followed quite closely, but the forecast is too low for the first half of the year and slightly too high for the last half of the year. The MAPE of the actual to the forecast is 9.2 percent. This might be suitable for some purposes, but probably not for performance evaluation, or fraud-detection in a business setting. These results are contrasted with a station with a MAPE close to the median of 70.4 percent. The results for station 2134500 are shown in Figure 14.16.

This station is on the Lumber River, at Boardman, North Carolina. This station had a MAPE of 71.8 percent, which was close to the median MAPE. The actual numbers and the fitted lines are shown in the left panel. This graph shows that there was much

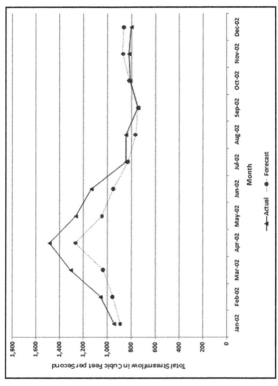

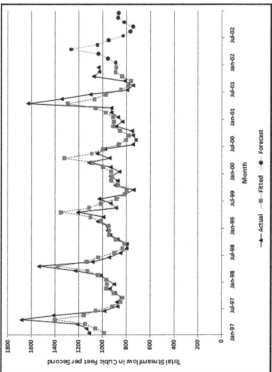

FIGURE 14.15 A Time-Series Analysis of Streamflow Data for Station 4124000

317

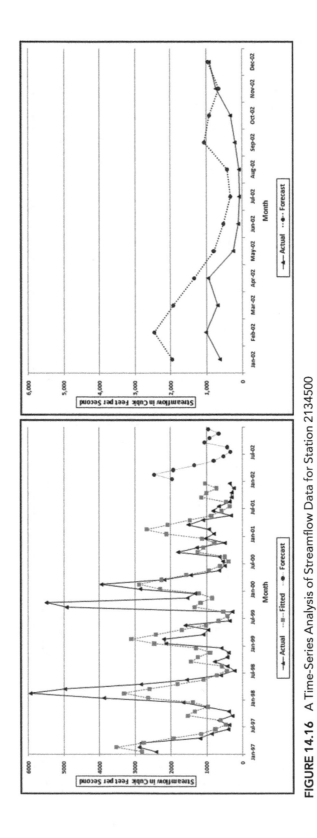

FIGURE 14.16 A Time-Series Analysis of Streamflow Data for Station 2134500

variability in the flow from year-to-year. The actual numbers show large flows in the second and the fourth year and an abnormal peak in September and October 1999. The September and October 1999 high was a near-record crest for the river and the abnormal activity was due to hurricanes Floyd and Irene, which slammed into North Carolina almost in succession. The streamflow patterns are erratic and because of this the time-series model cannot fit a curve with a low MAPE to the actual numbers and any forecasts are similarly unreliable. The forecast values in the right panel show an abnormal peak in September and October. This is because the abnormal peak in 1999 was so extreme that it caused a bump in the forecast values. While September and October is in the hurricane season it seems illogical to include an irregular event in a forecast. The MAPE of the actual to the forecast is about 200 percent. This level of error makes the forecast unsuitable for most purposes.

The streamflow application shows that the numbers have to be somewhat stable for the time-series model to be able to make any sort of reliable forecast. If the past data is erratic then the future data is also likely to be erratic and somewhat unpredictable. If the stakes are high, as in performance evaluations or fraud detection, then forecasts with high margins of error should not be used.

RUNNING TIME-SERIES ANALYSIS IN EXCEL

Time-series analysis is more complex than linear regression. The procedure begins by deseasonalizing the data. This is followed by calculating the regression line and then reseasonalizing the data. The final steps calculate the MAPE and the forecasts. Because the number of rows changes across the calculations and because of various scaling requirements, the flexibility of Excel is preferred over Access. Some of the calculations require formulas that look up or down a specified number of rows and it is difficult to program these formulas in Access. Time-series calculations will be demonstrated using the highway and street construction data in Figure 14.9. The Excel example uses 60 months of past data with a forecast horizon of 12 months. The original data and the first stage of the calculations are shown in Figure 14.17.

Figure 14.17 shows the first stage of time-series analysis. A description of columns **A** to **E** is given here:

A (*Blank*): This field is used when the analysis is performed on several forensic units such as the locations in a chain of stores, or auto dealers for a car manufacturer.

B (*Year*): This indicates the calendar year. The data should be organized so that the oldest year is at the top and the newest year is at the bottom. This column is not actually used in the calculations.

C (*Season*): This is a season indicator that goes from 1 to 12 for monthly data, or 1 to 24 for hourly data, or 1 to 7 for a weekly seasonal pattern.

D (*Amount*): This is the historical (past) data that will usually be denominated in dollars for financial data. Other possibilities include cubic feet per second for streamflow data, or people for passenger data.

	Home	Insert	Page Layout	Formulas	Data	Review	View	Develo

| | E2 | ▼ | f_x | =IF(D2>0,LN(D2),IF(D2=0,0,-LN(ABS(D2)))) | | |

	A	B	C	D	E	F
1	Blank	Year	Season	Amount	LnAmount	
2		2005	1	2978	7.999	
3		2005	2	3169	8.061	
4		2005	3	3636	8.199	
5		2005	4	4395	8.388	
6		2005	5	5632	8.636	
7		2005	6	6565	8.790	
8		2005	7	5815	8.827	
20		2006	7	8048	8.993	
21		2006	8	8358	9.031	
22		2006	9	7640	8.941	
23		2006	10	7073	8.864	
24		2006	11	6002	8.700	
25		2006	12	4431	8.396	
26		2007	1	3909	8.271	
27		2007	2	3817	8.247	
28		2007	3	4405	8.390	
29		2007	4	5419	8.598	
30		2007	5	6821	8.828	

Ⅰ◀ ▶ Ⅰ ConstructionData

FIGURE 14.17 The First Stage of the Time-Series Calculations

E (*LnAmount*): This is the natural logarithm (base *e*) of the *Amount* field. Because the logarithm of a negative number is undefined we need to use a formula that still works with negative numbers. The formula is

$$\text{E2: } =IF(D2>0,LN(D2),IF(D2=0, 0, -LN(ABS(D2))))$$

CALCULATING THE SEASONAL FACTORS

The second stage of the calculations is to calculate the seasonal factors. These factors calculate which months are higher and which are lower than average, and also the size of these differences. These formulas are not copied all the way down to the last row of the data. The completed second stage is shown in Figure 14.18.

The second stage of the time-series calculations is shown in Figure 14.18 in columns **F** through **L**. This stage calculates the seasonal factors for the data. None of the formulas in columns F through L are copied down to the last row of data. The formulas and notes are

$$\text{F7 } (MovingAvg): \ =AVERAGE(E2:E13)$$

	B	C	D	E	F	G	H	I	J	K	L
							F7	=AVERAGE(E2:E13)			
	B	C	D	E	F	G	H	I	J	K	L
1	Year	Season	Amount	LnAmount	MovingAvg	CenterMA	Diff	Smooth	PrelimExp	Normal	Month
2	2005	1	2978	7.999							
3	2005	2	3169	8.061							
4	2005	3	3636	8.199							
5	2005	4	4395	8.388							
6	2005	5	5632	8.636							
7	2005	6	6565	8.790	8.54						
8	2005	7	6815	8.827	8.55	8.54	0.286	0.296	1.344	1.289	M7
9	2005	8	7365	8.904	8.55	8.55	0.357	0.357	1.430	1.371	M8
10	2005	9	7383	8.907	8.56	8.56	0.351	0.330	1.391	1.334	M9
11	2005	10	6558	8.788	8.58	8.57	0.219	0.239	1.270	1.218	M10
12	2005	11	5505	8.613	8.59	8.58	0.030	0.049	1.050	1.007	M11
13	2005	12	4139	8.328	8.60	8.60	-0.269	-0.261	0.770	0.739	M12
14	2006	1	3288	8.098	8.62	8.61	-0.513	-0.490	0.612	0.587	M1
15	2006	2	3399	8.131	8.63	8.62	-0.492	-0.471	0.624	0.599	M2
16	2006	3	4150	8.331	8.63	8.63	-0.299	-0.313	0.732	0.701	M3
17	2006	4	5216	8.559	8.64	8.63	-0.075	-0.102	0.903	0.866	M4
18	2006	5	6729	8.814	8.65	8.64	0.173	0.098	1.103	1.057	M5
19	2006	6	7705	8.950	8.65	8.65	0.302	0.252	1.286	1.233	M6
20	2006	7	8048	8.993	8.67	8.66	0.335		sum		
21	2006	8	8358	9.031	8.67	8.67	0.361		12.515	12.000	
22	2006	9	7640	8.941	8.68	8.68	0.264				
23	2006	10	7073	8.864	8.68	8.68	0.183				
24	2006	11	6002	8.700	8.68	8.68	0.016				
25	2006	12	4431	8.396	8.68	8.68	-0.287				
26	2007	1	3909	8.271	8.68	8.68	-0.410				
27	2007	2	3817	8.247	8.68	8.68	-0.435				
28	2007	3	4405	8.390	8.69	8.69	-0.298				
29	2007	4	5419	8.598	8.70	8.70	-0.101				
30	2007	5	6821	8.828	8.71	8.71	0.119				

ConstructionData

FIGURE 14.18 The Calculation of the Seasonal Factors

This formula is a part of the procedure to determine which months are higher or lower than the annual average. This formula is copied down to row 55.

G8 (*CenterMA*): =AVERAGE(F7:F8)

This formula is a part of the procedure to determine which months are higher or lower than the annual average. This formula is copied down to row 55.

H8 (*Diff*): =E8−G8

This formula is a part of the procedure to determine which months are higher or lower than the annual average. This formula is copied down to row 55.

I8 (*Smooth*): =AVERAGE(H8,H20,H32,H44)

This formula calculates the average monthly seasonal deviation for the four-year period. There are 12 monthly averages, one average for each month. This formula is copied down to **I19**.

J8 (*PrelimExp*): =EXP(I8)

In this *Preliminary Exponent* field the EXP function "undoes" the conversion to logarithms in column **E** by getting back to the original number. This formula is copied down to **J19**. We need one more step to perfect our exponents, which is to get them to average 1. This is done by getting the sum of the 12 numbers to equal 12.

J20 (*sum*): sum

Enter the label "sum" in **J20**. This is to indicate that **J21** is the sum of the exponents.

J21: =SUM(J8:J19)

This formula sums the preliminary exponents. The sum of the exponents should equal 12 for monthly data.

K8 (*Normal*): =(J8/$J$21*12)

This formula normalizes the preliminary exponents and forces the sum to equal 12.00. This formula is copied down to **K19**.

K21: =SUM(K8:K19)

This formula is to check that the exponents sum to 12.00 for monthly data.

L8 to L19 (*Month*): These cells are given the labels M7 to M12 and M1 to M6.

The letter M stands for month and the numbers 1 to 12 are for January to December. These labels are not used in any formula.

The labels in column **L** complete the second stage. In the next stage, a linear regression is run on the deseasonalized data. The seasonal variations are removed and a forecast is made using linear regression.

RUNNING A LINEAR REGRESSION

This third stage calculates the long-term trend (upward or downward) using linear regression on the deseasonalized numbers. The seasonal factors will be used again in a later stage. The screenshot for the third stage is shown in Figure 14.19.

The third stage of the analysis in Figure 14.19 uses columns **M** through **V**. This stage uses the linear regression to calculate the long-term trend. The formulas and notes are

M(*Seasonals*): =$K14; =$K15; =$K16; =$K17; =$K18; =$K19; =$K8; =$K9; =$K10; =$K11; =$K12; =$K13.

This field repeats the seasonal factors from column K. These are listed starting with M1 and continuing to M12. Thereafter the M1 to M12 values are repeated so that the 12 values are repeated a total of five times from row 2 to row 61. The use of the $ sign before the column reference means that when the formulas are copied downward, they will continue to reference **K8:K19**.

N2 (*AmountDS*): =D2/M2

Month	Seasonals	AmountDS	X	X^2	Y^2	XY	SSXY	SSX	Slope	Intercept
	0.587	5071.6	1	1	25720639.0	5071.6	550760.8	17995.0	30.6	5312.9
	0.599	5293.3	2	4	28018535.0	10586.5				
	0.701	5183.2	3	9	26865623.6	15549.6				
	0.866	5076.0	4	16	25765450.0	20303.9				
	1.057	5327.5	5	25	28382633.6	26637.7				
	1.233	5323.9	6	36	28343682.9	31943.3				
M7	1.289	5287.2	7	49	27954807.7	37010.6				
M8	1.371	5372.7	8	64	28865481.1	42981.3				
M9	1.334	5536.4	9	81	30651524.9	49827.4				
M10	1.218	5385.6	10	100	29004640.8	53856.0				
M11	1.007	5467.2	11	121	29890214.6	60139.1				
M12	0.739	5604.1	12	144	31405730.4	67249.0				
M1	0.587	5599.5	13	169	31354218.8	72793.3				
M2	0.599	5677.4	14	196	32233189.0	79484.0				
M3	0.701	5915.9	15	225	34998172.8	88738.9				
M4	0.866	6024.2	16	256	36290682.7	96386.8				
M5	1.057	6365.2	17	289	40516176.6	108208.9				
M6	1.233	6248.4	18	324	39042004.4	112470.5				
	1.289	6243.8	19	361	38985286.0	118632.6				
	1.371	6097.0	20	400	37173891.9	121940.8				
	1.334	5729.1	21	441	32822606.5	120311.1				
	1.218	5808.5	22	484	33738982.6	127787.6				
	1.007	5960.8	23	529	35530913.1	137098.0				
	0.739	5999.4	24	576	35993290.0	143986.6				
	0.587	6657.1	25	625	44316321.8	166426.3				
	0.599	6375.6	26	676	40648569.4	165766.2				
	0.701	6279.4	27	729	39431291.6	169544.7				
	0.866	6258.6	28	784	39170424.2	175241.6				
	1.057	6452.3	29	841	41631637.9	187115.5				

FIGURE 14.19 The Third Stage of the Time-Series Analysis

This column calculates the deseasonalized amounts. This formula is copied down to **N61**.

O (X): This field is a counter that starts at 1 in O2 and increases by 1 as the row numbers increase.

This counter starts at 1 in **O2** and ends at 60 in **O61**, the 60th month. This counter is the x-axis in the linear regression calculations.

P2 (X^2): =O2*O2

This column calculates the x-squared values. The formula is copied down to **P61**.

Q2 (Y^2): =N2*N2

This column calculates the y-squared values. The formula is copied down to **Q61**.

R2 (XY): =O2*N2

This column calculates the xy-product values. The formula is copied down to **R61**.

S2 ($SSXY$): =SUM(R2:R61) − (SUM(O2:O61)*SUM(N2:N61)/COUNT(D2:D61))

This formula calculates the sum of the cross products. The last term divides by the number of records in the historical data, which in this case is 60.

T2 (*SSX*): =SUM(P2:P61)−(SUM(O2:O61)*SUM(O2:O61)/COUNT(D2:D61))

This formula calculates the sum of squares for x. The last term divides by the number of records in the historical data, which in this case is 60.

U2 (*Slope*): =S2/T2

This formula calculates the slope of the regression line. A positive value indicates that the long-term trend is upward.

V2 (*Intercept*): =SUM(N2:N61)/COUNT(D2:D61)
$$-(U2*SUM(O2:O61)/COUNT(D2:D61))$$

This formula gives the y-intercept value in the linear regression.

The third stage has now calculated the linear regression coefficients for the deseasonalized data. The fourth stage generates the fitted line and the fitted curve and calculates the MAPE.

FITTING A CURVE TO THE HISTORICAL DATA

The fourth stage of the time-series analysis is shown in Figure 14.20 and uses columns **W** through **Z**. This stage fits a straight line (giving us the trend) and the curved line (with the seasonal pattern), and also calculates the MAPE.

Figure 14.20 shows the fourth stage of the time-series analysis. The formulas and notes are

W2 (*FitLine*): =$V2+($U2*O2)

This formula applies the slope and the intercept to the x-values (the counter) in column **O**. This result is a straight line. This formula is copied down to **W61**. The formula in **W3** is =$V2+($U2*O3) and the formula in **W4** is =$V2+($U2*O4). Some manual work is needed to keep the **V** and **U** references constant and the **O** references relative.

X2 (*FitCurve*): =W2*M2

This is the fitted curve that takes into account the seasonal nature of the data. This formula is copied to **X61**. If there is no seasonal pattern then this line will equal the fitted line in column **W**.

Y2 (*MonthsBack*): 1/1/2005

Y3 (*MonthsBack*): 2/1/2005

This column will be used for the labels on the x-axis (the horizontal axis). The date is entered into **Y2** as 1/1/2005, and into **Y3** as 2/1/2005. Cells **Y2** and **Y3** are highlighted and the monthly increment is copied down to **Y61**. This field is formatted

	S	T	U	V	W	X	Y	Z	AA
1	SSXY	SSX	Slope	Intercept	FitLine	FitCurve	MonthsBack	AbsPctErr	MAPE
2	550760.8	17995.0	30.6	5312.9	5343.5	3137.7	Jan-05	5.36	3.40
3					5374.1	3217.6	Feb-05	1.53	
4					5404.7	3791.4	Mar-05	4.27	
5					5435.3	4706.1	Apr-05	7.08	
6					5465.9	5778.3	May-05	2.60	
7					5496.5	6777.9	Jun-05	3.24	
8					5527.1	7124.2	Jul-05	4.54	
9					5557.7	7618.7	Aug-05	3.44	
10					5588.3	7452.3	Sep-05	0.94	
11					5618.9	6842.1	Oct-05	4.33	
12					5649.5	5688.6	Nov-05	3.34	
13					5680.1	4195.2	Dec-05	1.36	
14					5710.8	3353.3	Jan-06	1.99	
15					5741.4	3437.3	Feb-06	1.13	
16					5772.0	4049.0	Mar-06	2.43	
17					5802.6	5024.1	Apr-06	3.68	
18					5833.2	6166.5	May-06	8.36	
19					5863.8	7230.8	Jun-06	6.15	
20					5894.4	7597.6	Jul-06	5.60	
21					5925.0	8122.2	Aug-06	2.82	
22					5955.6	7942.0	Sep-06	3.95	
23					5986.2	7289.4	Oct-06	3.06	
24					6016.8	6058.4	Nov-06	0.94	
25					6047.4	4466.4	Dec-06	0.80	
26					6078.0	3569.0	Jan-07	8.70	
27					6108.6	3657.2	Feb-07	4.19	
28					6139.2	4306.7	Mar-07	2.23	
29					6169.8	5342.1	Apr-07	1.42	
30					6200.5	6554.8	May-07	3.90	

W2 ▾ f_x =$V2+($U2*O2)

ConstructionData

FIGURE 14.20 The Fourth Stage of the Time-Series Analysis

as Date using the "Mar-01" Date format in Excel.

$$Z2 \ (AbsPctErr): \ =IF(D2<>0, ABS((D2-X2)/D2),1)*100$$

This field is the Absolute Percentage Error for the row. The IF function is used to avoid division by zero. This formula is copied to **Z61**.

$$AA \ (MAPE): \ =AVERAGE(Z2:Z61)$$

This formula calculates the average of the absolute percentage errors in column Z. The *Mean* Absolute Percentage Error indicates how well time-series was able to fit a curved line to the actual past data.

This completes the fourth stage and the final stage deals with the main objective of calculating forecasts. The next stage is shown below.

CALCULATING THE FORECASTS

The forecasts are calculated in the final stage. This stage also includes a MAPE for the forecast numbers.

FIGURE 14.21 The Calculation of the Forecasts and the MAPE

The final stage of the time-series analysis is shown in Figure 14.21 and uses columns **AB** through **AG**. The formulas for the forecasts and the MAPE are shown below:

> **AB2** (*FutureMonth*): This field is simply a counter that starts at 61 because we have 60 months of past data and the first forecast is for month "61." The counter starts at 61 and ends at 72 in cell **AB13**.
>
> **AC2** (*MonthFwd*): 1/1/2010

This column will be used for the labels on the *x*-axis (the horizontal axis). The date is entered into **AC2** as 1/1/2010, and into **AC3** as 2/1/2010. Cells **AC2** and **AC3** are highlighted and the monthly increase is copied down to **AC13**. This field is formatted as Date using the "Mar-01" Date format in Excel.

> **AD2** (*Forecast*): =($V2+$U$*AB2)*M2

The forecast uses the intercept and the slope times the counter in column **AB**. This forecast is then multiplied by the seasonal factor in column **M**. Because of the arithmetic gymnastics in columns **J** and **K**, the sum of the forecasts with the seasonal factor is equal to the straightline forecast (not shown). The formula for **AD3** is =($V2+$U2*AB3)*M3 and the formula for **AD4** is =($V2+$U2*AB4)*M4. Some manual work is needed to keep the **V** and **U** references constant and the **O** references relative.

AE (*Actual*): These are the actual numbers for the current period. In this case the source was the U.S. Census release dated September 1, 2010.

AF (*FAbsPctErr*): =ABS((AE2-AD2)/AE2)*100

This formula calculates the percentage error of the forecast expressed as a percentage of the actual numbers. The formula is copied down to the last row of data in column **AC**.

AG (*F-MAPE*): =AVERAGE(AF2:AF13)

This the average of the percentage errors calculated in column **AF**. A new column is used because we might want to sort the data according to the *F-MAPEs*.

Graphs of the data are shown in Figure 14.9. The left side graph of Figure 14.9 uses the data in,

> **D2:D61** (Actual data)
> **X2:X61** (Fitted numbers)
> **AD2:AD13** (Forecast numbers)
> **Y2:Y61** (*x*-axis labels)

	Home	Insert	Page Layout	Formulas	Data	Review	View
	E2	▾		f_x	=IF(D2>0,LN(D2),IF(D2=0,0,-LN(ABS(D2))))		

	A	B	C	D	E	F
1	Unit	Year	Season	Amount	LnAmount	
2	1010500	1997	1	1432	7.267	
3	1010500	1997	2	1029	6.936	
4	1010500	1997	3	1625	7.393	
5	1010500	1997	4	12200	9.409	
6	1010500	1997	5	26250	10.175	
7	1010500	1997	6	3346	8.116	
8	1010500	1997	7	1249	7.130	
9	1010500	1997	8	1097	7.000	
10	1010500	1997	9	1017	6.925	
11	1010500	1997	10	720	6.579	
12	1010500	1997	11	4025	8.300	
13	1010500	1997	12	696	6.545	
14	1010500	1998	1	871	6.770	
15	1010500	1998	2	1198	7.088	
16	1010500	1998	3	5860	8.676	
17	1010500	1998	4	24700	10.115	
18	1010500	1998	5	4482	8.408	
19	1010500	1998	6	1262	7.140	
20	1010500	1998	7	2755	7.921	
21	1010500	1998	8	922	6.827	
22	1010500	1998	9	2702	7.902	
23	1010500	1998	10	2034	7.618	
24	1010500	1998	11	2909	7.976	
25	1010500	1998	12	1612	7.385	

FIGURE 14.22 The Process to Run a Time-Series Analysis on Multiple Data Sets

The right side graph of Figure 14.9 uses the data in

> **AD2:AD13** (Forecast numbers)
> **AE2:AE8** (Actual data for 2010)
> **AC2:AC13** (*x*-axis labels)

Although it is useful to perform a time-series analysis on a single data set, the real power of the technique is when it is used on many data sets at the same time. The streamflow application used data from 639 stations for 1997 to 2001. The spreadsheet can be adapted to multiple data sets using strategically placed Copy and Paste commands. Figure 14.22 demonstrates the first step.

The first step to run time-series analysis on multiple data sets is shown in Figure 14.22. Column **A** is now used to show the unit reference (a location number, an account number, or a person's name, etc.). The only columns with new data (as compared to Figure 14.17) is **A** (the unit reference), **B** (the year references), and **D** (the Amount). The time periods in columns **Y** and **AC** will need to be updated.

The first-stage calculations (with the calculated fields in columns **B** and **E**) are copied downward for all subsets. In this case we have 639 stations, each with

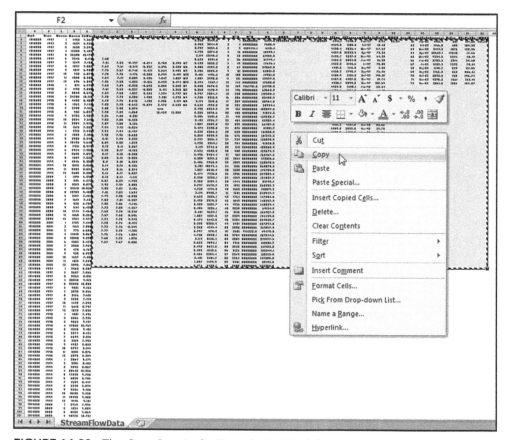

FIGURE 14.23   The *Copy* Step in the Time-Series Worksheet

60 months of streamflow, and so the first stage data and calculations will extend from the labels in row 1 to row 38341. The final row is 38341 because we use one row for the labels and $639 * 60$ rows for our data ($1 + 639*60 = 38341$). The next step is to copy the calculations starting in cell **F2** (which is blank) and ending in cell AG61 (which is also actually blank) down to the last row. On a much reduced scale, this is shown in Figure 14.23.

Figure 14.23 shows the first step in copying the formulas down so that the calculations are done for all units. Cells **F2:AG61** are highlighted and **Copy** is clicked. The formulas have been written so that the calculations to the right of each data set (each set of 60 rows) will pertain to that data set. The step is completed as is shown in Figure 14.24.

Figure 14.24 shows a portion of the spreadsheet where the formulas from **F2:AG61** are copied and pasted into **F2:AG38341**. The formulas have been set up so that they

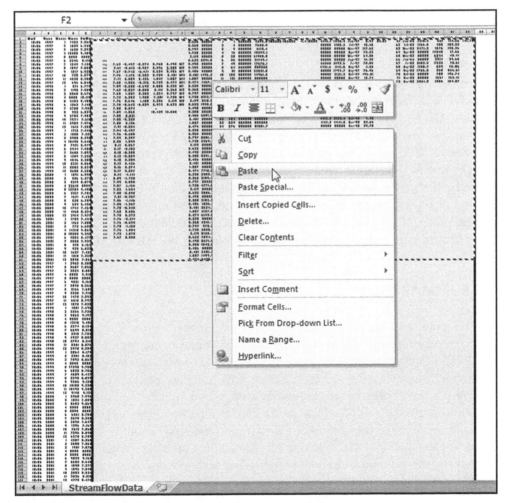

FIGURE 14.24 The *Paste* Step in the Time-Series Worksheet

	Home	Insert	Page Layout	Formulas	Data	Review	View	Developer	Add-Ins	Acrobat	
	AE2	▾	f_x	661							

	W	X	Y	Z	AA	AB	AC	AD	AE	AF	AG
1	FitLine	FitCurve	MonthsBack	AbsPctErr	MAPE	FutureMonth	MonthsFwd	Forecast	Actual	FAbsPctErr	F-MAPE
2	4441.1	1445.4	Jan-97	0.94	53.03	61	Jan-02	1418.9	661	114.66	141.75
3	4439.8	1188.3	Feb-97	15.48		62	Feb-02	1166.5	450	159.22	
4	4438.4	3536.4	Mar-97	117.62		63	Mar-02	3471.3	1576	120.26	
5	4437.0	21023.9	Apr-97	72.33		64	Apr-02	20637.1	17540	17.66	
6	4435.7	9397.5	May-97	64.20		65	May-02	9224.5	6344	45.41	
7	4434.3	2804.0	Jun-97	16.20		66	Jun-02	2752.3	3914	29.68	
8	4433.0	2192.6	Jul-97	75.55		67	Jul-02	2152.3	7322	70.61	
9	4431.6	1141.8	Aug-97	4.08		68	Aug-02	1120.7	529	111.86	
10	4430.2	1799.7	Sep-97	76.96		69	Sep-02	1766.5	265	566.61	
11	4428.9	2131.3	Oct-97	196.01		70	Oct-02	2092.0	705	196.74	
12	4427.5	4457.5	Nov-97	10.74		71	Nov-02	4375.3	1661	163.41	
13	4426.1	2099.8	Dec-97	201.69		72	Dec-02	2061.0	1006	104.87	
14	4424.8	1440.1	Jan-98	65.34							
15	4423.4	1184.0	Feb-98	1.17							
16	4422.1	3523.4	Mar-98	39.87							
17	4420.7	20946.5	Apr-98	15.20							
18	4419.3	9362.9	May-98	108.90							
19	4418.0	2793.6	Jun-98	121.37							
20	4416.6	2184.6	Jul-98	20.71							

FIGURE 14.25 The Comparison of the Actual Results to the Forecasts

are copied correctly. Each set of 60 rows and 28 columns will relate to one station. The final step is to insert the "Actual" numbers for 2002 (or whatever the case may be) into column **AE**. This might require a bit of spreadsheet gymnastics. The completed section for the first streamflow station is shown in Figure 14.25.

Figure 14.25 shows the comparison of the actual results to the forecast numbers. For the station 1010500 the MAPE is 141.75 percent. This shows a large difference between the past patterns and the current numbers. Care needs to be taken in this section of the worksheet (columns **AE**, **AF**, and **AG**) to only use the rows that are needed. If we have 12 months of actual data then we would use all 12 rows. If we only have seven months of actual data then we would only use **AE2** to **AF8**.

 ## SUMMARY

A time-series is a sequence of the successive values of an expense or revenue stream in units or dollars over equally spaced time intervals. There are many time-series graphs in the *Economist* where interest rates or inflation numbers are plotted over a period of time. A time-series graph is one where dates or time units are plotted on the x-axis (the horizontal axis). Time-series analysis is well suited to forensic analytics because accounting transactions always include a date as a part of the details. From a forensic analytics perspective the objectives when using time-series analysis are to (a) give a better understanding of the revenues or expenditures under investigation, and, (b) to predict the values for future periods so that differences between the actual and expected results can be investigated.

In a forensic setting the investigator might forecast the revenues, or items of an expenditure or loss nature for business or government forensic units. Loss accounts are costs but have no compensating benefit received and examples include (a) merchandise returns and customer refunds at store locations, (b) baggage claims at airport locations, or (c) warranty claims paid by auto manufacturers. A large difference between the actual and the predicted numbers would tell us that conditions have changed and these changes could be due to fraud, errors, or some other anomalies. Time-series analysis is most useful for data with a seasonal component and when the immediate past values of the series is a useful basis for a forecast.

Several examples are shown in the chapter. The first study looked at heating oil sales where the numbers are highly seasonal with high usage during the cold winter months and low usage during the warm summer months. The next study looked at stock market returns for 30 years to test for seasonality and the results showed a weak seasonal pattern. The results suggested, though, that time-series analysis cannot be used to generate superior investment returns. The third study looked at construction data where it would seem that time-series would work well on aggregate U.S. data. The results showed that 2010 brought in a change in conditions. The fourth study looked at streamflow data where the results showed that streamflows are highly volatile from a seasonal and from a trend perspective.

The chapter showed how to run time-series analysis in Excel. In the first stage the data is imported (copied) to the worksheet. The seasonal factors are calculated next. These factors indicate which months are above and below the average and the extent of these deviations. The data is then deseasonalized and normal regression techniques are applied to the long-term trend. In the fourth stage a curved line is fitted to the past data and the mean absolute percentage error (MAPE) is calculated as a measure of how well the curve fits to the past data. In the fifth stage the forecast numbers are calculated and the current numbers are compared to the forecasts. The process is completed by preparing a graph of the past data with the fitted curve and the forecasts, as well as a more detailed graph of the forecasts and the actual numbers for the current period.

CHAPTER FIFTEEN

Fraud Risk Assessments of Forensic Units

M ONITORING MEANS "TO WATCH, and keep track of, or to check for some special purpose." Continuous monitoring happens in many aspects of our personal life. Our water supply is continuously monitored, and all sorts of phenomena are monitored in commercial airplane flights. In hospitals, the monitoring of a patient's vital signs is taken for granted. In prisons, monitoring the activities and whereabouts of inmates is vital, and any escape is usually attributed to a lapse in monitoring activities. An Internet search for "continuous monitoring" will return results from applications such as monitoring storms, emissions, volcanoes, glucose for diabetics, perimeter activities for important installations, and foreign broadcasts for intelligence purposes. Since monitoring is so pervasive in everyday life it is puzzling that corporate transactions are not also the subject of continued monitoring to assess the risk of frauds or errors.

The 2006 edition of PricewaterhouseCoopers' (PWC) *State of the Internal Audit Profession* series reports that 81 percent of audit managers either had a continuous auditing or monitoring process in place, or that they were planning to develop one (PWC, 2006). Only one-half of audit managers had some actual form of continuous monitoring in place (possibly only one application). This low percentage might be due to a lack of guidance on methods and techniques that might be used in continuous monitoring applications. Of those that had a continuous monitoring application in place, 20 percent of these had fraud detection as the focus, and 10 percent focused their continuous monitoring activities on key performance indicators to identify deteriorating business activities. PWC (2006, 10) conclude that continuous auditing is still considered an emerging phenomenon, and is viewed by internal audit as a means to enhance their audit processes and to meet the stakeholder needs and demands for faster and higher-quality real-time assurance. PWC (2007a) paints a similar picture with 43 percent of respondents reporting the use of some form of continuous monitoring, but only 11 percent of respondents describing the process as fully operational. In 2006 and 2007 nearly one-fifth of audit managers did not have any form of continuous monitoring in place, nor did they have any plans to develop one. A lack of guidance on methods and techniques might be contributing to the low level of continuous monitoring. It is also possible that internal auditors expect the process owners to have a monitoring system in place.

PWC (2007b) predicts that over the next five years internal auditors will devote more time to risk management, fraud, internal controls, and process flows. Also, to remain relevant, auditors will need to adopt a comprehensive approach to audit and risk management, and will need to optimize the use of technology and conduct audits on a more targeted basis in response to specific risk concerns.

This chapter describes a system developed at a fast-food franchising company to monitor sales reports for errors, frauds, or omissions. The chapter describes the monitoring approach and includes some references to decision theory, fraud theory, and the deception cues literature. A case study is then described with a detailed description of the risk scoring method. Selected results and future plans for the system are then reviewed. The methodology could be adapted to other continuous monitoring and fraud risk assessment applications. The risk-scoring approach is developed further in the next chapter.

THE RISK SCORING METHOD

The *risk score* method was developed as a continuous monitoring system based on an adaptation of the IT-Monitoring framework of the International Federation of Accountants (IFAC, 2002). This adaptation gives the following steps in a continuous monitoring application:

- Determine the scope of the monitoring, and the methods and techniques to be applied
- Determine the indicators that will be used
- Design the system
- Document the system
- Record the findings
- Prepare management reports
- Update the system to improve the predictive ability of the system

One hurdle to getting started is that there are few, if any, documented methods and techniques. Without methods and techniques the rest of the steps in the framework cannot occur. Internal auditing standards state that in exercising due professional care the internal auditor should consider the use of computer-assisted audit tools and other data analysis techniques. The risk-scoring method is a computer-intensive forensic analytic technique.

The risk-scoring method uses a scoring system where the *predictors* are indicators of some attribute or behavior of interest. Examples of *behaviors of interest* include fraudulent baggage claims for an airline, check kiting by a bank customer, fraudulent vendors in a company, or fraudulent coupon claims against a manufacturer. The method applies to situations where the forensic investigator wants to score each *forensic unit* according to the risk of a specific type of fraud or error. A *unit* refers to one of the individuals or groups that together constitute a whole. A *unit* would also be one of a number of things that are equivalent or identical in function or form. A *forensic unit* is a unit that is being analyzed from a forensic perspective. Examples of forensic units could be:

- The frequent-flyer mileage account of an airline passenger
- A vendor submitting customer coupons to a manufacturer
- The sales reports of a franchisee
- The financial reports of operating divisions
- The income tax returns of individuals
- Bank accounts of bank customers
- An insurance adjuster at an insurance company
- A purchasing card of an employee

With the risk score method a risk score is calculated for each forensic unit. Higher scores reflect a higher risk of fraud or error. Forensic efforts can then be targeted at the highest scores.

The risk score method combines scores from several predictors. In the case study the behavior of interest was the underreporting of sales by fast-food franchise holders. A risk score of 0 is associated with a low risk of errors, and a risk score of 1 is associated with a high risk of errors. Each predictor is scored with a predictor risk score of 0 associated with a low risk of errors, and a predictor risk score of 1 is associated with a high risk of errors. Each predictor is weighted between 0 and 1 according to its perceived importance giving a final risk score based on the scores of the predictors and their weightings. This approach is similar to professors having various components in their classes (midterms, exams, quizzes, attendance, and assignments) with each component carrying a weight toward the final grade.

The predictors are chosen using professional judgment and industry knowledge. The goal is to try and capture mathematically what auditors are doing informally. The predictors are direct cues (clear signs of fraud) or indirect cues, which are similar to red flags. Red flag indicators are attributes that are present in a large percentage of fraud cases, although their presence in no way means that fraud is actually present in a particular case. For example, a vendor with the same address as an employee is a fact that is true in a large percentage of vendor fraud cases, but it does not mean that fraud is always present when a vendor has the same address as an employee. Risk-scoring applications usually target a very specific type of fraud.

Each predictor is scored so that each forensic unit ends up with a score from 0 to 1 for the predictor. The case study shows how the predictor values are converted to scores in the 0 to 1 range. The weights directly affect the final scores and because forensic units are ranked according to these scores, the weights affect the rankings and the fraud risk. The predictors can be seen to be the same as cues for decision making and the predictor weights to be the same as the weights given to the decision-making cues.

The weights used in decision making have been regularly discussed in psychological research studies. Slovic (1966) notes that little is known about the manner in which human subjects combine information from multiple cues, each with a probabilistic relationship to a criterion, into a unitary judgment about that criterion. A set of cues is consistent if the judge (decision maker) believed that the cues all agreed in their implications for the attributes being judged. Inconsistent cues would arise if the inferences that would be made from a subset of these cues would be contradicted by the implications of another set of cues. Consistency was seen to be a matter of degree and not an all-or-none matter. When a set of cues is consistent, each cue will be combined additively to reach a judgment. Inconsistent cues present a problem because the judge must either doubt the reliability of the cues or the belief in the correlation between the cues and the attributes being judged. In the risk-scoring methodology contradictory cues (predictors) would occur if one cue indicated a positive risk of fraud and another cue signaled "no fraud" with certainty. In the risk-scoring method, a score of 0 therefore means that the predictor seen alone suggests a *low risk of fraud* (and not a zero risk of fraud), and a score of 1 suggests a *high risk of fraud* (and not fraud with certainty). Because 0 and 1 mean *low* and *high* (and not zero risk, or certainty) we avoid contradictory cues.

The risk-scoring method also draws on the "theory of successful fraud detection" of Grazioli, Jamal, and Johnson (2006), which assumes that both the deceiver and the victim take into account the goals, knowledge, and possible actions of the other party. The deceiver cleverly manipulates the information cues. The detector also cleverly tries to reverse engineer the cues left by the deceiver and identifies them as symptoms of attempts to mislead. Detectors learn from experience to identify the deception tactics of the deceivers. These detection tactics are heuristics (trial and error methods) that evolve from (a) the discovery of an anomaly, (b) the belief that the anomaly is related to the goal of the deceiver, and (c), the belief that the anomaly could be the result of the deceiver's intentional manipulation. The risk-score method uses multiple predictors to assess the risk of fraud and also uses some reasonably sophisticated statistics including algebra, correlations, regressions, and mathematics related to Benford's Law.

The risk-score methodology combines scores from predictors into a final risk score from 0 to 1 with the scores closest to 1 indicating the highest risk of fraud. The predictors are based on various traits, which could be erratic numbers and deviations from expected patterns. A score of 0 indicates a low risk of fraud and a score of 1 indicates a high risk of fraud.

 THE FORENSIC ANALYTICS ENVIRONMENT

The risk-score method was used in a company that operates about 5,000 franchised restaurants. The franchisees are required to report their monthly sales numbers within a few days after the end of the month. Based on the sales numbers reported by the franchisees, the franchisor bills the franchisee for royalty and advertising fees of approximately 7 percent of sales. The sales reports of the franchisees are processed by the accounts receivable department and time is needed to follow up on missing values and obvious errors. By the end of the second week of the month, the sales file for the preceding month is finalized. There is a continual reconciliation process that occurs to account for sales adjustments identified by the franchisees. By the 20th day of the month the sales numbers for the preceding month can usually be audited. This gives a short window before the sales reports for the next month come rolling in.

Sales-reporting errors (intentional or unintentional) are usually in the direction of understated sales and cause a revenue loss for the franchisor. Using the Vasarhelyi (1983) classification of errors, these errors could be (a) arithmetic errors, (b) integrity errors (unauthorized deletion of transactions), (c) timing errors (incorrect time period), (d) deliberate fraud, or (e) legal errors (transactions that violate legal clauses) such as omitting nonfood revenues. The cost of a revenue audit on location is high and the full cost is not only borne by the franchisor, but also partially by the franchisee in terms of the costs related to providing data, documents, and access to the electronics of the cash registers. The company needed a system of identifying high-risk sales reports. This environment is similar to many other situations where forensic units self-report dollar amounts and other statistics, and the recipient has to evaluate which of these might contain errors (e.g., financial statements submitted to the SEC, hazardous waste reports submitted to the EPA, airline baggage claims, and insurance claims).

The risk-scoring system was developed by the franchise audit section of internal audit. The work was done by two people and included developing an understanding of the players and the processes, the selection of the predictors, and computer programming (a combination of Excel and Access), data analysis, and first and subsequent proposals for scoring the predictors, and downloading franchisee data from the company's systems.

The team realized that it was not necessary to conduct an on-site audit for each restaurant thought to be high risk. Audits could either be done as field audits or correspondence audits, much like the approach taken by the IRS. Correspondence audits or desk audits could be conducted when the questions were limited in scope. Such audits are useful when only one or two areas of concern need to be addressed. Field audits are typically more thorough and are also intended to identify opportunities for operational improvements as well as the detection of sales underreporting.

The data used for the risk-scoring system was extracted from various financial and marketing systems. No potentially useful predictors were discarded because of a lack of data. The required data was downloaded to Excel files. The Excel data was imported into Access and all the analysis work and the reports were done in Access. An Access switchboard was used so that users could easily run and view the reports.

A DESCRIPTION OF THE RISK-SCORING SYSTEM

Each franchised restaurant (called a location) was scored on 10 predictor variables. A score of 0 indicated a low risk of underreported sales, and a score of 1 indicated a high risk of underreported sales. The final result was a risk score between 0 and 1 based on a weighted average of the scores across the 10 predictors.

The original scoring objective for each predictor was to score one-third of the locations with 0, one-third of the locations with 1, and the remaining locations with evenly distributed scores from 0 to 1. This would give risk scores that were symmetrically distributed around the mean (something like the familiar bell-curve). The final scores would then also tend to be spread out as opposed to being clustered between (say) 0.40 and 0.44 where there is not much to distinguish the 50th highest score from the 500th highest score. The initial scoring objective was discarded in favor of a scoring system that more closely tracked low and high risks. The scoring objectives are shown graphically in Figure 15.1.

Figure 15.1 is a graphical depiction of the initial scoring objective and the final result for a typical predictor. The graphs in this chapter are a little more complex than usual and SigmaPlot 11 (www.sigmaplot.com) was used to prepare these graphics. It was not always possible to obtain a large (spread) variance for a single variable. For example, few locations actually used excessive round numbers and so relatively few locations would score 1.00 for that predictor.

Another scoring objective was to avoid the use of complex formulas (e.g., many nested "if" statements) because these are open to programming errors. In all cases where a formula included division (÷), care had to be taken to deal with the issues that arise when dividing by zero. Also, when a formula included taking either the log or square root of a number, care had to be taken to ensure that problems did not arise when trying to take the log or square root of a negative number. Division by zero or taking

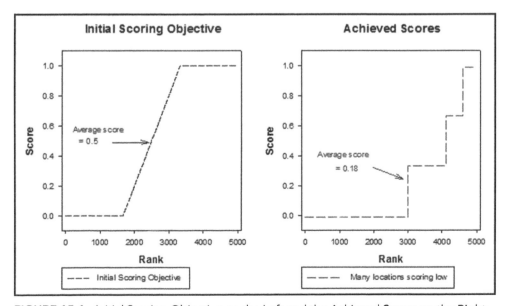

FIGURE 15.1 Initial Scoring Objective on the Left and the Achieved Scores on the Right

either the log or square root of a negative number gives an error message in Access and all subsequent uses of the calculated field have output errors.

The predictors and their weights were chosen based on the industry knowledge of the forensic investigators, their prior experiences, and to a small extent the available data. The system used 10 predictors and with hindsight, it seems that little would be added to the predictive value of the system if one or two more predictors were added. No predictors were considered as candidates for the risk scoring but then were later dropped because of a lack of data or other data issues such as data reliability. The predictors (abbreviated "P") are discussed in the next sections.

 ## P1: HIGH FOOD AND SUPPLIES COSTS

Franchisees are required to buy food and supplies (hereinafter "food") from a selection of approved vendors. The food cost percentage is a key performance metric used by the company. A high food percentage is an indicator that (a) sales might be underreported, or (b) there is some significant shrinkage occurring at the franchisee level (possibly sales not being rung up by employees). This predictor is based on *high values*. A *high values* predictor is one where the values are high as compared to some norm. To determine what constitutes the norm, an analysis was needed of the food cost percentages across all locations. Figure 15.2 shows the analysis of food cost percentages to determine what is normal and what is excessive.

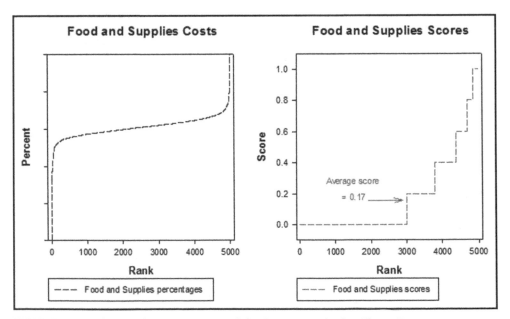

FIGURE 15.2 The Food Percentages and the Scores Applied to Those Percentages

TABLE 15.1 The Scoring Formula for the Food Cost Proportions

Food Proportion	Score	Notes
<= 0.31	0.0	Average or slightly lower than average
0.31 < Proportion <= 0.32	0.2	Slightly higher than average
0.32 < Proportion <= 0.33	0.4	Higher than average
0.33 < Proportion <= 0.34	0.6	Much higher than average
0.34 < Proportion <= 0.35	0.8	High
Above 0.35	1.0	Very high

The analysis of the food cost percentages in Figure 15.2 shows a small set of locations with abnormally low scores and abnormally high scores (the extreme left and right sides of the graph in the left panel). The calculations of the past percentages includes cases where a franchisee that owns more than one location purchases from a vendor for location x_1 and then later redistributes some of the food from location x_1 to other locations. This fact, together with the fact that purchases in one month might not be used until the next month gives us the cases at the left and the right with abnormally low or high food cost percentages.

The past data showed that the average food cost as a proportion of sales across all locations was 0.305 and the standard deviation of these costs was 0.043. The median food cost proportion was 0.315. The table with the final P1 scoring formula is shown in Table 15.1.

The graph of the P1 scores across all locations is shown in the right panel in Figure 15.2. About two-thirds of the locations scored a zero for P1 because they had food cost proportions that were close to average, or below average. The average score for P1 was just 0.17, because most restaurants had food costs near or below average.

P2: VERY HIGH FOOD AND SUPPLIES COSTS

Even with the issues introduced by food transfers between locations and inventory changes from month-to-month, the food cost predictor was seen as being a reasonably reliable means of identifying underreported sales. Before the risk-scoring system, this was the only criteria used to select locations for audits. It was believed that P1 by itself did not do an adequate job of significantly raising the final scores of locations with high and very high food cost proportions. With P1 scored as is shown above, if the location did not also get high scores on the other nine predictors then a location with a food cost of 0.345 might end up with an average final risk score. P2 was added to give an extra boost to the scores of high and very high food cost locations. The P2 scoring formula is shown in Table 15.2.

The P2 predictor was used to raise the final scores of the restaurants thought to be high risk locations. The average score for P2 was 0.136, which shows that not too many

TABLE 15.2 The Scoring Formula for the Second Predictor

Food Proportion	Score	Notes
<= 0.325	0.0	Higher than average
0.325 < Proportion <= 0.333	0.5	Much higher than average
Above 0.333	1.0	Very high

locations scored 0.5 or 1.00 on this predictor. It is possible to combine the scores from P1 and P2 into a single predictor. Keeping them as two predictors makes it clearer to an investigator which locations are in the stratosphere when it comes to the food cost predictors.

P3: DECLINING SALES

The logic behind using a declining sales trend as a predictor was that as a franchisee underreported an ever increasing percentage of sales, its sales trend would be below average. This predictor can be classified as an *opposite to expected* predictor. These types of predictors work well because fraudsters often take their frauds to levels that would be obvious to anyone looking at the analytics. The Charlene Corley shipping costs example in the first chapter is an example of an extreme fraud. In an application based on frequent-flyer miles the forensic analytics identified passengers that had completed (say) a Miami to Los Angeles flight, and New York to London flight on the same day. In the franchising example, in a time of economic growth and some inflation the expectation is that sales will increase over time, even if the increase is quite mild. For example, true sales might be increasing by 6 percent per year, but reported sales might only increase by 1 percent per year. The first step was to calculate the overall sales trend and these results are shown in Figure 15.3.

Figure 15.3 shows the sales changes for the past quarter against the same quarter one year earlier. The graph is truncated at −10 percent and +15 percent, which caused the two short straight lines on the left and right sides of the plotted line. About one-fifth of all locations had a sales decline and about four-fifths of the locations showed a year-on-year sales increase. All locations with sales changes that were below average were given a positive P3 score. The largest scores were for the largest quarter-on-quarter decreases. The P3 scoring formula is shown in Table 15.3.

The scoring formula for P3 is a step formula in that a sales decrease of 2.2 percent and 3.7 percent are both scored as 0.80. In Access the formula is programmed using the SELECT function. Table 15.3 is easy for management and other users to understand. The formula above is open to some improvements using a little algebra so that −3.7 percent is given a higher score that −2.2 percent. The highest and the lowest scores are for changes less than −4.00 percent and higher than 4.00 percent. A possible function-based formula is shown in Equation 15.1 with ΔS representing the change in Sales.

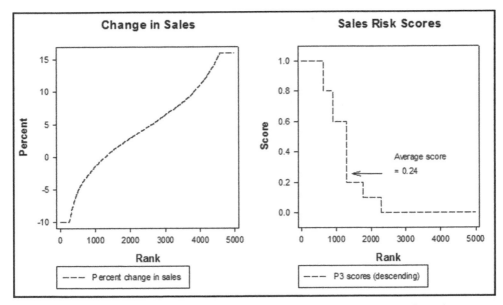

FIGURE 15.3 The Changes in Annual Sales and the P3 Scores Applied to the Sales Percentage Changes

$$P3 = 1 \quad where \ \Delta S < -0.04$$

$$= 0.5 - \frac{\Delta S}{0.08} \quad where -0.04 \leq \Delta S \leq 0.04 \qquad (15.1)$$

$$= 0 \quad where \ \Delta S > +0.04$$

Using Equation 15.1, a sales change of -2.2 percent would be given a P3 score of 0.7750 and a sales change of -3.7 percent would be given a P3 score of 0.9625. The formula in Equation 15.1 is more precise but it might be difficult for management to understand how sales changes are related to P3 scores.

TABLE 15.3 The Scoring Formula for the P3 Predictor Variable

Sales Change	Score	Notes
Less than −4 percent	1.00	Worst 15 percent of changes
−0.04 < Change <= −0.02	0.8	Close to the largest declines
−0.02 < Change <= 0.00	0.6	Slightly negative
0.00 < Change <= 0.02	0.2	Positive change, worse than average
0.02 < Change <= 0.04	0.1	Positive change, slightly worse than average
Above 4 percent	0	Better than average

P4: INCREASE IN FOOD COSTS

The goal for P4 was to score locations with an increasing food cost percentage as being high risk. The belief was that an upward shift in the food cost percentage over time is a sign of problems on the horizon or it could be an early stage fraud. This predictor is a *high values* predictor. The predictor uses the norm or average. In P4 *high* refers to a number being higher than the location's own historic averages.

For P4 the food cost proportion was based on the change over time. The monthly food cost percentages were quite variable because of food transfers and because large purchases in the final week of a month could distort the proportion for that month and for the following month. P4 was based on the slopes from linear regression equations run on several months of sales and food cost data.

A comparison of the slopes indicated whether the food cost proportion was nudging upward. The sales numbers were on average about three times as large as the food cost numbers and consequently the sales slope was usually about three times as large as the food cost slope. The slopes of the sales numbers indicated the average month-on-month change. A location with an average month-over-month increase of $1,000 would have a slope of 1,000. With a 30 percent food cost proportion, the slope of the food cost line would be $300. The sales would be increasing by $1,000 per month and the food costs would be increasing by $300 per month if the food cost proportion was constant at 30 percent. If the food costs were nudging upward then the food cost slope would be more than $300. A formula was developed using the sales slope, the food cost slope, and the intercept values (the intercept is where the line intersects with the y-axis and where x equals 0). The logic is shown graphically in Figure 15.4.

In the real application a formula was used that with hindsight was more complex than it needed to be, and a simpler approach is shown in the next few paragraphs. The result is that locations with food costs that have an increasing percentage are scored as high risk, and locations with a constant or a decreasing food cost percentage are scored as low risk. The food proportions were calculated for each location for each month (food cost divided by sales). The months were numbered 1 to 18. For each location the food proportion was regressed against the period (1 through 18). A positive slope in the regression (called either the slope or b_1 in statistics textbooks) would mean that the food proportion was increasing over time. The results are shown in Figure 15.5.

Figure 15.5 shows that about one-fifth of the locations had food proportion slopes that were negative. About 500 locations had food proportion slopes that were zero or near zero. These zero-slope locations included locations with zero sales for any month in the 18-month period because new locations and closed locations have volatile food costs. This left about 70 percent of the locations with positive food proportion slopes where the food costs as a proportion of sales were increasing over the period. P4 was scored as follows:

Food Proportion Slope	Predictor 4 score
Slope > 0.005	1
0.001 ≤ *Slope* ≤ 0.005	(*Slope* −0.001) * 250
Slope < 0.001	0

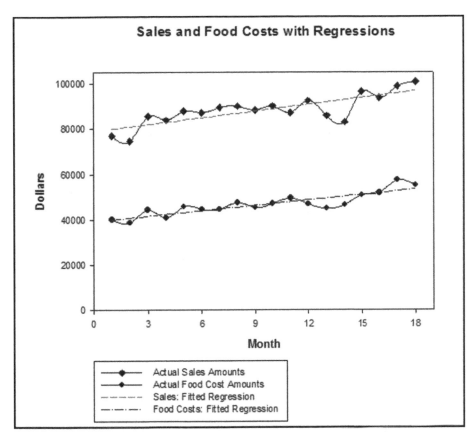

FIGURE 15.4 A Sales and Food Costs Pattern with a Fitted Regression Line

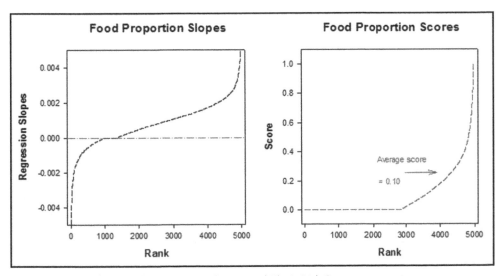

FIGURE 15.5 The Food Proportion Slopes and Their Risk Scores

The P4 formula gave high scores for high food proportion slopes. A food proportion slope of 0.005 (scored as 1, high risk) means that the food proportion is increasing by about one-half of 1 percent every month for 18 months. A food proportion slope of 0.001 (scored as 0, low risk) means that the food proportion is increasing by about one-tenth of 1 percent every month for 18 months.

P5: IRREGULAR SEASONAL PATTERN FOR SALES

P5 uses correlation as discussed in Chapter 13. The logic behind P5 was that sales numbers that deviated from the seasonal patterns were a higher risk for fraud or errors in the reported sales numbers. This predictor is an *erratic behavior* predictor. For this predictor the criteria is whether the sales numbers followed the seasonal norms. Figure 15.6 shows the typical sales pattern for a calendar year.

The left panel of Figure 15.6 shows the annual pattern of sales. The months with seasonally high sales are July, August, and December. February usually has the lowest sales because of winter and because it usually only has 28 days. The right panel of Figure 15.6 is a graph of the sales pattern of a hypothetical restaurant. The sales decrease significantly in the last two months of the year. The correlation between the sales for the specific restaurant and the seasonal pattern is 0.28.

Correlations by themselves are imperfect predictors of fraud risk. The association between underreported sales and a negative correlation is weak (but believed to be strong enough to be included in the risk scoring system), which is why multiple

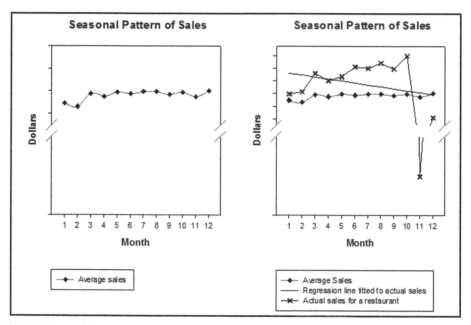

FIGURE 15.6 The Average Sales Pattern Together with the Sales of a Specific Location and a Fitted Regression Line

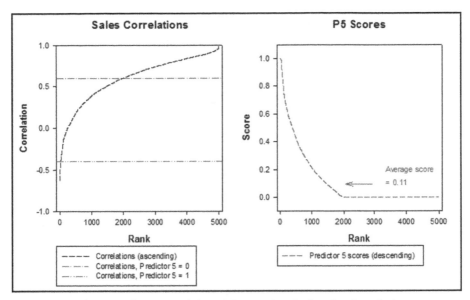

FIGURE 15.7 The Correlations and the P5 Scores Applied to the Correlations

predictors are used in the risk-scoring method. For example, a low correlation matched with an above average increase in sales suggests a low risk of reporting errors. Other predictors, including the trend in sales should be used together with the correlation to the seasonal pattern. The pattern shown on the right hand panel of Figure 15.6 is a high risk situation because of both the low correlation and the sharply decreasing trend. A graph of the ordered correlations and the P5 scores is shown in Figure 15.7.

The left-side panel of Figure 15.7 shows the correlations sorted from smallest to largest. The reference lines in the left panel relate to the way that the correlations were scored. Correlations *below* the lower horizontal reference line were scored as 1.00 (high risk), while correlations above the upper horizontal reference line were scored as 0.00 (low risk). Correlations between the two reference lines were scored with P5 values from 0.00 to 1.00. The P5 scoring formula is as follows:

Correlation	Predictor 5 score
Correlation < −0.4	1
−0.4 ≤ Correlation ≤ 0.6	(Correlation * −1) + 0.6
Correlation > 0.6	0

In the P5 scoring formula, correlations of 0.6 (and higher) were given a zero score, and correlations of −0.4 (or lower) were scored at 1.00. A correlation midway between −0.4 and 0.6 would be scored at 0.5. The reviews showed that locations on college campuses usually had negative correlations and high P5 scores. This was because July and August were usually low sales months because campuses are usually empty at that time, while February had high sales because the semester was in full swing at that time. A review of the actual sales numbers of locations that scored high on P5 always showed some odd sales pattern meaning that correlation was an effective tool to identify odd sales patterns.

P6: ROUND NUMBERS REPORTED AS SALES NUMBERS

The use of rounded numbers to identify data irregularities was first introduced to the auditing literature in Nigrini and Mittermaier (1997). The predictor P6 was based on the use of round numbers in the reported sales numbers. The assumption was that restaurants that reported round numbers as sales amounts were a higher risk for under-reported sales. This predictor is a part of the *other special situations* group of variables. Round number sales number might be an estimate and might be an indicator of rule-bending by the franchisor. Rule-bending in one area might signal a general disposition towards rules-bending.

The scoring of P6 required a rule as to what numbers constituted round numbers and also what constituted a high count of round numbers. The decision was that a round number would be a number with 0 in the unit position and zero cents after the decimal point. For example, $71,040.00 and $110,460.00 would be round numbers and $22,040.69 and 50,525.00 would not be round numbers. Round numbers ended with 00, 10, 20, . . . , 90 and these 10 two-digit combinations were one-tenth of the possible last two-digit combinations (00, 01, 02, . . . , 99). The expectation was that one-tenth of all reported numbers would be round numbers due purely to chance alone. Under Benford's Law the expected probabilities of the digits tend toward being uniformly distributed when moving from the left to right.

An analysis of the sales numbers showed that about three-quarters of all locations had either 0, 1, or 2 round numbers for the prior 18 monthly sales reports. The expectation was that each location would have 1.8 (one-tenth of 18) round numbers in an 18 month period. The round number counts and the P6 scores are shown in Table 15.4.

A count of either two or three round numbers exceeded the expected value of 1.8, but not by a large margin. Round number counts of four and higher were abnormally high. Only 8.7 percent of the locations had four or more round numbers, and consequently, a positive score for P6. There were not too many positive P6 scores, so the average score was only 0.032.

TABLE 15.4 The Distribution of Round Numbers in the Sales Numbers

Number of Round Numbers	Proportion	Predictor 6 Score
0, 1, or 2	0.764	0
3	0.149	0
4	0.062	0.25
5	0.019	0.50
6 and higher	0.006	1.00

P7: REPEATING NUMBERS REPORTED AS SALES NUMBERS

The use of repeated numbers to detect anomalies was introduced to the auditing literature in Nigrini and Mittermaier (1997) as the number duplication test. Because of the seasonal nature of the business, restaurants are unlikely to report exactly the same dollar amount more than once in an 18-month period. This predictor is an *other special situations* predictor. A location that duplicated a sales number in the past 18 months was seen to be a high risk for fraud or errors. A repeated number might come about when the franchisee reports a number for a prior period in error. In early September the franchisee reports July sales instead of August sales. The July number has already been reported, so the July number will show up as a duplicate.

The average range of the reported numbers was $16,250 over the 18-month period. The difference between the lowest month and the highest month was, on average, $16,250. The chances of an authentic duplicate are very small. The data analysis step for P7 included a calculation of the number of duplicate number locations and the results showed that 106 locations repeated a sales number in the 18-month period. An extract from the duplicate numbers table is shown in Table 15.5.

The location that duplicated the $1.00 was a college campus location that was closed during July and August. Presumably the owner wanted to report something because the reporting system does not allow sales of zero and so the owner reported $1.00 presumably just to submit a report and to avoid being classified as a nonfiler. A location was given a P7 score of 1.00 if any amount was duplicated during the 18-month period and zero otherwise. The average score for this predictor was very low at 0.02 because duplicates were quite rare.

P8: INSPECTION RANKINGS

The franchisor regularly carried out on-site inspections of franchised facilities. These inspections looked at a number of factors related to customer service, hygiene, and operating procedures. The inspection reports ranked the locations (from best to worst)

TABLE 15.5 An Extract from the Table Showing the Duplicated Sales Amounts

Restaurant Number	Amounts Duplicated
omitted	$ 1.00
omitted	$ 12,239.00
omitted	$ 27,915.00
omitted	$ 35,523.00
	. . .
omitted	$173,036.00
omitted	$344,986.00

TABLE 15.6 The P8 Scores Applied to the Inspection Rankings

Inspection Results	Score for V8
Poor scores	1.0
Worse than average	0.5
Average	0
Better than average	0

for the current month and for the year to date. This predictor is an *other special situations* predictor. The logic behind using the inspection rankings was the belief that a franchisee that was conscientious in following the operating procedures to the point of excellence was probably also doing the same with the sales reporting requirements. On the other hand, tardiness in operations was seen to have a high likelihood of spilling over into tardiness in reporting. A high inspection ranking was a sign of a positive attitude towards the franchisor and a desire to have a good relationship.

The score for P8 was based on a weighting of the restaurant's score for the most recent month and the score for the year to date. The P8 scores are shown in Table 15.6.

The scores in Table 15.6 were weighted 2/3 for the year-to-date and 1/3 for the most recent month. The year-to-date inspection scores were believed to be more important than the scores from a single month. A location with no score in the scorecard table was given a score of 1.00 because the lack of any score was seen to be a high-risk situation. The average P8 score was 0.30, which ties in with the fact that only locations with inspection scores that were worse than average were given a P8 score.

P9: HIGH RECEIVABLE BALANCE

This predictor tried to assess whether the franchisor had any pressure to underreport sales. A pressure could exist because the franchisor had a tight cash flow. There was no access to the franchisee's bank details, so an alternate (proxy) predictor was used. It was possible to see how up-to-date the franchisee was with paying the franchise fees. This cash flow predictor is an *other special situations* predictor that fits in with the pressure aspect of the fraud triangle (pressure, opportunity, and rationalization). P9 was scored based on whether there was a significant overdue balance shown in the accounts receivable listing. The P9 scores are shown in Table 15.7.

Table 15.7 shows the scoring formula for P9. If the days' outstanding reference point was (say) 60 days then all locations were tested against having a large, moderate, small, or zero balance that was 60 days overdue. The average score was 0.17, which means that most locations scored a zero for P9.

P10: USE OF AUTOMATED REPORTING PROCEDURES

The company provided an Internet-based reporting system to its franchisees. The system had options for other income sources, sales-related statistics, and permitted deductions.

TABLE 15.7 The P9 Scores Applied to the Accounts Receivable Data

Description	Score for P9
Significant balance over x days	1.00
Moderate balance over x days	0.75
Small balance over x days	0.50
Zero amount owing over x days	0.00

Full compliance was encouraged but was not required by the franchising agreement. The logic behind P10 was that if a franchisee voluntarily used the system and also reported all the small details, then this was a sign of voluntary cooperation and there was a reduced likelihood that the franchisee was engaging in willful sales underreporting. This predictor tried to measure the attitude of the franchisee toward having a cooperative relationship. This predictor is an *other special situations* predictor. The scoring of P10 took into account (a) whether the franchisee used the system in the immediately preceding month, (b) whether the franchisee had used the system for an extended period, and (c) whether the franchisee reported all or only some of the line-items requested.

The average score for this predictor was 0.38, which again means that the average location scored a zero for this predictor. The average score does not imply that most franchisees people complied perfectly with all information requests, rather it means that locations with below average compliance were given positive scores.

FINAL RESULTS

To calculate a final risk score for each location, each of the 10 predictors was weighted with a weighting that ranged from 0.05 to 0.20. Predictors were given low weights if the attributes that they measured were quite rare or if the predictor was seen to have a relatively low predictive ability. Examples of such predictors were P6 round numbers and P7 repeating numbers. A graph of the final risk scores (sorted from largest to smallest) is shown in Figure 15.8.

The left side panel of Figure 15.8 is a graph of the final risk scores. The results were very good in that only a small group of about 150 locations had scores that exceeded 0.50, and about 50 locations had scores that exceeded 0.60. The high-scoring locations were the focus of the company's audit efforts for the next year. About 270 locations, or 5.4 percent of the total, had scores of zero, which seems plausible. This means that about 5 percent of all restaurants did not display a single cue associated with a high risk of sales underreporting.

The final scores were compared to those of an earlier pilot study. The correlation between the pilot study risk scores and the current risk scores was 0.15. This means that there was virtually no relationship between the past scores and the current scores. The low correlations were because (a) there were different predictor weights in the current system, (b) the addition of new predictors and the deletion of some of the old predictors,

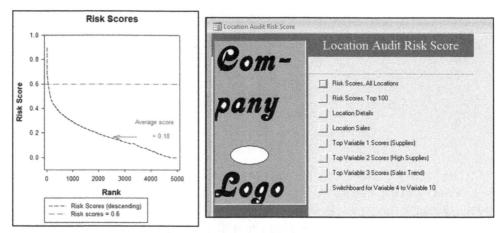

FIGURE 15.8 The Final Set of Risk Scores and the Switchboard Control of the System

and (c) changed conditions. The low correlation suggests that the risk-scoring system needs to be regularly updated with current data and with other changes that reflect changes in the environment.

 ## AN OVERVIEW OF THE REPORTING SYSTEM AND FUTURE PLANS

An Access database was created for each of the data-cleansing and data-manipulation steps needed to develop the risk-scoring system. The first database was used to import the data into Access and to change layouts and formats as needed. The second database was used for descriptive statistics and the data analysis work needed to calculate what the norms were for each predictor (e.g., the distribution of the food cost percentages). The third database was there for the users. This database calculated the scores for the individual predictors and the final risk score and also produced all the user reports. Several reports were available to the user:

- A report listing the risk scores for all locations.
- A report listing the risk scores of the locations with the 100 highest scores.
- A report for each of the 10 predictors listing the locations that scored high on that predictor only.
- A report where the user could enter a location reference (e.g., 45140) and the final score for that restaurant would be shown together with a list of the scores for that location for each of the 10 predictors. This report showed which predictors contributed the most to the location's overall score.
- An informative report where the user could enter a location number (e.g., 45140) to see the monthly sales history of the location together with other facts and figures related to that location.

The right side of Figure 15.8 shows the opening screenshot (with the company's logo removed) of the system. The system will be updated quarterly with the most recent data. Future system upgrades will probably be based on:

- Changes to the weights of the predictors.
- Changes to the scores associated with the values of the predictors (the equations shown in this chapter).
- Deletion of some predictors and the addition of other predictors.
- The inclusion of prior risk scores as an input to the current risk score.

The inclusion of prior risk scores in the calculation of the current risk score would mean that the risk scoring system has a memory. Prior high scores would linger. A prior score of 0.70 given a weight of 0.20 for the *past scores* predictor would give the location a starting score of 0.14 in the current period.

Assume that a location shows a large increase in food costs for 2009 to 2010. At the end of 2010 the very high food proportion stabilizes. A large increase in food costs and a large food cost proportion would probably cause the final risk score to be high. By including a prior score in the picture in 2011 we would capture the fact that the food cost percentage recently showed a large increase.

SOME FINDINGS

The reported numbers of the highest scoring locations were reviewed as a preliminary evaluation of the system. The highest risk score was 0.897. This location scored 1.00 on all variables except for the round numbers and repeated numbers variables, and marginally less than 1.00 on the sales correlation variable. The restaurant was located near a college, which explains the weak correlation. Colleges have vacations and have fewer people around in July, August, and December.

The round numbers predictor is given a low weight because only a few restaurants have excessive round numbers. However, this predictor is interesting when locations that score high on V6 only are reviewed. The sales numbers of a location with eight round numbers is shown in Table 15.8.

From Table 15.8 it would seem that some level of human intervention was active in the data. The location scored 1.00 on the round numbers predictor, and zero on all the other predictors. It might therefore be that the location is engaged in some innocent rounding and that in all other respects it is a low risk for underreported sales.

The repeating numbers predictor has a low weighting because the repeated numbers incidence is low. The stand-alone results are interesting. One restaurant had two numbers that were each duplicated (a double duplication in the 18-month period). A graph of these values is shown in Figure 15.9 together with the average sales per location.

The left-side panel of Figure 15.9 shows the sales pattern of a location that had a double duplication. This location reported the same dollar sales for November and

TABLE 15.8 The Sales Numbers of a Location

Month	Sales
1	96,907
2	91,537
3	100,920
4	106,640
5	111,242
6	108,740
7	109,159
8	110,035
9	107,762
10	112,012
11	110,300
12	115,070
1	101,850
2	90,908
3	106,252
4	107,539
5	152,390
6	157,780

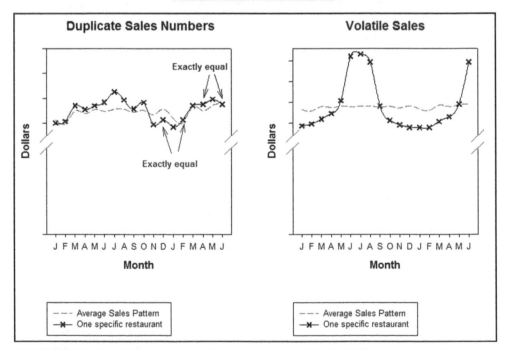

FIGURE 15.9 The Sales Numbers of a Location with Sales Duplicates and a High Standard Deviation

January and the sales for April and June were also equal. The final score for the location was about 0.40, which was higher than the average risk score and placed the restaurant in the seventh percentile. The location scored high on those predictors that related to compliance with policies and procedures (inspections, accounts receivable, and use of the reporting system). This error might be due to reporting sales for the incorrect month.

The right-side graph in Figure 15.9 is a sales pattern that was found as a part of some unstructured exploratory analysis. Locations were ranked by the volatility in their sales. The goal was to see whether a simpler metric would give essentially the same risk rankings. The location has highly volatile monthly sales. The risk score for the location was 0.38, which placed it in the ninth percentile. This risk score was high but an analysis of the data showed that (a) the location was at a seaside resort, which explained the high summer sales and low winter sales, and (b) the largest contributor to the risk score was that the location was not using the internal reporting system. The risk-scoring system painted a far more complete picture of the reporting patterns of the location than would be found by looking at sales volatility only.

DISCUSSION

The distinction between fraud *prevention*, which focuses on policies, procedures, training, and communication that stops fraud from occurring, and *detection*, which comprises activities and programs that detect frauds that have been committed is important. The risk-scoring system is a detection activity. Weaknesses in preventive controls are seen to increase the risk of fraud and place a greater burden on detective controls.

If a risk-scoring system was developed in which the weights of the predictors and the predictors themselves had no relationship to any predictive ability, then the system would function no worse or better than would a random selection of forensic units.

SUMMARY

This chapter describes the *risk-scoring method* and its application to the sales numbers reported by thousands of restaurant franchisees. The risk-scoring method functions well in a continuous monitoring environment. The *predictors* (of which there were 10 in the franchise application) are indicators of some attribute or behavior of interest. The risk-scoring system was used to detect underreported sales and so the *behavior of interest* was underreported sales. The risk-scoring predictors could also be called *cues* or *red flags*. A *forensic unit* is the entity or unit that is being scored. Examples could include fast-food restaurants, operating divisions, travel agents, or employees with active purchasing cards. The method works well with scoring hundreds or thousands of forensic units. Based on the numeric values of the predictors, a forensic unit would be seen to have either a *low risk of fraud* or a *high risk of fraud*. The *final risk score* is a score between 0 and 1 reflecting the risk that a forensic unit has engaged in the behavior of interest.

The case study is based on the monthly sales reports of franchisees. The company has only a short window within which to audit the sales numbers before the next wave of sales reports are submitted. The various types of frauds or errors include (a) arithmetic errors, (b) integrity errors (unauthorized deletion of transactions), (c) timing errors (incorrect time period), (d) deliberate fraud, or (e) legal errors (transactions that violate legal clauses) such as omitting nonfood revenues. The cost of a revenue audit by the company's auditors is high. The risk-scoring system was developed to identify high risk sales reports to minimize the costs of auditing locations that were compliant with respect to sales reporting.

The risk scoring system used 10 predictors to identify high-risk forensic units. The 10 predictors were related to (a) high food costs or a food cost percentage that was rapidly increasing, (b) a sales trend that was below average or a pattern of sales numbers that deviated substantially from the usual seasonal pattern, (c) irregularities in the numbers such as round numbers or repeating the same sales number in an 18-month period, (d) noncompliance with other aspects of the franchise agreement as evidenced by weak inspection rankings or incomplete reports submitted through the sales reporting system, or (e) pressure to minimize the franchise fee payments because of cash-flow problems. Each location was scored from 0 to 1 for each predictor. Scores of 1 were associated with a higher risk for sales underreporting.

For the final risk score, the predictors were weighted according to their importance and the final score was a weighted sum of the scores on the individual predictors. The locations with the highest final scores were the targets of franchise audits. The chapter included some of the future plans for improvements to the system. The logic and methodology could be adapted to other forensic analytic environments in which auditors or management wanted a formal system to evaluate the risk of a specific type of intentional or unintentional errors. The next chapter describes other examples and programming issues that need to be considered when using Access to program the system. The common thread in the applications is that the behavior of interest is very specific and the goal is a small set of audit targets that are a high risk for fraud or errors.

CHAPTER SIXTEEN

Examples of Risk Scoring with Access Queries

C HAPTER 15 DISCUSSED THE risk-scoring approach and the use thereof at a fast-food franchising company. This chapter is a continuation of the previous chapter with a review of other applications and an Access example. The chapter reviews the audit selection process used by the Internal Revenue Service (IRS) to demonstrate a highly sophisticated selection system. Other examples of the risk-scoring method are then reviewed. The examples include a banking fraud application, an airline ticketing fraud application, and a fictitious vendor fraud application. An example with financial statement fraud is presented in Chapter 17. The chapter concludes with an Access example showing a risk-scoring system designed to detect fraudulent vendors. Also discussed are general issues with using Access for these applications.

The risk-scoring model draws on the theory underlying decision-making cues. Using a psychology analogy, the predictors are the same as cues for decision making and the predictor weights are the same as the weights given to the decision-making cues. These weights have been addressed in psychological research studies. An early reference is Slovic (1966) in which he notes that little is known about the manner in which human subjects combine information from multiple cues, each with a probabilistic relationship to a criterion, into a unitary judgment about that criterion.

Slovic (1966) noted that a set of cues was consistent if the judge (decision maker) believed that the cues all agreed in their implications for the attributes being judged. Inconsistent cues would arise if the inferences that would be made from a subset of these cues would be contradicted by the conclusions from another set of cues. Consistency was seen to be a matter of degree and not an all-or-none matter. When a set of cues is consistent, each cue will be combined additively to reach a judgment. Inconsistent cues present a problem because in order to reconcile apparently contradictory information, the judge must either doubt the reliability of the cues or the belief in the correlation between the cues and the attributes being judged. In the risk-scoring method contradictory cues would occur if one cue indicated a positive risk of fraud and another cue signaled "no fraud" with certainty. The predictors are used to assess the risk of fraud and 0 and 1 simply indicate low risk and high risk as opposed to certainty.

THE AUDIT SELECTION METHOD OF THE IRS

One of the largest fraud detection applications is the system used by the IRS to detect tax evasion. A review of their system is valuable because it shows what can be done if cost is not that much of a concern. The IRS reviews its system in IRS (1979, 1989). The system uses discriminant analysis and requires a special audit called the Taxpayer Compliance Measurement Program (TCMP) of thousands of taxpayers on a regular basis.

The first step in the audit selection process is the TCMP that uses a stratified sample of approximately 50,000 income tax returns (IRS 1989, 24). Taxpayers are subjected to an intensive audit, and are subject to penalties and additional taxes in the event of noncompliance. The cost of the 1985 TCMP was $128 million. Of this amount, $42 million was the direct cost, and $86 million was an opportunity cost because the revenue yield from the random selection process is below that of the systems usually used to select returns for audit.

The IRS believes that the TCMP provides value because it provides them with an estimate of the level of noncompliance, the noncompliance trend, and the characteristics of delinquent returns. The results are used to improve efficiency and effectiveness in numerous areas, including the selection of returns for audit and general tax administration policy and systems (IRS 1989, 1). The steps in developing the audit selection process (IRS 1989, 10–13) are as follows:

1. **Preliminary planning.** The objectives of the audit are matched with available resources through sample planning, to ensure reliable compliance estimates and an effective audit selection formula.
2. **Sample design.** A system is developed to randomly select the returns according to the criteria formulated in the planning stage.
3. **Selection of returns.** Tax returns are selected for audit.
4. **Development of the progress reporting and control system.** A management information system is developed that enables management to monitor the progress of the project.
5. **Development of a checksheet and instructions.** The checksheet contains reported and corrected amounts for income, adjustments to income, exemptions, deductions, and credits, plus data that could lead to operational improvements, legislative recommendations, form changes, and enforcement strategies.
6. **Training and field orientations.** IRS auditors are trained to ensure consistent and credible results.

7. **Field examinations.** The selected returns are audited and the completed check-sheets are reviewed to ensure quality and accuracy.
8. **Checksheet processing.** The TCMP database is prepared after validity and consistency checks.
9. **Tables of results and Discriminant Index Function (DIF) development.** Tables summarizing the results are produced to estimate the level and types of noncompliance. The tables have multiple uses including the development of DIF formulas and methods to optimize the allocation of resources.

Once the TCMP data table has been completed, the IRS uses discriminant analysis to select returns for audit. The method uses discriminant analysis with some modifications to improve classification accuracy due to violations of the assumptions underlying the technique. The data violates the assumptions of equal covariance matrices and a normal distribution for the variable values (IRS 1979, 71). This causes the IRS to use a procedure called the *In-house approach*. Their method starts with a partition of the TCMP sample into two groups, on the basis of "profitable to audit" and "not profitable to audit." The cutoff numbers are (a) tax decrease of $25 or more, (b) tax increase or decrease of $25 or less, (c) tax increase of $25 to $400, and (d) tax increase of $400 and over. The IRS deletes all taxpayers from the sample that fall into either category (a) or (c). The two groups of interest are therefore those with only a small change to the balance due (within $25) because these returns are essentially unchanged, and taxpayers with a balance due of more than $400.

Separate DIFs are computed for each examination class where an examination class is basically a group of taxpayers. These groups help in improving the accuracy of the audit selection model. The two main groups are *nonbusiness* and *business returns* and within each of those two main groups there are five subgroups (also called classes). For *nonbusiness* returns the returns are classified according to total positive income. There are two classes for less than $25,000 returns (that end up getting audited at a very low rate), one class for $25,000 to $50,000, one class for $50,000 to $100,000, and one class for greater than $100,000 (which ends up getting audited at the highest rate). For business returns the classes are based on total gross receipts, and the dollar cutoffs are $25,000 and $100,000. There are five classes based on whether Schedule C or Schedule F was included in the return. The returns audited at the highest rates are those with total gross receipts above $100,000 with a Schedule F and total gross receipts above $100,000 with a Schedule C.

The 1985 results show that nonbusiness returns have a compliance rate of about 93 percent, and business returns have a compliance rate of about 77 percent. Stated differently, nonbusiness taxpayers evade about 7 percent of taxes due and business returns evade about 23 percent of the taxes due. Business taxpayers are therefore audited at a higher rate than nonbusiness returns.

To develop the selection formula, each of the 200 items on the checksheet is broken up into strata. The proportion of taxpayers in each of the two groups (no evasion and evasion) is calculated in each stratum. For example, 5 percent of taxpayers with three children had no evasion whereas 15 percent of taxpayers with three children had tax evasion. A *likelihood ratio* is then calculated at 3 (15 percent divided by 5 percent). These likelihood ratios are used to develop the formula. A statistical bonus would be a case where 100 percent of the taxpayers in stratum *x* were tax evaders whereas 0 percent of the taxpayers in the same stratum were compliant. This would mean that the stratum was a perfect predictor. Matters are unfortunately never so clear cut.

After solving a system of simultaneous equations, lambda (λ) values are obtained that represent the optimal weights to be assigned to the likelihood ratios. The preliminary weights are used to identify predictors with little or no discriminating power. Those predictors are discarded and the process is repeated until the model has a satisfactory predictive power with as few variables as possible.

The final model is an index score (Z-value) for each return of the form shown in Equation 16.1.

$$Z = \lambda_1 x_1 + \lambda_2 x_2 + \cdots + \lambda_n x_n \tag{16.1}$$

where the λ_1 are the optimal weights, and the x_1 are the predictors.

It is difficult to measure the efficiency of the DIF system, because such a measure would have to take into account the best non-DIF technique available. The statistics show that at the time of the first implementation, the average tax change per audit using the old selection method was $347, compared to $428 using the DIF selection algorithm. The "no tax change" percentage using the DIF system was 37.8 percent, compared to 42.0 percent using the prior method. The IRS also compared the DIF formulas on 1970 returns to a perfect selection method. A perfect selection method would have yielded 217 percent of the dollars assessed under the DIF formulas, and would have eliminated the 22 percent "no change" percentage.

Surprisingly, the DIF is not designed to rank returns according to the size of the expected tax change. At best, there is a positive correlation between the Z-score and the tax change in dollars. An improvement in the selection procedure is more cost-effective than an increase in the audit rate. The DIF is more effective in some districts than in others, which might be due to factors such as varying levels of voluntary compliance, staffing availabilities, and differences in audit practices.

The DIF system does not provide examiners with specific problematic areas or reasons for the high score. A manual examination at the district level determines whether the return will be audited, and the extent of the audit. The desired result is that the DIF model predicts taxpayer type (evasion or no evasion) better than the classification accuracy that could be achieved by chance alone (random selection). In the taxpayer audit selection context, the problem is more complex than usual because of the goals of predicting taxpayer type and also maximizing the revenue yield with a limited examination budget and within a limited time frame.

Unlike the coefficients in the classical linear regression model, the discriminant function coefficients are not unique; only their ratios are. It is not possible to test, as is the case with regression analysis, whether a particular coefficient is equal to zero or any other value. Also, seemingly unimportant variables on a univariate (stand-alone) basis may be important when combined with other variables. The IRS approach drops predictors that are highly correlated, and consequently, some predictors might be incorrectly deleted from the model. Discriminant analysis also assumes that the groups being investigated are discrete and identifiable. A violation of this assumption occurs when groups are formed by segmenting an inherently continuous variable (which is exactly what the IRS does). These segments are arbitrary and not truly distinct. Segmentation is only appropriate if natural breaks or discontinuities appear. Regression is the more appropriate statistical tool under these circumstances. The effect of arbitrary grouping schemes potentially includes a further source of error because a taxpayer might be misclassified giving errors in the input data. Another cause of statistical concern is when the analysis is based on data from one time period, and is then used to predict a future occurrence. This is because the relationships among the relevant variables (e.g., means, variances and covariances) change over time.

Congressional hearings were held in 1995 with witnesses from the IRS, the GAO (then called the U.S. General Accounting Office), the American Bar Association, and many other prominent persons. The hearings were held to assess the value of the TCMP program and to determine if there were less-burdensome alternatives available. The opening remarks included phrases such as "too costly, too time-consuming, and too burdensome." The witnesses used phrases such as "these unwarranted inconsistencies impose a hidden and vast burden on millions of taxpayers each year." Other statements along the same lines were that "TCMP audits are deeply invasive. They involve unearthing the most private aspects of a person's life."

The IRS has since stopped the TCMP audits and the DIF scores have not been updated for many years now. It is not clear whether the old formulas are still being used. In update IR-2007-113 dated June 6, 2007, the IRS notes that it will conduct audits of about 13,000 randomly selected tax returns as a part of its National Research Program. It would seem that this sample could be conducive to the development of a new DIF.

The following points compare and contrast the risk-scoring method and the DIF scoring procedure:

■ Both seek to score forensic units so that those with the highest risk of the behavior of interest have a score that reflects this risk.
■ Both use predictor variables and a model based on additive (addition) scores that come from multiplying certain values by weights (lambda values).
■ Both are used in an environment that has a relatively short auditing window after a report is submitted by a forensic unit.
■ Both are conducive to the auditor conducting a simple correspondence audit, office audits, or field audits.
■ Both need regular updates based on the predictors used, their weights, and how they are scored to take into account changes in conditions.
■ Both systems only use current data. Neither system has any *memory* of prior high scores. A forensic unit could therefore consistently have a risk score that is just below the threshold for an audit.
■ Both require a manual screening by a skilled investigator to decipher why the forensic unit was given a high score. This information is reasonably clear in the risk-scoring system.

- Both allow the company or agency to assert that forensic units were selected for audit based solely on the information and numbers in their reports. Forensic units were not selected for audit because of some personal bias on the part of the forensic investigator or revenue agent.
- The DIF system is based on two samples (low risk and high risk) because the IRS does not know what the predictor values are, or how to score them. Statistics based on discriminant analysis underlies the scoring model. The score is based on predictors, scores for the predictors, and weights. The risk-scoring method is based on predictors that might be red flags based on the experience and industry knowledge of the forensic investigator. The result is a score based on predictors, scores for the predictors, and weights.
- The DIF system is more expensive than the risk-scoring system.

Few private organizations have the ability to force forensic units to comply with audit directives. It is therefore difficult to get a "fraud" and a "no fraud" sample. Even if a fraud sample could be obtained, the *fraud* sample would be very small compared to the *no fraud* sample and the discriminant technique would not work well with a large difference between the sizes of the two groups. Also, we would be expecting a lot from a formula to use data from one time period to select forensic units (taxpayers) for audit in future time periods. The risk-scoring approach is a viable approach for organizations wanting to identify high risk forensic units.

 ## RISK SCORING TO DETECT BANKING FRAUD

Check kiting involves a bank account holder (the forensic unit) taking advantage of the fact that banks make deposits available to an account immediately while checks written take a few days to go through the banking system before being presented for payment. A customer with accounts at two different banks could therefore write a check for $8,000 from each account and deposit it into the other account. Each account will show a balance for perhaps two days before the checks are presented and the accounts each then show the correct balance of zero. For two days though, each account will show a balance of $8,000. The payout from this fraud occurs if the owner of the accounts can make a withdrawal from either or both accounts in the two-day window during which the accounts have balances. Check kiting and some variations on the theme are discussed in Wikipedia.

A banking software company had a successful software product that identified check kiting suspects according to a set of rules that it had developed. In the early hours of the morning of each business day the software would analyze checking account transactions and a listing would be printed of all the suspect accounts. This list was waiting for the "kiting researcher" when he or she arrived at work. The researcher would then review the details for each account and place a hold on the funds if it looked like a kite in the beginning stages or a kite in action. Other actions were also available. The researcher could place an exemption on the account meaning that it should be excluded from subsequent kiting reports. At one user in Pittsburgh, Pennsylvania, the average size of the check-kiting report was a printed report nearly 12 inches high. In this report the checking accounts were listed in account number order, which meant that (a) the list was far too long for anyone to possibly research in a day, and (b) the large and obvious kites were randomly scattered throughout the report. It was felt that the customer accounts should be ranked starting with the large obvious kites so that the researcher's efforts could be directed at the large and obvious cases. The risk scoring system was developed to create a ranked listing of the kite suspects.

The development of the system was a team effort with the author, a check-kiting specialist, and a programmer who would program the formulas and comment on what was feasible or not. The risk-scoring system allowed the user to have some control over the weighting of the predictors. The user could delete a predictor by giving it a weighting of zero. The seven predictors are described next.

P1: Deposits from the Same Routing Number

One predictor of check kiting is that the account holder continually makes deposits drawn on the same account. Evidence of this is frequent deposits with the checks drawn on the same bank with the same *routing transit number*. The risk-scoring approach uses a formula to determine whether deposits are continually being drawn on just one or two banks. The formula for the routing duplication factor is shown in Equation 16.2.

$$\text{P1, Routing Duplication} = \frac{\sum c^2}{n^2} \tag{16.2}$$

where c is the count for a specific routing number if the count is greater than 1 and n is the number of deposits. Both c and n are calculated for the preceding 10 days. By way of an example, P1 would be calculated as being 0.494 ((36+4)/81) for the following sequence of routing numbers: 100002204, 100002204, 100002204, 100002204, 100002204, 100002204, 100006340, 100006340, and 100110364.

If all the numbers are different then P1 would equal zero and if all the numbers are the same, then P1 would equal 1.00. A P1 score of zero is associated with a low risk of kiting and a P1 score of 1.00 is associated with a high risk of kiting.

P2: Deposits of Round Dollar Amounts

The logic behind predictor P2 was that kiters would tend to use round numbers in their deposits because round numbers are easier to track. For this predictor the proportion of round numbers was calculated. The formula is shown in Equation 16.3.

$$\text{P2, Round Proportion} = \frac{m}{n} \tag{16.3}$$

where m is the count of round numbers and n is the number of deposits. Both m and n are calculated for the preceding 10 days. By way of an example, P2 would be calculated as being 0.80 (8/10) for the following deposit amounts: $6,000, $8,200, $7,500, $6,000, $8,000, $7,800, $6,340, $8,000, $9,645, and $8,000.

Round numbers were defined to be numbers that could be divided by $100 without leaving a remainder. The belief was that round numbers were numbers that have been invented. Number invention does not always mean fraud (a painter might charge $200 to paint a room in a house) but it does signal that the number has been thought up as opposed to being the result of a calculation of some sort (such as a monthly electricity bill).

P3: Deposits of Equal Dollar Amounts

For predictor P3 the hypothesis was that kiters would tend to deposit the same amount repeatedly to the same account because a series of the same numbers would be easier to keep track of than a series of numbers that were different. The formula used for the number duplication factor is shown in Equation 16.4.

$$\text{P3, Number Duplication} = \frac{\sum c^2}{n^2} \tag{16.4}$$

where c is the count for a specific dollar amount if the count is greater than 1 and n is the number of deposits. Both c and n are calculated for the preceding 10 days. As an example, P3 would be calculated to be 0.81 (81/100) for the following sequence of deposits: $15,000, $15,000, $15,000, $15,000, $15,000, $15,000, $15,000, $15,000, $15,000, and $18,000.

If the deposit numbers are all different then P3 would equal zero and if all the numbers are the same, then P3 would equal 1.00. A P3 score of zero is associated with a low risk of kiting and a score of 1.00 is associated with a high risk of kiting.

P4: Deposit Frequency

For a kiting scheme to be successful, the fraudster needs to make regular deposits. Without regular deposits all the checks will clear and both bank accounts will show a zero balance. This predictor was based on the oldest date with a deposit in the last 10 banking days. If the bank date before the current date is designated as t_{-1} we would then count backward in time $t_{-2}, t_{-3}, \ldots, t_{-10}$. The range for the deposits over the past 10 days was calculated by counting backward from t_{-1} to the date of the first deposit in the 10-day window. For example, a report on June 1 might go backward in time as follows: May 29, May 28, May 27, May 26, May 22, May 21, May 20, May 19, May 18, and May 15, with May 29 being t_{-1} and May 15 being t_{-10}. The following deposit dates, May 13, 26, 27, and 29 would have a four-day range (the 26 is t_{-4}). May 13 is ignored because it falls before the 10-day range.

The formula for P4 is set out in Equation 16.5.

$$\text{P4, Deposit Frequency} = \frac{\sum Days\, Used}{Range} \tag{16.5}$$

For a $Range > 1$, the P4 predictor value for May 13, 26, 27, and 29 would be 0.75 (3/4).

One small tweak was needed for equation 16.05. For a Range = 1 (in this case a single deposit on May 29) the P4 predictor was set to equal 0 (even though it should be equal to 1.00 from equation 16.05). This override was needed to give a low risk score to a depositor that only used a single day in the last 10 days.

P5: Deposit Total

The logic for P5 was that the higher the deposit total, the higher the risk, all other things being equal. The more deposit activity in any account, the more the bank is at risk to lose. Deposit totals can be very high with no real upper bound, so some creativity was needed. There is a lower bound of zero but with no deposits the account would not be on the check-kiting suspect's report. The formula for P5 was based on the deposit total for the preceding four banking days. Checks usually clear within four days and so activity before t_{-4} is not really relevant. The formula is shown in Equation 16.6.

$$P5, \text{Deposit Total} = 0.5 \times (\log_{10}(DepositTotal) - 4) \tag{16.6}$$

where *DepositTotal* is restricted to the [10000,1000000] range. Deposit totals of less than $10,000 are raised to $10,000 for the P5 formula and deposit totals greater than $1,000,000 are reduced to $1,000,000 for the P5 formula. This range restriction uses its own formula, as is shown in Equation 16.7.

$$\text{DepositTotal} = \min(\max(Deposits, 10000), 1000000) \tag{16.7}$$

The use of logs has the effect that the P5 score does not increase in direct proportion to an increase in dollars of deposits. For example, a deposit total of $30,000 would have a score of 0.2386, a deposit total of $60,000 would have a P5 score of 0.3891, and a deposit total to $120,000 would increase the P5 score to 0.5396. The use of logs means that low values get relatively high scores ($60,000 is scored as 0.3891) and the deposit total has to increase to about $360,000 for the P5 score to double to 0.7782.

P6: Uncollected Funds

Predictor P6 was based on whether the account holder drew on uncollected funds in the past 10 days. This was an indicator with values of either 0 or 1. The predictor was called *UnCollect* and the formula is shown in Equation 16.8.

$$\begin{aligned} P6, \text{UnCollect} &= 1 \quad \text{\textit{where} Account Holder drew on uncollected funds} \\ &= 0 \quad \textit{otherwise} \end{aligned} \tag{16.8}$$

A kite is only "successful" if the account holder taps into uncollected funds. The use of uncollected funds increases the risk that the account is a kite in action.

P7: Returned Deposits

Predictor P7 was based on whether any deposits to the account had bounced in the past 10 days. A bounced deposit (insufficient funds on the part of the person that wrote the check) could be the first step in a kite unraveling. It could be because the "other" bank has detected the scheme as being a kite. Being the first of the two banks to uncover the kite has some advantages. This predictor assesses whether the account had a returned deposit and it is an indicator with values of either 0 or 1. The predictor was called *Return* and the formula is shown in Equation 16.9.

$$\text{P7, Return} = 1 \quad \textit{where} \text{ Account Holder had a returned deposit} \\ = 0 \quad \textit{otherwise} \tag{16.9}$$

P7 was the seventh and final predictor used to rank the check-kiting suspects. The final step was to weight the factors to compute a risk score for each account.

 ## FINAL RISK SCORES

The final risk score was based on a weighted average of the scores from P1 to P7. The weightings are shown in Table 16.1.

The seven predictors P1 to P7 were scored from 0 to 1 with 0 indicating a low risk of kiting and 1 indicating a high risk of kiting. The first installation of the risk-scoring kiting module was in Pittsburgh, Pennsylvania, and the feedback was that the risk-scoring method correctly identified the high-risk accounts and that they were able to focus their efforts on the high-risk forensic units (checking accounts).

 ## RISK SCORING TO DETECT TRAVEL AGENT FRAUD

This section describes a risk-scoring system developed for an organization associated with airline travel. The *behavior of interest* falls under the classification of *ownership change schemes*. In this scheme a fraudster would purchase a travel agency. The fraudster would then advertise specials for travel from the United States to various countries that have large emigrant populations (such as India, China, Vietnam, or Korea). After the passenger (victim) has purchased the ticket, the fraudster (who is now the owner of

TABLE 16.1 The Weightings Applied to the Check-Kiting Predictors

Predictor	Weight
P1, Deposits from the same routing number	0.20
P2, Deposits of round dollar amounts	0.08
P3, Deposits of equal dollar amounts	0.07
P4, Deposit frequency	0.15
P5, Deposit total	0.10
P6, Uncollected funds	0.20
P7, Returned deposits	0.20
Sum of Weights	1.00

the travel agency) would void the ticket and pocket the cash. Immigrants to the U.S. were generally the target of this scheme because they would tend to pay with cash or checks (which can be stolen) and there would generally be several weeks before the trip is eventually taken. By the time the victims found out that they did not really have valid tickets for their travel, the travel agency had closed its doors. The goal of this risk scoring was to identify travel agents who are in the starting phases of such a fraudulent scheme so that the organization could take corrective or preventive actions. Voided tickets occur regularly and for many valid reasons as a part of everyday business. The goal was to discover a void pattern that signaled the start of a fraudulent scheme.

There were some special challenges that needed to be dealt with. First, as the formulas were being developed they could not be run against the complete *tickets sold* data table. The test runs would have used up significant resources. The data analysis work was done against a "scratch file" with 2 million records. The program was run against this file until it was ready for deployment. Second, this was a mainframe environment requiring all the protocols for development work in a mainframe environment. The system took one week to develop and to program. The project was easier because the *behavior of interest* was clearly defined.

The predictors and some selected results are shown in the next sections. The formulas used were more complex than usual to capture some nonlinear relationships. A linear relationship would be where $2x$ was scored twice as high as x. A nonlinear relationship is where being 20 miles per hour over the speed limit is seen to be more than twice as bad as being 10 miles per hour over the speed limit.

P1: Average Void Amount

The forensic unit (travel agency) would be scored high on P1 if their average void was higher than average. The data analysis phase showed that the average void was around $500 and that $1,500 was a high void amount by industry standards. The formula for P1 is shown in Equation 16.10.

$$
\begin{aligned}
\text{P1, Average Void} &= 0 & &\text{where } AV < 500 \\
&= \frac{AV - 500}{1000} & &\text{where } 500 \leq AV \leq 1500 \\
&= 1 & &\text{where } AV > 1500
\end{aligned}
\tag{16.10}
$$

where AV is the average void amount for the past two weeks.

The equation for P1 is a linear equation in that the P1 score increases linearly with an increase in the average void (AV) above $500. An AV of $900 would have a P1 score that was double the P1 score for an AV of $700. Although this was an important risk predictor, it ended up being weighted with one of the lowest predictor weights.

P2: Cash Ticket Proportion

The funds used to purchase tickets with a credit card cannot be misappropriated by a travel agent because the funds are routed directly to the airline. Only cash or check payments could be stolen. The second predictor looked at the ratio of cash sales to total ticket sales for the prior four weeks to see if an agent was selling excessively for cash. The formula is shown in Equation 16.11.

$$P2, \text{Cash Tickets} = \sqrt[3]{\frac{\text{Count of Cash Tickets Sold}}{\text{Count of Tickets Sold}}} \qquad (16.11)$$

Equation 16.11 for P2 has a few interesting properties. The fraction within the cubed root sign will always be in the 0 to 1 range, which is what we want for the risk-scoring systems. Taking the cubed root *keeps* the calculated value in the 0 to 1 range but it has the effect of scoring low proportions with a higher P2 score. For example, the cubed root of 0.1 is 0.464, the cubed root of 0.2 is 0.584, and the cubed root of 0.3 is 0.669. The average cash tickets proportion was about 0.125 and so the agencies would on average score 0.50 for P2. The scoring objective in this application was to score the average agency at 0.50. That objective has since changed to score the average forensic unit at about 0.05 to 0.20 for each predictor.

P3: Void Count above Average

This predictor looked at whether the count of voids for the immediately past week was high when compared to the count of voids for the prior four weeks. A nonlinear function was used and the equation is shown in Equation 16.12.

$$P3, \text{Void Count} = \sqrt[3]{\frac{\text{Count of Voids this week}}{\text{Count of Voids for past four weeks}}} \qquad (16.12)$$

The cubed root in Equation 16.12 transforms a proportion of 0.25 to 0.63. If all weeks had an equal void count, the count for one week should be about one-quarter of the total count. With the cubed root the average agent would score 0.66 for P3. With hindsight it would seem that this predictor was not properly scored. A scoring formula that was based on the distance above 0.25 would have been more appropriate. Such a scoring formula is shown in Equation 16.13.

$$
\begin{aligned}
P3 \text{ (new)} &= 0 & &where\ VP < 0.25 \\
&= \left(\frac{\text{Count of Voids this week}}{\text{Count of Voids past four weeks}} - 0.25\right) \times 10 & &where\ 0.25 \leq VP \leq 0.35 \\
&= 1 & &where\ VP > 0.35
\end{aligned}
$$
$$(16.13)$$

where *VP* is the void proportion for the count of voids this week divided by the count of voids for the past four weeks.

The scoring formula in Equation 16.13 would score a void proportion of 0.26 (slightly higher than one-quarter) as 0.10, and a void proportion of 0.35 (much higher than one-quarter) as 1.00 indicating a high risk for the fraud scheme.

P4: International Ticket Proportion

The fraud scheme was focused on tickets to international destinations because foreign ticket prices are higher than normal, the flight date is usually further into the future, and the passenger is more likely to pay by cash or check. A high proportion of international tickets would suggest that the agency is a high-risk agency. The formula used to score P4 is shown in Equation 16.14.

$$\text{P4, International Sales} = \sqrt[3]{\frac{\text{Count of Foreign Tickets}}{\text{Count of all Tickets}}} \qquad (16.14)$$

Equation 16.14 uses the cubed root, which has the effect of giving the average agency a P5 score of about 0.50 because foreign sales were usually about 12 percent of total sales. More recent applications of risk scoring would use a scoring formula that assigns a lower score to the average forensic unit.

P5: High-Risk States

The target victims of the scheme were immigrants wanting to fly home on a bargain airfare. The fraudsters would therefore try to carry out a void fraud scheme from a location with many immigrants in the vicinity. P5 identified those states with (a) large immigrant populations, and (b) a history of such schemes being carried out or attempted. The result was that forensic units located in certain high-risk states were scored as high-risk for P5. The scoring formula is shown in Equation 16.15.

$$\text{P5, States} \begin{array}{l} = 1 \quad \textit{when } \text{Forensic Unit is in FL, IL, TX, CA, NJ, NY, VA, MA, or DC} \\ = 0 \quad \textit{otherwise} \end{array}$$

$$(16.15)$$

P5 uses an indicator variable with a score of 0 or 1. The indicator can work both ways. Forensic units can be scored with a 1 if they meet certain criteria and a 0 otherwise. Alternatively, forensic units can be scored with a 0 if they meet certain criteria and a 1 otherwise. The IRS might score certain taxpayers as 0 if it believes the taxpayers to be fully compliant. A reason for such a belief might be that the taxpayer has been audited more than once with no increases in taxes owed.

P6: Dollars at Risk

For P6 a forensic unit was given a high score if the sum of the cash voids for the prior week was high. The logic is that the more voids that are occurring, the higher the risk for the forensic unit. If there was only a small level of void activity measured by total dollars, the risk attached to that forensic unit would be small. Using the analysis of the average void activity, the scoring formula in Equation 16.16 was developed.

$$\text{P6, Dollars at risk} \begin{array}{l} = 0 \qquad\qquad\qquad \textit{where } \text{VS} < 5000 \\ = \log_{10}(VS) - 3.699 \quad \textit{where } 5000 \leq \text{VS} \leq 50000 \\ = 1 \qquad\qquad\qquad \textit{where } \text{VS} > 50000 \end{array} \qquad (16.16)$$

where VS is the Void Sum for the prior week.

The effect of using logs is that a forensic unit will be given a reasonably high score for a void sum that is not too much higher than $5,000. For example, a void sum of $10,000 will be given a P6 score of 0.301. A void sum of $15,000 will be given a P6 score of 0.477. The increase in P6 is at an ever-decreasing rate. At or above $50,000, the score will be 1.00. This predictor was seen to be very important and it ended up with the highest weight for any predictor.

P7: Nonreporting

This predictor looked at whether the forensic unit was guilty of any tardy behavior that might be a predictor that some or other scheme was in the works. This is similar to the belief in law enforcement that citizens who have a general contempt for the law will probably be breaking many different laws. This is why someone pulled over for speeding (a specific law) is given some general questioning and perhaps a search because the speeding offense could be a signal that the person has a contempt for law and order in general. For example, on April 19, 1995, Timothy McVeigh was stopped by a state trooper for driving without a license plate.

If a passenger arrives at the airport and the ticket sale was not reported to the carrier, this was a sign of tardy records and procedures. In this case a forensic unit was given a score of 1.00 if there were any unreported sales, and a score of 0 otherwise. These unreported sales were rare and P7 was given a relatively low weighting.

P8: Carrier Void Concentration

The P8 predictor gave a high score to forensic units that had most of their voids concentrated on one or two carriers only as opposed to having their voids spread across many carriers. It was a trademark of the scheme that specials were offered for one or two destinations and many tickets were sold for that overseas route. The scoring formula is shown in Equation 16.17.

$$\text{P8, Void Concentration} = \sqrt{1 - \frac{\text{Count of Carriers with Voids}}{\text{Count of Voids}}} \qquad (16.17)$$

The scoring formula in Equation 16.17 turned a fraction with a low proportion (one carrier and 10 voids, which gives one-tenth for the fractional part) into a high score (of 0.95). Some examples of P8 scores are shown below:

1 carrier and 10 voids: P8 score of 0.95
1 carrier and 25 voids: P8 score of 0.98
5 carriers and 10 voids: P8 score of 0.71
5 carriers and 50 voids: P8 score of 0.95

P8 will give high scores for many voids and fewer carriers. After the addition of P8 to the list of predictors, the scoring system was thought to have enough predictive capability.

FINAL RESULTS

The predictors were weighted for the final risk scores. This was a complex process and involved many iterations. The weighting method used five successful cases of the fraud. The data was then analyzed for the week in which it was felt that the fraud was well underway (usually the second week of the fraud). The analysis showed where that forensic unit was ranked in the rankings. The weightings were continually revised until the fraudulent agent was in the top 50 high-risk agents. The process went through many iterations with different weightings until the highest possible score across all five known past fraud cases was achieved.

Table 16.2 shows the predictors and their weights. The final objective was to identify the high-risk cases and to end up with scores where there were only a few high scores. Another consideration was that the distribution was somewhat stable from week to week. It seems logical that a risk-scoring system should generate scores that have similar patterns from week to week. The risk scores were calculated for three dates and the graph is shown in Figure 16.1.

Figure 16.1 shows that the pattern of the risk scores is very similar for the three dates selected. The results also show that there is only a small group of forensic units with high scores. In this case a high score seems to be a score of 0.70 and higher. The final reports used by the forensic investigators included some details relevant to the scoring procedure, such as average void in dollars, the number of voided carriers, and the total void percentage. The project was a success.

RISK SCORING TO DETECT VENDOR FRAUD

In 2009 this project was discussed with the auditors of an international conglomerate. The goal of the risk-scoring method was to detect vendor fraud. The project was given to an auditor but the system was never developed because it was just too difficult to get

TABLE 16.2 The Weightings of the Airline Fraud Predictors

Predictor	Weight
P1, Average void amount	0.100
P2, Cash ticket proportion	0.100
P3, Void count above average	0.150
P4, International ticket proportion	0.150
P5, High-risk states	0.125
P6, Dollars at risk	0.200
P7, Nonreporting	0.075
P8, Carrier void concentration	0.100
Sum of Weights	1.000

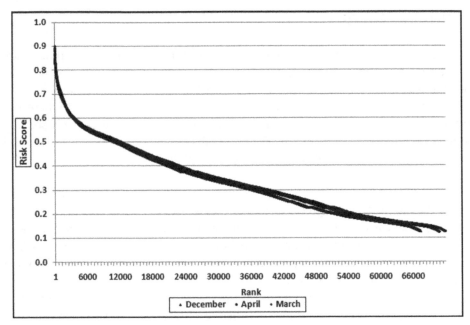

FIGURE 16.1 The Pattern of the Risk Scores on Three Different Dates

invoice-by-invoice data. Payments data was available as a part of a system to test for duplicate payments, but payments data (checks and wire transfers paid to vendors) could aggregate several invoices and payments data does not directly show credits. An invoice for $20,000 and a credit of $3,000 would end up as a single payment of $17,000. The details of the credit would be lost. The invoice data resided in too many different systems and was also simply too large (in terms of gigabytes) to download and analyze in Access. The formulas that would have been used are discussed below together with Access queries applied to the invoices data from Chapter 4. The predictor variables are discussed next.

P1: Invoice Count

The position was taken that a fraudulent vendor would not have too many invoices per month. Each invoice creates a risk for the fraudster and the belief was that they would try to at least keep that risk reasonable. The P1 scoring formula is a 0/1 indicator variable that scores a 0 if the vendor has more than six invoices in any single month and a 1 otherwise. This is set out in Equation 16.18.

$$\text{P1, Invoice Count} \begin{aligned} &= 1 \quad where \text{ Invoice Count is} \leq 6 \text{ invoices every month} \\ &= 0 \quad otherwise \end{aligned} \quad (16.18)$$

The scoring formula in Equation 16.18 would be quite easy to program in Access. If data from more than one year is being used, the equation could be changed to an invoice count of less than or equal to eight invoices to take account of the fact that the fraudster might occasionally deviate from the norm.

P2: Credits, Adjustments, and Reversals

The position was taken that a fraudulent vendor would not have any credits, adjustments, or reversals since no goods or services were actually provided. The fraudster would presumably try to have the invoice glide through the payments process with the absolute minimum of fanfare. Nigrini (1999) reviews an interesting case of vendor fraud, *State of Arizona* v. *Wayne James Nelson* (CV92-18841), where Nelson was found guilty of trying to defraud the state of $2 million. Nelson, a manager in the office of the Arizona State Treasurer, claimed that he had diverted funds to a bogus vendor to show the absence of safeguards in a new computer system. The amounts of the 23 checks are shown in Table 16.3.

TABLE 16.3 The Checks that a Treasurer for the State of Arizona Wrote to a Fictitious Vendor

Date	Amount ($)
October 9	1,927.48
	27,902.31
October 14	86,241.90
	72,117.46
	81,321.75
	97,473.96
October 19	93,249.11
	89,658.17
	87,776.89
	92,105.83
	79,949.16
	87,602.93
	96,879.27
	91,806.47
	84,991.67
	90,831.83
	93,766.67
	88,338.72
	94,639.49
	83,709.28
	96,412.21
	88,432.86
	71,552.16
Total	1,878,687.58

No services were ever delivered, so Nelson must have invented all the numbers in his scheme, and because people are not random, invented numbers are unlikely to follow Benford's Law. There are several indications that the data is made up of invented numbers. First, he started small and then increased the dollar amounts. The jumps were large, at least to the threshold of $100,000. Most of the dollar amounts were just below $100,000. It is possible that $100,000-plus amounts would receive additional scrutiny or that checks above that amount required human signatures instead of automated check writing. The digit patterns of the check amounts are almost opposite to those of Benford's Law. More than 90 percent of the amounts have a high first digit. Had each vendor been tested against Benford's Law, this set of numbers also would have had a low conformity to Benford as measured by the MAD.

The numbers seem to have been chosen to give the appearance of randomness. None of the check amounts were duplicated; there were no round numbers; and all the amounts included cents. Subconsciously though, the manager repeated some digits and digit combinations. Among the first-two digits of the invented amounts, *87, 88, 93,* and *96* were all used twice. For the last-two digits, *16, 67,* and *83* were duplicated. There was a general tendency toward the higher digits with *7* through *9* being the most frequently used digits. A total of 160 digits were used in the 23 numbers. The counts for the 10 digits from *0* to *9* were 7, 19, 16, 14, 12, 5, 17, 22, 22, and 26, respectively. An investigator familiar with Benford's Law would have seen that these numbers—invented to seem random by someone ignorant of Benford's Law—fall outside of the expected patterns and so merit a closer investigation.

Although the Arizona case violates the P1 predictor (there are more than six invoices), there are no credits and so the vendor would score a 1 on P2. The idea behind using multiple predictors is that no single predictor is, by itself, a perfect indicator. The P2 scoring formula is a 0/1 indicator that scores 0 if the vendor has any credits, adjustments, or reversals for the period under review and a 1 otherwise. This is set out in Equation 16.19.

$$\text{P2, Credits and Adjustments} \quad \begin{matrix} = 0 & where\ \text{Credits} \geq 1 \\ = 1 & otherwise \end{matrix} \qquad (16.19)$$

The scoring formula in Equation 16.19 would be quite easy to program in Access. Note that P1 and P2 are similar in that P1 scores 1 when the count is "low" (less than or equal to 6) and P2 also scores 1 when the count is "low" (zero). A low count of invoices and a low count of credits, adjustments, or reversals raise the risk of the vendor being fraudulent.

P3: Increase in Dollars over Time

A common theme in most frauds is that the fraudsters just do not know when to stop. The case of a large metropolitan housing authority that used an off-duty policeman to patrol its housing units is reviewed in Nigrini (1994). From 1981 to 1991 the head of security managed to embezzle about $500,000 by submitting phony time records and pay claims for work done by police officers. The policeman named on each timesheet were real people who worked for the authority, but the purported work done and hours worked were phony.

Each payday the security chief would go to the bank to cash checks for policemen who had worked, but were now back on regular duties in the city. There were usually one or two checks drawn for work done that were cashed and the cash kept by the security chief for his own use.

The security chief had to invent a fictitious work schedule, so the dollar amounts of the fraudulent checks lent themselves to an interesting application of Benford's Law. The time period of the fraud was divided into two five-year periods. Benford tests were designed to also see whether the security chief's number invention patterns changed over time or whether he was consistent over time.

The first-order test of the 273 fraudulent checks for the first five years of the fraud (1981 to mid-1986) is shown in the left panel of Figure 16.2. Some large positive spikes are evident and many different combinations were used. The fraudster used 52 of the possible 90 first-two digit combinations. The most frequently used numbers were $520, $540, $624, $312, $416, and $100. The check amounts ranged from $50 to $1,352 and totaled approximately $125,000. In the Arizona fraud case Nelson started off small and then quickly increased the fraudulent check amounts. This was also the case here in that the dollar amount tripled in the last five years.

The first-two digits of the 600 fraudulent checks for the last five years of the fraud (mid-1986 to 1991) are shown in the right panel of Figure 16.2. There are fewer significant spikes, and the significant spikes are larger. The MAD is larger for the right-hand side graph (the numbers for the last five years). Only 14 of the possible 90 first-two digit combinations were used, indicating that the security chief was gravitating toward using the same numbers over and over again. The most frequently used numbers were $600, $640, $560, $540, and $800. The check amounts ranged from $540 (much higher than the previous lows) to $1,120 and totaled approximately $375,000.

It is interesting that as time passed so the security chief gravitated toward reusing the same set of numbers. Over time the quantity and the amounts increased. The security chief used the names of valid policemen. An audit would have shown that the policemen often worked 40-hour weeks, yet there were no arrest or activity records for the energetic policemen working two full-time physically demanding jobs for that week. Given the size of the spikes on the 1986–1991 graph it is almost certain that these digit combinations would have spiked during an analysis of the general disbursements account (the account from which the policemen were paid).

This fraud would still be in progress had it not been that one Friday the security chief entered the bank to cash his usual package of checks. The teller happened to know one of the "prior-week" policemen whose check was cashed and who happened to be on-duty in the bank at the time. Later that afternoon she told the policeman that "security chief" had cashed his check and would probably have the cash at the station on Central Parkway soon. He was rather surprised by her statement because he had spent his off time that week working in the bank. The security chief was probably more surprised when he was arrested (probably not by the bank policeman) but none were as surprised as the management of the bank, which was sued for $100,000 for negligence by the

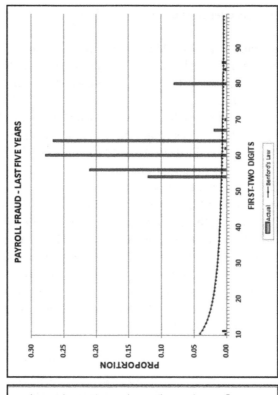

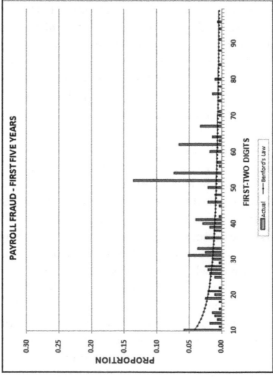

FIGURE 16.2 The Digit Patterns of the Fraudulent Payroll Amounts

housing authority. Using the fact that the fraud tripled in the past five years, an example of a scoring formula would be as shown in Equation 16.20.

$$\begin{aligned}
\text{P3, Increased Dollars} &= 0 && \textit{where } \text{Increase} < 0.20 \\
&= (\textit{Increase} - 0.20) * 1.25 && \textit{where } 0.20 \le \text{Increase} \le 1.00 \\
&= 1 && \textit{where } \text{Increase} > 1.00
\end{aligned}$$
$$(16.20)$$

where *Increase* is calculated as [(Current period)/(Prior period)] −1.00. A total for the current period of $6,000 and a total for the prior period of $4,000 would give an *Increase* of 0.50. Using the scoring formula in Equation 16.20, an increase of 0.50 would be scored with a P3 score of 0.625.

P4: Dollar Amounts

Another common theme in most frauds is that fraudsters do not just steal a small number of dollars, they tend to go so high that one is forced to wonder what they were thinking. This was definitely the case with the Charlene Corley fraud discussed in Chapter 3. The general rule is that no fraudster gets away with (say) $3,000 and then stops. P4 is there to keep forensic investigators focused on the large dollars, and vendors that are in the usual fraud range. Except for Charlene Corley, frauds are unlikely to be very large amounts. The scoring formula in Equation 16.21 discards vendors that are too small and also those that are too large.

$$\begin{aligned}
\text{P4, Material Dollars} &= 0 && \textit{where } \text{Total} < 5000 \\
&= [Log_{10}(Total) - 3.699] \div 2 && \textit{where } 5000 \le \text{Total} \le 500000 \\
&= 0 && \textit{where } \text{Total} > 500000
\end{aligned}$$
$$(16.21)$$

Where *Total* is the total dollars invoiced by the vendor over the past year. Ideally this equation should have a rapid increase to 1.00 (at a dollar value of $50,000) and then a gradual decrease to zero at $500,000. Such a formula would be too complex for this example.

P5: Round Number Dollars

A belief is that fraudsters use round numbers because these are easier to keep track of. Several years ago a Texas-based divisional controller believed that he was too busy to approve all the invoices for payment. He asked his administrative assistant whether she would approve all invoices under $5,000 for payment. She replied that she was happy to do this. Her fraud was detected about $500,000 later. The forensic investigation showed that almost all of the invoices were for round numbers (multiples of $100) that were less than $5,000. Some of the invoices were very primitive being, for example, an invoice for $2,800 for "office party." A possible scoring formula is shown in Equation 16.22.

$$\text{P5, Round numbers} = \sqrt{\frac{\text{Count of Round Numbers}}{\text{Count of Invoices}}} \qquad (16.22)$$

The square root has the effect of giving reasonably high scores to small round proportions. For example, a round proportion of 0.30 (perhaps 6 of 20 invoices are round) would be given a P5 score of 0.548.

P6–P14: Other Predictors

The predictors discussed in P1–P5 would be a good starting point. There are other possible predictors that could also be used and the logic would remain the same. Situations that are high risk would be scored as 1.00 and low-risk situations would be scored as 0.00. Each of these predictors would have a scoring formula and a weight in the final score. Examples of additional predictors are:

- Vendor's invoices are predominantly for services as opposed to goods for resale or for a production process.
- Vendor has invoices without purchase orders.
- Vendor has a regular pattern of invoices (e.g., one every week or two every month).
- Vendor has higher purchases just before Christmas holidays.
- Vendor's tax ID is a social security number.
- Vendor has excessive invoices just below key approval amounts or psychological thresholds.
- Vendor has many invoices dated on weekends or public holidays, or seems to favor one day of the week for invoicing.
- Vendor is consistently paid quickly or is paid in some way that is abnormal for the company.
- Vendor has a history of changes to the vendor master record (bank account changes or address changes).

The predictors listed above are not included in the Access demonstration in the next section. Access works well unless the number of forensic units is very large or there are many predictors with complex calculations.

 ## VENDOR RISK SCORING USING ACCESS

The risk-scoring method will be applied to the *Invoices* data from Chapter 4. The first step in the analysis is to create a table listing all the vendors that should be scored. This table will ensure that we have a score for each forensic unit and no null scores when it comes to calculating the final score. The make-table query and the results are shown in Figure 16.3.

This table should be used in any query when it is possible that the results do not end up with a score for all 26,166 vendors and it is necessary to force a score of 0 or 1 for the missing vendors. This will become clearer when the P3 queries are shown.

The query to score P1 is shown in Figure 16.4. A series of three queries is needed. The first query calculates the invoice month using the MONTH function. The second query counts the number of invoices for every month that the vendor actually has any

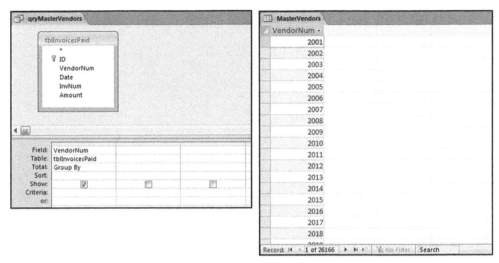

FIGURE 16.3 The Query to Generate a Master List of Forensic Units

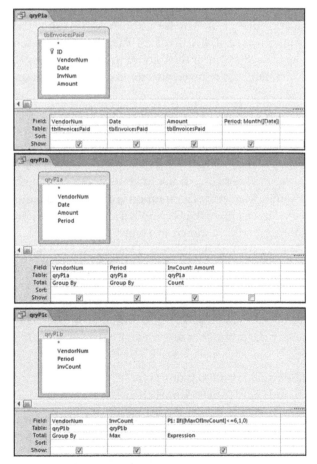

FIGURE 16.4 The Queries to Score P1

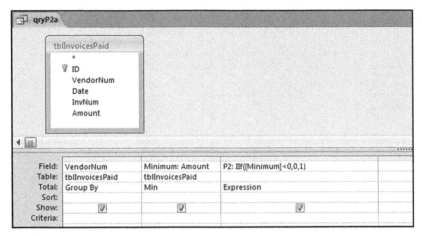

FIGURE 16.5 The Query to Score P2

invoice. The third query calculates the maximum for any month for each vendor. The third query also scores the vendor using the formula in Equation 16.18.

The series of queries for P1 is shown in Figure 16.4. The vendor is scored with a zero if the count in any month exceeds five invoices. The query used to score P2 is shown in Figure 16.5. The logic used is that if the minimum amount is less than zero then the vendor has a credit, adjustment, or reversal of some sort. The predictor P2 is then scored using the IIF function.

If the vendor has any amount less than zero then the vendor is scored with a zero. The series of queries needed to score P3 compares the total dollars for the last six months of the year (H2) with the total dollars for the first six months of the year (H1). It would seem that this would be an easy predictor to program. The issues arise when a vendor has transactions in either H1 or H2, but not in both periods. This makes the sum for H1 or H2 a null value rather than zero. The solution is to convert the null values to zeroes. The set of queries used to calculate the H1 and H2 sums are shown in Figure 16.6. The set of queries used to score P3 is shown in Figure 16.7.

The queries used to calculate the H1 and H2 sums uses the *Between* function in the Criteria. The *Between* function includes both of the numbers used in the *Between* statement. The query used for the comparisons and to score P3 is shown in Figure 16.7.

Figure 16.7 shows *qryP3c*, which is the query used to convert null values to zeroes. The use of the *MasterVendors* table makes sure that there is one record for each vendor. The query also changes the null values to zeroes with the following IIF functions and the *Is Null* criteria:

SumH1b: IIf([SumH1] Is Null,0,[SumH1])
SumH2b: IIf([SumH2] Is Null,0,[SumH2])

The final query to score P3 renames the *SumH1b* and *SumH2b* fields back to *SumH1* and *SumH2*. The increase from H1 to H2 is calculated using the following calculated field:

Inc: IIf([SumH1]<>0,Round([SumH2]/[SumH1]-1,4),1)

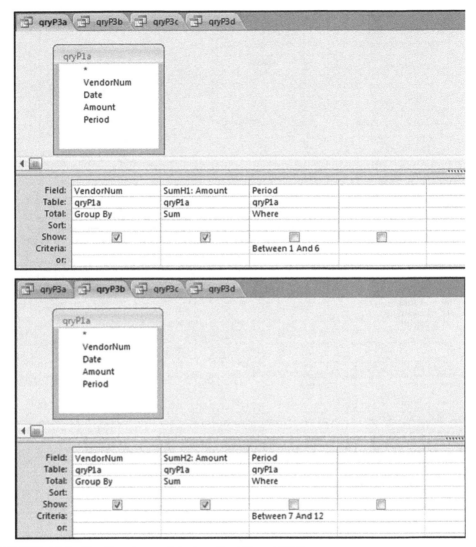

FIGURE 16.6 The Queries to Calculate the H1 and H2 Sums

The IIF function is used to calculate the increase from H1 to H2 to make sure that there is never a division by zero error. The last formula applies Equation 16.20 and is shown below:

P3: Val(Switch([Inc]<0.2,0,[Inc]<1,Round((([Inc]-0.2)*1.25,4),[Inc]>=1,1))

The P3 formula uses the SWITCH function in Access, which allows for multiple IIF criteria. The function applies the first true criterion when moving from left to right in the function. The results of the SWITCH function are shown as text and the use of VAL changes the text format to a numeric result. The ROUND function keeps the results neat.

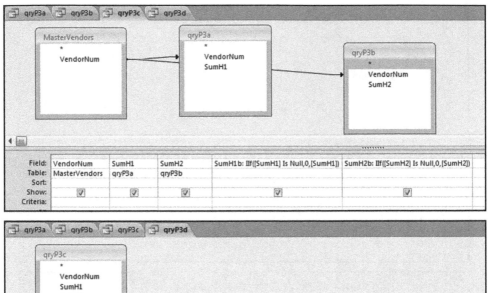

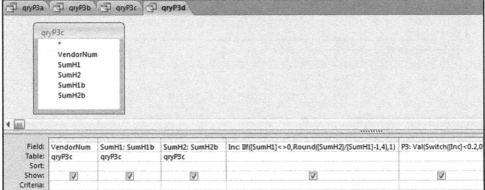

FIGURE 16.7 The Query to Score P3

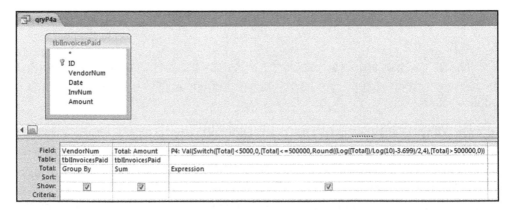

FIGURE 16.8 The Query with a SWITCH Function Used to Score P4

The query used to score P4 is shown in Figure 16.8 with the SWITCH function and the VAL function used to convert the text values to numeric values. The formula used is

P4: Val(Switch([Total]<5000,0,[Total]<=500000,Round((Log([Total])/Log(10)-3.699)/2,4),[Total]>500000,0))

The division by log(10) is there because Access calculates the natural log (base e) of a number using the LOG function. The division by log(10) converts the natural log (usually written as ln) to the log to the base 10. The queries used to score P5 are shown in Figure 16.9.

The first query calculates whether a number is round (neatly divisible by 100). The formulas used in query *qryP5a* are

Remain: [Amount]/100
Indic100: IIf([Remain]−Int([Remain])<0.0000001,1,0)

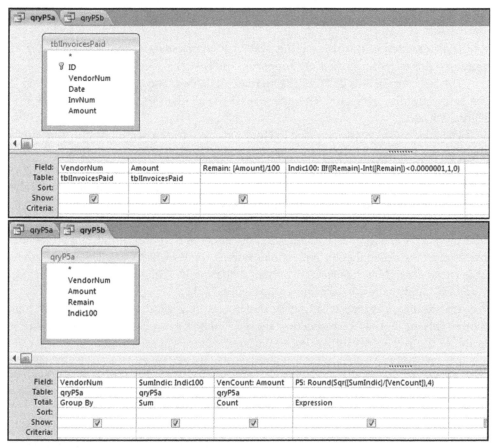

FIGURE 16.9 The Queries Used to Score P5

TABLE 16.4 The Weightings Applied to the Fraud Risk Predictors

Predictor	Weight
P1, Invoice count, not too large	0.15
P2, No credits, adjustments, or reversals	0.15
P3, Increase in dollars	0.40
P4, Total dollars, not small and not large	0.20
P5, Round numbers	0.10
Sum of Weights	1.00

A mathematically perfect formula would use an equals sign (=) instead of the less than (<) sign. The less than sign (<) is preferred because it takes account of possible problems with the limited precision of personal computers.

The formula used to score P5 in *qryP5b* uses the square root SQR function and also the ROUND function to keep the results tidy and is set out below:

P5: Round(Sqr([SumIndic]/[VenCount]),4)

The final step in the risk-scoring system is to calculate a final risk score for all vendors. The weightings used are shown in Table 16.4.

The largest weight is given to the increase in dollars. The lowest weight is given to the round number predictor. The query used to calculate the risk score is shown in Figure 16.10.

The final risk score is calculated in Figure 16.10. The risk score is simply the sum of the P-scores multiplied by their weights. The fields *SumH1* and *SumH2* are added to the query grid for informational purposes. For large files or for more predictors this query might not execute quickly. The solution is to create temporary tables (using make-table queries) of the predictors that require the most processing capacity (in this case it would be P3). The final step (not shown) is to sort the risk scores descending with a new query that only sorts *FinalRS* descending. The new query would also round *FinalRS* to four places after the decimal point and would rename the field *RiskScore*. The query would also show *SumH1* and *SumH2* in whole dollars only. This query was named *qry-Weighted2* and the results are shown in Figure 16.11.

The results in Figure 16.11 show that there are several vendors with very high scores. This means that these vendors "satisfied" almost every category of risk scoring. A graph of the risk scores sorted descending is shown in Figure 16.12.

The risk-scoring results show a small slice of high-scoring forensic units. In this case 91 vendors (0.3 percent) have risk scores that are greater than 0.80 and 366 vendors have risk scores that are equal to 0.80. The transactions of the two highest scoring vendors are shown in Figure 16.13.

The numbers in Figure 16.13 confirm that the risk-scoring system is calculating correctly. The H2 totals are significantly more than the H1 totals. There are no credits and the count for every month is six or fewer invoices. Many of the numbers are round

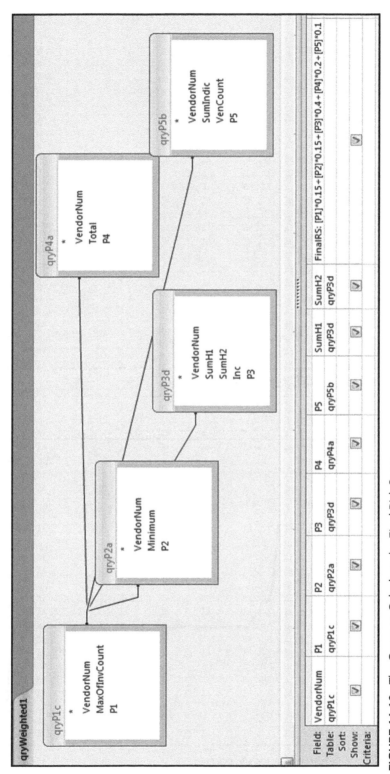

FIGURE 16.10 The Query to Calculate the Final Risk Score

VendorNum	RiskScore	SumH1	SumH2	P1	P2	P3	P4	P5
2098	0.9566	$1,623	$360,050	1	1	1	0.9297	0.7071
2764	0.9556	$1,915	$243,100	1	1	1	0.8451	0.866
3188	0.9437	$62,720	$205,715	1	1	1	0.8649	0.7071
15829	0.9398	$0	$125,000	1	1	1	0.699	1
3739	0.9388	$36,050	$150,250	1	1	1	0.7856	0.8165
17282	0.9365	$2,000	$114,000	1	1	1	0.6827	1
13832	0.9162	$89,415	$214,832	1	1	1	0.8921	0.378
3492	0.9079	$0	$60,000	1	1	1	0.5396	1
15817	0.9	$0	$50,000	1	1	1	0.5	1
3271	0.8939	$25,260	$60,000	1	1	1	0.6159	0.7071
2811	0.8925	$31,903	$101,210	1	1	1	0.7126	0.5
5426	0.89	$23,827	$101,883	1	1	1	0.7002	0.5
20886	0.8875	$0	$37,500	1	1	1	0.4375	1
14787	0.8872	$0	$372,556	1	1	1	0.9361	0
2332	0.8857	$0	$36,000	1	1	1	0.4287	1
7585	0.878	$81,325	$219,933	1	1	1	0.89	0
2465	0.8752	$6,481	$90,933	1	1	1	0.6448	0.4629
4234	0.8703	$7,200	$21,610	1	1	1	0.3803	0.9428
3429	0.8689	$0	$244,523	1	1	1	0.8447	0
16634	0.8651	$0	$22,400	1	1	1	0.3256	1
2495	0.8644	$31,982	$188,168	1	1	1	0.8219	0
3213	0.8643	$6,000	$16,000	1	1	1	0.3217	1
4886	0.8602	$0	$20,000	1	1	1	0.301	1
3493	0.8582	$0	$50,569	1	1	1	0.5024	0.5774
2879	0.8577	$300	$81,170	1	1	1	0.606	0.3651

Record: I◄ ◄ 1 of 26166 ► ►I ► ☒ No Filter Search

FIGURE 16.11 The Vendor Risk Scores

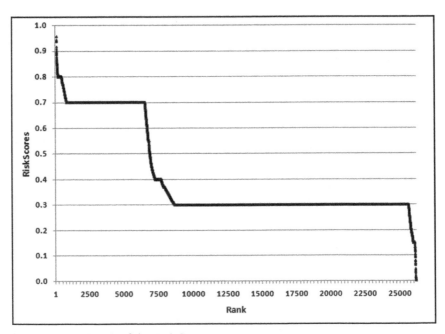

FIGURE 16.12 A Graph of the Risk Scores

qryVendorDetails			
VendorNum ▾	Date ▾	InvNum ▾	Amount ▾
2098	4/30/2010	904432	$1,272.70
2098	6/1/2010	01-00432-1	$350.00
2098	8/14/2010	808944	$60,000.00
2098	8/14/2010	808952	$150,000.00
2098	8/16/2010	01-004320050-1	$150,000.00
2098	8/31/2010	01-00432-3	$50.00
*			

qryVendorDetails			
VendorNum ▾	Date ▾	InvNum ▾	Amount ▾
2764	4/24/2010	374	$1,915.00
2764	10/29/2010	102910	$300.00
2764	11/19/2010	79	$77,800.00
2764	12/10/2010	A0001	$165,000.00
*			

FIGURE 16.13 The Invoices of the Two Highest Risk Vendors

and the totals are both above $250,000 but less than $500,000. A problem with the risk-scoring formula is that we seem to have one-third of the invoices being for more than $100,000. In accounts payable settings invoices for $100,000 or more are thoroughly audited before payment is made, even when the accounts payable function is outsourced. It would seem that refinements to the risk-scoring formulas could include a predictor that scores high if all invoices are less than $50,000, approximately 0.50 if some invoices are in the $50,000 to $100,000 range, and low if many invoices exceed $100,000 (as is the case in Figure 16.13). The third highest scoring vendor (vendor #3188 with a risk score of 0.9437) shows another interesting pattern of invoices. The transactions are shown in Figure 16.14.

The transactions for vendor #3188 warrant a closer look. The vendor has the right number of invoices (about four per month), there are no credits, there is a growth over time, many of the numbers are round, and the total is just about right at $270,000 per year. In addition, there are no "large" invoices (over $50,000). The investigation is made much easier if the images of the invoices are accessible.

 SUMMARY

The chapter reviewed the audit selection method of the Internal Revenue Service (IRS). The IRS scoring method analyzes the differences between those tax returns with an insignificant tax change and those tax returns with a significant tax due change. The analysis is based on an intensive audit of thousands of taxpayers. Discriminant analysis is used to distinguish between the two taxpayer groups. Returns are scored as to whether they more closely resemble the *no change* group or the *significant tax due change*

	A	B	C	D
1	**VendorNum**	**Date**	**InvNum**	**Amount**
2	3188	1/24/2010	1503	$4,700.00
3	3188	2/9/2010	1518	$880.00
4	3188	2/9/2010	157	$3,700.00
5	3188	2/16/2010	1528	$640.00
6	3188	2/24/2010	1535	$8,200.00
7	3188	2/24/2010	1536	$1,280.00
8	3188	3/10/2010	1555	$1,360.00
9	3188	3/10/2010	1556	$12,400.00
10	3188	4/26/2010	1083	$5,120.00
11	3188	4/28/2010	1091	$1,920.00
12	3188	5/12/2010	1114	$2,400.00
13	3188	5/24/2010	1132	$6,080.00
14	3188	6/7/2010	1146	$5,760.00
15	3188	6/24/2010	1170	$5,280.00
16	3188	6/28/2010	1178	$3,000.00
17	3188	7/1/2010	1192	$7,440.00
18	3188	7/1/2010	1193	$9,225.00
19	3188	7/22/2010	1222	$7,500.00
20	3188	7/28/2010	1232	$9,040.00
21	3188	7/31/2010	1254	$6,640.00
22	3188	8/5/2010	1234	$2,970.00
23	3188	8/5/2010	1239	$8,700.00
24	3188	8/23/2010	1263	$6,000.00
25	3188	8/23/2010	1264	$8,900.00
26	3188	8/27/2010	1271	$9,900.00
27	3188	8/27/2010	1278	$7,840.00
28	3188	9/22/2010	1288	$7,400.00
29	3188	9/22/2010	1290	$2,640.00
30	3188	10/7/2010	1326	$9,360.00
31	3188	10/7/2010	1331	$13,800.00
32	3188	10/25/2010	1355	$9,000.00
33	3188	10/25/2010	1356	$6,400.00
34	3188	11/5/2010	1375	$6,400.00
35	3188	11/5/2010	1376	$8,700.00
36	3188	11/23/2010	1405	$4,880.00
37	3188	11/23/2010	1406	$8,700.00
38	3188	12/9/2010	1423	$10,500.00
39	3188	12/9/2010	1425	$7,680.00
40	3188	12/23/2010	1452	$7,900.00
41	3188	12/23/2010	1453	$6,240.00
42	3188	12/31/2010	1478	$7,000.00
43	3188	12/31/2010	1479	$4,960.00

I◄ ◄ ► ►I qryVendorDetails

FIGURE 16.14 The Transactions for Vendor #3188

group. The method results in a DIF (Discriminant Index Function) score for each taxpayer. Both the risk-scoring and the DIF methods seek to score forensic units so that audit efforts are directed toward high-risk forensic units. Both methods use predictor variables, although the taxpayer predictors are "chosen" by the discriminant model, and in the risk-scoring method the predictors are chosen by industry experts. Both methods require regular updates and changes to the selection formulas.

A risk-scoring application for banking fraud was reviewed. Check kiting occurs when a bank account holder successfully withdraws funds from an account where the funds are made up of uncollected funds. The system was designed to rank bank accounts in terms of their check-kiting risk so that the bank investigators could focus their energies and efforts on the high-risk candidates. The system used seven predictors and the most important predictors were frequent deposits from the same routing number, drawing on uncollected funds, and recent returned (bounced) deposits.

A risk-scoring application to detect a type of travel agent fraud was reviewed. Agents sold airline tickets and then voided the tickets in the reservation system and pocketed the cash. The risk-scoring system used predictors such as the average voided amount, excessive voids in the current week, international sales, location of the forensic unit, and whether the voids were being carried out against just one or two carriers. This system was programmed on a mainframe computer. The system was judged a success by management and by the auditors.

A risk-scoring system to detect fictitious vendors was also reviewed. The predictors looked for vendors that were not too big and not too small, vendors that had no credits, adjustments, or reversals, vendors that showed an increase over time, and vendors with round dollar amounts. The equations were reviewed as well as the Access queries used to implement the risk scoring system. Access can calculate the final weighted scores as long as there are not too many forensic units or queries, and as long as there are no calculation errors (perhaps because of division by zero). The results showed a small group (0.3 percent) of high-risk vendors.

CHAPTER SEVENTEEN

The Detection of Financial Statement Fraud

THIS CHAPTER REVIEWS THE use of forensic analytics to detect financial statement fraud. The general belief is that analytic and analysis methods alone cannot detect fraudulent financial reporting. With this in mind, this chapter offers some methods and insights into the detection of some highly specific financial-reporting irregularities.

The first section of this chapter reviews the detection of financial statement fraud based on an analysis of the digit and number patterns of the reported numbers. The second section reviews the use of Benford's Law and other techniques to detect biases across many financial statements. Biases are a gravitation to some section or sections of the real number line, possibly for some psychological advantage. For example, retail store prices are biased toward being slightly below whole dollar amounts while gasoline prices in the United States are biased toward having an ending digit 9. The third section reviews the published financial statements of Enron, Inc. and the review shows that several suspect patterns were evident from those numbers. The final section reviews an application of the risk-scoring method to detect controller fraud at operating divisions. The risk-scoring method follows the same format and logic as is shown in the previous two chapters.

THE DIGITS OF FINANCIAL STATEMENT NUMBERS

Fraudulent financial reporting is the intentional misstatement of, or an omission from, the financial statements of a company, government agency, or other organization, made with the intent to deceive financial statement users. Most cases of financial statement fraud involve misstated revenue numbers in the financial statements. Fraud detection would be much easier if we could simply compare the patterns of a single set of financial statements to Benford's Law and then conclude that nonconformity means that the financial statements are misstated. However, fraudulent financial statements are rarely identified by analyzing the financial statements alone. Also, using Benford's Law is problematic because it is unlikely that changing only one or two numbers will cause the entire table of financial statement (FS) numbers to become nonconforming. With only a few numbers in a set of financial statements, we have to allow some extra leeway to the mean absolute deviation (MAD) when assessing conformity or nonconformity.

The combination of many financial statement numbers across many companies (known as a cross-sectional analysis) should give a close conformity to Benford's Law. Financial statements in general conform to Benford's Law, so it is reasonable to assume that a set of FS should by itself conform to Benford's Law. This is true, but because a set of FS only gives a small table of numbers, any set of FS numbers could deviate substantially from Benford's Law. The same logic would apply to income tax return numbers. If we omit those numbers that are fixed (standard deductions or exemptions), or are subject to maximums (child care allowance) then the remaining numbers, as a whole, should conform to Benford's Law. But because we only have a few numbers on any individual tax return, the return when analyzed alone could have a large departure from Benford and still be accurate and compliant.

To show how a Benford analysis might be performed on a set of financial statements, the reported numbers of a NYSE company were analyzed. The company was chosen because the financial statement numbers are presented in whole dollars making an analysis of the last-two digits meaningful. The primary business of the company is the exploration and production of oil and gas properties in Oceania. The following guidelines need to be followed when analyzing FS numbers:

Totals and subtotals should be ignored. For example, if an employee's travel claim is made up of three numbers ($545.18, $165.46, and $40.00) then the total ($750.64) should be excluded from the analysis. The total cannot be manipulated because it is an arithmetic operation applied to the three amounts.

Numbers brought forward from other schedules and pages should not be counted twice. In many places income tax returns require taxpayers to calculate certain numbers and then to carry the total (perhaps Schedule C Business Income) to the Form 1040. These numbers should not be double counted. An FS example is that the same net income number is copied from the income statement to the statement of changes in retained earnings.

Numbers that come from tables should generally be omitted in the analysis. Income tax examples are tax payable from the tax tables or the earned income credit from the earned income credit table. The *table* numbers cannot be manipulated. Table numbers in an employee travel claim could be the mileage allowance ($0.51 per mile) or a per diem for meals and incidental expenses ($52.00 per day).

Income and expense (or income and deduction) items need to be analyzed separately because they are manipulated in opposite ways. For income taxes, income is *omitted* or *understated* while deductions are *overstated*. In an FS context revenues would

	A	B	C	D	E	F
1	Details	2009	2008	2007	2006	2005
2	*Sales*	688,478,965	915,578,709	625,526,068	511,087,934	481,180,645
3	Interest	350,629	931,785	2,180,285	3,223,995	1,830,808
4	Other	4,228,415	3,216,445	2,666,890	3,747,603	528,270
5	Gain on LNG			6,553,080		
6	Foreign Exchange Gain		3,878,150	5,078,338	4,744,810	
7	Derivative gains	1,008,585	24,038,550			
8	Gain on sale of properties	7,364,468	11,235,084			
9	Income tax future	13,348,634	1,482,074	1,284,869		
10	Noncontrolling interest			22,333	263,959	368,312
11						
12	*Cost of Sales*	601,983,432	888,623,109	573,609,441	499,494,540	467,246,990
13	Admin expenses	33,254,708	31,227,627	31,998,655	20,728,618	14,672,793
14	Derivative losses			7,271,693		
15	Legal and Professional	9,067,413	11,523,045	6,532,646	3,937,517	3,606,415
16	Exploration costs	208,694	995,532	13,305,437	6,176,866	11,009,434
17	Exploration impairment		107,788	1,242,606	1,647,185	19,570,073
18	Short term borrowing	3,776,590	6,514,060	13,212,112	8,478,540	8,855,857
19	Long term borrowing	8,788,041	17,459,186	9,536,162	11,856,872	6,351,337
20	Depreciation	14,321,775	14,142,546	13,024,258	12,352,672	11,036,550
21	Loss on amendment PNGDV				1,851,421	
22	Foreign Exchange Gain	3,305,383				796,590
23	Loss on extinguishment IPI liability	31,710,027				
24	Noncontrolling interest	8,361	943			
25	Income tax current	2,272,645	1,564,038	2,491,761	1,232,487	2,605,265
26	Income tax future				1,110,386	226,729
27						
28	*Net Income*	6,082,627	-11,797,077	-28,912,908	-45,798,803	-62,069,998

FIGURE 17.1 The Reported Income and Expenses in a Consistent Format

be *overstated* and expenses might be *understated*. An analysis of income and expense items together would give a mix of numbers that were potentially manipulated upward with others that were potentially manipulated downward.

The start of the analysis was to enter the numbers into an Excel worksheet in a common format for all years. All income numbers are shown at the top of the table and all deduction and expense items are shown at the bottom of the table. The worksheet is shown in Figure 17.1.

The income statement items are shown in Figure 17.1. The numbers are interesting because the numbers are not rounded to the nearest thousand or million. The revisions were done so that all income items are now in the top section and all deduction items are now in the bottom section. The first digits of the income items (in **B2:F10**) and the expense items (in **B12:F26**) are shown in Figure 17.2.

The first digits in the left panel of Figure 17.2 do not conform to Benford's Law using the MAD criterion. However, because there are very few records, none of the differences are statistically significant using the z-statistic in Equation 6.1. To be statistically significant the deviation must be "large" and the data set must be "large." The right panel in Figure 17.2 also shows patterns that deviate from Benford's Law using the MAD criterion. However, again because there are very few records, none of the differences are statistically significant using the z-statistic in Equation 6.1.

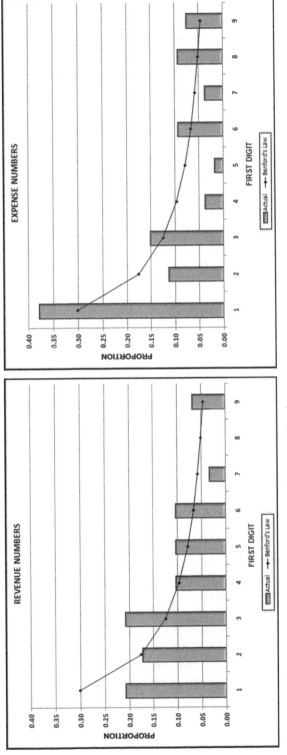

FIGURE 17.2 The First Digits of the Revenue and Expense Numbers

If the numbers represented by the graphs on Figure 17.2 were from a data table of 1,000 records then the individual digit differences would be statistically significant. Because the first digits have no significant differences this does not mean that there are no significant differences for the first-two digits. However, for the first-two digits there were also no significant differences (z-statistics > 1.96). For the expense numbers the 31 and 88 both had counts (of three and two respectively) that deviated significantly from Benford's Law. Some significant differences should arise just due to chance alone (5 percent at the 0.05 level) and there does not seem to be anything systematic in the 31 and 88 numbers. The 31 numbers were \$31,710,027, \$31,227,627, and \$31,998,655 and each of these numbers occurred in a different year. The digit patterns do not in and of themselves signal intentional or unintentional errors. The last-two digits are shown in Figure 17.3.

For the revenue numbers the last-two digits 34, 45, 50, 68, and 85 were significantly different from the 0.01 expectation. The last-two digits of the expense numbers had only the 90 that was significantly different from zero. The numbers with significant last-two digit combinations are highlighted in Figure 17.4.

Figure 17.4 shows that the expense numbers were relatively free of last-two digit duplications. The revenue numbers showed that 11 of the 29 numbers had last-two digits that were significantly in excess of the expectation. This is a reasonably surprising result. The chances of a duplicate or triplicate number can be calculated using the binomial distribution. The calculations are shown in Figure 17.5.

Figure 17.5 shows a binomial worksheet for the last-two digits. The binomial distribution is a discrete (dealing with whole numbers) probability distribution that can help to assess the conformity of the last-two digits. There is a good description of the binomial distribution in the *Engineering Statistics Handbook* (www.itl.nist.gov/div898/ handbook/). That discussion focuses on the formulas as opposed to applications to detect fraud or errors. The properties of a binomial experiment in the context of the income numbers are that each number can be seen to be:

▪ The result of a trial in an experiment to test whether the number has last-two digits of *yz*.
▪ With the outcomes being either a *success* where the last-two digits are *yz* or a *failure* where that is not the case.
▪ Where the probability of a success, *p*, is constant at 0.01 from number to number.
▪ Where the trials are independent (the outcome of one number does not affect the outcome of another number).

The values in C5:C9 were calculated using the BINOMDIST function in Excel. The formula for cell C5 is =BINOMDIST(B5,\$D\$1,\$D\$2,FALSE).

The interpretation of cell C5 is that when there are 29 trials (numbers) and the probability of any last-two digit combination is 0.01, then we expect 0 numbers with a specific last-two digit 74.72 percent of the time. There should be no last-two digit 27 numbers 74.72 percent of the time. There should be one occurrence of (say) 27, 21.89 percent of the time, two occurrences of 27, 3.1 percent of the time, and three occurrences of 27, 0.28 percent of the time.

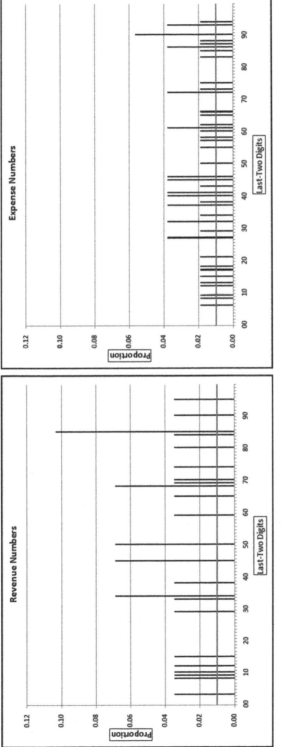

FIGURE 17.3 The Last-Two Digits of the Revenue and Expense Numbers

	A	B	C	D	E	F
1	Details	2009	2008	2007	2006	2005
2	Sales	688,478,965	915,578,709	625,526,068	511,087,934	481,180,645
3	Interest	350,629	931,785	2,180,285	3,223,995	1,830,808
4	Other	4,228,415	3,216,445	2,666,890	3,747,603	528,270
5	Gain on LNG			6,553,080		
6	Foreign Exchange Gain		3,878,150	5,078,338	4,744,810	
7	Derivative gains	1,008,585	24,038,550			
8	Gain on sale of properties	7,364,468	11,235,084			
9	Income tax future	13,348,634	1,482,074	1,284,869		
10	Noncontrolling interest			22,333	263,959	368,312
11						
12	Cost of Sales	601,983,432	888,623,109	573,609,441	499,494,540	467,246,990
13	Admin expenses	33,254,708	31,227,627	31,998,655	20,728,618	14,672,793
14	Derivative losses			7,271,693		
15	Legal and Professional	9,067,413	11,523,045	6,532,646	3,937,517	3,606,415
16	Exploration costs	208,694	995,532	13,305,437	6,176,866	11,009,434
17	Exploration impairment		107,788	1,242,606	1,647,185	19,570,073
18	Short term borrowing	3,776,590	6,514,060	13,212,112	8,478,540	8,855,857
19	Long term borrowing	8,788,041	17,459,186	9,536,162	11,856,872	6,351,337
20	Depreciation	14,321,775	14,142,546	13,024,258	12,352,672	11,036,550
21	Loss on amendment PNGDV				1,851,421	
22	Foreign Exchange Gain	3,305,383				796,590
23	Loss on extinguishment IPI liability	31,710,027				
24	Noncontrolling interest	8,361	943			
25	Income tax current	2,272,645	1,564,038	2,491,761	1,232,487	2,605,265
26	Income tax future				1,110,386	226,729
27						
28	Net Income	6,082,627	-11,797,077	-28,912,908	-45,798,803	-62,069,998

FIGURE 17.4 The Income Statements with the Significant Last-Two Digit Differences Highlighted

Column D in Figure 17.5 shows the actual probabilities. Cell D5 indicates that 77 percent of all the possible last-two digits were not used on the income statement. We expected 74.72 last-two digits not to be used, so this means that the data table contains more duplication than expected. At the extreme if 99 percent of all last-two digits were not used this would mean that one last-two digit was used 29 times, which exceeds the column C probabilities (29 is not shown) by a wide margin. The effect of the extra

	A	B	C	D
1			Number of trials (n)	29
2			Probability of Success (p)	0.01
3				
4		x	f(x)	Actual
5		0	0.7472	0.7700
6		1	0.2189	0.1800
7		2	0.0310	0.0400
8		3	0.0028	0.0100
9		4	0.0002	0.0000
10		Sum=	1.0000	1.0000

FIGURE 17.5 The Binomial Probabilities Related to the Last-Two Digits of the Income Numbers

duplication is that four last-two digits were used twice, and one last-two digit combination was used three times. The calculated chi-square statistic of 119.28 is just below the cutoff value for a significance level of 0.05 with 99 degrees of freedom. The extent of the duplication is not enough to reject the null hypothesis that the last-two digits are uniformly distributed.

Excessive duplication by itself would not necessarily prove fraud. The numbers would then be suspicious but the duplication would simply be a red flag. The usual practice in grocery stores is to price goods so that the ending digits are 9s. This does not signal fraud but rather that some human thought has gone into setting a selling price as a part of a marketing strategy. The question with FS numbers is whether any number invention was done with the intent to deceive, and whether the level of deception was material.

A few other factors in the financial statements are noteworthy. First, the company has restated some of the prior year numbers. Interestingly, the comparative figures on the 2009 income statement are not the same numbers that were originally reported. The net income of the prior years is unchanged but some formerly combined numbers were disaggregated. Second, the "other income" (revenue from sources other than sales to customers) and other types of gains grew almost exponentially from 2005 to 2008 and then showed a decline in 2009. The changes in the rate of large one-off gains make forecasting income from operations very difficult. Third, the five annual EPS numbers of (2.15), (1.55), (0.96), (0.35), and 0.15 includes of four numbers that are neat multiples of 5. Only one in five EPS numbers should be a multiple of 5.

Unusual patterns or ratios in reported numbers might be red flags to fraud but they are not guarantees of any sort. A red flag is an indicator that is present in a significant percentage of fraud cases, but their presence in no way means that fraud is actually present in a particular case. Many fraud schemes do not require any type of number invention. For example, improper cutoff procedures may show sales for (say) 55 weeks (the current year plus three weeks into the next year) as the sales for the current year.

 DETECTING BIASES IN ACCOUNTING NUMBERS

The Enron bankruptcy in December 2001 set off a chain of events that resulted in the Sarbanes-Oxley Act and brought the topic of corporate fraud and accounting to the attention of the financial press and television. The value of accounting and auditing was again questioned in 2008 with the bankruptcy of Lehman Brothers and the government bailout of the financial system. In 2002 the high visibility of accounting in a negative vein gave rise to the research question as to whether the level of earnings management around this time period was more or less than "normal." The approach taken in Nigrini (2005) was to look at the digit patterns of reported earnings for signs of biases in these reported numbers.

The *Wall Street Journal* (WSJ) includes a daily "Digest of Corporate Earnings Reports" that reports and summarizes the earnings releases of the previous day. The information reported includes:

TABLE 17.1 A Summary of Quarterly Earnings Numbers

	2001	2002
Quarter ended March 31	5,483	4,869
Quarter ended 12/31, 1/31, 2/28, or 4/30	624	547
New York Stock Exchange listing	1,747	1,633
AMEX or NASDAQ listing	4,360	3,783
Total number of records	6,107	5,416

- Company name, ticker symbol, and the stock exchange where the company is listed
- Reporting period (e.g., Q3/31 would indicate quarter ending 3/31)
- Revenue (in millions, with a percentage change)
- Income from continuing operations (in millions, with a percentage change)
- Net income (in millions, with a percentage change)
- Earnings per share (in dollars, with comparison to year-earlier period and percentage change)

The information is given a standard format for each company. The data studied included all the earnings reports published in the "Digest of Corporate Earnings Reports" from April 1 to May 31, 2001 (before the collapse of Enron), and from April 1 to May 31, 2002 (after the collapse of Enron). A summary of the earnings reports is shown in Table 17.1.

Table 17.1 shows that most of the earnings reports analyzed were for the quarter ended March 31, 2001, or March 31, 2002. About 30 percent of the companies were New York Stock Exchange (NYSE) listings, with the remainder of the companies being listed on the American Stock Exchange (AMEX) or Nasdaq exchanges. Toronto and foreign listings were omitted because the original numbers were not denominated in U.S. dollars. Also omitted were companies listed on the NYSE that were foreign and that did not report an earnings per share (EPS) number.

A test of the second digits was used to detect manipulations of revenues. Companies with less than $1 million in revenues were excluded from the analysis to avoid the situation where a company reported (say) $798,000 and this number was shown in the *WSJ* as $0.80 million (revenue numbers were shown in millions to two decimal places). This company would have a true second digit 9 that would be analyzed as if it were a second digit 0. In 2001 there were 182 companies with revenues under $1 million and in 2002 there were 186 such companies.

The first digits of the revenue numbers were tested as a preliminary test to check that Benford's Law was a valid expectation for the second digits. The results are shown in Figure 17.6.

The first digits of the net income numbers in Figure 17.6 show a close conformity to Benford's Law for both 2001 and 2002. The MAD for 2001 is 0.0052, which meets the criteria for close conformity and the MAD for 2002 is 0.0036, which also meets the criteria for close conformity. The second digits of the revenue numbers are shown in Figure 17.7.

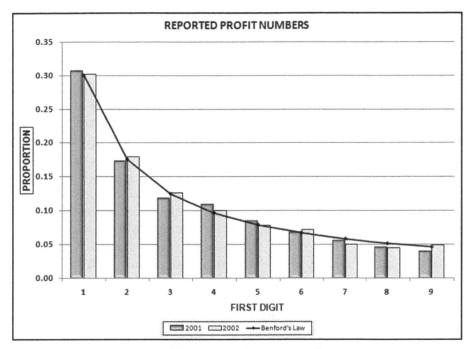

FIGURE 17.6 The First Digits of the Reported Income Numbers

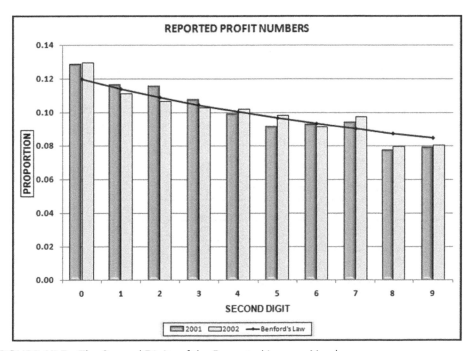

FIGURE 17.7 The Second Digits of the Reported Income Numbers

The second digits, as seen as a whole, have a close conformity to Benford's Law for each of the years in question. The calculated chi-square statistics of 14.56 and 10.58 are below the critical chi-square value (=CHIINV(0.05,9)) of 16.92. What is of interest is that for *both* 2001 and 2002 the digit 0 is overstated by an average of 0.9 percent while again for *both* 2001 and 2002, there is a shortage of 8s and 9s as compared to Benford's Law. These results are consistent with the belief that when corporate net incomes are just below psychological boundaries, managers would tend to round these numbers up. Numbers such as $798,000 and $19.97 million might be rounded up to numbers just above $800,000 and $20 million respectively, possibly because the latter numbers convey a larger measure of size despite the fact that in percentage terms they are just marginally higher. A clue that such *rounding-up* behavior was occurring would be an excess of second digit 0s and a shortage of second digit 9s in reported net income numbers. The direction of the deviations is consistent with an upward revision of revenue numbers where, for example, numbers with first-two digits of 79 or 19 are managed upward to have first-two digits of 80 and 20 respectively. The percentage of second digit 0s is 13.0 percent in 2002 and 12.8 percent in 2001, which suggests that rounding up behavior was more prevalent in 2002 than it was in 2001. This is puzzling given all the attention given to financial statement fraud in 2002 at the time that Arthur Andersen was in court because of the Enron saga.

AN ANALYSIS OF ENRON'S REPORTED NUMBERS

The preceding analysis looked at whether accounting numbers might have been influenced by psychological thresholds. Here the Enron numbers are analyzed to see whether they show signs of trying to make psychological thresholds. On November 11, 2001, Enron filed a Form 8-R in which it revised its results for 1997 to 2000 (four years) inclusive. Table 17.2 shows the original numbers as reported by Enron for 1997 to 2000.

Table 17.2 shows that for three of the four years from 1997 to 2000, Enron reported revenues that just exceeded a multiple of $10 billion, giving the revenues

TABLE 17.2 The Numbers Reported by Enron for 1997 to 2000

	2000	1999	1998	1997
Total Revenues (in $ millions)	100,789	40,112	31,260	20,273
Net income before cumulative effect of accounting changes (in $ millions)	979	1,024	703	105
Cumulative effect of accounting changes, net of tax (in $ millions)	–	(131)	–	–
Net income (in $ millions)	979	893	703	105
Earnings per share of common stock (diluted and in dollars)	1.12	1.10	1.01	0.16

numbers a second digit 0 for three of the four years. For three of the four years, Enron reported net income before the cumulative effect of accounting changes that just exceeded a multiple of $100 million, giving the income numbers a second digit 0 for three of the four years. Enron seemed to emphasize net income before the cumulative effect of accounting changes presumably because they wanted it to be clear that the effect of accounting changes were out of the control of management. The table shows that for the only year in which Enron's revenues did not just exceed a multiple of $10 billion, the reported EPS number is $1.01, which not only has a second digit zero, but it just makes a threshold of $1.00.

Table 17.2 shows 12 "headline" reported numbers (four each for total revenues, net income before the cumulative effect of accounting changes, and earnings per share). Of these 12 numbers, seven numbers have a second digit zero. The binomial probability distribution is used to calculate the chances of seven second digit zeroes. The BINOMDIST function (=BINOMDIST(7,12,0.11968,FALSE)) gives a result of 0.00016. The chances of seven or more second digit zeroes in 12 numbers is about 16 times in 100,000. Enron seemed to target numbers that just made psychological thresholds.

A look at the revenue numbers raises other questions. From 1999 to 2000 the revenues rose from $40 billion to $100 billion. This is dramatic for two reasons. First, at that time there were only a handful of companies with revenues over $100 billion. The common theme among those companies was that they were all international conglomerates founded more than 100 years ago (with the exception of Walmart). Second, the growth in revenues is difficult to understand. Seen in context, Enron's growth was slightly more than two times Microsoft's (Microsoft's revenues were about $25 billion per year at that time). Some reports suggested that most of this revenue increase came from the way that Enron booked its sales of derivative contracts.

AN ANALYSIS OF BIASED REIMBURSEMENT NUMBERS

A bias refers to individuals targeting, being predisposed toward, or inclined toward the numbers in one or more number ranges because of some real or perceived benefits or consequences. A plethora of minimums and maximums in the income tax code means that taxpayers are biased on a number of fronts. For example, to deduct charitable contributions of items valued at $500 or more, an additional form needs to be completed and attached to the tax return. An analysis of taxpayer *gifts to charity* other than by cash or check will presumably show "many" gifts in the $450 to $499 range and only a "few" gifts in the $500 to $550 range, because the $500 to $550 range would require the completion of Form 8283.

A small software company had a policy that for out-of-town travel employees need not include a receipt for breakfast costs of $10 or less. Management was considering raising the receipt amount to $15. An analysis of breakfast claims showed that the three most frequent amounts claimed for breakfast were $9.50, $9.90, and $10.00. The

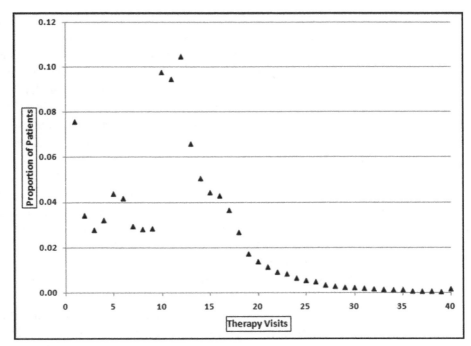

FIGURE 17.8 A Hypothetical Pattern of Therapy Visits

breakfast claims were influenced and biased by the receipt requirement for amounts over $10. However, believing that a financial threshold might create a bias, and statistically concluding that a set of numbers (perhaps financial statement numbers) are biased are two different things. This section shows how a bias might be evaluated statistically.

In April, 2010 the *Wall Street Journal* reported on an analysis of therapy visits and concluded that the number of therapy visits was influenced by the Medicare reimbursement formula. Medicare paid health services providers about $2,200 if a patient received from one to nine at-home therapy visits. The health services providers were paid an additional $2,100 if there were 10 or more at-home therapy visits. Medicare therefore paid an additional $2,100 for the 10th therapy visit and $0 for the 11th and subsequent visits. A hypothetical provider's therapy visit pattern is shown in Figure 17.8.

In most cases the forensic investigator would not know too much about therapy and therapy visits so we cannot really say that *x* percent of patients would normally have *y* number of visits. The assumption was made that the percentage of people having *y* visits should be approximately the same as the percentage having $y - 1$ visits and $y + 1$ visits. Similarly, we do not know what percentage of people have six dentist visits a year, but we can assume that the percentage must be close to the percentage of people having five or seven visits a year. There is no real reason for a spike at five unless many people have the same problem that is usually fixed in five visits. Also, the Facebook "friends" distribution is unknown, but it seems logical that the proportion of people with (say) 64 friends should be close to the proportion with 63 friends or 65 friends. The smooth pattern for y being close to $y - 1$ and $y + 1$ is the case for the 13 visits and higher section in Figure 17.8. The graph shows a consistent downward pattern to 39 visits. The proportion for 40 visits is actually the proportion for 40 and higher, hence the small upward jump. The assumption is that we should be able to fit a continuous function to the points and any discontinuities (abrupt changes) might signal biases.

Sigma Plot 11 was used to fit a curve to the points. Sigma Plot has formulas for smoothing sharp changes in two dimensional graphs. The software gives users a choice of smoothing methods that includes (a) negative exponential, (b) locally weighted scatterplot smoothing, (c) running average, (d) running median, (e) bisquare smoothing, and (f) inverse square smoothing. The results of all the smoothing methods are shown in Figure 17.9.

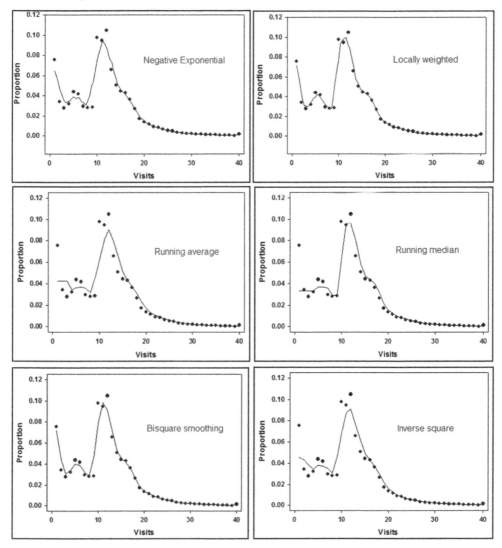

FIGURE 17.9 The Smoothing Functions Fitted to the Therapy Visit Data

The graphs in Figure 17.9 show that Sigma Plot's smoothing techniques can fit a neat curve to the line for 14 visits or more. The techniques cannot fit a close-fitting curve to the left side of the graph (1 to 13 visits). The largest deviations (fitted curve and actual proportions) are for therapy visits of 10, 11, and 12. In calculus terms the graphs seem to have a jump discontinuity. The hypothesis is that a jump discontinuity is evidence of a bias.

To determine how extreme the deviation was from the best-fitting smooth function, the chi-square statistic was calculated. Although the graphs show proportions, the chi-square statistic is calculated using the actual and the expected counts (from the fitted smooth line). The lowest two chi-square statistics and the highest chi-square statistic are shown below:

Negative exponential: 826.4
Bisquare smoothing: 1,261.7
Running median: 6,171.5

In each case the chi-square value for the 9 and 10 counts made a big impact on the chi-square statistics. In some cases the chi-square value for a count of one visit also contributed to the chi-square statistics. In all cases the fit was quite good for the counts of 14 through 40.

To determine the significance of the difference between the fitted smooth lines and the actual data, the chi-square statistics were calculated. The results using the CHIDIST function with 39 degrees of freedom were that the chances were less than 1 in 100,000,000 that the data as shown by the scatterplot points (the actual numbers) were drawn from the smooth distribution shown by the lines (the best fitting functions). There is therefore a clear bias evident in the data.

The same method was used on the 2002 accounting numbers reviewed in the previous section. The first and second digit counts, and the fitted smooth lines are shown in Figure 17.10.

For the first digits the smoothing technique fits a line with a slightly less dramatic difference between the low and high first digits. The first digit 6 shows up as a point above the line. For the second digits the technique manages to fit a function that starts at the overrepresented 0s and ends at the underrepresented 9s. The excess 7s and the shortage of 8s are evident from the graph.

The chi-square statistic for the first digits is 24.22 meaning that the actual data differs significantly from the fitted line. The digit 2 makes a large contribution to that value. The calculated chi-square statistic for the second digits of 6.09 means that there is not enough evidence to conclude that the actual data differs significantly from the fitted line. These results are in disagreement with what we know to be the case. It seems that the line-fitting technique did a good job (in fact too good) of fitting a line to the actual second digit counts. It seems that the technique is not too good at detecting peaks and valleys at the start or at the end of a series of numbers because it manages to fit the line close to these points.

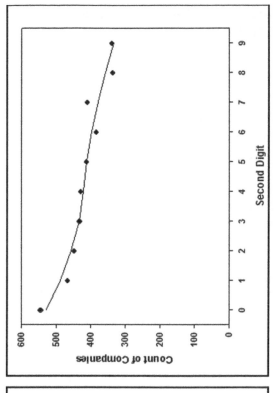

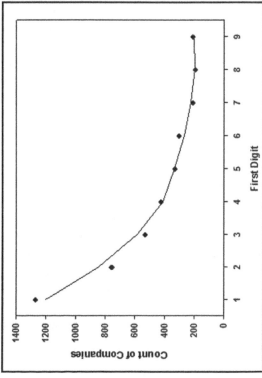

FIGURE 17.10 The Best Fitting Line Fitted to the First and Second Digit Counts

DETECTING MANIPULATIONS IN MONTHLY SUBSIDIARY REPORTS

This section describes a risk-scoring method to detect divisional fraud where the *predictors* are the reported monthly numbers. The behavior of interest is the overstatement of divisional profits or the creation of cookie jars for future use. The *forensic unit* is a division (or subsidiary or branch) of a company. The scoring system was designed to detect intentional and unintentional errors in the monthly reports. The forensic investigators wanted to proactively detect errors in the monthly reports.

It would seem that divisional controllers do commit fraudulent financial reporting. For example, on October 6, 2010, the *Wall Street Journal* reported that a subsidiary of Hitachi had been falsifying sales over the past five years. The subsidiary booked fictitious sales and profits between December 2005 and August 2010. The president of the unit had apparently been trying to "window dress" the division's earnings. The *Wall Street Journal* suggested that the company may be having difficulty in fully keeping track of the activities of its myriad units. On August 17, 2010, the *Wall Street Journal* reported that a division of Mercia Corporation had inflated profits by booking fictitious transactions since 2005.

The risk-scoring system was developed by a large company headquartered in the United States with most of its divisions located in the United States. There were about 500 divisions engaged in four similar types of products all requiring sophisticated manufacturing processes. The customers of the divisions were manufacturing companies that used the products in their end products. The company's fortunes were closely tied to the fortunes of the industry into which it sold. The results of the divisions were subject to large fluctuations.

The divisional controllers were required to report their prior month results by the fifth day of the following month. It took about 10 days to consolidate the results. Corporate accounting had systems and procedures in place to contact the controllers if they come across errors or questionable items. The head office review of the accounting numbers was a high-level scan using professional judgment. There was no formal systematic review of the numbers to detect intentional or unintentional errors. The company had a set of policies and procedures that were to be followed by the controllers. The divisions maintained their own accounting systems and they all had to use the same chart of accounts. The consolidation of the results was done with Oracle's Hyperion software. The uniform format of the reports and Hyperion's data retrieval capabilities meant that the team had access to archival data. The risk-scoring system had 27 predictors being scored on a 0 to 1 scale. The management reports include (a) a listing of the risk scores for all divisions, (b) the ability to call up and review the scores for all 27 variables for any single division, and (c) other high-level analyses of the reported numbers.

The risk scores were related to the following broad categories of predictors:

- Reported sales amounts
- Reported standard profits and net income

- Reported variances
- Selected expense amounts
- Reported accounts receivable, inventories, and prepaid expenses amounts
- The use of selected accounts in the general ledger
- Location
- Historical prior scores

The risk-scoring system sought to proactively and systematically evaluate the reported numbers for intentional and unintentional errors and violations of policies and procedures. The risk-scoring system had the following objectives:

- To assist in evaluating the risk of intentional and unintentional errors and biases in the reported numbers of the divisions.
- To function as an audit-planning tool for audit staff that were assigned to an audit of a specific division.
- To function as a planning tool to assist in the selection of divisions to audit in the coming year.
- As a tool for initiating contact (by phone or by letter) to alert controllers to the fact that the accounting numbers were being reviewed by corporate audit and to act as a mild deterrent to errors or biases in reported numbers.

The analysis required a systematic approach because each of the 500 divisions reported about 300 accounting numbers each period giving 150,000 data points each month. The analysis was further complicated by the fact that it could be relationships *between* the numbers that indicate the errors. For example, a decrease in sales might not be an abnormal event but a decrease in sales coupled with an increase in accounts receivable is suspicious. Access was used for data manipulation, calculations, and reporting. Excel was used to prepare neat graphs. A review of the predictors is given below.

P1: Erratic Sales

P1 gave a high score to divisions with erratic (volatile) sales. The belief was that large fluctuations in the sales numbers could be due to errors. The usual measure of dispersion (spread) is the variance, but the variance is not neatly bounded like correlation (from -1.00 to $+1.00$). Sales numbers that are all within 10 percent of $100,000 will have a larger variance than sales numbers that are all within 10 percent of $10,000, even though the percentage deviations are equal. The variance was therefore not a good measure of dispersion. The P1 formula is given in Equation 17.1.

$$\text{P1, Erratic Sales} = 1.5 * \frac{High - Low}{High} \qquad High \neq 0 \qquad (17.1)$$

The formula for P1 is shown in Equation 17.1. The formula uses the sales numbers for the past 12 months. If the highest sales number is zero (perhaps because the division is new) then P1 equals 0. A division with high sales of $160 and low sales of $100 will be scored as 1.00 because of the multiplication by 1.5. If the calculated P1 value is greater than 1.00 (perhaps with high sales of $180 and low sales of $100) then the P1 score was fixed at 1.00.

P2: Large Sales Change for Current Month

P2 was designed to give a high-risk score to divisions that had current month sales that were significantly different to the average for the prior 11 months. An example of this would be consistent sales of $100 per month with current month of (say) $150 or $50. The P2 formula is given in Equation 17.2.

$$\text{P2, Large Sales Change} = 4 * \frac{Abs(Current - Average)}{Average} \quad Average \neq 0 \quad (17.2)$$

The formula for P2 is shown in Equation 17.2. The formula uses the sales numbers for the past 12 months. The current month is the most recent month, and the average is calculated for the preceding 11 months. If the calculations were done for a calendar year then the current month would be December and the average would be calculated for January to November. If the average is zero (perhaps because the division is new) then P2 equals 0. A division with current sales of $120 and average sales of $100 will be given a P2 score of 0.80 because of the multiplication by 4. If the calculated P2 value is greater than 1.00 (perhaps with current sales of $75 and average sales of $100) then the P2 score was fixed at 1.00.

P3: Irregular Numbers Reported as Sales

P3 was designed to give a high risk score to divisions with irregular sales numbers. Irregular numbers were deemed to be zero, negative, or round numbers. P3 was based on the sales numbers for the preceding 12 months. The P3 formula is given in Equation 17.3.

$$
\begin{aligned}
\text{P3, Irregular Sales Numbers} \quad &\text{If Sales includes one zero} &&= 0.25 \\
&\text{If Sales includes} > \text{one zero} &&= 0.50 \\
&\text{If Sales includes any negative numbers} &&= 0.50 \\
&\text{If Sales includes any round numbers} &&= 0.50
\end{aligned}
$$

$$(17.3)$$

The score for the zeroes is added to the negative and round number scores. If the calculated score exceeds 1.00 then the score is capped at 1.00. Round numbers were defined to be multiples of $1,000.

P4: Increase in Sales Allowances

P4 scored increases in sales allowances. A large increase in allowances could be associated with fictitious or erroneous sales. This predictor was only based on the change in the sales allowances numbers. The P4 formula is similar to that of P2 and is given in Equation 17.4.

$$\text{P4, Sales Allowances Change} = 4 * \frac{Abs(Current) - Abs(Average)}{Abs(Average)} \quad Average \neq 0$$

$$(17.4)$$

The formula for P4 is shown in Equation 17.4. The formula is based on the sales allowances for the past 12 months. Sales allowances are negative numbers and the calculations use the absolute values of these negative numbers. Positive allowances, if any, were set equal to zero for the P4 calculations. The current month is the most recent month, and the average is calculated over the 11 months before the latest month. If the average is zero (perhaps because the division is new), then P4 equals 0. A division with current allowance of −$120 and average allowances of −$100 will get a P4 score of 0.80 because of the multiplication by 4. If the calculated P4 value is greater than 1.00, then the P4 score is fixed at 1.00.

P5: Irregular Numbers Reported as Allowances

P5 was designed to give a high-risk score to divisions with irregular sales allowances numbers. Irregular numbers were deemed to be zero, negative, or round numbers. P5 was based on the sales allowances numbers for the preceding 12 months. The P5 formula is given in Equation 17.5.

$$\text{P5, Odd Allowance Numbers} \quad \begin{array}{ll} \text{If Current equals zero} & = 0.50 \\ \text{If Current is round} & = 0.50 \\ \text{If Average equals zero} & = 0.50 \\ \text{If Current or Average is positive} & = 0.50 \end{array} \quad (17.5)$$

The formula for P5 is shown in Equation 17.5 with round numbers being numbers that are multiples of $1,000. Allowance numbers are negative numbers. The score for the zeroes is added to the positive and round number scores. If the calculated score exceeds 1.00, then the score is capped at 1.00.

P6: Excessive Sales Allowances

P6 was designed to score a large sales allowance percentage for the current month. The data analysis results showed that an allowance percentage above 2.5 percent was excessive. A high percentage could be due to weak sales work or even a misclassification of other expenses. This predictor used the allowances for the current month. The P6 formula is similar in form to P2 and is shown in Equation 17.6.

$$\text{P6, High Sales Allowances} = -40 * \frac{\text{Current Sales Allowances}}{\text{Current Gross Sales}} \quad Sales \neq 0 \quad (17.6)$$

The P6 formula is shown in Equation 17.6. The proportion is multiplied by −0.40 because sales allowances are negative numbers. P6 equals zero if sales allowances are zero. If the sales allowance proportion exceeds 0.025, then P6 is capped at 1.00.

P7: Quarter-End Pad

P7 was an innovative predictor designed to detect higher profit numbers in March, June, September, and December. This would presumably be because the controller was pushing hard to make or beat the budget. The P7 formula is given in Equation 17.7.

$$\text{P7, Quarter-End Pad} \quad 10^* \left(\frac{AvgQE}{AvgBetween} - 1 \right) \quad \text{If } Avg\,QE > Avg\,Between$$

$$Avg\,QE = Average(\text{Mar, Jun, Sept, Dec})$$

$$Avg\,Between = Average\,(\text{Jan, Feb, Apr, May, Jul, Aug, Oct, Nov})$$

$$(17.7)$$

The P7 formula in Equation 17.7 is based on the profit numbers for the preceding year, which should include four *quarter-end* months and eight *between* months. If the average of the quarter-end profits was $108, and the average of the between months was $100, then the calculated P7 value would be 0.80 (10 * (108/100−1)). The P7 values are bounded by the [0,1] range. If the quarter-end average was less than the average for the between months then the P7 score would be zero. The quarter-end pad was an important indicator of inflated profits.

P8: High Materials Price Variance

P8 was designed to detect a large price variance in an expense that was seen to reasonably controllable, namely the input prices for raw materials. The score for P8 used both positive (favorable) and negative (unfavorable) variances. The P8 formula is given in Equation 17.8.

P8, Materials Price, Past Year

$$10^* \left(\frac{SumMaterialsPriceVariance}{SumProfits} \right) \quad Min = 0, \; Max = 1$$

$$SumMaterialsPriceVariance = Abs(Sum(\text{Jan, Feb}, \ldots, \text{Dec}))$$

$$SumProfits = Sum(\text{Jan, Feb}, \ldots, \text{Dec})$$

$$(17.8)$$

The P8 formula in Equation 17.8 is based on the materials price variance and the profit numbers for the preceding year. The months shown above are January to December. Predictor P8 is not influenced by the sign of the materials price variance (positive or negative, favorable or unfavorable). The P8 scores are bounded by the [0,1] range. Large materials price variances were an anomaly because the divisions were expected to be in control (within a few percentage points) of the prices of their inputs.

P9: High Materials Price Variance for the Current Month

P9 was essentially the same as P8 except that the calculation was made for the immediately preceding month only. The P9 formula is given in Equation 17.9.

P9, Materials Price, Current Month

$$10 * \left(\frac{MaterialsPriceVariance}{Profit} \right) \quad Min = 0, \ Max = 1$$

$$MaterialsPriceVariance = Abs \,(Current\,Month)$$

$$Profits = Abs \,(Current\,Month)$$

(17.9)

The P9 formula in Equation 17.9 is based on the materials price variance and the profit numbers for the current month. Predictor P9 is not influenced by the sign of the materials price variance (positive or negative, favorable or unfavorable). The P9 scores are bounded by the [0,1] range. This predictor highlights a large variance for the current month in an area where the divisions were expected to be in control (within a few percentage points) of the prices of their inputs.

P10: Scrap Variance Is Extreme

P10 was based on the scrap variance, which was an account that could be used to smooth profits. The score for P10 used both positive (favorable) and negative (unfavorable) variances. The P10 formula is given in Equation 17.10.

P10, Scrap Variance, Extreme

$$10 * \left(\frac{SumScrapVariance}{SumProfits} \right) \quad Min = 0, \ Max = 1$$

or, if $SumScrapVariance = 0$, then $P10 = 0.50$

$$SumScrapVariance = Abs(Sum(\text{Jan, Feb}, \ldots, \text{Dec}))$$

$$Sum\,Profits = Sum(\text{Jan, Feb}, \ldots, \text{Dec})$$

(17.10)

The P10 formula in Equation 17.10 is based on the scrap variance and the profit numbers for the preceding year. The months illustrated are January to December. The predictor is not influenced by the sign of the scrap variance (positive or negative, favorable or unfavorable). The P10 scores are bounded by the [0,1] range. Also, a scrap variance of zero is also extreme and P10 equals 0.50 if the sum of the scrap variances is zero. The scrap variance account was an account that the controllers might use to smooth earnings.

P11: Warranty Variance Is Large

P11 was based on the warranty variance, which was an account that could be used by the controllers to smooth profits. The score for P11 used both positive (favorable) and negative (unfavorable) variances and the current profit number. The P11 formula is shown in Equation 17.11.

P11, Warranty Variance, Extreme

If $CurrentWarrantyVariance - AverageWarrantyVariance > 5000$

and, if $0.90 < \dfrac{CurrentProfits}{AverageProfits} < 1.10,$

then P11 equals 1, else P11 equals zero

$AverageWarrantyVariance = Average(\text{Jan, Feb}, \ldots, \text{Dec})$

$AverageProfits = Average(\text{Jan, Feb}, \ldots, \text{Dec})$

$$(17.11)$$

The P11 formula in Equation 17.11 is based on both the current warranty variance and the current profits. If the current warranty variance differs from the average by more than $5,000, then the first condition is met. The second condition is that the profits for the current month are within 10 percent of the average profits for the past year. If the warranty amount has changed by a large amount and the profits are normal, then P11 equals 1.00. If neither condition is met, then P11 equals zero. The results showed that about 15 percent of all divisions scored 1.00 for P11.

P12: Overhead Variance Is Erratic

P12 was based on whether the overhead variance was erratic. The usual measure of dispersion (spread) is the variance, but the variance is not neatly bounded like correlation (from -1.00 to $+1.00$). The range was used to measure dispersion and the P12 formula is shown in Equation 17.12.

P12, Overhead Variance, Erratic

$P12Factor = \dfrac{Range}{AverageOverheadVariance}$

if $P12Factor < 1.00$, then $P12 = 0$,

if $P12Factor > 3.00$, then $P12 = 1$, else

$P12 = \dfrac{P12Factor - 1}{2}$

$AverageOverheadVariance = Average(\text{Jan, Feb}, \ldots, \text{Dec})$

$Range = Maximum(\text{Jan, Feb}, \ldots, \text{Dec})$

$-Minimum(\text{Jan, Feb}, \ldots, \text{Dec})$

$$(17.12)$$

The formula for P12 in Equation 17.12 shows that the P12 score increases as the range increases and as the average decreases. The P12 result itself is restricted to the [0,1] range. Under normal circumstances the overhead variances should be quite stable. The average score for P12 was about 0.65 meaning that some two-thirds of divisions had "erratic" variances. Subsequent revisions will aim for a lower average score by the point at which the maximum is reached (when the *P12Factor* equals 3.00). An erratic overhead variance might be the result of smoothing or manipulating earnings.

P13: Overhead Variance Is High

P13 was based on a comparison between the current month's overhead variance and the current month's profits. The absolute value of the overhead variance was used because any high variance could signal issues with accuracy in budgeting. Issues with being able to budget expenses might be a motivation to resort to creative accounting to make up for profit shortfalls. The P13 formula is shown in Equation 17.13.

P13, Overhead Variance, High

$$P13Factor = Abs\left(\frac{OverheadVariance}{Profits}\right)$$

If $P13Factor \leq 1.00$, then $P13 = P13Factor$,
else if $P13Factor > 1.00$, then $P13 = 1.00$
OverheadVariance = Overhead Variance(Current Month)
Profits = Profits(Current Month)

$$(17.13)$$

The P13 formula in Equation 17.13 increases as the overhead variance increases and it also increases as the profit amount decreases. The P13 result itself is restricted to the [0,1] range. The ability to budget expenses accurately was a key performance measure for the company. The average P13 score was 0.21, which means that not too many, and not too few, divisions were scoring on this risk indicator.

P14: Overhead Variance Moving in the Wrong Direction

P14 was based on whether the current month's overhead variance was moving in the wrong direction. The expectation was that an increase in sales would cause the overhead variance to move in a *favorable* direction. Predictor P14 looked at the movement of the variance. The past data was for the 11 months before the current month. The P14 formula is shown in Equation 17.14.

P14, Overhead Variance, Opposite movement

SalesScore $= -2$ if $<$ Lower Bound or -1 if $<$ Average
SalesScore $= 2$ if $>$ Upper Bound or 1 if $>$ Average
OverheadScore = Same as SalesScore
UpperSales $= 1.25$*AvgSales or 1.25*CurrentSales
LowerSales $= 0.75$*AvgSales or 0.75*CurrentSales
OverheadBounds = Same as SalesBounds
AvgSales = *AverageSales*(Jan, Feb, . . . , Nov)
AvgOverhead = *AverageVariance*(Jan, Feb, . . . , Nov)
CurrentSales = Sales(Dec)
CurrentOverhead = Variance(Dec)

$$(17.14)$$

The P14 formula in Equation 17.14 shows that a *large* increase in sales (greater than 25 percent) would be coded as 2 and a *small* increase in sales would be coded as 1. A *large* decrease in sales would be coded as -2 and a *small* decrease in sales would be coded as -1. A *large* increase in the variance would be coded as $+2$ and a *small* increase in the variance would be coded as $+1$. A *large* decrease in the variance would be coded

TABLE 17.3 The Scores for the Sales and Overhead Changes

Sales Score (decrease is negative)	Overhead Score (unfavorable variance is positive)	P14
−1 or −2	−1 or −2	1
−1 or −2	+1 or +2	0
+1 or +2	+1 or +2	1
+1 or +2	−1 or −2	0

as −2 and a *small* decrease would be coded as −1. The cutoff percentage in each case is 25 percent. Changes that are larger than 25 percent are deemed *large* and changes that are smaller than 25 percent are *small*. Table 17.3 summarizes the scores for P14.

When the sales shows a decrease (−1 or −2) and the variance becomes more favorable, then P14 is scored as 1.00. When the sales shows an increase (+1 or +2) and the overhead variance becomes more unfavorable, then P14 is scored as zero. The extent of the change (greater than 25 percent or less than 25 percent) was not used because that would have made the programming unduly complex. The Access Switch function for P14 is shown below:

> V14f: Val(Switch([SDev]=−2 And [Bdev]=−2 Or [Bdev]=−1,1,[SDev]=−2 And [Bdev]=2 Or [Bdev]=1,0,[SDev]=−1 And [Bdev]=−2 Or [Bdev]=−1,1, [SDev]=−1 And [Bdev]=2 Or [Bdev]=1,0,[SDev]=2 And [Bdev]=−2 Or [Bdev]=−1,0,[SDev]=2 And [Bdev]=2 Or [Bdev]=1,1,[SDev]=1 And [Bdev]=−2 Or [Bdev]=−1,0,[SDev]=1 And [Bdev]=2 Or [Bdev]=1,1))

The result for P14 is restricted to the [0,1] range. The average P14 score was 0.50, which was too high for an average. Future refinements to the formula will only score divisions with 1.00 when the changes are more extreme. Predictor P14 is a good example of identifying amounts that were opposite to expectations.

P15: Other Income and Expenses Erratic

P15 was based on whether the *other income and expenses* amounts were erratic. The other income and expenses amounts could be used to dampen the effects of a very good or a very poor month. The usual metric for dispersion is the variance and in this case, the standard deviation (the square root of the variance) is used and is divided by the average amount to identify cases when the standard deviation is large relative to the norm. The P15 formula is shown in Equation 17.15.

P15, OtherIncome and Expenses, Erratic

$$P15Factor = \frac{\text{Standard Deviation}}{\text{Average}}$$

if $Abs(P15Factor) < 1.00$, or Standard Deviation < 1000 then $P15 = 0$,

if $Abs(P12Factor) > 5.00$, then $P15 = 1.00$, else

$$P15 = \frac{Abs(P15Factor) - 1}{4}$$

(17.15)

Average = $Avg(\text{Jan, Feb}, \ldots, \text{Dec})$

Standard Deviation = $StDev(\text{Jan, Feb}, \ldots, \text{Dec})$

The P15 score in Equation 17.15 increases as the standard deviation increases and it also increases as the average decreases. If the standard deviation is *small* (less than $1,000), then P15 is set equal to zero. P15 is restricted to the usual [0,1] range. As the dispersion increases, so the P15 score would also increase. The average score for P15 was about 0.48 indicating that one-half of the divisions had erratic other income and expenses numbers. Subsequent revisions would target a lower average score by increasing the lower bounds of 1.00 and 1,000.

P16: Increase in Supplies Manufacturing

P16 was based on increases in the supplies (manufacturing) account. Supplies and consumables accounts are often the targets for fraud because there is no control through an inventory account. One way to calculate an increase over time is by using linear regression but this is a bit complex to program so a simpler approach was used. The P16 formula is given in Equation 17.16.

P16, Supplies, Increase

$$P16Factor = \frac{PriorQ}{First3Q}$$

if $P16Factor < 0.333$, then $P16 = 0$,
if $P16Factor \geq 1.00$, then $P16 = 1.00$, else $\quad$ (17.16)
$P16 = (P16Factor - 0.3333)*1.5$
$PriorQ$ = Prior three months (Oct, Nov, Dec)
$First3Q$ = First nine months (Jan, Feb, ..., Sept)

The P16 formula in Equation 17.16 compares the supplies spending for the past three months with the spending for the first nine months of the year. If the spending is equal from month to month, then the ratio of the last three months to the first nine months should be one-third because 3/9 equals one-third. Factors (or ratios) above 1/3 result in a positive P12 score. The average score for P16 was 0.11, meaning that very few divisions showed large supplies increases and that the divisions with high scores were indeed quite odd.

P17: Net Income Smooth

P17 was based on whether the net incomes were perhaps just too smooth to be true. The R-squared statistic in a linear regression would indicate whether there was a close fitting straight line to the data points. The programming would be a bit complex in Access. A simpler approach was to use the standard deviation of the profit numbers. The P17 formula is given in Equation 17.17.

P17, Net Income Smooth

$$P17Factor = \frac{StDevProfit}{Abs(AverageProfit)}$$

if $P17Factor > 0.50$, then $P17 = 0$,
if $P17Factor \leq 0.50$, then,
$P17 = \sqrt{1 - (2*P17Factor)}$
$AverageProfit$ = Average Profit (Jan, Feb, ..., Dec)
$StDevProfit$ = Standard Deviation Profits (Jan, Feb, ..., Dec)

(17.17)

The P17 formula in Equation 17.17 uses the fact that a smooth profits stream would have a small standard deviation and a low ratio of the standard deviation divided by the profits. High ratios (above 0.50) are scored as a zero. The use of the square root gives a boost to low scores. The average score for P17 was 0.21 meaning that the scoring was just about right.

Figure 17.11 shows two sets of profit numbers. The vertical axis (the y-axis) is calibrated from $-\$800,000$ to $+\$1,000,000$ in each case. The numbers on the left are quite volatile and the P17Factor is 1.00 (giving a P17 score of 0.00) while the numbers on the right are quite smooth with a P17Factor of 0.15 (giving a P17 score of 0.832). The P17 formula does a good job of distinguishing between smooth and erratic profits.

P18: Accounts Receivable Increase

P18 was based on the fact that a large increase in the accounts receivable balance could be the result of overstated sales. A balance was seen to be high when it was compared to the prior norm for the division. The P18 formula is given in Equation 17.18.

P18, Accounts
Receivable High

$$P18Factor = \frac{\text{AR Proportion (Prior2M)}}{\text{AR Proportion (First10M)}}$$

if $P18Factor < 1.000$, then $P18 = 0$,

if $P18Factor \geq 2.00$, then $P18 = 1.00$, else

$P18 = P18Factor - 1.00$ $\qquad$ (17.18)

$$\text{AR Proportion} = \frac{\text{Sum AR}}{\text{Sum Sales}}$$

Prior2M = Prior two months (Nov, Dec)

First10M = First ten months (Jan, Feb, ..., Oct)

The P18 formula in Equation 17.18 uses the AR (Accounts Receivable) balance for the past two months and the AR balance for the prior 10 months. The AR numbers are scaled (divided) by sales. The average score for P18 was about 0.18 indicating that large increases were not the norm.

P19: Accounts Receivable Allowances Erratic

P19 was based on whether the AR allowances were erratic (volatile). This account could be used as a cookie jar account to smooth out low and high earnings. This formula is similar to P17 except that P19 looks for erratic numbers whereas for P17 looks for smooth numbers. The P19 formula is shown in Equation 17.19.

P19, Accounts Receivable
Allowances Erratic

$$P19Factor = \frac{\text{StDevARAllow}}{\text{Abs(Average AR Allowances)}}$$

if $P19Factor > 1.00$, then $P19 = 1$,

if $P19Factor \leq 1.00$, then,

$P19 = \sqrt{P19Factor}$

Average AR Allowances = Average AR (Jan, Feb, ..., Dec)

StDevARAllow = Std Deviation AR Allowances (Jan-Dec)

$\qquad$ (17.19)

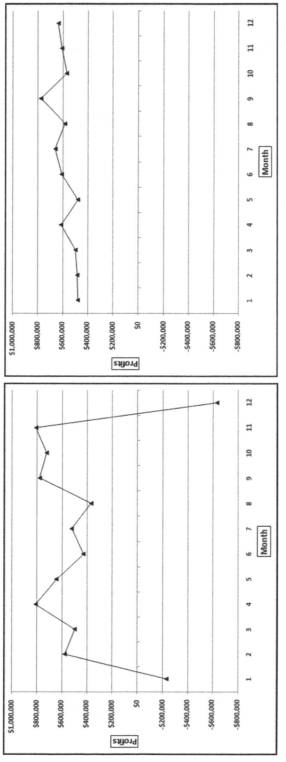

FIGURE 17.11 A Volatile Series of Profits and a Smooth Series of Profits

The P19 formula in Equation 17.19 is based on the standard deviation (dispersion) divided by the average AR allowance. A relatively high dispersion gives a high score for P19. The average score for P19 was about 0.31 meaning that the number of divisions with high volatility was on the high side. To illustrate the formula, two examples of AR allowances are shown in Figure 17.12.

The numbers should always be either negative or zero. The graphs in Figure 17.12 are calibrated from −$70,000 to $0 on the y-axis. The numbers on the left are quite volatile with the standard deviation being slightly greater than the mean giving a P19 score of 1.000. The allowance numbers in the right panel are neatly clustered in the −$58,000 to −$52,000 range. The formula can therefore distinguish between smooth and erratic allowance numbers. About one-half of the divisions had all allowance numbers equal to zero and consequently P19 scores of zero. The divisions were therefore inconsistent in their usage of the allowance account.

P20: Inventory Balance Erratic

P20 was based on erratic (volatile) inventory balances because this account could be used as a cookie jar account to smooth out low and high earnings. This formula is similar to the formula for P19. The P20 formula is shown in Equation 17.20.

P20,
Inventory,
Erratic

$$P20Factor = \frac{StDevInventory}{Abs(Average\ Inventory)}$$

if $P20Factor > 1.00$, then $P20 = 1$,

if $P20Factor \leq 1.00$, then,

$P20 = \sqrt{P20Factor}$

Average Inventory = Average Inventory (Jan, Feb, . . . , Dec)

StDevInventory = Std Deviation Inventory (Jan-Dec)

(17.20)

The P20 formula in Equation 17.20 is based on the standard deviation (dispersion) divided by the average inventory balance. The average score for P20 was 0.40 meaning that the number of divisions with high volatilities was again on the high side. Future revisions will revise the P19 and the P20 formulas to give average scores of about 0.20.

P21: Inventory Balance Increase

P21 was based on a large increase in the inventory balance because such an increase could be the result of understating cost of goods sold. A balance was seen to be high when it was compared to the prior norm for the division. The P21 formula is shown in Equation 17.21.

P21, Inventory
Increase

$P21Factor = Abs(Inventory\ Proportion)$

if $P21Factor \leq 0.3333$, then $P21 = 0$,

if $P21Factor \geq 1.00$, then $P21 = 1.00$, else

$P21 = \sqrt{P21Factor} * 1.5$

$$Inventory\ Proportion = \frac{Sum\ PriorQ}{Sum\ First3Q}$$

PriorQ = Prior three months (Oct, Nov, Dec)

First3Q = First nine months (Jan, Feb, . . . , Sept)

(17.21)

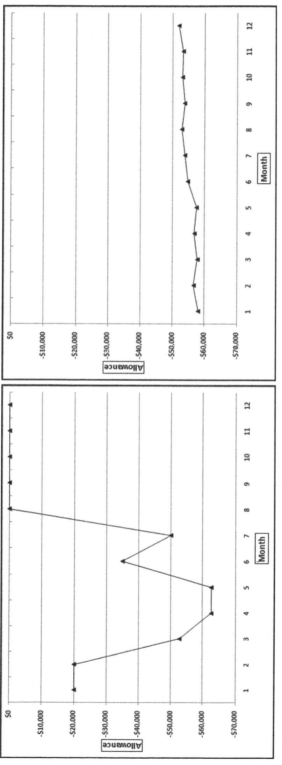

FIGURE 17.12 A Volatile Series of Allowances and a Smooth Series of Allowances

The P21 formula in Equation 17.21 uses the inventory balance for the past three months and the balance for the prior nine months. The average expected score for P21 was zero because the sum of the prior three months should be one-third of the sum for the first nine months. The actual average score for P21 was 0.19, meaning that the average did show an increase for a number of divisions.

P22: Prepaid Expenses Change

P22 was based on the change in prepaid expenses because this account could be used to smooth profits in times of shortages and surpluses as compared to budget. A balance was seen to be high when it was compared to the prior norm for the division. The P22 formula is shown in Equation 17.22.

$$
\begin{aligned}
&\text{P22, Prepaid} && P22 Factor = \frac{\text{Sum(Prior2M)}}{\text{Sum(First10M)}} \\
&\text{Expenses, Change} \\
&&& \text{if } P22 Factor \leq 0.000, \text{ then P22} = 1, \\
&&& \text{if } 0.00 < \text{P22 Factor} < 0.10, \text{ then} \\
&&& P22 = \sqrt{10^*(0.10 - P22 Factor)} \\
&&& \text{if } 0.10 \leq \text{P22 Factor} \leq 0.20, \text{ then P22} = 0, \qquad (17.22) \\
&&& \text{if } 0.20 < \text{P22 Factor} < 0.30, \text{ then} \\
&&& P22 = \sqrt{10^*(P22 Factor - 0.20)} \\
&&& \text{if } P22 Factor \geq 0.300, \text{ then P22} = 1.00, \\
&&& \text{Prior2M} = \text{Prior two months (Nov, Dec)} \\
&&& \text{First10M} = \text{First ten months (Jan, Feb, \ldots, Oct)}
\end{aligned}
$$

The P22 formula in Equation 17.22 gives a division a high score when the recent balances are higher than the average for the past balances. The sum of the balances for the two most recent months divided by the sum for the first ten months should be one-fifth (2/10) if the balances are consistent from one month to the next. The formula gives high scores when the ratio deviates from one-fifth. The P22Factors and the resulting P22 scores are set out in Figure 17.13.

Figure 17.13 shows the P22 scores (on the y-axis) applied to the P22Factors using the formulas in Equation 17.22. The expected score is 0.20 (two months divided by 10 months) and Figure 17.13 exposes an error in the scoring in that the P22 score of zero should be centered at 0.20 and not at 0.15. Despite the flaw, the graph shows that as we move to the left or right of 0.15, the score of zero increases to 1.00. The average score for P22 was 0.59, which was very high and it seems that P22 as it stands does not do a very good job of distinguishing between erratic prepaid expenses and the normal fluctuations in a business. The average score could be reduced by increasing the interval for a zero score for P22 to perhaps 0.10 to 0.30. The square root sign could also be removed which would make the slopes a straight line instead of the convex functions shown above. This predictor was given a low weighting and so the scoring issues actually had very little impact on the final risk scores.

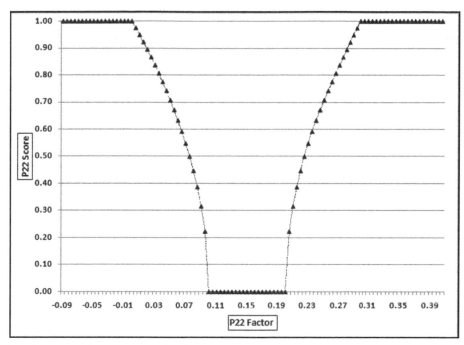

FIGURE 17.13 The Scores Applied to the Prepaid Expenses Predictor

P23: Prepaid Expenses Other

The company had chart of accounts of about 5,000 ledger accounts and every normal business transaction could be recorded using the available ledger accounts. The next three predictors deal with the use of certain vague and rarely needed accounts. Past experience showed that controllers were inclined to use these *rarely needed* accounts as cookie jar reserves for lean and fat times. Predictor P23 gave a high-risk score to any division that had used the Prepaid Expenses-Other account for anything more than insignificant amounts. The P23 formula is shown in Equation 17.23.

P23, Prepaid
Expenses, Other

$$P23Factor = \frac{\text{Std Dev Prepaid}}{\text{Abs(Average Prepaid)}}$$

if Prepaid(CurrentMonth) ≤ 0, then P23 = 1,
if $0 \leq$ Abs(Average Prepaid) ≤ 100, then P23 = 0,
if $0 \leq P23Factor \leq 1.00$, then P23 = $P23Factor$, else $\quad$ (17.23)
if $P23Factor > 1.00$, then P23 = 1.00.
Std Dev Prepaid = StDev(Jan, Feb, ..., Dec)
Average Prepaid = Average(Jan, Feb, ..., Dec)

The P23 formula in Equation 17.23 uses the Prepaid amounts for the prior year and gives a high score when there are large fluctuations in the prepaid account. Several conditions can cause a score of 1.00 or a score of zero and the conditions are not always consistent. The conditions listed in Equation 17.23 are listed in the order in which they are evaluated. If the prepaid balance for the current month is negative (which is irregular because the prepaid amounts should be positive), then P23 equals 1.00 without taking the amounts or the *P23Factor* into account. The average score for P23 was 0.61, which means that P23 does not do a very good job of distinguishing between using the account as a possible cookie jar and using the account in the normal course of business. As a test the upper bound (of $100) was changed to $5,000 and the average dropped to 0.51. A complete reevaluation of this formula is needed.

P24: Uninvoiced Trade Payables

The logic for P24 was the same as the P23 logic. The *Uninvoiced Trade Payables* account was created for an accrual for an expenditure that had not yet been invoiced by the supplier. This was a rarely needed account that controllers were inclined to use as cookie jar reserves. The P24 formula is shown in Equation 17.24.

$$
\begin{aligned}
&P24Factor = \frac{SumPayables3M}{SumProfits3M} \\
&\text{if } P24Factor < 0, \text{ then } P24 = 1, \\
&\text{if } 0 \le P24Factor \le 1.00, \text{ then } P24 = P24Factor, \text{ else} \\
&\text{if } P24Factor > 1.00, \text{ then } P24 = 1.00. \\
&SumPayables3M = SumPayables(Oct, \ Nov, \ Dec) \\
&SumProfit3M = SumProfit(Oct, \ Nov, \ Dec)
\end{aligned}
\tag{17.24}
$$

P24, Trade Payables, Uninvoiced

The P24 formula in Equation 17.24 uses the payables amounts for the prior three months and gives a high score when this is large in relation to the profits. P24 is scored as 1.00 if the ratio is negative. A review of the results showed that a negative P24Factor was usually due to the profits being negative. With hindsight it is not clear why a loss should generate a P24 score of 1.00. There were a few cases when the sum of the payables balances was negative, and this was a really odd situation. The average score for P24 was 0.44 and this high score again reflects a little too much zeal to score the payables predictor.

P25: Accrual Other Miscellaneous

The logic for P25 was the same as for P23 and P24. The *Accrual Other Miscellaneous* account was for "miscellaneous accrued liabilities awaiting final decision regarding their disposition and appropriate account classification." This was a rarely needed account that controllers were inclined to use as cookie jar reserves. The P25 formula is shown in Equation 17.25.

$$
\begin{aligned}
&P25Factor = SumAccruals1M \\
&\text{if } P25Factor < 0, \text{ then } P25 = 1, \\
&\text{if } P25Factor = 0, \text{ then } P25 = 0, \\
&\text{if } 1 \le P25Factor \le 5000, \text{ then } P25 = 0.50, \text{ else} \\
&\text{if } P24Factor > 5000, \text{ then } P24 = 1.00. \\
&SumAccruals1M = SumAccruals(Dec)
\end{aligned}
\tag{17.25}
$$

P25, Accruals, Other

The P25 formula in Equation 17.25 uses the Accruals amounts for the preceding month and gives a high score when the accruals exceed $5,000. A score of 1.00 is awarded if the accruals amount is negative. The average score for P25 was 0.16 and this average score seems just right for a seldom-used account. It is insightful that the simplest of the three formulas gives the best average result.

P26: Outside USA and Canada

The logic for P26 was that most of the prior issues that arose in the financial reporting arena were for divisions that were outside of the USA and Canada. The Hitachi example at the start of this section also concerned a distant subsidiary. The P26 formula is given in Equation 17.26.

$$
\begin{aligned}
&\text{P26, Outside} && \text{if Division is in USA or Canada then Location} = 0. \\
&\text{USA and Canada} && \text{Otherwise Location} = 1. \\
& && \text{P26Factor} = \text{Location}
\end{aligned}
\tag{17.26}
$$

The P26 formula in Equation 17.26 could be adapted so that the "outside USA and Canada" could include more or fewer countries or regions. The formula could also be adapted to score somewhat risky countries as 0.50 and very risky countries as 1.00. The average score for this predictor was about 0.50, which reflected the fact that about one-half of all divisions were outside of the United States and Canada. A more sophisticated scoring formula would aim to reduce the average to about 0.20.

P27: Prior Scores

The logic for P27 was that the effects of a prior high score would linger for several periods. P27 formula is given in Equation 17.27.

$$
\begin{aligned}
&\text{P27, Prior Scores} && \text{P27Factor} = \frac{\text{PriorScore1} + \text{PriorScore2}}{2} \\
& && \text{P27} = \text{P27Factor} \\
& && \text{PriorScore2} = \text{RiskScorePrior2Months(Oct)} \\
& && \text{PriorScore1} = \text{RiskScorePrior1Month(Nov)}
\end{aligned}
\tag{17.27}
$$

The formula for P26 is shown in Equation 17.26. This predictor keeps a prior high or low score tagging along for two more months. When the risk scoring model is first run it is not possible to have prior scores. Each forensic unit could be scored with a zero for the first run of the risk scoring model.

 PREDICTOR WEIGHTINGS

Each predictor was weighted according to its perceived influence on the total risk of the divisions. As with the prior applications the weights should sum to 1.00. With each predictor confined to the [0,1] range, the final scores are also bounded by the [0,1] range with high scores reflecting higher risks.

TABLE 17.4 The Weights Given to the 27 Predictors

Predictor #	Description	Weight	Notes
1	Erratic sales	0.05	
2	Large sales change	0.04	
3	Odd numbers reported as sales	0.02	Interesting, but not too predictive
4	Increase is sales allowances	0.03	
5	Odd numbers reported as allowances	0.03	Interesting, but not too predictive
6	Excessive sales allowances	0.04	
7	Quarter-end pad	0.06	Highly predictive
8	High materials price variance	0.03	Past year
9	High materials price variance	0.03	Current month
10	Scrap variance, extreme	0.03	Interesting, but not too predictive
11	Warranty variance large	0.04	Possible cookie jar account
12	Overhead variance is erratic	0.03	
13	Overhead variance is high	0.03	
14	Overhead variance, wrong direction	0.04	Possible result of manipulations
15	Other income and expenses, erratic	0.04	
16	Supplies manufacturing, increase	0.03	
17	Net income smooth	0.05	Predictive, fluctuations expected
18	Accounts receivable, increase	0.05	Possible result of manipulations
19	AR allowances, erratic	0.04	
20	Inventory balance, erratic	0.03	
21	Inventory balance, increase	0.01	Weighting should be increased
22	Prepaid expenses, change	0.01	Formula needs to be revised
23	Prepaid expenses, other	0.04	Irregular ledger account
24	Trade payables uninvoiced	0.04	Irregular ledger account
25	Accrual other miscellaneous	0.04	Irregular ledger account
26	Outside USA and Canada	0.02	Based on prior experience
27	Prior scores	0.10	Memory of past scores

The weights of the 27 predictors are given in Table 17.4. Highly predictive predictors were given higher weights. With 27 predictors the average weight is about 0.04. The profile of the final scores is shown in Figure 17.14.

The pattern of the risk scores shows that there is a small group of divisions with relatively high scores, with *high* in this case meaning 0.50 and higher. These divisions (about 8 percent of the divisions) scored above 0.5, *on average*, across all predictors. The highest score was 0.584. This high-risk division scored perfect 1s on 13 predictors. The

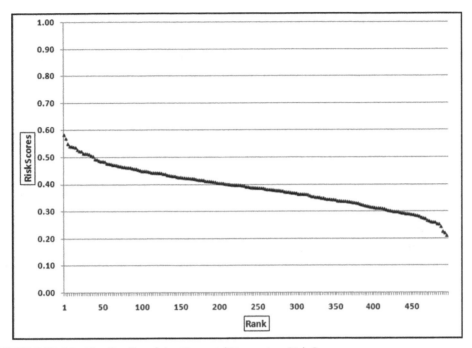

FIGURE 17.14 The Profile of the Financial Reporting Risk Scores

minimum score was 0.210, which means that the division that was seen to have the least financial reporting risk still scored perfect 1s on two predictors and positive scores on eleven variables.

 CONCLUSIONS

The 27 financial reporting predictors were based on (a) erratic behavior, (b) changes in balances, (c) changes in a direction opposite to expected, (d) balances that are relatively high or low, (e) targeted behavior such as increased profits in the quarter-end month, and (f) the use of obscure general ledger accounts.

The risk-scoring method added several layers of rigor to the audit process. It assisted with audit planning and it helped the auditors better understand the entity and its environment before any formal audits were started. Audit management had some reservations about the risk scoring approach correctly identifying the most high-risk divisions. Their belief was that a controller could be using only three manipulation methods. The division would end up with a low risk score because scoring 1s on three predictors each weighted 0.05 would only give a score of 0.15.

Future revisions will reduce the number of predictors to 10 predictors, plus the "outside USA" and the "prior scores" predictors, neither of which is directly based on the division's financial numbers. Each predictor could then be weighted from 0.05 to 0.125. The starting point for the deletion of predictors would be those predictors that currently have low weights. Another change could be to revise the formulas so that the average score is about 0.20 and that only extreme numbers are given positive scores. It is always easier to improve and upgrade a system that is already in place than it is to create a scoring system from scratch. The system would have been very difficult to design had it not been for the consistency of reporting due to the use of an enterprise resource planning (ERP) system.

SUMMARY

This chapter reviewed several ways to evaluate accounting numbers with a view to assessing their authenticity. The methods included (a) the analysis of the digit patterns in financial statement numbers, (b) detecting biases in accounting numbers, and (c) detecting high-risk divisional reports.

The analysis of the digit patterns in financial statement numbers started by rearranging the numbers to form a consistent set of reported numbers. Income and deduction numbers were analyzed separately. The analysis looked at the patterns of the leading and ending digits and compared these to Benford's Law. The binomial distribution was used to assess how unlikely the duplications were. The general rule is that most sets of financial numbers have too few numbers for a rigorous application of Benford's Law.

The detection of biases in accounting numbers focused on identifying an excess of second-digit zeroes that come about from inflating revenues of (say) $993 million to $1,008 million, or $798,000 to $803,000. These upward revisions were evident from an analysis of quarterly earnings reports. A review of Enron's reported numbers showed a strong bias toward reporting numbers that just exceeded psychological thresholds. This section included a method to identify biases in reported amounts. The method involved fitting the best-fitting smooth line to the data points and then assessing the magnitude of the difference between the fitted smooth line and the actual pattern. Biases are usually evident by large differences and clearly visible spikes. The technique was demonstrated on therapy visit data.

The chapter also demonstrated the risk scoring method on divisional reports. The *forensic units* were the divisions in an international manufacturing conglomerate and the predictors were based on the reported monthly numbers. The behavior of interest was whether the divisional controllers were reporting numbers that included intentional or unintentional errors. In general, the 27 predictors looked for (a) erratic behavior, (b) changes in balances, (c) changes in a direction opposite to expected, (d) balances that are relatively high or low, (e) targeted behavior such as increased profits in the quarter-end month, and (f) the use of obscure general ledger accounts. The final results showed that some divisions were apparently high risk. The scoring method needed to be simplified because the predictors allowed some questionable practices to remain hidden. The use of advanced detection techniques should act as a deterrent to fraudulent financial reporting.

CHAPTER EIGHTEEN

Using Analytics on Purchasing Card Transactions

T HIS CHAPTER SHOWS HOW the tests in the prior chapters could be used in a forensic analytics project related to purchasing card transactions. The first three chapters reviewed the use of Access, Excel, and PowerPoint in forensic analytics. These are the software programs used in this chapter. The next few chapters reviewed some high-level tests designed to analyze the internal diagnostics of transactional data. This was followed by more focused tests that identified small clusters of highly suspect items. The later chapters dealt with risk-scoring techniques to identify high-risk forensic units. These forensic units could be franchised locations, bank accounts, travel agents, or the controllers of distant divisions. This chapter now applies some selected tests to the high-risk environment of corporate purchasing cards. The methods and techniques in the book can be adapted to various environments by selecting a set of relevant tests, and perhaps even including innovative adaptations or revisions to the Nigrini Cycle of tests or the other tests discussed in the book.

The chapter starts by describing corporate purchasing cards. Examples of fraud, waste, and abuse are then listed. The examples are selected examples from forensic audits of the transactions. The work of the National Association of Purchasing Card Professionals is reviewed together with some results from a poll conducted by the association. An example of a purchasing card dashboard is then shown together with a discussion of using Excel for these applications. The chapter then reviews the results of selected tests run on a real-world data table of purchasing card transactions. The chapter ends with some concluding thoughts on various matters related to forensic analytics.

PURCHASING CARDS

A purchasing card (hereinafter "card") is a government or company charge card that allows an employee to purchases goods and services without going through the "rigors" of the traditional purchasing process. Cards are issued to employees who are expected to follow the policies and procedures with respect to card use. These procedures state which items may be purchased using the cards, the purchase approval process, and the reconciliation procedure required so that personal expenses can be reimbursed to the company. The use of cards is an efficient way of simplifying and speeding up the purchases of low-value transactions. The advantages are that employees can buy goods and services quickly, there is a reduction in transaction costs, there is the capability to track expenses, and the use of cards frees up the time of purchasing and accounts payable staff. The card issuer (a bank) typically invoices the agency or company on a monthly basis with an electronic invoice showing the total dollars per user and the grand total for the month. From a legal liability perspective it is important to understand that the organization assumes full liability for payment. The employee cardholder does not interact with the card issuer, but is expected to follow the company's policies and procedures relating to card usage. A typical statement in a set of policies and procedures is as follows:

> Under no circumstances is a cardholder permitted to use the P-Card for personal purchases. Using the P-Card for personal purchases may result in disciplinary action, up to and including termination from State employment and criminal prosecution. The Official code of Georgia, Annotated (O.C.G.A.), paragraph 50-5-80 states that any cardholder who knowingly uses the card for personal purchases under $500 is guilty of a misdemeanor. A cardholder who knowingly uses the card for personal purchases of $500 or more is guilty of a felony punishable by one to 20 years in prison. Supervisors or other approving officials who knowingly, or through willful neglect, approve personal or fraudulent purchases are subject to the same disciplinary actions as cardholders.

It would seem that with clear policies and effective audit procedures that a card program would make it easier for employees to do their jobs. Unfortunately, it seems that in some cases the card simply gives the employee the opportunity (one of the three parts of the fraud triangle) to commit fraud. Serious violations were documented in the U.S. General Accounting Office (GAO) audit of two Navy units and the Department of Education in 2002. The GAO is now known as the Government Accountability Office (www.gao.gov). In the report (GAO-02-676T dated May 1, 2002) the director notes that she supported the purchase card program because it resulted in lower costs and less red tape for the government and the vendor community. However, several GAO card audits in the early 2000s turned up instances of fraud, waste, and abuse. Selected examples are:

- A cardholder made over $17,000 in fraudulent transactions to acquire personal items from Walmart, Home Depot, shoe stores, pet stores, boutiques, an eye-care center, and restaurants over an eight-month period (Navy, GAO-01-995T, 2001).

- A military officer conspired with cardholders under his supervision to make nearly $400,000 in fraudulent purchases from five companies. He owned two of the companies and the other three companies were owned by family and friends. The purchased items included DVD players, Palm Pilots, and desktop and laptop computers (Navy, GAO-01-995T, 2001).
- A maintenance/construction supervisor made $52,000 in fraudulent payments to a contractor for work that was actually done by the Navy's Public Works Center (Navy, GAO-01-995T, 2001).
- A purchasing agent made about $12,000 in fraudulent purchases and planned to submit a further fraudulent $103,000 for expenses such as hotels, airline tickets, computers, phone cards, and personal items from the Home Depot (Navy, GAO-01-995T, 2001).
- A cardholder had transactions for $80,000 that was not supported by documentation. He admitted to making thousands of dollars of personal purchases including EZ-Pass toll tags, expensive remote-controlled helicopters, and a dog (Navy, GAO-03-154, 2002).
- A cardholder used his card to purchase $150,000 in automobile, building, and home improvement supplies. The cardholder then sold some of these items to generate cash (Navy, GAO-03-154, 2002).
- Two cardholders conspired with seven vendors to submit about $89,000 in fictitious and inflated invoices. The cardholders sold, used, and bartered the illegally obtained items (Navy, GAO-03-154, 2002).
- The Navy inappropriately issued five cards to individuals who did not work for the government (Navy, GAO-03-154, 2002).
- The audit report also identified other issues such as (a) purchases that did not serve an authorized government purpose, (b) split purchases, and (c) purchases for vendors other than the specifically approved vendors for certain categories of expenses (Navy, GAO-03-154, 2002).
- Cardholders and approving officials bought items for $100,000 that were for personal use, including a computer game station, a computer, a digital camera, and a surround sound system (Army, GAO-02-732, 2002).
- One cardholder bought fraudulent items for $30,000 including a computer, rings, purses, and clothing from vendors such as Victoria's Secret, Calvin Klein, and others (Army, GAO-02-732, 2002).
- A cardholder bought fraudulent items for $30,000 including various items for personal use and cash advances (Army, GAO-02-732, 2002).
- A cardholder bought fraudulent items including cruises, cell phones, hotels, Payless Car Rental, and Extended Stay America. The cardholder claimed that the card was stolen and that the card thief had made the purchases (Army, GAO-02-732, 2002).
- The Army audit showed many examples of fraud including a card that had $630 charged to it for escort services (Army, GAO-02-732, 2002).
- The audit of the Veterans Affairs and the Veterans Health Administration identified more than $300,000 in purchases that were considered wasteful including movie gift certificates of $30,000, and an expensive digital camera for $999 when many

cheaper models were available. The vendors used included Sharper Image, Baltimore Orioles, Daddy's Junky Music, Eddie Bauer, Gap Kids, Hollywood Beach Country Club, Harbor Cruises, and Christmas Palace (VHA, GAO-04-737, 2004).

■ Control issues raised in the VHA audit included (a) untimely recording (where the cardholder does not notify the agency that a purchase has been made), (b) late reconciliations (where the goal is to detect invalid transactions, billing errors, and unauthorized purchases) or signing off that a reconciliation was done when it was not actually done, and (c) lack of a review by an approving official (so as to identify fraudulent, improper, or wasteful transactions) (VHA, GAO-04-737, 2004).

■ In a sample of 1,000 transactions the GAO identified 17 purchases for $14,000 for clothing, food, and other items for personal use. One transaction was for winter jackets for warehouse employees, another purchase was for 18 pairs of jeans that the cardholders claimed were employee uniforms, and there were several purchases of food that should have been the personal responsibility of the employees. About 250 transactions lacked documentation and the GAO could not determine what was actually purchased and the cost of each of the items purchased, and whether there was a legitimate need for the items (VHA, GAO-04-737, 2004).

■ An Air Force audit showed (a) a down payment of a $10,000 sapphire ring for $2,400 at E-Z Pawn, (b) suitcases, garment bags, flight bags, and briefcases for $23,760 from 1-800-Luggage, Patagonia, and Franklin Covey, (c) clothes for parachutists and pilots for $23,600 from REI, L.L.Bean, Old Navy, and Nordstrom, (d) two reclining rocking chairs with vibrator-massage features from La-Z-Boy Furniture, (e) tractor rentals for $52,500 from Crown Ford, and (f) a dinner party and show for a visiting general including $800 for alcohol from Treasure Island Hotel and Casino for $2,141 (Air Force, GAO-03-292, 2004).

■ Other Air Force findings included a cardholder who purchased $100,000 in helmets by splitting the purchase into four parts to stay within their $25,000 transaction limit. The goods were not needed, but the cardholder wanted to spend the funds before the end of the budget period. The cardholder then returned the items and used the credits to purchase other items. This effectively converted fiscal year 2001 appropriations to a fiscal year 2002 budget authority, which was a violation of appropriation law (Air Force, GAO-03-292, 2004).

■ Department of Homeland Security findings included (a) more than 100 laptops missing and presumed stolen for $300,000, (b) unauthorized use of a card by a vendor to purchase boats for $200,000, (c) more than 20 missing and presumed stolen printers for $84,000, and (d) three Coast Guard laptops missing and presumed stolen for $8,000 (DHS, GAO-06-1117, 2006).

■ Other Department of Homeland Security cases of abuse included the purchase of a beer brewing kit, a 63-inch plasma television set for $8,000, which was found unused in its box six months later, and tens of thousands of dollars for training at golf and tennis resorts (DHS, GAO-06-1117, 2006).

■ The Forest Service also had its share of wasteful purchases that included (a) extravagant digital cameras, (b) premium satellite and cable TV packages including HBO, Cinemax, NFL, and NBA games for their recreation facilities, (c) employee awards, which included hats, mugs, backpacks, and blankets from Warner Brothers, Eddie Bauer, and Mori, Luggage and Gifts, (d) two fish costumes, Frank and Fanny fish, from the Carol Flemming Design Studio at $2,500 each, and 14 high-end PDAs from vendors such as Palm when there were many economical alternatives available (Forest Service, GAO-03-786, 2003).

▪ Housing and Urban Development came in with (a) $27,000 spent at Dillard's, JCPenney, Lord & Taylor, Macy's and Sears, (b) $74,500 spent at Ritz Camera, Sharper Image, Comp USA, and PC Mall, (c) $9,700 spent at Legal Sea Food, Levis Restaurant, Cheesecake Factory, and TGI Fridays, and (d) $8,900 spent at music and audio stores such as Sound Craft Systems, J&Rs Music Store, and Guitar Source (GAO-03-489, 2003).

▪ The FAA audit showed (a) purchases of personal digital assistants, keyboards, and leather cases for $66,700, (b) individual subscriptions to Internet providers for $16,894, (c) store gift cards for $2,300, and (d) retirement and farewell gifts including Waterford crystal, a glass clock, and an engraved statue for $1,200 (GAO-03-405, 2003).

In March 2008 the GAO reported on the use of cards across all government agencies. This report was based on an audit of a sample of card transactions for fiscal 2006. The results were that about 40 percent of all transactions sampled and audited did not meet the basic internal control standards of the purchase being authorized, the goods or service being received, and that a third party vouched for such receipt. Also, for large transactions (more than $2,500) the agencies could not show that these large purchases met the standards of proper authorization, and independent receipt and acceptance.

Table 18.1 shows a select list of fraudulent cases and other acts similar in nature to fraud. One way for a cardholder to avoid a fraud "issue" is to claim that the card was stolen or compromised. The examples indicate that effective monitoring and internal controls are absolutely vital to detect and deter fraud. Table 18.2 lists several improper and abusive charges. Here the goal should be to detect these charges early so as to warn the cardholder against their recurrence. Abusive charges are more difficult to detect because a charge is only abusive because of the circumstances. It might be allowed by company policy for the marketing vice-president of a high-end luxury yacht company to treat a potential customer, or a celebrity endorser, to a lavish meal with alcohol. The same meal enjoyed by a federal government employee, while at a conference, would be abusive. If Live Nation Entertainment hired a chauffeured limousine to drive a professional comedian from the airport to her hotel then this would be an acceptable business charge, whereas it would be extravagant for a federal government employee going to a conference. Some abusive charges are described in Table 18.2.

The improper and abusive purchases listed in Table 18.2 are blatant and therefore not too difficult to detect. There are many other purchasing card fraud cases and an Internet search of "sentenced for purchasing card fraud" will list thousands of hits showing that purchasing card fraud is serious and pervasive.

TABLE 18.1 Fraudulent Acts Discovered during a GAO Purchasing Card Audit (GAO, Report GAO-08-333, 2008)

Activity	Vendor	Agency	Amount	Brief Details
Fraudulent use of convenience checks	None	Forest Service	$642,000	Over a period of six years cardholder wrote 180 checks to a person with whom they lived and shared a bank account.
Potentially fraudulent transaction	CompUSA	Navy	$ 2,200	Cardholder purchased 19 items, of which 18 were lost and presumed stolen.
Compromised account	Tina Nails	NSF	$ 1,800	Card was used to transact purchases at a nail salon. Cardholder disputed transactions when they were brought to their attention.
Fraudulent card use	Online dating and pornography	USPS	$ 1,100	Over a 15-month period a postmaster used the card at online dating and pornographic sites.
Fraudulent charge	Foreign airline	Dept. State	$ 890	Airfare was fraudulently charged to card. Cardholder did not dispute charge until it was brought to their attention.
Fraudulent charges	Various	Dept. State	$ 735	Charges from vendors such as Match.com, Old Navy, and a camera store were charged to card. See above.
Fraudulent claim	Ritz Carlton	GSA	$ 380	GSA purchased breakfasts for 18 conference attendees. Sixteen of these claimed reimbursement for the meal that was already paid for.
Fraudulent charges	Grape and Wine conference	Treasury	$ 280	Cardholder used card to purchase extravagant meals.
Fraudulent claim	Radisson	GSA	$ 150	Five conference attendees claimed reimbursement for meals that were provided at the conference.
Compromised account	Match.com	Army	$ 83	Fraudulent charges appeared on a cardholder's account. Cardholder did not dispute charge until it was brought to their attention.

Abuses such as buying goods from vendors that are quite normal for the cardholder (e.g., Home Depot for someone working in maintenance) and then reselling the goods through an auction site or classified adverts will be very difficult to detect. Also, an issue with the approval of charges is that neither the approver, nor the cardholder gets to see the big picture. Given all the complexities of a card program it is not surprising that there is an association for those employees charged with administering the card programs. This is discussed next.

TABLE 18.2 Examples of Improper and Abusive Purchases (GAO, Report GAO-03-333, 2008)

Activity	Vendor	Agency	Amount	Brief Details
Multiple improper charges	Tire store	Forest Service	$115,000	Superior 24 Hour charged a card 91 times for tire installations that were not performed.
Improper use of convenience checks	Toyota dealer	USDA	$ 80,000	Cardholder purchased 2 Toyota vehicles by check without obtaining a waiver. Circumvented policy by splitting purchase. The convenience check fee was $1,000.
Improper use of card	Brook Bros, Talbot's, Johnston Murphy	DOD	$ 77,700	Four cardholders purchased expensive clothing and accessories for service members.
Violation of agency policy	Relocation services	Dept. Energy	$112,000	Cardholder paid relocation expenses for two employees using convenience checks. Card policy limits checks to $3,000 except for emergencies.
Improper cash advances	Automatic teller machines	Dept. Interior	$ 24,300	Cardholder withdrew $24,300 through cash advances for personal gain.
Purchases in violation of agency policy	Internet merchants	USPS	$ 15,700	USPS officials purchased employee awards such as briefcases, iPods, and music systems. Agency policy prohibited noncash awards larger than $50.
Excessive cost	Ruth's Chris Steakhouse	USPS	$ 13,500	Cardholder charged dinner for 81 people at $160 per person that included steaks, crab, and alcohol.
Excessive cost	Ritz Carlton	FBI	$ 11,000	Cardholder charged conference coffee and light refreshments for 55 people at $50 per day for four days.
Questionable need	Apple Computer	NASA	$ 800	Cardholder purchased two 60 GB iPods claiming that they were needed to store official information. Audit showed that the iPods contained music, photos, and videos.
Questionable need	Seduction Boutique	Dept. State	$ 360	Cardholder purchased women's underwear/lingerie for use during jungle training by trainees of a drug enforcement program.

THE NATIONAL ASSOCIATION OF PURCHASING CARD PROFESSIONALS

The National Association of Purchasing Card Professionals (NAPCP) is an association that provides services and guidance to purchasing card managers. NAPCP provides continuing education and networking through conferences and seminars. The association undertakes and sponsors research in the form of white papers and survey results related to purchasing card matters. They administer the Certified Purchasing Card Professional (CPCP) designation, which requires applicants to pass an exam and to maintain the designation through a process similar to continuing professional education for public accountants and internal auditors. The association's website is www.napcp.org.

The NAPCP regularly polls its members with interesting questions related to purchasing cards. One poll asked members to indicate the percentage of transactions that were audited. The survey defined an audit as an independent review by someone other than the cardholder or the cardholder's manager with or without of the supporting documentation. The results cannot be generalized because the survey was not based on a random sample. Approximately 40 percent of managers said that they audited 100 percent of transactions, about 20 percent of managers audited 25 percent, and about 20 percent of managers audited 10 percent of transactions. The remaining 20 percent of managers were evenly spread across the remaining percentages. The graphical results show a large spike at 100 percent and two medium spikes at 10 percent and 25 percent. The audit rate seems to depend on the organization. Selected written responses are shown here:

- We start with 10 percent and if there are a lot of issues, we increase that percentage.
- We audit 50 different cardholders in detail each month.
- We don't have the personnel available.
- I would like to audit more by using electronic methods. I haven't developed these tests yet.
- Random selection as well as an ad hoc review of out of the ordinary transactions.
- We randomly select the cardholders. We choose new cardholders, cardholders with large monthly purchases, or cardholders that have strange activity of some sort.
- We have about 500,000 transactions annually. We select random departments and random cardholders and all statements are reviewed monthly by managers.
- Because of a lack of resources we do not have a regular audit procedure.
- We have 2,000 cardholders and 130,000 transactions per year. We audit 25 percent and run many high-level reports to look for suspicious activity.
- We look at 2 percent of transactions because of a lack of resources.
- We try to identify risky transactions first and focus on those using this selective approach.
- We go through the cardholder report on a monthly basis looking for split purchases or other issues.

Industry practice varies widely suggesting that the field might be open to the development of Standards of Professional Practice, along the lines of the standards that are applicable to external or internal auditors. The next section shows an example of a purchasing card dashboard.

A FORENSIC ANALYTICS DASHBOARD

The internal auditors of a global technology company recently developed an operational dashboard to continuously monitor their purchasing card data. The project was a joint effort between internal audit and the IT support staff. The goal was to monitor several aspects of the program on a continuous basis. The first page of the dashboard was a high-level overview that shows that the monthly amount spent using the cards was about $8 million. The dashboard was created in Excel and a screen shot is shown in Figure 18.1.

Figure 18.1 shows the summary page of an Excel dashboard. The summary shows the dollar totals and the transaction totals for the preceding six months. Additional statistics regarding plastic cards, strategic cards, and ghost cards are provided. In the lower half of the screen the results are shown graphically. The dashboard shows that plastic cards account for a little more than one-half of the spending. The lower half of the dashboard is shown in Figure 18.2.

The second-level analysis of the purchasing card transactions is shown in Figure 18.2. This analysis deals with the plastic card purchases. The table shows the number of employees with a total monthly spend in each of the six ranges. Not surprisingly, most of the dollars are spent by employees with monthly totals above $5,000. Other worksheets in the dashboard system contain more detailed information including reports of a forensic nature. The dashboard was developed by an internal auditor who had an excellent knowledge of the policies and procedures and also the controls related to the use of the purchasing cards. The data procurement and the analysis tasks were done by IT staff, but the process was under the control of the auditor. The company has had its fair share of past instances of fraud and waste and abuse. The dashboard will be updated monthly within three weeks of the end of the month.

AN EXAMPLE OF PURCHASING CARD DATA

Card data seldom requires extensive data cleansing. The data tables provided by the card issuers include an extensive amount of descriptive data. In Figure 18.3 the transactions were extracted from the company's Oracle accounting system. There were extra fields that were relevant to accounting and other fields that would have been useful that were omitted.

Figure 18.3 shows the Access table of card transactions imported from an Oracle system. Several useful data fields are missing (transaction time and vendor codes) and also several irrelevant rows are included courtesy of double-entry bookkeeping and the

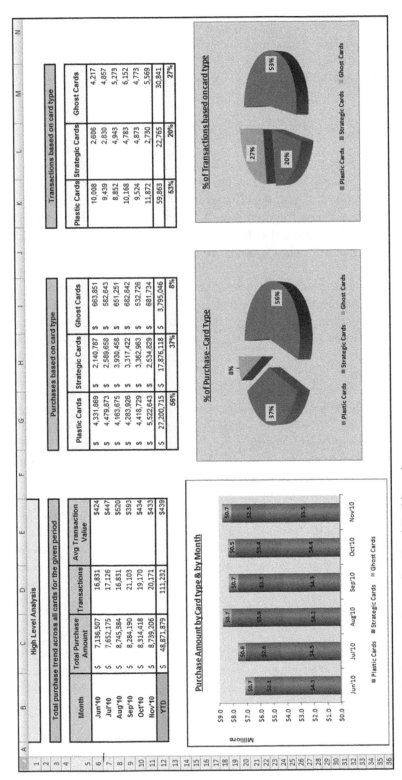

FIGURE 18.1 The Summary Page of an Excel Dashboard

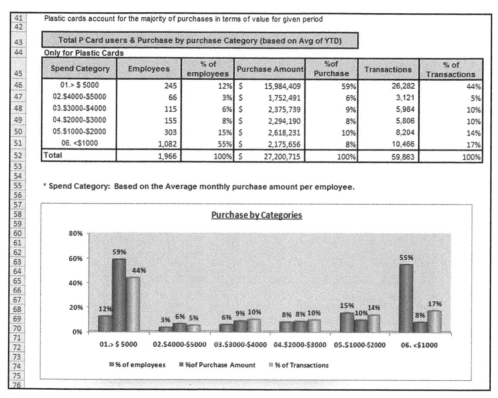

	Spend Category	Employees	% of employees	Purchase Amount	%of Purchase	Transactions	% of Transactions
46	01.> $ 5000	245	12%	$ 15,984,409	59%	26,282	44%
47	02.$4000-$5000	66	3%	$ 1,752,491	6%	3,121	5%
48	03.$3000-$4000	115	6%	$ 2,375,739	9%	5,984	10%
49	04.$2000-$3000	155	8%	$ 2,294,190	8%	5,806	10%
50	05.$1000-$2000	303	15%	$ 2,618,231	10%	8,204	14%
51	06. <$1000	1,082	55%	$ 2,175,656	8%	10,466	17%
52	Total	1,966	100%	$ 27,200,715	100%	59,863	100%

FIGURE 18.2 A Second-Level Analysis in the Excel Dashboard

Oracle system. The first step was to delete all records where *Account* equals 30135 and also where *Debit* equals $0.00. The result was a table with 276,000 card transactions totaling $75,000,000. This data table has no credits and it would seem that the accounting system only enters the net amount of each purchase. Although this table would work adequately for a forensic analysis, the best data source is the full set of transactions in electronic form as prepared by the card issuer.

 ## HIGH-LEVEL DATA OVERVIEW

The data used for the case study is a table of card transactions for a government entity. The entity was the victim of fraud in the prior year and management wanted an analysis of the current transactions to give some assurance that the current year's data was free of further fraud. The focus was on fraud as opposed to waste and abuse. The first test was the data profile and this is shown in Figure 18.4.

The data profile in Figure 18.4 shows that there were approximately 95,000 transactions totaling $39 million. The total should be compared to the payments made to the card issuer. It is puzzling that there are no credits. This might be because there is a field in the data table indicating whether the amount is a debit or credit that was deleted

FIGURE 18.3 A Typical Table Layout of Purchasing Card Data Extracted from an Oracle System

PurchCard2010

ID	Year	Month	Day	Source	Ledger	Legal	Account	Dept	Product	Inter	Debit	Credit	DebitUSD	CreditUSD	LastName	Merchant
1	2010	1	1	2 Procard	4	100	30135	0	0	3	$0.00	$0.00	$118.00	$0.00		
2	2010	1	1	2 Procard	3	100	30135	0	0	4	$118.00	$0.00	$0.00	$0.00		
3	2010	1	1	2 Procard	3	100	21100	40412	0	0	$0.00	$0.00	$118.00	$0.00		
4	2010	1	1	2 Procard	4	100	66184	0	0	0	$48.00	$0.00	$48.00	$0.00		
5	2010	1	1	2 Procard	4	100	30135	0	0	3	$0.00	$0.00	$0.00	$0.00		
6	2010	1	1	2 Procard	3	100	30135	0	0	4	$48.00	$0.00	$48.00	$0.00		
7	2010	1	1	2 Procard	3	100	21100	0	0	0	$0.00	$0.00	$0.00	$0.00		
8	2010	1	1	2 Procard	4	100	62327	40286	0	0	$111.45	$0.00	$111.45	$0.00		
9	2010	1	1	2 Procard	4	100	30135	0	0	3	$0.00	$0.00	$0.00	$0.00		
10	2010	1	1	2 Procard	3	100	30135	0	0	4	$111.45	$0.00	$111.45	$0.00		
11	2010	1	1	2 Procard	3	100	21100	0	0	0	$0.00	$0.00	$0.00	$0.00		
12	2010	1	1	5 Procard	4	100	62507	40548	0	0	$289.88	$0.00	$289.88	$0.00		
13	2010	1	1	5 Procard	4	100	30135	0	0	3	$0.00	$0.00	$0.00	$0.00		
14	2010	1	1	5 Procard	3	100	30135	0	0	4	$289.88	$0.00	$289.88	$0.00		
15	2010	1	1	5 Procard	3	100	21100	0	0	0	$0.00	$0.00	$0.00	$0.00		
16	2010	1	1	5 Procard	4	100	62507	40544	0	0	$19.51	$0.00	$19.51	$0.00		
17	2010	1	1	5 Procard	4	100	30135	0	0	3	$0.00	$0.00	$0.00	$0.00		
18	2010	1	1	5 Procard	3	100	21100	0	0	4	$19.51	$0.00	$19.51	$0.00		
19	2010	1	1	5 Procard	3	100	62507	40341	0	0	$0.00	$0.00	$0.00	$0.00		
20	2010	1	1	5 Procard	4	100	30135	0	0	0	$72.75	$0.00	$72.75	$0.00		
21	2010	1	1	5 Procard	4	100	30135	0	0	3	$0.00	$0.00	$0.00	$0.00		
22	2010	1	1	5 Procard	3	100	21100	0	0	4	$72.75	$0.00	$72.75	$0.00		
23	2010	1	1	5 Procard	3	100	62507	40341	0	0	$0.00	$0.00	$0.00	$0.00		
24	2010	1	1	5 Procard	4	100	30135	0	0	0	$41.60	$0.00	$41.60	$0.00		
25	2010	1	1	5 Procard	4	100	30135	0	0	3	$0.00	$0.00		$0.00		

Record: 1 of 944156 No Filter Search

▲	A	B	C	D	E	F	G	H	I	J
1						DATA PROFILE				
2										
3	Details			Count		% of Total		$		% of Total
4	Amounts	10.00 and over		81,842		86.08		$38,976,906		99.84
5	Amounts	0.01 to 9.99		13,234		13.92		60,516		0.16
6	Amounts	equal to zero		0		0.00		0.00		0.00
7	Amounts	-0.01 to -9.99		0		0.00		0.00		0.00
8	Amounts	-10.00 and under		0		0.00		0.00		0.00
9				--------------		--------------		--------------------		--------------
10				95,076		100.00		$39,037,422		100.00
11				=========		=========		=============		=========
12										
13	Low-value Amounts									
14	Amounts	0.01 to 50.00		29,469		31.00		$516,653		1.32
15				=========		=========		=============		=========
16										
17	High-value Amounts									
18	Amounts	100,000 and higher		1		0.00		$3,102,000		7.95
19				=========		=========		=============		=========

FIGURE 18.4 The Data Profile for the Card Purchases

before the analysis. It might also signal that cardholders are not too interested in getting credits where credits are due. The data profile also shows that about one-third of the charges are for amounts of $50.00 and under. Card programs are there to make it easy for employees to pay for small business expenses. The data profile shows one large invoice for $3,102,000. The review showed that this amount was actually in Mexican pesos making the transaction worth about $250,000. This transaction was investigated and was a special circumstance where the Mexican vendor needed to be paid with a credit card. This finding showed that the *Amount* field was in the source currency and not in U.S. dollars. Another query showed that very few other transactions were in other currencies and so the *Amount* field was still used "as is." There were some Canadian transactions in Canadian dollars but this was not expected to influence the results in any meaningful way. The second high-level overview was a periodic graph. This graph is shown in Figure 18.5.

Because the "$3,102,000" purchase was an abnormal event, this number was excluded from this graph. The graph shows that August and September had the largest transaction totals. The entity's fiscal year ends on September 30th. The August/September spike might be the result of employees making sure that they are spending money that is "in the budget." The average monthly total is $3 million. The two spikes averaged $4.2 million, which is a significant amount of money. An earlier example of abuse was a cardholder buying unnecessary helmets in one fiscal year, only to return them the next fiscal year and then to use the funds for other purchases. The transactions for 2011 should be reviewed for this type of scheme. In another card analysis a utility company found that it had excessive purchases in December, right around the festive season. This suggested that cardholders might be buying personal items with their corporate cards.

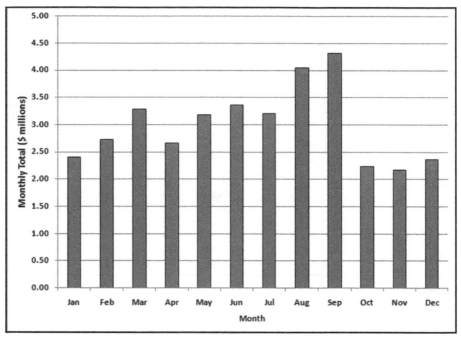

FIGURE 18.5 The Monthly Totals for Card Purchases

The data profile and the periodic graph are high-level tests that are well-suited to purchasing cards. The high-level overview could also include a comparative analysis of the descriptive statistics which would use the data for two consecutive years.

 ## THE FIRST-ORDER TEST

The Benford's Law tests work well on card transactions. It would seem that the upper limit of $2,500 on card purchases would make the test invalid, but this is not the case because most of the purchases are below $1,000 and the $1,000-plus strata is dwarfed by the under $1,000 purchases. Also, the $2,500 limit can be breached if the purchase is authorized. The purchase might also be in another currency and the analysis can be run on the "transaction currency" as opposed to the amounts after converting to USD. The first-order test results are shown in Figure 18.6.

The first-order results in the first panel of Figure 18.6 show a large spike at 36. A review of the number duplication results (by peeking ahead) shows a count of 5,903 amounts in the $3.60 to $3.69 range. These transactions were almost all for FedEx charges and it seems that FedEx was used as the default mail carrier for all documents larger than a standard first class envelope. Although this was presumably not fraud it might be wasteful because USPS first class mail is cheaper for small documents. It is also noteworthy that a government agency would prefer a private carrier over the USPS. The test was run on all purchases of $10 and higher and the results are shown in the second panel of Figure 18.6.

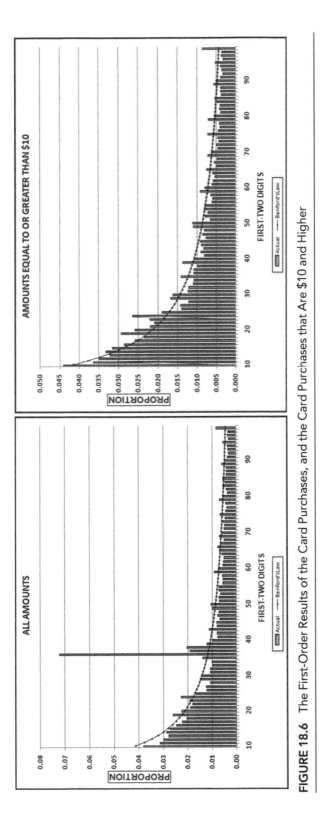

FIGURE 18.6 The First-Order Results of the Card Purchases, and the Card Purchases that Are $10 and Higher

The first-order test in the second panel in Figure 18.6 shows a reasonably good fit to Benford's Law. The MAD is 0.0015, which gives an *acceptable conformity* conclusion. There is, however, a large spike at 24, which is the largest spike on the graph. Also, there is a relatively large spike at 99 in that the actual proportion is about double the expected proportion. The spike at 24 exists because card users are buying with great gusto for amounts that are just less than the maximum allowed for the card. The first-order test allows us to conclude that there are excessive purchases in this range because we can compare the actual to an expected proportion. The number duplication test will look at the "24" purchases in some more detail. The "99" purchases showed many payments for seminars delivered over the Internet (webinars) and it seemed reasonable that the seminars would be priced just below a psychological boundary. There were also purchases of computer and electronic goods priced at just under $100. This pricing pattern is normal for the computer and electronics industry. The purchases also included a payment to a camera store for $999.95. This might be an abusive purchase. The procurement rules state that a lower priced good should be purchased when it will perform essentially the same task as an expensive item. The camera purchase was made in August, which was in the two-month window preceding the end of the fiscal year.

THE SUMMATION TEST

The summation sums all the amounts with first-two digits 10, 11, 12, . . . , 99. The test identifies amounts with the same first-two digits that are large relative to the rest of the population. The results so far have highlighted the large 3.102 million transaction, and the fact that there is an excess of transactions just below the $2,500 threshold. The summation graph is shown in Figure 18.7.

The summation test in Figure 18.7 shows that there is a single record, or a group of records with the same first-two digits, that are large when compared to the other numbers. The spike is at 31. An Access query was used to select all the 31 records and to sort the results by *Amount* descending. The query identified the transaction for 3,102,000 pesos.

The summation test was run on the *Amounts* greater than or equal to $10. The summation test could be run on all the positive amounts in a data set. The expected sum for each digit combination was $433,077 ($38,976,906/90). The 24 sum is $2.456 million. The difference is about $2 million. The drill-down query showed that there were eight transactions for about $24,500 and about 850 transactions for about $2,450 each summing to about $2,250,000. There is a large group of numbers that are relatively large and that have first-two digits of 25 in common. So, not only is the spike on the first-order graph significant, but the transactions are for large dollar amounts.

THE LAST-TWO DIGITS TEST

The last-two digits test is usually only run as a test for number invention. The number invention tests are usually not run on accounts payable data or other types of payments

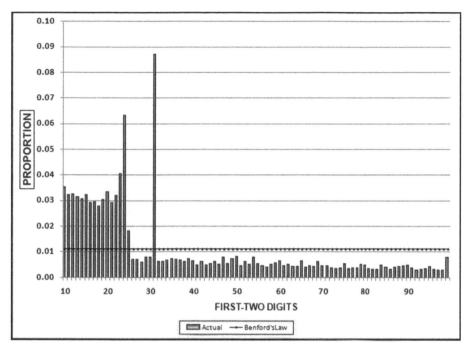

FIGURE 18.7   The Results of the Summation Test Applied to the Card Data

data because any odd last-two digits results will be noticeable from the number duplication test. For purchase amounts this test will usually simply show that many numbers end with "00." This should also be evident from the number duplication test. The results are shown in Figure 18.8.

The result of the last-two digits test is shown in Figure 18.8. There is a large spike at 00, which is as expected. The 00 occurs in amounts such as $10.00 or $25.00. An interesting finding is the spike at 95. This was the result of 2,600 transactions with the cents amounts equal to 95 cents, as in $99.95.

The last-two digits test was run on the numbers equal to or larger than $10. If the test was run on all the amounts there would have been large spikes at 62 and 67 from the FedEx charges for $3.62 and $3.67. The large spike in the left graph of Figure 18.6 was for amounts of $3.62 and $3.67, which have last-two digits of 62 and 67 respectively. The 62 and 67 spikes are there not because of fraud but rather because of the abnormal duplications of one specific type of transaction.

 THE SECOND-ORDER TEST

The second-order test looks at the relationships and patterns found in data and is based on the digits of the differences between amounts that have been sorted from smallest to largest (ordered). These digit patterns are expected to closely approximate the expected frequencies of Benford's Law. The second-order test gives few, if any, false positives in

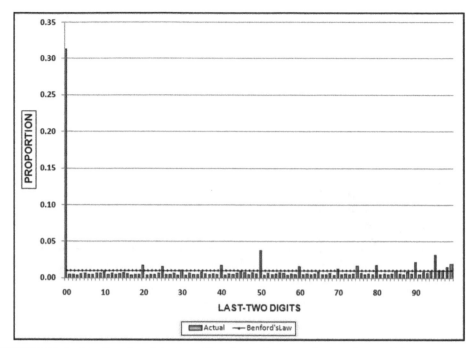

FIGURE 18.8 The Results of the Last-Two Digits Test Applied to the Card Data

that if the results are not as expected (close to Benford's Law), then the data do have some characteristic that is rare and unusual, abnormal, or irregular. The second-order results are shown in Figure 18.9.

The graph has a series of prime spikes (10, 20, . . . , 90) that have a Benford-like pattern and a second serious of minor spikes (11–19, 21–29, ...) that follow another Benford-like pattern. The prime spikes are large. These results are as expected for a large data set with numbers that are tightly clustered in a small ($1 to $2,500) range. The second-order test does not indicate any anomaly here and this test usually does not indicate any anomaly except in rare highly anomalous situations.

 THE NUMBER DUPLICATION TEST

The number duplication test analyzes the frequencies of the numbers in a data set. This test shows which numbers were causing the spikes in the first-order test. This test has had good results when run against bank account numbers and the test has also been used with varying levels of success on inventory counts, temperature readings, health-care claims, airline ticket refunds, airline flight liquor sales, electricity meter readings, and election counts. The results are shown in Figure 18.10.

The number duplication results in Figure 18.10 show four amounts below $4.00 in the first four positions. A review showed that 99.9 percent of these amounts were for FedEx charges. The charges might be wasteful, but they were presumably not

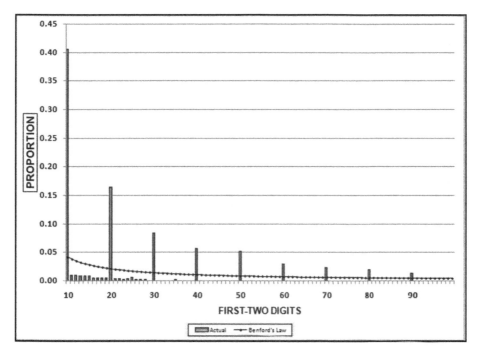

FIGURE 18.9 The Second-Order Results of the Card Purchases Amounts

fraudulent. A second number duplication test was run on the numbers below $2,500. This would give some indication as to how "creative" the cardholders were when trying to keep at or below the $2,500 maximum allowed. Purchases could exceed $2,500 if authorized. The "just below $2,500" table is shown in Figure 18.11.

The $2,495 to $2,500 transactions in Figure 18.11 show some interesting patterns. The large count of "at the money" purchases of $2,500 shows that this

qryNumberDuplication	
Amount	Frequency
$3.62	4283
$3.67	1620
$3.74	913
$3.80	827
$4.37	378
$3.85	271
$100.00	252
$75.00	242
$6.62	219
$19.95	209
$150.00	208
$50.00	205
$99.00	200

FIGURE 18.10 The Results of the Number Duplication Test

qryNumberDuplication	
Amount ▾	Frequency ▾
$2,500.00	157
$2,499.99	5
$2,499.97	3
$2,499.96	1
$2,499.95	2
$2,499.90	1
$2,499.89	1
$2,499.83	1
$2,499.80	1
$2,499.61	1
$2,499.57	1
$2,499.50	2
$2,499.45	2
$2,499.25	1
$2,499.15	1
$2,499.12	1
$2,499.10	1
$2,499.05	1
$2,499.00	42
$2,498.99	1
$2,498.96	1
$2,498.93	1
$2,498.88	1
$2,498.40	1
$2,498.35	1
$2,498.00	8

$2,497.90	1
$2,497.50	1
$2,497.25	1
$2,497.04	8
$2,497.00	5
$2,496.95	1
$2,496.90	1
$2,496.74	1
$2,496.72	1
$2,496.71	1
$2,496.50	1
$2,496.29	1
$2,496.00	10
$2,495.85	1
$2,495.70	1
$2,495.56	1
$2,495.53	1
$2,495.48	1
$2,495.28	1
$2,495.00	26

FIGURE 18.11 The Purchase Amounts in the $2,495 to $2,500 Range

number has some real financial implications. Either suppliers are marginally reducing their prices so that the bill can be paid easily and quickly, or some other factors are at play. Another possible reason is that cardholders are splitting their purchases and the excessive count of $2,500 transactions includes partial payments for other larger purchases. Card transaction audits should select the $2,500 transactions for scrutiny. Also of interest in Figure 18.11 is the set of five transactions for exactly $2,499.99 and the 42 transactions for exactly $2,499.00. There are also 21 other transactions in the $2,499.04 to $2,499.97 range. It is surprising that people think that they are the only ones that might be gaming the system. The review of the eight transactions of $2,497.04 showed that these were all items purchased from GSA Global Supply, a purchasing program administered by the General Services Administration. It seems that even the federal government itself takes the card limit into account when setting prices.

 THE LARGEST SUBSETS TEST

The largest subsets test uses two fields in the data table and tabulates the largest subsets (or groups). The subsets could be vendors, employees, bank account holders, customer refunds, qryLargestMerchants

MerchantName	TotalPurchases
"Name Deleted"	$3,102,000.00
DELL MARKETING L.P.	$1,177,917.91
CDW*GOVERNMENT INC	$626,706.02
MWI*MICRO WAREHOUSE	$532,226.56
SIGMA-ALDRICH	$456,323.25
FISHER SCI ATL	$423,066.00
PC *PC CONNECTION	$338,642.84
GTSI	$336,838.87
BUY.COM	$296,840.49
FISHER SCI CHI	$282,798.32
VWR SCIENTIFIC PROD VCTS	$280,646.01
AMC SYSTEMS	$260,964.06
GOVERNMENT SCIENTIFIC SOU	$229,573.27
STAPLES #941	$227,150.45
C & C PRODUCT SERVICES	$213,380.54
GSA-FSS-ADV	$204,478.69

FIGURE 18.12 The Largest Merchants for Card Purchases in 2010

or shipping charges per vendor. This test has produced some valuable findings, despite the fact that it is neither complex nor difficult to program. The test can be run in Excel using pivot tables or it can be run in Access using a **Group By** query. With purchasing cards the subset variable could be cardholders, vendors, dates (a monthly or daily graph of purchases), vendor codes, vendor zip codes, or cardholder by type of purchase (convenience checks or gift cards).

The merchants with purchases of $200,000 or more for 2010 are listed in Figure 18.12. The name of the Mexican vendor for 3,102,000 MXN has been deleted. The largest merchants are all suppliers of technology, scientific, or other business-related products. Some vendors, such as Buy.com also sell items that could be for home use. Internet purchases of home items are easier to detect because the electronic records are reasonably easily accessible. In another analysis of purchasing card transactions the purchasing vice president looked at their equivalent of Figure 18.12 and remarked that there was a vendor on the largest subsets list for $31,000 that was a "hole in the wall restaurant next to the manufacturing plant." Company employees would have no reason to charge any meals in that restaurant as valid business expenses. Fraud and abuse is therefore not confined to merchants at the top of this list but that a careful look at all the vendors above $10,000 should be done by someone with institutional knowledge.

The total annual dollars for each card is shown in Figure 18.13. The table shows cards with dollar totals above $200,000. This report should be more detailed by adding the cardholder's names and perhaps some other details (department or job description) to assess the amounts for reasonableness. The second largest amount of $1.433 million should be carefully reviewed. The program had 1,634 active cards and if the total dollars per card (of which the largest amounts are shown above) are tested against Benford's Law then the card totals have a MAD of 0.00219. This result implies marginally

qryLargestSpenders	
CardNumber	TotalPurchases
5142134797	$3,131,023.52
5142189945	$1,433,899.98
5142184598	$425,329.72
5142121593	$288,286.81
5142223373	$270,988.96
5142260984	$270,796.18
5142189108	$243,921.34
5142289546	$242,465.38
5142257356	$234,820.96
5142183210	$228,697.43
5142234471	$220,283.78
5142176897	$218,244.15
5142182128	$214,165.61

FIGURE 18.13: The Total Dollars for the Individual Cards for 2010

acceptable conformity. For this test the auditors would need to know the cardholders and their jobs and responsibilities to assess these numbers for reasonableness. In another analysis the vice president of purchasing saw an amount of $650,000 for a cardholder and immediately recognized that the cardholder was the person that paid the company's cell phone bills by credit card.

THE SAME-SAME-SAME TEST

The same-same-same duplications test does not usually have any interesting findings because most payment systems have ways to detect and prevent accidental duplicate payments. This uncomplicated test has shown many interesting results when applied to card transactions. The test was set up to identify (a) *same* cards, (b) *same* dates, (c) *same* merchants, and (d) *same* amounts and the results are shown in Figure 18.14.

The rightmost field is the count and most cases were for two identical purchases. The exceptions were one case of three identical purchases, two cases of four identical purchases, and one case of six identical purchases. The two largest purchases (for $23,130 and $24,845) would merit special attention because they not only exceed the card limit, but they are close to the limit for convenience checks. Also of special interest would be the purchase labeled "Retail Debit Adjustment." The initial review showed that the four hotel payments for $2,500 were a $10,000 deposit (to secure a conference venue) split into four payments of $2,500. There were 786 duplicates on the report after limiting the output to dollar amounts greater than $100.

THE SAME-SAME-DIFFERENT TEST

It would seem that this test would give few, if any, results. The test was run to identify (a) *different* cards, (b) *same* dates, (c) *same* merchants, and (d) *same* amounts. The test

CardNumber	Date	MerchantName	Amount	PurchaseCount
5142189945	12/28/2010	GE REUTER-STOKES, INC	$24,845.00	2
5142189945	9/18/2010	DELL MARKETING L.P.	$23,130.00	2
5142121593	12/22/2010	DELL MARKETING L.P.	$6,296.00	2
5142288601	9/11/2010	CHEM-TECH CONSULTING GR	$3,144.00	2
5142189945	5/10/2010	LYNDE-ORDWAY CO, INC.	$3,115.00	2
5142117663	8/18/2010	INORGANIC VENTURES INC	$2,542.68	2
5142123687	10/13/2010	RETAIL DEBIT ADJUSTMENT	$2,500.00	2
5142131721	5/11/2010	FBM COMPUTER & OFFICE SU	$2,500.00	2
5142149042	3/13/2010	CROWN PLAZA HOTEL	$2,500.00	4
5142153646	3/22/2010	INFORMATION MAPPING	$2,500.00	4
5142251068	4/11/2010	COLE INDUSTRIAL INC	$2,500.00	2
5142251068	4/24/2010	COLE INDUSTRIAL INC	$2,500.00	2
5142257356	2/28/2010	BFS SOLUTIONS	$2,500.00	2
5142122592	8/3/2010	PC *PC CONNECTION FED	$2,499.00	2
5142205500	4/5/2010	MICRON GOVERNMENT SYSTE	$2,499.00	2
5142196337	7/22/2010	MWI*MICRO WAREHOUSE	$2,494.90	2
5142221788	9/12/2010	DELL MARKETING L.P.	$2,494.00	2
5142289869	6/7/2010	LABSOURCE INC	$2,492.00	3
5142196337	2/16/2010	DELL MARKETING L.P.	$2,490.00	2
5142278415	11/15/2010	COMBINED DIGITAL	$2,485.00	6

FIGURE 18.14 Cases of Identical Purchases on the Same Dates by the Same Cardholder

provided some remarkable results in another application when it showed many cases where purchases were split between two different employees (usually a manager and their subordinate) to avoid detection with a simple same-same-same test.

Amount	Date	MerchantName	CardNumber	ID
$3,040.00	5/11/2010	STORK SWL INC	5142288601	88380
$3,040.00	5/11/2010	STORK SWL INC	5142181708	36585
$2,500.00	9/18/2010	CAVINS	5142211180	54064
$2,500.00	9/18/2010	CAVINS	5142204798	52134
$2,500.00	8/9/2010	SANS/NETWORK SCRTY	5142152700	24910
$2,500.00	8/9/2010	SANS/NETWORK SCRTY	5142146548	18596
$2,500.00	7/20/2010	ENVIRONMENTAL SAFETY PROF	5142213087	54807
$2,500.00	7/20/2010	ENVIRONMENTAL SAFETY PROF	5142195081	46923
$2,499.00	12/10/2010	DELL MARKETING, L.P.	5142150217	23057
$2,499.00	12/10/2010	DELL MARKETING, L.P.	5142144478	17624
$2,499.00	3/1/2010	PC *PC CONNECTION	5142127070	6716
$2,499.00	3/1/2010	PC *PC CONNECTION	5142122592	3394
$2,490.00	3/29/2010	AMC SYSTEMS	5142151962	23737
$2,490.00	3/29/2010	AMC SYSTEMS	5142123514	4056
$2,475.00	6/8/2010	SENTINEL, INC.	5142289665	88812
$2,475.00	6/8/2010	SENTINEL, INC.	5142288601	88388
$2,453.84	9/29/2010	FRANK PARSON PAPER CO INC	5142152700	24931
$2,453.84	9/29/2010	FRANK PARSON PAPER CO INC	5142147836	19433

FIGURE 18.15 The Largest Cases of Identical Purchases Made on Different Cards

The same-same-different results are shown in Figure 18.15. Each match is shown on two lines because there are two different card numbers. Each match has the same amount, date, and merchant, but different card numbers. The near-duplicates could be coincidences and they could also be cleverly split purchases. Split purchases are a willful circumvention of internal controls, and a split purchase might just be a red flag for other fraudulent or wasteful or abusive acts. The transactions above are all interesting and the most interesting near duplicate is the last match because it occurred one day before the end of the federal fiscal year-end, and it is the type of purchase (paper products) that cardholders might use to spend "what's in the budget."

THE RELATIVE SIZE FACTOR TEST

The relative size factor (RSF) test uses the ratio of the largest amount divided by the second largest amount. This test has had valuable findings in many areas including accounts payable amounts and health care payments. Experience has shown that the findings in a purchasing card environment are limited. Even with limited findings, the test is still recommended for inclusion in the set of forensic analytic tests for purchasing card data.

The relative size factor results are shown in Figure 18.16. The results are not very interesting, but the full table should be looked at with a skeptical eye. For this application there were 6,642 merchants. The list could be pruned to 3,300 records by only listing the merchants where the maximum exceeded (say) $500. The most interesting records in Figure 18.16 are the Rampy Chevrolet purchase because auto expenses were prohibited expenses, and the FedEx payment for $1,801.14 because this was a very large amount to pay to FedEx. The payment might be employee relocation costs, which were prohibited under the card rules.

qryRelativeSizeFactor11b				
Merchant Name ▾	LargestAmount ▾	SecondLargest ▾	CountForMerchant ▾	RelativeSizeFactor ▾
LIBERTEL ASSOCIATES	$2,474.03	$2.41	2	1026.57
RAMPY CHEVROLET NISS	$2,430.57	$4.06	2	598.66
PLATT ELECTRIC 0026	$2,087.06	$3.64	2	573.37
MICRON GOVERNMENT	$2,499.00	$6.66	2	375.23
FEDEX SHP 11/23/10 AB#	$1,801.14	$8.31	21	216.74
ONSET COMP SHIPPING,	$2,441.00	$12.00	2	203.42
THE ASPEN INSTITUTE	$2,370.00	$12.00	2	197.50
RYDER WOBURN STRG D	$869.65	$5.25	2	165.65
HOTEL MONACO-SEATTL	$2,208.13	$14.75	2	149.70
AIRLIE FOUNDATION	$875.00	$7.67	2	114.08
EMBASSY SUITES 6323	$850.00	$8.55	2	99.42
BIOELECTROMAGNETICS	$554.40	$5.60	2	99.00

FIGURE 18.16 The Results of the Relative Size Factor Test

CONCLUSIONS WITH RESPECT TO CARD PURCHASES

The forensic analytic tests run on the card data would fit in well with a continuous monitoring program. The data format would stay the same from period to period and these tests would show valuable results. The test interval could differ among the various tests. The data profile, the periodic graph, the digit-based tests, and the relative size factor test could be run quarterly. These high-level tests work best with a longer time interval. The number duplication test, the largest merchants, and the largest card spenders could be run monthly. Finally, the same-same-same and same-same-different tests could be run every week to quickly discover anomalies such as purchase splitting.

The analytic tests are efficient and effective at detecting large errors and anomalies and large changes in behavior (where a small spender suddenly becomes a large spender). The tests are not very effective at detecting waste and abuse. The tests cannot identify that a $125 limo ride from the airport to a hotel was wasteful. This would require a close scrutiny of the largest vendors report and the ability to see possible waste when XYZ Limo Service appears on the report. Other tests to detect waste and abuse would be to search for specific vendors or vendor codes that might indicate issues. For example, Best Buy sells a range of products that are aimed at people rather than government agencies. A review of the Best Buy purchases might therefore yield some results. The test could extract all purchases where the vendor's name is like "Best Buy." The results sorted by dollars descending are shown in Figure 18.17.

The Best Buy card purchases are shown in Figure 18.17. The dollar amounts suggest that sales tax was not paid on many of the purchases. Even if a cardholder later reimburses the agency for the purchases, they would have evaded sales tax by using a government purchase card. The $1,749.99 purchases would be of interest to a forensic investigator. These purchases were made just before the end of the fiscal year and the three purchases were made using only two cards.

Other more sophisticated tests could also be used. For example, we could look for split purchases where we have the same merchant, same date, different cards, and *different* amounts. This differs from the earlier tests where we assumed that the split purchase would be split equally between the two different cardholders. This query would be more complex than the usual same-same-different query. Another test would be to use the largest growth test to identify cardholders with large increases from 2010 to 2011.

The fraud triangle is made up of (1) pressure, (2) opportunity, and (3) rationalization. Without an opportunity the other two components (pressure and rationalization) may exist in vast quantities and there would still be no fraud because the individual would not be able to commit a fraud without opportunity. Purchasing cards give individuals with pressure and rationalization the means (the opportunity) with which to commit fraud. Management that are aware of the relationship among the three components will have an effective and efficient fraud, waste, and abuse program in place to detect and deter employees from making illicit use of their opportunities.

Card	Date	MerchantName	MerchantZip	Amount
5142236765	11/18/2010	BEST BUY 00000976		$2,410.00
5142119607	6/10/2010	BEST BUY 00002105	80123	$2,349.98
5142197614	9/28/2010	BEST BUY 00002998	27612	$2,249.98
5142237805	11/10/2010	BEST BUY 00000976		$2,070.00
5142211809	8/18/2010	BEST BUY 00002998	27612	$1,999.99
5142159706	2/3/2010	BEST BUY 00005116	30622	$1,968.89
5142267106	6/14/2010	BEST BUY 00000430	55811	$1,819.96
5142199302	9/28/2010	BEST BUY 00002998	27612	$1,749.99
5142199302	9/27/2010	BEST BUY 00001602	27707	$1,749.99
5142197614	9/27/2010	BEST BUY 00001602	27707	$1,749.99
5142207493	8/24/2010	BEST BUY 00001602	27707	$1,734.82
5142180307	8/18/2010	BEST BUY 00002774	66211	$1,695.75
5142267106	6/15/2010	BEST BUY 00000430	55811	$1,609.97
5142207493	8/7/2010	BEST BUY 00001602	27707	$1,607.23
5142207493	8/31/2010	BEST BUY 00001602	27707	$1,477.62
5142207493	1/7/2010	BEST BUY 00001602	27707	$1,401.68
5142158945	2/24/2010	BEST BUY 00005116	30622	$1,399.93
5142297011	6/15/2010	BEST BUY 00002998	27612	$1,349.98
5142207493	8/17/2010	BEST BUY 00001602	27707	$1,327.03
5142202304	9/29/2010	BEST BUY 00001602	27707	$1,273.79
5142260984	12/21/2010	BEST BUY 00002691	22150	$1,134.89
5142260984	12/29/2010	BEST BUY 00002691	22150	$1,074.90
5142211809	5/18/2010	BEST BUY 00002998	27612	$1,049.87
5142297011	7/26/2010	BEST BUY 00002998	27612	$1,029.97
5142276356	12/6/2010	BEST BUY 00004267	30519	$959.94

Record: I◄ ◄ 1 of 210 ► ►I ► No Filter Search

FIGURE 18.17 A Series of Best Buy Card Purchases

A NOTE ON MICROSOFT OFFICE

The Office suite allows forensic analytics to be carried out on data tables large enough for most uses. Excel is limited by the row count of 1,048,576 rows and the memory limitations of personal computers while Access is limited to databases up to 2GB in size. These two products are adequate for most forensic applications. It is problematic to continually add new data to Excel worksheets and to add new reports and new functionalities down the road, but it is easy enough for most people to use and is a firm favorite among forensic investigators. In Excel it is difficult to distinguish between data, formulas, and the results of formulas, whereas Access has all of these components neatly compartmentalized. Excel has some advanced reporting features and references to Excel dashboards have become more and more commonplace.

A longtime issue with the digit-based tests is because of the computer's use of floating point arithmetic. In general, 9 is close enough to 8.9999999999999999 for most purposes except for taking the first digit, which is 9 in the first case and 8 in the second case. Data analysts should be aware of this issue and should program accordingly when using any data analysis program mentioned in the book and also any others such as SAS or SPSS.

The size restrictions of Excel and Access can be overcome with the use of more specialized auditing software such as IDEA (www.caseware.com/products/idea). IDEA tables and databases are only limited in size by the user's memory and processing speed. IDEA also has a number of the tests referred to in the book (e.g., correlation, time-series, the summation test, and the second-order test) built in as preprogrammed routines.

The combination of PowerPoint and Word contain many powerful features that make them highly effective for the preparation and presentation of forensic reports. Many aspects of a forensic presentation are important, including the actual content, the color schemes used, the ability to copy from Word and Excel, the ability to copy images to the presentation, and the use or misuse of animations. PowerPoint also acts as a distraction and presenters should work to make themselves, as opposed to their slides, the center of attraction.

Several contenders are coming forward to challenge the dominance of the Office suite. These include Google Docs (http://docs.google.com) and OpenOffice (www .openoffice.org). At the time of writing these two suites lack the processing power and the broad range of functions of the Office suite. The Office suite has many tools that lend themselves to forensic analytics and the ability to send data, document, and presentation files to almost anyone else is a very important consideration.

A NOTE ON THE FORENSIC ANALYTIC TESTS

The book reviewed a series of forensic analytic tests in Chapters 4 through 16. Benford's Law forms the theoretical basis of the tests. Benford's Law dates back to 1938 and sets out the expected patterns of the digits in tabulated data. The four main Benford-related tests are the first-two digits test, the summation test, the second-order test, and the last-two digits test. These tests, together with the high-level data overview and the number duplication tests, make up the Nigrini Cycle and it seems that these tests should be applicable to almost every data analysis project.

Several tests are geared toward identifying abnormal duplications. These tests are the largest subsets test and the tests that identify the same-same-same and same-same-different conditions. The tests that use some advanced statistical methods include the relative size factor test, correlation, and time-series analysis. Chapters 15 and 16 showed examples of risk scoring where forensic units are scored for fraud risk.

The tests described in this book range from being quite straightforward to being reasonably complex. The suite of tests is both efficient and effective at detecting many types of fraud, errors, biases, and other anomalies. New tests are currently being developed. One new test that is close to completion is a test to assess by how much a set of numbers has changed from one period to the next. This test will allow an analyst to conclude that the financial statements for fiscal 2011 differ from the 2010 statements by a magnitude of x. The belief is that large changes signal large changes in conditions and could be red flags for errors or fraud. Another test under development assesses by how much a transaction differs from the normal transactions in the data table. The belief again is that it is the high-risk transactions that stand out from the crowd. The tests in the domain of forensic analytics are continually evolving and with the passage of time new tests will be added to the arsenal and perhaps even replace some of the older tests that might be losing some steam in the detection and deterrence of fraud.

The increase in computing power over the past 20 years has made it possible to run complex queries on large data tables. These tests are now not only possible on a personal computer but can be done reasonably inexpensively. This has allowed auditors and investigators to become much more efficient and effective at detecting data issues. These tests can play an active and useful role as detective controls that detect errors or incidents that bypassed the preventative controls.

 ## CONCLUSION

Fraud is here to stay. The only really surprising fact is that people are still surprised by the discovery of fraud. The financial press and the popular press regularly report on the largest cases. It seems that when people are given the opportunity to commit fraud, many do indeed commit fraud. A few general comments are listed below:

- Forensic analytics is only one part of the forensic investigations process. An entire investigation cannot be completed with the computer alone. The investigation would usually include a review of paper documents, interviews, reports and presentations, and concluding actions.
- It is best to collect and analyze the data at the start of the investigation, and long before the suspect suspects that an investigation is underway. In a proactive fraud detection project the data is automatically analyzed before the suspect has any wind of an investigation.
- Incomplete and inaccurate data might give rise to incorrect and incomplete insights. Data should be checked for completeness and accuracy before being analyzed.
- The data should preferably be analyzed together with a subject-matter expert. Such a person would know company policies and procedures and would prevent valuable hours being wasted by investigating apparent anomalies. For example, the rules, policies, and procedures related to airline baggage claims, and frequent-flyer mileage programs are numerous. What may seem to be an anomaly can often be explained by the subject matter expert. Without a subject matter expert the analysis of something as complex as trader's mark-to-market activities is nearly impossible.
- The legal environment should be in the forefront of the investigator's mind in any forensic investigation. The evidence obtained should meet the standard for admissible evidence. The legal environment is especially complex when dealing with data that spans national boundaries.

Forensic analytics is the analysis of a large number of records to identify signs of fraud, errors, and biases. This is far more efficient than combing through documents.

The analysis usually starts with an investigation question or with a mission to proactively look for signs of fraud or errors. The GAO studies reviewed at the start of this chapter were proactive investigations where the auditors went looking for waste and abuse without having a specific suspect in mind.

The first analytics-related task is to identify the data that is easily available. The next task is to identify the additional skills available to the forensic investigator (besides their own abilities). The next consideration is how the forensic analytics phase fits into the investigation as a whole. In a proactive fraud investigation the investigator might want access to the employee master file, payroll data, the vendor master file, the customer master file, cash disbursements, check registers, customer invoices, vendor invoices, and general ledger detail. The investigator should not be surprised if managers along the way simply refuse to provide the data requested. It is quite normal for a marketing manager to refuse to supply customer data, a human resources manager to refuse to supply employee data, and a coupon payments manager to refuse to supply systems data related to access to their payments system. Another important point is that investigators should limit their requests to only relevant data and should take into account the demands usually placed on IT staff. It is usually best to request data in a format that is easy for IT personnel to supply and then for the investigator to do some data-cleansing work before the analysis can proceed, than to ask IT to take time getting the format perfect.

Certain technical skills are expected from forensic investigators. These technical skills include accounting skills, information technology skills, reporting skills, and a healthy dose of patience. A forensic analytics project is an iterative process. If an analysis of card payments shows significant gift card purchases then this might signal a significant type of fraud and abuse. Drilling deeper and deeper into those purchases would be warranted. The investigator might then discover that these cards can easily be sold on Internet auction sites and that might lead to the next step of trying to try to find employees listed as sellers on Internet auction sites.

Forensic analytics is an evolving subdiscipline of forensic accounting. Changes in fraudulent behavior, software upgrades and enhancements, changes in the way that data is accumulated and stored, and changes in priorities will all call for changes in the forensic analytics landscape by way of new and improved detection techniques. There is also a changing corporate environment with managers and directors becoming more aware of the risks of fraud and their ever-increasing obligations to deter, to detect, and to combat corporate fraud. Managers are becoming aware that the costs are not just financial, but also reputational, too. As the world becomes more global, so the ability to conduct fraud across national boundaries increases. These changes make the science of forensic analytics both interesting and in-demand. These changes not only require forensic practitioners to keep up with trends and techniques through publications, training, and conferences, but they also require practitioners to be willing and able to share their successes and best practices with others in the field. This concluding sentence is not the end of the road, but rather the beginning of the trip with exciting findings, an ever-improving technology, and more new techniques in the years ahead.

References

Acker, K., Moller, D., Marquardt, W., Bruggemann, E., Wieprecht, W., Auel, R., & Kalas, D. (1998). Atmospheric research program for studying changing emission patterns after German unification. *Atmospheric Environment*, 32 (20), 3435–3443.

Adhikari, A. (1969). Some results on the distribution of the most significant digit. *Indian Journal of Statistics, Sankhya Series B*, 31, 413–420.

Adhikari, A., & Sarkar, B. 1968. Distribution of most significant digit in certain functions whose arguments are random variables. *Indian Jnl. of Statistics, Sankhya Series B*, 30, 47–58.

Alexander, J. (2009). *Remarks on the use of Benford's Law*. Working paper, Case Western Reserve University, Department of Mathematics and Cognitive Science.

American Institute of Certified Public Accountants. (1988). *Statement on Auditing Standards No. 56, Analytical Procedures*. New York, NY: Author.

American Institute of Certified Public Accountants. (2002). *Statement on Auditing Standards No. 99, Consideration of Fraud in a Financial Statement Audit*. New York, NY: Author.

American Institute of Certified Public Accountants. (2006). *Statement on Auditing Standards No. 106, Audit Evidence*. New York, NY.

Association of Certified Fraud Examiners, American Institute of Certified Public Accountants, and The Institute of Internal Auditors. (2008). *Managing the Business Risk of Fraud: A Practical Guide*. Altamonte Springs, FL: Author.

Becker, P. (1982). Patterns in listing of failure-rate and MTTF values and listings of other data. *IEEE Transactions On Reliability* R-31, 2 (June), 132–134.

Benford, F. (1938). The law of anomalous numbers. *Proceedings of the American Philosophical Society*, 78, 551–572.

Bolton, R., & Hand, D. (2002). Statistical fraud detection: A review. *Statistical Science*, 17 (3), 235–255.

Boyle, J. (1994). An application of Fourier Series to the most significant digit problem. *The American Mathematical Monthly*, 101 (9): 879–886.

Brady, W. (1978). More on Benford's Law. *Fibonacci Quarterly*, 16, 51–52.

Buck, B., Merchant, A., & Perez, S. (1993). An illustration of Benford's first digit law using alpha decay half lives. *European Journal of Physics*, 14, 59–63.

Burke, J., & Kincanon, E. (1991). Benford's Law and physical constants: The distribution of initial digits. *American Journal of Physics*, 59 (October), 952.

Busta, B., & Weinberg, R. (1998). Using Benford's Law and neural networks as a review procedure. *Managerial Auditing Journal*, 13 (6), 356–366.

Carslaw, C. (1988). Anomalies in income numbers: Evidence of goal oriented behavior. *The Accounting Review*, 63 (April), 321–327.

Christian, C., & Gupta, S. (1993). New evidence on "secondary evasion." *Journal of the American Taxation Association*, 15 (1), 72–92.

Cleary, R., & Thibodeau, J. (2005). Applying digital analysis using Benford's Law to detect fraud: The dangers of type I errors. *Auditing: A Journal of Practice and Theory*, 24 (1), 77–81.

Craig, T. (1992). Round-off bias in earnings per share calculations. *Journal of Applied Business Research*, 8, 106–113.

Das, S., & Zhang, H. (2003). Rounding-up in reported EPS, behavioral thresholds, and earnings management. *Journal of Accounting and Economics*, 35 (1), 31–50.

Daugherty, B., & Pitman, M. (2009). Auditing the auditors: A case on PCAOB inspection reports of registered public accounting firms. *Current Issues in Auditing*, 3 (1), B1–B18.

Dettinger, M., & Diaz, H. (2000). Global characteristics of stream flow seasonality and variability. *Journal of Hydrometeorology*, 1 (4), 289–310.

Drake, P., & Nigrini, M. (2000). Computer assisted analytical procedures using Benford's Law. *Journal of Accounting Education*, 18, 127–146.

Ettredge, M., & Srivastava, R. (1999). Using digital analysis to enhance data integrity. *Issues in Accounting Education*, 14 (4), 675–690.

Feller, W. (1966). *An introduction to probability theory and its applications*. New York, NY: John Wiley & Sons.

Flehinger, B. (1966). On the probability that a random integer has initial digit "A." *The American Mathematical Monthly*, 73 (10), 1056–1061.

Fleiss, J. (1981). *Statistical methods for rates and proportions*. New York, NY: John Wiley & Sons.

Furry, W., & Hurwitz, H. (1945). Distribution of numbers and distribution of significant figures. *Nature*, 155, 52–53.

Golden, T., Skalak, S., & Clayton, M. (2006). *A guide to forensic accounting investigation*. Hoboken, NJ: John Wiley & Sons.

Good, I. (1965). Letter to the editor. *The American Statistician*, 19, 43.

Goudsmit, S. (1977). Pitfalls in elementary probability. *Proceedings of the American Philosophical Society*, 121, 188–189.

Goudsmit, S., & Furry, W. (1944). Significant figures of numbers in statistical tables. *Nature*, 154, 800–801.

Gramling, A., & Watson, M. (2009). Analysis of peer review reports: A focus on deficiencies of the Top 20 triennially inspected firms. *Current Issues in Auditing*, 3 (2), A1–A14.

Grazioli, S., Jamal, K., & Johnson, P. (2006). A cognitive approach to fraud detection. *Journal of Forensic Accounting*, 7 (2), 65–88.

Grisso, T. (2010). Guidance for improving forensic reports: A review of common errors. *Open Access Journal of Forensic Psychology*, 2, 102–115.

Hamming, R. (1970). On the distribution of numbers. *Bell System Technical Journal*, 49, 1609–25.

Herrmann, D., & W. Thomas. (2005). Rounding of analyst forecasts. *The Accounting Review*, 80 (3), 805–824.

Hill, T. (1988). Random number guessing and the first digit phenomenon. *Psychological Reports*, 62 (3), 967–971.

Hill, T. (1995). A statistical derivation of the significant-digit law. *Statistical Science*, 10 (4), 354–363.

Hsu, E. (1948). An experimental study on "mental numbers" and a new application. *The Journal of General Psychology*, 38, 57–67.

Institute of Internal Auditors. (2005). *Global technology audit guide: Information technology controls*. Altamonte Springs, FL: Author.

Internal Revenue Service. (1979). *Discriminant function (DIF) handbook (Document 6588)*. Washington, D.C.: U.S. Department of the Treasury.

Internal Revenue Service. (1989). *Taxpayer compliance measurement program handbook (Document 6457)*. Washington, D.C.: U.S. Department of the Treasury.

International Federation of Accountants (IFAC). (2002). *IT Monitoring*. New York, NY: Author.

Ittig, P. (2004). Comparison of efficient seasonal indexes. *Journal of Applied Mathematics and Decision Sciences*, 8 (2), 87–105.

Knuth, D. (1969). *The art of computer programming volume 2: Seminumerical algorithms*. Reading, MA: Addison Wesley.

Miller, S., & Nigrini, M. (2008). Order statistics and Benford's Law. *International Journal of Mathematics and Mathematical Sciences*, Volume 2008, Article ID 382948, 19 pages.

Mosimann, J., Wiseman, C., & Edelman, R. (1995). Data fabrication: Can people generate random digits? *Accountability in Research*, 4 (1), 31–55.

Nelson, L. (1984). Technical aids. *Journal of Quality Technology*, 16, 175–176.

Newbold, P., Carlson, W., & Thorne, B. (2010). *Statistics for business and economics 7th Edition*. Upper Saddle River, NJ: Prentice-Hall.

Nigrini, M. (1994). Using digital frequencies to detect fraud. *The White Paper*, (April), 3–6.

Nigrini, M. (1996). A taxpayer compliance application of Benford's Law. *The Journal of the American Taxation Association*. 18 (1), 72–91.

Nigrini, M. (1999). Fraud detection: I've got your number. *Journal of Accountancy*, May 1999, 79–83.

Nigrini, M. (2005). An assessment of the change in the incidence of earnings management around the Enron-Andersen episode. *Review of Accounting and Finance*, 4 (1), 92–110.

Nigrini, M. (2006). Monitoring techniques available to the forensic accountant. *Journal of Forensic Accounting*, 7 (2), 321–344.

Nigrini, M., & Johnson, A. (2008). Using key performance indicators and risk measures in continuous monitoring. *Journal of Emerging Technologies in Accounting*, 5, 65–80.

Nigrini, M., & Miller, S. (2007). Benford's Law applied to hydrology data—results and relevance to other geophysical data, *Mathematical Geology*, 39 (5), 469–490.

Nigrini, M., & Miller, S. (2009). Data diagnostics using second-order tests of Benford's Law, *Auditing: A Journal of Practice and Theory*, 28 (2), 305–324.

Nigrini, M., & Mittermaier, L. (1997). The use of Benford's Law as an aid in analytical procedures, *Auditing: A Journal of Practice and Theory*, 16 (2): 52–67.

Pinkham, R. (1961). On the distribution of first significant digits. *Annals of Mathematical Statistics*, 32 (4), 1223–1230.

PricewaterhouseCoopers. (2006). *State of the internal audit profession study: Continuous auditing gains momentum.* New York, NY: Author.

PricewaterhouseCoopers. (2007a). *State of the internal audit profession study: Pressures build for continual focus on risk.* New York, NY: Author.

PricewaterhouseCoopers. (2007b). *Internal Audit 2012.* New York, NY: Author.

Raimi, R. (1969a). On the distribution of first significant figures. *The American Mathematical Monthly*, 76 (4), 342–348.

Raimi, R. (1969b). The peculiar distribution of first digits. *Scientific American*, 221 (6), 109–120.

Raimi, R. (1976). The first digit problem. *The American Mathematical Monthly*, 83 (7), 521–538.

Raimi, R. (1985). The first digit phenomenon again. *Proceedings of the American Philosophical Society*, 129, 211–219.

Sentence, W. (1973). A further analysis of Benford's Law. *Fibonacci Quarterly*, 11, 490–494.

Slovic, P. (1966). Cue-consistency and cue-utilization in judgment. *The American Journal of Psychology*, 79 (3), 427–434.

Stewart, I. (1993). *The law of anomalous numbers.* Working paper, Mathematics Institute, University of Warwick. Published in *Spektrum der Wissenschaft*, April, 1994.

Stigler, G. (1945). *The distribution of leading digits in statistical tables.* Working paper. University of Chicago, Regenstein Library Special Collections, George J. Stigler Archives.

Thomas, J. (1989). Unusual patterns in reported earnings. *The Accounting Review*, 64 (October), 773–787.

Tootle, G., Piechota, T., & A. Singh. (2005). Coupled oceanic-atmospheric variability and United States streamflow. *Water Resources Research*, 4, W12408, DOI:10.1029/2005Wr004381.

Tsao, N. (1974). On the distribution of significant digits and roundoff errors. *Communications of the ACM*, 17, 269–271.

Varian, H. (1972). Benford's Law. *The American Statistician*, 23 (June), 65–66.

Vasarhelyi, M. (1983). A framework for audit automation: Online technology and the audit process. *The Accounting Forum*.

Wall Street Journal. (1998). *Tax Report: An IRS blooper startles thousands of taxpayers*, February 18, 1998. Front page.

Wilk, M., & Gnanadesikan. (1968). Probability plotting methods for the analysis of data. *Biometrika*, 55 (1), 1–17.

Williams, M., Moss, S., Bradshaw, J., & Rinehart, N. (2002). Brief report: Random number generation in autism. *Journal of Autism and Developmental Disorders*, 32 (1), 43–47.

Wlodarski, J. (1971). Fibonacci and Lucas numbers tend to obey Benford's Law. *Fibonacci Quarterly*, 9, 87–88.

Index